FORM AND FABRIC

FORM AND FABRIC

*Studies in Rome's material past
in honour of B. R. Hartley*

Edited by Joanna Bird

Oxbow Monograph 80
1998

Published by
Oxbow Books, Park End Place, Oxford OX1 1HN

ISBN 1 900188 35 X

This book is available direct from
Oxbow Books, Park End Place, Oxford OX1 1HN
(Phone: 01865–241249; Fax: 01865–794449)

and

The David Brown Book Company
PO Box 511, Oakville, CT 06779, USA
(Phone: 860–945–9329; Fax: 860–945–9468)

*The cover illustration shows samian in the Fosse Malaval, La Graufesenque
Photo, Alain Vernhet*

Frontispiece, photo Arthur MacGregor

*Printed in Great Britain at
The Alden Press, Oxford*

Editor's Foreword

The range of papers presented in this volume demonstrates the wide scope of Brian Hartley's interests and the fields of archaeological scholarship with which he has been involved. The number of them shows, too, the affection and esteem in which he is held. I have attempted to group the papers in a logical order, though several of them have inevitably escaped too strict an ordering. After appreciations by his friends and a bibliography of Brian's own publications, the book begins with studies on Roman Britain, particularly the military history which has been the subject of much of Brian's own fieldwork; this is followed by the largest category, papers on samian ware, the specialist study for which Brian is best known, especially abroad. Papers on other types of Roman pottery, also one of Brian's key interests, follow, arranged chronologically where possible; and the book ends with a group of papers on various classes of other finds, all of them relevant to the history and life of Roman Britain.

I am grateful to Geoffrey Dannell, Brenda Dickinson and Kay Hartley for inviting me to edit this collection; it has been an honour to prepare such a book for one who is both a friend and a mentor. I would also like to thank David Bird, Thomas Bird and Michelle Willoughby for their assistance.

JOANNA BIRD

Contents

Editor's foreword v

List of contributors ix

Brian Rodgerson Hartley: an appreciation, with contributions by his friends and relations   *Geoffrey Dannell* xi

B. R. H.   *S.S. Frere* xvii

A bibliography of the works of B. R. Hartley   *Josephine Dool and John Pentney* xix

1   *Inde opes et rerum secundarum luxus*, Stanwick and Melsonby   *Leon Fitts* 1

2   Tacitus on Agricola: truth and stereotype   *R. H. Martin* 9

3   Agricola and Roman Scotland: some structural evidence   *Gordon Maxwell* 13

4   Camelon and Flavian troop-movements in southern Britain: some ceramic evidence
     Vivien G. Swan and Paul T. Bidwell 21

5   Units doubled and divided and the planning of forts and fortresses   *Mark Hassall* 31

6   The dating of town walls in Roman Britain   *John Wacher* 41

7   William Stukeley's *Caesaromagus*, its basis in fiction and fact   *Raphael M. J. Isserlin* 51

8   Romano-British art and Gallo-Roman samian   *Martin Henig* 59

9   Ovolos on Dragendorff form 30 from the collections of Frédéric Hermet and Dieudonné Rey
     Geoffrey Dannell, Brenda Dickinson and Alain Vernhet 69

10   Three stamped decorated bowls from Gloucester   *Felicity Wild* 111

11   Old wine in new bottles. Reflections on the organization of the production of terra sigillata at
      La Graufesenque   *Marinus Polak* 115

12   Un vase moulé de Montans au décor volontairement effacé   *Jean-Louis Tilhard*............123

13   Lezoux – La Graufesenque et la Romanisation   *Hugues Vertet*............127

14   A collection of samian from the legionary works-depot at Holt   *Margaret Ward*............133

15   An unusual decorated jar from Northamptonshire   *Graham Webster*............145

16   Zur Verwertbarkeit von Reliefsigillaten des 2. und 3. Jahrhunderts   *Ingeborg Huld-Zetsche*............147

17   A decorated samian dish from the London waterfront   *Joanna Bird*............151

18   Die Datierung der Rheinzaberner Reliefsigillata   *Klaus Kortüm und Allard Mees*............157

19   Samian from the City of Lincoln: a question of status?   *Margaret J. Darling*............169

20   Expert systems in sigillata and numismatic studies   *George Rogers*............179

21   Un dépôt pré-flavien à Tongeren (Belgique)   *M. Vanderhoeven*............183

22   Where did Cen, Reditas and Sace produce pots? A summary of the range and distribution of
     Romano-British stamped wares   *Val Rigby*............191

23   The incidence of stamped mortaria in the Roman Empire, with special reference to imports
     to Britain   *Kay Hartley, with illustrations by Malcolm Stroud*............199

24   Early Roman amphorae from Le Mans   *Patrick Galliou*............219

25   Pottery production at Corbridge in the late 1st century   *J. N. Dore*............227

26   Une enfance de Dionysos: moule d'applique de la collection Constancias   *Colette Bémont*............235

27   From Katendrecht back to Nijmegen: a group of pottery moulds and relief-tablets from
     Ulpia Noviomagus   *J. K. Haalebos and L. Swinkels*............241

28   Second-century pottery from Caerleon derived from metal and samian prototypes
     Janet and Peter Webster............249

29   Hoards of Roman coins found in Britain: the search and the byways   *Anne S. Robertson*............263

30   Do brooches have ritual associations?   *Grace Simpson and Beatrice Blance*............267

31   A hoard of late Roman ironwork from Sibson, Huntingdonshire   *W. H. Manning*............281

32   A sling from Melandra?   *John Peter Wild*............297

33   Early occupation at St. Mary's Abbey, York: the evidence of the glass   *H.E.M. Cool*............301

34   A glass drinking cup with incised decoration from Newton Kyme, North Yorkshire   *Jennifer Price*............307

List of contributors

COLETTE BÉMONT
21 Rue Henri Mürger
F–75019
Paris

PAUL T. BIDWELL, LL.B, MA, FSA
28 Kingsley Place
Heaton
Newcastle upon Tyne NE6 5AN

JOANNA BIRD, BA, FSA
14 Kings Road
Guildford
Surrey GU1 4JW

BEATRICE BLANCE (CLAYRE), MA, PH.D
Green College
Woodstock Road
Oxford OX2 6HG

H. E. M. COOL, FSA, MIFA
16 Lady Bay Road
West Bridgford
Nottingham NG2 5BJ

G. B. DANNELL, FSA
28–30 Main Street
Wood Newton
Peterborough PE8 5EB

MARGARET J. DARLING, M.PHIL, FSA, MIFA
3 Club Yard
Blacksmiths Lane
Harmston
Lincoln LN5 9SW

BRENDA DICKINSON, BA, FSA
6 Parkland Terrace
Leeds LS6 4PW

JOSEPHINE DOOL, BA, AMA
18 Tristram Drive
Creech St. Michael
Taunton
Somerset TA3 5QU

J. N. DORE, BA, FSA
27 Malcolm Street
Newcastle upon Tyne NE6 5PL

PROFESSOR LEON FITTS, PH.D, FSA
Dickinson College
Carlisle,
Pennsylvania 17013–2896
USA

EMERITUS PROF. S. S. FRERE, CBE, MA, LITT.D, D.LITT, FBA
Netherfield House
Abingdon
Oxfordshire OX13 6NP

PATRICK GALLIOU, DR.PHIL, FSA
Université de Bretagne Occidentale
Brest
France

PROFESSOR J. K. HAALEBOS, DR.PHIL
Etudestraat 62
NL–6544 RT Nijmegen
Netherlands

KAY HARTLEY, BA, FSA
Flat A
22 Shire Oak Road
Leeds LS6 2DE

MARK HASSALL, MA, FSA
Institute of Archaeology
University College London
31–34 Gordon Square
London WC1H 0PY

MARTIN HENIG, MA, D.PHIL, D.LITT, FSA
Institute of Archaeology
36 Beaumont Street
Oxford OX1 2PG

INGEBORG HULD-ZETSCHE, DR.PHIL
Museum für Vor- und Frühgeschichte
Karmelitergasse 1
D–60311 Frankfurt am Main
Germany

RAPHAEL M. J. ISSERLIN
School of Classics
University of Leeds
Leeds LS2 9JT

KLAUS KORTÜM, DR.PHIL
Landesdenkmalamt in Stuttgart
Silberburgstrasse 193
D–70178 Stuttgart
Germany

PROFESSOR W. H. MANNING, PH.D., FSA
School of History and Archaeology
University of Wales Cardiff
P O Box 909
Cardiff CF1 3XU

EMERITUS PROFESSOR R. H. MARTIN
School of Classics
University of Leeds
Leeds LS2 9JT

GORDON MAXWELL, MA, FSA, FSA SCOT
Micklegarth
72a High Street
Aberdour
Fife KY3 0SW

ALLARD MEES, DR.PHIL
Römisch-Germanisches Zentralmuseum
Ernst-Ludwig-Platz 2
D–55116 Mainz
Germany

JOHN PENTNEY, MA
18 Tristam Drive
Creech St. Michael
Taunton
Somerset TA3 5QU

MARINUS POLAK, DR.PHIL
Aldenhof 38–14
NL-6537 BD Nijmegen
Netherlands

JENNIFER PRICE, BA, PH.D, FSA
Department of Archaeology
University of Durham
South Road
Durham DH1 3LE

VAL RIGBY
Department of Prehistoric and Romano-British Antiquities
The British Museum
London WC1B 3DG

PROFESSOR ANNE S. ROBERTSON, MA, D.LITT., FMA, FSA, FSA SCOT
31 Upper Glenburn Road
Bearsden
Glasgow G61 4BN

GEORGE ROGERS, FSA
243 Avénue Général Leclerc
06700 St. Laurent-du-Var
France

GRACE SIMPSON, D.PHIL., FSA
73 Butler Close
Oxford OX2 6JQ

MALCOLM STROUD
63 Park Street
Armley
Leeds LS12 3NW

VIVIEN G. SWAN, BA, FSA
Research Centre for Roman Provincial Archaeology
Department of Archaeology
University of Durham
South Road
Durham DH1 3LE

L. SWINKELS, DR.PHIL
Museum G. M. Kam
NL-6522 GB Nijmegen
Netherlands

JEAN-LOUIS TILHARD
Chercheur associé, UMR 126.3 du C.N.R.S.
1 Rue Froide
F–16000 Angloulême
France

M. VANDERHOEVEN
Repenstraat 8
B–3700 Tongeren
Belgium

ALAIN VERNHET
Centre Archéologique de la Graufesenque
F–12100 Millau
France

HUGHES VERTET
66 Boulevard Saint Exupéry
F–03400 Yzeure
France

PROFESSOR JOHN WACHER, BSC, FSA, MIFA
Rosewin
Gwinear Road
Hayle
Cornwall TR27 5JQ

MARGARET WARD, MA, MIFA
2 Woodfields
Christleton
Chester CH3 7AU

GRAHAM WEBSTER, OBE, MA, PH.D., D.LITT, FSA, HON. MIFA
The Old Post Office
Sevenhampton, nr. Highworth
Swindon
Wiltshire SN6 7QA

JANET WEBSTER, BA
8 Cefn Coed Avenue
Cyncoed
Cardiff CF2 6HE

PETER WEBSTER, BA, M.PHIL, D.LITT, FSA
Department for Continuing Education
University of Wales Cardiff
38 Park Place
Cardiff CF1 3BB

FELICITY WILD, MA, FSA
30 Prince's Road
Heaton Moor
Stockport SK4 3NQ

JOHN PETER WILD, MA, PH.D, FSA
30 Prince's Road
Heaton Moor
Stockport SK4 3NQ

Brian Rodgerson Hartley

An appreciation, with contributions by his friends and relations

Brian Rodgerson Hartley was born in Chester on the 31st of December, 1929, the youngest of the four surviving children of Henry and Gertrude Hartley, and the only boy. Both of his parents had connections with South Africa, and the pioneering spirit of that colony seems to have rubbed off on their son. He was brought up within a strongly Methodist tradition, among a close and happy family, where the importance of personal relationships was highly valued.

His early interests included 'train-spotting' on Crewe Station, and philately – both hobbies requiring the use of catalogues and the compilation of lists, a trait which has remained part of his character ever since. Brian appears to have first taken to archaeology at the age of seven, when, after a school lesson about Roman Britain, he took a bucket and spade and went to work on the garden, producing a piece of crenellated white pottery which he was sure was part of a Roman's upper set. The first samian ware of which he was cognisant (aged five) were two Drag. 32s in the foyer of the Regal Cinema, Chester (it is typical that even now he can remember that only one was stamped).

His education started modestly at the local primary school in Victoria Road, Chester, from which he won a scholarship to the King's School Chester, which then, as now, maintained an extremely high academic standard. He was apparently more willing to lead from the front in those days: appointed captain of Shepherd's House in 1946 and then school captain in 1947/8. His House note for 1946 laments an unsuccessful sporting year, 'House cricket was of poor standard...Much practice will be needed to improve on this result...' (one can hear him now). Brian remains, if not devoted, certainly interested in the game, whereas, although he played soccer, he was more keen on participating than in following. Walking was another passion; Alistair Jenkins tells how expeditions to the Lake District were led by a teacher, 'Johnny' Walsh, who frequented the Kardomah café in Chester and there plied his charges with cups of tea, while discussing current matters of interest, and splitting matches (an old wartime economy). Extra-curricular activity included his interest in railways, as a member of the King's School Railway Club, and of course archaeology. He was clearly an active teenager ; among other

exploits, his sister notes that on one occasion while working at the Post Office, he was party to stuffing the Headmaster's son in a mail-sack, and delivering him down the mail-chute.

His education was wide; by nature a classicist and linguist (teaching even extended to a little Hebrew), he was also persuaded to embrace the sciences, which was to lead to a small impasse later. Indeed in the report of the Prefectorial Society meeting in 1948 he was referred to, tongue-in-cheek, as 'that eminent Scientist and Archaeologist'. Among other records of the time are his six years of voluntary work on the 'drains' of the River Dee Catchment Board, an essentially physical activity, and particularly, his report in 1946 of the excavations at Heronbridge, directed by W. J. ('Walrus') Williams, in which he assisted. Brian wrote in the King's School magazine: 'The finds in pottery have been excellent, both in rough-ware and in fine red-glazed ware (misnamed 'Samian'). In rough-ware, cooking pots, storage-jars, wine-jars, bottles and mortaria (heavy bowls studded inside with grit) were plentiful. The red-glazed ware has included decorated bowls and plain bowls, cups and platters (examples of this ware are to be seen in the Grosvenor Museum). About fifteen potter's stamps have been recovered on this type of pottery. Although the work has certainly been hard at times, it has also been well worth the energy expended'. Heronbridge was reported elsewhere (*J. Roman Stud.*, **37**, 170 and 38, 85ff., where for the 1946 excavations he contributed a plan, and for 1947 he is acknowledged as co-director). The 1947–48 season was reported in full in his own name (Hartley 1952a), complete with his drawings of the samian and the coarse pottery. It is noteworthy that all of the pottery was published there in its own archaeological groups – making the dating evidence far easier to assimilate. Brian obtained comments from Eric Birley about some of the samian. Family history recalls that at that time Brian slept with a sack of Roman pottery under his bed.

Chester was of course a prime site for any young person interested in Roman Britain. The richness of its 'red-glazed wares' provided the basis for two papers which recorded and analysed samian stamps. These cannot have escaped Brian's attention, nor indeed the possibilities of the use of samian in archaeological research generally (Williams 1902; Hayter

1926). In 1948 he was involved in excavations directed by Graham Webster and the late Sir Ian Richmond (Webster & Richmond 1951): 'Lastly, very special thanks to Messrs. D. Barker, B. Hartley and S. Kay, all of whom rendered valuable assistance in the trenches themselves particularly in the delicate work of cleaning up details.' The friendship and association with Graham Webster has been long-lasting, while Ian Richmond was to be a decisive influence for the future in forming Brian's practical and academic approach to archaeology, and in the development of not a few imitative mannerisms.

In 1948 he also gained admission to Trinity Hall, Cambridge, to read Natural Sciences. National Service intervened (RAF, AC1 (2110323); unfortunately regulations still require that, 'Service details can only be given on receipt of the airman's written consent', so this history records only that Brian was in a stores unit, and perhaps reinforced his cricketing interests while serving for a time with J.B. Statham), and he actually went up in 1950. He found the course somewhat trying, particularly the physics, and on gaining his first degree, took the Diploma in Prehistoric Archaeology, for which he was awarded a distinction. His academic career had commenced, and when Sheppard Frere took a lectureship at Manchester, instead of a Research Assistantship under Grahame Clark, Brian was given that post. He lectured and supervised in Romano-British Archaeology, in the course of which he developed both a style and technique which has proved invaluable to his later students. Joyce Reynolds recalls '...his admiration for Ian Richmond – on whose lecturing style he based his own at that stage (and what better model could one have!)'. A photograph of Richmond ('Dad') remains in a prominent place on Brian's desk. It is true that his deliberate delivery in the lecture-hall still recalls that of Richmond; it is also unaffected by whichever language he is speaking, much to the endearment of his closest friends.

The Cambridge years were clearly formative and extremely active. Prehistory was not Brian's primary love (Ian Longworth observes: 'Grahame had little time for Roman archaeology and Brian was not entirely convinced about prehistory!'), although he wrote the report of the excavation at Wandlebury (Hartley 1956b) with an easy competence. He also returned to Heronbridge in 1953 and 1954 for two seasons, the latter being aborted due to bad weather (Hartley 1954c, written with K.F. Kaine ('K'), and Hartley 1955e). He became acquainted with an increasingly wide group of teachers, colleagues and students which included the late Glyn Daniel, W.H.C. (Bill) Frend, Roy Hodson, Ian Longworth and Ian Stead, and he quickly expanded his field activities and ceramic studies. Roy Hodson, who studied for the diploma at the same time as Brian, says: 'he was already an experienced archaeologist, and the rest of us real amateurs, and not on his wave-length!', while Ian Stead records that: 'Brian taught me a lot about writing an excavation report for publication'.

Brian provided reports for the Arbury Road excavations (Hartley 1954f and 1955d, where he very competently drew a signed Drag. 37 by Mercator i). Bill Frend observes: '...our short description was dwarfed by his scholarly account of the

coarse pottery, which became the "Bible" for future local archaeology', a demonstration of his emerging mastery of matters relating to Romano-British coarse pottery and samian ware. Excavations were undertaken at High Wycombe (Hartley 1955f and 1959a), and notes of excavations appeared under his name at Barley and Pampisford (*J. Roman Stud.*, **46**); travel was effected by Vespa.

In 1951 Graham Webster had encouraged him to join in the activities of the summer school excavations organised by the extra-mural department of Nottingham University (Corder (ed.) 1951; 1954; 1961), and he met an influential teaching staff, which included the late Philip Corder, John Gillam and Maurice Barley. 'Uncle' Philip (Corder 1928 and *Antiq. J.*, **21**, 271–98), and John Gillam (Gillam 1957) were already deeply involved in systematic appraisals of Romano-British coarse pottery, to which Brian's increasing specialist knowledge of samian added a neat counter-point, and he joined the teaching staff of the school in 1958. It was also at Great Casterton that he had met Katharine Kaine ('K'). They were married in 1955.

A photograph taken at Heronbridge in 1953 shows a long-jawed, aquiline Hartley, fiercely gripping his beloved pipe, a rival for the late Basil Rathbone in the part of Sherlock Holmes. This allusion is not casual. Like many archaeologists Brian found the logical deductive process of the classical English detective story basic to the interpretation of evidence, and is an aficionado of the genre (Hartley 1989f).

In 1956 Brian succeeded William V. Wade in the lectureship in Romano-British Archaeology within the Department of Latin Language and Literature in the University of Leeds and moved to Headingley. Ronald Martin writes: 'The title of the Department reflected the strong literary and linguistic bias it had always had hitherto. Brian's main task was to offer, as a two-year Special Subject within the Department, an option which (it was expected) might appeal primarily to students whose abilities were not markedly linguistic. In the upshot "Roman Britain" quickly established itself within the Department as the most popular option and it attracted a good number of students (Brenda Dickinson was one) who were equally at home in the linguistic and non-linguistic aspects of our courses'.

His arrival in Yorkshire is marked by information about excavations at Ferry Fryston, Castleford (*J. Roman Stud.*, **47**, 210). This was also the period during which Sheppard Frere started his excavations at Verulamium, and Brian would go to the Institute of Archaeology in London each autumn to look over the season's samian and provide a preliminary dating. The operation was a veritable 'production line' with paper bags being unpacked at one end of a long table, Brian commenting, while his amanuensis tried to keep up with the flow, the bags being repackaged after each batch was recorded. The room would grow fuggier by the hour under the combined outputs of the Frere and Hartley pipes; the sessions ended in total exhaustion only to be relieved by Brian's legendary capacity at that time for black coffee. He also took over the University Training Excavation at the Roman fort of Brough by Bainbridge, a programme of work which went on for a further ten years. Reports appeared regularly in the 'Roman Britain' section of the *Journal of Roman Studies* from 1958 onwards (and see below for the excavations of 1957–59).

In 1957 recognition of his academic advancement came in his election as a Fellow of the Society of Antiquaries of London (his 'Blue paper' was signed from personal knowledge by, among others, Sheppard Frere, Graham Webster, M.V. Taylor, Ian Richmond, Jocelyn Toynbee, John Gillam, and W.F. Grimes, and from general knowledge by Eric Birley). He directed the excavation of a pottery kiln at Stibbington (Hartley 1958i), and the ensuing close friendship with Eric Standen, the then Secretary of the Peterborough Museum Society Field Club, and his wife Aileen, has happily continued. Eric Standen tells of Stibbington: 'at the end of the first day, Brian finished off with a cross section of the kiln stoke-hole, in the face of which a complete folded beaker came to light which Brian (observing strict etiquette), left there for the next day. Unfortunately a well known local solicitor and antiquary went down to the site, and removed it for his private collection!'. Eric and Aileen Standen's hospitality encouraged Brian to give a number of free lectures to the Museum Society. Eric recalls one: '... before the lecture commenced Brian went out with one of his colleagues for light refreshments. He commenced the lecture looking very pleased and happy with life, and it was not long before we all realised that he was "whistled". In spite of this he gave an excellent talk and it will never be forgotten in the Nene Valley.' Eric Standen subsequently undertook the logistical organisation for the much larger Water Newton excavations of 1958, directed with John Gillam and Graham Webster, and greatly assisted by the magnetometer of Martin Aitken (*J. Roman Stud.,* **50**, 117–18).

The 1960 season at Bainbridge proved a triumph for Brian's thorough methods. In excavating the east gateway, he came across a large stone (Hartley 1961h) , which had been photographed previously in situ by R.G. Collingwood; it was turned over, and revealed a dedicatory inscription to C. Valerius Pudens, a hitherto unknown Governor (in getting it into the site hut, it fell and cracked Brian's toe. He claims that his hand slipped, others blame sheer excitement. His reward was the heaviest plaster application ever devised for such an insignificant injury, a far greater incapacity than the toe itself and according to 'K' a lasting source of merriment). He also published a type series of Nene Valley wares (Hartley 1960a) following his field-work in the area. The 1961 season at Bainbridge added another inscription, this time of the Cohors VI Nerviorum (Hartley 1962j), and he returned to excavate in the Nene Valley (Hartley 1962k). In 1963 work began seriously on collecting the material for a revision of Felix Oswald's corpus of potter's stamps on samian ware (Oswald 1937).

The next few years were very busy in the field; attention in Yorkshire turned to the Roman fort at Ilkley (Hartley 1963g) and a series of four excavations at the samian production site of Lezoux was commenced (Frere 1966). Memories of Lezoux are recalled by Sheppard Frere with relish: '...the horse-meat sandwiches and *gaperon*', and that 'on one of the progressions through France in the Rolls, Brian overdosed on oysters and missed visiting Chartres Cathedral'. None who worked on

those excavations will forget the evening meals at the Hôtel des Voyageurs, where Sheppard and Brian held court at a baronial table, while the preparation of rubbings went on late into the night, with Brian strictly invigilating their quality. Nor indeed M. Martignat the chef, who cooked on a coal range, and who was known to run through the streets of Lezoux with a platter of *croquettes de volaille*, which arrived at the site in the same superb condition as those served in his restaurant; or Malcolm Todd's avowed intention to sample the contents of every bottle on the shelves of the Voyageurs' saloon.

There was further work in the Nene Valley at both Castor and Stanground Park Farm (Hartley 1966k). In 1966, Ilkley was published (Hartley 1966d) as well as a paper in *Northern History* (Hartley 1966c). Work with Sheppard Frere commenced at Bowes in 1967 (*J. Roman Stud.,* **58**, 179; Britannia, **2**, 251); and from 1968 Brian investigated Kirk Sink (Gargrave) (Hartley 1969j; Hartley 1970i; Hartley 1974n; Hartley 1975f; Hartley 1976i). Work also took place at Slack (Hartley 1969k). 1969 saw the initial publication of 'Roman samian ware' (Hartley 1969a).

Throughout this period it is clear that his interest in coarse pottery was also being deepened: cf. Hartley 1959h in which he quotes: 'As Dr Philip Corder has recently observed, one of the most urgent needs in Romano-British studies is the publication of kiln-groups from local potteries'. It was an opinion with which Brian has always kept faith. His studies into Romano-British coarse pottery had the objectives of adding a parallel dating tool to that of samian ware, to providing information about local and long-distance trade, and not least to investigating ceramic technology (Hartley 1961a). He was therefore an enthusiastic supporter of 'The Study Group for Romano-British Coarse Pottery', which Graham Webster sponsored and nurtured so effectively. The format was essentially that of the seminar at which information was freely exchanged between participants, in which Brian was totally at ease, talking to, rather than at, people, and leading to practical results.[1] He even drafted a paper to propose an 'Institute of Roman Pottery Studies'. The kite alas, never flew; if it had, many of the current problems associated with the costs of post-excavation, and the standard of reports about Roman pottery, might have been averted.

In 1967 Brian had been promoted to a Readership, still within the Department of Latin,[2] and combined with 'The Index' (as the new corpus of samian stamps became known), the work-load slowly began to reduce his field activity. He enjoyed a sabbatical year in 1972, which saw the seminal publication of 'The Roman occupations of Scotland: the evidence of samian ware' (Hartley 1972a) in which he was able to demonstrate how far the advance in the study of samian ware could be used to draw much wider inferences than the mere individual dating of sites, and how it could contribute evidence to the historical record of the province as a whole.

In 1973 Brian married Elizabeth Blank, and moved to York, where they began an extensive renovation of an 18th-century house in Bootham. Work started with Leon Fitts in 1976, on what was to be the last excavations to date, at the fort of Lease Rigg (Hartley 1977n; Hartley 1979i; Hartley

1980e; Hartley 1981d). The demands of teaching, 'The Index', and the blessing of a son in 1977, put a stop to fieldwork. However, two major publications were completed: first, 'The enclosure of Romano-British towns in the second century AD' (Hartley 1983b), and a book, 'The Brigantes' (Hartley 1988a), written with Leon Fitts.

All of Brian's academic work draws on three strengths: first, the width of his reading (his personal library would be the envy of many university departments);[3] secondly, the happy endowment of a retentive memory (if not quite in the class of Ian Richmond, who could do party tricks, Brian could frequently quote page references from memory), and finally, a scientific methodology. Their combination in the study of samian potters' stamps (and signatures) has been particularly successful. Brian also has remarkable eyesight, although it is almost certainly the link to his retentive memory which enables him to make sense of the most fragmentary letters. Brenda Dickinson remarks how often with the offending sherd held close to his face, Brian utters the measured words 'But... Can't you see? It's perfectly clear!' He is rarely wrong.

Oswald's pioneering volume (1931) was based on much secondary evidence and in some cases important kiln sites themselves were unknown, unrecognised or unpublished at the time (as Les Martres-de-Veyre: cf. the introduction to Stanfield & Simpson 1958, and Terrisse 1968). By the 1960s it was clear that a reassessment of Oswald's work was indispensable to the history of the development of the western Roman Empire, over its first two and a half centuries at least. It would offer the possiblity of a currency of far greater precision than coins themselves, if only the minor nuances in the development of the potter's workshops could be properly recorded and interpreted.[4] Brian had long realised that many of Oswald's recorded readings and attributions were doubtful, undermining the validity of their dating, and the tremendous growth of archaeological activity in post-war Europe, as its cities were rebuilt and redeveloped, offered fresh examples of historically attested strata, vital to making sense of the potters' working lives. He also sought to pay close attention to the epigraphy, lettering, design and condition of the stamps, realising that each stamp was the product of an individual die, which degraded over its life, offering possibilities of exactitude hitherto ignored.[5]

The decision to embark on re-examining as much evidence as possible *de novo* was carefully calculated to eliminate the inevitable confusions of site attribution and terminology which plagued Oswald's reliance on his disparate sources. The project was designed to last for twelve years. Field collection started in 1963, principally by Felicity Wild and Brenda Dickinson, while 'K' recorded much material in combination with her own parallel work on the stamps on mortaria. The sheer volume of data explains why the twelve-year project is only now reaching its conclusion (much to the disappointment of some, who see in this a certain lack of self-discipline). The truth is that a manuscript, some 1m in height, was ready in 1975, but was subject to certain vital *lacunae*, such as the collection of stamps from La Graufesenque, which had been unavailable for study up to then; to publish without them (over

30,000 entries on their own) would have vitiated much of the interpretative analysis, particularly for those South Gaulish potters for whom external evidence was scarce. This delay was fortunate, because it allowed the whole project to be transferred from manuscript to computer using an image-scanner, thus making it possible to extract statistical information, to compose special fonts for individual characters, and to make the whole work capable of revision as future evidence should accumulate. While many have fretted at the mine of information which they have seen as being stuck firmly in the Leeds files, it should be remembered that it has often been their own material which has been the cause of lengthy digressions in writing up samian reports to their excavations (in reply to a carping letter at the slowness of the project in the early 1970s, Brian pointed out that he was already working 75 hours a week, 50 related to his teaching commitments, and 25 on 'The Index'). That work-load probably increased thereafter. Additionally there has been the huge correspondence responding to enquiries, and the numerous visitors who have come to have their queries resolved. Few have been turned away empty-handed.

However, scrupulous recording of the stamps was but one small facet of the task, and then only a means to an end; samian stamps offer an important source of evidence for differentiation both in time and space, and often point to patterns of historical behaviour which cannot be detected by other means. For Brian, mastery of this evidence in its historical context is the real attraction.[6] At the same time, the stamps offer a means of working out the socio-economic fabric of the industry in which the potters worked (cf. Hartley 1977a).

Away from his professional life Brian's interests are truly catholic. He delights in music of the baroque period. Once, at a concert in the Leeds Town Hall in the 1960s, Brian was faced with a piece by Martinu. He retreated under the current ubiquitous duffel-coat until he considered that it was safe to emerge at the interval. His sympathies are with that other Methodist, Organ Morgan in Dylan Thomas' *Under Milkwood*, who replied to his wife's enquiry of 'Who do you like best, Organ?', with 'Oh, Bach without any doubt. Bach every time for me'. He has also explored personal interests in art and architecture (Hartley 1994b; forthcoming b); criminology (Hartley 1989f), and more latterly both his own, and his wife's ancestry. The Hartley family seem to have originated in the north-west, and were active in shipping out of Whitehaven in the 18th century, where some were involved in the slave trade (Richardson & Schofield 1992), while the Blanks appear to have had an interesting and convoluted history in continental Europe. As with his professional work, each of these relaxations is not just to be enjoyed, but forms the basis of intellectual challenge. It is interesting that many are involved with, or are made to involve, the manipulation of data and the formation of lists (one little project was to see how many Italian composers could be found (without reference books), the surnames of whom *did not end in 'i'*, another, those Scottish surnames which do end in 'o').

He has never been content merely to assemble facts for their own sake. His dictum to his students that 'It's not the pots that count: it's the chaps' is a leitmotif to his conversation, which all who have studied, worked with him, or shared his friendship can attest (from Alec Taylor, who also recalls other little Hartley catch-phrases: 'Ve-ry odd, ve-e-re-ey odd!', a regular incantation when faced with a problem not capable of instant resolution, and 'Interesting and curious!' (an echo of Ian Richmond) which was applied to the walls of Le Mans, among other posers temporarily shelved in a mental Hartley pigeon-hole for further reflection). He has always been intensely concerned with his fellows, and over the years supported a teaching load which has horrified many of his colleagues. Yet time and effort have been given freely, because without effort Brian believes nothing can be achieved (not everyone is aware that he suffers acute asthma attacks, especially in the pollen season, which can not only lead to being 'confined to barracks', but make any work at all very laborious, if not impossible), and *disciplina* required that his students received only the best of which he was capable, at all times. Patrick Roberts writes of the Bainbridge excavations: 'Countless students must have benefited from his careful and clear instruction: although the pace was good, Brian always had time to explain to everybody exactly what the plan was, what they were finding and what interpretation was justified'.

Brian is essentially a social person with a breadth of humanity which his students have enjoyed and recognised (Mrs Betty Oxby writes of the excavations at Gargrave, '... But what he excelled at was conversation...we used to sit outside in the evening before supper enjoying a glass of sherry and some spirited exchanges. His dry dead-pan wit made us all sharpen *our* wits and it was great fun.' If his courses and excavations have not bred the next generation of archaeologists, as those remarkable Frere years at Verulamium did, correspondence from his pupils tells how much Brian has clearly enriched other people's lives. Patrick Roberts again: 'I can see Brian now, as a young man, sitting in his armchair with his pipe on, leading some discussion in his gentlemanly but rigorous way, with flashes of impish humour, illuminating almost any topic touched on. Of course this was around 1960 and they [the students] responded wonderfully to his gentle paternalism'. By nature a listener and a private person, he has always found it important to extract and mentally file away information about his acquaintances, while on the other hand, few know much about *his* personal life (including his nearest and dearest); part modesty, part empathy.

At home family ranks first in importance. Naturally interested in whatever they are doing, he has offered intellectual, moral and practical support to their various endeavours, and is clearly delighted in their achievements; ease with children has made Christopher a friend as much as a son. Practicality stretches to handicrafts, such as carpentry, and the considerable work of restoring 39, Bootham. It also embraces a determined interest in food (cf. W.C. Sellars & R.J. Yeatman, *1066 and All That*, according to Mrs. Betty Oxby, '...the book he quoted most frequently': 'Napoleon's armies always used to march on their stomachs, shouting: Vive l'Intérieur'). Probably more of a cook in the Victorian or Edwardian mode than *chef de cuisine,* his soups, curries and sauces are renowned among

those lucky enough to visit his table. He also has more than a passing interest in the fruits of the vine. No account of his households can be complete without reference to Messrs. Gingerpuss and Pounce, imperious feline assessors of those friendly paunches on which to perch, nor more recently of William the chinchilla, shoe-chewer extraordinaire.

Brian has had the uncomfortable burden over the last few years of being 'a legend in his own time' within his own academic specialisation (the extensive bibliography assembled by Josephine Dool and John Pentney is an explanation in itself). He has worn it lightly. Unfailing patience, kindness and hospitality have won him friends across many disciplines and many countries. He has consistently contributed to courses and day-schools (particularly those organised by Graham Webster and Peter V. Webster, for the Extra-mural Departments of Birmingham and Cardiff Universities respectively), to disseminate knowledge of samian ware to any who might wish to learn more. Without doubt his personality has contributed greatly to getting more information for 'The Index' than others might have achieved. The loss of teaching responsibilities, and they will be a loss to him, should happily allow the completion of 'The Index', as well as other projects.

GEOFFREY DANNELL

Notes
1. Cf. *Romano-British coarse pottery: a student's guide*, Council for British Archaeology, Research Report, **6**, to which Brian contributed.
2. In 1973 the title was changed to that of 'Reader in Roman Provincial Archaeology' and in 1974 he was appointed as first head of the newly constituted Department of Archaeology. He had the headship for five years, but when the University decided that it could not afford a major expansion in archaeology, he returned to the School of Classics, a position which suited him ideally, because it avoided excessive administrative work, which he has always found irksome. Committee rooms were not his natural habitat, although Sheppard Frere recalls that Brian served for some years as an Administrator of the Haverfield Bequest, where 'his presence was very useful, as at least some of the Administrators needed some knowledge of the value of applicants and their projects.'
3. Sherlock Holmes speaking in 'The adventure of the five orange pips': 'Well, he said, I say now, as I said then, that a man should keep his little brain attic stocked with all the furniture that he is likely to use, and the rest he can put away in the lumber room of his library, where he can get it if he wants it.' Sir Arthur Conan Doyle, *The Adventures of Sherlock Holmes*, London, 1892.
4. Holmes: 'I have no data yet. It is a capital mistake to theorise before one has data. Insensibly one begins to twist facts to suit theories, instead of theories to suit facts.' 'The adventure of a scandal in Bohemia', *op. cit.* in note 3.
5. Holmes again: 'It has long been an axiom of mine that little things are infinitely the most important.' 'The adventure of a case of identity', *op. cit.* note 3.
6. Cf. Mrs. Bradley: 'An axiom among historians and great detectives is to be aware of the bit of evidence which refuses to fit. These little awkward facts are keys to mysteries', in Gladys Mitchell's *The Mystery of a Butcher's Shop*, London, 1929.

Bibliography
For the references to Brian Hartley's own publications, see the bibliography on pp. xvii–xxvi.
Corder, P., 1928 *The Roman pottery at Crambeck, Castle Howard*, Roman Malton and District Rep., **1**

Corder, P., 1941 A Roman pottery of the Hadrian-Antonine period at Verulamium, *Antiq.J.,* **21**, 271–98

_____, (ed) 1951 *The Roman town and villa of Great Casterton, Rutland, interim report 1,* Univ. Nottingham

_____, (ed) 1954 *The Roman town and villa of Great Casterton Rutland, interim report 2,* Univ. Nottingham

_____, (ed) 1961 *The Roman town and villa of Great Casterton Rutland, interim report 3,* Univ. Nottingham

Frere, S.S., 1966 Fouilles de Lezoux (Puy-de-Dôme) en 1963, *Cahiers de Civilisation Médiévale,* IXe. année, **4**

Gillam, J.P., 1957 Types of coarse pottery vessels in northern Britain, *Archaeol. Aeliana,* 4 ser., **35**, 180–251

Hayter, A.G.K., 1926 Report on Roman potters' marks found at Chester, *J. Chester North Wales Archaeol. Soc.,* **26**, 1–42

Oswald, F. 1931 *Index of potters' stamps on terra sigillata, 'samian ware'* (Margidunum)

Richardson, D., & Schofield, M.M., 1992 Whitehaven and the eighteenth-century British slave trade, *Trans. Cumberland Westmorland Antiq. Archaeol Soc.,* **92**, 183–204

Stanfield, J.A., & Simpson, G., 1958. *Central Gaulish potters* (London)

Terrisse, J-R., 1968 *Les céramiques sigillées gallo-romaines des Martres-de-Veyre (Puy-de-Dôme),* Gallia Supplément, **19** (Paris)

Webster, G., & Richmond, I.A., 1951 Excavations in Goss Street, Chester, 1948–9, *J. Chester North Wales Archaeol. Soc.,* **38**, 3

Williams, F.H., 1902 An extended list of potters' stamps on the red-glazed Roman ware (popularly known as samian) found at Chester, with the chief forms of stamping briefly classified, *J. Chester North Wales Archaeol. Soc.,* **8**, 170ff.

B. R. H.

S. S. Frere

Having spent the seven years since 1988 working full-time on the publication of *Roman inscriptions of Britain* ii, I have found my files awkwardly bare of any unpublished paper which I might offer in honour of Brian Hartley; but pressure from the editor as well as a sense of deep obligation to the recipient have compelled me to contribute a few words. They must be few, for the story of his life supported by the appropriate anecdotes has already been set out above.

Any serious student of Roman Archaeology must be aware of Brian's great contribution to the subject, and I in particular owe much to him, not merely for his professional contributions on samian ware, many of them lengthy, to all my published reports since 1956, but also to the stimulus of his conversation on matters of mutual interest; various nights spent under his hospitable roof, restfully dividing the long drive each year from Oxford to Strageath and back, produced talk and ideas which were often inspirational. The wisdom of his historical judgement was never more apparent to me than in the care which he devoted to the revision of the original draft chapters of my *Britannia: a history of Roman Britain*. One of his most endearing characteristics is his willingness to respond to requests for help. In this, indeed, he follows the example of Felix Oswald, to whom long ago I with many other field archaeologists used to turn with sherds. That the study of samian has developed so enormously since Oswald's pioneering days is due very largely to Brian's own work, and not least to the insights gained from his monumental analysis of the potters' stamps. Its eventual publication will be a land-mark in Roman provincial archaeology.

Geoffrey Dannell has already hinted at the extraordinarily busy life that Brian has always led, never allowing his overloaded teaching programme to stand in the way of his research, but at the same time never allowing other calls to distract him from the service of his pupils. This volume is a tribute to a great scholar and a great teacher.

A bibliography of the works of B. R. Hartley

Compiled by Josephine Dool and John Pentney

Whilst every effort has been made to trace all significant books, papers and contributions by Brian Hartley, it cannot be claimed that this is a comprehensive listing; and in particular, a number of short pottery identifications contributed to certain excavation reports together with summary excavation reports in more ephemeral publications such as newsletters may have been overlooked. All relevant sources published up to January 1995 have been searched. Some short contributions are not separately sub-titled in articles, and where this is the case, they are not cited within quotation marks. In some instances, it is not clear to what extent Brian Hartley's specialist report has been used verbatim by the principal author(s) of an article. Where his contribution appears as a sub-section in a subsidiary contributor's report, the subsidiary author has not been cited.

Standard CBA journal and monograph series title abbreviations are used, with volume numbers in **bold**. Journal articles are listed under the year *for* which the volume or part was published where this differs from the actual year of publication – usually the following year, but occasionally up to several years later. Where journal volumes embrace more than one year e.g. 1971–73, and separate annual parts cannot be identified, articles are listed under the last year of the range cited on the title page. For instance, item 1984(b) was published in volume 85 of the *Transactions of the Birmingham and Warwickshire Archaeological Society* for 1983–84, which did not appear until 1989.

Titles are quoted as they appear in the journals and books, and accordingly reflect inconsistencies in punctuation, the hyphenation of place-names like Brough-under-Stainmore and the italicization or otherwise of Roman place-names.

The compilers are grateful to the librarians of the Somerset Archaeological and Natural History Society, the University of Exeter and the Society of Antiquaries of London for access to their collections, and without whose willing assistance this bibliography would not have been possible. Thanks are also due to Brenda Dickinson for details of forthcoming publications and certain additional references.

1952

(a) 'Excavations at Heronbridge, 1947–48', *J. Chester N. Wales Archaeol. Soc.*, **39**, 1–20

1953

(a) 'Decorated samian ware from Sanvey Gate', and identifications of plain samian in R.G. Goodchild, 'Leicester city wall in Sanvey Gate: excavations in 1952', *Leicestershire Archaeol. Hist. Soc. Trans.*, **29**, 26–7, 20–3 *passim*

1954

(a) 'A fragment of samian ware from York with a figure in "cut-glass" technique', *Antiq. J.*, **34**, 233–4

(b) 'Heronbridge excavations: bronze-worker's hearth', *J. Chester N. Wales Archaeol. Soc.*, **41**, 1–14

(c) With K. F. Kaine, 'Heronbridge excavations: Roman dock and buildings', *J. Chester N. Wales Archaeol. Soc.*, **41**, 15–37

(d) 'Samian pottery', in R. Goodchild & J. R. Kirk, 'The Romano-Celtic temple at Woodeaton', *Oxoniensia*, **19**, 31–3

(e) 'Samian ware', in E.J.W. Hildyard, 'Excavations at Burrow in Lonsdale', *Trans. Cumberland Westmorland Antiq. Archaeol. Soc.*, **54**, 91–3

(f) 'The pottery', in W.H.C. Frend, 'A Romano-British settlement at Arbury Road, Cambridge', *Proc. Cambridge Antiq. Soc.*, **48**, 26–39

(g) Summary excavation report on Heronbridge in 'Roman Britain in 1953', *J. Roman Stud.*, **44**, 89

1955

(a) Review of E. Delort, *Vases ornés de la Moselle* (Nancy, 1953), *Antiq. J.*, **35**, 100–101

(b) 'Samian', in G. Webster, 'A section through the Roman fort at Kinvaston, Staffordshire', *Birmingham Warwickshire Archaeol. Soc.*, **73**, 103

(c) 'Report on the piece of samian', in G. Webster, 'A section through the legionary defences on the west side of the fortress', *J. Chester Archaeol. Soc.*, **42**, 47

(d) Note on a samian bowl and Appendix I: 'Pottery from pit 9', in W.H.C. Frend, 'Further Romano-British burials found at Arbury Road in 1953', *Proc. Cambridge Antiq. Soc.*, **49**, 25, 27

(e) Summary excavation report on Heronbridge in 'Roman Britain in 1954', *J. Roman Stud.*, **45**, 129–30

(f) Summary excavation report on High Wycombe villa in 'Roman Britain in 1954', *J. Roman Stud.*, **45**, 136

1956

(a) Review of G. Chenet & G. Gaudron, *La céramique sigillée d'Argonne des II et III siècles*, Supplément à *Gallia*, **6** (Paris, 1955), *Antiq. J.*, **36**, 106–7

(b) 'The Wandlebury Iron Age hill fort, excavations of 1955–6', *Proc. Cambridge Antiq. Soc.*, **50**, 1–27

1957

(a) 'The samian pottery', in E. E. Pickering, 'Roman Walton-le-Dale: excavation report for the years 1947–1957', *Trans. Hist. Soc. Lancashire Cheshire*, **109**, 25–37

(b) 'Samian', in D. R. Shearer, 'A note on the discoveries at Market Hall site, Worcester, 1955–56', *Trans. Worcestershire Archaeol. Soc.*, new ser., **34**, 56–9

(c) 'Samian', in G. Webster, 'A section through the Romano-British defences at Wall, Staffordshire', *Birmingham Warwickshire Archaeol. Soc.*, **75**, 27–8

(d) 'The pottery', in J. Liversidge, 'Roman discoveries from Hauxton', *Proc. Cambridge Antiq. Soc.*, **51**, 16–7

1958

(a) Report on samian ware in S. C. Stanford, 'Excavations at the Roman camp of Bravonium (Leintwardine) ', *Trans. Woolhope Natur. Field Club*, **36.1**, 97–8

(b) 'Samian pottery', in M. U. Jones, 'Excavations at Stanton Low, in the Upper Ouse Valley, during March, 1957', *Rec. Buckinghamshire*, **16.3**, 205

(c) Opinion on samian sherd in F.G. Keys & M. J. Thomas, 'Excavations of the defences of the Romano-British town at Kenchester', *Trans. Woolhope Natur. Field Club*, **36.1**, 114

(d) 'The samian ware: St. Martin's', in P. A. Rahtz, 'Dover: Stembrook and St. Martin-le-Grand, 1956', *Archaeol. Cantiana*, **72**, 131–3

(e) 'Pottery from the Exning well', in D.E. Johnston, 'A Roman well at Exning, Suffolk', *Proc. Cambridge Antiq. Soc.*, **52**, 16–20

(f) With E. Standen, 'A group of Romano-British pottery with an owner's mark', *Proc. Cambridge Antiq. Soc.*, **52**, 21–2

(g) Summary excavation report on Brough-by-Bainbridge fort in 'Roman Britain in 1957', *J. Roman Stud.*, **48**, 135

(h) Summary excavation report on Adel near Leeds in 'Roman Britain in 1957', *J. Roman Stud.*, **48**, 136

(i) Summary excavation report on Stibbington in 'Roman Britain in 1957', *J. Roman Stud.*, **48**, 139

(j) 'Samian ware', in I. Walker, 'Excavations on a Romano-British site at Astley, 1956–58', *Trans. Worcestershire Archaeol. Soc.*, new ser., **35**, 41–2

1959

(a) 'A Romano-British villa at High Wycombe', *Rec. Buckinghamshire*, **16.4**, 227–57

(b) 'Samian ware', in C. M. Daniels, 'The Roman bath house at Red House, Beaufront, near Corbridge', *Archaeol. Aeliana*, **37**, 158–60

(c) 'Pottery', in R. F. Tylecote & E. Owles, 'A second-century iron smelting site at Ashwicken, Norfolk', *Norfolk Archaeol.*, **32.2**, 156–9

(d) Pottery identifications in N. S. Smedley & E. Owles, 'Some Suffolk kilns: I – a Romano-British pottery kiln at

Homersfield', *Proc. Suffolk Inst. Archaeol. Hist.*, **28.2**, 168–84 *passim*

(e) Review of A. L. F. Rivet, *Town and country in Roman Britain* (London, 1958), *Antiq. J.*, **39**, 302

(f) Report on a samian sherd in J. W. G. Musty, 'A pipe-line near Old Sarum: prehistoric, Roman and medieval finds including two twelfth century lime kilns', *Wiltshire Archaeol. Natur. Hist. Mag.*, **57.2**, 186

(g) Dating of samian ware in B. J. Philp, 'Reculver: excavations on the Roman fort in 1957', *Archaeol. Cantiana*, **73**, 110

(h) 'Notes on pottery from some Romano-British kilns in the Cambridge area', in H. J. M. Green, 'Roman Godmanchester', *Proc. Cambridge Antiq. Soc.*, **53**, 23–8

(i) Summary excavation report on Brough-by-Bainbridge fort in 'Roman Britain in 1958', *J. Roman Stud.*, **49**, 108

(j) Summary excavation report on Water Newton in 'Roman Britain in 1958', *J. Roman Stud.*, **49**, 116–8

(k) 'Samian ware', in I. Walker, 'Excavations on a second Romano-British site at Astley and reports from the first site, 1958–59', *Trans. Worcestershire Archaeol. Soc.*, new ser., **36**, 54

1960

(a) *Notes on the Roman pottery industry in the Nene Valley*, Peterborough Museum Soc. Occas. Papers, **2** (reprinted 1972)

(b) 'The Roman fort at Bainbridge: excavations of 1957–59', *Proc. Leeds Phil.. Lit. Soc.*, **9.3**, 107–31

(c) 'Samian ware', in H. J. M. Green, 'Roman Godmanchester', *Proc. Cambridge Antiq. Soc.*, **53**, 12–14

(d) Pottery identifications in N. Smedley & E. Owles, 'Some Suffolk kilns: II – two kilns making colour-coated ware at Grimstone End, Pakenham', *Proc. Suffolk Inst. Archaeol. Hist.*, **28.3**, 203–25 *passim*

(e) Samian identifications in N. Smedley, 'Roman Long Melford', *Proc. Suffolk Inst. Archaeol. Hist.*, **28.3**, 272–89 *passim*

(f) Samian identifications in G. Webster, 'The discovery of a Roman fort at Waddon Hill, Stoke Abbott, 1959', *Dorset Natur. Hist. Archaeol. Proc.*, **82**, 93

(g) 'Samian pottery' and 'Decorated samian pottery', in A. W. J. Houghton, 'The Roman road and other Roman remains at Whitchurch, Shropshire', *Trans. Shropshire Archaeol. Soc.*, **56.3**, 232

(h) 'The samian ware', in D. F. Petch, 'Excavations at Lincoln, 1955–58', *Archaeol. J.*, **117**, 55–6

(i) Identification of a samian sherd in E. Greenfield, 'A Neolithic pit and other finds from Wingham, East Kent', *Archaeol. Cantiana*, **74**, 69

1961

(a) 'The firing of kilns of Romano-British type: archaeological notes', *Archaeometry*, **4**, 1–3

(b) 'The samian pottery', in G. Webster, 'An excavation on the Roman site at Little Chester, Derby', *Derbyshire Archaeol. J.*, **81**, 95–104

(c) 'Samian ware from Causeway site', in H. J. M. Green, 'Roman Godmanchester, Part II: The town defences', *Proc. Cambridge Antiq. Soc.*, **54**, 77–8

(d) 'Samian pottery', in K. M. Richardson, 'Excavations in Lewis's Gardens, Colchester, 1955 and 1958', *Trans. Essex Archaeol. Soc.*, 3 ser., **1.1**, 18–19

(e) 'The samian ware', in F. H. Lyon, 'A section through the defences of the Roman forts at Wall, Staffordshire', *Birmingham Warwickshire Archaeol. Soc.*, **79**, 20–22

(f) 'The samian ware', in K. A. Steer, 'Excavation at Mumrills Roman fort, 1958–60', *Proc. Soc. Antiq. Scotland*, **94**, 100–10

(g) 'Decorated samian ware', in A. D. Saunders, 'Excavations at Park Street, 1954–57', *Archaeol. J.*, **118**, 125

(h) Summary excavation report on Brough-by-Bainbridge fort in 'Roman Britain in 1960', *J. Roman Stud.*, **51**, 167, 192–3 (note on inscription)

(i) Identification of samian pottery in J. M. T. Charlton, 'Excavations at the Roman site at Holditch 1957–1959', *N. Staffordshire J. Field Stud.*, **1**, 42

1962

(a) Opinion on stamped samian ware in D. J. Smith, 'The shrine of the nymphs and the *genius loci* at Carrawburgh', *Archaeol. Aeliana*, 4 ser., **40**, 77–9

(b) 'The samian pottery', in J. A. Ellison, 'Excavations at Caister-on-Sea, 1961–2', *Norfolk Archaeol*, **33.1**, 101–2

(c) 'Decorated samian', in R. H. Hayes, 'Romano-British discoveries at Crayke, N. R. Yorks.', *Yorkshire Archaeol. J.*, **40**, 111

(d) Notes on samian in G. Webster, 'Excavations on the Roman site at Rocester, Staffordshire, 1961', *N. Staffordshire J. Field Stud.*, **2**, 43–7 *passim*

(e) 'The samian', in F. G. Keys & M. J. Thomas, 'Excavations on the defences of the Romano-British town at Kenchester: final report, *Trans. Woolhope Natur. Field Club*, **37.2**, 175–6

(f) 'The samian ware', in K. M. Richardson, 'Excavations in Parsonage Field, Watermoor Road, Cirencester, 1959', *Antiq. J.*, **42**, 167–9

(g) 'The samian ware', in C. M. Bennett, 'Cox Green Roman villa', *Berkshire Archaeol. J.*, **60**, 78–80

(h) Samian ware identifications in K. A. Steer & R. W. Feachem, 'The excavations at Lyne, Peeblesshire, 1959–63', *Proc. Soc. Antiq. Scotland*, **95**, 212–13

(i) 'Samian pottery'; and samian ware identifications in 'Appendix II: the dating evidence for site A', in S. S. Frere, 'Excavations at Dorchester on Thames, 1962', *Archaeol. J.*, **119**, 133, 137–143 *passim*

(j) Summary excavation report on Brough-by-Bainbridge fort in 'Roman Britain in 1961', *J. Roman Stud.*, **52**, 165

(k) Summary excavation report on Castor in 'Roman Britain in 1961', *J. Roman Stud.*, **52**, 169

(l) Identification of samian pottery in J. M. T. Charlton, 'Excavations at the Roman site at Holditch 1960–1961', *N. Staffordshire J. Field Stud.*, **2**, 68–9

1963

(a) 'Samian ware', in D. Fennell, 'The excavation of a Romano-British enclosure at Hawford, Worcestershire', *Trans. Worcestershire Archaeol. Soc.*, new ser., **40**, 7

(b) 'Samian', in E. Greenfield, 'The Romano-British shrines at Brigstock, Northants.', *Antiq. J.*, **43**, 254–5

(c) 'Samian pottery', in P. A. Rahtz, 'A Roman villa at Downton', *Wiltshire Archaeol. Natur. Hist. Mag.*, **58.3**, 334

(d) 'Samian ware', in D. A. White, 'Excavations at the War Ditches, Cherry Hinton, 1961–62', *Proc. Cambridge Antiq. Soc.*, **56 & 57**, 24

(e) 'Samian ware', in D. A. White, 'Excavations at the War Ditches, Cherry Hinton, 1949–51', *Proc. Cambridge Antiq. Soc.*, **56 & 57**, 39

(f) 'Decorated ware' and 'Plain ware', in A. W. J. Houghton, 'A Roman pottery factory near Wroxeter, Salop', *Trans. Shropshire Archaeol. Soc.*, **57.2**, 107

(g) Summary excavation report on Ilkley fort in 'Roman Britain in 1962', *J. Roman Stud.*, **53**, 129

1964

(a) Samian identifications in G. Webster, 'Further investigations on the site of the Roman fort at Waddon Hill, Stoke Abbott, 1960–62', *Dorset Natur. Hist. Archaeol. Soc. Proc.*, **86**, 140

(b) 'The samian ware', in J. Gould, 'Excavations at Wall (Staffordshire), 1961–63, on the site of the early Roman forts and of the late Roman defences', *Lichfield S. Staffordshire Archaeol. Hist. Soc. Trans.*, **5**, 23–9

(c) Samian ware identifications in K. J. Barton, 'Star Roman villa, Shipham, Somerset', *Somerset Archaeol. Natur. Hist.*, **108**, 73

1965

(a) 'Samian ware', in T. Potter, 'The Roman pottery from Coldham clamp and its affinities', *Proc. Cambridge Antiq. Soc.*, **58**, 15–17, 30–2

(b) 'Samian pottery', in D. B. Kelly, 'Excavations at Watergate House, Chester, 1959', *J. Chester and N. Wales Archaeol. Soc.*, **52**, 12–13

(c) With F. Pearce, 'Report on decorated samian', in M. E. Burkett, 'Recent discoveries at Ambleside', *Trans. Cumberland Westmorland Antiq. Archaeol. Soc.*, new ser., **65**, 93–101

(d) Samian identifications in C. Woodfield, 'Six turrets on Hadrian's Wall', *Archaeol. Aeliana*, 4 ser., **43**, 87–200 *passim*

(e) 'Samian ware', in N. H. Field, 'Romano-British settlement at Studland, Dorset', *Dorset Natur. Hist. Archaeol. Soc. Proc.*, **87**, 186–8

(f) With F. Pearce, 'The samian ware', in J. Gould, 'Excavations in advance of road construction between Shenstone and Wall' (Staffordshire)', *Lichfield S. Staffordshire Archaeol. Hist. Soc. Trans.*, **6**, 8–10

(g) 'Samian', in E. Greenfield & G. Webster, 'Excavations at High Cross 1955', *Leicestershire Archaeol. Hist. Soc. Trans.*, **40**, 15–20

(h) 'The samian ware', in R. R. Inskeep, 'Excavations at *Ad Pontem*, Thorpe Parish, Notts.', *Trans. Thoroton Soc. Nottinghamshire*, **69**, 33–4

(i) 'Samian', in N. P. Bridgewater, 'Romano-British iron making near Ariconium', *Trans. Woolhope Natur. Field Club*, **38.2**, 135

(j) 'Samian ware found in 1960', in C. I. Walker, 'Excavation at the Roman fort at Walltown Farm, Shropshire, 1960–1961', *Trans. Shropshire Archaeol. Soc.*, **58.1**, 13–14

(k) 'Samian ware', in A. W. J. Houghton, 'A water cistern at Viroconium (Wroxeter)', *Trans. Shropshire Archaeol. Soc.*, **58.1**, 25

(l) Summary excavation report on Brough-by-Bainbridge fort in 'Roman Britain in 1964', *J. Roman Stud.*, **55**, 203

1966

(a) 'Dating town buildings and structures', in J. Wacher (ed.), *The civitas capitals of Roman Britain*, Leicester Univ. Press, 52–9 (reprinted 1975)

(b) 'Gaulish potters' stamps', *Antiq. J.*, **46**, 102–3

(c) 'Some problems of the Roman military occupation of the north of England', *Northern Hist.*, **1**, 7–20

(d) 'The Roman fort at Ilkley: excavations of 1962', *Proc. Leeds Phil. Lit. Soc.*, **12**, 23–72

(e) 'The samian pottery', in J. A. Ellison, 'Excavations at Caister-on-Sea, 1962–63', *Norfolk Archaeol.*, **34.1**, 62–4

(f) Review of M. H. Callender, *Roman amphorae* (Oxford Univ. Press, London, 1965), *Antiq. J.*, **46**, 124–5

(g) Review of M. Durand-Lefebvre, *Marques de potiers gallo-romains trouvées à Paris et conservées principalement au Musée Carnavalet* (Histoire générale de Paris) (Paris, 1963), *Antiq. J.*, **46**, 125–6

(h) Samian ware identifications in A. Fox & W. L. D. Ravenhill, 'Early Roman outposts on the North Devon coast, Old Burrow and Martinhoe', *Devonshire Archaeol. Soc. Proc.*, **24**, 34

(i) 'Samian pottery' and 'Colour-coated ware', in P. A. Rahtz, 'Cheddar Vicarage 1965', *Somerset Archaeol. Natur. Hist.*, **110**, 74–5

(j) 'The samian', in N. Smedley & E. Owles, 'A Romano-British bath-house at Stonham Aspal', *Proc. Suffolk Inst. Archaeol. Hist.*, **30.3**, 241–3

(k) Summary excavation report on Stanground in 'Roman Britain in 1965', *J. Roman Stud.*, **56**, 206

1967

(a) 'The samian ware', in M. Todd, 'The Roman site at Little Chester, Derby: excavations in 1966', *Derbyshire Archaeol. J.*, **87**, 79–80

(b) 'Samian', in D. Charlesworth, 'Excavations on the Carrawburgh car park site, 1964', *Archaeol. Aeliana*, 4 ser., **45**, 6–16

(c) With B. M. Dickinson, 'Samian', in M. Brassington, 'Roman material recovered from Little Chester, Derby, 1965', *Derbyshire Archaeol. J.*, **87**, 47–51

(d) Samian identifications in M. Forrest, 'Recent work at Strutt's Park, Derby', *Derbyshire Archaeol. J.*, **87**, 164

(e) Samian identifications in C. J. S. Green, 'Roman remains in Durngate Street, Dorchester, *Dorset Natur. Hist. Archaeol. Soc. Proc.*, **89**, 127–32 *passim*

(f) With B. M. Dickinson, 'The samian ware', in J. Gould, 'Excavations at Wall, Staffs., 1964–6, on the site of the Roman forts', *Lichfield S. Staffordshire Archaeol. Hist. Soc. Trans.*, **8**, 17–23

(g) Opinion on samian potters' stamps in M. Biddle, 'Two Flavian burials from Grange Road, Winchester', *Antiq. J.*, **47**, 234–7

(h) With B. M. Dickinson, 'Samian', in B. Hobley, 'A Neronian-Vespasianic military site at "The Lunt", Baginton, Warwickshire', *Birmingham Warwickshire Archaeol. Soc.*, **83**, 85–99 *passim*

(i) 'Samian stamps from Tripontium', in H. Cameron & J. Lucas, 'Tripontium: first interim report on excavations by the Rugby Archaeological Society at Caves' Inn near Rugby ...', *Birmingham Warwickshire Archaeol. Soc.*, **83**, 172–5

1968

(a) With B. M. Dickinson & F. Pearce, 'The samian stamps', in B. W. Cunliffe (ed.), *Fifth report on the excavations of the Roman fort at Richborough, Kent*, Rep. Res. Comm. Soc. Antiq. London, **23**, 125–48

(b) 'The samian ware', in M. Todd (ed.), *The Roman fort at Great Casterton, Rutland*, Univ. Nottingham, 41–2

(c) 'Potters' stamps on samian ware as evidence for the date of the fort at Chester-le-Street', in J. P. Gillam & J. Tait, 'The Roman fort at Chester-le-Street', *Archaeol. Aeliana*, 4 ser., **46**, 91–6

(d) 'Samian ware', in S. C. Stanford, 'The Roman forts at Leintwardine and Buckton', *Trans. Woolhope Natur. Field Club*, **39.2**, 235–6, 249–51, 253–4, 299–305

(e) Identification of samian potters' stamps in A. C. C. Brodribb, A. R. Hands & D. R. Walker, *Excavations at Shakenoak Farm, near Wilcote, Oxfordshire – Part I: Sites A & D*, privately printed, Oxford, 43–4

1969

(a) 'Samian ware or *terra sigillata*', in R. G. Collingwood & I. A. Richmond, *The archaeology of Roman Britain*, Methuen, 235–251 (Reprinted as *Roman samian ware* (terra sigillata), Hertfordshire Archaeol. Soc., 1970)

(b) 'Samian', in E. Greenfield, 'The Romano-British settlement at Little Paxton, Huntingdonshire', *Proc. Cambridge Antiq. Soc.*, **62**, 49

(c) With B. M. Dickinson, 'Samian potters' stamps', in M. Brassington, 'Roman pottery from Little Chester', *Derbyshire Archaeol. J.*, **89**, 108–9

(d) Samian pottery identifications in G. C. Boon, 'Belgic and Roman Silchester: the excavations of 1954–8 with an excursus on the early history of Calleva', *Archaeologia*, **102**, 59

(e) 'The sherd of decorated samian', in P. J. Woods, *Excavations at Hardingstone, Northants, 1967–8*, Northamptonshire County Council, Northampton, 36

(f) 'Samian', in S. E. Rigold, 'The Roman haven of Dover', *Archaeol. J.*, **126**, 97

(g) 'The samian pottery', in J. S. Wacher, *Excavations at Brough-on-Humber 1958–1961*, Rep. Res. Comm. Soc. Antiq. London, **25**, 107–132

(h) Information on samian potters' stamps in L. Murray Threipland, 'The Hall, Caerleon, 1964: excavations on the site of the legionary hospital', *Archaeol. Cambrensis*, **118**, 111–13

(i) Summary excavation report on Brough-by-Bainbridge fort in 'Roman Britain in 1968', *J. Roman Stud.*, **59**, 206–9 *passim*

(j) Summary excavation report on Kirk Sink villa, Gargrave, in 'Roman Britain in 1968', *J. Roman Stud.*, **59**, 207

(k) Summary excavation report on Slack fort, Huddersfield in 'Roman Britain in 1968', *J. Roman Stud.*, **59**, 207

(l) Identification of a samian sherd in F. H. Goodyear, 'The Roman villa site at Hales, Staffordshire: an interim report', *N. Staffordshire J. Field Stud.*, **9**, 115

1970

(a) With K. F. Hartley, 'Pottery in the Romano-British Fenland', in C. W. Phillips (ed.), *The Fenland in Roman times*, Roy. Geological Soc. Research Memoir, London, 165–9

(b) 'Samian pottery', in P. A. Rahtz, 'Excavations on Glastonbury Tor, Somerset, 1964–6', *Archaeol. J.,* **127**, 61

(c) 'Potters' stamps on samian', in I. M. Stead, 'A trial excavation at Braughing, 1969', *Hertfordshire Archaeol.,* **2**, 44

(d) 'The samian ware', in A. A. Round, 'Excavations at Wall (Staffordshire), 1966–7, on the site of the Roman forts (Wall excavation report No. 9)', *S. Staffordshire Archaeol. Hist. Soc. Trans.,* **11**, 16–8

(e) 'Samian', in G. Webster & C. Daniels, 'A street section at Wroxeter in 1962', *Trans. Shropshire Archaeol. Soc.,* **59.1**, 19–21

(f) With B. M. Dickinson, 'The samian pottery', in C. Mahany, 'Excavations at Manduessedum, 1964', *Birmingham Warwickshire Archaeol. Soc.,* **84**, 26–8

(g) With G. Simpson, notes on the samian in S. S. Frere, 'The Roman theatre at Canterbury', *Britannia,* **1**, 93–112 *passim*

(h) Summary excavation report on Brough-by-Bainbridge fort in 'Roman Britain in 1969', *Britannia,* **1**, 279

(i) Summary excavation report on Kirk Sink villa, Gargrave in 'Roman Britain in 1969', *Britannia,* **1**, 280–1

(j) Summary excavation report on Slack fort *vicus*, Huddersfield in 'Roman Britain in 1969', *Britannia,* **1**, 281

(k) 'The dating evidence for the end of the Saalburg Erdkastell', in H. Schönberger, 'Die Namenstempel auf glatter Sigillata aus dem Erdkastell der Saalburg', *Saalburg Jahrbuch,* **27**, 28–30

1971

(a) 'Roman York and the Roman military command to the third century A.D.', in R. M. Butler (ed.), *Soldier and civilian in Roman Yorkshire,* Leicester Univ. Press, 55–70

(b) 'The samian ware', in A. C. C. Brodribb, A. R. Hands & D. R. Walker, *Excavations at Shakenoak Farm, near Wilcote, Oxfordshire – Part II: Sites B & H,* privately printed, Oxford, 59–70

(c) 'Report on the samian pottery', in M. Brassington, 'A Trajanic kiln complex near Little Chester, Derby, 1968', *Antiq. J.,* **51**, 44–6

(d) Notes on the samian in S. S. Frere, 'The forum and baths at Caistor by Norwich', *Britannia,* **2**, 23–5

(e) 'Samian ware', in M. U. Jones, 'Aldborough, West Riding, 1964: excavations at the south gate and bastion and at extra-mural sites', *Yorkshire Archaeol. J.,* **43**, 63–4

(f) Report on a samian stamp in G. J. Wainwright, 'The excavation of prehistoric and Romano-British settlements near Durrington Walls, Wiltshire, 1970', *Wiltshire Archaeol. Natur. Hist. Mag.,* **66**, 114

1972

(a) 'The Roman occupations of Scotland: the evidence of samian ware', *Britannia,* **3**, 1–55

(b) 'Samian', in A. Fox & W. Ravenhill, 'The Roman fort at Nanstallon, Cornwall', *Britannia,* **3**, 100–2

(c) 'The samian ware', in S. S. Frere, *Verulamium excavations I,* Rep. Res. Comm. Soc. Antiq. London, **28**, 216–62

(d) 'Samian pottery', in D. J. Breeze, 'Excavations at the Roman fort of Carrawburgh, 1967–1969', *Archaeol. Aeliana,* 4 ser. **50**, 119–24

(e) 'Samian', in B. Rawes, 'Roman pottery kilns at Gloucester', *Trans. Bristol Gloucestershire Archaeol. Soc.,* **91**, 50–6

(f) Comments on samian and orange wares in D. I. Higgins, 'Three groups of Romano-British coarse pottery from Caister-on-Sea, Norfolk', *Norfolk Archaeol.,* **35.3**, 283, 290

(g) 'Samian ware', in P. Wenham, 'Excavations in Low Petergate, York, 1957–58', *Yorkshire Archaeol. J.,* **44**, 104–6

(h) 'Samian ware', in A. Fox, 'Excavations at the South Gate, Exeter 1964–5', *Devonshire Archaeol. Soc. Proc.,* **26–30**, 14–7

(i) 'Samian ware', in A. C. C. Brodribb, A. R. Hands & D. R. Walker, *Excavations at Shakenoak Farm, near Wilcote, Oxfordshire – Part III: Site F,* privately printed, Oxford, 53

(j) Notes on colour-coated wares, 'Decorated samian ware' and 'Potters' stamps on undecorated samian ware', in P. J. Woods, *Brixworth excavations – vol. 1: the Romano-British villa, 1965–70,* J. Northampton Mus., **8**, 39, 44–5, 47, 49–52

1973

(a) 'Samian', in B. Hobley, 'Excavations at "The Lunt" Roman military site, Baginton, Warwickshire, 1968–71: second interim report', *Birmingham Warwickshire Archaeol. Soc.,* **85**, 45–50

(b) 'The samian potters' stamps', in H. Chapman & T. Johnson, 'Excavations at Aldgate and Bush Lane House in the City of London', *Trans. London Middlesex Archaeol. Soc.,* **24**, 54–5

(c) 'Samian ware', in F. H. Thompson & J. B. Whitwell, 'The gates of Roman Lincoln', *Archaeologia,* **104**, 172–3

(d) 'Samian ware' and 'Samian stamps', in H. Cameron & J. Lucas, 'Tripontium: second interim report on excavations by the Rugby Archaeological Society at Caves' Inn near Rugby...', *Birmingham Warwickshire Archaeol. Soc.,* **85**, 121–5, 125–7

(e) Dating of a samian sherd in K. Scott, 'A section across the defences of a Roman fort at Mancetter, Warwickshire, 1968', *Birmingham Warwickshire Archaeol. Soc.,* **85**, 212, 213

(g) 'Samian ware', in F. Pemberton, 'A Romano-British settlement on Stane Street, Ewell, Surrey', *Surrey Archaeol. Collect.,* **69**, 18–9

(h) 'The samian ware', in A.C.C. Brodribb, A.R. Hands & D. R. Walker, *Excavations at Shakenoak Farm, near Wilcote, Oxfordshire – Part IV: Site C,* privately printed, Oxford, 47–50

(i) Note on a Dr. 27 cup in R. Ling & L.A. Ling, 'Excavations at Loughor, Glamorgan: the NE and SE angles of the Roman fort', *Archaeol. Cambrensis,* **122**, 130

1974

(a) 'The samian', in S. S. Frere & J. K. St. Joseph, 'The Roman fortress at Longthorpe', *Britannia,* **5**, 91–6

(b) 'The samian ware', in D. J. Breeze, 'The Roman fortlet at Barburgh Mill, Dumfriesshire', *Britannia,* **5**, 155–6

(c) 'The decorated samian' and 'Samian potters' stamps', in A. Rae & V. Rae, 'The Roman fort at Cramond, Edinburgh, excavations 1954–1966', *Britannia,* **5**, 199–206

(d) With G. B. Dannell, 'The samian pottery', in C. J. Ainsworth & H. B. A. Ratcliffe-Densham, 'Spectroscopy and a Roman cremation from Sompting, Sussex', *Britannia,* **5**, 312

(e) 'Samian potters' stamps', in M. Hassall & J. Rhodes, 'Excavations at the new Market Hall, Gloucester, 1966–7', *Trans. Bristol Gloucestershire Archaeol. Soc.,* **93**, 37–9

(f) Information on samian potters' stamps in A. R. Budge, J. R. Russell & G. C. Boon, 'Excavations and fieldwork at Charterhouse-on-Mendip, 1960–67', *Proc. Univ. Bristol Spelaeol. Soc.*, **13.3**, 341–3

(g) 'The samian stamps', in A. Down, *Chichester excavations II*, Phillimore, Chichester, for Chichester Civic Soc. Excav. Comm., 5–6, 123–4

(h) 'Potters' stamps on samian', in D. S. Neal, *The excavation of the Roman villa in Gadebridge Park, Hemel Hempstead, 1963–8*, Rep. Res. Comm. Soc. Antiq. London, **31**, Thames and Hudson, London, 211

(i) 'The samian ware', in A. A. Round, 'The bath-house at Wall, Staffs.: excavations in 1971 (Wall excavation report No. 10)', *S. Staffordshire Archaeol. Hist. Soc. Trans.*, **15**, 21–3

(j) 'Samian pottery from the mound', in S. C. Stanford, *Croft Ambrey (excavations carried out for the Woolhope Naturalists' Field Club (Herefordshire) 1960–66)*, privately published by the author, Leominster, 150–2

(k) 'The samian potters' stamps', in H. Sheldon, 'Excavations at Toppings and Sun Wharves, Southwark, 1970–1972', *Trans. London Middlesex Archaeol. Soc.*, **25**, 39–41

(l) With B. M. Dickinson, 'Index of samian potters' stamps', in K. J. Evans, 'Excavations on a Romano-British site, Wiggonholt, 1964', *Sussex Archaeol. Collect.*, **112**, 149

(m) Comments on some samian sherds in P. J. Casey, 'Excavations outside the north-east gate of Segontium, 1971', *Archaeol. Cambrensis*, **123**, 62

(n) Summary excavation report on Kirk Sink villa, Gargrave, in 'Roman Britain in 1973', *Britannia*, **5**, 416–7

1975

(a) 'The samian ware', in V. G. Swan, 'Oare reconsidered and the origins of Savernake ware in Wiltshire', *Britannia*, **6**, 59

(b) Reports on samian ware in B. D. F. Hutty, 'Hob Ditch Causeway, final excavation report', *Birmingham Warwickshire Archaeol. Soc.*, **87**, 99–109 *passim*

(c) With B. M. Dickinson & H. Pengelly, 'Samian ware', in V. A. Maxfield & A. Reed, 'Excavations at Ebchester Roman fort 1972–3', *Archaeol. Aeliana*, 5 ser., **3**, 80–88

(d) Pottery identifications in D. F. Petch, 'Excavations in Eaton Road, Eccleston, Chester, 1972', *J. Chester Archaeol. Soc.*, **58**, 35–7 *passim*

(e) Samian potter's stamp identification in P. Marsden, T. Dyson & M. Rhodes, 'Excavations on the site of St. Mildred's Church, Bread Street, London, 1973–74', *Trans. London Middlesex Archaeol. Soc.*, **26**, 199

(f) Summary excavation report on Kirk Sink villa, Gargrave, in 'Roman Britain in 1974', *Britannia*, **6**, 238

1976

(a) With J. Morris, 'Samian ware', in F. H. Thompson, 'The excavation of the Roman amphitheatre at Chester', *Archaeologia*, **105**, 200–209

(b) 'Samian pottery', in S. S. Frere, 'The Silchester church: the excavations by Sir Ian Richmond in 1961', *Archaeologia*, **105**, 299

(c) 'Samian pottery', 'Samian stamps' and 'Additional report on samian stamps', in K. M. Kenyon, 'Excavations at Viroconium in insula 9, 1952–3', *Trans. Shropshire Archaeol. Soc.*, **60**, 18–25, 25–6, 27–8

(d) 'Samian ware', in K. Jarvis & V. Maxwell, 'The excavation of a first-century Roman farmstead and a late Neolithic settlement, Topsham, Devon', *Devonshire Archaeol. Soc. Proc.*, **31–34**, 229–32

(e) With B. M. Dickinson, notes on the samian potters' stamps in D. S. Neal, 'Northchurch, Boxmoor and Hemel Hempstead station: the excavation of three Roman buildings in the Bulbourne Valley', *Hertfordshire Archaeol.*, **4**, 104–5

(f) Samian potters' stamps identifications in P. Marsden, 'Two Roman public baths in London', *Trans. London Middlesex Archaeol. Soc.*, **27**, 55–7

(g) With H. Pengelly, 'Samian ware', in I. M. Stead, *Excavations at Winterton Roman villa and other Roman sites in North Lincolnshire*, Department Environment Archaeol. Rep., **9**, HMSO, London, 102–16

(h) 'Samian ware', in S. E. West with J. Plouviez, 'The Romano-British site at Icklingham', *E. Anglian Archaeol. Rep.*, **3**, Suffolk County Council, Ipswich, 86

(i) Summary excavation report on Kirk Sink villa, Gargrave, in 'Roman Britain in 1975', *Britannia*, **7**, 317–8

(j) Information on samian potters' stamps in T. W. J. Potter, 'Excavations at Stonea, Cambs: sites of the Neolithic, Bronze Age and Roman periods', *Proc. Cambridge Antiq. Soc.*, **66**, 44

1977

(a) 'Some wandering potters', in J. Dore & K. Greene (eds), *Roman pottery studies in Britain and beyond*, BAR Supplementary Series 30, Oxford, 251–61

(b) With B. M. Dickinson, 'The samian', in T. Potter, 'The Biglands milefortlet and the Cumberland coast defences', *Britannia*, **8**, 172–3

(c) With G. C. Boon, 'The samian ware', in P. A. Rahtz & E. Greenfield, *Excavations at Chew Valley Lake, Somerset*, Department Environment Archaeol. Rep., **8**, HMSO, London, 206–16

(d) Report on two stamped samian pieces in B. Rawes, 'A Roman site at Wells' Bridge, Barnwood', *Trans. Bristol Gloucestershire Archaeol. Soc.*, **95**, 27

(e) Notes on the samian stamps in M. J. Jones, 'Archaeological work at Brough under Stainmore 1972–77: 1. The Roman discoveries', *Trans. Cumberland Westmorland Antiq. Archaeol. Soc.*, **77**, 37–8

(f) 'Potters' stamps' and 'Decorated ware', in M. E. Burkett, 'Rescue dig in Ambleside', *Trans. Cumberland Westmorland Antiq. Archaeol. Soc.*, **77**, 179–80

(g) 'Samian ware', in P. J. Foster, R. Harper & S. Watkins, 'An Iron Age and Romano-British settlement at Hardwick Park, Wellingborough, Northamptonshire', *Northamptonshire Archaeol.*, **12**, 80–2

(h) 'Report on the samian stamps' (with B. M. Dickinson), 'Samian wares' and 'Samian stamps from the River Rib', in C. Partridge, 'Excavations and fieldwork at Braughing, 1968–73', *Hertfordshire Archaeol.*, **5**, 83–4, 98–102, 103

(i) With B. M. Dickinson, information on samian potters' stamps in C. J. S. Green, 'Excavations on the Roman kiln field at Brampton, 1973–4', *E. Anglian Archaeol. Rep.*, **5**, Norfolk Archaeol. Unit, Gressenhall, 59–63 *passim*

(j) With B. M. Dickinson, 'The samian ware', in A. Rogerson, 'Excavations at Scole, 1973', *E. Anglian Archaeol. Rep.*, **5**, Norfolk Archaeol. Unit, Gressenhall, 155–72

xxv

(k) 'The samian', in C. Smith, 'A Romano-British site at Binscombe, Godalming', *Surrey Archaeol. Collect.*, **71**, 33–6

(l) With B. M. Dickinson, 'Samian stamps', in T. R. Blurton, 'Excavations at Angel Court, Walbrook, 1974', *Trans. London Middlesex Archaeol. Soc.*, **28**, 55

(m) Samian sherd identification and 'The samian potters' stamps', in A. Gentry, J. Ivens & H. McClean, 'Excavations at Lincoln Road, London Borough of Enfield, November 1974–March 1976', *Trans. London Middlesex Archaeol. Soc.*, **28**, 130, 134

(n) Summary excavation report on Lease Rigg fort, North Yorkshire, in 'Roman Britain in 1976', *Britannia*, **8**, 381–2

(o) 'Roman camp, Lease Rigg', *Scarborough Archaeol. Hist. Soc. Trans.*, **20**, 42–3

1978

(a) With R. L. Fitts, 'Comments on some Roman material from Stanwick', *Antiq. J.*, **57**, 93–4

(b) With B. M. Dickinson, 'The samian', in G. H. Smith, 'Excavations near Hadrian's Wall at Tarraby Lane 1976', *Britannia*, **9**, 37–41

(c) 'Decorated samian ware and potters' stamps', in D. A. Jackson & T. M. Ambrose, 'Excavations at Wakerley, Northants.,1972–75', *Britannia*, **9**, 184, 191

(d) 'The samian', in J. Collis, *Winchester excavations II: 1949–1960*, Winchester City Museum, 83–5; (with G. B. Dannell) 98–101, 107

(e) With B. M. Dickinson, 'The samian stamps', in A. Down, *Chichester excavations III*, Phillimore, Chichester, for Chichester Civic Soc. Excav. Comm., 234–41

(f) Notes on samian potters' stamps in G. C. Boon, 'Excavations on the site of a Roman quay at Caerleon and its significance', in G. C. Boon (ed.), *Monographs and collections I: Roman sites*, Cambrian Archaeol. Assoc., Cardiff, 17–8

(g) With B. M. Dickinson, 'Stamped samian', in Southwark and Lambeth Archaeological Excavation Committee, *Southwark Excavations 1972–1974*, Joint Publication, **1**, London & Middlesex Archaeol. Soc. and Surrey Archaeol. Soc., 95–6, 199, 225, 233–4, 261–2, 332–3, 436–7, 469–70, 481

(h) 'Roman fort at Lease Rigg: interim report', *Scarborough Archaeol. Hist. Soc. Trans.*, **21**, 31–2

1979

(a) With B. M. Dickinson, 'Samian' in W. S. Hanson, C. M. Daniels, J. N. Dore & J. P. Gillam, 'The Agricolan supply base at Red House, Corbridge', *Archaeol. Aeliana*, 5 ser., **7**, 35–42

(b) With G. B. Dannell, 'Plain samian' (from Walcot Street), in B. Cunliffe (ed.), *Excavations in Bath, 1950–1975*, Comm. for Rescue Archaeol. in Avon, Gloucestershire and Somerset, Bristol, 107

(c) 'The samian ware', in G. Webster, 'Final report on the excavations of the Roman fort at Waddon Hill, Stoke Abbott, 1963–69', *Dorset Natur. Hist. Archaeol Soc. Proc.*, **101**, 84–5

(d) 'Report' (on samian ware), in P. A. Rahtz, *The Saxon and medieval palaces at Cheddar: excavations 1960–62*, BAR Brit. Ser., **65**, Oxford, 304–7

(e) 'The samian stamps from Chilgrove', in A. Down, *Chichester excavations IV*, Phillimore, Chichester, for Chichester Excav. Comm., 199

(f) With B. M. Dickinson, 'The potters' stamps', in J. N. Dore & J. P. Gillam, *The Roman fort at South Shields: excavations 1875–1975*, Soc. Antiq. Newcastle upon Tyne Mono. Ser., **1**, 98–106

(g) Samian ware identifications in D. J. Turner & C. R. Orton, '199 Borough High Street, Southwark: excavations in 1962', *Res. Vol. Surrey Archaeol. Soc.*, **7**, 6–20 *passim*, microfiche *passim*

(h) With B. M. Dickinson, 'Stamped samian', in W. McIsaac, I. Schwab & H. Sheldon, 'Excavations at Old Ford, 1972–1975', *Trans. London Middlesex Archaeol. Soc.*, **30**, 62

(i) Summary excavation report on Lease Rigg fort, North Yorkshire in 'Roman Britain in 1978', *Britannia*, **10**, 287

1980

(a) 'The Brigantes and the Roman army', in K. Branigan (ed.), *Rome and the Brigantes*, Univ. Sheffield, 2–7

(b) 'Potters' stamps', in B. Rawes, 'The Romano-British site at Wycomb, Andoversford: excavations 1969–1970', *Trans. Bristol Gloucestershire Archaeol. Soc.*, **98**, 26

(c) With B. M. Dickinson, 'Samian ware', in I. MacIvor, M. C. Thomas & D. J. Breeze, 'Excavations on the Antonine Wall fort of Rough Castle, Stirlingshire, 1957–61', *Proc. Soc. Antiq. Scotland*, **110**, 243–7

(d) With B. M. Dickinson, notes on the samian potters' stamps in G. Lambrick, 'Excavations in Park Street, Towcester', *Northamptonshire Archaeol.*, **15**, 70–6 *passim*

(e) Summary excavation report on Lease Rigg fort, North Yorkshire in 'Roman Britain in 1979', *Britannia*, **11**, 363

(f) 'Samian ware', in D. J. Breeze & J. N. Graham Ritchie, 'A Roman burial at High Torrs, Luce Sands, Wigtownshire', *Trans. Dumfriesshire Galloway Nat. Hist. Antiq. Soc.*, **55**, 81

(g) 'Roman fort at Lease Rigg: interim report', *Scarborough Archaeol. Hist. Soc. Trans.*, **22–3**, 8–11

1981

(a) 'The early Roman military occupation of Lincoln and Chester', in A. C. Anderson & A. S. Anderson (eds), *Roman pottery research in Britain and north-west Europe. Papers presented to Graham Webster*, BAR Int. Ser., **123** (i), Oxford, 239–47

(b) With B. M. Dickinson, 'The samian stamps', in C. Partridge, *Skeleton Green: a Late Iron Age and Romano-British site*, Britannia Mono. Ser., **2**, Soc. Promotion Roman Stud., London, 266–8

(c) 'Stamps on plain samian ware', in M. Todd, *The Roman town at Ancaster: the excavations of 1955–1971*, Universities Nottingham and Exeter, 50

(d) Summary excavation report on Lease Rigg fort, North Yorkshire in 'Roman Britain in 1980', *Britannia*, **12**, 328

(e) Information on samian potters' stamps in B. Philp, *The excavation of the Roman forts of the Classis Britannica at Dover, 1970–1977*, Kent Mono. Ser., **3**, Kent Archaeol. Rescue Unit, Dover, 178–202 *passim*

(f) With B. M. Dickinson, 'The samian stamps', in A. Down, *Chichester Excavations V*, Phillimore, Chichester, for Chichester Excav. Comm., 269–74

(g) With B. M. Dickinson, 'The samian stamps', in M. G. Jarrett & S. Wrathmell, *Whitton: An Iron Age and Roman*

Farmstead in South Glamorgan, Univ. Wales Press, Cardiff, 104–5

(h) With B. M. Dickinson, 'Catalogue', in J. R. Perrin, *Roman pottery from the Colonia: Skeldergate and Bishophill*, The Archaeology of York, **16/2**, CBA for York Archaeol. Trust, York, 70–3

1982

(a) 'Military activity', in D. A. Spratt (ed.), *Prehistoric and Roman archaeology of north-east Yorkshire*, BAR Brit. Ser., **104**, Oxford, 210–14; rev. edn published as CBA Res. Rep., **87**, York, 1993, 160–6

(b) 'Samian', in A. Poulter, 'Old Penrith excavations 1977 and 1979', *Trans. Cumberland Westmorland Antiq. Archaeol. Soc.*, **82**, 60

(c) 'The samian', in S. S. Frere, 'The Bignor villa', *Britannia*, **13**, 184

(d) With B. M. Dickinson, 'The samian', in J. Wacher & A. McWhirr, *Cirencester excavations I: early Roman occupation at Cirencester*, Cirencester Excav. Comm., Cirencester, 133–42

(e) With B. M. Dickinson, 'The samian', in A. McWhirr, L. Viner & C. Wells, *Cirencester excavations II: Romano-British cemeteries at Cirencester*, Cirencester Excav. Comm., Cirencester, microfiche 1/5 C08

(f) 'Samian ware' in G. Webster & L. Smith, 'The excavation of a Romano-British rural establishment at Barnsley Park, Gloucestershire, 1961–1979, Part II: *c*. AD 360–400+', *Trans. Bristol Gloucestershire Archaeol. Soc.*, **100**, 169–74

(g) With B. M. Dickinson, 'The samian stamps', in R. Leech, *Excavations at Catsgore 1970–1973: a Romano-British village*, Excav. Mono., **2**, Western Archaeol. Trust, Bristol, 151–2

(h) Roman pottery identifications in D. B. Taylor, 'Excavation of a promontory fort, broch and souterrain at Hurly Hawkin, Angus', *Proc. Soc. Antiq. Scotland*, **112**, 241–4 *passim*

(i) With B. M. Dickinson, 'The samian', in G. Parnell, 'The excavation of the Roman city wall at the Tower of London and Tower Hill, 1954–76', *Trans. London Middlesex Archaeol. Soc.*, **33**, 106–7, 121–3

(j) Notes on the samian potters' stamps in W. J. Wedlake, *The excavation of the shrine of Apollo at Nettleton, Wiltshire, 1956–1971*, Rep. Res. Comm. Soc. Antiq. London, **40**, Thames and Hudson, London, 154–76 *passim*

(k) With B. M. Dickinson, 'Stamped samian', in P. Bennett, S. S. Frere & S. Stow, *The archaeology of Canterbury – volume I: excavations at Canterbury Castle*, Kent Archaeol. Soc., Maidstone, for Canterbury Archaeol. Trust, 93–4

(l) Report on some samian stamps, in S. S. Frere, S. Stow & P. Bennett, *The archaeology of Canterbury – volume II: excavations on the Roman and medieval defences of Canterbury*, Kent Archaeol. Soc., Maidstone, for Canterbury Archaeol. Trust, 126

(m) 'The samian,' in T. W. Potter & C. F. Potter, *A Romano-British village at Grandford, March, Cambridgeshire*, Brit. Mus. Occas. Paper, **35**, 81–90

(n) 'Samian ware', in S. M. Elsdon, 'Iron Age and Roman sites at Red Hill, Ratcliffe-on-Soar, Nottinghamshire: excavations of E. Greenfield, 1963 and previous finds', *Trans. Thoroton Soc. Nottinghamshire*, **86**, 31–2

(o) 'The samian pottery', in A. A. Round, 'Excavations at Wall (Staffordshire), 1968–1972 on the site of the Roman forts (Wall excavation report No. 12)', *S. Staffordshire Archaeol. Hist. Soc. Trans.*, **23**, 17–26

1983

(a) Co-edited with J. S. Wacher, *Rome and her northern provinces. papers presented to Sheppard Frere in honour of his retirement from the Chair of the Archaeology of the Roman Empire, University of Oxford, 1983*, Alan Sutton, Gloucester

(b) 'The enclosure of Romano-British towns in the second century A.D.', in B. R. Hartley & J. S. Wacher (eds), *Rome and her northern provinces*, Alan Sutton, Gloucester, 84–95

(c) 'The samian', in J. Collis, 'Excavations at Silchester, Hants., 1968', *Proc. Hampshire Field Club Archaeol. Soc.*, **39**, 64–5

(d) With B. M. Dickinson, comments on samian pottery in R. G. J. Williams, 'Romano-British settlement at Filwood Park, Bristol', *Bristol Avon Archaeol.*, **2**, 15

1984

(a) 'Figured samian', in R. L. Bellhouse, 'Roman sites on the Cumberland coast: the new tower on Rise How', *Trans. Cumberland Westmorland Antiq. Archaeol. Soc.*, **84**, 47

(b) With B. M. Dickinson, samian ware identifications in P. Booth, 'Excavations at 64 Bleachfield Street, Alcester, Warwickshire, 1981', *Birmingham Warwickshire Archaeol. Soc.*, **93**, 25

(c) With B. M. Dickinson, 'The samian stamps', in K. R. Crouch & S. A. Shanks, *Excavations in Staines, 1975–6: the Friends' Burial Ground site*, Joint Publication, **2**, London & Middlesex Archaeol. Soc. and Surrey Archaeol. Soc., 34–8

(d) 'Unusual [samian] forms', in S. S. Frere, *Verulamium excavations volume III*, Oxford Univ. Comm. Archaeol. Mono.. **1**, 197–9

(e) 'Samian pottery', in F. Ball & N. Ball, '"Rescue" excavation at Wall (Staffordshire), 1980–81 (Wall excavation report No. 13)', *S. Staffordshire Archaeol. Hist. Soc. Trans.*, **25**, 17–20

(f) With B. M. Dickinson, 'The samian', in M. J. Darling, *Roman pottery from the upper defences*, The Archaeology of Lincoln, **XVI/2**, CBA, 50–1, Microfiche Appendices I–III

1985

(a) 'The samian ware', in L. F. Pitts & J. K. St. Joseph, *Inchtuthil: the Roman legionary fortress – excavations 1952–65*, Britannia Mono. Ser., **6**, Soc. Promotion Roman Stud., London, 314–22

(b) With B. M. Dickinson, 'The samian ware', in J. Dool, 'Derby Racecourse: excavations on the Roman industrial settlement, 1974', *Derbyshire Archaeol. J.*, **105**, 181–8

(c) With B. M. Dickinson, note on a signed samian bowl in A. G. Hunter, 'Building-excavations in Southgate Street and Quay Street, Gloucester, 1960', *Trans. Bristol Gloucestershire Archaeol. Soc.*, **103**, 62–4

(d) Samian identifications in C. J. Bailey, 'The Romano-British site at Walls, Punknowle, Dorset', *Dorset Natur. Hist. Archaeol Soc. Proc.*, **107**, 74

(e) With B. M. Dickinson, 'Samian ware', in A. R. Wilmott & S. P. Q. Rahtz, 'An Iron Age and Roman settlement outside Kenchester (*Magnis*), Herefordshire, excavations 1977–1979', *Trans. Woolhope Natur. Field Club*, **45.1**, 134–41 and Microfiche Section 3, Sheet 1, frames 60–77

(f) Identification of some samian ware in B. J. N. Edwards & P. V. Webster (eds), *Ribchester excavations – part 1: excavations within the Roman fort 1970–1980*, University College, Cardiff, 48–58 *passim*

(g) With B. M. Dickinson, 'The samian pottery from Anglo-Saxon contexts', in S. E. West, *West Stow: the Anglo-Saxon village volume 1*, East Anglian Archaeol. Rep., **24**, Suffolk County Council, Ipswich, 82

(h) With B. M. Dickinson, 'Samian stamps', in R. B. White, 'Excavations in Caernarfon 1976–77', *Archaeol. Cambrensis*, **134**, 78–9

(i) With B. M. Dickinson, 'The stamps', in H. R. Hurst, *Kingsholm*, Alan Sutton, Gloucester, 57–8

1986

(a) 'The samian', in P. A. Rahtz, C. Hayfield & J. Bateman, *Two Roman villas at Wharram le Street*, York Univ. Archaeol. Publ., **2**, ¶12.14.3 (no pagination), micro-fiche 26.10.4

(b) Identification of samian potters' stamps in J. D. Zienkiewicz, *The legionary fortress baths at Caerleon – II: the finds*, National Museum of Wales and Cadw, Cardiff, 49

(c) 'Samian', in T. Gregory & D. Gurney, *Excavations at Thornham, Warham and Caistor St. Edmund*, East Anglian Archaeol. Rep., **30**, Norfolk Archaeol. Unit, Dereham, 10, 29–30

(d) With B. M. Dickinson, 'The samian stamps', in M. Millett & A. Graham, *Excavations on the Romano-British small town at Neatham, Hampshire, 1969–1979*, Hampshire Field Club & Archaeol. Soc. and Farnham & District Museum Soc. Mono., **3**, 66–7

1987

(a) *Roman Ilkley*, Olicana Museum, Ilkley

(b) 'The samian', in S. S. Frere, 'Brandon Camp, Herefordshire', *Britannia*, **18**, 80–4

(c) 'Samian ware', in C. J. Webster, 'Ernest Greenfield's excavations at Exning Roman villa', *Proc. Cambridge Antiq. Soc.*, **76**, 59

(d) With B. M. Dickinson, 'The samian stamps from Boudiccan groups', in M. Millett, 'Boudicca, the first Colchester potters' shop, and the dating of Neronian samian', *Britannia*, **18**, 113–6

(e) 'Decorated and stamped samian', in N. Holbrook & A. Fox, 'Excavations in the legionary fortress at Bartholomew Street East, Exeter, 1959', *Devonshire Archaeol. Soc. Proc.*, **45**, 39–41

(f) 'The [samian] stamps', in G. B. Dannell & J. P. Wild, *Longthorpe II: the military works depot: an episode in landscape history*, Britannnia Mono. Ser., **8**, Soc. Promotion Roman Stud., London, 125

(g) With B. M. Dickinson, 'The samian', in R. Buckley & J. Lucas, *Leicester town defences: excavations 1958–1974*, Leicestershire Museums, Art Galleries and Records Service, Leicester, 75–8

1988

(a) With R. Leon Fitts, *The Brigantes*, Peoples of Roman Britain, Alan Sutton, Gloucester

(b) '*Plus ça change...*', or reflections on the Roman forts of Yorkshire', in J. Price & P. R. Wilson (eds) *Recent research in Roman Yorkshire: studies in honour of Mary Kitson Clark*, BAR Brit. Ser., **193**, Oxford, 153–9

(c) With B. M. Dickinson, 'Samian pottery', in E. Martin, 'Burgh: Iron Age and Roman enclosure', *East Anglian Archaeol. Rep.*, **40**, 30–4

(d) 'The Arretine', in T. W. Potter & S. D. Trow, 'Puckeridge-Braughing, Herts.: the Ermine Street excavations, 1971–1972', *Hertfordshire Archaeol.*, **10**, 94–6

(e) With B. M. Dickinson, 'Samian ware stamps', in P. Hinton (ed.), *Excavations in Southwark 1973–76, Lambeth 1973–79*, Museum of London, Department of Greater London Archaeology, Joint Publication, **3**, London & Middlesex Archaeol. Soc. and Surrey Archaeol. Soc., 217, 227–9, 233, 263–7

(f) With B. M. Dickinson, 'Samian potters' stamps from Corbridge' and 'Selected Dr. 29's', in M. C. Bishop & J. N. Dore, *Corbridge: excavations of the Roman fort and Town, 1947–80*, Engl. Heritage Archaeol. Rep., **8**, Historic Buildings and Monuments Commission, London, 221–8, 243–6

(g) Identification of potters' stamps in K. A. Rodwell, *The prehistoric and Roman settlement at Kelvedon, Essex*, CBA Res. Rep., **63**, CBA and Chelmsford Archaeol. Trust, 92–3

(h) Identification of some samian ware in B. J. N. Edwards & P. V. Webster (eds), *Ribchester excavations – part 3: excavations in the civil settlement 1968–1980*, Univ. College, Cardiff, 9–50 *passim*

1989

(a) 'The Romans', in D. A. Spratt & B. J. D. Harrison (eds), *The North York Moors: landscape heritage*, David & Charles, Newton Abbot, 45–54 (chap. 3)

(b) 'The samian pottery', in W. F. Moore & M. S. Ross, 'The Romano-British settlement, Common Mead Lane, Gillingham, Dorset', *Dorset Natur. Hist. Archaeol Soc. Proc.*, **111**, 59–62

(c) 'The samian ware', in C. Woodfield (with C. Johnson), 'A Roman site at Stanton Low, on the Great Ouse, Buckinghamshire', *Archaeol. J.*, **146**, 180–3

(d) With B.M. Dickinson, 'The samian stamps', in T.J. O'Leary, *Pentre Farm, Flint, 1976–81: an official building in the Roman lead mining district*, BAR Brit. Ser., **207**, Oxford, 99

(e) 'List of samian sherds' and 'Samian potters' stamps and decorated ware', in S. S. Frere & J. J. Wilkes, *Strageath: excavations within the Roman fort, 1973–86*, Britannia Mono. Ser., **9**, Soc. Promotion Roman Stud., London, 204–18

(f) With J. Bull, M. Houghton, P. Northover & R. Williams, *Penguin crime fiction, 1935–1988: a bibliographical checklist*, The Dragonby Bibliographies, **5**, Dragonby

1990

(a) With B. M. Dickinson, 'Samian ware', in J. R. Perrin, *Roman pottery from the colonia – 2: General Accident and Rougier Street*, The Archaeology of York, **16/4**, CBA for York Archaeol. Trust, York, 264–5, 275–303

(b) Samian ware identifications in P. A. Rahtz, 'Bower Chalke: excavations at Great Ditch Banks and Middle Chase Ditch', *Wiltshire Archaeol. Natur. Hist. Mag.*, **83**, 32

(c) With B. M. Dickinson, 'Samian', in S. West, *West Stow, Suffolk: the prehistoric and Romano-British occupations*, East Anglian Archaeol. Rep., **48**, 89–92

1991

(a) With B. M. Dickinson, reports on samian potters' stamps in B. Rawes, 'A prehistoric and Romano-British settlement at Vineyards Farm, Charlton Kings, Gloucestershire', *Trans. Bristol Gloucestershire Archaeol. Soc.*, **109**, 74–8

(b) 'Samian pottery', in V. A. Maxfield, 'Tiverton Roman fort (Bolham): excavations 1981–1986', *Devon Archaeol. Soc. Proc.*, **49**, 61–7

(c) 'Report on samian stamp on base fragment from F59', in P. A. Barker, R. Haldon & W. E. Jenks, 'Excavations on Sharpstones Hill near Shrewsbury, 1965–71', *Trans. Shropshire Archaeol. Hist. Soc.*, **67**, 38–9

(d) With B. M. Dickinson, 'The samian ware', in J. Hinchliffe & J. H. Williams, *Roman Warrington: excavations at Wilderspool 1966–9 and 1976*, Brigantia Mono. Ser., **2**, Univ. Manchester Department Archaeol., 31–41

(e) With B. M. Dickinson, notes on the samian potters' stamps in B. Philp *et al.*, *The Roman villa site at Keston, Kent*, Kent Mono. Ser., **6**, Kent Archaeol. Rescue Unit, Dover, 180–91 *passim*

(f) 'The new index of potters' stamps on samian ware (*terra sigillata*)', *Annales de Pegasus*, 1990–1991, 18–25

1993

(a) With B. M. Dickinson, 'The samian', in R. H. Leech, 'The Roman fort and *vicus* at Ambleside: archaeological research in 1982', *Trans. Cumberland Westmorland Antiq. Archaeol. Soc.*, **93**, 56, 58–60

(b) With B. M. Dickinson, 'Samian ware' and 'Illustrated samian', in J. Monaghan, *Roman pottery from the fortress: 9 Blake Street*, The Archaeology of York, **16/7**, CBA for York Archaeol. Trust, York, 722–5, 745–69

(c) 'Potters' stamps', in W. J. Rodwell & K. A. Rodwell, *Rivenhall: investigations of a Roman villa, church and village, 1950–77, Vol. 2*, CBA Res. Rep., **80**/Chelmsford Archaeol. Trust Rep. **4.2**, 71–2

(d) With B. M. Dickinson, information on samian potters'

stamps in A. Hannan, 'Excavations at Tewkesbury 1972–74', *Trans. Bristol Gloucestershire Archaeol. Soc.*, **111**, 49–51

(e) With B. M. Dickinson, 'The samian stamps', in W. H. Manning (ed.), *Excavations at Usk 1965–1976: the Roman pottery*, Univ. Wales Press, Cardiff, 205–15

(f) With B. M. Dickinson, 'Samian', in D. A. Gurney, J. Neve & F. M. M. Pryor, 'Excavations at Plants' Farm, Maxey, Cambridgeshire', in *The Fenland Project number 7: excavations in Peterborough and the Lower Welland Valley 1960–69*, East Anglian Archaeol. Rep., **61**, Fenland Archaeol. Trust, Peterborough, 89–90

(g) 'Samian', in W. G. Simpson, 'The excavation of Romano-British aisled buildings at Barnack, Cambridgeshire', in *The Fenland Project number 7: excavations in Peterborough and the Lower Welland Valley 1960–69*, East Anglian Archaeol. Rep., **61**, Fenland Archaeol. Trust, Peterborough, 122

1994

(a) With B. M. Dickinson, 'The samian ware', in P. Bidwell & S. Speak, *Excavations at South Shields Roman fort vol.1*, Soc. Antiq. Newcastle upon Tyne Mono. Ser., **4**, 206–8

(b) 'Thomas Griffith of York, "once Governor of the Castle and now a Debtor of the Same"', *York Historian*, **11**, 40–55

(c) With H. Pengelly & B.M. Dickinson, 'Samian ware', in C. Mahany (ed.), *Roman Alcester: southern extra-mural area, 1964–1966 excavations, 1*, CBA Res. Rep., **96**, 93–119

Forthcoming
(Publication details provisional or not known)

(a) With B. M. Dickinson & F. Wild, *Index of potters' stamps on samian ware* (provisional title)

(b) 'The Palazzo Balbi on the Rialto, or reflections on Canaletto's architectural accuracy'

(c) Samian ware reports, all with B. M. Dickinson, for the following sites: (i) Camelon; (ii) Castleford; (iii) Catterick (also with H. Pengelly); (iv) Cramond; (v)Wanborough, Wilts.

1   *Inde opes et rerum secundarum luxus,*
Stanwick and Melsonby

Leon Fitts

Brian Hartley and I share a mutual interest in the Brigantes, Cartimandua, their queen, and Stanwick, North Yorkshire. Since 1986 I have pursued our common interest, not only in the field at Stanwick, excavating with Colin Haselgrove of Durham University and Percival Turnbull, but in the archives of the Duke of Northumberland at Alnwick where key information concerning the Stanwick hoard and its provenance came to light. Subsequently, work (again with Colin Haselgrove) at Low Langdale, Melsonby, North Yorkshire commenced, based on that information (fig. 1). What follows is an assessment of some insights gained from both sites, although much of what is said about Low Langdale is at present largely conjecture as only a small fraction of the place has been excavated. Still, I know Brian will appreciate the attempt to understand the material, as well as the degree to which our knowledge of the Brigantes has increased almost out of all recognition since the time we first began to write about them.

The excavation at Stanwick has immensely advanced our knowledge of the Brigantes and their relationship to Rome. Whereas Wheeler excavated Stanwick in the 1950s, interpreting the site as materially poor and, based on Tacitus' narrative of Cartimandua, the place of Venutius' last stand, current excavations now show the material culture to be rather long-lived and wealthy, and the site not directly involved with the Roman advance under Cerialis (Wheeler 1954; Turnbull 1984; Haselgrove *et al.* 1990a). In fact, instead of a monument of resistance to Rome, Stanwick seems to have enjoyed a friendly relationship with her, and many of the remains are decidedly philo-Roman. Roman tile has been found in some quantity, as well as a ceramic assemblage that includes imported Roman table wares, with special emphasis on drink, glass and amphorae for wine. Because of their appearance on a northern native site in a pre-Flavian setting, and their exceptional quality and unusual forms, the imports have been deemed too special to be the result of trade alone and are thought to represent high-value gifts derived through diplomatic channels (Haselgrove *et al.* 1990b; Turnbull & Fitts 1988). Certainly the Roman building material may be on site too early to have arrived with the Roman army and suggests the presence of

a Roman building or the intent to build one, as well as Roman engineers to assist (Hartley & Fitts 1988, 8).

These imports, dated to the mid-1st century AD, are contemporary with dramatic changes in the landscape at Stanwick (Haselgrove *et al.* 1989, 44; Turnbull 1984, 45). A vast area of the place was surrounded by earthworks, much like a park wall, while massive fortifications with an impressive gateway on the north-west end encircled a subdivision of the marked-off area, apparently to designate the focus of the site. These massive fortifications, built as much to impress as to defend and in an architecture that is British and vernacular, indicate that in its local setting Stanwick was of the highest importance (Higham 1987, 13–16); the imports show it had importance enough to figure in the 'Roman geography' of Britain. Moreover, it would be naive to think, based on the mid-1st century AD date for the fortifications, imports, and the treaty between the Brigantes and Rome, that Roman authority was ignorant of the defenses at Stanwick. Perhaps the construction, but certainly the maintenance, of them was done with Roman knowledge and approval, as on the Continent where the Belgic élite after Caesar's conquest maintained their defended sites by privileges granted by Rome (Haselgrove 1987, 115). Thus, the imports, the fortifications and Roman interest portray Stanwick as a place of unusual distinction belonging to the Tiberian-Neronian era; and current speculation is that, at the very least, Stanwick is the seat of power of a leader of some standing, at the very best, perhaps of Cartimandua herself.

Stanwick's special standing makes it clear that it would be a target of Roman diplomatic largess; however, in a field near Low Langdale farm, Melsonby, *c.*2 km south-east from the Tofts at Stanwick and outside the fortifications, similar artifacts appear on an open settlement site, where a magnetometer survey in 1992 revealed various anomalies and 19th-century estate maps indicate the findspot of the 'Stanwick hoard' (Haselgrove *et al.* 1990a, 7–14). A trial excavation in 1994 (Fitts *et al.* 1994) produced a rather splendid circular building of Iron Age tradition, along with a work area represented by intercutting pits with burned material (fig. 2). Two

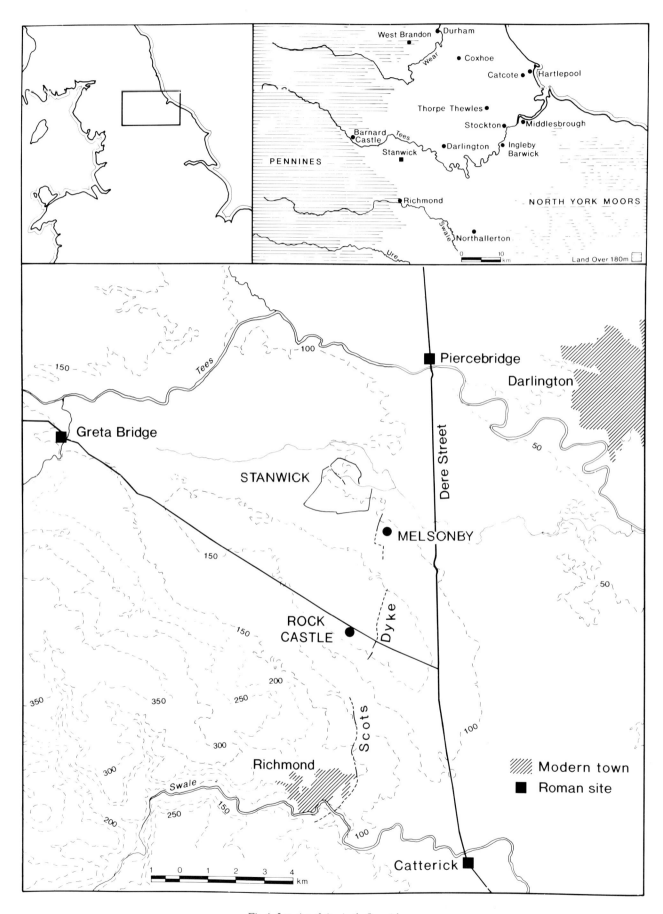

Fig. 1. Location of sites in the Stanwick area.

phases of ditches cut across the site at oblique angles to the circular building. Material recovered from ditch fills and gullies consists of Roman tile, Dressel 20 amphorae, mortaria of local fabric and mid-1st century South Gaulish samian, including decorated pieces, all of which suggests Langdale is contemporary with the floruit of Stanwick, or slightly longer in duration. Very little other pottery of either Roman or Iron Age tradition was found.

The parallel between Stanwick and Low Langdale is (as Alice says) curious and raises issues of their relationship and the meaning of the spread of Roman material in a pre-Flavian setting. That said, nothing from the excavation yet pinpoints Low Langdale's *raison d'être*. It is distinctly probable that the discovery of intercutting pits and dumps of burnt material east of the house corroborates information from the 19th century concerning the find-spot of the hoard, thus indicating not only an Iron Age context for the cache but Brigantian industrial activity. The location of Low Langdale would have enjoyed access to the metalliferous ores of the upland to the west via the Stainmore pass, and copper was available in the area; and, along with the minerals, Stanwick, a place of Brigantian élite, was a ready-made market (Haselgrove *et al.* 1990a, 89). The hoard may be evidence for a specialist/s in metal-working residing nearby Stanwick for the production and sale of native luxury items to the élite (Hartley & Fitts 1988, 14).

MacGregor in her publication of the Stanwick hoard lists three other possible uses of the find-spot: a chariot burial, a founder's hoard or a votive offering (MacGregor 1962, 19–20). Based on current information, it is difficult to choose between the three. A chariot burial seems unlikely, however. Concealment of the hoard for future recovery is a possibility, given the existence of a building on site. The site may have had a religious nature. The Stanwick hoard comprises five incomplete sets of chariot fittings and horse harness, and a set of weapons dating to the first century AD. Among the items, some are defective, broken and distorted pieces which show signs of burning for unknown purposes (MacGregor 1962, 20). At Carlingwark, Blackburn Mill and Eckford in southern Scotland (Powell 1980, 178–9; Piggott 1953) a ritual significance attaches to similar broken native objects (but they come from proven votive deposits); at Lexden near Colchester, iron-mail from the tumulus (similar to that in the hoard) is mangled, perhaps in a ritualistic manner (Dunnett 1975, 17); and from Llyn Cerrig Bach in Anglesey weapons and decorative harness metalwork are items of a watery votive offering (Fox 1946).

Moreover, there is some evidence that religious practice among the Britons and Celts was conducted in formal settings (Chadwick 1982, 163–5). Often such sites were surrounded by ditches and had within them deep shafts for timber uprights and pits for ritual, as at Frilford in Berkshire (Powell 1980, 170–71; Bradford & Goodchild 1939). At St. Margarethen-am-Silberberg in Austria a circular postbuilt hut has been interpreted as a native temple (Powell 1980, 171). None of these ingredients are blatant at Low Langdale, but as mentioned above only a small portion of the site has been dug. The Langdale building is large, *c.*10m in diameter, and eastward facing. Paralleling the interior of the wall trench of the house itself is a series of small holes apparently forming a continuous wall of sorts, and in the north-west sector of the interior is a pit. However, the pit produced no artifacts, and the interior of the hut is basically devoid of any evidence of habitation, which leaves any determination of its use as guesswork. The ditches that cut obliquely across the site are perhaps consecutive rather than contemporary and seem not to form a perimeter for the hut, but as only three have been partially recovered that possibility cannot be ruled out. Two of the ditches, west of the hut, running in a north-west/south-east direction to the axis of it, are roughly parallel and *c.*9m apart; the third ditch is *c.*60m to the east beyond the house and basically on the same course. The magnetometer survey shows them to be somewhat extensive in length, and other ditches are indicated in the unexcavated portion of the field. Taken all together, their set-up is much akin to the field boundaries found on the Roman villa at Gargrave (Hartley & Fitts 1988, 82–3), but given the proposed date of mid-1st century AD for them that possibility seems moot. Only further geophysical survey and excavation will hopefully solve this problem.

Failing any religious significance in Low Langdale itself, recent geophysical and topographical work at nearby Stanwick (Haselgrove *et al.*, forthcoming) may corroborate a sacred function of the general area. A lake/pond of some antiquity, from which skulls and other animal bones found in the 19th century may come, is suggested in the area east of the Tofts, near the Wild Mary Beck. Use of water in Celtic ritual in Britain is well known – Llyn Cerrig Bach stands as the supreme example – and the presence of water at Stanwick may help to explain its high status, as well as the presence of the Low Langdale site and its unusual hoard.

In the final analysis the house *et al.* only represent a settlement of unknown purpose and a place of someone or something that was kept tidy, as were the circular buildings at Stanwick nearby (Haselgrove *et al.*, forthcoming). The site must be distinct from the oppidum, unless one wishes to reinterpret, in the manner of the 19th-century antiquarians, Scots Dyke, which runs a few hundred metres west of the site, as part of the fortifications of Stanwick; and, in any case, as an unenclosed site outside Scots Dyke, it must be secondary compared to the enclosed oppidum. North of the Stanwick ramparts at Cat Wood, another extramural settlement of some importance may also have existed (Haselgrove *et al.* 1990b, 55–8). It has not been excavated, but coupled with Low Langdale, Cat Wood now suggests satellite settlements around Stanwick. Perhaps the inhabitants simply wanted the security of living near the extensive fortifications, had obligations to the oppidum or sought to share in the ambience of power and wealth which Stanwick represented (much like living 'within the Beltline' of Washington D.C. for many in the United States today!). In sum, Stanwick, Low Langdale and Cat Wood collectively represent a Brigantian enclave of some size in the upper northern end of the Vale of York which in its growing complexity greatly resembles the extensive oppidum at Colchester, where Sheepen, Lexden and Gosbecks made up the Trinovantian tribal capital (Dunnett 1975).

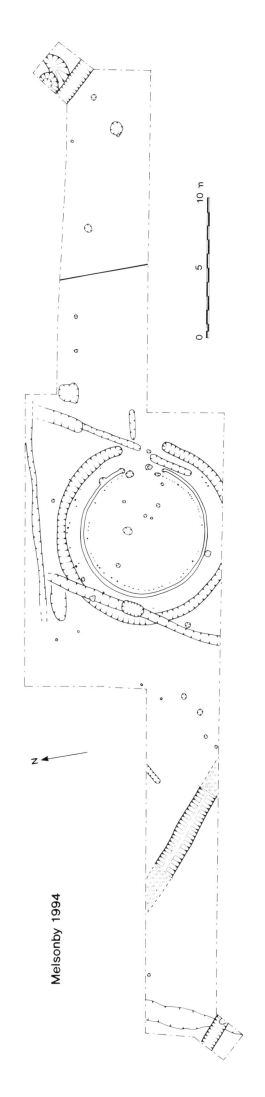

Melsonby 1994

10 m
5
0

Fig. 2. Low Langdale, Melsonby: features excavated in 1994.

5

It is clear that the ceramic assemblage from Low Langdale is pivotal to any interpretation of the site. The imports are identical to the finds at Stanwick, which implies that either the settlement at Low Langdale was important enough to be included in the diplomacy and trade aimed at Stanwick, or its proximity to Stanwick is the reason for the imports. As nothing proves the former, probability favors the latter. The hoard may represent commodities of trade, but trade, one suspects, drawn to Stanwick rather than to Low Langdale independently. Samian pottery was also recovered from the ditch (Site A of Wheeler) fronting the ramparts at Cat Wood near to the putative settlement (Wheeler 1954, pl. 23a, 10; Hartley & Fitts 1977; Haselgrove *et al.* 1990b, 55–8); if the pottery originally came from the Cat Wood settlement, then conceivably all settlements close to Stanwick shared in the luxury goods coming to it. Conversely, the more distant a native site was from Stanwick, the less likely for the appearance of Roman material on it. Rock Castle (Fitts *et al.*, forthcoming), a sub-rectangular enclosure with one or two round-huts dated to the mid- to later Iron Age, some seven miles to the south of Stanwick and Low Langdale, certainly lacks such finery. Although it is uncertain whether Rock Castle was abandoned before the Roman military intervention in AD71–2 or much earlier still, it is thought to overlap Stanwick and, given the uncertainty of its disappearance, that it shares nothing of the material culture of Stanwick or Low Langdale before the Flavian period is telling. Its distance from the epicenter of the Brigantian tribe, in some respects, may be responsible. Coxhoe in Co. Durham, north of Stanwick, likewise produces no Roman pottery (Haselgrove & Allan 1982). The few fragments of Roman pottery from the native sites of Teesdale, Thorpe Thewles, Ingleby Barwick and Catcote (Heslop 1983; 1984; 1987; Long 1988; Vyner & Daniels 1989), at great distances east of Stanwick, are often viewed as 'goods distributed more through a patron-client relationship than by trade' (Higham 1987, 15); surely the same holds true for Low Langdale next to Stanwick.

In any case, the imports tell us that both sites once enjoyed Roman delicacies, which is not too surprising since the Celtic love for wine and feasting is legendary. That tradition, which is often viewed as a commonplace, appears proven by the export of wine amphorae to Britain starting in the 1st century BC (Rankin 1987, 49–82; Peacock 1971; Fitzpatrick 1985). One can hardly doubt that wine was an important component of the ethos of ancient British society. If, as suggested above, the imports at Langdale derive from Stanwick, perhaps more than common tastes may be assumed. There is a strong tradition that the Celtic élite used wine and food as a means to retain a role of dominance or to form close bonds. In fact, Theopompus, quoted by Athenaeus, reports that Celts utilized ceremonial feasts to drug their guests in order to kill them easily. Athenaeus (151e-152f) speaks of a milder use and tells of a Louernius, who courted others for the leadership of his Galatian tribe by fencing in a space *c.*12 stadia square, within which he provided wine and vast quantities of food; Ariamnes (150b-f) also did the same by building banquet halls, each holding 400 people and continuously

stocked with food and drink. That said, anthropologists find that communities without money use drink and feasting as a means of promoting social solidarity and economic status, accomplishing projects requiring a larger communal effort, and augmenting individual power and prestige (Dietler 1990). Examples are available worldwide, but the Tarahumara of Mexico, who employ the tesqüinada (a beer party) as a 'standard method of mobilizing co-operative labor' and the Fur of the Sudan, who have a strong reluctance to exchange labor for anything but beer, illustrate the point (Dietler 1990, 365, 366). The 'feast-driven mechanism of labor mobilization' is also seen by anthropologists as nearly universal for societies with an agricultural subsistence base (Dietler 1990, 365).

It cannot be stated with certainty that the Galatian social habits were present in Celtic Britain. But, as noted above, wine was heavily imported to Britain from the Roman world, and in neighboring Gaul at least an understanding of the disrupting potential of wine and luxury items in society is certainly implied by the Nervii who forbade their importation (Caesar, *Gallic War* ii, 15). Irish tales of a later period make much of feasts and their place in that Celtic society, especially with regard to competition of warriors (Rankin 1987, 60). In sum, it is a fairly safe conclusion that manipulation of wine and/ or feasts for ulterior purpose was fairly ubiquitous among all western Celts and Britons (cf. Haselgrove 1987, 108–9).

The socio-economic circumstances of the late Iron Age at Stanwick certainly parallel those stressed by anthropologists: Roman wine and delicacies are there and at Low Langdale; the Brigantes had no currency based on metal; and pastoralism/agriculture dominated their economy (Hartley & Fitts 1988, 10–12). Moreover, the Stanwick defenses were built relatively quickly and obviously by means of corvée labor, which the leaders at Stanwick in some way had to gather and which may have been not only novel in the political world of the Brigantian confederacy, but a cause of resentment among certain tribal members (Higham 1987, 167). No doubt physical force could be used by the leadership to counteract the problem; but, given the delicacy of the confederacy, as the analogies mentioned above suggest, the élite at Stanwick may also have enticed participation. The need for labor and the need to generate power and prestige for the élite in charge thus could be reflected in the imports at Low Langdale (cf. Dietler 1990, 385–6). They may be evidence of the use of potlatch as a primary tool in tribal politics, whereby Cartimandua, or whoever, shared the material benefit from Rome with her neighbor for ulterior purposes. In that vein, the settlements at Low Langdale and Cat Wood perhaps housed part of the forces who helped build the fortifications.

Pottery aside, Roman building material at Low Langdale is especially intriguing. No other native site in Brigantia, excepting Stanwick, produces Roman tile in a pre-conquest context. As yet there is no petrological evidence that the tiles from Stanwick and Low Langdale are from a common source, nor anything to suggest a common building from which they all might come. The sites are *c.*2 km apart, and the existence of a building between them is possible, perhaps one that housed Roman forces, either in a pre-Flavian context or later

(Hartley & Fitts 1977; Higham 1987, 15). Equally, there could be a Romanised building on each site. At Stanwick, the tribal centre, such a building takes on symbolic purpose in face of the politics implied, but at Low Langdale the reason for one is more difficult to guess. Again the Stanwick hoard offers a slim clue: the hoard includes pieces made of Roman brass, which like the building materials themselves possibly hint at the presence on site of workmen skilled in Roman metallurgy (D. Dungworth, pers. comm.). In any case, a building at each site looks suspiciously like the 'grace and favour' houses built for friendly native rulers on the Continent around the borders of the empire (Turnbull & Fitts 1988, 377–8; Mócsy 1974, 89).

The assemblages from Stanwick and Low Langdale thus reveal a sympathy with the ideals of *Romanitas* that results either from trade and exchange or from deliberate policy on the part of Rome. The latter seems as probable as the former. In general, foreign dignitaries were often bestowed gifts when formally recognized by Rome, and examples from eastern parts of the empire are plentiful (Braund 1983, 27–37). The nature of such gifts varied, but all were tokens of recognition appropriate for the situation and undoubtedly served the purpose of publicly binding foreign rulers to Roman ideals. Such occasions involving British élite are little known, save in the unusual instance of Caratacus in Rome (Tacitus, *Annals* xii, 37). In AD 43 several British tribes became allies of Rome, though nothing of the nature of the official treaty is known save that it followed Roman protocol of the time in being initially created in the presence of the emperor (Millar 1988, 349). It may be the case that Cartimandua was in charge of the Brigantian confederacy by that time, and it was her decision to link her group with Rome. Certainly the Brigantes were allied to Rome by AD 47 when Ostorius Scapula, during his movement towards northern Wales, entered into Brigantia itself to quell disturbances within the tribe (Hartley & Fitts 1988, 15–16). If Cartimandua was honored with gifts in AD 43 or 47 we are not told. Tacitus (*Histories* iii, 45), however, hints that in AD 51 Cartimandua gained material rewards when she handed over Caratacus, *inde opes et rerum secundarum luxus*. In other words, Tacitus apparently viewed the situation as *quid pro quo*: Cartimandua acts with loyalty and is rewarded in return.

Tacitus supplies nothing to illustrate or substantiate his claim, nor is the precise meaning of his remark clear. Richmond long ago maintained that the Cartimandua-Caratacus episode is used by Tacitus for didactic effect to display an act done more from expediency than from passion, as if the historian wanted to underscore a moral well known to the nobility of Rome (Richmond 1954, 52). Moreover, what Tacitus says about the Celts is often colored by his view of them as noble savages whose heroic code is uncorrupted by urban civilization (Rankin 1987, 147–50); and such may obtrude in this instance. His use of *ops* and *res secunda* insinuates resources and prosperity out of the ordinary, items to be calculated as foreign in the native definition of the terms. *Luxus* for the historian means excess or extravagance, and he generally uses the term in both the *Histories* and *Annals* to vilify,

not compliment, members of the highest social rank. Tacitus may have accepted the tradition (Diodorus v, 22) that the Celts had no contact with 'luxury produced by wealth,' or the oft-repeated commonplace that people, absent from the monied worlds of Greece and Rome, were less open to temptations of evil and had a primal purity (Rankin 1987, 49). Tacitus thus perhaps compares the rustic world of the Brigantians and the cosmopolitan one of Rome to show that Cartimandua, a product of barbarism living on the periphery of the Roman world, was subject to the frailties of her own innocence in the face of Roman decadence.

Regardless of Tacitus' prejudices or ulterior motives, it seems likely that Rome honored Cartimandua in tangible ways. Not only was it the proclivity of Rome to bestow gifts, she surely kept abreast of the tenuous nature of Cartimandua's confederacy and its internal troubles, which included, *inter alia*, the possible resentment about the building and/or maintenance of the fortifications at Stanwick. No doubt Roman authority also recognized the importance of luxury items within a tribal setting that practiced potlatch and where power and prestige were based on outward manifestations, 'prestige goods', and they supplied them or at least seriously promoted them. Such goods are difficult to distinguish in the archaeological record, but in a continental context it is suggested that they will probably be artifacts which require rare materials, considerable technical skills and foreign trade goods (Haselgrove 1982, 82). The imports from Stanwick and Low Langdale easily fall into these categories and begin arriving at Stanwick around AD 43 and continue until the conquest by Cerialis; in part they must represent the *opes et rerum secundarum luxus* mentioned by Tacitus

ACKNOWLEDGEMENTS

My thanks to Robert Sider, C.C. Haselgrove, Steve Willis, Pam Lowther and David Dungworth who read the draft of this paper; Pam Lowther also kindly provided figs. 1 and 2. I owe a lot to them for their suggestions and corrections, but I remain responsible for the contents of the paper.

Bibliography
Primary sources
Athenaeus, *Deipnosophistae*
Gaius Julius Caesar, *The Gallic war (BG)*
Diodorus Siculus, *World history*
Publius Cornelius Tacitus, *Annals*
Publius Cornelius Tacitus, *Histories*

Bradford, J.S.P., & Goodchild, R.G., 1939 Excavation at Frilford, Berkshire. 1937–8, *Oxoniensia*, **4**, 170
Braund, D. C., 1983 *Rome and the friendly king*
Chadwick, N., 1982 *The Celts* (Harmondsworth)
Dietler, M., 1990 Driven by drink: the role of drinking in the political economy and the case of early Iron Age France, *J. Anthropol. Archaeol.*, **9**, 352–406.
Dunnett, R., 1975 *The Trinovantes* (London)
Fitts, R.L., Haselgrove, C.C., & Willis, S., 1994 Excavations at Melsonby, North Yorkshire, 1994, *Durham Archaeol. Rep.* (forthcoming)
————, ————, Lowther, P.C., & Turnbull, P., forthcoming An Iron

Age farmstead at Rock Castle, Gilling West, North Yorkshire, *Durham Archaeol. Rep.*

Fitzpatrick, A., 1985 The distribution of Dressel 1 amphorae in north-west Europe, *Oxford J. Archaeol.,* **4.3**, 305–40

Fox, C., 1946 *A find of the early Iron Age from Llyn Cerrig Bach, Anglesey* (Cardiff)

Hartley, B.R., & Fitts, R.L. 1977 Comments on some Roman material from Stanwick, *Antiq. J.* **57**, 93–4

_____, & _____, 1988 *The Brigantes* (Gloucester)

Haselgrove, C.C., 1982 Wealth, prestige and power: the dynamics of late Iron Age political centralization, in *Ranking, resources and exchange* (eds C. Renfrew & S. Shennan), 79–88 (Cambridge)

_____, 1987 Culture process on the periphery: Belgic Gaul and Rome during the late Republic and early Empire, in *Centre and periphery in the ancient world* (eds M. Rowlands, M. Larsen, & K. Kristiansen), 104–24 (Cambridge)

_____, & Allen, V.L., 1982 An Iron Age settlement at West House, Coxhoe, County Durham, *Archaeologia Aeliana*, 5 ser, **10**, 25–51

_____, Willis, S.H., Fitts, R.L., & Turnbull, P., 1989 Excavations in the Tofts, Stanwick, North Yorkshire, *University of Durham Archaeol. Rep. 1989*, 40–5

_____, Turnbull, P., & Fitts, R.L., 1990a Stanwick, North Yorkshire, Part 1: Recent research and previous archaeological investigations, *Archaeol. J.*, **147**, 1–15

_____, Lowther, P., & Turnbull, P., 1990b Stanwick, North Yorkshire, part 3: excavations on earthworks sites 1981–86, *Archaeol. J.*, **147**, 37–90

_____, *et al.*, forthcoming Excavations in the Tofts, Stanwick, North Yorkshire, 1984–9, *Archaeol. J.*

Heslop, D., 1983 The excavation of an Iron Age settlement at Thorpe Thewles, in *Recent excavations in Cleveland*, 17–26 (Cleveland)

_____, 1984 Initial excavations at Ingleby Barwick, Cleveland, *Durham J. Archaeol.*, **1**, 23–34

_____, 1987 *The excavation of an Iron Age settlement at Thorpe Thewles, Cleveland, 1980–1982*, Counc. Brit. Archaeol. Res. Rep., **65**

Higham, N.J., 1987 Brigantia revisited, *Northern Hist.*, **23**, 1–19

Long, C., 1988 The Iron Age and Romano-British settlement at Catcote, Hartlepool, Cleveland, *Durham Archaeol. J.*, **4**, 13–35

MacGregor, M., 1962 The early Iron Age metalwork hoard from Stanwick, North Riding of Yorkshire, England, *Proc. Prehist. Soc.*, **28**, 17–57

Millar, F., 1982 Emperors, frontiers and foreign relations, 31 BC to AD 378, *Britannia*, **13**, 1–23

_____, 1988 Government and diplomacy in the Roman empire during the first three centuries, *Internat. Hist. Rev.*, **10.3**, 345–516

Mócsy, A., 1974 *Pannonia and Upper Moesia* (London)

Peacock, D.P.S., 1971 Roman amphorae in pre-Roman Britain, in *The Iron Age and its hill-forts* (eds D. Hill & M. Jesson), 161–88 (Southampton)

Piggott, S., 1953 Three metal-work hoards of the Roman period from southern Scotland, *Proc. Soc. Antiq. Scotland*, **87**, 1–50

Powell, T.G.E., 1980 *The Celts* (London)

Rankin, H.D., 1987 *Celts and the classical world* (London and Sydney)

Richmond, I.A., 1954 Queen Cartimandua, *J. Roman Stud.*, **44**, 43–53

Turnbull, P., 1984 Stanwick in the northern Iron Age, *Durham Archaeol. J.*, **1**, 41–51

_____, & Fitts, L., 1988 The politics of Brigantia, *BAR*, **193**, 377–86 (Oxford)

Vyner, B., & Daniels, R., 1989 Further investigation of the Iron Age and Romano-British settlement at Catcote, Hartlepool, Cleveland, *Durham Archaeol. J.*, **5**, 1–10

Wheeler, R.E.M., 1954 *The Stanwick fortifications, North Riding of Yorkshire*, Rep. Res. Comm. Soc. Antiq. London, **17** (Oxford)

2   Tacitus on Agricola: truth and stereotype

R. H. Martin

Fifty years ago Ian Richmond wrote a short account of the life and career of Gnaeus Iulius Agricola (*J. Roman Stud.*, **34** (1944), 34–45); his appraisal was both judicious and generous.[1] Today a more overtly critical stance is favoured by many scholars: Agricola is seen as no more than 'a man of honest mediocrity',[2] whose reputation owes much to 'the clear bias of the author Tacitus in favour of the subject of his biography'.[3] In a volume offered as a tribute to Brian Hartley there is no need to state that the validity of Tacitus' statements about Agricola's career in Britain must continue to be rigorously scrutinised by archaeologists; in particular the task of determining what is to be ascribed to Agricola and what to his immediate predecessors and successors still leaves a significant margin of uncertainty. And, with regard to Tacitus' biography of his father-in-law, it is undeniable that both the conventions of the genre and the claim of *pietas* encouraged a substantial degree of enhancement. It is with two aspects of that enhancement that I wish to deal here: first I shall argue that the belief that Tacitus sought to promote that enhancement by disparaging the achievements of Agricola's predecessors is ill-founded; then I shall consider briefly some of the ways in which Tacitus did in fact seek to heighten the picture he draws of Agricola.

It is particularly regrettable that we have lost all those books of Tacitus' *Histories* that would have included an account of Britain under the governorships of Cerialis, Frontinus and Agricola himself. But not all points of comparison are lost to us; in the cases of Suetonius Paullinus and Petillius Cerialis, under both of whom Agricola served in Britain, there is enough material in the surviving books of *Histories* and *Annals* to make possible a direct comparison with the treatment Tacitus gives them in *Agricola*. It is simpler to begin with Cerialis, since the material has already been assembled and discussed by A. R. Birley. Birley rightly concludes that 'Tacitus can be seen ... to have viewed Cerialis' career ... in a critical light'.[4] In the *Histories* Cerialis is described as *incautus* (3.79.1) and characterised by *temeritas* (4.76.3, 77.2), while in *Annals* 14.32.3 his dash to the defence of Camulodunum, which ended with the rout of the ninth legion and his retreat within the safety of his camp, is described as a disaster (*clades*). But

what Tacitus says of Cerialis in the *Agricola* is much more favourable. In 8.2 he is spoken of as a governor under whom 'habuerunt uirtutes spatium exemplorum'. In chapter 17 he appears as the first of the series of governors appointed by Vespasian, of whom Tacitus says 'magni duces, egregii exercitus', while the statement 'magnamque Brigantum partem aut uictoria amplexus est aut bello' is, both by virtue of its context and the striking and unparalleled verbal phrase,[5] expressive of praise, not disparagement of a task begun but not completed. This is the first mention in the *Agricola* of the Brigantes ('numerosissima [sc. *ciuitas*] prouinciae totius'), and Cerialis' success, Tacitus says, was such that only Frontinus could match or surpass it. It is perhaps significant too that, though there is an allusion to Cerialis' debacle with the ninth legion during the Boudiccan revolt, it is done anonymously, by means of a rhetorical plural (5.2 'trucidati ueterani, incensae coloniae, intersaepti [intercepti *Puteolanus*] exercitus'). It seems incontrovertible, then, that Tacitus' treatment of Cerialis in the *Agricola* is more, not less, favourable than in his other writings. Incidentally, it is clear that the single sentence that Tacitus accords to Iulius Frontinus (17.2) is also one of praise, not depreciation; he matched the attainments of Cerialis and, by his subjugation of the 'pugnacem Silurum gentem', earned the right to be regarded as 'uir magnus' – a powerful phrase, whose connotation is discussed further below.

Evaluation of the judgement that Tacitus makes in the *Agricola* on Suetonius Paullinus is more difficult; for in addition to his prominent role on the Othonian side during the civil wars of AD 69 we have in book 14 of the *Annals* an extended account of the Boudiccan revolt that occurred in the last year of his governorship (AD 61 or 60). Thus a direct comparison is possible between Suetonius' role as depicted in the *Agricola* and – some twenty years later – in the *Annals*. When allowance is made for the shorter compass that the biography allows to the affair, one is at first struck by the similarities between the two accounts. In both cases Boudicca's revolt takes place when Suetonius is engaged in reducing Mona (Anglesey), which he sees as 'uires rebellibus ministrantem' (*Agricola* 14.3), or as a 'receptaculum perfugarum' (*Annals* 14.29.3); in both cases he hurries back to the mainland and wins a decisive battle ('unius proelii fortuna' (*Agricola* 16.2); 'clara et antiquis uictoriis par ea die laus parta' (*Annals* 14.37.2)); in both cases his determination to exact revenge for the revolt leads to his replacement by a less harsh successor, Petronius Turpilianus (*Agricola* 16.3 *mitior*, *Annals* 38.3 *clementer*). Admittedly the version in the *Annals* develops the idea, missing in the *Agricola*, that Suetonius' recall was engineered by the intrigue of the procurator Iulius Classicianus and Nero's freedman adviser, Polyclitus, but in essence the two versions can be regarded as covering the same ground in virtually the same way. Yet there is a difference that may be of some significance. Though Suetonius is elsewhere described as 'cunctator natura' (*Histories* 2.25.2), according to the version in *Annals* 14 his decision to attack Anglesey was motivated by a desire to rival the fame that Corbulo had won by his re-conquest of Armenia (*Annals* 14.29.2 'rumore populi ... Corbulonis concertator, receptaeque Armeniae decus aequare domitis perduellibus cupiens' – the strikingly unusual words *concertator* and *perduellibus* emphasise the importance Tacitus attaches to the phrase). In the *Agricola* the description of Suetonius at 5.1 as 'diligenti ac moderato duci' and the insistence at 14.3 that it was only after successes during the first two years of his governorship and after strengthening his position with garrisons among the defeated peoples ('subactis nationibus firmatisque praesidiis') that he felt the confidence ('quorum fiducia') to invade Anglesey are more in keeping with the description of him at *Histories* 2.25.2 as one 'cui cauta potius consilia cum ratione quam prospera ex casu placerent'. I can see no evidence that Tacitus treated Suetonius less favourably in the *Agricola* than in his later works; if anything, the contrary is the case.

If, then, Tacitus does not seek to enhance Agricola's stature by disparagement of his predecessors, how does he achieve that end? Among the ways open to him two in particular seem to deserve attention: the overall structure of the work and the use of linguistic cross-references. It is to these that I now turn.

It is natural that the attention of the archaeologist should focus on the chapters that deal with Agricola's years in Britain (chapters 5, 8, 18–38), but those chapters need to be seen in relation to the structure of the biography as a whole; for the historical core of the work is set within a framework that helps to throw light on the manner in which the portrait of Agricola is drawn. The opening words, 'Clarorum uirorum facta moresque *posteris tradere*' are balanced by the final words, 'Agricola *posteritati* narratus et *traditus* superstes erit' (46.4), while the theme of chapters 1–3, that the times are hostile to the display of excellence (*uirtus*), is developed in the concluding chapters (39–46), where Agricola's *uirtutes* are portrayed as having incurred the suspicion and enmity of Domitian. But, whereas in the opening chapters this theme is broached only in general terms (Domitian is never mentioned by name and Agricola only in the final sentence (3.3), where it forms a link to the first words of the next section (4.1: 'Gnaeus Iulius Agricola...')), Agricola and Domitian are both named repeatedly in the closing chapters.

The structure of the historical core of the *Agricola* is straightforward: biographical details of Agricola's life before he became governor of Britain (chapters 4–9); a survey of the geography and ethnography of the island (10–12); a brief account of the earlier history of Roman Britain from Julius Caesar to the governorship of Frontinus (13–17); there then follows an extended account of Agricola's own governorship of the province (18–38). This section, which constitutes the 'core of the core' of the work, is itself significantly split in two by the account of the astonishing voyage of the Usipi (28), which marks off in roughly equal halves Agricola's first six campaigns from his final campaign and the victory of Mons Graupius. The disproportion of the space allotted to the first six years and the final year of Agricola's term of office is designed to signalise the victory of Mons Graupius as the climax of Agricola's career and as effectively marking the completion of the conquest of Britain. Even more striking to the modern reader is the fact that half of the space of the final year's narrative is given over to the respective speeches of the opposing generals – Calgacus on the British side (chapters 30–32, about 70 lines) and Agricola on the Roman side (chapters 33–34, just under 40 lines). Neither speech – as Tacitus' readers were well aware – makes the slightest claim to reproduce what (if anything) either leader said before the battle; instead, both draw heavily on ideas and language to be found in the speeches (equally fictitious) in comparable situations in Sallust and Livy, and, to a lesser extent, Caesar. Tacitus' choice of the invented speech as a way of emphasising the significance of Agricola's final year in Britain carries an important implication for our understanding of the narrative of the earlier years' campaigns in Britain: where we should have welcomed a greater number of factual details, Tacitus has preferred to elevate the subject of his biography by generalising his role.

Tacitus' description of the ensuing battle led Mommsen to castigate him as 'this most unmilitary of all writers'.[6] In fact Mommsen to a large extent was rebuking Tacitus for failing to do what he never set out to do. Like so much else in the *Agricola* the battle of Mons Graupius is an amalgam of the specific and the commonplace. Tacitus must have heard from his father-in-law – probably more than once – an account of the decisive battle of his career, and despite many conventional motifs there are clearly also a number of details, such as those of the terrain and the Roman strategy, that seem to reproduce with some accuracy what actually occurred. But – perhaps significantly as an indication of what interested Tacitus and how he handled his material – the most graphic portion of the narrative is that which describes the carnage that met the eye as the Roman forces pressed home their victory: 'tum uero patentibus locis grande et atrox spectaculum: sequi uulnerare capi' (37.2). We cannot say that this is not what actually happened, but Tacitus' description is directly modelled on Sallust, *Jugurtha* 101.11, where, as the enemy are routed, the scene is described as follows: 'tum spectaculum horribile in campis patentibus: sequi fugere, occidi capi'.

This echo of Sallust affords a convenient point of transition to the second method by which Tacitus enhances Agricola's role, namely the use of verbal cross-references. These may be within the *Agricola* itself or to other authors (as to Sallust immediately above), and may consist of the significant repetition of individual words (e.g. *uirtus*) or of the echoing of extended phrases (as Sallust *Jugurtha* 101.11, quoted above). This technique, which persists in all Tacitus' writings from *Agricola* to *Annals*, is used in various ways and contexts, but common to all instances is that it adds emphasis and resonance. A notable example is afforded by the *Agricola*'s opening words: 'clarorum uirorum facta moresque' is a double allusion to the elder Cato's *Origines*, commonly regarded as inaugurating Latin historiography (the earlier history of Fabius Pictor being written in Greek), sc. 'clarorum uirorum atque magnorum' (Cato, *Origines* fr.2 = Cicero, *Pro Plancio* 66) and 'clarorum uirorum laudes atque uirtutes' (Cato fr. 118 = Cicero, *Tusculan Disputations* 4.3). On Tacitus' purpose in beginning his biography of Agricola with the allusions to Cato, Ogilvie[7] *ad loc.* writes: 'Tacitus is … acknowledging his agreement with Cato's belief that success in life is to be won by personal achievement (*uirtus*) rather than by circumstances, birth or position. This was one of the themes of the *Origines*: it was illustrated by the career of Agricola'. What, however, Ogilvie does not note is that these opening words also point forward to a statement within the *Agricola*'s historical core, when, after Agricola's successes during his first campaigning season, Tacitus says, 'ita … clarus ac magnus haberi Agricola' (18.5). This statement is doubly significant: (i) *clarus ac magnus* ascribes to Agricola those qualities that the elder Cato regarded as worthy of a historian's praise. Here Ogilvie's assertion that the two adjectives are 'a frequent collocation' is misleading. Though Cicero has *clari et* (not *ac* or *atque*) *magni* at *de Oratore* 2.19 and *Philippics* 14.33, the normal order (Cicero, Sallust, *Jugurtha* 92.1, Livy, Pliny, *Epistulae* 1.10.8) is *magnus … clarus*. Only at Sallust, *Catiline* 53.1 do we have *clarus atque magnus*, where the word order and the following *habetur* make it certain that Tacitus is here making a specific allusion to the Sallustian passage; (ii) the allusion is given further resonance by the fact that in Sallust the phrase is predicated of Cato, the great-grandson of the elder Cato.[8] We have no means of knowing whether, in fact, people at Rome *were* talking of Agricola in those terms, but Tacitus' use of the Sallustian allusion has a different purpose – to affirm his conviction that, by the end of his first season as governor of Britain, Agricola had already done enough to justify his inclusion in the ranks of those to whom the title of greatness could be applied.

The achievements which, according to Tacitus, had caused Agricola to be regarded as 'clarus ac magnus' are against the Ordovices and in Anglesey. In neither case does Tacitus claim that Agricola had been breaking new ground, and when he claims that in the former case an engagement resulted in 'the almost total annihilation of the people' (18.3), some allowance needs to be made for the biographer's *amplificatio*. A further point remains to be noted about the year's narrative. At the outset of the engagement with the Ordovices Tacitus says of Agricola (18.2) 'ipse ante agmen … erexit aciem', which combines a clear reminiscence of Sallust, *Catiline* 59.1 with a Livian phrase (*aciem erigere*). On this Ogilvie notes that this is a gesture that 'conventional rhetoric commonly expected of a brave general', and expressed it as unlikely that 'many generals (or Agricola on this occasion) did lead their troops in person'. If

that scepticism is justified we have the first of many instances (amply noted by Ogilvie) of a commonplace being used to enhance Agricola's fame. Though it may oversimplify matters, there may be some truth in saying that in at least four of Agricola's first five campaigns the narrative contains three similar elements, sc. (i) a small factual element, mostly expressed without identifying features; (ii) one or more commonplaces identifying Agricola as a model general; (iii) some further comment, often by other people, informed or not, on Agricola's actions or opinions.

In the narrative of Agricola's second campaign (chapter 20) that technique is again employed. Tacitus neither mentions the fact that Agricola was traversing ground which, at least in part, Cerialis had covered before him nor names the people in whose territory he was operating. In fact, it is the extensive territory of the Brigantes in northern England that Agricola brought under control during that season. That substantial achievement is indicated by no more than the statement that 'multae ciuitates … datis obsidibus iram posuere et praesidiis castellisque circumdatae …' (20.3). But Agricola's own actions are enhanced by a series of commonplaces that are characteristic of an outstanding general; so, especially in 20.2, the actions described have analogues, sometimes with verbal echoes, in Sallust and Livy (and Statius!).[9]

Agricola's third season saw him for the first time moving into wholly unknown territory (22.1 'nouas gentes aperuit'), and we are given a name to mark the northern limit of his advance ('usque ad Taum'). But, that apart, we are given only generalisations, often expressed in commonplaces. So, when (22.2) Tacitus says that experts noted that no fort (*castellum*) set up by Agricola was ever stormed or unwillingly abandoned, that too is a *topos*. But that does not necessarily mean that the statement is untrue. The matter is further complicated by Ogilivie's assertion that *adnotabant periti* 'implies that Tacitus consulted written sources' (sc. written by military experts). However, the seemingly documentary assurance of the phrase may be illusory; compare the same phrase at *Annals* 12.25.2 with Suetonius, *Claudius* 39.2, and cf. *Histories* 3.37.2.

The fourth year was marked by consolidation along the Clyde-Forth line. Though it is the shortest of the narratives of any year (seven lines in all), paradoxically it is, in topographical detail, more specific than any other year's narrative. We are not only given the names of the Firths of Clyde and Forth (23.1 'Clota et Bodotria'), but the picture of the deep intrusion of the waters of the opposing firths is more exact than that of any other physical feature in the *Agricola* apart from the vivid description of the western sea-lochs in the geographical section at 10.6. The short chapter also contains one interesting comment: the Clyde-Forth line, Tacitus says, would have provided a permanently defensible line, 'had that been permitted by the valour of the army and the glory of the Roman name' (si uirtus exercitus et Romani nominis gloria pateretur'). The oblique wording at the same time excuses the relative inactivity of the fourth summer and alludes to the unquenchable enthusiasm of Agricola and his army for further advance.

The fifth season, unlike the year just passed, saw further advance into, and conquest of, 'ignotas ad id tempus gentes'

(24.1). Contrary to the impression we had gained from the previous chapter, sc. that everything up to the Clyde-Forth isthmus had been secured, it now transpires that the peoples hitherto unknown in fact consisted of the tribes of south-west Scotland, sc. Ayrshire and Galloway. But beyond a short initial statement that Agricola subdued these unknown tribes 'crebris simul ac prosperis proeliis' (24.1) the narrative of the year is devoted exclusively to the fact that it was from the coast here that Agricola looked across the sea to Ireland and expressed the option that Ireland could be occupied and held 'legione una et modicis auxiliis' (24.3). 'Saepe ex eo audiui' (24.3) appears to tell us that we here have the explicit, and frequently repeated (*saepe*), testimony of Agricola himself. However, the statement in Strabo 4.5.3 that a single legion with some cavalry would have sufficed for a successful invasion of Britain in the time of Augustus suggests that here too we may be dealing with a *topos* rather than the *ipsissima uerba* of Agricola. Statements of the type 'saepe audiui' (cf. *Annals* 3.16.1 'audire me memini'; 3.50.2 'saepe audiui principem nostrum conquerentem' (in an invented speech)) present problems which cannot be entered into here. On balance it seems likely that, as at *Agricola* 4.3 ('memoria teneo solitum ipsum (sc. *Agricolam*) narrare ...'), we do in fact have a genuine utterance of Agricola.

The broad outline of Agricola's sixth campaign is clear: first a move beyond the Firth of Forth (25.1), in which the army was supported by the fleet, and then the initial contacts with the inhabitants of 'Caledonia'. A surprise attack on the camp of the ninth legion is repulsed in the nick of time by the arrival of Agricola with 'uelocissimos equitum peditumque' (26.1); a battle was fought outside the gates of the camp, 'in ipsis portarum angustiis' (26.2), and the enemy were overwhelmingly defeated. The attack on the ninth legion's camp and a Roman victory may be taken as authentic. How much else of the military detail is factual we have no means of telling. But much of the military description draws on phraseology already to be found in comparable situations in Livy. Moreover this cameo of a disaster narrowly averted is framed by the observations of the 'ignaui specie prudentium' before the event (25.3) and their loud-mouthed acclamations at its successful outcome – the adjective *magniloquus* (27.1) is used by no other classical prose author.

One further point (though it is simple and obvious) deserves to be noted. The narrative of Agricola's sixth campaign occupies almost fifty lines – more than the total of the three previous years. Tacitus is already building up to the climax of Agricola's final year in Britain and the battle of Mons Graupius; but the greater space he accords to the penultimate year's narrative is not used to introduce a greater amount of factual detail, but to develop a more dramatically organised account of the action. As in the narrative of the previous years of Agricola's governorship a relatively small factual kernel is embellished by the addition of commonplaces and resonant echoes of earlier writers, especially Sallust and Livy. That is

a technique well-known from the prescriptions of rhetorical handbooks for the handling of the themes of praise and blame. It also corresponds exactly to the request that the younger Pliny makes in a famous letter to Tacitus (7.33), in which he asks to be included in the historical work on which Tacitus was currently engaged (the work we know as the *Histories*). In paragraph 10 of that letter Pliny writes: 'haec (sc. Pliny's own actions) ... notiora clariora maiora tu facies'. Pliny is talking of history, but his remarks will apply equally to the writing of biography. That Tacitus has made Agricola's achievements *maiora* is not in question; whether in so doing he has 'exceeded the limits of truth' (the words again are Pliny's) is another matter. But what I have tried to show is how Tacitus has attained a significant degree of enhancement, not by a resort to falsehood, but by uniting a small, but significant core of factual achievements to a broader spread of laudatory generalisation. The resulting portrait is a fitting tribute to Tacitus' dead father-in-law, and one that may lead the reader to echo Tacitus' own words: 'bonum uirum facile crederes, magnum[10] libenter' (44.2) – 'you could easily believe him a good man, gladly a great one'.

Notes

1. The best modern commentary on the *Agricola* remains that of R.M. Ogilvie & I. A. Richmond (Oxford, 1967); there is some valuable additional linguistic material in H. Heubner, *Kommentar zum Agricola des Tacitus* (Göttingen, 1984). Volume II.33.3 of *Aufstieg und Niedergang der römischen Welt* (Berlin/New York, 1991) has four articles on the *Agricola*; those by W.S. Hanson ('Tacitus' *Agricola*: an archaeological and historical study', pp.1741–84) and M.-Th. Raepsaet-Charlier ('Cn. Julius Agricola: mise au point prosopographique', pp. 1807–57) have substantial bibliographies. The full Latin text of the *Agricola*, with Ogilvie's revision of Hutton's translation, is contained in the revised Loeb edition of the minor works of Tacitus (Cambridge, Mass., & London, 1970).

     A brief conspectus of the evidence of Tacitus and archaeology can now be found in Brenda Dickinson & Brian Hartley, 'Roman military activity in 1st century Britain: the evidence of Tacitus and archaeology', *Papers Leeds Internat. Latin Seminar*, **8** (1995), 241–55.

2. Hanson, W.S., *Agricola and the conquest of the north* (London, 1987), 187.

3. Hanson, W.S., *ANRW* II.33.3 (1991), 1778.

4. Birley, A.R., *The Fasti of Roman Britain* (Oxford, 1981), 69 (summarising *Britannia*, **4** (1973), 179ff.).

5. *Agricola* 25.1 'amplexus ciuitates trans Bodotriam sitas' has a similar use of the accusative after *amplector*, but there seem to be no exact parallels for the ablatives 'uictoria ... aut bello'.

6. The quotation is given *in extenso* by K. Wellesley in note 1 (p.95) in his chapter on 'Tacitus as a military historian', in *Tacitus* (ed. T.A. Dorey, London, 1969).

7. All references to 'Ogilvie' are to the edition by R. M. Ogilvie & I.A. Richmond (Oxford, 1967). The relationship between the opening words of the *Origines* and the *Agricola* is a complex one, since Cato is referring to himself as one who both performed deeds of merit and was now writing about such deeds, whereas in the *Agricola* the performer (Agricola) and the writer (Tacitus) are different persons.

8. The whole phrase (an authorial statement) in Sallust is 'Cato clarus atque magnus habetur'.

9. Cf. Statius, *Siluae* 5.2.41ff. (quoted by Ogilvie *ad loc.*).

10. Again the use of the *magnus* is significant (see above and note 8). But note that the second person potential subjunctive and the adverb *libenter* invite the reader rather than coerce him into endorsing Tacitus' judgement.

3   Agricola and Roman Scotland: some structural evidence

Gordon Maxwell

The contribution made by pottery studies to our understanding of the activities of the Roman army in Scotland has always been considerable. From an early stage, the value of not only a close examination of such artefactual evidence but also a keen awareness of its wider context was fully appreciated by Scottish excavators. In the hands of sympathetic scholars it transformed excavation reports, like the seminal publication on five years' work at Newstead (Curle 1911), from mere finds-lists into reasoned assessments, indicating far more than the chronological context of the sites investigated. The refinement of pottery studies in more recent years, however, has been instrumental in enhancing our ability to distinguish sensibly between not just the three main periods of occupation which can be recognised, in structural terms, on Roman military sites in the North, but even the various sub-phases. In this process of enhancement, it is pleasant to be able to acknowledge the special role played by Brian Hartley with respect to samian ware: thirty years ago, the debate about the dating of the first and second Antonine occupation periods in Scottish forts was dominated by his opinion on the samian from Mumrills on the Antonine Wall (Steer 1961, 100–10; cf. also Steer 1964, *passim*); a little later his survey of the totality of samian evidence, including fresh examination of material in a number of private collections, led to a magisterial pronouncement on the chronological structure of Roman Scotland (Hartley 1972); since then the fruits of his experience and scholarship have continued to embellish many of the most significant reports to appear in print.

Scottish sites nevertheless still furnish problems of dating which even the most sensitive reading of pottery evidence may not avail to solve; indeed it would not be fair to expect a solution in some cases, given the uncertainty or the complexity of the data upon which the formulation of the problem is based. This stricture applies most pertinently to any appraisal of the Flavian period in Scotland. As Hartley himself observed (1972, 1), although referring specifically to the Antonine period, there are bound to be difficulties of dating where contemporary literary and epigraphic testimony is so sparse. We might add that those difficulties are accentuated where there is a requirement to harmonise archaeological data with his-

torical evidence which, though not sparse, lacks definition in vital areas.

Such, certainly, is the case with the Flavian period. The account furnished by Tacitus allows us to envisage two years of expansion into Scotland (probably AD 79–80), a season of consolidation (AD 81), and two more campaigns of conquest, culminating in a decisive battle (AD 82–83). Archaeological studies extending over the past century provide evidence of the primary troop-movements which can reasonably be assigned to this five-year period, i.e. various categories of temporary camps, as well as the sites of a number of permanent installations – forts, fortlets, and a series of watchtowers. However, there is also an appreciable amount of archaeological evidence for activity in the years immediately following the Agricolan advance, on which Tacitus is less than helpful, having been taken to imply by his comment *perdomita Britannia et statim omissa* (*Histories* 1, 2) that the great victory at Mons Graupius was followed straightaway by abandonment of most of the northern conquests. The existence of the legionary fortress at Inchtuthil, whose evacuation and demolition can hardly have occurred less than three years after Agricola's return to Rome (Pitts & St. Joseph 1985, 263–79), is just one element that gives the lie to such a simplistic interpretation. Moreover, even with regard to only those structures which might conveniently have been built or planned during Agricola's governorship, there are several widely divergent interpretations of their specific relationships currently proposed (e.g. Breeze 1982, 62–72; Hanson 1987, 84–173 *passim*; Daniels 1989; Breeze & Hanson 1994). The problem here is that the complexity of the structural evidence has generated hypothesis with a degree of resolution somewhat finer than the capacity of any of our current dating mechanisms.

It is thus impossible to be absolutely certain, for example, how the watchtower system first recognised on the Gask Ridge relates to the Outer *Limes* forts; or how the Outer *Limes* forts relate, in turn, to the legionary fortress at Inchtuthil; or even how the major Outer *Limes* forts in Strathmore relate to the intercalated fortlets at Cargill and Inverquharity. Suggestions continue to be made (e.g. Maxwell 1990; Woolliscroft 1993), but final solutions remain elusive, partly because of the scarcity of datable material recovered from excavation, partly as a result of the evidential ambiguity of that material.

Paradoxically, it is not the purpose of this brief paper to resolve these problems. On the contrary, what is presented here may initially produce further complications, although it is to be hoped that the eventual result will be to clarify. The evidence in question is almost entirely structural, and the approach morphological – hardly an innovation in the study of the Flavian period (cf. Breeze 1981, 16–20; Hanson 1987, 177–9), but two possible links between early Flavian temporary and permanent works of distinctive character are here identified for the first time.

The character and distribution of late 1st-century temporary camps in Roman Scotland have become much better understood through the operations of aerial archaeologists, notably those of the late Professor J.K.S. St. Joseph (for useful summaries, see St. Joseph 1976; Maxwell 1981; Frere & St. Joseph 1983, 19–31). Securely identified marching-camps, which can be taken to illustrate the preliminary phases of the Flavian conquest, when large bodies of troops were brigaded together in campaigns of movement or consolidation, are still relatively few in number. The largest and most distinctive group of these is that distinguished by the external gateway-defence involving an oblique traverse and *clavicula*, and called the Stracathro type, after the site where the defensive device was first aerially recorded. The group embraces camps of widely differing size: the south-western cluster – Castledykes, Dalswinton and Beattock – average 25ha; the 'central' group, comprising Camelon (2), Malling, Bochastle and Dalginross range from about 10 to 20ha; and the northern examples – Stracathro, Ythan Wells and Auchinhove – average 14ha or so. There are also four Stracathro camps of much more humble proportions: Inverquharity (in Strathmore); Malling (to the north of the large example); Dalswinton (overlapped by the larger camp); and Woodhead (where Dere Street crosses the Lothian Tyne). The last-named site is the only instance of a Stracathro-type camp on the eastern side of the country, south of the Forth. There are, as yet, no examples recorded elsewhere in Britain.

Because of this exclusively northern distribution, it has occasionally been suggested that Stracathro camps should be closely, indeed personally, associated with Agricola, but scholars are, for the most part, unhappy with so specific an attribution, preferring to see it as the 'badge' of a single legion or legionary work-group (Wilson 1974, 344; Breeze 1981, 17–18; Hanson 1987, 178). As such, the presence of a Stracathro gate indicates no more than the possibility of assigning the relevant work to the 'expansionist' phase of Flavian operations in the north, i.e. up to *c.* AD 86/87, three or four years after Agricola ceased to be governor of Britannia. Nevertheless, there would be a presumption in the case of sites which occupy the best ground or the ground nearest to the river-crossing, as at Dalswinton, Camelon, or Castledykes, for instance, that an Agricolan attribution is fully justified. Equally, and this holds good for certain non-Stracathro camps, it is inherently more likely that clusters or series of camps in Scotland south of the Forth, apparently pre-dating the road-system, and displaying

either squarish plan-form or other clavicular gateway defences, will also have originated in the Agricolan phase; the 16ha series extending from mid-Clydesdale to Lothian (Maxwell & Wilson 1987, 32–4), the examples at Oakwood, to the south-east of the fort at Newstead, and disposed along Dere Street from the Cheviots to the Forth, are cases in point. If we add to these the *c.* 45ha camps marking the advance of an early battle-group down the right bank of the Earn in Perthshire, as well as the scattered traces of temporary camp activity recorded along the main east-west route through upper Tweeddale, mid-Clydesdale and via Avondale to the Ayrshire coast, it is remarkable how complementary the distribution-patterns of the Stracathro and non-Stracathro categories are.

Such mutually exclusive patterns are all the more noteworthy in view of the probability that the central Scotland Stracathro group is composed mainly of sites which lie adjacent to permanent Flavian forts and have therefore sometimes been identified as labour-camps, intended to accommodate legionary construction parties. However, it has also been suggested (Maxwell 1981, 35) that there are grounds for viewing these camps as bases of more than ephemeral nature, housing troops employed in the exploration and pacification of the surrounding area. Their close proximity to permanent *castella* had nevertheless led some to examine the latter as possible examples of the forts located by Agricola himself (Tacitus, *Agricola* 22). Whether or not this is true, commentators on the forts in question (e.g. Breeze 1981, 18; Hanson 1987, 178) have tended to be more concerned with refuting earlier claims that the character of the forts confirmed Tacitus' picture of Agricola as a paragon of military innovation; in consequence, certain interesting points have escaped general notice.

The most important of these is that gateways with inturned rampart-terminals are not identical with gateways with inturned multiple ditch-terminals. The former feature, reflecting a desire for greater defensive strength at the entrances of fortified enclosures, is a recurrent theme in castrametation generally, an early example being the inturned ramparts of the Neronian gateways at Vetera. Occasionally, the two elements may coincide, as aerial photography (fig. 1) and excavated data confirm at the fort of Bochastle, near Callander (Anderson 1956). Elsewhere this occurrence appears to be infrequent, so that the two elements could perhaps be described as inheritors of different architectural traditions. The developed form of the ditched version, to which the term 'parrot's beak' terminal has been given (Maxwell 1984, 217), is best illustrated by air photographs of the fort at Malling, possibly Ptolemy's *Lindum* (fig. 2), on the west shore of the Lake of Menteith. In this example, at each gate the outer ditch curves inward as it approaches the entrance to unite with the inner, both then continuing a little further towards the *angustiae portarum*. The gate is thus approached down an ever-narrowing funnel, with no access being granted to the platform between the ditches. In rectilinear form, the same feature can be seen in much earlier works, e.g. at the south and east gates of Claudian Hod Hill (Richmond 1968), and similar expressions of the theme are provided at forts as different in date and purpose as Claudian Great Casterton and Antonine Bar Hill.

That the Scottish and other examples are more numerous than most scholars are aware is perhaps due to the fact that many can only be seen as cropmarks, in some cases with difficulty, while the presence of a few has to be deduced from vestigially-preserved earthwork evidence. It must be said that 'parrot's beaks' are, not inappositely, polymorphic, and several do not present the extreme form noticed at Malling; in these (for example, both sites at Cargill) the innermost ditch does not display an inward curve (see figs. 3, 4).

The *indubitable* Scottish examples, all of Flavian date, are thirteen in number:

1. **Cardean** (NO 288 460): the most northerly instance, known from both excavation and aerial photography (Robertson 1972; 1979); north, south and east gates recorded; only the two innermost ditches appear to be linked, and, at all of these, the rampart appears to be inturned.

2. **Cargill 1** (the fortlet, NO 163 376): at both of the centrally-placed entrances, on the north-west and south-east, air pho-

tographs reveal the outer ditch curving to join the inner (RCAHMS 1994, 84–5).

3. **Cargill 2** (the fort, NO 166 379): recorded by aerial photography at the north-east, south-east, and south-west entrances; at the first, both outer ditches are linked in a curve to the straight innermost (RCAHMS 1994, 84–5).

4. **Bochastle** (NN 613 081): excavation (Anderson 1956) demonstrated that the ramparts inturned at each entrance; later air photographs reveal a developed, double-ditched 'parrot's beak' at east entrance.

5. **Malling** (NN 564 000): developed, inswinging 'parrot's beak' recorded by aerial photography (St. Joseph 1973, 222–3) at north and south entrances of uniformly double-ditched perimeter.

6. **Drumquhassle** (NS 484 874): defensive perimeter, faintly visible in parched pasture, recorded from the air in 1977 (Maxwell 1983, 168–72); subsequent interpretation reveals a plain 'beak' on the north side of the south-west entrance.

7. **Doune** (NN 727 012): south-east defences, very faintly

Fig. 1. Roman fort at Bochastle, Central Region: oblique air photograph showing in-turned 'parrot's-beak' ditch terminal at the fort's east gate (right). The oblique line of cropmark immediately west (left) of the fort represents the east side of the adjacent 'Stracathro'-type temporary camp. (Copyright RCAHMS)

visible in parched pasture, recorded from the air in 1983 (Maxwell 1984); triple ditches on north side of entrance in that side unite in a developed 'parrot's beak'.

8. **Barochan** (NS 413 690): excavation of the west gate in 1986 (Frere 1987, 311–13) confirmed that the double ditches terminated there in a plain 'beak'; the adjoining rampart was not found to be inturned.

9. **Castle Greg** (NT 150 592): Handsomely preserved fortlet, scene of the earliest Roman excavation in Scotland (Wilson 1851); at the single north-east entrance double ditches unite in a plain 'beak', first noticed on aerial photograph of the site under snow.

10. **Crawford** (NS 954 214): simple 'parrot's beak' identified during 1961–66 excavations (Maxwell 1972, 162) at double-ditched south gate, where rampart is most unlikely to be inturned; the fort was abandoned, after one period of occupation, c. AD 86/7.

11. **Tassiesholm-Milton** (NT 091 011): excavation over a number of years (see especially Clarke 1947) revealed two successive Flavian forts, both displaying the 'beak' feature;

aerial survey over the intervening years has refined observations then made, indicating that, in each case, the double ditched, plain version was employed; there was no evidence, however, of the rampart-terminals being inturned, in either structural phase.

12. **Dalswinton** (NX 933 849): Bankhead, the smaller of two Flavian forts occupying the same river-terrace site, displays a plain, double ditched 'beak' at its north-east entrance; excavation (Richmond & St. Joseph 1957) demonstrated that the 'parrot's beak' fort was the earlier.

13. **Broomholm** (NY 379 816): discovered on vertical photographs; subsequent excavation (Wilson 1965, 202) revealed that the earlier of the two superimposed Flavian structures was provided with a plain-ditched 'beak'.

In addition to these Roman Scotland can furnish another four sites, where the existence of a 'beaked' entrance may possibly await confirmation:

14. **Stracathro** (NO 615 656): the cropmark evidence recorded on aerial photographs is not entirely clear, but the outer

Fig. 2. Roman fort and temporary camps at Malling, Central Region: oblique air photograph showing in-turned 'parrot's-beak' ditch terminals at the north and south entrances of the fort (centre), as well as the 'Stracathro entrance' of the larger camp (left). (Copyright RCAHMS)

ditches appear to curve inwards on either side on the south entrance.

15. **Ardoch** (NN 839 099): the presence of a 'parrot's beak' at Ardoch is based upon the observation that, at the east gate, the visible innermost ditch displays a small, but perceptible, inward curve (as was noticed by Roy in the 18th century: cf. *Military antiquities*, pls. 10, 30); since it has been argued (Maxwell 1989, 115–16, 165–8) that this ditch follows the same line as the outer member of a pair of Flavian ditches, there is a likelihood that the surviving curve denotes the former existence of a 'beak' at this gate.

16. **Drumlanrig** (NS 852 989): the east side of a plain, double-ditched example has been tentatively identified (Maxwell & Wilson 1987, 19–20) at the south entrance, but the aerial record needs to be confirmed on the ground, in view of the site's evidently complex structural sequence.

17. **Glenlochar** (NX 735 645): despite the considerable degree of exposure in publications (e.g. Frere & St. Joseph 1983, pl.76), the curving arcs of cropmark linking the middle pair of ditches on either side of the fort's south gate do not appear to have been accorded the significance they appear to warrant; a *prima facie* case for another 'beak'.

Doubtless the ditch systems of other sites in Scotland may yet yield traces of this type of gateway defence. For example, the outlying double-ditched terminal which the original excavators of Camelon identified on the western limit of the 'South Camp' defences (Christison & Buchanan 1901, 370, pl. 2) bears a strong resemblance to a plain 'beak'. However, more recent investigations (Maxfield 1981) have made it possible that this appearance is illusory, being composed of two intersecting

elements of widely differing date. The complexity of structures at this much refurbished site makes it difficult to be absolutely certain either way. Similarly, at Castledykes in Clydesdale, the complexity of the structural sequence precludes certainty, but if, as has been argued (Hanson 1987, 103–4), the Agricolan fort was roughly coextensive with the Antonine, the linked ditches on the north side of the east entrance (Robertson 1964, 28–9, pl. 48) may possibly have had a Flavian precursor.

Even without the addition of the probable or possible sites, the frequency of occurrence of the 'parrot's beak' terminal is quite remarkable, roughly half of the known Flavian forts in Scotland displaying at least one example. Several significant relationships can be observed: at Cargill, it appears in both the fort and the fortlet, neither of which is likely to be later than AD 86/87; at Crawford, coin evidence indicated that the fort was deliberately demolished around AD 86, and it was probably also at this time that the early fort at Dalswinton, Bankhead, was replaced by a larger successor, whose ditches lacked 'beaked' terminals; at Milton, on the other hand, both the secondary and the primary Flavian forts display the feature. The last-named site does not necessarily prove an exception to the general presumption of an 'Agricolan' origin (i.e. in execution or conception); for there is evidence that the latest Flavian phase at Milton may be represented by a smaller enclosure, which was constructed in the interior of the second fort.

The apparent unanimity of dating is less remarkable, however, than the pattern of distribution, which resolves itself, for the most part, into three distinct areas: a Strathmore group, a central Scotland group, and a south-western group. About the structure of Flavian forts located elsewhere in Scotland, complementing this distribution, there is less that can

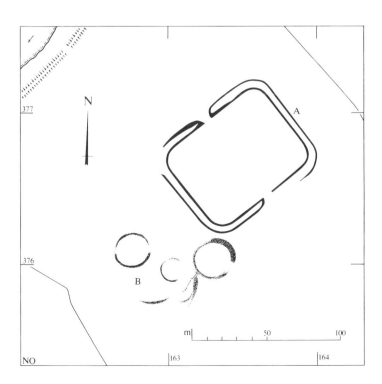

Fig. 3. Roman fortlet (A) at Cargill Mains, Tayside Region: adjacent ring-ditches (B) represent an unenclosed native settlement. (Copyright RCAHMS)

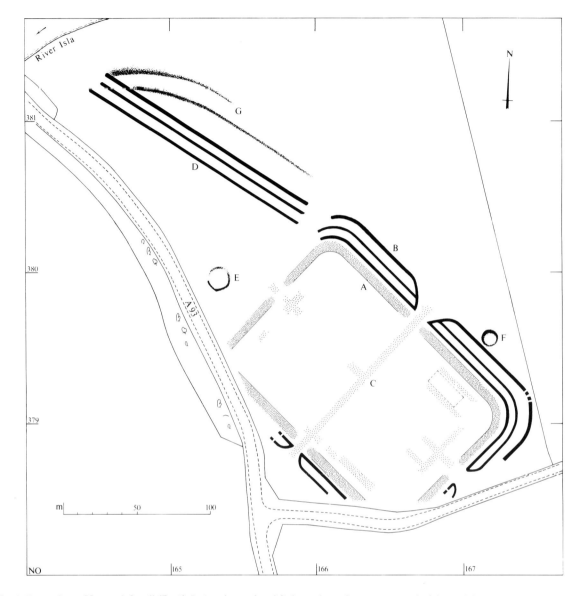

Fig. 4. Roman fort at Hatton of Cargill, Tayside Region: the complex of ditches to the north-west represents the defences of the fort annexe (D) intersected by post-Roman hollow-ways (G). (Copyright RCAHMS)

as yet be said. Inturned *rampart* terminals, unaccompanied by incurved ditches, have been recorded during excavation at Strageath, Elginhaugh, and Oakwood; complementary crop-mark evidence, on air photographs, in the form of observable narrowing or inswinging of the intervallum street, as it approaches what may be presumed to be an inturned gateway, can be adduced at Easter Happrew and Dalginross. At all the other known Flavian sites of any size, the structural evidence is either too complex, too obscure, or too limited to permit even rudimentary categorisation. Yet once again, as with temporary camps, the sites on the Dere Street corridor, on the main east-west Clyde-Tweed route, and in the main Tay basin, furnish no secure instances of the relevant type of ditch-terminals. The significance of the closely comparable distribution-patterns of 'parrot's beak' and Stracathro entrances will be examined presently.

First, it may be of interest to consider the parallels for the former elsewhere in Britain. The distribution, as known at

present on the basis of evidence similar to that presented above, is striking. The best known example, Pen Llystyn in north-west Wales, was long ago shown to be of an Agricolan origin (Hogg 1968), probably constructed *c.*AD 79; at three of its four entrances developed 'parrot's beak' terminals can be seen; at the fourth, the single ditch curves inwards in a regular quarter circle. The rampart terminals, however, are in each case undeviatingly straight. In 1975, excavation of the fort of Hayton, by Pocklington, in Yorkshire (Johnson 1978), confirmed the evidence of air survey, revealing that at least two of its gates were flanked by plain, double-ditched 'beaks'; pottery evidence suggested that Hayton had been built *c.*AD 70–71 and abandoned in the early 80s. At Ribchester, excavation showed that the north gate of the pre-Agricolan fort (Frere 1992, 276–7) was flanked on the one side by a triple-ditched 'beak'; again, neither here nor at Hayton was the rampart terminal inturned.

In addition to the explicit testimony of excavation, there

are a number of sites where either scrutiny of relevant air photography, or consideration of the surviving earthworks, suggests – as we have already seen in Scottish examples above – that the presence of a 'parrot's beak' can be recognised, or perhaps inferred. The first example, at Greensforge, Staffordshire, is the most southerly so far recorded. Known primarily from air photographs (cf. Frere & St. Joseph 1983, 96–9), the feature is displayed in the larger of the two forts which belong to the early period of campaigning in the Welsh Marches. At each of its gates, the fort's double-ditched perimeter terminates in a plain 'beak', and the rampart terminals are straight; Claudian pottery has been recovered from the site, but occupation could conceivably have continued until early Flavian times. The second, recorded from the air in 1991 (Bewley & Macleod 1993), can be seen at the fort of Roall, lying on the south bank of the River Aire, and some 30km south-west of the fort at Hayton described above; the cropmarks of the ditch-system are intermittent, but there is a marked curving of the outer ditch on the east side of the south-west gate, while magnetometer survey appears to show similar evidence at the north-east gate. Though no artefactual dating-evidence has yet been recovered from the site, its position, off the known road-system, may indicate an early origin, possibly contemporary with the establishment of the legionary base at York.

Interestingly enough, the early fort at Newton Kyme, situated near Tadcaster, in South Yorkshire, and little more than 20km distant from Roall, may also fall into the same category. Air photographs (e.g. CUCAP print CEI 85) show possible 'beaked' terminals at the south gate; about the other entrances, being incorporated within the defensive perimeter of the later, larger fort, nothing can be said, but finds suggest an occupation which also began in the early Flavian period.

It will be obvious that most forts with a long occupation-sequence are unlikely to furnish superficially accessible evidence of this kind, the later defences usually overlying and obscuring the details of the earlier perimeter. Nevertheless, as we have seen at Ardoch, vestigial traces may still survive. The search for these demands a more intensive scrutiny of excavation reports and site-plans than has yet been possible, but initial appraisal has so far revealed a number of intriguing possibilities. Mention might be made of Bainbridge, in North Yorkshire, where the undoubted Agricolan occupation is yet to be associated with a defensive system; the visible earthworks are thought to belong mainly to the later Flavian-Trajanic period, but at the south gate the incurving of the ditch-system on the east side may betoken the adaptation of an earlier 'beak'. The same can be said of the ditches at the north-east gate of Tomen-y-Mur in north-west Wales (cf. Nash-Williams 1969, 111–13), where an originally double ditch was soon replaced by a single, larger ditch, and at the west gate of Coelbren in Glamorgan (Nash-Williams 1969, 81–3), which provides a much closer resemblance to the cropmark form of the 'beaked' feature.

As to their dating, with the exception of Greensforge, which could have been constructed at any stage in the Claudian-Neronian period, all the southerly examples appear to be Flavian, being built, at a guess, in the governorships of

Cerealis, Frontinus, and Agricola – with a bias towards the earlier half of the bracket (AD 71–84). The distribution pattern is, however, not just acceptably comparable with the main fields of military activity within that period. Yorkshire and north-west Wales/Lancashire are most significant areas, if one reckons that structural idiosyncrasies are more likely to reflect the predilections of a particular legionary workforce or *praefectus castrorum*, rather than the hand of a specific provincial governor (Breeze 1981, 17–18). Given the evidence of date and location, the identity of the originating force is not hard to seek. The transfer of Legio II Adiutrix in AD 71 from Nijmegen on the Lower Rhine to Lincoln, gave Petillius Cerealis the troop re-enforcement required to undertake the subjugation of Brigantia and the establishment of a legionary presence, if not yet a full-blown fortress, at York. Assuming, on the evidence of the size of the labour-camp at Inchtuthil (Pitts & St. Joseph 1985, 223–44), that a legion's building capacity would be devoted entirely to the construction of its own fortress, then most of Legio IX Hispana would have been engaged in building-operations at the bases of Malton or York (Hartley 1966, 10–11); construction of auxiliary works in the surrounding area might thus have fallen to the troops of the nearest supporting legion, i.e. Legio II Adiutrix, by whom the 'beaked' ditch-system of Hayton, Roall and Newton Kyme would have been produced. The transfer of II Adiutrix to Chester in the 70s provides ample reason for the examples at Pen Llystyn, Ribchester, and possibly Tomen-y-mur, all of which could in fact have been built in the aftermath of Agricolan campaigning in AD 77–78.

Turning to the northern sites, it would be reasonable to argue that they show the primary areas of responsibility of Legio II Adiutrix in Scotland: in terms of 'parrot's beaks', the supervision of the construction of permanent forts. However, it would not be unreasonable to go further and suggest that the roughly co-terminous distribution of Stracathro camps indicates that these areas were the same legion's zones of responsibility in the campaigning phase. If that were so, it would cast useful light on a phase of Roman military activity that history and archaeology have hitherto found relatively obscure, and its relevance would extend far beyond the confines of late 1st-century Britain.

Returning to a consideration of the problems of site-dating with which we started, it can be seen that, rather than providing an answer, identifying the possible context of Stracathro gates and 'parrot's beaks' has only reformulated the original question and inspired many more; at least it can be admitted that, if the relevant forts and camps indicate the influence of Legio II Adiutrix, their absence as structural elements from later field-works in north Britain is entirely comprehensible, since we know that by around AD 89, if not before, the legion had been transferred to the Danube. But precisely how long did the legion remain active in the north? The occurrence of 'beaks' in the presumably successive works at Cargill, argues for its presence or influence persisting into the period 84–86, after Agricola had demitted office, but before the abandonment of Inchtuthil. The testimony of Milton is less easy to read. If the major reshaping of the defences there parallels the structurally comparable process at Dalswinton, the continuing use of the beaked ditch-terminals might suggest that II Adiutrix still had a hand in the construction of frontier posts *after* the decision to give up the northernmost conquests; moreover, such participation might be taken to indicate that the legion's eventual withdrawal from Britain was the result of, and not the reason for, the Domitianic retrenchment on the northern frontier. So crucial an interpretation may not, however, be allowed to rest on evidence of such manifest fragility. The most that can be said is that, in Scotland, most 'parrot's beaks' (and all Stracathro camps) are likely to denote activity in the period 79–86.

The comparable exclusivity of the distribution patterns of both seems to tell us something about the way in which legionary roles were allocated by a commander-in-chief, as well as offering, more specifically, the hope of understanding a little more clearly how the Flavian conquest of north Britain was planned and executed. Because the character of the temporary works is still not fully understood, we cannot yet claim that territorial responsibilities assigned to legions in the campaigning phase inevitably remained with the assignees in the subsequent phase of consolidation. Nevertheless, it is encouraging to see evidence that what would have been an advantageous arrangement may in fact have been occasionally in force. To go beyond that and suggest that we can identify theatres of operation and supervision for two or three main battle groups (comprising say, most of II Adiutrix and XX Valeria Victrix together with a detachment of IX Hispana) is tempting, but not justifiable. There would, however, be ample justification for expecting II Adiutrix to have played a major part in the conquest of the North. Though much attention has been paid to the links between Agricola and Legio XX – he had commanded it during Cerealis' invasion of Brigantia – less thought has been given to the ties that could have been established a little earlier, when he oversaw the recruitment of II Adriutrix at Ravenna (Tacitus, *Agricola* 7,4). Whatever the character of those links, the presence of the isolated Stracathro camps at Ythan Wells and Auchinhove (St. Joseph 1978, 278–9) demonstrates that II Adiutrix retained the confidence of Agricola or his successor in the final trial of strength with the defenders of Caledonia. Not for the first time, the quality and character of field monuments in Roman Scotland provide insights with a potential interest and value far beyond their local context. As clues at the beginning of another campaign of archaeological exploration, which could extend from Inchtuthil to the gates of Aquincum, it is a pleasure to offer them to such an experienced explorer as Brian Hartley.

Addendum

The list of southern fort-sites with 'parrot's beaks' may be expanded by the inclusion of the proven example at Marton, Lincolnshire (SK 832 821) and a possible identification at Lancaster.

Bibliography

Anderson, W.A., 1956 The Roman fort at Bochastle, Callander, *Trans. Glasgow Archaeol. Soc.*, **15**, 35–63

Bewley, R.H., & Macleod, D., 1993 The discovery of a Roman fort at Roall Manor Farm, North Yorkshire, *Britannia*, **25**, 243–7

Breeze, D.J., 1981 Agricola the builder, *Scottish Archaeol. Forum*, **12**, 14–24

————, 1982 *The northern frontiers of Roman Britain* (London)

Christison, D., & Buchanan, M., 1901 Account of the excavation of the Roman station of Camelon near Falkirk, Stirlingshire, *Proc. Soc. Antiq. Scotland*, **35** (1900–1), 329, 417

Clarke, J., 1947 The forts at Milton, Beattock (Tassiesholm), *Trans. Dumfriesshire Galloway Natur. Hist. Antiq. Soc.*, **25**, 10–26

Curle, J., 1911 *A Roman frontier post and its people; the fort of Newstead in the parish of Melrose* (Glasgow)

Daniels, C.M., 1989 The Flavian and Trajanic northern frontier, in Todd, M. (ed.), *Research on Roman Britain 1960–89*, 31–6

Frere, S.S., 1987 Roman Britain in 1986, *Britannia*, **18**, 301–59

————, 1992 Roman Britain in 1991, *Britannia*, **23**, 256–308

————, & St. Joseph, J.K.S., 1983 *Roman Britain from the air* (Cambridge)

Hanson, W.S., 1987 *Agricola and the conquest of the north* (London)

Hartley, B.R., 1966 Some problems of the Roman occuation of the north of England, *Northern Hist.*, **1**, 7–20

————, 1972 The Roman occupation of Scotland: the evidence of the samian ware, *Britannia*, **3**, 1–55

Hogg, A.H.A., 1968 Pen Llystyn: a Roman fort and other remains, *Archaeol. J.*, **125**, 101–92

Johnson, S., 1978 Excavations at Hayton Roman fort, *Britannia*, **9**, 57–114

Maxfield, V., 1981 The Flavian fort at Camelon, *Scottish Archaeol. Forum*, **12**, 69–78

Maxwell, G.S., 1972 Excavations at the Roman fort at Crawford, Lanarkshire, *Proc. Soc. Antiq. Scotland*, **104** (1971–2), 147–200

————, 1981 Agricola's campaigns: the evidence of the temporary camps, *Scottish Archaeol. Forum*, **12**, 25–54

————, 1983 Recent aerial discoveries in Roman Scotland: Drumquhassle, Elginhaugh and Woodhead, *Britannia*, **14**, 167–81

————, 1984 New frontiers: the Roman fort at Doune and its possible significance, *Britannia*, **15**, 217–23

————, 1989 *The Romans in Scotland* (Edinburgh)

————, 1990 Flavian frontiers in Caledonia, in Vetters, H., & Kandler, M. (eds), *Akten des 14. Internationalen Limeskongresses 1986 in Carnuntum*, 353–65 (Vienna)

————, & Wilson, D.R., 1987 Air reconnaissance in Roman Britain, 1977–84, *Britannia*, **18**, 1–48

Nash-Williams, V.E. (ed. M.G. Jarrett), 1969 *The Roman frontier in Wales* (Cardiff)

Pitts, L.F., & St. Joseph, J.K.S., 1985 *Inchtuthil: the Roman legionary fortress* (London)

RCAHMS (Royal Commission on the Ancient and Historical Monuments of Scotland) 1994 *South-east Perth: an archaeological landscape* (Edinburgh)

Richmond, I.A., 1968 *Hod Hill 2: excavations carried out between 1951 and 1968* (London)

————, & St. Joseph, J.K.S., 1957 The Roman fort at Dalswinton, *Trans. Dumfriesshire Galloway Natur. Hist. Antiq. Soc.*, **34** (1955–6), 1–21

Robertson, A.S., 1964 *The Roman fort at Castledykes* (Edinburgh)

————, 1972 The watch-tower at Roundlaw, and the Cardean barrack block, *Roman Northern Frontier Seminar*, **7**, 25–28

————, 1979 The Roman fort at Cardean, in Breeze, D. J. (ed.), *Roman Scotland: some recent excavations*, 42–4 (Edinburgh)

St. Joseph, J.K.S., 1973 Air reconnaissance in Roman Britain, 1969–72, *J. Roman Stud.*, **63**, 214–46

————, 1976 Air reconnaissance of Roman Scotland, 1939–75, *Glasgow Archaeol. J.*, **4**, 1–28

————, 1978 The camp at Durno, Aberdeenshire, and the site of Mons Graupius, *Britannia*, **9**, 271–87

Steer, K.A., 1961 Excavations at Mumrills fort, 1958–60, *Proc. Soc. Antiq. Soctland*, **94**, 84–132

————, 1964 John Horsley and the Antonine Wall, *Archaeol. Aeliana*, 4 ser., **42**, 1–39

Wilson, D., 1851 Roman camp at Harburn, *Proc. Soc. Antiq. Scotland*, **1** (1851–54), 58–9

Wilson, D.R., 1974 Roman camps in Britain, in Pippidi, D.M. (ed.), *Actes du IXe Congrès International d'Études sur les Frontières Romaines*, 341–50 (Bucharest)

Woolliscroft, D.J. 1993 Signalling and the design of the Gask Ridge system, *Proc. Soc. Antiq. Scotland*, **123** (1992–93), 291–314

4   Camelon and Flavian troop-movements in southern Britain: some ceramic evidence

Vivien G. Swan and Paul T. Bidwell

Between 1975 and 1979, five seasons of rescue excavations, in advance of re-development, were conducted by Dr Valerie Maxfield for the then Scottish Development Department (Ancient Monuments), on the southern part of the Roman forts at Camelon, Central Region (*Britannia*, **7** (1976), 300; **8** (1977), 362–4; **9** (1978), 411; **10** (1979), 275). Over 211kg of Flavian and Antonine pottery (excluding mortaria and amphorae) was recovered, and in the early 1980s Andrew King, a former student of Dr Maxfield, processed this, and prepared catalogues of fabrics and forms. More recently, a fortunate coincidence of Dr Maxfield's work towards the publication with the first author's (VGS) personal research on Roman pottery in northern Britain,[1] has resulted in a fresh consideration of some of this material. In 1994, in tandem with editorial work on King's archive, VGS briefly examined a selection of vessels in Falkirk Museum. Among the pottery of particular interest, several jars of distinctive and unusual type caught her attention (fig. 1, B-D), and she decided to seek the opinion of the second author (PTB). This paper has been a collaborative effort in many respects, but we hope that the recipient of this *Festschrift* will enjoy guessing which of the more individual strands have been contributed by each of us!

The Roman forts at Camelon, now lying within the north-west suburbs of Falkirk, occupy the level corner of a north-north-west-projecting sand and gravel plateau. The ground is more or less level to the south and west, but to the north and east, the site is protected by a steep scarp which falls 15–18m to the valley of the Carron. This river flows into the Forth Estuary almost 7km to the east, a location which is, in fact, visible from the Camelon forts. An outline history of the probable sequence of occupation, based on a reconsideration of the excavations of 1899–1900 (Christison & Buchanan 1901) and subsequent aerial photography, was published in 1963 by the Royal Commission on the Ancient and Historical Monuments of Scotland (RCAHMS 1963, 107–12, no. 122). This has since been supplemented by the published summaries of the results of Dr Maxfield's excavations (Maxfield 1979; 1981), and by the report on the small excavation of 1961–3 (McCord & Tait 1978).

The two-phase Antonine fort had an annexe on both its northern and its southern sides, and underlying the latter there was evidence of Flavian occupation. This consisted of two structural phases; the first, an irregularly-shaped defended enclosure, apparently lacked any substantial internal buildings. The second phase was represented by a fort of more conventional layout, on the lines of but larger than the overlying Antonine annexe, and probably occupying at least 4ha; its interior contained permanent timber buildings. To the north-west, west, and west-south-west of the forts, indications of at least ten temporary camps have been recorded from the air (RCAHMS 1963, 111–2; Maxwell & Wilson 1987, 29, 39). Most are undated, but two of the north-western group (Lochlands), sited within a buckle of the river close to its crossing point, may be attributed to the Flavian period, from the plans of their gates (Maxwell 1991). In 1993, excavation by Geoff Bailey within the complex immediately west of the forts (Three Bridges) suggested a Flavian date for one of the camps, and, like the Lochlands complex, more than one phase of activity (*Britannia*, **25** (1994), 257; Bailey forthcoming).

The course of the River Carron is known to have changed considerably in the past two millennia (Bailey 1992). In the Roman period it was evidently much wider and deeper, almost certainly tidal and navigable as far as Camelon, at which point it probably flowed at the foot of the scarp immediately east of the forts. There may well have been a harbour in that vicinity (Tatton-Brown 1980).[2] The Antonine fort, indeed, seems to have faced east, though the lowest bridging point of the Carron lay about 1km to the north-west. The road which utilised this crossing-point in the Antonine period, and perhaps in the Flavian period too, would have been following what was then the main practical land-route between the south of Scotland and Strathmore.

The topographical evidence, therefore, suggests that the forts at Camelon were intended to guard the harbour, and thus they presumably had a role in the reception of supplies and troops for the conquest and garrisoning of Scotland. Moreover, the exceptional concentration of camps in the vicinity is unlikely to be purely coincidental. As several authors have pointed out (Frere & St Joseph 1983, 129; Keppie 1986, 144; Maxwell 1991), the whole locality was evidently of considerable strategic importance as the jumping-off point for campaigns further north. It thus follows that the topography of Camelon and its probable role in the occupation of Flavian Scotland are both highly relevant to the interpretative study of the pottery from the forts.

The Flavian pottery from Dr Maxfield's excavations at Camelon has already received mention in print by several authorities (Maxfield 1981; Dore 1981). These have pointed out its relatively early character, seemingly earlier than any other Flavian assemblage in Scotland. For example, it includes the largest quantity of terra nigra yet recorded from Scotland (twelve to fifteen vessels of true TN, plus several copies), as well as a few sherds of Lyon ware, and a fragment of a barbotine cup in Central Gaulish colour-coated ware has resulted in a fresh consideration of some of this material. One or two of the mortaria are 'unexpectedly early' for their context, including a 'late Claudian' wall-sided form (K. F. Hartley, pers. comm.); the emphasis of the samian assemblage is early rather than mid-Flavian (inf. A. Mees); the glass, in general, gives a similar 'early' impression (J. Price, pers. comm.). Inevitably, however, the earliest possible date for Camelon is dictated more precisely by the historical evidence, that is Tacitus' account of Agricola's campaigns; the site thus cannot pre-date AD 79/80.

Dore (1981, 67–8) has drawn attention to similarities between the Flavian ceramic assemblages from Camelon and Newstead, and their marked contrast with the pottery from the Agricolan campaign-base at Red House, Corbridge. The Red House pottery has a decidedly utilitarian air, its style apparently representing a fusion of Roman and native southern British traditions, whereas very many of the vessels from Camelon and Newstead exhibit 'a more direct derivation from Belgic pottery types in southern Britain'. Dore thought that Camelon's pottery supply should, therefore, be seen 'more in the *post*-campaign context of a static frontier', where some kind of long-distance supply-system, operated either by the military or by entrepreneurs, was bringing in a substantial amount of the pottery from a large number of long-distance sources, some 'more adherent to Belgic pottery traditions'. This, however, does not accord with the pattern of pottery supply characteristic of a number of Flavian northern military installations with secure post-campaign contexts. Where known, these are usually marked by a significant dependence on pottery produced locally, probably by, or under the direct control of, the military. Such was the case in Scotland, at Inchtuthil fortress on the Tay (Darling 1985; Williams 1985), and at Elginhaugh, just south of the Forth (inf. J. Dore and K. F. Hartley), and at a number of established Flavian sites in northern England, including Malton, York and Carlisle. More examples are probable, but the relative scarcity of Flavian pottery on Scottish sites makes certainty impossible. In contrast, at Camelon, few Flavian vessels appear to be local products (possibly excepting a small number of flagons), though the raw materials were certainly available nearby, as the Antonine assemblages imply (inf. D. F. Williams, in Camelon Archive). An alternative interpretation of the Camelon pottery is therefore offered here, which takes into account both

the context of the site, and more recent research into the sources of some of the pottery.

Three jars (B-D) of a distinctive type suggest a link with military sites in south-west England. The flat-topped rim, with a lid-seating formed by a slight projection of the inner edge of the rim over the convex inner surface, is characteristic of the jars produced by the Exeter Fortress Ware industry (Holbrook & Bidwell 1991, fig. 52, type 10, fig. 53, type 2). The Camelon vessels are in a gritty grey fabric with much quartz, apparently identical to Exeter Fortress Ware Fabric B (Holbrook & Bidwell 1991, 149). A tripod bowl (E), a reeded-rim bowl (F) and a beaker (A) also occur in this fabric. The tripod bowl is an uncommon type, and the jars are generally confined to other south-western military sites, where they are in Fortress Ware fabrics. At Dorchester, a single example of this type of jar represents an outlier from the main distribution of Fortress Ware (Woodward *et al.* 1993, fig. 131, type 602). The only other examples known to the authors are from York[3] and possibly from the fort at Ebchester, County Durham (Gillam 1975, fig. 11, no. 5;[4] these also appear to be in Fortress Ware Fabric B.

Although the Second Augustan Legion had left Exeter in *c.* 75, production of Fortress Wares seems to have continued. They were well represented in a group of *c.* 75–80 from Lower Coombe Street at Exeter (Holbrook & Bidwell 1991, Table 1), and in rubbish tipped into the ditch of the fort at Tiverton, on its abandonment in the early to mid-80s (Maxfield 1991, 56–7). It is possible that in these contexts the Fortress Wares occurred residually, but continuing military occupation in the south-west, after the departure of the legion (see below), would have provided a reason for maintaining pottery production at Exeter; mortaria certainly continued to be made there after *c.* 75 (Holbrook & Bidwell 1992, 65).

A slightly larger element in the Flavian ceramic assemblage at Camelon comprises vessels which seem almost certainly to have originated within a broad area coincident with the present East Anglia and the littoral of the Thames estuary. The material is diverse, ranging from vessels of local fabric but Romanised form and technique (e.g. fig. 2, no. 8) to native, hand-made utilitarian types, which probably rarely travelled outside their immediate production-locality and which may even represent the output of domestic or small-scale pottery-making (fig. 1, nos. 2, 3, 5). A substantial number of forms and fabrics seem to be related quite closely to the indigenous Late Iron Age 'Belgic' traditions of the region, or to be strongly influenced by the Gallo-Belgic wares which had been imported to the south-east for over half a century before the Claudian invasion. In the decades following the conquest, these general traditions were apparently spread outside the region by the Roman army and its potters, but such derivative products are usually characterised by devolved vessel profiles and almost always have Roman or Romanised culinary fabrics. At Camelon, however, there are East Anglian regional types which scarcely ever appeared outside their district of origin. Moreover, a significant number of the fabrics of these Belgic-derived vessels are quite untypical of military potting. Most are reduced grey or black. Several are tempered with coarse grog

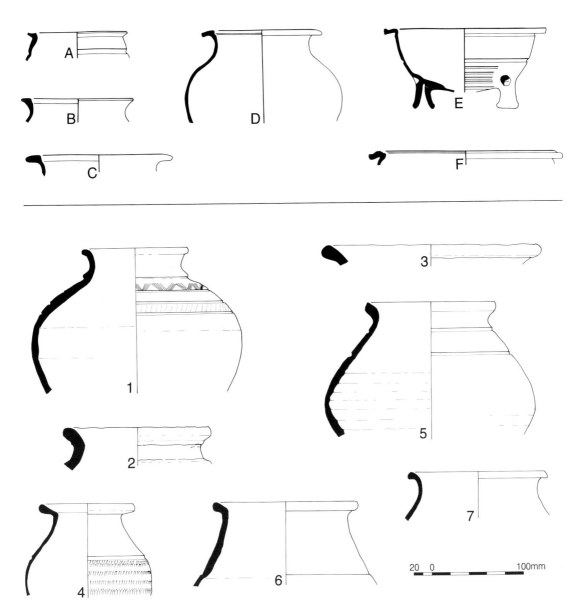

Fig. 1. Camelon, Falkirk. **A–F:** *Exeter Fortress Ware; nos.* **1–7:** *probable products of East Anglia or the environs of the Thames Estuary. Scale 1:4.*

or organic matter and relatively few have the distinctive sandy texture and relatively light surface smoothing of Romanised wares. In many examples, the surface finish, a seamless overall burnishing with a silky feel, is characteristically Belgic or Gallo-Belgic. In short, the techniques of their manufacture – always a good indicator of affinities or origins – often embody Belgic or Gallo-Belgic traditions.

Another point of reference concerns a natural inclusion apparent in a number of these Camelon fabrics, and one which is particularly characteristic of East Anglia, that is, particles of fine silver mica in varying quantities. A preliminary examination of the output of most of the Romano-British kiln sites in Norfolk, Suffolk and Essex (Swan 1984, MF and unpublished archive) noted that the pottery fabrics from within a broad belt extending roughly west to east across central East Anglia (from Hacheston in the Deben Valley to West Stow in the Lark Valley, and including Wattisfield, Pakenham and the

Little Ouse and Waveney Valleys) are very frequently loaded with fine silver mica. The relative proportions of such inclusions can, in fact, vary within an individual kiln site. On the fringes of that zone, from southern Essex (including Colchester) to the Bure and Nar Valleys of Norfolk, such mica may indeed be present, but in lesser quantities (Swan 1984, map 15). Nevertheless, it is usually quite conspicuous, being relatively fine and always silver, a feature in marked contrast to the gold or black mica which characterises Romano-British ceramics in a number of other regions of England, and the large white mica platelets in the 'céramiques micacées' of north-western France. Thus, the varying combinations of distinctive inclusions, characteristic Belgic or Gallo-Belgic techniques of fabric and finish, and often diagnostic forms, some intrinsic to the region, make an attribution to East Anglia a reasonable probability for many of the vessels catalogued below. If a significant portion of the Camelon pottery had originated in this region, this might also explain the unusually large number of platters of terra nigra and imitation TN from the site. These would have been readily available there at a number of centres, particularly at Colchester, which was both a receiving point for such imports, as well as the site of workshops making imitations of these and other Gallo-Belgic tableware forms (Swan 1984, MF 287, Kilns 34–5).

As already mentioned, one of the most striking features of the eastern and south-eastern pottery under discussion, and indeed, of the Flavian pottery from Camelon as a whole, is its great diversity, with little more than one example of each vessel-type (for a statistical estimate of the frequency of individual forms, see the Camelon Site Archive). Very few duplicates of forms or fabrics are apparent, even for those vessels evidently from the same general region. A very substantial number of production sources seems probable. Such variety is not what might be expected of pottery shipped to Scotland in bulk, as a component in the official military supply of Agricola's campaigns; nor is it what might be expected to have been brought by merchants peddling a selection of forms from a limited number of workshops. One or two of the more utilitarian vessels are, indeed, of a quality too poor for them to have been appropriate for long-distance trade. Nevertheless, if sold in the locality in which they had been made, they would have had the merit of being cheap to purchase, and just about adequate for the basic needs of a neighbouring military establishment. Many forts in Britain apparently opted to buy local pottery of very variable quality just for essential basic functions such as storage and cooking; the use of native calcite-gritted hand-made cooking-jars by the Flavian-Trajanic garrison at Malton is just such a case.

It has long been known that soldiers, either as individuals or in groups, were supplied with military equipment, clothing, tents and other items, for which deductions were made from their pay. It now seems likely that pottery vessels for basic cooking and eating may also have been issued by the army quartermasters, either for individual use, or to be shared (as with food rations) by groups of soldiers, such as the occupants of a *contubernium*,[5] or a complete barrack-block (i.e. a century).[6] Whether such a fragile commodity as pottery, which had a limited life, would have been pay-deductable seems doubtful. Even so, the fact that communal vessels were sometimes labelled with ownership graffiti could well suggest that the joint owners were expected to take reasonable care of their shared property, and that it was not replaceable at the drop of a hat. It therefore seems logical to assume that troops would have sometimes included such pots in their baggage when orders came to transfer to other locations. Such vessels could also have served as containers for rations, and for packing a wide variety of other items, such as the household goods of officers. A substantial part of the Camelon pottery may, therefore, have arrived on the site with individuals (e.g. the face-pot, fig. 2, no. 8), or, in the case of some cooking-vessels (e.g. fig. 1, B-D), perhaps in the baggage of groups of soldiers. If this was so, it might explain the rather 'early' appearance of the Camelon assemblage, since some pottery might have originally been requisitioned by the army, then kept in military

stores for several years before the quartermasters issued it, and subsequently been in use for some time before being transported to Camelon. A striking collection of objects from the fort at Caistor-on-Sea, Norfolk, probably resulted from the movement of troops from the area of the Danube and Upper Rhine in the mid-4th century (Darling & Gurney 1993, 247). It comprised a hoard of 24 coins put together 'somewhere to the north or east of Italy' (Darling & Gurney 1993, 63), a glazed mortarium from the region between Raetia and Pannonia, and a steatite bowl from the Danubian frontier area, or possibly Upper Germany or Switzerland (Darling & Gurney 1993, fig. 159, no. 717 and fig. 65, no. 351 respectively).

Another possible interpretation is that some of the pots at Camelon may have constituted the residue of the stores of forts which were being evacuated, though there is evidence from several military sites that such pottery was sometimes deliberately jettisoned rather than be carried elsewhere when a fort was abandoned.[7] The course of action taken by a departing quartermaster may, in fact, have depended on a number of factors: whether transport was likely to be easy (i.e. sea rather than land-transport), whether there was room in the baggage-train,[8] how many vessels were needed as transit-containers for supplies and equipment, whether or not pottery was likely to be freely available in the location to which the unit was being transferred, or whether it could be easily and conveniently made there. In the vicinity of Camelon, there would have been little or no local native pottery suitable for use by the army, or available in sufficient quantity, nor would military production have been a realistic option in the early campaigning stages of Agricola's operations.

There is also a possibility that some pottery may have reached Camelon with other goods. At a time when the northeast was not yet pacified, East Anglia would have constituted an obvious source of the grain supply so essential for a campaigning army. As seems likely at the later supply depot of South Shields, some pottery vessels might have been shipped to Camelon as make-weight components of other cargoes. This, however, would not constitute a satisfactory explanation for all the East Anglian pottery, and is certainly not appropriate for the Exeter Fortress Ware.

Yet another possible interpretation for some of the Camelon pottery is that new recruits to the Roman army or levies might have brought vessels with them as personal possessions, perhaps to avoid having to pay inflated prices for official issue. The *vici* and *canabae* of forts and fortresses were traditional military recruiting grounds, particularly for the sons of veterans and serving soldiers (Dobson & Mann 1973, 202), and Agricola must have been hard-pressed to muster forces large enough for his expansionist policies. Perhaps the Iceni were subject to conscription in the decades following the Boudiccan revolt; it was certainly routine at this period to raise units in newly-conquered areas (Dobson & Mann 1973, 194, 198–9, n. 37). Tacitus mentions the presence of Britons in Agricola's army on several occasions (*Agricola* 29.1, 32.1 and 3), and the British leader Calgacus is made to complain of the *dilectus* (*Agricola* 31.1). Although some men raised through the *dilectus* at this general period were sent to serve outside their province of origin (e.g. in the *cohortes Britannorum*), it is likely that any *dilectus* held in Britain specifically for the purpose of Agricola's campaigns would have probably been used to provide men for units which had dropped below strength.

Possible corroborative evidence for the recruitment, at about this period, of at least one auxiliary from Icenian territory comes in the form of two very small joining fragments of a military diploma found immediately outside and south of the south gate of Caistor St. Edmund, the *civitas* capital of *Venta Icenorum* (RMD **3**, no. 145, pl. 1a and b). Though of insufficient size to be precisely dateable, Dr Margaret Roxan considers from the style of the formulae, that it should belong within the period AD 91 to 105, and most probably to between 100 and 105 (excluding 103). On less certain ground, it may, in fact, have been a parallel issue to the diplomas of May 105, already known from Sydenham, Kent and Middlewich, Salop (CIL XVI, 51 = RIB **2.1**, 2401.2; RMD **1**, 8 = RIB **2.1**, 2401.3). If this last attribution is correct, and if the veteran to whom the Caistor diploma belonged had been discharged after 25 years service (the norm for most of the 2nd century), the man may have been recruited in *c.* AD 80 or shortly before. However, as Margaret Roxan has pointed out to us, the length of service of pre-Hadrianic auxiliaries was not standard, and some served a few years longer.[9] Even so, a recruitment date for our man of AD 75 to 77 would still be well within the bounds of possibility.[10] Most discharged soldiers either settled at their existing or previous station, or returned to the general vicinity of their original home, presumably in the area where they had been recruited, if the latter was not too distant (Roxan 1981, 279–82, Table 3a). Thus *Venta Icenorum* or its *civitas* may perhaps have been the *origo* of the man to whom the diploma was issued,[11] for local recruitment in Britain was quite common at this period. It has been argued, from a range of evidence, that there was probably a Nero-Flavian (post-Boudiccan) military establishment somewhere in the vicinity of the later town (Swan 1981, 124–35), so the veteran in question could well have been recruited at this fort or even perhaps have been the offspring of a military liaison, as the sons of soldiers often joined the army. However, the last proposition can be no more than speculation!

To return to Camelon, the possibility, therefore, that at least some of the pottery reached the site through direct shipment with soldiers evacuated from forts in distant parts of Britain, or through other transfers of men and goods, would, indeed, be compatible with its topographical situation. Its potential as a primary landing point for sea-borne troops, and also as a springboard where land and sea forces might congregate in anticipation of campaigns further north, has already been discussed here and elsewhere (Maxwell 1991). This is just the sort of situation to which Tacitus is probably referring in the *Agricola* (25.1), when he mentions the early use of the fleet, and the sharing of rations by infantry, cavalry and marines, all meeting up in the same camp.

Finally it is worthwhile examining the historical contexts for troop evacuations in the areas from which the Camelon pottery appears to have been derived, that is, the south-west and East Anglia. The fortress at Exeter was abandoned in *c.* 75,

when the legion moved to Caerleon (Holbrook & Bidwell 1991, 6–8). The fort at Tiverton continued in occupation until the early to mid-80s (Maxfield 1991, 56–7), and the forts at Okehampton and Nanstallon were certainly held into the early Flavian period, if not later (Holbrook & Bidwell 1991, 8). The evacuation of Tiverton has been tentatively associated by Dr Maxfield with the major troop movements in 86–7 caused by the Danubian wars. However, the dating evidence, most importantly the samian ware, would allow an earlier terminal date in *c.* 80, when troops were needed in northern Britain.

In East Anglia, a number of military installations had been established in the early 60s, in the wake of the Boudiccan revolt. These are thought to have included Chelmsford, Great Chesterford, and possibly Stanway (Gosbecks) near Colchester, in Essex; Pakenham, Coddenham, and possibly Long Melford in Suffolk; and in Norfolk, probably Caistor St. Edmund, Swanton Morley and Scole, and possibly somewhere in the vicinity of Ashill and Morley St. Peter. The occasion for the removal of such garrisons has been the subject of some discussion, although the evidence from some forts, such as Pakenham (inf. J. Plouviez) and Chelmsford (Reece 1988, 93) suggests only a very short period of occupation. Frere argued persuasively that Agricola's northern offensive was the trigger for the pulling out of the last troops from this area, and that Agricola's urbanisation policy was implemented as a deliberate concomitant of this process (1987, 99). Similarities between some of the products of probable military Nero-Flavian kilns at Caistor St. Edmund, and pottery types in Flavian Scotland (from sites excluding Camelon), lead Swan to suggest independently an Agricolan context for the stripping from Icenian territory of the last garrisons (1981, 131–2).[12] Some Camelon vessels certainly seem Icenian in origin, but the Colchester face-pot (fig. 2, no. 8) and the North Kent bowls (fig. 2, nos. 10–11) might have been acquired nearer the Thames Estuary. Unfortunately nothing is known of the dating of the fort at Stanway, but the inhabitants of the nearby *colonia* at *Camulodunum* would have included numerous sons of legionary veterans, and must have constituted an important recruiting-ground for both legions and the auxilia (Dobson & Mann 1973, 202). This is, indeed, epigraphically attested on the tombstone of a legionary who had originated there, apparently in the late 1st century (CIL III, 11233).

If there is a lesson to be learnt from the Camelon pottery, it is the great relevance of the regional pottery of southern Britain to our understanding of the garrisons in the north. In turn, those studying pottery in southern Britain would do well to appreciate that the most precise dates for their local products may sometimes be derived from northern military assemblages!

CATALOGUE OF
ILLUSTRATED POTTERY FROM CAMELON

The numbers of the Camelon Forms, Fabric groupings and Feature-Contexts listed at the end of each catalogue entry refer to those in the Camelon Excavation Archive.[13] Many of the excavated deposits produced chronologically mixed assem-

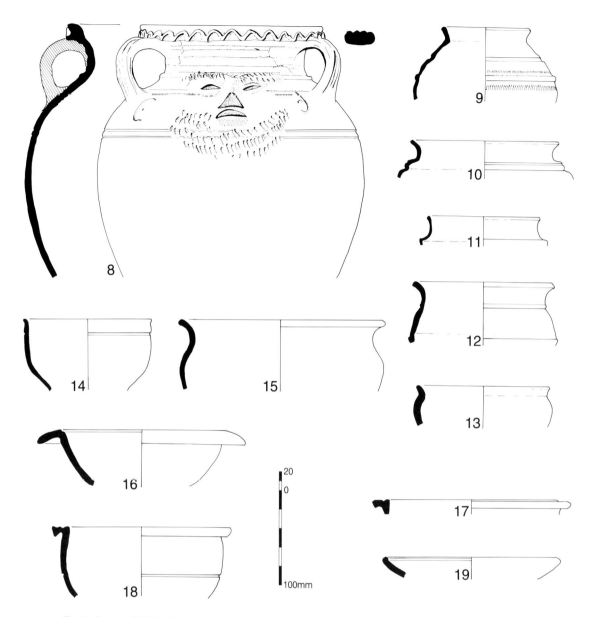

*Fig. 2. Camelon, Falkirk. Nos. **8–19**: probable products of East Anglia or the environs of the Thames Estuary. Scale 1:4.*

blages, due to the disturbance of Flavian features by Antonine structures and other later activities on the site.

Exeter Fortress Wares (fig. 1, A-F)

The following vessels are in a fabric with abundant small quartz grits usually less than 1mm across. The surfaces vary from light to mid-grey and the interior is usually lighter in colour; the harder, more highly-fired example (D) has a dark grey core. A similar range of colour and firing temperature is evident in Exeter Fortress Ware Fabric B.

A. Beaker with slightly cupped rim. No precise parallel is known in Fortress Ware Fabric B, but cupped rims occur on beakers of Types 19 and 20, and Type 22 is a beaker with deep horizontal grooves on the body, although with a simple everted rim (Holbrook & Bidwell 1991, fig. 54). Camelon Form 124, Fab-

ric-group 10, Context A101 (Flavian pit with Antonine contamination).

B-D. Jars with a slight protuberance on the inner edge of the rim; the feature is characteristic of Fortress Ware Fabric B, Type 2, and Fabric A, Type 10 (Holbrook & Bidwell 1991, figs. 52–3). B: Camelon Form 113, Fabric-group 10, Contexts A101, A143 (Flavian with Antonine contamination); C: Camelon Form 110, Fabric-group 10, Flavian Contexts A71, A137.6, A177; D: Camelon Form 115, Fabric-group 10, Context A101 (Flavian pit with Antonine contamination).

E. Tripod bowl. The one foot preserved has been roughly luted onto the underside of the bowl over a zone of horizontal grooves; above the foot, there is the impression of an implement with a rounded end. This is the first complete profile of a tripod bowl recorded in Fortress Ware, but three examples of hollow, trumpet-shaped feet are known from Exeter in Fabric B, two of them associated with sherds with bands of horizontal grooves (Holbrook & Bidwell 1991, fig. 54, Type 32). The closest parallel is a vessel at Richborough, again with trumpet-shaped feet luted on to a zone of horizontal grooves (Pearce 1968, pl. 75, no. 577, 'pale grey ware with blue-grey surface'). The vessel had two handles, and it is possible that the examples in Fortress Ware, including that from Camelon, also had handles. Camelon Form 231, Fabric-group 10, Context Flavian pit A137.2.

E. Reeded-rim bowl, as Exeter Fortress Ware Fabric B (Holbrook & Bidwell 1991, fig. 54), Type 25, especially Type 25.2. Camelon Form 232, Fabric-group 10; mixed Contexts A91, A152.

Probable products of East Anglia or the Thames Estuary (figs. 1–2, nos. 1–19)

Fabric descriptions have been deliberately kept relatively short, but more details can be found in the Camelon Excavation Archive.

1. Narrow-mouthed jar in a fairly hard, light-grey fabric, with mid-grey surfaces, and inclusions of very fine sand and some fine silver mica; the raised shoulder cordons are decorated with combed chevrons and oblique stabbing, both evidently executed with the same implement. Though the general type occurred throughout eastern and south-eastern England in the mid- to late 1st century, the rim profile of this example, the shortish neck, proportionally squat, rather globular body, high shoulder, and decorative techniques in combination are most closely paralleled in Norfolk, in particular, among the Flavian material at Ashill (Gregory 1977, fig. 7, nos. 1, 3, and 9). Camelon Form 66, Fabric-group 80, Context A161 (Flavian with Antonine contamination).

2. Narrow-mouthed jar in a crude, dark brown-black, fairly soft, unevenly fired, hand-made fabric, containing sparse but large inclusions of grog, and abundant voids left by burnt-out organic matter. This typical native 'Belgic' fabric would be not be out of place in south-eastern or eastern England. Camelon Form 180, Fabric-group 218, Context: residual in Antonine pit G3.

3. Rim of a wide-mouthed storage-jar in a hard, smooth, dark grey, unevenly fired fabric, with abundant irregular cavities left from the burning-out of organic temper: another 'native Belgic' south-eastern fabric. Generally comparable vessels (Camulodunum 270A–271) in closely similar fabrics are common on settlements in Essex, for example in the Heybridge area (unpublished). Camelon Form 182, Fabric-group 157, residual in Antonine Context A73.

4. Butt beaker with light rouletting, in a fairly soft, fine, powdery grey fabric containing some silver mica. The fabric and its 'silky'-smooth surface texture, reminiscent of terra nigra, are clearly in a Gallo-Belgic tradition, and most probably emanate from Essex, Suffolk or south Norfolk, areas where butt beakers were widely imitated in such fabrics at this period. Grey copies of butt beakers with a similar rather elongated rim and a fabric containing abundant silver mica were made at the Flavian-Trajanic kiln site at Pear Tree Farm, Wattisfield (unpublished in Ipswich Museum). Close parallels were also probably made at Colchester (Symonds & Wade forthcoming, fig. 182, no. 469). Camelon Form 100, Fabric-group 61, Flavian Context E8.

5. Jar in fairly hard, fine, pale buff, burnished fabric with abundant inclusions of very fine quartz, and some fine silver mica. The fabric and smooth 'soapy' surface of the vessel are reminiscent of butt-beakers, though slightly coarser, but the craftsmanship is not particularly competent. The interior of the vessel is very roughly finished; it sags at the girth, and may perhaps have been hand-formed, but wheel-finished. Narrow-mouthed jars and bowls of this general type were widespread, but the short, gen-

tly everted rim, markedly sloping shoulder and rather angular girth of this example tend to be more characteristic of Norfolk and Suffolk than of Essex, where the detailing of rim and neck differs. General similarities in profile occur at Thetford (Gregory 1991, fig. 142, no. 55). Camelon Form 97, Fabric-group 130, Flavian contexts A145, A235.

6. Large copy of a butt beaker in a very rough-textured dark brownish grey fabric, containing abundant very coarse sand, and a moderate amount of fine silver mica; the darker grey surface of the fabric has an orange tinge. Though the neck shows some evidence of horizontal burnished lines, this does not appear to be North Gaulish grey ware. The colour and coarse fabric texture are more reminiscent of the products of the Nar Valley, Norfolk (e.g. at Pentney and Shouldham: Swan 1984, MF 503–6), where imitations of Gallo-Belgic-inspired vessels were evidently already being made by the last decades of the 1st century AD (inf. M. de Bootman). These sometimes have a partially oxidised exterior surface. Camelon Form 67, Fabric-group 15, Contexts A45, A143 (Flavian with Antonine contamination), Context A239 (Flavian).

7. S-shaped jar or bowl in fabric similar to no. 6, and perhaps from the same general source. Camelon Form 121, Fabric 90/197, Contexts A38, A101, C layer 6 (Flavian features with Antonine contamination).

8. Face-jar with two ribbed handles, in a fairly soft, powdery-textured yellowish-buff fabric. The eyebrows, eyes, nose, mouth and beard have been formed by modelling, stabbing, or cutting slits in clay added separately to the shoulder of the vessel. In style and fabric, this vessel belongs to the group of face-pots apparently made at Colchester (Braithwaite 1984, 105, fig. 5, nos. 1 and 2; fig. 9, no. 1). Their production seems to have spanned the mid-1st to the mid-2nd century (May 1930, pls. 51A and 52, also 289, pl. 90, grave group 13; Hull 1963, 133, fig. 71, no. 18, not a product of the published kilns), but the Camelon example was sealed in a Flavian pit, so its early date is not in doubt. Face-jars, introduced to Britain by the army of conquest, and mostly occurring in military contexts, or on sites with military origins, are never common finds. The elaboration of such vessels suggests that most were probably made to special order. Colchester face-jars rarely occur outside the *colonia* and its immediate environs, so the Camelon vessel was probably acquired in the locality and carried north as a personal possession. Camelon Form 33, Fabric-group 56, Flavian Context A228.

9. Rouletted jar, in a fairly soft, orange, powdery fabric containing small quantities of fine silver mica. The ovoid form, upright rim, and raised cordons are a little reminiscent of barrel beakers, and the 'soapy' exterior surface and general fabric texture also hint at Gallo-Belgic ancestry; for a similar fabric, see no. 16. Camelon Form 99, Fabric-group 32, Flavian Context E8.

10. Bowl, in a fine, fairly soft, mid-grey fabric with small inclusions of iron oxide and a dark grey, smooth burnished surface – a very competently potted table-vessel, with clear Gallo-Belgic ancestry (see also fig. 2, no. 11). The details of profile and fabric suggest a source in the North Kent Marshes, at Cliffe or Upchurch (Monaghan 1987, Form 4J1.3 and 7). Such products occur in London, Colchester, Canterbury and Richborough, at the last of which at least four examples are known; this may be no coincidence, as it was the major supply-base of the fleet at this period.[14] Camelon Form 116, Fabric-group 77, Context A, layer 8 (Flavian).

11. Cordoned jar, possibly a variant of the preceding (no. 10), and in a generally similar fabric. Camelon Form 259, Fabric-group 61, Flavian Context A254.

12. Bowl in a fairly soft, light grey fabric, with a slightly gritty texture and a darker surface – a version of the so-called Icenian bowl, in a somewhat Romanised fabric. Similar forms were produced in the probable Nero-Flavian kilns at Caistor St. Edmund (Atkinson 1932, pl. 9, Fi; Swan 1981). Camelon Form 255, Fabric-group 90/138, Contexts C8 and C49 (Antonine with some residual Flavian pottery).

13. Bowl with simple S-shaped profile in a thick, fairly soft, light grey 'Belgic-type' fabric with a darker smoothed surface. Similar forms occur in Essex and Suffolk, e.g. at Sheepen, Colchester (Niblett 1985, fig. 26, no. 95) and at Scole (Rogerson 1977, fig. 76, no. 75). Camelon Form 250, Fabric-group 90, Context A17 (Antonine with several residual sherds).

14. Bowl probably imitating samian form Drag. 29, in a fine soft greyish fabric of Gallo-Belgic character, with a small amount of fine silver mica and a smooth black surface. Camelon Form 260, Fabric-group 2, Context A101 (predominantly Flavian with some intrusive Antonine material).

15. S-shaped bowl in a fabric generally similar to that of the preceding vessel; a source somewhere in East Anglia or the south-east seems probable. Camelon Form 252, Fabric-group 61, Flavian Context A101 (a predominantly Flavian assemblage with some Antonine contamination), and A254 (Flavian).

16. Flanged bowl in a soft, orange, powdery ware containing fine silver mica; the fabric, apparently in a Gallo-Belgic tradition, ressembles in general that of the jar, fig. 2, no. 9. Detailed contemporary parallels to this Romanised form are uncommon, but similar bowls, with a shallow groove just inside the rim, were made at the kiln site at Pear Tree Farm, Wattisfield (unpublished in Ipswich Museum), and were well represented in Flavian-Trajanic deposits at neighbouring Scole (Rogerson 1977, fig. 76, nos. 74 and 76). Camelon Form 244, Fabric-group 32, Flavian Context A101.

17. Bowl, probably hemispherical or carinated, with a flattened and grooved rim, in a fine pale brownish-grey fabric loaded with fine particles of silver mica, and with dark grey-black smoothed surfaces; the texture is similar to terra nigra. This fabric would not be out of place in the Waveney Valley, where similar forms were made at Common Barn, Rickinghall Inferior, part of the Wattisfield industry (unpublished in Ipswich Museum). Camelon Form 241, Fabric-group 75, Context D27 (Antonine with residual Flavian material).

18. Hemispherical bowl with a reeded rim, in a fine, soft, grey powdery-textured fabric containing much fine silver mica, and with darker grey surfaces; probably a product of one of the industries of central East Anglia such as Brampton (Green 1977, fig. 30, no. 78). Camelon Form 226, Fabric-group 7, Flavian Contexts A234 and A239.

19. Platter copying terra nigra form, Camulodonum 16, in a fairly fine, light grey, TN-related fabric, containing some silver mica, and with a darker, 'silky' smooth surface. Such vessels were widely imitated in the late 1st century, but centres with products containing silver mica include Brampton, Norfolk (Green 1977, figs. 27–8, nos. 27, 48–9) and the Waveney Valley (Rogerson 1977, fig. 56, nos. 82, 83, 86). Camelon Form 343, Fabric-group 158, Context A120 (Antonine with intrusive Flavian material)

Acknowledgements

The authors would like to thank Val Maxfield most warmly for permission to publish a selection of the Camelon pottery in advance of her full excavation report, and for supplying additional information on the site and its archive. Thanks are also due to Andrew King for the originals on which the present pottery illustrations have been based, except for fig. 2, no. 8, which has been traced from a drawing by Sean Goddard. Our particular gratitude is due to Geoff Bailey (Falkirk Museum) for providing transport, information and encouragement and for facilitating our access to the Camelon pottery on more than one occasion. Ailsa Mainman (York Archaeological Trust) kindly made selected York pottery available to us for mention in this paper, and Jason Monaghan provided contextual information. We are also indebted to Gordon Maxwell for his helpful comments on an early draft of this paper, to his collegue Graham Ritchie and staff at RCAHMS, Edinburgh, for providing data from the National Monuments Record, and last, but not least to Margaret Roxan, for her helpful discussion and guidance on the possible significance of the Caistor diploma, and for reading a draft of the relevant section of the text.

Notes

1. This work has been made possible through the late John Gillam's card index of pottery vessels, now expanded and updated in collaboration with John Dore in preparation for a new edition of *Types of Roman coarse pottery vessels in northern Britain*. Thanks are due to the Societies of Antiquaries of London and Scotland, and the Administrators of the Haverfield Bequest, for grants in this connection, and to Brian Hartley for his early encouragement of the project.

2. In the 18th century an anchor was found at Dorrator near an old course of the Carron, just over 1km north-east of the Camelon forts (Maitland 1757), but the object, not now extant, is undated (RCAHMS National Archaeological Record, NS 88 SE 94). I am grateful to the staff of RCAHMS for drawing my attention to this find.

3. A jar of a type characteristic of Exeter Fortress Ware was found at 9 Blake Street, York, in a context dated to *c.* 100–140/160 (Monaghan 1993, fig.292, no. 2904); two other jars, classified as being in the same fabric (Monaghan 1993, fig. 292, no. 2905; fig. 300, no. 3056), do not appear to be in Fortress Ware. There is also a lid from the excavations by York Archaeological Trust in The Bedern (Y.A.T. no. SY-31; 1979.14), as Holbrook & Bidwell 1991, fig. 53, Fabric A, Type 28, and another unpublished lid from Y.A.T. work on the 'Lion and Lamb' site, Blossom Street, as Holbrook & Bidwell 1991, fig. 55, Type 33.1 (illustrated as a bowl but more probably a lid).

4. The Ebchester vessel came from a Flavian-Trajanic context and is a jar, apparently as Holbrook & Bidwell 1991, fig. 53, Type 2.

5. At the Neronian fortress at Usk, a mortarium waster, inscribed before firing *[Pel]v(e)is Contub(e)rnio Messoris*, had evidently been locally commissioned for a contubernium (Hassall 1982, 57–8, fig. 6, no. 44; RIB **2.6**, 2496.3); Johnson (1983, 202) lists evidence from Germany for samian dishes shared on this basis.

6. A Claudian mortarium from Colchester was inscribed before firing '> IVSTI SVPIIRI', '(property) of the century of Iustius Super' (*J. Roman Stud.*, **34** (1944), 91, no. 23; RIB **2.6**, 2496.2). A mortarium, with a graffito cut after firing, belonged to a century at Catterick (RIB **2.6**, 2497.5). Samian vessels, also marked as the property of a century, are recorded at Chester and Castleford (RIB **2.7**, 2501.2 and 4). At the Caerleon fortress, an inscription cut *ante cocturam* on an early 3rd-century casserole (not a butt-jar as published) indicated that it had been made for the century of Aelius Romulus (Boon 1966, 54–7, fig. 1 and pl. 3, no. 2). VGS plans to publish a reconsideration of the historical context of this vessel. Bronze *trullae* were evidently shared on a similar basis (RIB **2.2**, 2415.41, 57–9, and 66).

7. A deposit of unused pottery, both tablewares and culinary vessels, found in the ditch of the fort at Leaholme, Cirencester, is thought to represent material dumped from the military stores when the garri-

son moved on (Wacher & Mcwhirr 1982, 58; Rigby 1982, 179ff). A quantity of pottery, used and unused, and demolition material, tipped into the ditch terminals flanking the west gate of the Tiverton fort, is another example of this phenomenon (Maxfield 1991, 29–33, 67–9).

8. Roman military equipment, particularly that needing repair, was also sometimes discarded; the Corbridge hoard of armour and other items appears to have been packed in a chest ready for transport, but then left behind, perhaps as a last minute decision, because there was insufficient room for it in the baggage train when the garrison left (Allason-Jones & Bishop 1988, 109–110; Bishop & Coulson 1993, 37–7).

9. Dr Margaret Roxan has contributed the following information: Diplomas up to the reign of Hadrian invariably give the years of service as 25+, that is, they include the word *plurave* or *pluribusve* (or similar) in the formula. This could simply be to cover men being kept in service a little over the 25 years. However, Géza Alföldy (1968, 215–17) has drawn together a considerable body of epigraphic evidence in the tombstones of the Julio-Claudian period, indicating that individual auxiliary soldiers had served much longer terms, some as much as 40, and one even 50 years, although some allowance should be made for the tendency to 'round up' figures on tombstones. However, for the Flavian and early Trajanic periods, less evidence was found for such long periods of service (four cases of between 26 and 32 years). In addition, there are some altars which were set up in Rome at the time of their discharge by *equites singulares Augusti* (who, having been drawn from the ranks of the auxilia, received the same diplomas), which show that even in the Hadrianic period, they could serve as much as 28 or 29 years; e.g. CIL VI, 31140 = ILS 2181, where men recruited in AD 103 and 104 were recording their discharge in 132.

10. The evidence of auxiliary diplomas in general indicates that the Flavian period was a time of intense recruitment, evidently in order to raise the additional auxiliary units necessary to garrison newly conquered territory (Roxan 1981, 275). Expansionist policies in northern Britain from *c.* AD 70 to the early 80s would undoubtedly have contributed to a pressing need for more troops. Epigraphic evidence from outside the province, drawn together by Dobson & Mann (1973, 199, n.42), indicates several Britons who were enlisted in auxiliary units between the late 70s and *c.* AD 85, but who ended up serving in the Danube provinces.

11. Though diplomata were sometimes collected as scrap metal for melting down (e.g. at Banasa in Mauretania Tingitana, inf. M. Roxan), it is likely that such material would not have been moved far from its place of origin – in this case, probably in the town of *Venta* itself, or nearby within the *civitas Icenorum*.

12. There is a clear need for a systematic re-examination of pottery from Flavian sites in Scotland in order to identify additional vessels from East Anglia and elsewhere in the south-east. For example, a Flavian jar with an unusual collared rim from Castledykes fort, Scotland (Robertson 1964, 221, fig. 37, no. 10) has a profile identical in detail to that of a probably local vessel from Brampton, Norfolk (Green 1977, 69, fig. 29, no. 61).

13. At the time of writing, it has not always been possible to determine from the Camelon archive which vessel, of several pots catalogued under the same Form/Type number, is actually that selected for illustration; in such cases, alternative context numbers have been listed.

14. The occurrence of probable Exeter Fortress Ware at Richborough (see Catalogue, vessel D), may indicate that the site served as a trans-shipment point for troops from the south-west, as well as for goods drawn from elsewhere.

Bibliography and abbreviations

Alföldy, G., 1968 Zur Beurteilung der Militärdiplome der Auxiliarsoldaten, *Historia*, **17**, 215–27

Allason-Jones, L., & Bishop, M. C., 1988 *Excavations at Roman Corbridge: the hoard*, English Heritage Archaeol. Rep., **7**, HBMCE (London)

Atkinson, D., 1932 Three Caistor pottery kilns, *J. Roman Stud.*, **22**, 33–46

_____, 1937 Roman Pottery from Caistor-next-Norwich, *Norfolk Archaeol.*, **26**, 197–230

Bailey, G. B., 1992 Along and across the River Carron. A history of communications on the lower reaches of the river, *Calatria*, **2**, 49–84

_____, forthcoming Excavations on the Roman temporary camps at the Three Bridges, Camelon, *Proc. Soc. Antiq. Scotland*

Bishop, M. C., & Coulson, J. C. N., 1993 *Roman military equipment from the Punic Wars to the fall of Rome* (London)

Boon, G. C., 1966 'Legionary' ware at Caerleon?, *Archaeol. Cambrensis*, **115**, 45–66

Braithwaite, G., 1984 Romano-British face pots and head pots, *Britannia*, **15**, 99–131

Camulodunum: vessel type numbers in Hawkes, C. F. C., & Hull, M. R., 1947 *Camulodunum*, Rep. Res. Comm. Soc. Antiq. London, **14**

Christison, M. D., & Buchanan, M., 1901 An account of the excavation of the Roman station of Camelon near Falkirk, Stirlingshire, undertaken by the Society in 1900, *Proc. Soc. Antiq. Scotland*, **35**, 329–417

CIL: *Corpus Inscriptionum Latinarum* (Berlin 1863–), cited by volume and item number

Darling, M. J., 1985 The other pottery, in Pitts & St Joseph 1985, 323–38

_____, & Gurney, D, 1993 *Caister-on-Sea: excavations by Charles Green, 1951–55*, East Anglian Archaeol., **60**.

Dobson, B., & Mann, J. C., 1973 The Roman army in Britain and Britons in the Roman army, *Britannia*, **4**, 191–205

Dore, J. N., 1981 Flavian coarse pottery in Northern Britain, in *Early technology in North Britain*, Scottish Archaeol. Forum, **11**, 62–9

Frere, S. S., 1987 *Britannia, a history of Roman Britain*, 3 edn

_____, & St Joseph, J. K., 1983 *Roman Britain from the air* (Cambridge)

Gillam, J. P., 1975 The coarse pottery, in Maxfield, V. A., & Reed, A. H., Excavations at Ebchester Roman Fort 1972–3, *Archaeol. Aeliana*, 5 ser., **3**, 88–101

Green, C., 1977 Excavations in the Roman kiln field at Brampton, 1973–4, *East Anglian Archaeol.*, **5**, 31–95

Gregory, A., 1977 The enclosure at Ashill, *East Anglian Archaeol.*, **5**, 9–30

_____, 1991 *Excavations in Thetford, 1980–1982, Fison Way, 1*, East Anglian Archaeol., **53**

Hanson, W. S., 1987 *Agricola and the conquest of the north* (London)

Hassall, M. W. C., 1982 Inscriptions and graffiti, in Boon, G. C., & Hassall, M. W. C., *The coins, inscriptions and graffiti: report on the excavations at Usk 1965–76* (ed. W. H. Manning), 45–58 (Cardiff)

Holbrook, N., & Bidwell, P. T., 1991 *Roman finds from Exeter*, Exeter Archaeol. Rep., **4** (Exeter)

_____, & _____, 1992 Roman pottery from Exeter 1980–1990, *J. Roman Pottery Stud.*, **5**, 35–80

Johnson, A., 1983 *Roman forts of the 1st and 2nd centuries AD in Britain and the German provinces* (London)

Keppie, L., 1986 *Scotland's Roman remains* (Edinburgh)

McCord, N., & Tait, J., 1978 Excavations in the north annexe of the Roman fort at Camelon, near Falkirk, 1961–3, *Proc. Soc. Antiq. Scotland*, **109**, 151–65

Maitland, W., 1757 *The history and antiquities of Scotland, from the earliest account of time to the death of James the First, anno 1437*

Maxfield, V. A., 1979 Camelon 'south camp' excavations, 1975–79, in Breeze, D. J. (ed.), *Roman Scotland, some recent excavations*, 28–32 (Edinburgh)

_____, 1981 The Flavian fort at Camelon, in *Agricola's campaigns in Scotland*, Scottish Archaeol. Forum, **12**, 69–78

_____, 1991 Tiverton Roman fort (Bolham): excavations 1981–1986, *Proc. Devon Archaeol. Soc.*, **49**, 25–98

Maxwell, G. S., 1991 Springboards for invasion: marching-camp concentrations and coastal installations in Roman Scotland, in Maxfield, V. A., & Dobson, M. J., *Roman frontier studies 1989. Proceedings of the XVth International Congress of Roman Frontier Studies*, 111–13 (Exeter)

May, T., 1930 *Catalogue of the Roman pottery in the Colchester and Essex Museum* (Cambridge)

Monaghan, J., 1987 *Upchurch and Thameside Roman pottery*, BAR Brit. Ser., **173** (Oxford)

_____, 1993 *Roman pottery from the Fortress: 9 Blake Street*, The Archaeology of York, The Pottery, **16/7**

Niblett, R., 1985 *Sheepen: an early Roman industrial site at Camulodunum*, CBA Res. Rep., **57**

Pearce, B. W., 1968 Roman coarse ware, in Cunliffe, B. W. (ed.), *Fifth report on the excavations of the Roman fort at Richborough, Kent*, Rep. Res. Comm. Soc. Antiq. London, **23**, 117–24

Pitts, L. F., & St Joseph, J. K., 1985 *Inchtuthil, the Roman legionary fortress: excavations 1952–65*, Britannia Monograph Ser., **6** (London)

RCAHMS 1963 *Stirlingshire: an inventory of the ancient and historical monuments* (Edinburgh)

Reece, R., 1988 Roman coins, in Drury, P. J., *The mansio and other sites in the south-eastern sector of Caesaromagus, Chelmsford,* Chelmsford Archaeol. Trust Rep., **3.1**, CBA Res. Rep. **66**, 91–3 (London)

RIB **2**: Collingwood, R. G., & Wright, R. P., 1990–95 *The Roman inscriptions of Britain, vol 2: inscriptions on material other than stone,* seven fascicules, (eds Frere, S. S., *et al.*)

Rigby, V, 1982 The coarse wares, in Wacher & McWhirr, 153–200

RMD **1**: Roxan, M. M., 1978 *Roman military diplomas 1954–1977,* Inst. Archaeol. Occas. Publications, **2** (London)

RMD **3**: Roxan, M. M., 1994 *Roman military diplomas 1985–1993,* Inst. Archaeol. Occas. Publications, **14** (London)

Robertson, A. S., 1964 *The Roman fort at Castledykes* (Edinburgh)

Rogerson, A., 1977 Excavations at Scole, 1973, *East Anglian Archaeol.,* **5**, 97–224

Roxan, M. M., 1981 The distribution of Roman military diplomas, *Epigraphische Studien,* **12**, 265–86

Swan, V. G., 1981 Caistor-by-Norwich reconsidered and the dating of Romano-British pottery in East Anglia, in Anderson, A. C., & Anderson, A. S. (eds), *Roman pottery research in Britain and north-west Europe,* BAR Int. Ser., **123**, 123–155 (Oxford)

——————, 1984 *The pottery kilns of Roman Britain,* RCHM Suppl. Ser., **4** (London)

Symonds, R. P., & Wade, S. (eds P. T. Bidwell & A. Croom), forthcoming *Roman pottery from excavations in Colchester 1971–85,* Colchester Archaeol. Rep., **10**

Tatton-Brown, T. W. T., 1980 Camelon, Arthur's O'on and the main supply base for the Antonine Wall, *Britannia,* **11**, 340–43

Wacher, J. S., & McWhirr, A. D., 1982 *Cirencester excavations I, early Roman occupation at Cirencester* (Cirencester)

Williams, D. F., 1985 Fabric examination, in Pitts & St Joseph 1985, 339–40

Woodward, P. J., Davies, S. M., & Graham, A. H., 1993 *Excavations at the Old Methodist Chapel and Greyhound Yard, Dorchester, 1981–1984,* Dorset Natur. Hist. Archaeol. Soc. Mon., **12**

5   Units doubled and divided
and the planning of forts and fortresses

Mark Hassall

Over thirty years ago the author had the delightful experience of attending the excavations co-directed by Sheppard Frere and Brian Hartley at the samian potteries at Lezoux. Since then he has had the opportunity of expressing his appreciation of the former by contributing to the Frere *Festschrift*, edited by Brian and John Wacher (Hartley & Wacher 1983), and it is a renewed satisfaction, therefore, to have the chance now to pay a similar compliment to Brian himself. The paper offered to Sheppard Frere was concerned with the internal planning of Roman auxiliary forts, primarily forts which appear to have been designed for single units. It is not inappropriate that the present study picks up where the previous one left off and deals with topics either only briefly touched upon earlier, such as the planning of forts like Pen Llystyn which appear to have housed two distinct cohorts, or else which were only hinted at: the planning of forts for several units, or subdivisions of units, particularly the infantry or cavalry elements of *cohortes equitatae* (Hassall 1983, 120). However, unlike the earlier one which was confined to a simple analysis of fort plans, I wish here to take a somewhat broader view and examine the plans as a reflection of two fundamental aspects of Roman military practice: the pairing or combining of military units for organisational or tactical reasons, and, conversely, the division of others for similar reasons. Various combinations and divisions are considered and only then are the practical implications for the interpretation of Roman fort and fortress plans examined.

DOUBLED UNITS OF IDENTICAL TYPE

The doubling or pairing of identical units was a long-standing phenomenon in the Roman army: traditionally under the Republic each of the two consuls commanded two legions enrolled annually from the citizen body (Parker 1958, 13). By the time of the early Empire the legions consisted of men who had permanently enlisted, and the consuls no longer lead them into battle, but the concept of paired legions remained. Thus, in his account of the military dispositions of the Empire in AD 23, Tacitus (*Annals* iv, i, 5) lists the legionary strength in each province, and inscriptions and literary references allow us to identify the legions and locate most of their fortresses.

Of a total of 25 legions, probably a dozen, or just under half, were based in double legionary fortresses. Gradually the practice was abandoned. Suetonius (*Domitian* vii, 3) says that it finally came to an end under Domitian when the governor of Upper Germany, Antonius Saturninus, used the savings of the two legions based at Mainz to finance an abortive coup. After the revolt had been suppressed, Domitian reduced the garrison there to a single legion. Henceforth, pairs of legions were no longer brigaded together, the exception that proves the rule being the double legionary fortress at Nicopolis outside Alexandria, which accommodated Legions III Cyrenaica and XXII Deiotariana. These two legions were under the sole command of the equestrian camp prefect whose relatively low status will have made the temptation to stage a coup in the province of Egypt – critically important as the granary of Rome – less likely. Archaeologically the best example of a double legionary fortress is provided by Castra Vetera at Xanten in the lower Rhineland, where the earlier fortress of the Claudio-Neronian period housed legions V Alaudae and XV Primigenia (von Petrikovits 1975, 153, Taf. 5a). Tile stamps of the two legions show that each confined its building activities to what in Roman terms will have been thought of as the *dexter* and *sinister* side of the fortress, i.e. to right and left of the long access as one faces the front gate (*porta praetoria*), and this should correspond to the way in which their accommodation within the fortress was also assigned. Thus the senior legion, V Alaudae, built and occupied the more honourable *dexter* side, and the junior, XV Primigenia, the less honourable or *sinister* (CIL XIII.6, pp. 14 and 47). A similar phenomenon is observable at the double legionary fortress at Mainz where tile stamps of the senior legion, IV Macedonica, are again found in the *dexter* side of the fortress, and of XXII Primigenia in the *sinister* (CIL XIII.6, pp. 12 and 56). The arrangements for the joint headquarters building (*principia*) at Xanten (fig. 1, no. 4) are of interest and show how, although there was a common central shrine opposite the short axis of the 'cross hall' or basilica, each legion also had its own shrine (*aedes*), where its standards were lodged and the savings of the soldiers stored, at either end.

This arrangement, with *aedes* at each end of the basilica, is

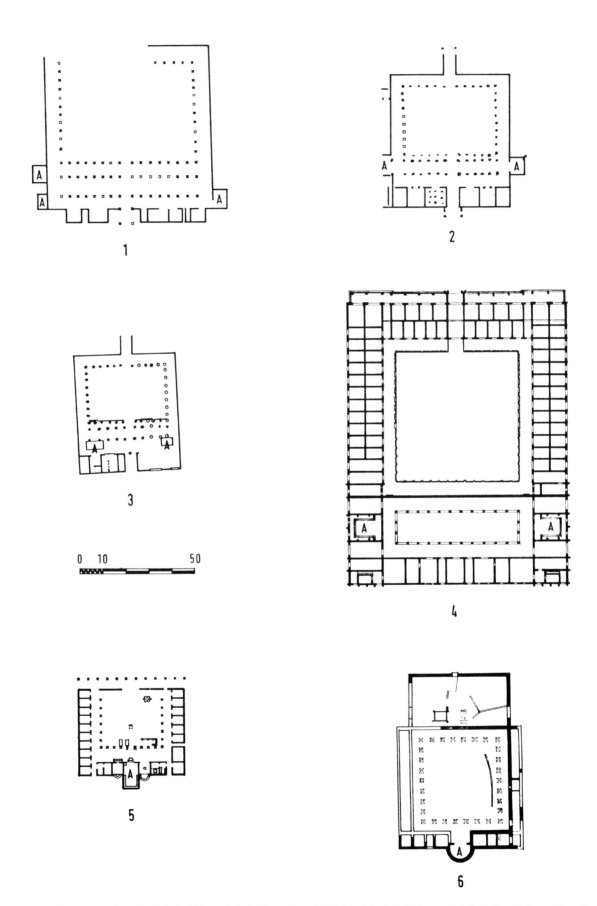

Fig. 1. Comparative plans of principia *('A' =* aedes*): 1. Neuss, Camp 'C'; 2. Marktbreit; 3. Haltern, period 2; 4. Castra Vetera (Xanten);
5. Gemellae; 6. Niederbieber. (Drawn by Digby Stevenson: Nos. 1–3 after Pietsch 1993; nos. 4–5 after Fellmann 1983; no. 6 after Fabricius 1937)*

reminiscent of the second period *principia* at Haltern (fig. 1, no. 3) where there was no cenral shrine, its place being occupied by a rear entrance to the basilica, but where two separate underground strongrooms have been located which will have corresponded to the two *aedes* of two units or detachments in garrison (von Schnurbein 1974, 57ff., Beilage 7, IV). At Haltern, as at Xanten, it is perhaps also possible to recognise two courtyard houses serving as the quarters (*praetoria*) for the two commanding officers, to the rear of the *principia* and to its north-east (von Schnurbein 1974, 59, 61 ff.), which would support the notion that there were indeed two units or detachments in garrison. Augustan headquarters buildings similar to that discussed at Haltern, i.e. with an axially aligned rear entrance to the basilica, have also been identified at Neuss, Camp C (fig. 1, no. 1) and Marktbreit (fig. 1, no. 2). Camp C at Neuss may, it is thought, have possibly accommodated four legions, but the location of four distinct *aedes* cannot be identified with certainty, though two rooms projecting from the *sinister* side end of the basilica and one from the *dexter* may have served this purpose. At Marktbreit a single room projects from each end of the basilica and these would appear to have been the *aedes* for two distinct units. Behind the *principia* and linked to its rear door by a covered porch, is a house with peristyle courtyard, identified, surely correctly, as a *praetorium*. On its dextral side is a second courtyard building identified as an 'administrative block' (Pietsch 1993, 356, Abb. 1), but perhaps in reality a second *praetorium*. Again this would lend support to the notion that two units or detachments are in garrison.

Though this all appears to make good sense, it should be pointed out that the *principia* at other Augustan fortresses, such as Oberaden and first period Haltern, also have axially aligned rear entrances to their basilicas, but apparently no *aedes* at all (Pietsch 1993). A discussion of this question is beyond the scope of this paper, though a possible clue to the answer may be provided by Cagnat in his discussion of a curious exedra-like paved area on the *dexter* side of the fore hall (*groma*) at the fortress of Legion III Augusta at Lambaesis (Cagnat 1908, 47–8; 1913, 497–8). This area, lying between the front of the *principia* and the *via principalis*, but separated from it by a sort of rail or screen, is explained by Cagnat as a sort of covered tribunal from which orders of the day were issued on the basis of a passage in Hyginus (*de munitionibus castrorum* 20) where such a function is ascribed to an apparently similar location (though the meaning is not altogether clear) in his specimen temporary camp, and where it is stated that this lay *contra aquilam* – 'over against the Eagle'. The exedra-like feature has more recently been explained by Rakob (1979) as the site of a nymphaeum, but even if he is correct, the passage cited by Cagnat from Hyginus might be taken to indicate a position near the front entrance to the commander's tent for the eagle in temporary camps. Some of the scenes on Trajan's Column clearly show the standards set up in the open and outside large frame tents which certainly look as if they served as officers' or administrative quarters. If this is correct then a similar position near the front entrance to the *principia* may have been assigned to the standards in some of the Augustan fortresses.

Within the legion also, the principle of pairing also existed.

During the middle Republic the basic subdivision of the legion was a maniple of two centuries. Under the Empire, though the maniple had ceased to exist for tactical purposes, it survived for organisational ones in the *prior* and *posterior* centuries within legionary cohorts. This pairing is, of course, reflected in the three pairs of barrack blocks assigned to the six centuries that formed the regular legionary cohorts. There may also be another and less obvious example of the principle of pairing in the internal organisation of the legions. After the tactical division of the legion into maniples had been abandoned, it was replaced by a division into ten cohorts. It is often stated, or implied, that there were no cohort commanders among the officers of the legion (Parker 1958, 30, 201). Though this is formally true, there were six tribunes of which five, the equestrian *tribuni angusticlavii*, were relatively mature men who had previously exercised independent commands of auxiliary units. It is tempting to regard the equestrian tribunes as in some sense the commanders of *paired* cohorts, and though this cannot be proved, it is certainly true that under the Empire tribunes were often put in charge of legionary vexillations, so that they sometimes exercised a command role and did not function merely as staff officers (Saxer 1967, 120). Just as whole legions might operate in pairs, so too auxiliary cohorts. Tacitus (*Annals* xii, 39), in describing the operations in south Wales during the last months of the governorship of Ostorius Scapula and the period immediately following his death in AD 53, describes the destruction of two auxiliary cohorts that were presumably operating as a pair. In AD 66 Josephus (*Jewish War* ii, 318) states that two cohorts had been summoned to Jerusalem by the procurator Florus from their camp at Caesarea, while three years later, at the other end of the Empire, the Frisii attacked the *hiberna* of two cohorts stationed near the coast (Tacitus, *Histories* iv, 15). Finally the Vindolanda tablets also hint at the brigading of units or at least parts of units if not actual pairing, for the tablets attest the presence there of *Cohortes III* and *IX Batavorum* and *Cohors I Tungrorum* (as well as a detachment at least of *Cohors I Fida Vardullorum equitata civium Romanorum*) and it may well be that some or part of some of these units were in garrison at the same time (Bowman & Thomas 1994, 22–4). What might have been true of Vindolanda could also have applied to other forts in the area, since one of the tablets seems to show the presence of two commanding officers, Brocchus and Niger, at one of them (Bowman & Thomas 1994, no. 248).

Archaeologically the clearest example of an auxiliary fort designed for two cohorts is Flavian Pen Llystyn (Nash-Williams & Jarrett 1969, 101–3; Hassall 1983, 118–9), with its twelve barrack blocks, appropriate to the twelve centuries of two quingenary cohorts. It is tempting to interpret Rottweil, Fort III, as another example (Filtzinger *et al.* 1986, 69, Abb. 16): the plan is incomplete, but there are two sets of four barracks in the rear part of the fort (*retentura*) and it is very likely that these were complemented by two further pairs of barracks in the front part of the fort (*praetentura*) for a total of twelve. At Rottweil there are two courtyard houses (if not three!) in the area flanking the *principia* (*latera praetorii*), which could have housed the two cohort commanders (and a *praefectus castrorum*?). Alternatively the fort could have housed two legionary cohorts, an interpretation favoured by the relatively generous dimensions of the barrack blocks (cf. Davison 1989, 203–4). The fact that the *principia* at both Rottweil and Pen Llystyn are of conventional type, and not provided with two *aedes* as in the examples noted above, is not a difficulty since at Niederbieber and Gemellae (both discussed below) where there were certainly two units, there were only single shrines. There is perhaps a difficulty, though, in the presence of only one *praetorium* at Pen Llystyn.

Another possible candidate for an auxiliary fort designed for two cohorts is Flavian Elginhaugh just south of Edinburgh, which appears to have four barrack blocks in the *retentura* and eight in the *praetentura* for a total of twelve, again the appropiate accommodation for two quingenary cohorts. However one of the 'barracks' in the *praetentura* may in fact be a long stores shed, while two of those in the *retentura* could have housed cavalry troops (*turmae*). The difficulties of interpretation are well discussed by Davison (1989, 193–4, 460, fig. 10), but a definitive interpretation – if one is possible – must await the imminent pubication of the site by its excavator, Bill Hanson.

One certain case where two units of similar type were stationed in the same fort is provided by Niederbieber on the German frontier, occupied in the 3rd century by the *Numerus Exploratorum Germanicorum Divitensium* and a *Numerus Brittonum*. Here both units again shared a single *principia* (fig. 1, no. 6), but unlike the early headquarters buildings at Haltern, Neuss Camp C, Marktbreit and Xanten, there was only one *aedes* (fig. 1, no. 6). However, the evidence of epigraphy shows that the rooms on its sinistral side were occupied by the *Brittones*, and it is reasonable to assume that those on the dextral side were allocated to the *Germanici* (Fabricius 1937, 19–25; Fellmann 1983, 65, Abb. 40 and 76). Another probable case of paired units is that of the (*Numerus*) *Brittonum Stu*(...) and the (*Numerus*) *Brittonum Dediticiorum Alexandrianorum* associated together on an inscription in the work of rebuilding a bathouse at the small fort of Walldürn on the Outer *Limes*. Here, however, lack of space makes it likely that the last named unit occupied a separate fortlet, perhaps nearby Haselburg (Baatz 1993, 222–4).

The principle of pairing units is, if anything, better attested in the field army units (*comitatenses*) of the late Empire, when units were enrolled and subsequently operated as pairs. Under the tetrarchy two such newly enrolled legions were called Ioviani and Herculiani after Jupiter and Hercules, the two patron deities of the two senior tetrarchs, Diocletian and Maximian, while another pair, the Solenses and Martenses, were named after Sol and Mars, the patrons of the junior tetrarchs, Constantius and Galerius. Among the units called *auxilia* were other pairs, the Cornuti and the Bracchiati, and the Iovii and the Victores. Again among Constantine's new 'legions', the Divitenses were paired with the Tungrecani, and among the cavalry, the Equites Cornuti with the Equites Promoti (Tomlin 1981, 249ff.; Hoffmann 1969–70). There is a hint that limitanean units may sometimes have been paired also. In the Notitia (*Not. Dig. Occ.* xxviii), the order in which the forts of the Saxon Shore in south-eastern England are listed appears to be on the basis of geographically paired units (Hassall 1977, 8; Stevens 1940, 138 n.2).

THE COMBINATION OF DISSIMILAR UNITS

So far only the pairing of identical types of units has been considered. This, it can be suggested, reflects a deep-seated predilection on the part of the Romans for pairing units deriving from the traditional two-legion consular armies of Republican times and the way in which the legionary maniples were formed from paired centuries. However, there is, hardly surprisingly, considerable evidence for a more flexible approach whereby units of different type could on occasion, operate together or share the same camp. An interesting case is the legionary fortress at Neuss. Here the original fortress layout is obscured by subsequent rebuilding, but the plan of *c.* AD 50 can be reconstructed (Nissen 1904, 33). The reconstruction, though highly speculative, is nevertheless convincing and accords with what is known of the garrison from literary and epigraphic evidence. The fortress would appear to have been designed for a legion, an auxiliary *ala* and two auxiliary cohorts. The legion, consisting of ten cohorts, all of six centuries, occupied the *retentura* and *latera praetorii* of the fortress, while the auxiliary units were all housed in the *praetentura*. From the account of Tacitus (*Histories* iv, 62) we know that, in AD 70, the cavalry regiment was the *Ala Gallorum Picenti(a)na* and that there were other unspecified troops, and though their identity is not given, these, on the Nissen interpretation, should be two auxiliary cohorts. Such an arrangement would have precedents under the Republic. Polybius' description of the ideal camp of a consular army of two legions in the 2nd century BC includes Italian allies (Fabricius 1932, 79, fig. 12), while the contemporary camp at Renieblas near Numantia in Spain (Schulten 1929, plan 17, 2) will have housed just such a force. Under the Empire other legionary fortresses in the Rhineland apart from Neuss also included accommodation for auxiliary units (von Petrikovits 1975, 57; Alföldy 1968, 144), one example being Mainz where the *Ala Indiana* may have been stationed in the legionary fortress along with Legion XXII Primigenia in the late 2nd century (Baatz 1962, 87). Reconstructed plans of early legionary fortresses in Britain such as those of Legion XX at Colchester and Legion II Augusta at Exeter, would appear to have had room for more than the number of barracks required for the legion in garrison, so that auxiliary units may have formed part of the garrison at these sites also. In the case of Colchester the discovery of a fine tombstone of a trooper in *Ala I Thracum* (RIB **1**, 201) may indicate the unit in question, though it is possible that the regiment was based at the nearby auxiliary fort at Gosbecks. The presence of a skillet stamped with the name of the same or an identically named unit (RIB **2**, 2415. 39) at Caerleon, could also indicate that at one period the regiment was stationed in the fortress along with Legion II Augusta.

The same flexibility is shown where auxiliary units alone are concerned. It has been demonstrated above that auxiliary cohorts sometimes operated as a pair and shared the same fort. But it was also possible for auxiliary regiments of different types, e.g. *alae* of cavalry and cohorts of infantry, to share accommodation in this way. Such mixed garrisons can be suggested on the basis of fort plans, of inscriptions naming units, or both. At Heddernheim in the first Flavian period two cohorts and an *ala* are attested, *Cohors IV Vindelicorum, Cohors XXXII Voluntariorum,* and *Ala I Flavia Gemina* (thought at this period to be quingenary rather than milliary as it was later). The regular garrison may, it has been suggested, have been an *ala* and a cohort (Baatz & Herrmann 1982, 279 ff.; Abb. 207, 208). The same combination has been suggested for Echzell, where one cohort but three different *alae* are known, the *Ala Indiana Gallorum, Ala Moesica Felix Torquata,* and *Ala I Flavia Gemina* (Baatz & Hermann 1982, 261 ff.). In both cases other units, apart from those actually attested, may have helped form part of the garrison at different periods. If this is so, the association of specific *alae* and cohorts may sometimes have been maintained when the garrison as a whole was changed.

A rather similar situation may have existed at Gemellae, established by Hadrian south of the legionary fortress at Lambaesis as a key fort associated with one section of the Fossatum Africae in Algeria (Baradez 1967, 205). At Gemellae two (successive?) *alae* are known, *I Thracum* and *I Pannoniorum,* as well as a milliary part-mounted cohort, *I Chalcidenorum equitata,* and it seems likely that one of the *alae* and the part-mounted cohort were in garrison at the same time. In support of this interpretation may be the name of the fort, Gemellae, which means 'Twins' (another fort in Algeria, incidentally, was called Dimidi, 'Half', which might suggest that the unit in garrison there was not at full strength but had been subdivided in the manner to be discussed below). It is noteworthy that at Gemellae, the combined strength of the *ala*, with its 16 *turmae*, and the cavalry element of part-mounted cohort, with its eight, would come to 24 *turmae*, or precisely the equivalent of a milliary *ala*, a rare type of unit and one of which no example is known in Numidia. It is almost as if Gemellae was being singled out to receive the next best thing, a sort of *ersatz* milliary *ala* made by increasing the strength of a quingenary *ala* with the eight *turmae* of the mixed unit. As at Niederbieber a single *aedes* was provided in the *principia* for the standards of the two units in garrison (fig. 1, no. 5).

In some cases we know that auxiliary units were joined not by other *alae* and cohorts but by *numeri*. There are examples of this on the frontiers in north Britain and southern Germany. In the 3rd century several – perhaps a majority – of the outpost forts north of Hadrian's Wall were garrisoned in this way, including the two major outposts of Risingham and High Rochester on Dere Street. At Risingham *Cohors I Vangionum milliaria equitata* was, as we know from epigraphy (RIB **1**, 1235), united in garrison with the *Raeti Gaesati* and the *Exploratores Habitancenses,* while further to the north another milliary part-mounted unit, *Cohors I Fida Vardullorum C.R.* was combined with the *Exploratores Bremenienses* (RIB **1**, 1279 and 1270). On the wall itself during the same period, Housesteads was garrisoned by *Cohors I Tungrorum milliaria,* attested by many inscriptions, together with the *Numerus Hnaudifridi* (RIB **1**, 1576). A third unit, the *Cuneus Frisiorum Ver(coviciensium)* (RIB **1**, 1594)

will either have been replaced by, or replaced the *numerus,* or, possibly, have formed a third unit in garrison on the analogy of Risingham where, as we have seen there were three units.

A similar situation obtained in southern Germany where we find *Cohors III Aquitanorum* and the *Numerus Brittonum Elantiensium* associated with each other at Neckarburken, though actually accommodated in separate forts (Filtzinger *et al.* 1986, 279–85). When in *c.* AD 160, the cohort moved eastwards to Osterburken on the Outer *Limes,* the *numerus* probably moved too, when it was accommodated (though possibly not initially) in an annexe physically attached to the new cohort fort at Osterburken (Filtzinger *et al.* 1986, 468–71; Speidel 1986).

In a number of other forts, for example Künzing in Raetia, built *c.* AD 90 for a quingenary part-mounted cohort, *Cohors III Thracum,* an extra barrack block over and above the expected number suggests the presence of extra troops, possibly a *numerus* of scouts, or a detachment from such a unit (Schönberger 1975, 112; Hassall 1983, 105, 107–8). In relation to the frontier in southern Germany, Baatz (1993, 31) has pointed out that even when there are no inscriptions and little of the plan of a fort is known, its size alone can suggest multiple occupancy, either by more than one auxiliary unit, or by an auxiliary unit and an associated *numerus.*

Finally, in discussing composite forces, there is the question of mixed garrisons of auxiliaries and legionary vexillations, that is detachments as distinct from whole legions. There is possible literary evidence for this practice. Thus, according to Josephus (*Jewish War* iv, 486), during the revolt of AD 66–71 camps were established at Adida and Jericho for garrisons drawn from both 'Romans' and allied forces, presumably legions and auxiliaries, though 'Romans' could, in theory, mean legions and/or auxiliaries, and 'allied forces' the contingents supplied by client kings such as we know fought on the side of the Romans duing the revolt. Another possible example is given by Tacitus (*Annals* xii, 45) when he refers to the fort at Gorneae in Armenia as 'under the command of Caelius Pollio and the centurion Crepereius'. One would naturally assume that Pollio was the commander of an auxiliary unit and that Crepereius was in charge of legionaries, but this is not necessarily so: Arrian (*Ektaxis* 2) provides an example of auxiliary troops being commanded by an officer of the same rank as Crepereius when he refers to 'Celtic' (i.e. German) cavalry being under the command of a centurion 'as they are at base camp'. In fact there are numerous cases known from epigraphy of this practice. To quote two examples only, both from the north British frontier, Julius Marcellinus, a centurion of Legion II Augusta, was in charge of *Cohors I Aelia Dacorum* at Birdoswald on Hadrian's Wall (RIB **1**, 1880), while Julius Candidus, centurion (designate) of Legion I Italica, had command of all or part of *Cohors I Baetasiorum* at Old Kilpatrick on the Antonine Wall (*Britannia,* **1** (1970), 310, no. 20). Cases like these bring into question the garrisons of forts such as 2nd-century Newstead. Here inscriptions attest the presence of a cavalry regiment, the *Ala Vocontiorum* and one of its decurions (RIB **1**, 2121), as well as two centurions of Legion XX, Arrius Domitianus (RIB **1**, 2122–4) and

Maximius Gaetulicus (RIB **1**, 2120, cf. AÉ 1985, 735). Richmond (1949–50, 50, 20) assumed that the presence of the legionary centurions indicated that the troops they commanded were legionaries and, on the basis of the accommodation available, suggested a garrison of two cohorts of Legion XX quartered there alongside the cavalry of the Vocontii. If true, Domitianus and Gaetulicus would have been just two of twelve centurions, presumably under the command of a tribune seconded from the legion, but, from the examples quoted above, it is equally possible that they were each in command of a single auxiliary cohort. However, the relatively generous proportions of the barrack blocks for the two cohorts, as at Rottweil III discussed above, might suggest that legionaries were present (Davison 1989, 81). A similar situation may have obtained at Ardoch where the dimensions of the barracks in the *praetentura* have been thought to indicate that a legionary cohort was stationed there along with *Cohors I Hispanorum* attested there by an inscription (RIB **1**, 2213) in the Flavian period (Breeze 1983, 233–4).

If a mixed legionary and auxiliary garrison cannot be proved at either Newstead or Ardoch, such a garrison is even less certain at other sites such as Hod Hill (Richmond 1968, 117 ff.) and, as Maxfield has shown (1986, 66–71), is certainly not proved by finds of *lorica segmentata*. This is not to say that small numbers of legionaries may not on occasion have been present in auxiliary forts for specific purposes, as indeed we know that they were at Vindolanda in the early 2nd century (Bowman & Thomas 1994, no. 214).

THE DIVISION OF UNITS – LEGIONS

Whatever the situation at Newstead, the legions certainly did supply vexillations. The present writer, however, does not regard the so called 'vexillation fortresses', of which some dozen or so are known from lowland Britain dating to the middle years of the 1st century, as the bases for half legions, as has been claimed, notably by Sheppard Frere, but suggests that they served perhaps as the winter quarters for concentrations of auxiliary units (Hassall forthcoming). Nevertheless there is good evidence that the legions, if not normally divided in this way, did provide smaller bodies of troops. However, even the removal of two of the ten cohorts of a legion, as may have been done to provide the garrison at Antonine Newstead, will have had serious consequences for the effectiveness of the parent unit. A less damaging way of providing troops for service elsewhere, was to send a force drawn from the legion as a whole. We know from Hadrian's speech to the army of Africa (ILS, 2487) that Legion III Augusta had recently contributed reinforcements to Legion III Cyrenaica, and that these consisted of one complete cohort together with four men drawn from each of the remaining centuries of the legion. It may well be that in the case of the small numbers of men drawn from the legionary centuries, the measure was designed to replace losses in Legion III Cyrenaica, while the transfer of the whole cohort was thought of only as a temporary expedient. In the course of time, however, the permanent transfer of legionary cohorts gradually

became more common. From the point of view of surviving fort plans, Flavian Rottweil III, probably accommodating two cohorts, would, if they were legionary, be the earliest example, and Antonine Newstead perhaps the second (both discussed above). The earliest certain examples are the three 3rd-century desert outposts of Legion III Augusta in Libya, Gadames, Gheria el-Garbia and Bu Ngem (Goodchild 1954). Of the three most is known about Bu Ngem (Rebuffat 1989, 162–3), though even here, despite a relatively complete plan, it is not certain how many barracks were originally provided (fig. 2): it is clear that there were eight barracks of half the normal length in the *praetentura*, between them sufficient to have held four centuries, and it is tempting to suppose that there were originally four more in the *retentura* to accommodate two more centuries, thus six in all and so a full legionary cohort, but certainty is not possible.

By the late Empire, the permanent division of the legions into their constituent cohorts or groups of cohorts had become standard. Thus in the province of Pannonia Prima, Legion XIV Gemina was divided into two, and Legion III Italica into three parts, each with its own permanent fortified base (*Not. Dig. Occ.* xxxiv), while in the neighbouring province of Valeria, Legion II Adiutrix was split into as many as seven different sections similarly accommodated (*Not. Dig. Occ.* xxxii).

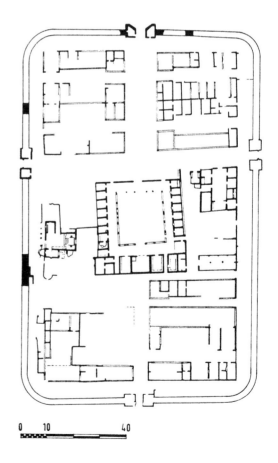

Fig. 2. Bu Ngem
(restored plan, drawn by Digby Stevenson after Rebuffat 1989).

THE DIVISION OF UNITS – AUXILIARIES

Turning briefly to the auxiliary units, the epigraphic evidence, particularly that provided by the military diplomas, shows that cohorts, *alae* and *cohortes equitatae*, either individually or collectively, all supplied vexillations for service elsewhere. Where part-mounted cohorts are concerned, such as *Cohors IV Tungrorum* and *Cohors III Batavorum*, both milliary units, the division was probably made between the ten infantry centuries on the one hand and the eight *turmae* of cavalry on the other. Sometimes composite forces were made up from several different auxiliary units such as the *vexillatio equitum Illyricorum*, comprising small numbers of men from the *alae* and/or *cohortes equitatae* in Illyricum and attested in Dacia Inferior in AD 129 (CIL XVI, 75). The epigraphic evidence shows that this force was never disbanded but became a regular unit in the Roman army, though with several changes of title. Where individual units were called upon to supply vexillations, the option existed of either detaching individual centuries or *turmae*, or detaching small numbers of men from all the centuries or *turmae* in the unit – or combining both principles, as happened in the case already discussed above of the reinforcements sent from Legion III Augusta to Legion III Cyrenaica. A possible example of this could be the Hadrianic fort at Wallsend, the eastern terminal of Hadrian's Wall (*Britannia*, **16** (1985), 269, fig. 11). Unfortunately there is no independent epigraphic evidence for the type of unit in garrison there, though the consensus of opinion seems to be now that it was a *cohors quingenaria equitata* (e.g. Davison 1989, 206). If, however, the garrison was, as the author of this paper once thought, a *cohors milliaria*, one barrack block out of an expected total of ten is missing, as is one *contubernium* from each of the remaining nine barracks, accommodation appropriate for almost another complete century. The explanation could be that the two centuries that are missing were permanately detached from the unit in garrison, perhaps for service in the mile-castles and turrets of Hadrian's Wall. Such an explanation will be condemned as over ingenious – and correctly – but explanations *like* this, if only we had the evidence, would surely explain the anomalies that are found in so many auxiliary fort plans.

THE DIVISION OF PART-MOUNTED UNITS
(*COHORTES EQUITATAE*)

In conclusion it is worth looking more closely at the subdivision of *cohortes equitatae*, such as *Cohors IV Tungrorum* and *Cohors III Batavorum*, both of which, as mentioned above, are known from diplomas to have supplied vexillations. When this happened and the division was a straight one between the infantry and cavalry sections, the larger infantry element would continue to be commanded by its prefect or tribune, but the smaller cavalry element would require a commander. This would usually be one of the decurions, and, to indicate his enhanced authority he often received the additional title of *princeps*, a title, however, which was also used for other *ad hoc* commanders (Speidel 1981). The practice of dividing the part-mounted units in this way is particularly interesting, and will have been especially common since the cavalry and infantry sections could each be used in different tactical roles. This comes over clearly in *The order of march against the Alani (Ektaxis)* written by Arrian, Hadrian's govenor of Cappadocia, and the subsequent description in the same work of his intended dispositions on the battlefield if the invading Alans should offer battle. Arrian had at his disposal ten auxiliary cohorts, of which as many as eight were part-mounted units, and the cavalry element from these regularly operated with the cavalry *alae* rather than with the infantry. This has implications for our interpretation of Tacitus' account of the battle of Mons Graupius where he says that Agricola had at his disposal, in addition to the legions and auxiliary infantry, a cavalry force of 3,000, exclusive of four *alae* which he kept in reserve. From what has been said above, it would be wrong to assume, with Richmond, that this force was necessarily all made up of six quingenary *alae* (Ogilvie & Richmond 1967, 271, cf. 78).

The semi-permanent division of part-mounted units, and the recognition that the constituent parts could operate either independently or in conjunction with other units, is obviously relevant to attempts at deducing the nature of the garrisons of forts from their plans and sizes. Thus in the case of the 3rd-century fort of Castlesteads on Hadrian's Wall where the attested garrison, *Cohors II Tungrorum milliaria equitata* is too large, E. Birley (1961, 138 ff.; cf. Speidel 1981, note 29) has suggested that part of the unit may have been in garrison elsewhere, perhaps at Old Church. Again, it is likely that most or all part-mounted cohorts stationed on the Antonine Wall in Scotland in the 2nd century were similarly divided, although the number of such units may not have been large. This would help to explain the wide variation in fort area, most of them too small to have housed complete units: to the six regular types of auxiliary unit (or five if one ignores the rare milliary *ala*), it would be necessary in effect to add two more, a cavalry detachment of 240 men supplied by a part-mounted milliary cohort, and one of 120 men supplied by the smaller part-mounted quingenary regiment, a half and a quarter the size respectively of a regular quingenary *ala*. There are possible, though perhaps not very convincing, hints from inscriptions that two of the part-mounted units attested on the Wall may have been divided in this way. At Castlecary, *Cohors I Fida Vardullorum*, a milliary part-mounted regiment, was commanded by a prefect on one inscription (RIB 1, 2149) instead of by a tribune, as would be normal for a unit of this size. The inferior status of the commander suggests that some of his men may have been detached, though if so, it is perhaps odd that the milliary sign qualifying the unit has been retained. In the case of *Cohors IV Gallorum*, a part-mounted quingenary cohort based at Castlehill, the unit lacks the epithet *eq(uitata)* on the inscription that attests its presence there (RIB 1, 2195). This might be taken to indicate that the cavalry section was elsewhere, although the ommision may, of course, have no particular significance. However, the evidence of archaeology suggests that, irrespective of the above argument, this may indeed have been the case: the nearby fort at Bearsden is too small to have contained a complete unit and also lacks a *principia* and it is reasonable to suppose that part of the unit, including the headquarters staff, was in garrison somewhere else, almost certainly Castlehill (Breeze 1984, 26–7). One part-mounted unit that may at one time have been divided was the Fourth Cohort's sister unit, *Cohors III Gallorum (quingenaria) equitata*, but by the removal of both infantry and cavalry. This unit was based in early Claudian times at Valkenburg where it has been argued (Glasbergen & Groenman-van Waateringe 1974, 20) that there was only accommodation sufficient for four of the unit's centuries and two of its four *turmae*, but the matter is not certain and the unit may have been present at full strength after all (Hassall 1983, 108–10; Davison 1989, 201–3).

The splitting of a part-mounted unit could explain the barrack accommodation for the first stone period at Hofheim, built *c*. AD 75 (Baatz & Herrmann 1982, 354, Abb. 297). This fort apparently had twelve barracks but also stables, whose presence might be thought to rule out a garrison of two quingenary cohorts, the suggested garrison of the fort at Pen Llystyn (though in fact there is some provision for sheds or stables there also). One explanation may be that Hofheim was designed for a *cohors milliaria peditata*, its ten centuries occupying ten barracks, with the addition of the four *turmae* from a *cohors quingenaria equitata* accommodated in the two extra barracks. Alternatively it could have housed a *cohors milliaria equitata* which had lost half its cavalry, which would again result in a force of ten centuries of infantry and four *turmae* of cavalry. However, it is not certain that milliary cohorts existed so early and other explanations are certainly possible, such as the presence of six legionary centuries as part of the garrison (Davison 1989, 203; cf. Nuber 1983, 229).

If the cavalry *turmae* of part-mounted cohorts became permanently detached, they would, as pointed out above, become, in effect, independent cavalry units of 120 or 240 men. This may become relevant to the origin of some of the cavalry units of this size in the armies of the late Empire, e.g. the *Ala Hiberorum* of 116 men (Tomlin 1981, 251) or the *Equites Sagittarii* of 121 (Tomlin 1981, 253). Margaret Roxan, in examining the survival of pre-Severan auxiliary regiments in the lists of troops preserved in the Notitia Dignitatum, has pointed to the phenomenon of *alae* which are apparently converted cohorts, and cites eight probable and four possible examples (Roxan 1976, 75, Table II; 77, Table III). In some cases at least, it seems more likely that they are the cavalry elements of part-mounted cohorts which had been given independent status.

Like the study of samian pottery, the study of the organisation of the units of the Roman army, and the forts that provided the permanent accommodation for them, whether combined or in part, is a technical subject with its own technical vocabulary. As one who has not the sensibility to appreciate the aesthetics of the girth groove on a Drag. 33, or mastered the niceties in the variations in the ovolo of the potter Cinnamus, I could not reasonably expect Brian, if he has got this far, to throw up his hands in delight at the suggested explanation of how cohorts in the early Empire became *alae* in the later, or why there were only 116 troopers in the *Ala*

Hiberorum and not 480; and yet, I seem to recall that Brian, too, has on occasion, and that to great effect, turned to the forts and garrisons of the frontier districts of Roman Britain (Hartley 1966; 1972), and, indeed was the director of the excavations at Brough by Bainbridge in his own Yorkshire. Moreover Legend has it that he was (to his cost – the stone fell on his foot in the moment of discovery and resulted in a sprained ankle) the discoverer there of the famous gateway inscription recording a new governor, Valerius Pudens, set up by *Cohors VI Nerviorum* (*J. Roman Stud.*, **51** (1961), 192 = AÉ 1963, 281), so that perhaps he is more broad-minded than the author of this note can claim to be. But whether he has actually read this far or not, this paper comes with the respect due to a great scholar and a good man from one who once – very long ago – dug under his direction.

ACKNOWLEDGEMENTS

An earlier, unpublished, version of this paper was given at the 1986 Limeskongress at Carnuntum. For help and advice with the original version I would like to thank Robin Birley, Jonathan Henderson, David Kennedy, John Mann, Valerie Maxfield and Margaret Roxan, and for constructive comments and encouragement at the congress and subsequently to Dietwulf Baatz, Eric Birley, Brian Dobson, Rudolf Fellmann, Ilse Kromer, Marie-Louise Münker, Hans-Ulrich Nuber and Michael Speidel. Digby Stevenson redrew the comparative plans of *principia* and the plan of Bu Ngem.

Abbreviations

AÉ	*L' Année Épigraphique* (cited by year and item number)
CIL	*Corpus Inscriptionum Latinarum* (cited by volume and item number)
ILS	H.Dessau (ed.), *Inscriptiones Latinae Selectae* (cited by item number)
MDAI(R)	*Mitteilungen des deutsches archäologischen Instituts* (Röm. Abt.)
Not. Dig. Occ.	*Notitia Dignitatum...in partibus occidentis* (Seeck, O.(ed.) 1876, reprinted 1972)
ORL	*Der obergermanisch-raetische Limes*
PBSR	*Papers of the British School at Rome*
RIB **1**	Collingwood, R.G., & Wright, R.P. (eds), *The Roman inscriptions of Britain, Vol. 1: Inscriptions on stone*, 1965 (cited by item number)
RIB **2**	Collingwood, R.G., & Wright, R.P. (eds), *The Roman inscriptions of Britain, Vol.2: Inscriptions on material other than stone*, seven fascicules, 1990–95 (eds Frere, S.S., & Tomlin, R.S.O.) (cited by item number)

Bibliography

Alföldy , G., 1968 *Die Hilfstruppen in der römischen Provinz Germania Inferior*, Epigraphische Studien, **6**

Baatz, D., 1962 *Mogontiacum*, Limesforschungen, **4** (Berlin)

————, 1993 *Der römische Limes: archäologische Ausflüge zwischen Rhein und Donau*, 3 edn (Berlin)

————, & Herrmann, F-R., 1982 *Die Römer in Hessen* (Stuttgart)

Baradez, J., 1967 Compléments inédits au Fossatum Africae, *Vorträge des 6. internationalen Limeskongresses in Süddeutschland*, Beihefte der Bonner Jahrbücher, **19**, 200–10

Birley, E., 1961 *Research on Hadrian's Wall*

Bowman, A.K., & Thomas, J.D., 1994 *The Vindolanda writing tablets (Tabulae Vindolandenses* II)

Breeze, D.J., 1983 The Roman forts at Ardoch, in O'Connor, A., & Clarke, D.V. (eds), *From the Stone Age to the 'Forty-Five'* (Essays in honour of R.B.K.Stevenson), 224–36

————, 1984 The Roman fort on the Antonine Wall at Bearsden, in Breeze, D.J. (ed.), *Studies in Scottish antiquity presented to Stewart Cruden*, 32–67

Cagnat, R., 1908 *Les deux camps de la Légion IIIe Augusta à Lambèse,* Mémoires de l'Académie des Inscriptions et Belles-Lettres, **38.1**

————, 1913 *L'Armée Romaine d'Afrique et l'occupation militaire de l'Afrique sous les Empereurs* (Paris)

Connolly, P., 1981 *Greece and Rome at war*

Davison, D.P., 1989 *The barracks of the Roman army from the 1st to the 3rd centuries A.D.,* Brit. Archaeol. Rep. Int. Ser., **472** (3 vols.)

Fabricius, E., 1932 Some notes on Polybius's description of Roman camps, *J. Roman Stud.,* **22**, 78–87

————, 1937 No.1 a: Das Kastell Niederbieber, ORL, Abteilung B, Band **1**

Fellmann,R., 1958 *Die principia des Legionslagers Vindonissa und das Zentralgebäude der römischen Lager und Kastelle* (Brugg)

————, 1983 *Principia Stabsgebäude : kleine Schriften zur Kenntnis der römischen Besetzunggeschichte Südwestdeutschlands,* **31**

Filtzinger, P., Planck, D., & Cämmerer, B., 1986 *Die Römer in Baden-Württemberg,* 3 edn (Stuttgart & Aalen)

Glasbergen, W., & Groenman-Van Waateringe, W., 1974 *The pre-Flavian garrisons of Valkenburg Z.H.* (Amsterdam & London)

Goodchild, R.G., 1954 Oasis forts of *Legio III Augusta* on the routes to the Fezzan, PBSR, **22**, 30–80 = Reynolds, J.(ed.), *Libyan Studies: select papers of the late R.G.Goodchild* (1976), 46–58

Hartley, B. R., 1966 Some problems of the Roman military occupation of the north of England, *Northern History,* **1**, 7–20

————, 1972 The Roman occupation of Scotland: the evidence of the samian ware, *Britannia,* **3**, 1–55

————, & Wacher,J. (eds) 1983 *Rome and her northern provinces: papers presented to Sheppard Frere*

Hassall, M., 1977 The historical background and units of the Saxon Shore, in Johnston 1977, 7–10

————, The internal planning of Roman auxiliary forts, in Hartley & Wacher 1983, 96–131

————, forthcoming Pre-Hadrianic legionary dispositions in Britain, in Brewer, R. J. (ed.), *Roman fortresses and their legions: papers in honour of G.C. Boon*

Hoffmann, D., 1969–70 *Das spätrömische Bewegungsheer,* Epigraphische Studien, **7**

Johnston, D.E. (ed.), 1977 *The Saxon Shore,* Counc. Brit. Archaeol.Res. Rep., **18**

Maxfield, V.A., 1986 Pre-Flavian forts and their garrisons, *Britannia,* **17**, 59–72

Nash-Williams, V.E., & Jarrett, M.G. (eds), 1969 *The Roman frontier in Wales,* 2 edn

Nissen, H., 1904 Geschichte von Novaesium, *Bonner Jahrbücher,* **111/112**, 1–96

Nuber, H.-U., 1986 Das Steinkastell Hofheim (Main-Taunus-Kreis), *Studien zu den Militärgrenzen Roms,* **3**: *internationaler Limeskongress Aalen 1983,* Forschungen und Berichte zur Vor-und Frühgeschichte in Baden-Württemberg, **20**, 226–34

Ogilvie, R.M., & Richmond, I.A., 1967 *Tacitus' Agricola*

Parker, H.M.D., 1958 *The Roman legions,* rev. edn

Pietsch, M., 1976 Die Zentralgebäude des augusteischen Legionslagers von Marktbreit und die Principia von Haltern, *Germania,* **71.2**, 355–68

von Petrikovits, H., 1975 *Die Innenbauten römischer Legionslager während der Prinzipatzeit* (Opladen)

Rakob, F., 1979 Das Groma-Nymphaeum in Legionslager Lambacsis, MDAI(R), **86**, 375–89

Rebuffat, R., 1989 Notes sur le camp romain de *Gholaia* (Bu Njem), *Libyan Studies,* **20**, 155–67

Richmond, I.A., 1949–50 Excavations at the Roman fort of Newstead 1947, *Proc. Soc. Antiq. Scotland,* **84**, 1–38

————, 1968 *Hod Hill, vol. 2. Excavations carried out between 1951 and 1958*

Roxan, M.M., 1986 Pre-Severan auxilia named in the Notitia Digitatum, in Goodburn, R., & Bartholomew, P. (eds), *Aspects of the Notitia Dignitatum,* BAR Suppl. Ser., **15**, 59–79

Saxer, R., 1967 *Untersuchungen zu den Vexillationen des römischen Kaiserheeres von Augustus bis Diokletian,* Epigraphischen Studien, **1**

von Schnurbein, S., 1974 *Die römischen militäranlagen bei Haltern,* Bodenaltertümer Westfalens, **14**

Schönberger, H., 1975 *Kastell Künzing – Quintana: die Grabungen von 1958 bis 1966,* Limesforschungen, **13** (Berlin)

Schulten, A., 1929 *Numantia IV: die Lager bei Renieblas* (Munich)

Speidel, M., 1981 Princeps as a title of ad hoc commanders, *Britannia,* **12**, 7–13 = *Mavors,* **1** (M. Speidel *Roman army studies,* 1) 1984, 189–95.

————, 1986 Die *Brittones Elantienses* und die Vorverlegung des Obergermanischen Limes, *Fundbericht aus Baden-Württemberg,* **11**, 309–11 = *Mavors,* **8** (M. Speidel, *Roman army studies,* 2), 1992, 145–8, updated

Stevens, C.E., 1940 The British sections of the Notitia Dignitatum, *Archaeol. J.,* **97**, 125–54

Tomlin, R.S.O., 1981 The mobile army, in Connolly 1981, 249–59

6 The dating of town walls in Roman Britain

John Wacher

In the recently-revised edition of *The towns of Roman Britain* (Wacher 1995, 75–8) the present writer has raised serious doubts about the validity of the current methods of dating town walls in Roman Britain. Space did not there permit a full and detailed treatment, and it seems appropriate to offer an expanded version to Brian Hartley, who for long has been interested in the problems of dating all manner of structures. It must be emphasised at once that this offering cannot propose any durable solutions. But it may make people stop and think before pontificating about the dates of town walls. Stated briefly these methods rely on a series of sections being cut across the lines of the walls and ramparts, with the latest artefacts from the cumulative, relevant stratified deposits providing a date for the whole circuit. The tendency has been often to cause a gradual progression in the date of construction, as each fresh section contributed later artefacts to the sum total. But these methods were also dependant on one fundamental assumption: that all circuits were homogeneous and uniformly synchronous in construction. This may well apply to earth ramparts, which were presumably erected in a comparatively short space of time, and enjoyed but a short life, thus obviating the need for repairs or embellishments. But it is becoming increasingly apparent that the same criterion cannot always be applied to masonry walls with a longer time-span of construction and length of life to be envisaged.

In a number of towns, where lengths of the defences have been excavated – in contrast to sections of limited width cut across them – a complex sequence of construction of the masonry walls has often been revealed; the four most notable examples are London, Gloucester, Lincoln and Cirencester. In others where excavations have been confined to traditional sections, variations in the structures have sometimes been observed between one section and another; this is certainly the case at Chichester and Winchester, and may also be true at Colchester and Caerwent, while Dorchester presents its own specific problem. At Brough-on-Humber, interruptions in the construction of the masonry fortifications have been clearly proved (Wacher 1969, 34–55), if indeed the wall protected a town and not some military or naval establishment. The apparently isolated single internal tower known

at Canterbury (Frere *et al.* 1982, 61–2) and the two similar examples on the southern wall of Verulamium (Wheeler & Wheeler 1936, 59–68) must surely indicate changes in plan during the course of construction, although other variations have yet to be identified. In some other towns where the wall appears to have been totally robbed, such as Leicester (Buckley & Lucas 1987) and Wroxeter (Webster 1962, 27) we shall probably never be able to ascertain the true state of affairs. This is also unfortunately true of most small towns; but in one of the few cases of survival, at Catterick, the extraordinary discrepancy between the widths of cobble foundation and the masonry superstructure (fig. 1), which had been set slightly askew on it, would seem to point again to a radical change in plan during construction (Wilson, P.R. (ed.), forthcoming).

Probably the most complicated sequence of defences in Britain is that surrounding Lincoln, with its two separate, though linked, enclosures. Even for the first-phase wall of the upper enclosure there is a lack of consistency in dating, ranging from the Flavian-Trajanic period for northern parts of the circuit to Hadrianic-Antonine for that south of the East Gate (summarised by Jones 1980, 51). But these differences in date cannot, as yet, be firmly related to differences in construction, except perhaps for the unexplained stone pitching found at the Westgate; it may therefore be suggested that the translation of the first defences of the *colonia* from timber to masonry took place over perhaps as much as 50 years. The addition of internal towers is no more clearly defined, since here some differences in construction between one tower and another have been observed. Moreover, to assume that they were provided at regular intervals round the circuit is perhaps unwise, given the examples of Verulamium and Canterbury quoted above. Jones has argued that the towers were added in the Hadrianic-Antonine period, but if parts of the wall were not constructed until then, it must mean that, in places, the two are virtually contemporary. This modification of the fortifications appears to have been followed by rebuilding of some of the gates and a supposed heightening of the wall and rampart: but everywhere? Dated to Antonine-early 3rd century, it is quite feasible to propose a continuing programme of construction, which may have begun as early as the 1st cen-

Fig. 1. South-west wall at Catterick showing the diverging cobble footings. (Reproduced by permission of Raymond Hayes)

tury and continued with only slight (if any) interruptions for over a hundred years. What hope then of obtaining precise dating for these defences?

As already noted, the situation at Lincoln is doubly complicated by the fortifications of the lower enclosure, which in

themselves also embrace several phases of construction. So far it has not been possible to examine the junctions between them and the walls of the upper enclosure, so that strictly and for the time being each must be considered as a separate entity. What is more, the walls of both enclosures were further modi-

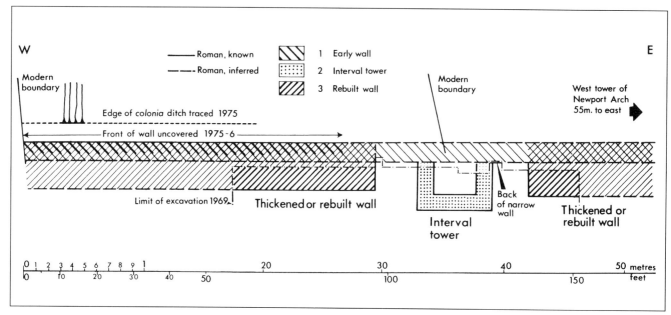

Fig. 2. Lincoln. Wall thickening and internal tower of the upper town in Temperance Place.
(Reproduced by permission of M.J. Jones and the City of Lincoln Archaeological Unit)

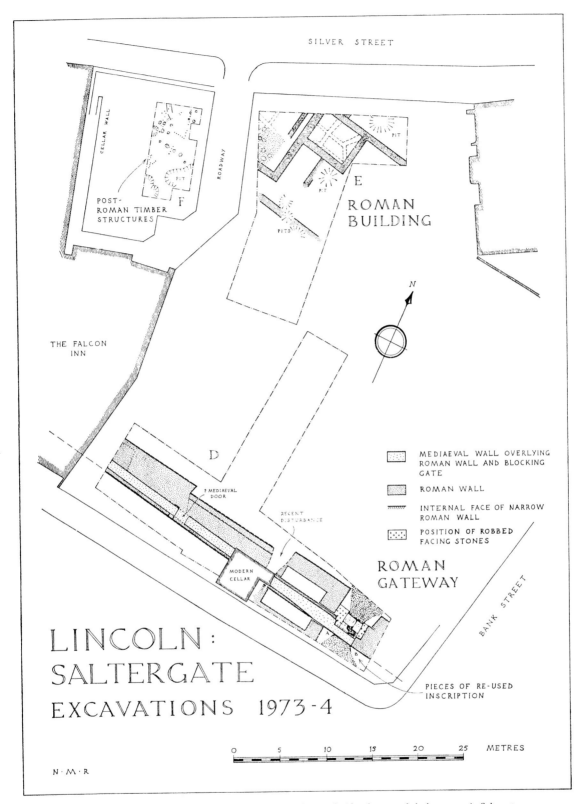

Fig. 3. Lincoln. Wall thickenings, and internal and external towers beside a late gate of the lower town in Saltergate.
(Reproduced by permission of the Society of Antiquaries of London and the City of Lincoln Archaeological Unit)

fied by thickening and possibly heightening. For some un-known reason this work was not always carried right up to the internal towers (figs. 2, 3); moreover, some of the latter ap-pear to have been replaced with solid stone platforms. Al-though these alterations are so far broadly dated to the 4th century, there is nothing to show that all were contemporary. We are possibly dealing with a single, conceptual plan, initi-ated within a very small time span, but executed in a series of consecutive, but almost continuous, stages, over a period of time which could be as much as a hundred years or more; it would hardly be appropriate to call the first and last stages contemporary with one another! Alternatively, a far more likely state of affairs can be envisaged beginning with no pre-conceived, detailed plan, beyond the intention of fortifying the *colonia*, which was then executed by a sequence of prag-matic decisions made from time to time, as the work pro-gressed and developed, with new ideas and changes in plan being incorporated as necessary. In the circumstances, it is probably wrong to do as Jones has done (Jones 1980, 50) and try and force the different structural methods so far observed into a series of discrete building phases.

A second example where considerable variations in con-struction have been observed is Cirencester, although here the complexities are, if anything, greater since they embrace not only far more differences in styles of masonry, but also probable combinations of masonry and earthwork; the cur-rent situation has recently been summarised, with references, by Holbrook (1994, 65) while a full definitive survey will shortly be forthcoming (Holbrook 1997).

The masonry wall at Cirencester was everywhere pre-ceded by one, and possibly two, earthworks, dating probably from the late 1st to early 2nd century and late 2nd century

respectively. Associated with the second, but not necessar-ily strictly contemporary with it, were masonry gates and internal towers, although one timber tower is suspected. Arguments relating to their structural sequence are only peripherally relevant in the present context (Hartley 1983, 84; Frere 1984, 69, n. 44; Wacher 1995, 74–5): work was perhaps originally planned in masonry but an interruption for an unknown reason caused the completion of the cur-tain in earthwork.

It is usually assumed that this earthwork was ultimately fronted by a narrow-gauge wall 1.2m wide along its entire length to unite the existing masonry gates and towers. Sub-sequently this wall, so it is argued, was thickened in places, up to 2.3–2.7m, but by no means round the entire circuit (fig. 4). There are some indications, normally to be seen only where the superstructure has been entirely robbed, that the narrow wall was demolished to the foundations before being recon-structed to the wider gauge, the front of the rampart being further cut back to accommodate it (fig. 5). But generally, where the superstructure of the wide wall survives to any height, it is impossible to say that it was necessarily preceded by the narrow wall. Consequently, there is nothing to prevent

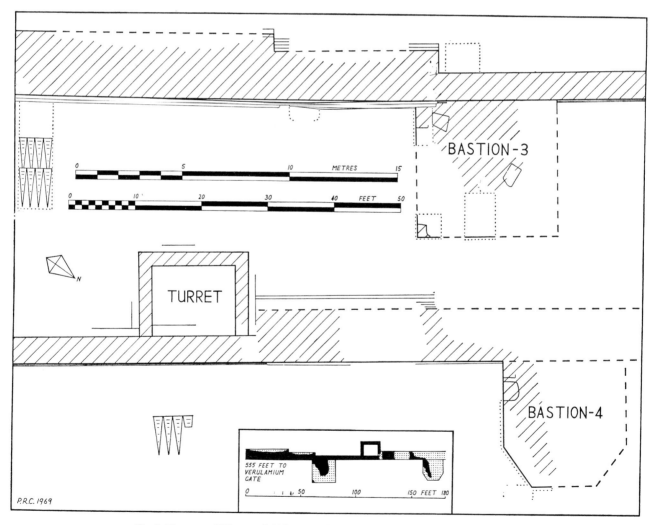

Fig. 4. Cirencester. Different wall thicknesses and internal and external towers in the Abbey Park.
(Reproduced by permission of the Cirencester Excavation Committee)

Fig. 5. Cirencester. Robber trench of the wall in the Abbey Park, showing the divided foundation.
(Reproduced by permission of the Cirencester Excavation Committee)

some of the lengths of wide wall from being primary construction, and therefore in existence at the same time as the narrow wall. One might imagine a scenario, therefore, where work on the curtain began with the wider gauge, but for reasons of economy or haste this was reduced to about half the width for much of the circuit. The latter is, after all, the second longest (*c.* 3.6km) of any town of Roman Britain, and even the longest (*c.* 5km), at London, was not completed in one stage (see below). Moreover the widths of most town walls in Britain approximate more to the wider gauge at Cirencester than to the narrow. To continue the scenario, once the circuit was completed, the narrow wall could then be converted to the wider gauge at leisure as labour and money became available; but even this work was never completed in its entirety, and the piecemeal approach could account for the variations in width found on excavation. Additionally, there is evidence for numerous minor repairs and no less than five or six different styles of masonry have been observed in a length of only 50m.

The initial date of the masonry curtain is difficult to assess, but because of the constrictions caused by the earlier earthwork, it seems unlikely to have been begun much before the early 3rd century. Thereafter, it may be envisaged, as at Lincoln, that work at Cirencester went on almost continuously for perhaps more than a century if the addition of external, polygonal towers in the 4th century is included.

So far little has been said about the ramparts which were normal adjuncts of the walls. Although there are some indications at Lincoln that the wall rampart of the upper town was added to at least once, it otherwise reflected very little of the

greater number of alterations which took place to the wall. Much the same can be said of Cirencester. But at Chichester it seems to have played a more significant part.

A number of sections have been cut across the wall at Chichester at different parts of the circuit. Wilson (1957, 15) argued from his researches that the rampart and wall were contemporary. Holmes excavated a section on the south side and concluded that there was a cut in the rampart for insertion of the wall foundations (Holmes 1962, 80). Magilton examined the defences on the west side and found that the cut in the front of the rampart only penetrated to about half its depth, the lower layers apparently being contemporary with the masonry (fig. 6). Obviously the existence of a free-standing earthwork still cannot be ruled out, but if these three different sets of interpretations are taken at their face value there is only one explanation. It is obvious that the masonry wall was in some parts extensively rebuilt, even perhaps from foundation level, as at Cirencester, which may have also involved radical alterations to the rampart. Moreover, construction of the wall suffered interruptions as has now been confirmed by excavations on the north-east sector in 1993 (*Britannia*, **25** (1994), 289) when horizontal silt layers were revealed in the core of the wall between 1m–1.5m apart. In addition, different types of face have been observed behind two external towers; in one case it was of flint, in the other small dressed stone. Furthermore, wider foundations were used for some of the rebuilt sections. To quote Magilton (Down & Magilton 1993, 108): 'The implication would appear to be that where the wall needed to be entirely rebuilt it was constructed on broader foundations, at least in the Cawley Priory area. Ad-

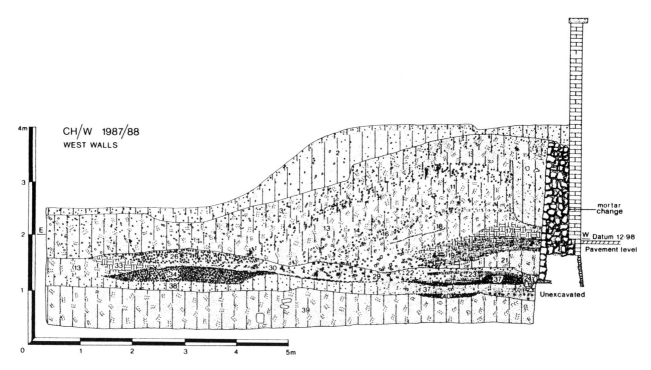

Fig. 6. Chichester. Section through the western defences in the Avenue de Chartres, showing the partial cut in the rampart. (Reproduced by permission of Chichester District Council and John Magilton)

ditional confirmation that stretches were rebuilt comes from examination of the bastions'.

The problems here, therefore, seem to be: (1) how long were the interruptions during construction; (2) how much of the wall was rebuilt; (3) whether all the rebuilding was carried out at the same time or in a piecemeal fashion; (4) how much was rebuilt from foundation level; and (5) the extent to which the rampart was affected. Neither is it yet possible to be absolutely certain which lengths of wall represent the genuine primary work, and consequently its relationship with the rampart(s) must still be a matter for speculation.

There is furthermore a crucial detail which does not perhaps receive sufficient weight in Down & Magilton 1993, 99–109. This section (fig. 6) across the west wall showed a 'rebuild' which had involved partly cutting down into the rampart behind. One of the layers (4) in the rampart, which had been cut, contained coarse pottery of the late 3rd to 4th century; Magilton argued that it might be intrusive. But if taken at its face value it must reflect on the date of the primary wall *on this part of the circuit*, but not necessarily elsewhere. Consequently the 'rebuild' here cannot be earlier than the 4th century.

Partly underlying the tail of the rampart in the same place were two superimposed gravel surfaces (layers 34 and 26). In the summary of the dating evidence (Down & Magilton 1993, 106) a late 4th-century coin (? Valentinian II) is recorded as coming from (26). Unfortunately it is not given a closer context, but if it was found in the body of the layer it would make the rampart and consequently the wall in this sector even later

in the 4th century. If, on the other hand, it was found on the surface of the layer beyond the tail of the rampart, it would have no bearing on the date of the latter. Confusion, though, is compounded by the text (Down & Magilton 1993, 107) which dismisses the coin altogether as more likely coming from the higher layer (3). On the balance of probability, the interface between the two layers would seem to be its correct context. Be that as it may, there is clearly much still to be done at Chichester.

An almost identical state of affairs has been observed at Winchester, where Biddle noted that at Wolvesey the rampart and wall seemed to be contemporary (Biddle 1975, 112). But his published section of the defences at the South Gate (Biddle 1975, fig. 7) shows a cut in the front of the rampart, which, on first impression, was intended for the wall; however the cut does not penetrate as far down as the foundation, so closely resembling the section across the west wall at Chichester.

The situation at Gloucester is very similar to that at Lincoln, although much depends on whether Hurst's interpretation that the first masonry fortifications belonged to the fortress, not to the succeeding *colonia*, is correct. This is not the place to argue this particular hypothesis, but it is worth pointing out that his late 1st-century date for these defences ignores at least one sherd of early 2nd-century samian. Consequently, whatever the date for the start of the work, it may have dragged on into the 2nd century, by when it must incontrovertibly have belonged to the *colonia* (Heighway 1983, 3; Hurst 1986, 104–13), which cannot have been founded later than AD 98 (CIL VI, 3346).

Thereafter the defences of Gloucester seem to have been subject to a series of modifications which included the rampart as well as the wall and which, by analogy with some other towns, might have extended in time from the 2nd century, certainly until the end of the 3rd, if not into the 4th.

According to Hurst's (1986, 99–115) interpretation the first *colonia* (or as he would have it the last legionary) defences consisted of a wall of *opus quadratum*, backed by rubble, inserted into the front of the legionary rampart. Internal masonry towers were added later and the rampart was augmented both in height and width. There followed a piecemeal replacement of the original ashlar and rubble wall, in which two different styles of masonry can be identified, and where in some places the second style actually replaced lengths of the first (fig. 7). Later still, external towers were added at irregular intervals.

The complexity of the 'finished' defences therefore matches the examples already quoted above; on present evidence, apart perhaps for the first phase, it is quite impossible to say how long the complete process took and the precise way in which the rebuilds were carried out round the whole circuit.

Colchester also presents problems. Crummy's most recent views have now placed the initiation of work on the wall into the period immediately after the Boudiccan rebellion (Crummy 1992, 14–18). At first the wall was free-standing, but seemingly during the second half of the 2nd century a rampart was thrown up behind it (Crummy 1984, 14–15): '... it seems possible that the wall and rampart were conceived of as a single scheme in which the building of the wall was the priority which had to be achieved before work could begin on the rampart. Probably this was done partly for the logistical

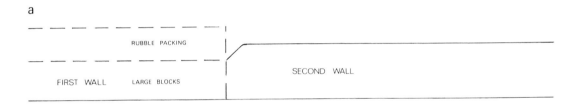

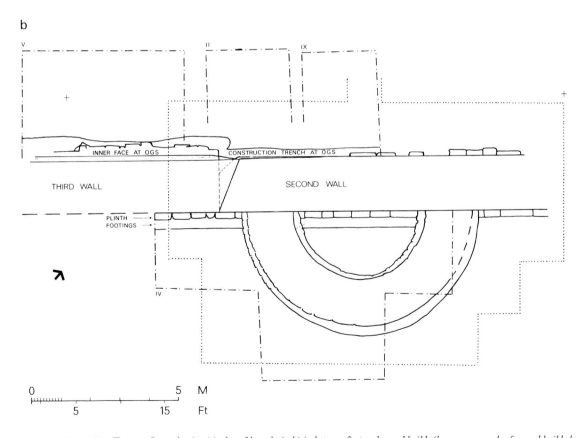

Fig. 7. Gloucester. The wall in Eastgate Street showing (a) plan of hypothetical join between first and second builds (lower courses only of second build shown);
(b) second and third builds and medieval tower as found. (Reproduced by permission of Henry Hurst)

reasons ... and partly to re-establish an effective defensive circuit as quickly as possible'. This seems to be something of a contradiction since, as almost every other town in Roman Britain has demonstrated, the quickest method of defence is an earthwork, or at best a narrow gauge wall. Crummy (1984, 14) also observed that the rampart had been built up in stages. Why could not these stages have gone hand-in-hand with the raising of the curtain? To quote again twice from the same reference: 'The whole project may have taken many decades to complete'; '... but it may well have taken many years'. Quite. A time span stretching from the Boudiccan rebellion to the mid-2nd century is not inconceivable and would explain some other recorded features, such as the two-period (temporary?) street sealing a wall construction level beneath the rampart; also the mortar spreads recorded by Miss Richardson in 1951 (Hull 1958, 26) at different levels in the body of the rampart. The modern tendency has been to ignore the latter as erroneously inconvenient, but there seems no good reason why the observations of a competent excavator should be summarily dismissed without adequate explanation (Crummy 1984, 15 is not entirely convincing). Inconsistencies of this sort are to be expected in the circumstances here being explored. Work might start on the wall in several places at once but not proceed to the full height; then a bit of rampart might be added, not necessarily everywhere, followed by a bit more masonry, and so on until the circuit was complete; there is scope for many permutations. Then there is the worrying question of the westward extension, presumbably of earthwork, dated by Crummy to the 1st century (Crummy 1984, 11). Why go to the trouble of building a wall along the west end of the town, only to negate its effectiveness a few decades later, even if it was temporary?

The landward wall of London appears perhaps more homogeneous than those of most towns. It may be that the presence of the governor and the treasury caused the work to be expedited with the provision of financial aid and drafts of skilled labour. Maloney lists the very considerable quantity of materials required for this 3000m of wall (Maloney 1983, 97), the provision of which must have been a mammoth task in itself. But is it really feasible for the work to have been completed in the four years between 193–7, as he claims (Maloney 1983, 104) especially since building must have been delayed during winter because of frost? But undoubtedly the greater problem of London concerns the riverside wall. Recent orthodoxy had it that this section of the defences was not built until the second half of the 4th century (Hill *et al.* 1980, 69), although this has now been revised, following further work on dendrochronological specimens, to the mid- to later 3rd century (Sheldon & Tyers 1983, 361). But this still leaves an uncomfortable gap between Maloney's putative date of the landward wall and that fronting the river. Another curious feature lies near the south-east corner in the Tower of London, where there was either a rebuild on a different alignment, or else a dog-leg was incorporated to provide a postern. But perhaps it is best to extend Maloney's abbreviated scale for the landward wall and see the whole work as part of a continuous planned construction extending over nearly a

hundred years. The alternative is to envisage an original scheme in which a riverside wall played no part. It seems most unlikely that a town of the importance of London would have been deliberately left unenclosed on its most vulnerable side. No other riverside town in the Empire appears to have been so treated.

The defences of Carmarthen have only been investigated properly in the last few years; here there seems to be an analogy with Cirencester. On the north-west sector the wall is reported as having been only 5ft (1.5m) wide (Jones 1964–69, 3), in contrast to the south-west part where, near the south corner, it was found to be 10½ft (3.2m) (James 1978, 63). Obviously, this very large variation needs to be accounted for.

The last town to be considered in this appraisal, where there is indisputable evidence for a change of plan during construction, is Dorchester. Here at two places on the southern part of the circuit, an early foundation trench for a curtain wall, 3m wide and packed with flints, has been located, sealed beneath the earthwork defences (Davies & Farwell 1990, 53). Consequently, when the curtain wall was finally completed it lay some distance in front of the original foundations.

The seven or so examples quoted above represent nearly a 40% sample of the major towns of Roman Britain. At the very least they provide a strong argument against the presumption of homogeneity for wall circuits and favour an extended period of construction, or reconstruction for masonry defences. In addition there are one or two others, such as Caerwent and Caister-by-Norwich where there are suspicions that all is not as straightforward as was once thought. All-in-all, it is probably sufficient to conclude that the present standard methods used to explore masonry defences are no longer adequate. Much more attention must be paid to apparently minor variations in construction, which can no longer be automatically dismissed as the errors of observation of earlier excavators, or, as is more normal, to the work of different gangs of builders. Most urgently it is obviously necessary to examine extended lengths of the defences rather than just cutting narrow sections across them. But above all the extraordinary confidence with which some excavators, the present writer included, have in the past proclaimed the date of an entire town wall on the evidence from perhaps only one or two sections, can no longer be justified. The most glaring example must surely be the attempt by Casey to tie the date of the whole circuit at Caerwent to a single coin of 330–5 found by Nash-Williams (Casey 1983, 122).

In terms of volumes of masonry, of quarrying and transporting stone and removal of earth, a defensive circuit represented a building project probably larger than any town had yet met, larger than a forum or a basilica or baths, even larger probably than an amphitheatre. A rough calculation has shown that the fifty or so fortified towns in Britain possessed in sum about 80km of wall, mostly averaging 2–3m in width in their final states; this is well over half the length of Hadrian's Wall. It is usually assumed that the latter, in its composite form, was mostly finished during the governorship of A. Platorius Nepos, although the turf wall was not completely replaced by masonry until somewhat later. As a comparison it is not entirely apposite as it included subsidiary works such as forts and milecastles, which town walls did not possess. But it is the only major, finite, building work in Britain for which a time-scale can be approximately gauged. So also can the labour force. If three legions were totally involved, a minimum of some 15,000 men must have been employed, most of whom were more or less skilled in construction work; that is an average of 127 men per kilometre although it is unlikely that they would have been so regularly spaced out, but concentrated into sections where need was greatest. Nevertheless it is important to remember that only about half the masonry wall was completed during the four years of Nepos' governorship. To have finished the full length in a continuous operation might well have doubled or even trebled the time taken. It might also be argued that Hadrian's Wall is not a good analogy for urban fortification, because factors were at work which would not have applied to towns; but if anything, such factors would probably have militated against the latter. But at least the comparison provides a useful yard-stick against which to match the towns. Thus on the above basis London alone could have taken eight years or more to build the 3km of landward wall, always providing 400 or so skilled or semi-skilled labourers could have been obtained. Were there as many in London? It seems doubtful. Moreover, to have started work on all defended towns in Britain at the same time would have required something in the region of 10,000 similarly qualified workers in order to have completed the programme in a reasonable time of say ten years. It seems hardly surprising that the entire scheme of urban fortification took very much longer, probably over a hundred years.

The second inhibiting factor controlling this type of building work must have been the cost. While there is a considerable amount of information relating to the financial management of the construction of public works and buildings in other provinces, there is unfortunately none in Britain. For this province, therefore, it is only possible to draw some most general analogies, at the same time acknowledging the dangers involved in doing so, in an area containing many variables and with a uniquely individualistic structure.

The most commonly-quoted references to building costs, delays and errors are contained in the younger Pliny's letters to Trajan (*Epistulae* 10, 37–40) and in his adoptive father's comment about Crinas, the physician, who apparently spent 10 million sesterces on the wall of Massilia (*Naturalis Historia* 29, 9). Jouffroy collected and compared sources – mainly inscriptions – for Africa and Italy (Jouffroy 1986), while Mangas did so for the evidence from Spain (Mangas 1971, 105). For Gaul reliance must be placed on the somewhat dated account in Blanchet 1900. There is also the more general survey of the Empire contained in Jacques 1984. Most of the references, though, apply to public works such as fora, baths, aqueducts, statues and roads; specific references to walls are much rarer. Certainly walls could be erected, or repaired, with rapidity. An inscription from the Borsarian gate at Verona,

dated to AD 265, refers to their completion in nine months (CIL V, 3329 = ILS 544). There is also evidence for major restoration work financed by private individuals, notably at Castulo in Hispania Tarraconensis (CIL II, 3270 = ILS 5513; Duncan-Jones 1974, 79–85) and at Sala in Mauretania (AE 1931, 38). But, mainly, public works seem to have been financed, to take Italy and Africa as examples, by municipalities, chiefly from the revenue obtained from office-holders on their appointments (Jouffroy 1986, 462). Occasionally, personal intervention by an emperor is attested, but here fiscal means were usually employed, such as the remission or lightening of taxes.

Delays in the construction of public works, though, were by no means uncommon, and might exceed ten years; they appear to increase, in Africa at least, in number towards the end of the 2nd century (Jacques 1984, 735), but the reasons are not entirely clear. Overall, delays must have been caused by irregular 'cash-flow' in municipal finances. It has for instance often been claimed that town walls in Gaul were the immediate product of the barbarian invasions of the second half of the 3rd century, but King has now pointed out that the period of construction may have been extended, as in Britain, over a period of 150 years so (King 1990, 177).

To what extent this information can be applied to Britain is arguable, but if it is taken in conjunction with the evidence reviewed above, it would not be unreasonable to suppose that delays were just as common as in other provinces. Much would have depended on the two factors referred to above: labour and cost. Presumably if the state paid, and could conscript sufficient labour, the whole scheme of fortification could have been completed within a reasonably short space of time. Such, though, was evidently not the case, since the process was strung out from about the end of the 2nd until the early 4th century. Consequently, it might be argued that the state did not pay, although some contributions may have been made. Failing that source, the cost must have been borne primarily by the *civitates*. There is, of course, no more information from Britain about their local revenues than there is about building costs, but few can have been wealthier than the municipalities where it is known that delays occurred.

Duncan-Jones (1990, 174–84) has matched annual revenues against building costs for some towns in Africa and has concluded for instance that, at Thubursicu, a small forum would have absorbed at least eleven years revenue before it was finished, a theatre as much as 33 years, while it might have taken as much as 140 years income before all essential buildings were completed in some towns. He has also collected together (1982, *passim*) the sources for the known instances of building costs for Africa and Italy. There were quite wide variations between the two areas and clearly costs in Britain would almost certainly have been very different, but the figures provide a useful back-drop for relative values. Costs everywhere must be in direct proportion to revenues, so that if we argue that the cost of a circuit of a town-wall with gates, towers, rampart and ditches lay somewhere between a small forum and a theatre, then it follows that it might have taken some twenty or so years to build, providing that there were no significant changes in plan during this period, which was not always the case, and providing also that there was an adequate supply of labour. Nor must it be forgotten that a *civitas* might be responsible for walling the small towns in its territory, as well as its own capital. Thus the *civitas Dobunnorum*, as well as being responsible for Cirencester, may also have had to provide Kenchester and Dorn, and possibly Bath and Worcester and even perhaps Droitwich and Alcester with fortifications, in all an operation of considerable magnitude. It is not surprising that it covered many decades, the wall at Cirencester being started probably in the early 3rd century, while that at Alcester (*Britannia*, **17** (1986), 393) seems not to have been completed until the 4th. Neither can it be assumed that work proceeded at an even rate at each site, or between one site and another, due to possible fluctuations in the provision of finance and labour. Indeed, on reflection, there are so many imponderables to be taken into account, all of which must have affected the construction work, that nothing can be taken for granted in the future with regard to the proclaimed dates of town walls.

Bibliography and abbreviations

AE *L'Année Épigraphique*; cited by year and item number

Biddle, M., 1975 Excavations at Winchester, 1971, *Antiq. J.*, **55**, 96–126

Blanchet, A., 1900 *Les trésors de monnaies romaines et les invasions germaniques en Gaule*

Buckley, R., & Lucas, J., 1987 *Leicester town defences*

Casey, J., 1983 Imperial campaigns and 4th-century defences in Britain, in Maloney, J., & Hobley, B. (eds), *Roman urban defences in the west*, 121–4

CIL *Corpus Inscriptionum Latinarum*, 1863– (Berlin); cited by volume and item number

Crummy, P., 1984 *Excavations at Lion Walk, Balkerne Lane, and Middleborough, Colchester, Essex*

_____, 1992 *Excavations at Culver Street, the Gilberd School and other sites in Colchester, 1971–85*

Davies, S.M., & Farwell, D.E., 1989 The South Walks Tunnel sewers, Dorchester – archaeological watching brief, *Proc. Dorset Natur. Hist. Archaeol. Soc.*, **111**, 51–6

Down, A., & Magilton, J., 1993 *Chichester excavations, 8*

Duncan-Jones, R., 1974 The procurator as civic benefactor, *J. Roman Stud.*, **64**, 79–85

_____, 1982 *The economy of the Roman Empire*

_____, 1990 *Structure and scale in the Roman economy*

Frere, S.S., 1984 British urban defences in earthwork, *Britannia*, **15**, 63–74

_____, Stow, S., & Bennett, P., 1982 *Excavations on the Roman and medieval defences of Canterbury*

Hartley, B.R., 1983 The enclosure of Romano-British towns in the second century AD, in Hartley, B., & Wacher, J. (eds), *Rome and her northern provinces*, 84–95

Heighway, C., 1983 *The East and North Gates of Gloucester*

Hill, C., Millett, M., & Blagg, T., 1980 *The Roman riverside wall and monumental arch in London*

Holbrook, N., 1994 *Corinium Dobunnorum*: Roman *civitas* capital and Roman provincial capital, in Darvill, T., & Gerrard, C. (eds), *Cirencester: town and landscape*, 57–86

_____ (ed.), 1977 *Cirencester: the Roman town defences, public buildings and shops, vol. 1*

Holmes, J., 1962 The defences of Roman Chichester, *Sussex Archaeol. Collect.*, **100**, 80–92

Hull, M.R., 1958 *Roman Colchester*

Hurst, H., 1986 *Gloucester, the Roman and later defences*

ILS Dessau, H. (ed.), *Inscriptiones Latinae Selectae*; cited by item number

Jacques, F., 1984 *Le privilège de liberté*

James, H.J., 1978 Excavations in Church Street, Carmarthen 1976, in Boon, G.C. (ed.), *Cambrian Archaeological Association Monographs and Collections I. Roman Sites*, 63–106

Jones, G.D.B., 1964–69 Excavations at Carmarthen 1968, *Carmarthenshire Antiq.*, **5**, 2–5

Jones, M.J., 1980 *The defences of the upper Roman enclosure*

Jouffroy, H., 1986 *La construction publique en Italie et dans l'Afrique Romaine*

King, A., 1990 *Roman Gaul and Germany*

Maloney, J., 1983 Recent work on London's defences, in Maloney, J., & Hobley, B. (eds), *Roman urban defences in the west*, 96–117

Mangas, J., 1971 *Hispania Antiqua*, **1**, 105–46

Pliny (the elder) *Naturalis Historia*

Pliny (the younger) *Epistulae*

Sheldon, H.L., & Tyers, P., 1983 Recent dendrochronological work in Southwark and its implications, *London Archaeol.*, **4**, 355–61

Wacher, J., 1969 *Excavations at Brough-on-Humber, 1958–1961*

_____, 1995 *The towns of Roman Britain*, 2 edn

Webster, G., 1962 The defences of Viroconium (Wroxeter), *Trans. Birmingham Archaeol. Soc.*, **78**, 27–39

Wheeler, R.E.M., & Wheeler, T.V., 1936 *Verulamium. A Belgic and two Roman cities*

Wilson, A.E., 1957 *The archaeology of Chichester city walls*, Chichester Papers, **6**

Wilson, P.R. (ed.), forthcoming [*Catterick excavations*]

7   William Stukeley's *Caesaromagus*, its basis in fiction and fact

Raphael M. J. Isserlin

SUMMARY

Past and present attitudes to the archaeology of the area underneath medieval Chelmsford, Essex, are explored. Stukeley considered this the site of a Roman town, and his motives for doing so are examined. Limited fieldwork offers a different verdict, in which the rural hinterland of a Roman 'small town' can be identified with some success.

INTRODUCTION

Sometime in the 18th century, a traveller en route from London to Colchester alit from his stage-coach at Chelmsford, and looked around. He saw a triangular market-place, a church at its head, and timber-framed building after timber-framed building, their tiled roofs glowing in the sunshine. Ahead of him, the High Street curved downhill to the bridge crossing the river Can, built by Henry Yevele in 1372, and led to the hamlet of Moulsham. Doctor William Stukeley, antiquary extraordinary, had come to town.

Or so we may imagine. 18th-century travellers praised the inns, the court and the jail of Essex's county town (Grieve 1994, 113), but that we know so much of the appearance of pre-industrial Chelmsford is in fact due to John Walker. His coloured maps of 1591 depict streets and buildings in quite astonishing detail (Essex Record Office ERO D/DM P1,2; D/DGe M50), many recognisable today. Chelmsford was a medieval town, founded by the Bishop of London in 1199, north of the river Can. South of it, Moulsham grew up at about the same time on fields owned by the Bishop of Westminster, where once Roman *Caesaromagus* had stood (Grieve 1988). Details of the growth of neither medieval settlement need detain us here, but excavation has proved beyond doubt that a Roman settlement with a *mansio* and a temple built of stone lay **south** of the Can, under Moulsham. This is usually identified as *Caesaromagus* (Drury 1988; Wickenden 1992; Isserlin & Wickenden forthcoming).

It is well to remember, however, that for a place with such a grand name, we lack a single Roman inscription to clinch the matter (indeed, any *in-situ* Roman architectural stonework whatsoever). Though the Antonine Itinerary established that *Caesaromagus* lay between London and Colchester, a lack of control points other than these two explains the many candidates for the honour. Basic survey teaches that two fixed points are inadequate to tie in a location, though to find Dunmow (between Colchester and Braughing, on the road to St. Albans) among them is unexpected (Table 1).

Table 1: 'Caesaromagus' through the ages
(Sources: Drury 1988, 1–2, amended; Ordnance Survey)

Settlement	NGR	Authority	Date
Brentwood	TQ 5993	Camden	1610, 442
Burstead	TQ 6892	Camden	1610, 442
Chelmsford	TL 7006	Stukeley	1776, 13
Writtle	TQ 6706	Morant	1768, 61
Dunmow	TL 6222	Drake	1779, 13–7–9
Moulsham	TL 7006	Brinson	1963, 63
Widford	TL 6905	Rivet	1970, 47, 52
Witham	TL 8215	Gale	n.d., 91

Even Camden (who used modern English place- and river names as a check) confessed defeat: 'Heere I am at a stand, and am in halfe a doubt whether I should now slip as an abortive fruite that conjecture, which my minde hath travailed with. Considering there hath beene in this tract the City CAESAROMAGUS... What if I should say that CAESARO-MAGUS did stand neare unto Brentwood, would not a learned reader laugh at me, as one soothsayer doth when he spieth another? Certes, no ground I have to nor reason to strengthen this my conjecture from the distance thereof, seeing the numbers of the miles in Antonine be most corruptly put downe, which nevertheless agree well enough with the distance from COLONIA and CANONIUM.... Neither verily ther remaineth heere so much as a shadow or any twinkling shew of the name CAESAROMAGUS, unless it be (and that is but very slender) in the name of an Hundred, which of old times was called Ceasford, and now Cheasford Hundred... If in this quarter heereby, there be not CAESAROMAGUS, let others seeke it after me: It passeth my wit, I assure you, although I have diligently laid for meet to with net, and toile, both of eares and eies.' (1610, 442).

However, he did not quite give up: 'Burghsted, & more short, Bursted, that is, the place of a Burgh, which name our forefathers used to give unto many places that were of greater antiquity. This I once supposed to have been CAESAR-OMAGVS: and what ever it was in old time, it is at this day but a good country towne neere unto Byliricay, a mercat town of very good resort' (1610, 442).

If then Burstead was *Caesaromagus*, what was Chelmsford? 'But now returne we to Chelmer, which by this time speedeth it selfe to Chelmersford commonly Chemsford (where by the distance of the place from CAMVLODUNVM, it may seeme that old CANONIUM sometimes stood). This is a good bigge towne situate in the heart of the shire betweene two rivers, who, as it were, agreed heere to joyne both their streames together: to wit Chelmer from the East, and another from the south, the name whereof if it be Can, as some would have it, we have no reason to doubt, that this was CANONIUM' (1610, 445).

TWO COUNTY HISTORIES

Beguiled by the Roman tile reused in Writtle church, Philip Morant located *Caesaromagus* there instead, 3km further west of Moulsham (1768, 61). Perhaps he discussed this with his friend Stukeley (their correspondence survives: Piggott 1985, 147, and n. 401; British Library Add. MSS 3722). Thomas Wright (perhaps better known as an early investigator of Roman Wroxeter) adopted a more rational approach. He weighed up the thoughts of various editors of the Peutinger Table and Antonine Itinerary (who followed these dismal traditions) against hard physical evidence (Wright 1836, 37, esp. 165ff.). He ignored the reused brick in Writtle church and instead noted the lack of Roman remains, coins or antiquities from the settlement, reducing its claim merely to its distance from Colchester (Gibson considered Writtle was *Canonium/ Kelvedon*; Gale thought it was *Caesaromagus*). He dismissed Gibson's claims for Dunmow as *Caesaromagus* without comment, and pointed out that Widford had been suggested by Reynolds because of the quantity of Roman bricks and tiles (a familiar argument). He also mentioned that Gale had thought that Witham might be another candidate because he linked modern local place-name evidence (the river Bar) with a reading in a corrupt ms. (*Baromagus* for *Caesaromagus*) and had been further misled by the presence of earthworks at Witham (either a hillfort or a *burh*: Rodwell 1994).

Current wisdom assumes Writtle's masonry was robbed from Chelmsford's *mansio*. Recently a revival of the Widford location, to the south-west of Chelmsford, was attempted (Drury 1988, 1–2). Moulsham is now the accepted location (Rivet & Smith 1979, 162, 169, 287–8). Frederic Chancellor discovered Chelmsford's *mansio* baths in the middle of Moulsham well after Wright's history had been published (Drury 1988, 1, 5).

One other location is notable because it is so close to the mark: Chelmsford itself, which Wright favoured on the grounds of historical geography. Wright's geography was based on reason. Not so Stukeley, who decided on Chelmsford through a remarkable topographical analogy.

STUKELEY'S VISION

Volume II of *Itinerarium Curiosum* was published posthumously, together with other works. Stukeley suggested that The Brill in London ('Caesar's Camp at Pancras') was a meticulously-planned Roman earthwork. He reinforced this by analogy with Chelmsford:

> 'I am very much confirmed by the opinion, by the ground-plot I have made of *Caesaromagus*, now Chelmsford, built by Mandubrace's nephew the great king Cunobeline, to the honour of Augustus, his great friend and ally; for that city was of exactly the same form and disposition' (Stukeley 1776, 12).

It had the form of a 'playing-card' Roman camp, with parallel streets, and a fountain, forum, temple and palace (fig. 1). Having gone on to discuss *Camulodunum*'s earthworks, Stukeley concluded:

> 'Thus we see a great conformity between old London and Cunobeline's *Caesaromagus*, especially as to the general distribution and design; the four gates of the sides correspond to different streets obliquely' (1776, 13).

The Brill (destroyed by St. Pancras railway-station) was no such site (Celoria & Spencer 1968; Piggott 1985, 99), while by the 18th century the area Stukeley describes as *Caesaromagus* had been covered by the medieval town for nigh on 600 years (figs. 2, 3). Stukeley's 'ground-plot' cannot be reconciled with the natural terrain, or with Walker's accurate maps drawn 185 years earlier. As has been said, subsequent research places *Caesaromagus* south of the river under Moulsham, and before rescue excavation took place Stukeley's map was dismissed out of hand (Brinson, in Richmond 1963, 63). The good Doctor located *Caesaromagus* north of the River Can, presuming 'urban continuity' – where there was a medieval town, there once had been a Roman one. Was his depiction the result of a visit to Chelmsford?

STUKELEY AND THE ROMAN KNIGHTS

Stukeley was a member of the Society of Roman Knights, constituted in 1722 (motto: '*Temporis utriusque vindex*'). He resolved to promote Romano-British antiquities, not the voguish medieval, through site visits (Piggott 1985, 55). Though he visited Chesterford and Colchester in that very year, he omits Chelmsford in his *Iter V* (1776, 78–9). Perhaps he gave the area a wide berth in 1722, only to go there when he visited Colchester in 1759 (Piggott 1985, 147).

Chelmsford does not feature in a reconstruction of his journey for Volume I of his *Itinerarium* (Piggott 1985, appendix 1). If the plan was drawn up as far back as 1722 it must have relied on second-hand information from a local source. A fellow Knight, Nicholas Hayn, lived at '*Caesaromagus*' – presumably at or near Chelmsford (Piggott 1985, 53–5 and fig. 4). Hayn's nom-de-plume ('*Varro*') suggests a gentry-farmer but a search of the Essex Record Office surname index reveals no trace of this particular individual (though the surname is known). Stukeley's judgment may have been swayed by the arguments of a fellow knight with an intense local pride, but it is difficult to see why the 'information' was not included in Volume I of his *Itinerarium* if he was supplied with it. We may either acquit '*Varro*' or give a verdict of not proven, but Stukeley does not get off so easily, for he states that the 'ground-plot' was his own work, and he had done this kind of work before.

STUKELEY THE SURVEYOR OR
STUKELEY THE VISIONARY?

Though Stukeley's 1722 survey of Chesterford was good, Thomas Hearne savaged him for reducing the (octagonal) defences of Silchester to a parallelogram. Aubrey had committed the same mistake, but Hearne ignored this – and said the defences were nonagonal! Hearne disbelieved Stukeley's discovery of Silchester's amphitheatre and called him conceited (Boon 1974, 24, 330; Piggott 1985, 73, 145). This onslaught provoked a deep inner crisis in a man whose vocation had been questioned – soon he took up holy orders.

When (if?) he visited Chelmsford, it was as an older man who had turned to religion for comfort, gathering material for a projected second volume of his *Itinerarium* (which never really saw the light of day). An account exists of a visit by an unknown person in 1759 (the year of Stukeley's visit to Colchester) together with the Rev. Mr. Kilner to sites including Romford, nearby Writtle and *Caesaromagus* (*Bodl. Ms. Gough Prints and Drawings*, f. 35 b, r-h, reverse). In the same folio is Stukeley's plan of *Caesaromagus*, sundry items of antiquarian interest, and a sketch of the south porch of St. Mary's Parish Church (since 1917, Chelmsford Cathedral). Possibly the author of the account was Stukeley himself. An interest in ecclesiology (which once would have been incredible for a member of a society which had condemned '*Gothic Remnants*': Piggott 1985, 55) would be quite appropriate in a man who was now a vicar.

His *Caesaromagus* was really self-justification: the insight he had applied to The Brill *was* superior! Certain aspects of Stukeley's work provided inspiration for poets such as Thomas Gray and that sublime visionary, William Blake (Piggott 1985, 145, 149, 156–8). It is equally clear that his own work had visionary overtones. His revelation strongly foreshadows Samuel Taylor Coleridge's poem *Xanadu*, written in 1798. Of the topographical motifs present in the first ten lines of Coleridge's original first draft, only woodlands and gardens are not present in Stukeley's engraving of *Caesaromagus* (fig. 1; Table 2):

Table 2. Topographical motifs in symbolic landscapes
(Source: Coleridge, Xanadu, 1798; Stukeley, undated)

	Stukeley	*Coleridge*
Monarch	Cunobeline	Kublai Khan
Residence	palace	stately pleasure dome
Water	fountain	fountain
River	Can	Alph (sacred)
Fortification	walls, gates	walls, towers

Such common motifs are intriguing. Coleridge's essay *The Friend* written in 1809 demonstrates a passing knowledge of (American) burial mounds, but we cannot assume Coleridge had read Stukeley's posthumous volume (diffusionism!). Other factors may be at work. Coleridge's familiarity with certain aspects of pharmacopeia is well-known. Stukeley's medical training at St. Thomas's Hospital, London should not be forgotten either (Piggott 1985, 32). Was this vision the side-effect of self-medication, a cure for depression? Or were others indulging the fancies of a sick man, even taking advantage of him to perpetrate some sort of hoax?

STUKELEY'S AUDIENCE

Apart from Kilner, two other fellow clerics in Chelmsford were interested in antiquities. The Rev. Dr. Foote Gower, who lived just opposite the town church which Stukeley sketched, hoped to improve Philip Morant's *History and Antiquities of Essex* (Grieve 1994, 223). For Morant, beyond mentioning Writtle as an alternative to Camden's Bursted as a location for *Caesaromagus*, prudently gave the whole affair a wide berth (1763, 61, 196). Foote Gower undertook fieldwork on Roman roads in the year of Stukeley's death (1765), together with the Rev. Benjamin Forster. Stukeley's work in north-west Essex in 1722 seems to have bulked little in Foote Gower's fieldwork, to judge from his archaeological table-talk (Green 1907).

While Stukeley is more likely to have visited Chelmsford in 1759 than in 1722, proving it is far from easy (a sketch of the kitchen of the Dominican Friary may be by him: *Bodl. MS* Top. Gen. e. 61 fol.40) – ironically, in Moulsham. His local contacts were clearly good. Had Volume II of his *Itinerarium* been published in his lifetime, it would have found an appreciative local audience. Six subscribers to the two-volume *County History* written by his friend Philip Morant came from Chelmsford (some quite influential: Grieve 1994, 223). In addition, as we have seen, Nicholas Hayn ('*Varro*'), the Rev. Kilner, and the Rev. Gower all played an active antiquarian role in Chelmsford. None of these (nor, one imagines, the Rev. Forster) would have been sorry to see a decent Roman town on their doorstep – and Stukeley's reputation would have been restored. Perhaps this was the motive behind his 'Dissertation on *Caesaromagus* to Charles Gray, M.P.', written in 1751 (*BM Add. MS* 5261) – a barrister who was to be five times Member for Colchester (Grieve 1994, 152) might be a useful ally (we can suspect the hand of his constituent Morant here). It is tempting to say that, unwittingly, Stukeley was on the verge of committing something akin, in archaeological terms, to the perfect victimless crime, from which everyone stood to gain. The reaction of a national audience to his claims would have been a very different matter. The same sort of critics who attacked him over Silchester would soon have caught up with him, and unfortunately this time their attacks would have been justified.

ROADS AND THE WALKER MAP

Though poor Stukeley is gone, the problem of ferreting out Roman activity north of the river is with us still. It has never

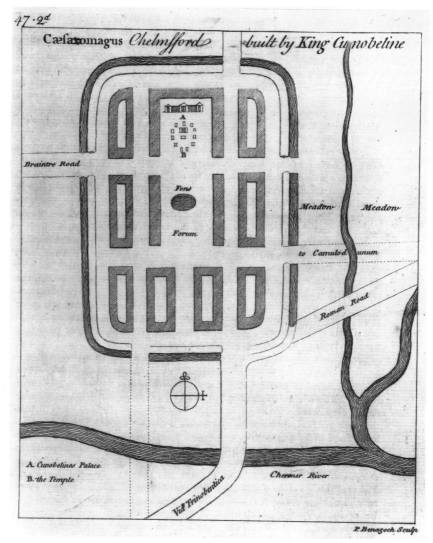

Fig. 1. William Stukeley's 18th-century ground-plot of Caesaromagus *(Bodl. Gough Gen. Top.2). Compare fig. 2.*

been the subject of systematic investigation, for information comes from chance survival of Roman features at sites dug for their medieval deposits. But this newer information on boundaries and routes can only really be understood if the fruits of analysis of the Walker map (fig. 2), and of topographical tradition since Stukeley, are brought to bear (Walker's 1591 map of Chelmsford was presumably not available for him to study, any more than the 1653 estate map of Silchester: Boon 1974, 24).

South of the Can, the London-Colchester road bisects the 'small town' of *Caesaromagus*. It underlies Moulsham Street. North of the Can, however, its course disappears. Earlier this century, Miller Christy speculated that the street-pattern of the medieval town-centre was based on a Roman road system. The London-Colchester road became the lower part of the medieval High Street and, turning off it to the north-east, Springfield Road. The upper end of the High Street, he argued, forked off it as a route running north to Braintree, underneath New Street (Christy 1921, 207–8).

Seventy years later, his theory is confirmed (fig. 3). The London-Colchester road does not continue the straight course

of Moulsham Street, up to Springfield Road. Instead, it curves, for only flood-silts were observed in a watching-brief along a portion of this presumed course (**Site CF 25**). The inference is that the High Street follows the course of the Roman road meticulously, avoiding marshy lower ground, and that the Roman road curved at this point. At **Site W 72** west of the High Street lay a ditch containing 3rd-century pot and tile (see below). Possibly the eastern portion of a long-lived boundary shown on the Walker Map, it could have gone up to Christy's road-junction, and suggests a precursor for the High Street at least as far as this point. At **Site GBC 82** a boundary-ditch ran at right-angles to Springfield Road; it dates to AD 120/150, and a gravelled yard lay nearby. Presumably it ran up to the major denominator in the landscape – Springfield Road, or rather, its Roman precursor. Close to the High Street, a tile hearth and sequence of surfaces was observed. Such hearths are familiar enough in Caesaromagus, though here undated. A structure by the High Street, perhaps even fronting onto its precursor may be mooted. Another (undated) hearth was recorded in a trench at **Site CC 83**. Roman tile was incorporated into the foundations of the earliest stone building on this site, Chelmsford Cathedral, and one may ask how far it wandered. Recent excavations outside the Cathedral have also revealed only single sherds of pottery. Further north at **Site CF 23**, Roman and Saxon material came from the fill of a ditch flanking New Street, implying a road and flanking ditches. As we have seen, evidence is now emerging for Roman roads and activity north of the Can. A century ago the only sign of Roman activity north of the Can was a ditch at a quarry-site to west of the area of the Walker map, full of 'black earth, fragments of bones, iron and pottery...thought to be Roman' (Corder 1887, 92), so there have been advances. In essence, approaches to understanding settlement across the river from *Caesaromagus* must be similar to those used in understanding the topography of Southwark, across the river from Londinium.

FIELDS AND THE WALKER MAP

These roads crossed a landscape more bucolic than Roman Southwark's. Transcription and analysis of the Walker map of 1591 for the area around Moulsham/*Caesaromagus* detected a fossilised pre-medieval field-system (Drury & Rodwell 1980,

59–62; Drury 1988, 125–6). The same procedure, applied to the sheet of the Walker map for north of the Can, produces the same result: a 'brickwork' field-system (fig. 2). Further along the London-Colchester road, whole tracts of field-systems can be traced around Witham (Rodwell 1993, 58–9). The Chelmsford example may be an outlier of this system. Dating fields from boundary-ditches – let alone entire field-systems – is a notoriously ticklish matter, to which we must now turn.

It is easiest to deal with the London-Colchester road first for its date and now its course (under Springfield Road) are known. It was built *c*. AD 60/65, as excavation at Moulsham demonstrated (Drury 1988, 128). Some fields plotted at Witham were co-axial with this road (Rodwell 1993, 58). This implies that the co-axial landscape was reorganised only when or after the road was built – at Chelmsford north of the Can, 60 years after. There is a 'time-lag' between the construction of the road and occupation alongside it.

The road under New Street leading to Braintree is on a completely different axis. But the field-boundaries portrayed on the Walker Map are nevertheless co-axial with it, so here too the fields were laid out only when or after the road was built. A portion of ditch flanking the road at **Site CF 23**

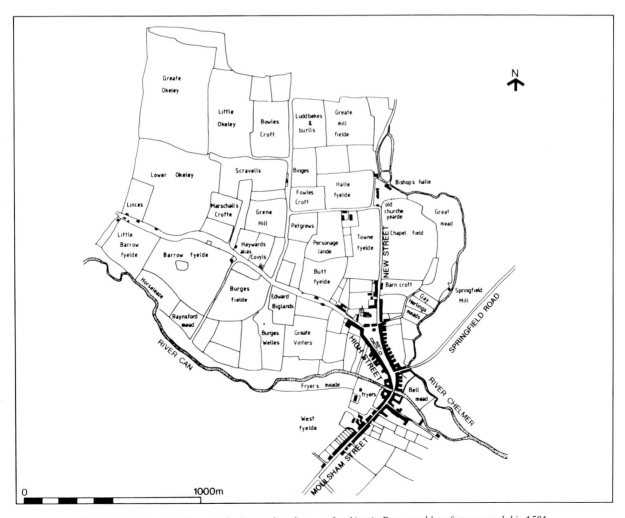

Fig. 2. The Walker Map (transcribed), showing the palimpsest of prehistoric, Roman and later features recorded in 1591 (reproduced by permission of the Essex Record Office).

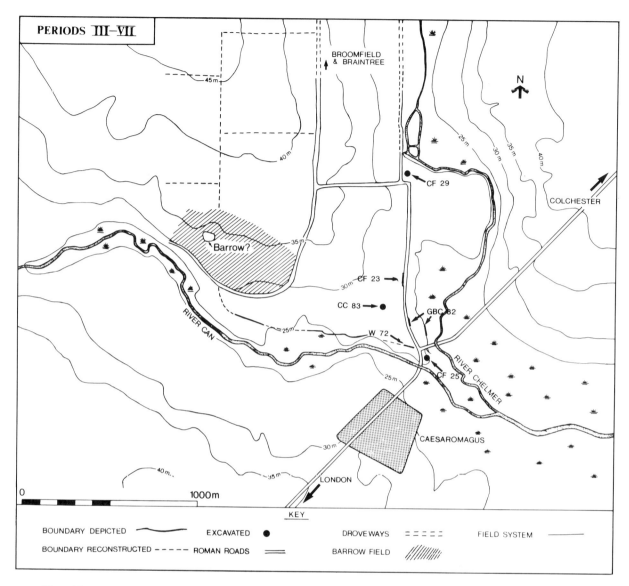

Fig. 3. The Roman landscape: extracted features from the Walker Map; excavated portions ringed; the walled Roman town has been added.

yielded abraded material, but cannot be claimed as a formal road-ditch.

It has been suggested that dating-evidence from ditches tends to be deposited only after the fill has been cleared out for the last time. Portions of silt may collapse back into the ditch from a bank of material cast up by cleaning, only to be shovelled out again. Pottery becomes progressively more abraded as the cycle of ditch-dredging repeats itself. If pottery comes from an intact primary deposit, matters should be much clearer (Pryor 1984, 110–12). Abraded Roman and Saxon material from the ditch at **CF 23** shows that the field-system the ditch bounded was maintained in the Roman and Saxon periods, not that it was necessarily dug in either: there was no sequence of fills – only uniform silt from the last episode of dredging. Conversely, material recovered from the 'supernatural' may reflect the range of activity in the neighbourhood more accurately, though usually considered a result of manuring. The absence of Late pre-Roman Iron Age pot in either ploughsoil or ditch-fill is however conclusive, for

Late pre-Roman Iron Age material is not known south of the Can either. South of the river in Moulsham, fields had been argued to be pre-Roman on grounds of alignment, but the same cannot necessarily hold good north of the river in Chelmsford: they may be Roman or later.

Presumably these reflect two distinct tenurial units, for south of the River Can, an early Roman Iron Age settlement is known to underlie the Roman town (Isserlin & Wickenden forthcoming). Conversely, a Middle Iron Age settlement was found at Little Waltham (on the uplands north of the study-area: Drury 1978). The surprising lack of Roman pottery from even the little excavation under medieval Chelmsford may possibly indicate pasture, rather than arable land. As Late pre-Roman Iron Age sites are not known from under the medieval town, perhaps we should imagine limited gravel-terrace settlement exploiting field-systems on either side of the River Can, the result of pastoral intensification only starting shortly before the Roman occupation. Grazing would be suited to the more marginal, wetter soils.

PRE-ROMAN MONUMENTS?

While this agricultural landscape can be rationally reconstructed if it is assumed that the 'brickwork' field system employed units of more or less equal size, laid out in 'English bond', there is one anomaly. The Walker Map also depicts a kidney-shaped area (Burges Welles Field and *Barrow* Field) respected by most later tracks and roads. Together with *Little Barrow* Field it is likely to have formed a single unit originally, and represent a prehistoric funerary landscape. At Rivenhall, Essex, the term 'Barrow Field' was taken to indicate a barrow cemetery (Rodwell & Rodwell 1985, 32–33), and in other parts of England also (Field 1972, 14). It may be significant that the Walker map shows the 16th-century town gallows near 'Barrow Field': such a juxtaposition has a long antiquity.[1] A blob depicted in Barrow Field may represent the barrow itself.[2] One corner of this brickwork field-system was aligned exactly on the site of the ?barrow. If it still existed, it would have been a useful sighting-point for those laying out the fields. The field-system is clearly a small part of a larger whole, which, presumably, being skirted by what are clearly droveways, this 'unit' predated. When gravel was quarried to the west of the medieval town (in the area of Admirals Park) antiquarians recovered an Early Bronze Age flint dagger, suggesting high-status burial (Grimes 1931, 352), an impression which the discovery of a ring-ditch by aerial photography reinforces. Analysis of the cartographic evidence suggests that high-status burials in barrows may have been widespread on fringes of the flood-plain, and Walker's 'Barrows' may have been an extension of the barrow-field which finds and aerial photography suggest existed further west.

Just as this represents the major episode of change in the landscape, so it was itself transformed in the Roman period. A boundary-ditch, aligned east-west, referred to earlier (**Site W, Period VII**) can be identified as the eastern portion of a boundary shown on the Walker Map. This would originally have extended up to the junction of the London-Colchester and Braintree roads, and almost up to Barrow Field. It suggests an attempt at reclamation of marginal land, and the division of arable land to the north from the floodplain of the River Can and water-meadows to the south. It dates to the 3rd century. Environmental evidence from **Site GBC 82** during **Period III** suggests that the landscape was one of mixed wetlands and grassland, and that the River Can was prone to flood. The drainage ditch dug and redug several times at this same site (**Periods VI.1–VII.2**; 2nd-4th centuries) may be an early version of the medieval *conduit*, an artificial water-channel, depicted on the Walker Map (Grieve 1988, 120–2). If so, this could be an attempt at flood-control, or perhaps even part of a mill-leat. A suitable site for a mill would be nearby, as in the Middle Ages. The area can be viewed either as a suburb – for the unwalled town spread north towards the river – or a separate settlement, part of a dispersed pattern of landholdings, as part of a farm or villa; observation at Bishop's Hall Lane (**Site CF 29**) in 1993 revealed part of a curvilinear gulley, alas undated. Was this part of a round-house? The extensive chemical and heavy-metal pollution which precluded proper investigation means we shall never know.

CONCLUSIONS

The first part of this essay showed how accumulated layers of conjecture have forced us away from examining aspects of 'settlement hinterland', of the sort most frequently associated with rural archaeology, primarily because of the difficulties in locating a documented settlement. Now that this problem has been solved, a more impersonal view can be taken.

The second part showed how analysis of very limited results from urban sites can pay dividends in formulating a land-use model. Such a model embraces evidence for a Roman road, and evidence for a barrow-field which may have survived into the Roman period, incorporated into a rectilinear field-system. It suggests the increasing formalisation of activity with the passage of time. Such a situation is, on reflection, hardly surprising. Water Newton is another example of a Romano-British 'small town' with its barrow-field, revealed by aerial photography.

Major settlement, or at least something on the scale of activity underneath present-day Moulsham, is not yet known underneath medieval Chelmsford, despite Stukeley's efforts. That we know as much as we do is only because excavators have examined earlier levels – and because of the pioneering efforts of John Walker in 1591. The best may, however, be yet to come. Let us hope that it is too, for Brian, to whom this *lanx saturna* is dedicated.

ACKNOWLEGEMENTS

I am grateful to the British Library, London, for access to Stukeley material and to the Bodleian Library, Oxford for permission to reproduce fig. 1; and to the Essex Record Office, especially Janet Smith and June Beardsley for access to the Walker map, and to Christopher Lambert for permission to reproduce illustrations based thereon; to the late Miss H. Grieve for discussion on field-names; and to L. Collett and N. Nethercoat for illustration. I am most grateful to C.R. Wallace for discussion of Stukeley, and to N.P. Wickenden for discussion of the topography of Roman Chelmsford – and to the various site directors for digging some of their sites down to natural! A more detailed site-specific text together with the excavation reports is at County Hall, Chelmsford, pending full publication of the sites.

Notes

1. Alternatively the name marks the site of a gravel pit – 'borrow field'. Certainly the earliest Ordnance Survey map shows the position of a gravel quarry here. It is likely that first there was a mound and then quarrying, as happened further west.
2. Within the context of monuments and ritual activity, one other kind of evidence should be mentioned, namely hoarding. A watching-brief was undertaken at the confluence of the Rivers Can and Chelmer, but no prehistoric metalwork was recovered. A human jawbone was retrieved however. Human skulls feature in some Bronze, Iron Age and Roman ritual deposits, associated in the Thames with metalwork (Marsh & West 1981; Bradley & Gordon 1988). Bronze Age hoards are known from elsewhere in the Chelmer Valley (Buckley *et al.* 1986).

Bibliography

Allen, P.T., *et al.* forthcoming *Caesaromagus: excavations of Roman Chelmsford, 1980–1988, East Anglian Archaeol.*

Bradley, R., & Gordon, H., 1988 Human skulls from the River Thames, their
dating and significance, *Antiquity*, **62**, 503–9

Bristow, C.R., 1985 Geology of the country around Chelmsford, *Mem. British
Geol. Surv.*, Sheet 241 (London)

Buckley, D.G., & Major, H., 1983 Quernstones, in Crummy, N. (ed.), *Colchester Archaeological Report 2: The Roman small finds from excavations in
Colchester 1971–9*, 73–6 (Colchester)

_____, Brown, N., & Greenwood, P., 1986 Late Bronze Age Hoards
from the Chelmer Valley, Essex, *Antiq. J.*, **66**, 248–66

Camden, W., 1610 *Britain, or a chorographicall description of England, Scotland and
Ireland* (trans. Philemon Holland)

Celoria, F., & Spencer, B., 1968 Eighteenth century fieldwork in London and
Middlesex: some unpublished drawings by William Stukeley, *Trans.
London Middlesex Archaeol. Soc.*, **22**, 23–31

Christy, M., 1921 Roman roads in Essex, *Trans. Essex Archaeol. Soc.*, new ser.,
15, 196–227

Corder, H., 1887 Gravel-pits and ancient pottery near Chelmsford, *Essex
Naturalist*, **1**, 1887

Drake, W., 1779 Observations on two Roman stations in Essex, *Archaeologia*,
5, 137–42

Drury, P.J., 1978 *Excavations at Little Waltham, Essex*, CBA Res. Rep., **26**,
Chelmsford Excav. Comm. Rep., **1** (London)

_____, 1988 *The mansio and other sites in the south-eastern sector of
Caesaromagus*, CBA Res. Rep., **66**, Chelmsford Archaeol. Trust Rep., **3.1**
(London)

_____, & Rodwell, W., 1980 Settlement in the later Iron Age and
Roman periods, in Buckley, D.G. (ed.), *Archaeology in Essex to AD 1500*,
CBA Res. Rep., **34** (London)

Field, J., 1972 *English field names: a dictionary* (London)

Gee, M., 1986 Broomfield Borrowpit, *Essex Archaeol. Hist.*, **17**, 141–55.

Going, C.J., 1987 *The mansio and other sites in the south-eastern sector of
Caesaromagus: the Roman pottery*, CBA Res. Rep., **62**, Chelmsford Archaeol.
Trust Rep., **3.2** (London)

Green, J.J., 1907 The Rev. Benjamin Forster, B.D., and his account of Roman roads in North Essex and Saffron Walden, *Essex Rev.*, **16**, 165–73

Grieve, H.M., 1988 *The sleepers and the shadows: Chelmsford: a town, its people and
its past. Vol. 1 the medieval and Tudor story* (Chelmsford)

_____, 1994 *The sleepers and the shadows: Chelmsford: a town, its people and
its past. Vol. 2 from market town to Chartered Borough, 1608–1888* (Chelmsford)

Grimes, W.F., 1931 The Early Bronze Age flint dagger in England and Wales,
Proc. Prehist. Soc. East Anglia, **6**, 340–55

Harris, A.P., & Isserlin, R.M.J., forthcoming Excavations in medieval and
post-medieval Chelmsford, *East Anglian Archaeol.*

Hedges, J.D., & Buckley, D.G., 1981 Springfield Cursus and the cursus problem, *Essex County Council Occas. Paper*, **1** (Chelmsford)

Isserlin, R.M.J., 1995 Roman Coggeshall II; excavations at 'The Lawns',
1989–93, *Essex Archaeol. Hist.*, **26**, 82–104

_____, & Wickenden, N.P., forthcoming *Frontage sites in the northern
sector of Caesaromagus*, CBA Res. Rep.

Kenward, H.K., Hall, A.R., & Jones, A.K.G., 1980 A tested set of techniques
for the extraction of plant and animal macrofossils from waterlogged
archaeological deposits, *Science Archaeol.*, **22**, 3–15

Marsh, G., & West, B., 1981 Skullduggery in Roman London?, *Trans. London Middlesex Archaeol. Soc.*, **32**, 86–102

Morant, P., 1768 *The history and antiquities of the County of Essex*

Robinson, M.A., & Lambrick, G.H., 1984 Holocene alluviation and hydrol-
ogy in the upper Thames basin, *Nature*, **308**, 809–14

Morris, R., & Roxan, J., 1980 Churches on Roman buildings, in Rodwell, W.
(ed.), *Temples, churches and religion: recent research in Roman Britain*, Brit.
Archaeol. Rep. British Ser., **77** (Oxford)

Myres, J.N.L., 1977 *A corpus of Anglo-Saxon pottery of the pagan period* (Oxford)

Piggott, S., 1985 *William Stukeley. An eighteenth-century antiquary* (London, 2
edn)

Pryor, F., 1984 Excavation at Fengate Peterborough, England: the fourth
report, *Northamptonshire Archaeol. Soc. Monograph*, **2**

Read, C.H., 1894 A Saxon grave at Broomfield, *Proc. Soc. Antiq. London*, **15**,
250–55

Rippon, S., 1991 Early planned landscapes in south-east Essex, *Essex Archaeol.
Hist.*, **22**, 46–60.

Rivet, A.L.F., 1970 The British section of the Antonine Itinerary, *Britannia*,
1, 34–82

Rodwell, W.J., 1993 *The origins and early development of Witham, Essex: a study in
settlement and fortification, prehistoric to medieval* Oxbow Monograph, **26**
(Oxford)

_____, & Rodwell, K.A., 1985 *Rivenhall: investigations of a villa, church,
and village, 1950–1977*, CBA Res. Rep., **55**, Chelmsford Archaeol. Trust
Rep., **4** (London)

Stukeley, W., 1776 *Itinerarium Curiosum*, cent. ii

Wickenden, N.P., 1992 *The temple and other sites in the north-eastern sector of
Caesaromagus*, CBA Res. Rep., **75**, Chelmsford Archaeol. Trust Rep., **7**
(London)

Wright, T., 1836 *The history and topography of the County of Essex, comprising its
ancient and modern history...*, **1** (London, 2 vols.)

8   Romano-British art and Gallo-Roman samian

Martin Henig

Although for many students throughout the world, Brian Hartley's name is virtually synonymous with samian ware, his interests extend far beyond pottery studies. For example, over the years he has kindly brought to my attention a number of engraved gemstones amongst which one in particular stands out in my memory. It was an old find from South Shields, which had long been thought to have been lost. Its subject was two confronted masks (Henig 1974, no. 526), presumably with a Bacchic connotation; its material the opaque red stone known as red jasper. The colour is that of blood and of fire (Webster 1991b, 12–14), perhaps too it was associated with gold (Vickers 1994; Vickers & Gill 1994). In any case the Romans loved it, and 'Pompeian red' is the most familiar tone on Roman walls including the walls of houses in Roman Britain, especially in the 2nd century (Ling 1991; for Britain, Davey & Ling 1982). It is also the colour of samian ware which was contemporary with it.

Samian ware has not often been treated as art. However any decorated object deserves to be examined in that context and Anthony King rightly included it in his brief survey (1983, 183–5) where he sketches the main features of development but avoids the more contentious question of how it was received by the customer. This contribution takes up that challenge and muses on the response of the Roman and Romanised inhabitants of Britain to a table-ware produced in quantity far away and traded in bulk to the province. It is in some sense an appendix to the author's *The art of Roman Britain* (1995) and takes as its point of departure a thesis first voiced ten years ago (Henig 1985) which runs counter to the depressing analysis of R.G. Collingwood (1937, 247–60) by maintaining that Roman Britain had a vibrant artistic culture throughout the period. If people of taste were well able to distinguish between what was good and what was not, how did they react to samian at its various stages of development in the 1st and 2nd centuries? It needs to be stated that this is not essentially involved with quantitative analysis such as that of Marsh (1981). The reasons for such fluctuations in supply were probably largely occasioned by economic factors. However the 1st-century peak in samian importation corresponds with what I shall call the period of 'samian as current art' and even the 2nd-century

florescence in Verulamium certainly occurs at a time when red assumed especial prominence on the walls of the town's houses and when red jasper signets were very much *à la mode*.

The artistic sources of samian have always been clear and are given by Oswald & Pryce (1920, 6 and 131, pl. 22). They lie especially in silver-ware. Not many such silver vessels are known from Britain, but even before the conquest silver cups like those from Welwyn (Stead 1967, 2–22; Henig 1995, 36, pl. 16) were in circulation and were copied and adapted in bronze as testified by two examples from Norfolk (Henig 1995, 37, pl. 17). More relevant to our purpose are the decorated cups from Hockwold, especially cup 1 with its rich frieze of vine-foliage admixed with olive (Johns 1986)(fig. 1). Such decoration is typical of the plate (bowls and dishes as well as cups) found throughout the Empire (Strong 1966, 133–55; Baratte & Painter 1989, esp. 63–75). A *ministerium* of silver would surely have been used by a Romanised aristocrat such as King Cogidubnus or by anyone else who inhabited the palatial *domus* at Fishbourne. No such service has survived, of course, but the partly silvered handle of a bronze *askos* or water-jug does (Down & Henig 1988). Like the Hockwold cups its ornament is essentially vegetal, its satyr-mask escutcheon emphasising the Bacchic world of the feast. Other materials represented were glass (Harden & Price 1971), valued for its translucency, as is implied by Pompeian still lifes (Ling 1991, 157, fig. 167), and lack of flavour as even the boor Trimalchio admits in the *Satyricon* (Petronius, XV, 50), 'if only it wasn't breakable', and of course samian ware (Dannell 1971), both plain forms and figured. Figured forms associated with the period of the first masonry building (the 'proto-palace') and the Flavian building contain many fragments of bowls with rich vegetal ornament, Dragendorff forms 29 (fig. 2a) and 30; it would be surprising if they did not, for such meandering, repeating scrolls provided the basic repertoire of South Gaulish potters whose wares were ubiquitous in the Romanised centres of southern Britain including Camulodunum (fig. 2b), London and Verulamium (Marsh 1981; see King 1983, 184–5, ill. 152). The designs are in lower relief than contemporary plate and also more formal and less naturalistic, though some of the leaves will bear comparison with

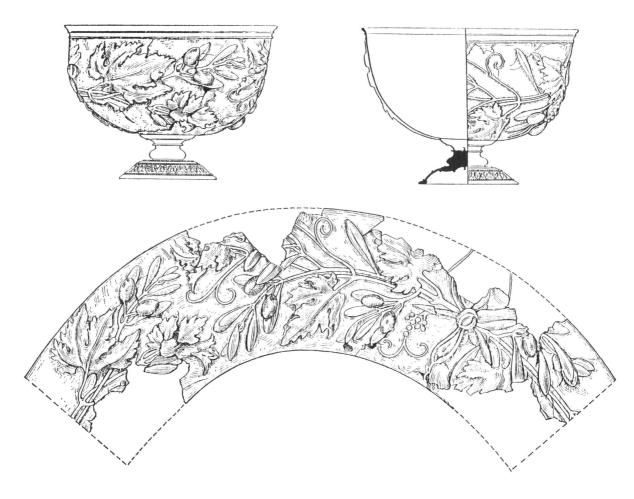

Fig. 1. Hockwold Treasure, silver cup no. 1 (after Johns 1986, fig. 2).

vegetable ornament executed *en repousée* in precious metal; in the dim, artificial light of dining-rooms the gloss on the vessels may have reflected the gleam of the lamps of torches to give a hint of the effect of light on silver or even of the heavy gilding to be seen on some silver vessels (Baratte & Painter 1989, 71, no. 12, and col. pl. on p. 30). Michael Vickers has even suggested that the ultimate source of red-gloss pottery in the Mediterranean world lay in gold vessels (Vickers 1994), and further that the main centres of samian manufacture in Gaul lay in the proximity to gold-bearing regions (Vickers 1994, 245–7; Vickers & Gill 1994, 175–6). It is an intriguing idea that some of the richest inhabitants of Gaul (and perhaps even of Britain) owned gold plate, but it is not one susceptible of proof, and in any case is seems to me unlikely to have been a major factor in the artistic development of the western provinces.

The decoration of early samian is a 'current' taste, whether we look at silver or other metalwork such as military belt-buckles, at mosaic, painting or stone reliefs. It is easy to understand that running scrolls probably had an especial fascination to Celts whose own art was curvilinear. We can still see their appeal in the 2nd century in the rich vegetal ornament of a silver *trulla* from Backworth, Northumberland (Walters 1921, 46–7, no. 183) (fig. 3) and two simpler silver

vessels from Bath (Sunter & Brown 1988, 16, nos. 24, 25) the former dedicated to the Matres by Fabius Dubitatus and the latter to Sulis, again in all probability by people of native origin. Moreover in Gaul as late as the 3rd century silver vessels like those in the Chaourse (Baratte & Painter 1989, 111–2, no. 48; 127–8, no. 74) and Graincourt-lès-Havrincourt (Baratte & Painter 1989, 144–5, no. 90; 147–9, no. 94) treasures display superb scrollwork. Certainly 3rd-century is the great silver mirror from Wroxeter, comparatively plain but with its simple but gorgeous vegetal wreath-frame recalling South Gaulish samian (Toynbee 1964, 334–5, 78c) but at a distance of time which ensures that while there was no direct link, we can see how confidently the Roman style it represented was now part of the accepted artistic vocabulary of the western provinces. Vegetal scrolls were very much 'current' in Roman Britain on a larger scale as demonstrated by a peopled scroll on the wall of a house in Verulamium (Davey & Ling 1981, 171–3, no. 41, A) and similar scrolls on mosaic pavements like that from Middleborough, Colchester (Smith 1984); these exemplify a continuing tradition which we can indeed take forward throughout the artistic life of Roman Britain, to the lovely bi-coloured scrolls of the Woodchester, Chedworth and Stonesfield mosaics, long after the samian industry had expired (Henig 1995, 125).

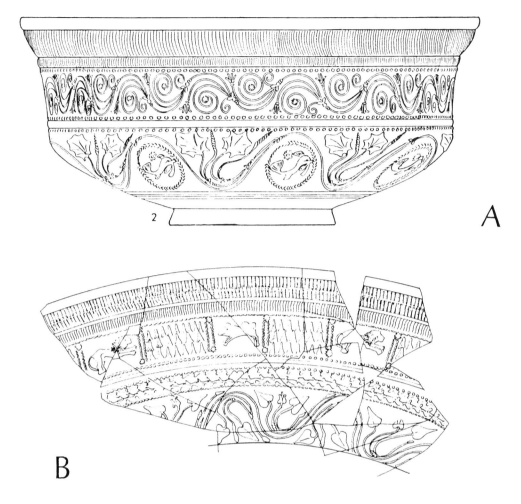

Fig. 2. South Gaulish vessels (form 29): **A**, Flavian, from Fishbourne (after Dannell 1971, fig. 131, no. 50); **B**, Claudio-Neronian, from Camulodunum (after Hawkes & Hull 1947, pl. 31, no. 2).

Beside these masterpieces the scrolls of the Central Gaulish potters Sacer (Stanfield & Simpson 1990, 203–6, pl. 83, no. 8) in the reign of Hadrian, or of Paternus (Stanfield & Simpson 1990, 235–9, pl. 107, nos. 26–8, 30–1) or Cinnamus (Stanfield & Simpson 1990, 303–10, pl. 162, nos. 57–64) (fig. 4) in the second half of the century appear decidedly coarse and are certainly less rich than those on earlier South Gaulish vessels; moreover there is a tendency in Central Gaulish pottery to place the decorative element too low on the body of the vessel, leaving a disturbingly deep rim which rather spoils the composition.

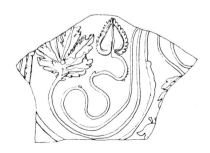

Fig. 3. Silver-gilt trulla from Backworth, Northumberland (after Walters 1921, fig. 47b).

Fig. 4. Central Gaulish vessel by Cinnamus (form 30) from Fishbourne (after Dannell 1971, fig. 131, no. 55).

*Fig. 5. South Gaulish vessel (form 37) from Fishbourne
(after Dannell 1971, fig. 133, no. 69).*

Samian ware, although largely made in Gaul, does not really reflect local culture either in content or in taste and after the Flavian period not even the social aspirations of Romanised Britons. Attractive scrolls persist as the dominant ornamentation for a while, but around the beginning of the reign of Vespasian there was a marked shift towards panels containing figures of men or animals within schemae where the vegetal ornament was held in check (Oswald & Pryce 1920, 74–5, 77, 91–2) (fig. 5). As King (1983, 184) puts it, 'the *horror vacui* of the earlier styles continued, but the well-spaced and well-composed scenes of the earlier period were abandoned'. An intermediate stage is shown by a form 30 bowl where a frieze serves to demarcate gladiatorial scenes (Oswald & Pryce 1920, pl. 8, no. 4) (fig. 6), the latter a theme attested in a fragment from a Colchester fresco (Ling 1984), and of

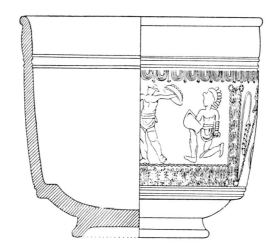

Fig. 6. South Gaulish vessel (form 30) from Richborough (after Bushe-Fox 1932, pl. 27).

Fig. 7. Handle of silver trulla from Capheaton, Northumberland (after Walters 1921, fig. 49).

The general cramped decoration and avoidance of empty spaces (except in the plain band below the rim) observable on the majority of figured samian vessels, with their lack of proper design, carefully executed figure-types and narrative interest, suggest a craft that was losing its way artistically however much it may have remained successful commercially for a time. The situation appears to be analogous to that of 'blue and white' Wedgwood since its *floruit* in the 18th century. Although it is still made, neither its style nor its quality are likely to appeal to the discriminating. In fact the decline in samian style was not inevitable and some Central Gaulish potters made bold attempts to reverse it. Some employed relief appliqués to excellent effect, especially in the Hadrianic period when they may stand as not unworthy examples of the minor art of the period. We may note, for example, two superb pots of the form Déchelette 72 from London, one from Cornhill depicting a frieze of standing figures separated by vines (Oswald & Pryce 1920, 230–1, pl. 84, esp. no. 1) (fig. 8) and another from New Guy's House, Southwark showing cupid huntsmen (Marsden 1965, 129 and pl. 1, d). Black-gloss wares were particularly attractive products of the Central Gaulish samian factories and were often the medium for distinctive appliqué designs, which 'appealed to the taste of but a small *clientèle*' in the first half of the 2nd century, so once again belonging to the phase of Hadrianic classicism (see Toynbee 1964, 393–4); perhaps following the Vickers thesis we can see them as trying to imitate silver though it should be noted that at least in the 3rd century *niello* was much used to contrast with the whiteness of silver (Baratte & Painter 1989, 27, and see for example 168, no. 113). The taste for black is shown also in native colour-coated vessels including wares from the Nene Valley and the New Forest as well as in objects made from jet and shale.

course a commonplace in the uneducated tastes of Trimalchio's Puteoli. The separation of figures or groups of figures into panels with little relationship one to another is to be found on some silver of the Middle Empire, notably *trullae* like those found in the Rhône between Arles and Tarascon (Baratte & Painter 1989, 227–8, nos. 185, 186) and others from the Capheaton treasure (Walters 1921, 48–50, nos. 189, 190) (fig. 7) but the figured decoration of these vessels is confined to the limited space provided by their flat handles and besides their subject matter is special, undoubtedly concerned with religious ritual. A third *trulla* from Capheaton in fact depicts Minerva presiding over a sanctuary (Walter 1921, 50–1, no. 192). We long to find a similar consistency on the walls of samian vessels but consistent iconographies are very rare and for the most part limited to subjects of lesser importance such as *venationes*.

The arrangement of panels on samian pots is generally far too cramped for the field available, and this is accentuated in much Central Gaulish figured ware by the deep plain band between the rim of the vessel and the band of ovolos. Here there is a marked contrast with contemporary frescoes. Even with regard to stylistic organisation of wall-surfaces, where there was the precedent of Italian wall-painting of the third and fourth styles, the Hadrianic and Antonine frescoes from London, Verulamium, Cirencester and Leicester do not on the whole become over-fussy (Davey & Ling 1982).

Fig. 8. Vessel of form Déchelette 72 from Cornhill, London (after Oswald & Pryce 1920, pl. 84, no. 8).

Another technique was incision, as employed also on cut-glass ware (Oswald & Pryce 1920, 223–6, pls. 77; 78; 79, no. 7; 80, nos. 1–4). Black-gloss vessels are also known (see Toynbee 1964, 395, pl. 89, a). Barbotine ornament with decoration trailed onto the surface is much more of a style unique to pottery and it was, indeed, employed on the New Guy's House vase. It was especially popular at the northern limits of samian production in East Gaul (Oswald & Pryce 1920, 226–30, pls. 62; 79, nos. 8–14; 80, nos. 5–8; 81, nos. 2–4). All these techniques added novelty to the product but did not forestall the marginalisation of samian as an art. Barbotine, for example, was used more effectively by the makers of 'Rhenish' beakers (King 1983, 187–8, and especially Symonds 1992) and similar wares were also produced in Roman Britain (see below).

For the present writer, returning to samian after twenty years and to the new edition of Stanfield & Simpson's classic work now re-issued as *Les potiers de la Gaule Centrale* (1990) there remain questions to ask. A comparison of samian ware with gems (1974, 177–9) suggested to me that in both cases the student is dealing with a 'Roman' art which remained largely distinct from the world of Romano-Celtic art and cult. I see no reason to change my views now after more research on gems, and my attitude to samian has been confirmed by Jeanne-Marie Demarolle (1994). There is nothing really local here. However Antonine and Severan glyptic does have an attractiveness and a personality of its own and its use of rich patterning and texture gives it a place in the 'current' art of the time. Amongst conventional samian, on the other hand, real merit as art is almost confined to pots showing hunting scenes (e.g. Stanfield & Simpson 1990, 82–7, pl. 26, the Trajanic 'Potier à la Rosette; 109–13, pl. 57, 653, the Hadrianic Butrio (fig. 9); 250–2, pls. 117, 118, the early to mid-Antonine Criciro). They may be compared to certain metal vessels like a silvered-bronze one from Valence (Walters 1921, 20, no. 75; Baratte & Painter 1989, 226, no. 184) (fig. 10), though this has rather been related to African sigillata, but they lack the liveliness of 'hunt cups' from the Nene Valley. While most fig-

Fig. 10. Silver-plated bronze bowl from Valence, Drôme, France (after Walters 1921, fig. 42a).

ures who are not huntsmen or gladiators are mythological and satyrs, pans, cupids and several deities may be distinguished, there is not even a hint of a coherent programme such as we find in native figured pots, such as friezes of deities (Webster 1989, 10; 1991c, 140–3), the Labours of Hercules (Webster 1989, 11–15; 1991c, 143–57) or religious rituals (Webster 1989, 5–9; 1991c, 135–40).

The contrast is shown most poignantly in the samian and other pottery produced in kilns at Colchester (Hull 1963). The potters show 'a fine disregard for detail and accuracy' (Hull 1963, 50). However it is notable that within the tired conventions of samian design or lack of design the animal figures are distinctive and 'belong to the native style so well known to us from the 'hunt cups' of Castor and similar potteries' (Hull 1963, 72). In a bowl like that of the hunting scene of a mould of Potter B (Hull 1963, fig. 29, 2) (fig. 11) we see an approximation to *venationes* on colour-coated vessels as were also made at Colchester (Hull 1963, 93, 95, fig. 52, and see 168–31, figs. 96, 97 for kiln 32) (fig. 12).

It is very possible that samian had slipped downwards in social acceptability (Millett 1980), though this is hard to prove, and even if it had it would not of itself explain the samian potters' lack of initiative. While not a luxury ware in any real sense, it was certainly used in respectable and even wealthy households as suitable ware for dining in 1st-century Britain as elsewhere. The second peak in the Antonine period espe-

Fig. 9. Central Gaulish vessel showing hunting scene , style of Butrio, from Richborough (after Bushe-Fox 1949, pl. 83, no. 59).

Fig. 11. Colchester samian, mould of potter B (after Hull 1963, fig. 29, no. 2).

Fig. 12. Colchester barbotine hunt-cup (after Hull 1963, fig. 52, no. 6).

cially at Verulamium, argues, indeed, that it had *not* been banished from fashionable dining. A group of 22 items of samian from a stone building at Towcester (Pengelly 1980), all but one of them from Central Gaul and mainly plain forms but including a couple of bowls of form 37 and an appliqué black-slip vase of form Déchelette 74 depicting hounds chasing stags (Simpson 1980), was associated with fragments from at least eighteen glass vessels, which have been regarded as a set (Price 1980). Whether these vessels are to be regarded as the possessions of a fairly wealthy family or as belonging to

a public building is uncertain (Lambrick 1980, 47, 49). Brian Hartley (1980) shows that the samian dates on the whole to the second quarter of the century but it is clear that it was not deposited until the decade 155–65.

Plain samian too has its part to play in assessing the value placed on the ware as art. At Alton (Millett 1986) samian vessels were present in two of the graves, one of which was clearly of 'high status' as it contained a gold ring. However, the greater part of the pottery found was Farnham ware, both oxidised and reduced fabrics, so that here at least as Millett comments 'the purchasers were not concerned by the colour' (1986, 79). We find a *ministerium* largely of plain samian from a Flavian grave at Winchester (Biddle 1967) and it is present in burials of Hadrianic and Antonine age from Skeleton Green, Puckeridge (Partridge 1981, 258–68). We should bear in mind that even though they were not in the same category as metal vessels they may have been acceptable symbols of the deceased person's importance. Even the relatively poor vessels of the Antonine period still had their colour to recommend them for it is during this period that we have the best evidence from Britain of the popularity of red in the decor of houses as well as on objects as various as enamelled cups and red jasper gemstones. Red pottery was of course easy to produce and inevitably native potters, for example in the Oxford area (Young 1977), were able to continue this aspect of the traditon.

The art historian can no longer regard contemporary samian as being important evidence for 'current' [bad] taste. More important as indicators of culture are locally produced drinking vessels, some with hunting scenes, others showing deities or having an erotic connotation. Their manufacture and distribution may have been further limited by the fact that they were intended as New Year presents or for use at religious festivals (Webster 1989) but unlike samian some vessels do figure native Celtic deities in a recognisably Romano-British style; others like the Horsey Toll pot (Webster 1989, 9, fig. 9, no. 15) make use of sexual humour with the directness of a modern cartoonist (Webster 1991c, 157–62).

The majority of pots (the plain forms) imitate the forms and perhaps the shine of plain metal vessels. This is interesting because the indication we get from pewter vessels, the earliest perhaps 2nd-century but most of them 4th-century, is that the British gentry liked using simple vessels sometimes with a patterned centre-piece (Henig 1995, 133, pl. 81). The silver Water Newton Treasure, most of it certainly of insular manufacture (as made for dedication at a specific church) and probably of the later part of the 4th century but conceivably earlier, demonstrates the same restraint. One jug is however covered with a rich acanthus ornament (Painter 1977b, 26 and 31, no. 5). Of course the Mildenhall Treasure presents a number of geometric, vegetal and above all figural, themes but this is exceptional in every way (Painter 1977a).

The character of Romano-British art may be defined in its simplicity, its regard for textures and for pattern, for colour and coherence (Henig 1985). Had the manufacturers of samian been interested in supplying the artistic needs of the British market such would have been a major consideration. It was not, and like the Wedgwood ware of modern times samian ware was more or less inflicted on a market where there was no other source of fine ware in a popular colour. One cannot help wondering whether such samian, Gaulish though it is, encouraged Professor Collingwood (1937) in his diatribe against Romano-British art as it certainly led his predecessor Francis Haverfield to see the *characteristic* of Roman art as being that of mechanical production (1915, 48–51). When the samain industry finally collapsed it had, in truth, nothing left to contribute to the artistic life of the province

but that does not mean we should forget or ignore that enormous influx of glossy red pottery in the years after the conquest and its possible impact as a source of inspiration at those elegant banquets of which Tacitus writes (*Agricola* 21), where the Britons enslaved themselves to the good life.

ACKNOWLEDGEMENTS

I would like to thank Joanna Bird, Anthony King and George Lambrick for comment and helpful information.

Bibliography

Anderson, A.C., & Anderson, A.S. (eds), 1991 *Roman pottery research in Britain and North-West Europe*, BAR Int. Ser., **123** (Oxford)

Baratte, F., & Painter, K., 1989 *Trésors d'orfèvrerie Gallo-Romains*, Exhibition catalogue (Paris)

Biddle, M., 1967 Two Flavian burials from Winchester, *Antiq. J.*, **47**, 224–50

Bushe-Fox, J.P., 1932 *Third report on the excavation of the Roman fort at Richborough, Kent*, Rep. Res. Comm. Soc. Antiq. London, **10** (Oxford)

_____, 1949 *Fourth report on the excavation of the Roman fort at Richborough, Kent*, Rep. Res. Comm. Soc. Antiq. London, **16** (Oxford)

Collingwood, R.G., 1937 Art, in R.G. Collingwood & J.N.L. Myres, *Roman Britain and the English settlements*, 2 edn, 247–73 (Oxford)

Crummy, P., (ed.) 1984 *Colchester Archaeological Reports 3. Excavations at Lion Walk, Balkerne Lane and Middleborough, Colchester, Essex* (Colchester)

Cunliffe, B. (ed.), 1971 *Excavations at Fishbourne 1961–1969. II. the finds*, Rep. Res. Comm. Soc. Antiq. London, **27** (Leeds)

_____, (ed.) 1988 *The temple of Sulis Minerva at Bath 2*, Oxford Univ. Comm. Archaeol. Monograph, **16**

Dannell, G.B., 1971 The samian pottery, in Cunliffe 1971, 260–316

Davey, M., & Ling, R., 1981 *Wall-painting in Roman Britain*, Britannia monograph, **3** (London)

Demarolle, J.-M., 1994 Des dieux et des motifs: à propos de la sigillée ornée au Haut-Empire, in C. M. Ternes & P.F. Burke (eds), *Roman religion in Gallia Belgica and the Germaniae*, 14–33 (Luxembourg)

Down, A., & Henig, M., 1988 A Roman *askos* handle from Fishbourne, *Antiq. J.*, **68**, 308–10

Harden, D.B., & Price, J., 1971 The glass, in Cunliffe 1971, 317–68

Hartley, B.R., 1980 Comment on the stamped vessels, in Lambrick 1980, 73

Haverfield, R., 1915 *The Romanization of Roman Britain*, 3 edn (Oxford)

Hawkes, C.F.C., & Hull, M.R., 1947 *Camulodunum. First report on the excavations at Colchester 1930–1939*, Rep. Res. Comm. Soc. Antiq. London, **14** (Oxford)

Henig, M., 1974 *A corpus of Roman engraved gemstones from British sites*, BAR Brit. Ser., **8** (Oxford)

_____, (ed.) 1983 *A handbook of Roman art. A survey of the visual arts of the Roman world* (Oxford)

_____, 1985 Graeco-Roman art and Romano-British imagination, *J.Brit. Archaeol. Assoc.*, **138**, 1–22

_____, 1995 *The art of Roman Britain* (London)

Hull, M.R., 1963 *The Roman potters kilns of Colchester*, Rep. Res. Comm. Soc. Antiq. London, **21** (Oxford and Colchester)

Johns, C., 1986 The Roman silver cups from Hockwold, Norfolk, *Archaeologia*, **108**, 1–13

King, A., 1983 Pottery, in Henig 1983, 179–90

Lambrick, G., 1980 Excavations in Park Street, Towcester, *Northamptonshire Archaeol.*, **15**, 35–118

Ling, R., 1984 The wall-plaster from Balkerne Lane, in Crummy 1984, 147–53

_____, 1991 *Roman painting* (Cambridge)

Marsden, P.R.V., 1965 A boat of the Roman period discovered on the site of New Guy's House, Bermondsey, 1958, *Trans. London Middlesex Archaeol. Soc.*, **21.2**, 118–31

Marsh, G., 1981 London's samian supply and its relationship to the development of the Gallic samian industry, in Anderson & Anderson 1981, 173–230

Millett, M., 1980 Aspects of Romano-British pottery in West Sussex, *Sussex Archaeol. Collect.*, **118**, 57–68

_____, 1986 An early Roman cemetery at Alton, Hampshire, *Proc Hampshire Field Club*, **42**, 43–87

Oswald, F., & Pryce, T.D., 1920 *An introduction to the study of terra sigillata* (London)

Painter, K.S., 1977a *The Mildenhall Treasure. Roman silver from East Anglia*, British Museum (London)

_____, 1977b *The Water Newton early Christian silver*, British Museum (London)

Partridge, C., 1981 *Skeleton Green. A late Iron Age and Romano-British site*, Britannia Monograph, **2** (London)

Pengelly, H., 1980 The samian, in Lambrick 1980, 69–76

Price, J., 1980 The glass, in Lambrick 1980, 63–8

Simpson, G., 1980 An appliqué metallic slip vase from Central Gaul, in Lambrick 1980, 73, 75

Smith, D.J., 1984 The mosaic of the wrestling cupids in Room 7, in Crummy 1984, 168–74

Stanfield, J.A. & Simpson, G., 1990 *Les potiers de la Gaule Centrale,* Revue Archéologique Sites (Gonfaron)

Stead, I.M., 1967 A La Tène burial at Welwyn Garden City, *Archaeologia*, **101**, 1–62

Strong, D.E., 1966 *Greek and Roman gold and silver plate* (London)

Sunter, N., & Brown, D., 1988 Metal vessels, in Cunliffe 1988, 9–21

Symonds, R.P., 1992 *Rhenish wares. Fine dark coloured pottery from Gaul and Germany*, Oxford Univ. Comm. Archaeol. Monograph, **23**

Toynbee, J.M.C., 1964 *Art in Britain under the Romans* (Oxford)

Vickers, M., 1994 Nabataea, India, Gaul, and Carthage: reflections on Hellenistic and Roman gold vessels and red-gloss pottery, *Amer. J. Archaeol.*, **98**, 231–48

_____, & Gill, D., 1994 *Artful crafts. Ancient Greek silverware and pottery* (Oxford)

Walters, H.B., 1921 *Catalogue of the silver plate in the British Museum* (London)

Webster, G., 1989 Deities and religious scenes on Romano-British pottery, *J. Roman Pottery Stud.*, **2**, 1–28

_____, 1991a *Archaeologist at large* (London)

_____, 1991b Colour symbolism: an anthropological diversion, in Webster 1991a, 6–17

_____, 1991c Romano-British scenes and figures on pottery, in Webster 1991a, 129–62

Young, C.J., 1977 *The Roman pottery industry of the Oxford region*, BAR Brit. Ser., **43** (Oxford)

9 Ovolos on Dragendorff form 30 from the collections of Frédéric Hermet and Dieudonné Rey

Geoff Dannell, Brenda Dickinson and Alain Vernhet

Over the past seven years, a team of friends and colleagues, among them Brian Hartley, has been working on a reassessment of the collections of decorated samian from la Graufesenque, published in 1934 by the late Abbé Frédéric Hermet (Hermet 1934, hereafter referred to as Hermet). That publication is now outdated, due to an accumulation of subsequent evidence. It is also difficult to use, both because of the way Hermet chose to present the decoration of his bowls (for instance, he disassociated the upper and lower zones of the Dr. 29s, and listed rather less than a third of the extant stamps), and because the illustrations are not sufficiently accurate to allow confident ascriptions to be made, quite apart from the use of two-thirds scale for a number of plates. It was clear from remarks made at recent samian study courses,[1] that most students were unable to use Hermet's material as he had presented it, and needed guidance to find their way among the different sections of the book. Sometimes the teachers were equally perplexed, and so it seemed timely to take a fresh look at the pottery itself.[2]

The first three seasons were spent in washing, rubbing, recording and attempting to reassemble the bowls of form Dr. 29. Perhaps the most important fact to emerge from this work was that, in addition to the few bowls published by Hermet which came from the same mould, but were stamped by different bowl-makers (Hermet, pl. 106, nos. 12–18), the collections contained many other bowls sharing groups of decorative details, but stamped internally with different names (Dannell 1995; Dannell forthcoming).

Study of the Dr. 30s began in 1994, with three main objectives in mind: first, to see whether there was any correspondence with the decoration on the Dr. 29s; secondly, to record the ovolos and their associated decoration and to attribute them to workshops, mould-makers and/or bowl-makers; finally, to produce a concordance to the Hermet volume. The two-letter codes used to identify each ovolo are for convenience of reference in this article. They are not suggested to form a permanent reference structure for South Gaulish ovolos.

Despite the difference in shape between Dr. 29 and Dr. 30, which would seem to require two distinct sets of figure-types and motifs, it soon became clear that some groups of decorative details were common to both forms. This usefully confirmed a previous suspicion that at least some of the moulds were made in the same workshops. When we turned to the ovolos on the Dr. 30s, a new problem arose. It is unfortunate that almost all drawings of ovolos are unsatisfactory. While a number of Hermet's ovolos can be recognised from his illustrations, many cannot be distinguished from others which are only marginally different, and the same applies to most other people's drawings of South Gaulish ovolos. Perhaps only Robert Knorr, in his many publications, has managed to capture these ovolos with sufficient accuracy to inspire some confidence.

The ovolos proved to have an interesting morphology. Most of the earlier series comprised an egg with a plain tongue, to which a terminal was attached as a secondary process, sometimes on the poinçon itself, sometimes in the mould. More work needs to be done on these traits, to see how common they were at la Graufesenque as a whole, and in which periods. The two methods can be distinguished by looking at the repeat pattern of the ovolo round the pot, though it is rarely possible to construe the use of a roller with a number of ovolos on it. Clearly, where the ovolo terminal is applied to the poinçon, or run of poinçons, its position relative to the tongue remains constant within the repeat pattern; however, when the terminal is applied in the mould, its position is likely to vary with each impression.

A clear example of the first method is ovolo GG, which appears elsewhere on bowls with mould-signatures of **Masclus** with four other tips (see remarks under MM). Unfortunately, it is rare to have a sufficiently large collection of decorated ware to be able to make exact comparisons between ovolos. For an example of the second method, where the tip of the tongue is added in the mould, see ovolo EA.

Not all of the ovolos on Dr. 30 in the Hermet/Rey collection are represented in their unadorned versions. For instance, ovolos JJ (used by **Lupus ii**) and FG (used by **Sabinus iii**), are, so far, known only with rosettes added to the their tongues.

It seems likely that matrices existed in the workshops, from which multiple copies of the more frequently-used ovolos could be struck. Different terminals might then be added to the ovolos with plain tongues, either on the poinçon or in the mould. Why this process should have been necessary is another question. Clearly, it would be much easier, as a practical matter, to cut the egg and tongue, and then apply the terminal, if the ovolo was applied by a roller. The maker would otherwise have been faced with cutting a number of similar tips; but hardly a single ovolo shows any sign of being put on with a roller. For the most part they are struck singly, sometimes in pairs, and more rarely in threes. Then there is the question of why the same egg and tongue should receive a number of different tips. There are two fairly straightforward solutions. First, it may simply represent different stages in the life of the ovolo, reflecting whichever tip happened to be around and available when it was re-struck. The alternative is that these differences in tips reflect some working arrangement within the workshop – a tempting insight into workshop organisation.

Unfortunately, the present sample is too small to test this theory, and we must wait for statistical analysis of the decoration from substantial populations of bowls before we can be more sure. This is some way off, not the least of the problems being the difficulty of comparing published illustrations directly with rubbings or pots. Indeed, even with many examples of the same ovolo to hand at la Graufesenque, it was not always possible to pick out minute distinguishing features. It was only after rubbings of the clearest examples of the ovolos had been enlarged several times by a photocopier, that such details could be seen clearly.

The bulk of the Hermet/Rey collection, as evidenced by the potter's stamps on the plain ware, is Neronian, falling mainly c. AD 50–65/70. However, fortunately for us, Hermet also touched upon a number of areas with Flavian and Trajanic deposits. In the small collection of Dr. 30s from this later period a distinct change can be seen, not only in the decorative schemes as a whole, but in the ovolos themselves, though this is a gradual process which was not completed before the 80s of the 1st century.

The first change came in the late 60s or early 70s, when the decorated forms 29 and 30 were joined by two new moulded decorated bowls, the hemispherical Dr. 37 and the cup, Knorr 78. Both had an ovolo and Dr. 37 shared with Dr. 30 the advantage of a large, unbroken surface area which could be decorated with bigger figure-types and motifs than were possible on Dr. 29. In practice, the potters' *horror vacui* persisted for some time, and early Flavian Dr. 37s continued to be decorated in much the same way as Dr. 29, with a multiplicity of zones, involving relatively small details (cf. Atkinson 1914, pl. 7). The tradition of applying terminals to the tongues of ovolos survived into this period (or the ovolos themselves did), on both Dr. 30 and Dr. 37, but the tips gradually became simplified, with trident or four-pronged tips replacing the former, rather intricate rosettes, circles and blobs (cf. Atkinson 1914, pl. 11).

The more radical changes which took place in the late 70s and 80s involved both plain and decorated samian. Several new forms were added to the plainware repertoire, some of which were deliberately left unstamped. The strictness of the production control was such that among these new unstamped forms, vessels which had accidentally been stamped had their stamps excoriated, or smeared over. The accompanying change in the decorated range involved phasing out Dr. 29 (both an inherently more intricate shape to produce, and more fragile to transport) and the drastic simplification of the decoration of Dr. 30 and Dr. 37, by dividing their surfaces into panels rather than zones, and by the addition of more large figure-types and motifs. The introduction of ovolos with integral tongue and terminal appears to be part of this sweeping change which overtook the samian industry at la Graufesenque in the early Flavian period.

Another feature which developed at about this time was the emergence of (large?) firms who had stamps cut in bold retrograde letters, which were stamped into the moulds to appear the right way round on the bowl (cf. **M. Crestio**, K52, Taf. 19, on forms 30 and 37). Whilst this practice was common at Arezzo, where it began (cf. Oswald & Pryce 1920, pl. 2, nos. 2, 4, 5), it went out of use at la Graufesenque in the Tiberio-Claudian period (cf. K52, Taf. 63 B & E, by **Volus**), and it was not revived until late into Nero's reign. It was accompanied by an increase in the use of plainware stamps impressed in the mould, appearing in sunken letters on the pot, usually retrograde.

The recognition of a change in the style of the ovolos used on Dr. 30, coming just at the time that other major changes were overtaking the industry, is a significant result for this, still preliminary, work on the Dr. 30s. The reasons which may have occasioned all of the changes in the output of the la Graufesenque workshops in the later 1st century AD are a separate topic, which will be discussed further after the next stage in our project, which will take in the Dr. 37s and the more rare decorated forms.

THE OVOLOS

The ovolos are both illustrated and described, in an attempt to clarify both the good impressions and the many poor impressions which can occur. The list of parallel occurrences is not meant to be exhaustive – it is heavily weighted in favour of British evidence, because that is available for the most part as rubbings, and the attributions are thus more secure. The ovolos were all enlarged by means of making photocopies for comparative study, but even then the trident-tipped tongues of the Flavian period proved very difficult to ascribe with certainty – and this *caveat* should be borne in mind. The principal figures are noted in Table 2; they are those which could be attributed with some confidence. Not all of the bowls illustrated by Hermet were seen (see Table 1), and attributions of the ovolos made from his drawings are noted.

THE FIGURE-TYPES

The large number of variants and differences in size in the figure-types published by Oswald (Oswald 1936–37) raises the problem of the way in which he collected and published his evidence. There is a suspicion that many of his drawings are reproduced at slightly (4–6%) oversize, based on type examples where rubbings are available for comparison. At the same time, some of the drawings are simply not accurate, based again on comparison with rubbings of figure-types from the same bowls which he drew; there are also quite clearly versions of the same type which were not available to him, as well as entirely new figure-types.

Table 2 reflects numerous instances where the general shape of the type is shown by Oswald, but the detailed treatment appears different (marked **V**); then there are the cases where the size varies from that given in Oswald's catalogue (**TS** = type but smaller, **TL** = type but larger).

This is not to denigrate Oswald's pioneering work in any way. He was not able to see a lot of the original material, and relied on re-drawing it; he was unsure of the number of variants, because he could not compare the mass of material available at one time, as Hermet would have done. Note typically Hermet, pl. 26, nos. 35, 36, 37, which Oswald shows as his O. 1968; we have distinguished five variants on Dr. 30 alone, ranging from 15–20 mm in length, and with different features of head and tail. Clearly something has got to be done about this problem in the near future, by re-publishing the standard corpora using modern technology. Two methods are worth considering: first the technique of publishing photographs of casts adopted for Rheinzabern (cf. Ricken & Fischer 1963), and the method employed for the forthcoming publication of Colchester samian (Dannell forthcoming) where rubbings are scanned. This is an extension of Thomas May's method of publishing his rubbings of decorated samian from Colchester, Silchester, and Templeborough (May 1930; 1916; 1922, respectively). One other technique which may be worthy of examination is to photocopy rubbings at 2:1 or greater, and then block-shade the highlights (as for Valkenburg, cf. Glasbergen 1940–44), finally reducing back to 1:1.

Examples of inaccurate drawings are legion and are inevitable, even given the new guide-lines recently proposed (Rigoir & Rivet 1994). We would say categorically that any interpretation by an artist is unlikely to give an entirely satisfactory result, and that line drawing should be abandoned as a future means of publication in favour of more direct methods of illustration. There is then the question of scale. Catalogues of details need to be at 1:1; it should then be easier to compare details from different bowls, even if the bowls are illustrated at a smaller scale (cf. M 1995[3], where the decoration is quite recognisable as an ensemble, but fine comparison of details is much more difficult).

In the discussion of the bowls that follows, numbers (No.) refer to the series of numbered plastic bags in which the Dr. 30s from the Hermet/Rey collection have been repackaged.

Ovolo	AA
Borders	Single, slightly curved to the left at the bottom.
Core	Full.
Tongue	Left; Z-twist cord, but often appears as plain.
Terminal	Applied eight-petalled, hollow rosette; often touches the borders to the right.

This ovolo appears on two Dr. 30s from London (ML 12188L). A number of the details are idiosyncratic: a gladiator, O. 1019 type (No. 320), and a lion, similar to O. 1447, but with the front paws together, and a smaller version of the bear, O. 1614 (both No. 322). None of the vegetal details appear among the Dr. 29s from the collection. There appears to be a plain version of the ovolo (ML 1184G) and one with a circle tip (ML 11726G).

Ovolo	BA
	T-1
Borders	Single, slightly flared towards the top.
Core	Full.
Tongue	Right; S-twist cord.
Terminal	Applied ten-petalled rosette, placed to the left.

The eight examples all have decoration composed of details associated with the T-1 mouldmaker(s) and the group of potters using the moulds (Dannell forthcoming, GBSA 1400; and see Hermet, pl. 69, nos. 7, 13). Many of the details are known on Dr. 30s with the KK ovolo (see discussion below). Among the vegetal motifs, note the trilobe (K19, Taf. 13, no. 4), the frond (K19, Taf. 13, no. 22) and the small serrated frond (K52, Taf.10), attributed there to **Bassus & Coelus, Coelus, Seno**, all members of the T-1 group of potters stamping Dr. 29. It is interesting that Knorr (K52, Taf. 9) attributes a large lobed leaf to **Bassus & Coelus** on the basis of the small oak leaf there; the lobed leaf appears on No. 6. Two Dr. 30s from London (ML 11734G and 11743G) have the warrior, O. 164A, and one from Colchester (Dannell forthcoming, GBSA 1400) has an arcade which appears on Nos. 1, 3, 4, 5 and 6, either as part of a wreath, or as an arcade.

Ovolo	BB
	(Sabinus?)
Borders	Double, slightly flared towards the top. The outer border is serrated at the bottom, although this is often blocked, leaving a thickening.
Core	Short.
Tongue	None.
Terminal	None.

This is a very well known ovolo, which has been attributed to **Sabinus iii;** however it has not yet been recorded on signed bowls or moulds (Stanfield 1937, 174). Nevertheless, the association is fairly secure because the large lotus bud, and bordered leaf (No. 188 = Hermet, pl. 69, no. 14) appear on a *lagena* signed by **Sabinus** (Stanfield 1937, pl. 22, no. 4). The ovolo appears at York (Dickinson & Hartley 1993, no. 2663), where a useful reference is made to Dr. 29s stamped by **Albus i, Macer i**, and **Melainus**, all of whom are recorded in the Hermet/Rey collection. Indeed **Macer** and **Melainus** share a curious Dr. 29 mould (Hermet, pl. 106, no. 15), which has this ovolo in the upper zone; moreover the lower zone palisade appears on No. 184. These three Dr. 29 bowl-makers all appear to have used moulds from diverse sources. A Dr. 30 from Colchester (Dannell forthcoming, 1.81E 656) has the figure with a bird, Hermet, pl. 18, no. 11.

Besides the bowls illustrated by Stanfield (1937) others come from: Colchester (Dannell forthcoming 1.81E 656; May 1930, pl. 17, no. 87); la Graufesenque (G69 A32.2); London (Regis House, ML 1932.196 and 11797G); Sheepen (Dannell 1985, fig. 42, no. 21).

Ascribed, but not seen: Hermet, pl. 75, nos. 1, 2.

Ovolo BC
Secundus, cf. Hermet pl. 28, no. 22
Borders Single, curved to the left.
Core Full, placed to the right.
Tongue None.
Terminal None.

Only one example comes from the collection. Two, more complete, vessels come from Colchester (Dannell forthcoming, 1.81K 373 and BKCT 518); the former has a full-height vine scroll with an uncatalogued bird, similar to O. 2229, and the latter an uncatalogued Abundance facing left, holding a serrated wreath and long corn-stalk. A Dr. 30 from la Graufesenque (G 1968 [16] III) has part of a vine scroll, and there is a small sherd from London (ML 11757G).

Ovolo BD
Sabinus iii
Borders Double, flared towards the top. The ovolo is frequently cut off short, so that the remainder gives a slightly ovular shape.
Core Pointed.
Tongue None.
Terminal None.

This ovolo is very well linked to the signatures of **Sabinus iii** (Hermet pls. 71, no. 9; 77, no. 11, on Dr. 30; Stanfield 1937, fig. 8, no. 12, on the Hartlip *lagena*; and three from Narbonne-la Nautique (Fiches *et al.* 1978, fig. 15, nos. 1, 3, 5, on Dr. 30)). There is also a curious small Dr. 30 with a very small signature from la Graufesenque (VAYSS 85), which has the large lotus bud and a large seed-pod (see No. 188, and York no. 2663, discussed under ovolo BB above).

Unstamped material comes from la Graufesenque (G71.54 and G77); London (ML 11790G and B 30/2); Rheingönheim (Ulbert 1959, Taf.7, nos. 11a & b (incidentally almost the only ovolo drawn there which can be recognised with confidence)); and Sheepen (Dannell 1985, figs. 42, no. 20; 44, no. 50).

Ascribed, but not seen: Hermet, pls. 70, no. 12; 77, no. 12; 77, no. 15.

Ovolo CA
Borders Single.
Core Full.
Tongue Left; thin, the end turned to the right.
Terminal None.

There are no significant clues as yet to the mouldmaker for this ovolo. It is just possible that ovolo CA is the same as that on a Dr. 30 from Neuss (Mary 1967, Taf. 6, no. 10).

Ascribed, but not seen: Hermet, pl. 72, no. 6.

Ovolo CC
T-1 = Calvus i
Borders Double, slightly flared outwards at the top, cf. CG and SX.
Core Thin, pointed.
Tongue Right; the top is pointed.
Terminal Applied hollow(?), eight-petalled rosette. The petal at six o'clock' is larger, and square-tipped.

This is the ovolo which is on moulds signed by **Calus i = Calvus i** (see KK below). There are a number of examples: Augst (M 1995, Taf. 16, no. 7); Leibnitz-Flavia Solva (Weber-Hiden 1987–8, Taf. 1, no. 1.); Mainz (K19, Taf. 16, no. 15a; Taf. 17); Roanne (K42, Abb.1). An unsigned Dr. 30 from Mainz (K52, Taf. 67, A) and a bowl from Utrecht (Brunsting & Kalee 1989, Afb. 80.18) show many of the vegetal motifs used with this ovolo, and on the Dr. 29s of the T-1 group. A Dr. 30 from la Graufesenque has a complete design, again with T-1 group motifs (G54 NW 192).

Ovolo CD
OFMO?
Borders Double.
Core Thin, perhaps tapering towards the top.
Tongue Right, probably.
Terminal Perhaps a broken seven-petalled, centred rosette, placed to the left. This tip seems always to be blurred and looks a bit like a frond.

Only two examples of this ovolo are present, and it is not entirely certain that they have the same tip, although the egg and tongue do appear to be the same. Records for Dr. 30 come from: Colchester (Dannell forthcoming, MID 2421); Gorhambury (Dannell 1990, fig. 161, no. 11); la Graufesenque (G190 & G60 H61.11); London (ML 6544L, 11773G and 11815G); Silchester (May 1916, pl. 17, no. 9); Verulamium (1959, XI (29), Buildings 1 and 2 X, XI (12), and 'Selfridge 1', Ins. V); and Vindonissa (30.21809). There are four other Dr. 30s with similar decoration, which almost certainly have this ovolo: Augsburg (Roger 1913, Taf. 1, no. 1, which is probably from the same mould as that from York (Dickinson & Hartley 1993, nos. 2672 (cf.) and 2675)), Dammartin-les-Pesmes (*Gallia,* **28**, 360), and Baginton (Hartley 1973, fig. 13, no. 18).

A small fragment of a Dr. 37 from London (ML 6205L) has a mould-stamp **OFMO** (retrograde), and an ovolo which is the same or very similar (K19, Taf. 59, A). The style of these Dr. 37s seems somewhat earlier than that with the same stamp from Pompeii (Atkinson 1914, pl. 13, no. 65). The stamp also appears on a Dr. 29 from Rodez.

Ovolo CE
Borders Double.
Core Well rounded.
Tongue Right; corded Z-twist.
Terminal Blocked, solid rosette?

Only one sherd, almost entirely filled with pinnate leaf-tips.

Ovolo	CF
	T-1/2a = Calvus i?
Broders	Double, the borders close together on the left.
Core	Normally applied obliquely top left to bottom right.
Tongue	Right; pointed at the top, shorter than the borders.
Terminal	Applied, centred, six-petalled rosette.

This ovolo has habitually been associated on stylistic grounds with **Calvus i** (Dickinson & Hartley 1993, no. 2681 for a recent ascription), however no signature has been found with it. On the other hand it has strong associations with the T-1 mouldmaker(s), through the use of the bud (K52, Taf 10, stamped by **Bassus & Coelus**, and Droitwich, 1003.3B, stamped by **Senicio**), and the ubiquitous trifid (K19, Taf. 13, no. 4, at Leicester (1969, 164, I, 79 and GHS, B86), both on Dr. 37). Dickinson & Hartley (1993, no. 2861) record a marbled Dr. 37H, and this form with the ovolo occurs at Asciburgium (Vanderhoeven 1978, 665), too.

There are also links to the T-2a group (unpublished, but comprising Dr. 29s stamped internally by **Lucceius i** and **Mommo**), through a trifid motif (Hermet. pl. 14, no. 22). It is noticeable that there are very few, if any, human figure-types associated with this ovolo.

Ascribed, but not seen: Hermet, pl. 72, no. 7.

Ovolo	CG
	T-1 = Calvus i?
Borders	Double, slightly flared outwards at the top. In a clear example the very tops of each border are turned to the right, cf. CC and SX.
Core	Thin, slightly curved to the right.
Tongue	Right; the top has a point.
Terminal	Applied solid, seven-petalled rosette, with that at four o'clock' very faint, and that at eleven o'clock' broken.

Another difficult ovolo to identify positively when blurred, and easy to confuse with ovolo CD. It does not appear to have been used on Dr. 37, but does appear on a *lagena* from Gadebridge (Dannell 1974, fig. 93). A similar scene appears on two Dr. 30s from Cologne (Wittkamp Coll., 60) & Ribchester (Wild 1988, fig. 13, no. 142). Other Dr. 30s come from: Bingen (Behrens 1920, Taf. 11, no. 2); Colchester (Dannell forthcoming, 1.81G 1292); la Graufesenque (G65, G66 48 -170, G69 A52 III and G81/92, and Coll. Artières); Leicester (1993, 15.90 (269); London (ML 11723G, 11812G, 12240L); Verulamium (VCP, A IV (15N), B III (23); York (Dickinson & Hartley 1993, no. 2670).

Linking motifs to the T-1 group are a vine leaf (Hermet, pl. 8, no. 14) and a trifid motif (Hermet, pl. 14, no. 25), which appear frequently on Dr. 29s from the Hermet/Rey collection (stamped internally by **Niger ii**), and a small oak leaf (Hermet, pl. 6, no. 18), which appears there on stamped bowls of **Cabucatus**, **Felix i**, **Lucceius i**, **Niger ii**, **Regenus** and **G. Salarius Aptus**.

The scene on another Dr. 30 (Hermet, pl. 76, no. 9) is very similar to the Verulamium VCP bowl (B III (23)), but is drawn with a single-bordered ovolo with a rosette tip to the tongue. This has not been recorded from the collection, so no parallel is available. A warrior (O. 164A) appears without a spear (Hermet, pl. 79, no. 12), and is drawn with a small leaf above his right hand; this is more likely to be the version on the Gadebridge *lagena*, and if so, the ovolo is probably also not as drawn, because there is no parallel for the rosette. The figures have not been put in the table because of these uncertainties.

Ascribed, but not seen: Hermet, pls. 74, no. 8; 75, no. 9).

Ovolo	CH
	Caerleon, Catterick Racecourse
Borders	Double, angle top right to bottom left.
Core	Vertical, as opposed to borders, chamfered to right at bottom.
Tongue	Right; plain, follows alignment of borders, and thickens towards the end, which is turned to left.
Terminal	Applied solid rosette, which appears to have been damaged so that a number of petals to top right are missing, and that at eight o'clock' is reduced to a stub.

Just the one example (Hermet, pl. 74, no. 4, no. 422); the ovolo, used on both Dr. 30 and Dr. 37, can be confused with one used by **Frontinus**, where the large rosette is placed to the right of the tongue, and is often blurred or reduced in size, but the **Frontinus** egg is less pointed. Recognition is not helped by the fact that ovolo CH does appear to have a version with a rosette tip as well. Two other examples have been noted on Dr. 37: London (ML 11953G); Silchester (May 1916, pl. 15, A).

Ovolo	DA
Borders	Single.
Core	Slightly asymmetrical.
Tongue	Left; plain, pointed at the top, where it often fades out, thickened towards the bottom.
Terminal	Applied solid, eight-petalled rosette.

The ovolo with this tip has not been noted elsewhere, and only one example comes from the collection.

However, what appears to be the same ovolo, but with a small, hollow, seven-petalled rosette, in addition to version DB below, is found more widely. Frustratingly, none of the following examples has much surviving decoration: Fishbourne (Dannell 1971, fig. 129, no. 36); Leicester (GHS); Sheepen (Dannell 1985, fig. 44, no. 49); Verulamium (1959, Ins. XXVII, Buildings 1 and 2, IX (12), and X, XIV (12)).

Two other Dr. 30s appear to have this ovolo. The first, with a tongue with roulette tip from Colchester (Dannell forthcoming, BKCD 422), has an uncatalogued Apollo with lyre in an arcade; on top of the arcade column there is a pair of pinnate leaves (see the basal wreath on Hermet, pl. 60, no. 13, incompletely illustrated; it is in fact a stamped Dr. 29 of **Mommo**). The second is from Mainz (K19, Textbild 31), which has a

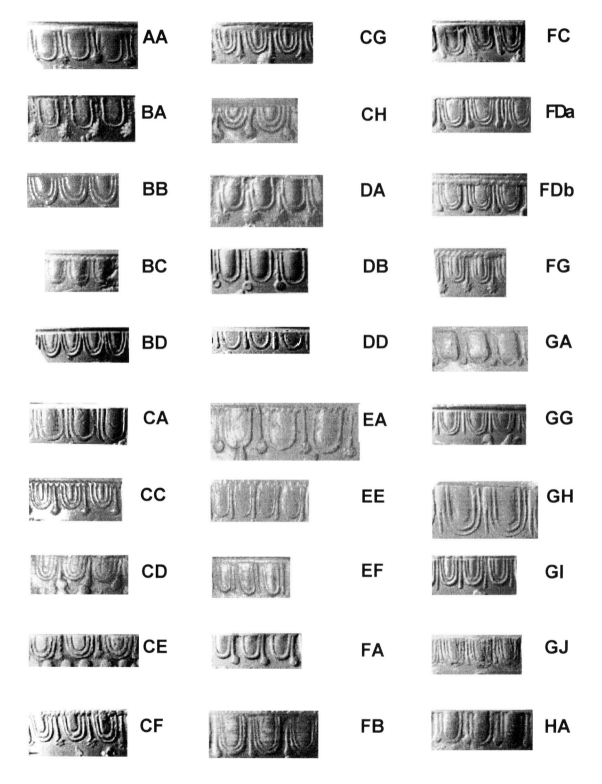

Fig. 1. Ovolos on Dragendorff 30: AA–HA. Scale 1:1. (Photographs by Alain Vernhet and Peter Webster)

tongue with hollow, multi-petalled rosette tip, a wreathed medallion over the altar, and the same columns as the Colchester vessel. Knorr ascribed this to the earliest work of **Calvus**, which is interesting in terms of the composition of the Hermet/Rey collection.

Ovolo DB
Borders Single, cf. DA.
Core cf. DA.
Tongue cf. DA.
Terminal Applied plain circle.

Three examples from the collection, but none recorded from elsewhere.

Ovolo DD
Sabinus iii
Borders Single.
Core Full.
Tongue Right; the end turned sharply to the right.
Terminal None.

Two Dr. 30s from la Graufesenque certainly have this ovolo: G90 [39].150 and Hermet, pl. 76, no. 1, which has a curious footring, more like Dr. 24. Hermet, pl. 71, no. 5 is also identified as this ovolo, although less certainly because it was not seen. Two other vessels from la Graufesenque may have it: a Dr. 30 (Millau Museum, unmarked) has a swollen tip to the straight tongue, which does not occur on the type example; the other, interestingly, is a Dr. 11 signed by **Sabinus iii** (Bémont et. al. 1987, pl. 11, right). The only recorded parallel to the ovolo from elsewhere is also on a Dr. 11: Sheepen (Dannell 1985, fig. 43, no. 26).

Ovolo EA
Borders Single, the shape is irregular, but generally inturned at the top.
Core Irregular, but full.
Tongue Right; pointed at the top, thickened at the bottom, where it appears to end in a wedge. Shorter than borders.
Terminal Applied, six-beaded, centred rosette

Another ovolo recorded only once; the irregularity in the position of the rosette on the tongue, and the lack of consistency in the application of the ovolo itself, suggest that the rosette tip was added in the mould. The finial, Hermet, pl. 22, no. 224, which appears on this piece has the leaf bent like a banana to the left, which may be a useful diagnostic.

Two interesting Dr. 29s may be related: from Peyrestortes (Fiches 1978, fig. 4, no. 6), and d'Ennsérune (Fiches 1978, fig. 4, no. 7). Both have ovolos, which is rare enough, and the one from d'Enssérune is stamped internally by **Cantus**, and is drawn clearly enough to show the beaded rosette tip to the tongue. The style of these vessels is not particularly early, perhaps c.AD 50–65, and **Cantus** might have been buying in moulds, or the workshop may have passed into other hands

by this time (see EE below for other connections with **Cantus**).

The irregularity in the application of the ovolo on the Dr. 30, Hermet, pl. 70, no. 2, which was not seen, suggests ovolo EA.

Ovolo EE
T-2
Borders Single, flared towards the top, chamfered at bottom left.
Core Full.
Tongue Right, thickened towards bottom.
Terminal None

This ovolo appears together with decorative detail which is shared among a number of bowlmakers of Dr. 29, temporarily assigned the identification code T-2 (with internal stamps of: **Ardacus**, **Cantus**, **Felix i**, **Matugenus ii**, **Mommo**, **Regenus**, and one with a signature, **MOD[ESTUS?**). The linking motif is a distinctive tendril binding (Hermet, pl. 69, no. 1 on Dr. 30, pl. 37, no. 28 on Dr. 29), although the group shares many others. The predominant Dr. 29s in the Hermet/Rey collection are by **Mommo**. The small bird O. 2284A, which appears in the scroll of Hermet, pl. 69, no. 1, and a cluster of berries (Hermet, pl. 13, no. 35), on the same bowl but not drawn, are other common motifs which appear on his stamped Dr. 29s. Note the trifid motif Hermet, pl. 14, no. 22, referred to for ovolo CF, which appears on Hermet, pl. 73, no. 1 with the present ovolo.

Apart from the figure-types illustrated on Hermet, pl. 75, no. 5 (Penelope, O. 909A, and gladiator, O. 1013A) the only other which appears with any frequency is a hunched hare, O. 2109. It is noteworthy that one of the Dr. 29s stamped by **Mommo** with the T-2 style of decoration, is present in the Pompeii Hoard (Atkinson 1914, no. 21).

Ascribed, but not seen: Hermet, pls. 70, no. 6; 73, no. 2.

Ovolo EF
T-3?
Borders Single, chamfered at bottom left.
Core Pointed.
Tongue Right; plain, tapered towards bottom, ends in point.
Terminal None

An ovolo which is singly impressed (Hermet, pl. 69, no. 6 understates the misalignments). The decoration contains a number of very characteristic leaves, including Hermet, pl. 7, no. 47; pl. 8, nos. 48 and 49; pl. 70, no. 7; pl. 6, no. 34.

The first appears on a Dr. 29 from the Hermet/Rey collection, with a straight wreath in the upper zone (Hermet, pl. 45, no. 28); this is from the same mould as a Dr. 29 stamped by **Amandus ii** (K19, Taf. 6, B). **Amandus** probably worked rather too early for the same mould-maker to have supplied him and the maker of the Dr. 30s with ovolo EF, but note that the leaf (K19, Taf. 6, no. 16) appears to be the same as that used by **Sabinus iii** and **Murranus** (K52, Taf. 45); perhaps the poinçons were handed down.

Ovolo   FA
              Lupus ii
Borders   Single, flared outwards at top, incurved on right.
              Aligned slightly top right to bottom left.
Core   Ovular.
Tongue   Right; hangs vertically, so away from border at
              bottom.
Terminal Probably a circle set to the right, but often blocked
              to show as a blob.

The ovolo is well known and associated with **Lupus ii**
through a small lunate intra-decorative stamp in the mould,
which reads positively on the bowl. Dr. 30s with both ovolo
and stamp come from: la Graufesenque (Hermet, pls. 72, no.
4; 73, no. 12); Narbonne-la Nautique (M 1995, Taf. 99, no. 4,
from the same mould as Hermet pl. 73, no. 12); Oberstimm
(Simon 1978a, Taf. 51, C184); Richborough (Davies Pryce
1932, pl. 25, no. 2); Vertault (Hermet pl. 117, no. 16); Vindonissa (K35, Abb. 1, no. 7). There is also a signed Dr. 30 with
this ovolo from la Graufesenque (G7. A65), although the
signature appears not to be that of **Lupus ii**; the same three
letters, **CAL**? (blind A), also occur on a sherd of Dr. 30 with
the dog, O.1968.

Unstamped Dr. 30s come from: Colchester (Dannell forthcoming, BKCV 1271); la Graufesenque (Hermet, pl. 70, no.
5; G71A 85, G72 35–2, G76 5.2.2 and unpub. (5 examples);
London (ML 12237L from the same mould as Hermet, pl.
73, no. 12?); Zwammerdam (Haaalebos 1977, Taf. 33, no. 43).

Ovolo   FB
              Malaval MA 22/3
              Sabinus iii?
Borders   Double, slightly pointed at the bottom.
Core   Chamfered at bottom left.
Tongue   Left; shorter than borders.
Terminal Blob, placed to right.

Two examples of this ovolo come from the collection, but
nine others, also on Dr. 30 (Fosse Malaval, A. Bourgeois,
report in prep.), and a tenth from the Collection Artières,
come from la Graufesenque. Figure types from the Hermet/
Rey collection on no. 95 include: a prisoner, O. 1139A, an
uncatalogued *bestiarius*, and a seated dog similar to that on the
grande lagène' (Balsan & Vernhet 1971). The figures on the
Malaval (MA) vessels are recorded in Table 2.

Some of the vegetal motifs occur on unattributed sherds
of Dr. 29 from the Hermet/Rey collection, and further analysis may provide clues to their mould-makers. The leaf,
Hermet, pl. 6, no. 15 (ovolo BD, no. 45) appears on one of
the Malaval Dr. 30s in a version about 5% larger, suggesting
that the user of ovolo FB may have copied it, by taking a pull
from an existing mould.

Ovolo   FC
Borders   Double, slightly asymmetrical, the outer border
              flattened at the bottom right.
Core   Slightly pointed towards bottom.
Tongue   Left; plain.

Terminal Applied very small, solid, five-petalled rosette,
              placed to right. It is so small as to look like a swell-
              ing to the tongue.

Just two examples; the decoration is unhelpful to attribution.

Ovolo   FDa
              Albinus i
              Masclinus
Borders   Double, the outer border slightly chamfered at
              bottom left. Borders meet at top right. Both bor-
              ders slightly incurved at top.
Core   Placed to right, where it impinges on inner bor-
              der; short.
Tongue   Left; plain.
Terminal Applied small, centred circle, placed to right, usu-
              ally blocked.

Ovolo   FDb
              Martialis i
              Masclinus
              Masclus
Borders   cf. FDa, but inner border broken on lower right.
Core   cf. FDa.
Tongue   cf. FDa.
Terminal cf. FDa.

The fact that signatures of **Masclinus** in the genitive
appear to be associated with both versions of the ovolo suggests that the small fault in the border may not be wholly
significant for attribution, and probably not for date, other
than as a phase. His signature with ovolo FDa comes from
Kingsholm (Wild 1985, fig. 21, no. 3); (?)Martigny (M 1995,
Taf. 104, no. 2); (?)Rottweil (K19, Taf. 98, A). With FDb, it
occurs at: Canterbury (Bird 1995, no. 647); Hofheim-Erdlager
(M 1995, Taf. 104, no. 5). Two other bowls have been ascribed
to **Masclinus** on the basis of the style of the signatures: Mainz,
FDb? (Behrens 1915, Abb. 18) and Valkenburg (Glasbergen
1940–44, Afb. 59, no. 2).

The **Albinus** signature in the genitive apparently only
occurs with FDa: la Graufesenque (Hermet, pl. 69, no. 5; pl.
76, no. 8); Mainz (K19, Taf. 5); Silchester (May 1916, pl. 17,
no. 2).

Martialis i, with FDb, is represented by both a mould-
stamp, at Usk (Boon 1962, fig. 1) and a signature with the *'fecit'*
ending (Entraigues: Jospin 1989, 46) and so he must be favoured to be an actual mould-maker. His stamp (?) appears
on a Dr. 37 with handles from Ruscino (Fiches & Genty 1980,
299 no. 351). There is a probable **Martialis i** signature associated with ovolo Fda from Hofheim (K19, Taf. 87); it is
incomplete, but appears to read]ISF (the F reversed) as on
the Entraigues bowl.

A bowl from Schifferstadt (K19, Textbild 41, with FDb)
is a problem; it only has M extant, but the lettering is close
to that on a Vienna bowl, (see LL below) signed by **Masclus**.
There does not appear to be a bar in the A in the manner of
Martialis i.

Ovolo FDa apparently is also associated with two **MAS** signatures, probably from the same mould, with clear and completely barred A : London (Lambert 1915, fig. 24) and Mainz (Esser *et. al.* 1969–70, Taf. 38b).

Unsigned Dr. 30s with FDa come from: Colchester (Dannell forthcoming, COC 16, GBSA 569/693, BKCD 217 and BKCD 329); Exeter (Oswald 1952, fig.9, no. 3; Dannell 1991, fig. 13, no. 40; LCS 90, 2030); Fishbourne (1969, F61/ F61A); Kingsholm (Wild 1985, fig. 21, no. 1); la Graufesenque (G47–46 IV, G 1950–54, 54 SE, 1 à 2, G54 NE 1 à 2, G66 A 21.2 (very similar to Stanfield 1930, fig. 5, X), G66 58–150 & 5–25–II, G68 [15–35] & [16] & 16. II, G69 40 III, G71 A71 & A-21–2, G72 [34] II, G81 968, G75–75 1 à 2, G81/G68, G81/G92, G87 531, G7a A-95 1–2, G1901, G1950–4 and Collection Artières, Cyl. Nos. 2, 4, 6 & 16, plus 3, unmarked); London (Stanfield 1930, fig. 5, X; ML 11089G; 11750G; 11759G; 11765G; 11764G; 11808G; 11809G; 11811G; 12189L; 12212L; 12216L; 12220L; 12225L; Leadenhall Court, LCT 84 4313 & 4329); London (Southwark) (CB 1298); Verulamium (VCP BIII (23).

Unsigned Dr. 30s with ovolo FDb come from: Colchester (Dannell forthcoming, BKCJ 183, 188 & 222, GBSA 1793 and May 1930, pl. 16, nos. 77, 83); Fishbourne (1985, E2); Kreuznach (K52, Taf. 69, B, note the uncatalogued Pan); la Graufesenque (Collection Artières (5)); London (ML 11730G & Leadenhall Court LCT 84 4313/4329); Silchester (May 1916, pl. 17, no. 5); Zwammerdam (Haalebos 1977, Taf. 33, no. 38). One curiosity, No. 351, has a rouletted rim.

One of the FDa bowls (No. 273) has a berry motif (Hermet, pl. 13, no. 35) which is a 'marker' for the products of the T-2 group (see EE above, **Mommo**).

Among Dr. 30s of the Neronian and early Flavian periods, this ovolo, with its various tongue-tips, is probably among the most frequently found. One of the problems with illustrated sherds is that the fault in the borders is rarely observed, even when present. One of the clearest illustrated examples to show the fault is that from Zwammerdam (Haalebos, 1977, Taf. 33, no. 38).

It is not entirely clear whether the Dr. 30s, Hermet, pl. 69, no. 5; 73, nos. 4, 14; 74, nos. 11, 12, which were not seen, have ovolo FDa or FDb, but they have one or the other.

Ovolo FG
           Sabinus iii
Borders Double, chamfered on bottom right.
Core Narrow, chamfered to follow borders.
Tongue Right; angle top right to bottom left.
Terminal Solid eight-petalled applied rosette.

The rosette-tip appears to be multi-petalled, but it is quite often blocked. However, careful examination will often reveal the two lower-most petals ('five and seven o'clock') sticking out from the blurred mass. It also seems to appear in different sizes, and may well have been copied during its lifetime. There are four Dr. 30s with this ovolo signed by **Sabinus iii**: Le Mans (Ribemont 1977, 203); Narbonne-la Nautique (Fiches *et al.* 1978, figs. 14, no. 1 and 15, no. 3); Narbonne-

Montfort (M 1995, Taf. 168, no. 7). Other, unsigned Dr. 30s come from Asciburgium (Vanderhoeven 1978, 578); Bath (unmarked); Colchester (Dannell forthcoming, BKCE 944/946, BKCT 286, 1.81E 779, GBSA 952, 1.81E 1194, 1.81 H627; May 1930, pl. 16, no. 80 (cf. Oswald & Pryce 1920, pl. 10, no. 3)); Hofheim (Ritterling 1912, Taf. 27, no. 19); la Graufesenque (G1901, G68 I-II [25] & [35]; Leicester (Stanfield 1937, pl. 8, no. 75); London (ML 11739G, 11802G); Silchester (May 1916, pl. 17, no. 3); Usk (Johns 1993, fig. 92, no. 52; fig. 93, no. 55).

There are two related ovolos: one which is very similar, but which appears to have a rather smaller rosette tip, appears on a Dr. 37 with the mould signature of **Pontus** (Alchester B5280; B. Dickinson, report in prep.); it shows an accentuated chamfer to the bottom left of the borders. There is then a much smaller version, possibly a *surmoulage* of the ovolo, which appears at Leicester (1973, I 64, 302 & Causeway Lane, 13937.02 & 16118. 01; G. Dannell, report in prep.), London (ML 11732G) and Richborough (AML 78305053).

The Dr. 30, Hermet, pl. 77, no. 9 almost certainly has ovolo FG, despite being drawn with a single bordered one, as most of the vegetal details appear elsewhere with it, and FG is the only ovolo with such a long tongue, while Hermet, pl. 78, no. 7 also looks as if it has ovolo FG; neither of these vessels was seen.

Ovolo GA
Borders Single, worn (or just badly impressed) at bottom, concave on left.
Core Full, placed to right.
Tongue Left; overlaps left border, and sharply turned to left at bottom.
Terminal Applied blob.

Just one example; the curious deformation of the tongue may be a quirk of impression, wear, or re-cutting.

Ovolo GG
           Malaval
Borders Double, ovular, slightly incurved on left, cf. MM.
Core Pointed.
Tongue Left; plain, thin, the end tends to block out in a wedge.
Terminal None.

Almost certainly the ovolo which, with decorated tongue, appears on moulds signed by **Masclus** (see MM below for discussion). Dr. 30s with this ovolo appeared in the Fosse Malaval (A. Bourgeois, report in prep.), one of which shows that Oswald has not drawn the gladiator, his O. 1020, correctly; the shield is actually carried horizontally, as on the Dr. 30 from Valkenburg (Glasbergen 1940–44, Abb. 59, no. 1), and the *retiarius*, O.1043, is a much scrawnier individual that any that Oswald shows.

Three other Dr. 30s have been noted: London (ML 12223L); Leicester (Causeway Lane, 13937.03; G. Dannell, report in prep.); and Zwammerdam (Haalebos 1977, Taf 33, no.

39). But, more interestingly, the ovolo is associated with other vessel shapes. It appears on four Hermet form 7s from la Graufesenque (area around the Fosse Malaval); on a *lagena* (unprovenanced), and on a small Dr. 37H (with a large and clumsy strap-handle) from Cirencester (1980/137 (40))

Note that a gladiatorial scene very similar to those of the Fosse Malaval and Valkenburg vessels occurs with a different ovolo at Hofheim (Ritterling 1912, Abb. 51).

Ovolo   GI
             Secundus
Borders Double, asymmetrical, chamfered to the right. Frequently cut off short at the top.
Core   Thin, chamfered to the left.
Tongue   Right; slightly curved to the left.
Terminal None.

The signature **SIICVNDI M** appears with this ovolo from la Graufesenque (Hermet, pl. 72, no. 12). That illustration does not show the ovolo correctly (cf. the same ovolo, Hermet. pl. 78, no. 15). It can be distinguished from ovolo GG by the core, which is thin, and has parallel sides, rather than the ovular shape of GG. It also suffers frequently from being cut off short at the top by the bowl finisher, which can totally change its appearance (5mm, against 9mm at full height). Examples come from Fishbourne (FB 85, D1021); Hofheim (Ritterling 1912, Taf. 26, no. 3); la Graufesenque (Fosse Malaval; A. Bourgeois, report in prep.); London (ML 11795G); Usk (unpub.); Verulamium (Hartley 1972, D2); Wiesbaden (Ritterling 1915, Taf. 6); Wroxeter (Atkinson 1942, pl. 65, no. S22, which has a trifid motif, which is apparently one of the 'markers' for the T-2 group of mould-makers: see ovolo CF).

Ascribed, but not seen: Hermet, pls. 33, no. 37; 78, no. 10; 78, no. 11.

Ovolo   GJ
             Masclus?
Borders Double, slightly flared out at the top, chamfered on bottom right.
Core   Aligned top left, bottom right, slightly pear-shaped.
Tongue   Left; plain, shorter than borders.
Terminal None.

This looks like the ovolo frequently found on bowls signed by **Masclus**, but without any decoration to the tongue; see ovolo LL. There are just two examples.

Ovolo   HA
             Malaval MA 34
Borders Single, very slightly flared out at the top.
Core   Full; the edges are parallel, therefore leaving space between the core and the border at top.
Tongue   Left; plain.
Terminal Probably a blocked ring.

Three examples; another from la Graufesenque (G75 T 70/2) shows a slave, quite similar to O. 975, carrying an am-phora, following his elderly master who is leaning heavily on a cane in his left hand. Hermet, pls. 71, no. 4; 73, no. 11, which were not seen, have been attributed to this ovolo. It looks as if it was also used on Dr. 11 (cf. Haalebos *et. al.* 1991, Abb. 2, no. 2)

Ovolo   HH
Borders Single, symmetrical.
Core   Full.
Tongue   Right; split, placed tight against border, open at bottom.
Terminal None.

One example of this split-tongued ovolo comes from the Hermet/Rey collection.

Ovolo   HI
             Malaval MA 31
Borders Single, slightly flared at top, more to left.
Core   Full.
Tongue   Right; split, placed tight against border, closed at bottom.
Terminal None.

One example from the Hermet/Rey collection, but a number recorded from the Fosse Malaval, one other from la Graufesenque (G71 A B3 (3)) and one from Canterbury (Bird 1995, no. 664) on a *lagena*.

Ovolo   HJ
Borders Single.
Core   Full.
Tongue   Left; split, tight against border, closed at bottom.
Terminal None.

Again a single example from the Hermet/Rey collection.

Ovolo   IA
Borders Single, everted at top
Core   Full
Tongue   Left; plain
Terminal Applied hollow, seven-petalled rosette, often blocked to look solid.

Apart from the five examples in the Hermet/Rey collection, there are two others from la Graufesenque (Collection Rey, 1901–06, No. 348 & G72–4). The ovolo may be the same as one on a Dr. 30 from Hofheim (Ritterling 1912, Taf. 26, no. 5).

Ovolo   IIa
             M. Crestio
Borders Double, the outer strongly pear-shaped, and chamfered at bottom left.
Core   Pear-shaped.
Tongue   Right; plain.
Terminal Applied (?) trident, turned to left, often blocked as blob.

One aspect of this ovolo came rather as a surprise. It has been known for a long time on Dr. 30 with the mould-stamp of **M. Crestio** from Verulamium (Dickinson 1984, fig. 71, no. 9) on which, curiously, his usual mould-stamp has been contracted to fit a small space, giving **MCTO**, by impressing only the beginning and the end of the die; it also appears on Dr. 37 with the mould-stamp of **C. Val[erius] Alb[anus]** at Colchester (Hull 1958, fig. 48, no. 3). However, the trident tip was not recognised, and it is difficult from illustrations to know whether IIa or IIb is recorded (see below). Nor is it clear whether IIb is a worn, recut, or different version of IIa. The Verulamium example is IIa, and it may be that **M. Crestio** was the original owner. On this basis, IIa has been associated with him alone.

Other clear examples come from London on Dr. 37 (ML 4673G & 5114G), and another from Leicester (1973, 295, I, 148). There must be more awaiting identification.

Ovolo   IIb
            C. Val. Alb.
            IVCV
            Patricius
Borders Similar shape to IIa, but borders appear to be more separated, although this could be variability of impression.
Core   cf. IIa.
Tongue cf. IIa.
Terminal Applied (?) broken rosette. There is a horizontal petal at the top left which shows clearly, and seems to differentiate this tip from IIa.

The ovolo in this form has been found associated with the mould-stamp of **C. Val[erivs] Alb[anvs]**: Augst (M 1995, Taf. 2, no. 7); Colchester (Hull 1958, fig. 48, no. 3); Orange (M 1995, Taf. 2, no. 8); Wroxeter (Atkinson 1942, pl. 68, no. 51A), and **Patricius**, la Graufesenque (G59, with a Dr. 29 footring), all on Dr. 37. There are also two pieces with fragmentary signatures which could be attributed to an Albanus: from Geneva (see M1995, Taf. 3, no. 3 and comments, pp. 67–8), and Vechten? (M1995, Taf. 3, no. 6), again on Dr. 37. Another related Dr. 37 with this ovolo comes from Heerlen (van Giffen & Glasbergen 1948, Afb. 3, no. 1) with a signature below the decoration **IVCV**. The fact that names are only associated with Dr. 37 so far, may turn out to be a useful marker (although it should be noted that signatures on Dr. 30 are rare at all times), but cf. the bowl from Sint-Michielgestel (M 1995, Taf. 41, no. 5), which needs to be seen to confirm whether it really has ovolo IIa.

A clear unstamped example on Dr. 30 can be seen from Wroxeter (Atkinson 1942, pl. 66, no. S28). Others come from Gorhambury (Dannell 1990, fig. 161, no. 11); la Graufesenque ('L' & G54 SE 1–2).

Ovolo   IJ
            C. Val. Alb./M . Crestio
Borders cf. IIa/b. Not enough survives to be sure, so distinguished as a different type.

Core   cf. IIa.
Tongue cf. IIa
Terminal Applied (?) blob.

Merely separated because it is not clear whether these bowls have ovolo IIa or IIb. Note the Dr. 30 from Verulamium (Hartley 1972, D34, where it seems that the attribution to **OFMO=Mommo** may not be correct).

Ovolo   JA
Borders Double, flared at top left.
Core   Full, angled top right to bottom left.
Tongue Left?; plain.
Terminal Applied, blob or blocked rosette.

A well recorded ovolo, which remains obstinately anonymous. It appears not to have been used very often on Dr. 30; most of the records are for Dr. 37. Three other Dr. 30s have been recorded: London (ML 11958G and ML unmarked); Silchester (May 1916, pl. 17, no. 12). There are a number of examples on Dr. 37: Colchester (Dannell forthcoming, GBSA 275, 1.81D 1076); Fishbourne (Dannell 1971, pls. 128, no. 19; 129, no. 41; 13, no. .90); London (ML 4467G, 4510G, 4518G, 4528G, 4586G, 5760G, 5861G, 5869G, 5867G, 5876G, 5924G, 71819, Walbrook 218/2,3), Margidunum (Oswald 1948, pl. 14, no. 2); Ribchester (Wild 1988, fig. 3, no. 40); Vechten (Mees 1990, Abb. 16, no. 9; 31, no. 5); Winchester (WP 67 [402]).

There are also two Dr. 29s: from Caerleon (British Telecom site, D8; B. Dickinson, report in prep.) and London (Southwark), Calvert's Buildings (CB 521/982/1001/1060, J. Bird, pers.comm.), which look as if they come from this mouldmaker. In general, the decoration of these vessels uses a limited, but individual, range of poinçons, and the design of the Dr. 37s suggests they are early examples of the form.

Ovolo   JJ
            Lupus ii
            Sabinus iii
Borders Double, well flared at top.
Core   Pointed.
Tongue Left; plain, aligned top left to bottom right.
Terminal Applied solid , eight-petalled rosette

The connection with **Lupus ii** is through the same lunate mould-stamp which appears with ovolo FA. Examples on Dr. 30 come from: Colchester (Dannell forthcoming, BKCK 425); la Graufesenque (Hermet, pl. 73, no. 12); Narbonne-la Nautique (M 1995, Taf 99, no. 4, from the same mould as that at la Graufesenque).

Unstamped vessels include: Colchester (May 1930, pls. 15, D (from the same mould as Dannell forthcoming, 1.81B 1182; pl. 16, no. 74) and Castle Museum 32/1964/8; Dannell forthcoming, CPS 1002 (from the same mould as Hermet, pl. 70, no. 15), BKCE 1278, BKCT 1, & GBSA 938); Exeter (LCS 90.879 & WC 690); Hofheim (Ritterling 1912, Taf. 26, no. 2); la Graufesenque (G1901, G54, SE 192, G54 SE 1–2, G 54 NW 1–2, S54 NW, 2–3, G54 NE 1–2, G54 NE 2–3, G54 SW

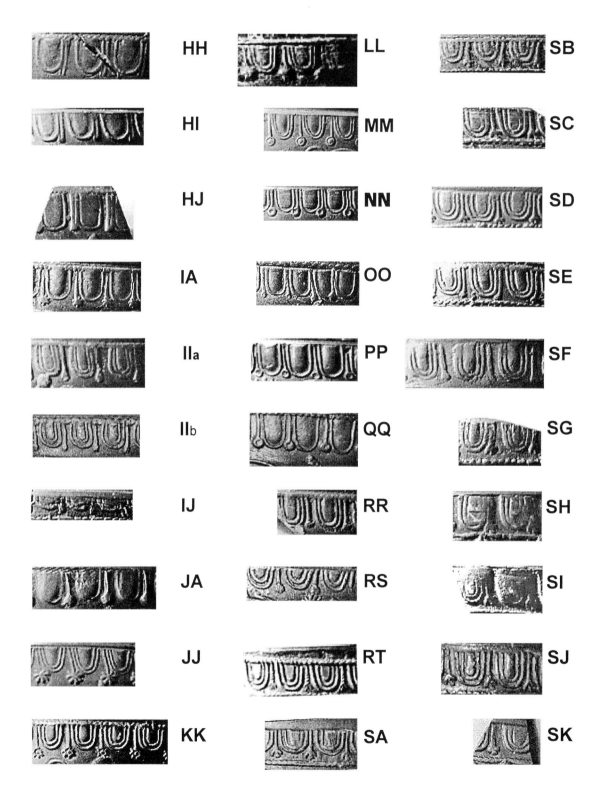

Fig. 2. Ovolos on Dragendorff 30: HH–SK. Scale 1:1. (Photographs by Alain Vernhet and Peter Webster)

1–2, G67 [46] IV, G67 50 & 55 IV, G68 SG III and Hermet, pls. 69, no. 12; 70, no. 15; 77, no. 2); London (ML 11689G, 11742G, 12231L A 2841/8, 17.926, 16794G); London (Southwark) (Bird & Marsh 1978, fig. 115, no. 104); Verulamium (1930 Site A, Ins. 1, B1, 70.3, & Ins. I Bldgs. 1 & 2); Winchester (WP 1944).

The same ovolo appears on a Dr. 11 from la Graufesenque (G78 E77), and also on two *lagenae* (Fosse Malaval 64, & Bémont *et al.* 1987, pl. 11 left), both signed by **Sabinus iii**. What relationship, if any, existed between **Lupus ii** and **Sabinus iii** is not clear.

While the mould-maker of the Dr. 30s associated with ovolo JJ employed figures, it is the large leaves which attract attention – beautiful is, in this case, not an overstatement!

There is a larger ovolo with a very similar shape (K19, Taf. 95, D), but it has not been recorded on signed or stamped bowls.

Ovolo	KK
	T-1 'Potter of the large rosette', said to be Calus
Borders	Double: the outer border is slightly flared at the top, the inner more parallel sided.
Core	Placed slightly to the right.
Tongue	Left; plain.
Terminal	Applied centred, seven-petalled rosette. On some impressions the centre is blocked. The central dot is placed to the bottom right.

The association of this ovolo with **Calus i** is assured by the rare discovery of four Dr. 30s signed **Calus f**, apparently from the same mould, but from different sites: Bregenz (K42, Abb. 1, A); Martigny (Wiblé 1981, fig. 52); Nijmegen-Ulpia (M 1995, Taf. 15, no. 2); Nijmegen-Canabae (M 1995, Taf. 15, no. 4). The same ovolo also appears with a Gaulish inscription, **Calvo,** on a Dr. 37H from la Graufesenque (M 1995, Taf. 17, no. 1), with a plain-ware stamp of **Patricius i** on a handle. A substantial amount of a bowl from the same mould comes from Fishbourne (Dannell 1971, fig. 130), but the signature and stamp are missing.

The known quantity of moulds and bowls with this ovolo is probably the greatest for any in the 1st century, and it would appear to have had a relatively long life. Whether the association with Patricius means that it was passed on by some means to another workshop is open to speculation, but that might account for its longevity. The large number of vessels on which it was used raises the question of whether there were multiple copies of an original die. The potter's name is another matter, but the view taken here is that the **Calus** and **Calvo** signatures belong to the same man, i.e. **Calus i.**

There is then the matter of associations; the small trifid leaf (Hermet, pl. 70, no. 13) appears on a Dr. 30 with the JJ ovolo (G54, NE 1–2); the small warrior, O. 162, is on Dr. 29s stamped by **Lucceius i**, a user of moulds by the T-1 mould-maker(s) (cf. K19, Taf. 48, A). The large leaf and the lyrate bud (Hermet, pl. 70, no. 1) are also found frequently on T-1 moulds, as is the ubiquitous trifid (see ovolo CC above). It is clear from the table of figure-types, that the ovolo is asso-

ciated with the pool available to other makers of Dr. 30. Clearly, there is much analytical work to do in the future, and a re-examination of the work of **Calus i** is overdue. Because there are so many known examples, space does not allow a comprehensive list of bowls, but one or two are noteworthy: the Dr. 30, Stanfield 1937, fig. 10, no. 40, attributed by him to **Sabinus iii**, has ovolo KK, and a leaf (his no. 94), which appears in the Hermet/Rey collection (No. 199); the four Dr. 30s shown by Knorr (K19, Taf. 96,C; 98,C; 99, A; 99,G) all have ovolo KK. The Mainz bowl which Knorr ascribes to **Calus i** (K42, Abb. 1, F) is probably not his work, and almost certainly has a **Masclus** group ovolo, with a hollow rosette tip (see ovolo MM below).

Ascribed, but not seen: Hermet, pl. 78, no. 14.

Ovolo	LL
	Masclus
Borders	cf. GJ.
Core	cf. GJ
Tongue	cf. GJ.
Terminal	Applied centred, seventeen (?) petalled rosette, which often impinges on the outer and/or inner border of the ovolo to the right. The rosette is so fine that it frequently blocks out to a blob.

Again an ovolo with a good pedigree; there are about thirty examples on Dr. 30s with signatures, reading **MASCLUS F** or **MASCLUS**.

Bowls with both ovolo and signature come from: Asberg (M 1995, Taf. 106, no. 1); Augst (Steiger *et al.* 1977, Abb. 70, no. 4; Englert 1925, 63); Avenches (M 1995, Taf. 109, no. 2); Colchester (Dannell forthcoming, 1.81E 922); Ehl (Helmer 1991, pl. 13, no. 1); Hofheim-Steinkastell (M 1995, Taf. 105, no. 5); la Graufesenque (M 1995, Taf. 105, no. 2, unmarked); London (Southwark) (Bird & Marsh 1978, fig. 28, no. 2) London (ML 1172G, 12201L; Smith 1859, pl. 27, no. 6; Walters 1908, M444); Narbonne-la Nautique (Fiches *et al.* 1978, figs. 12, no. 4; 14, no. 5); Nuits-Saint-Georges (M 1995, Taf. 112, no. 2); Richborough (Davies Pryce 1949, pl. 75, no. 11; Simpson 1968, pl. 80, no. 8); Sheepen (Dannell 1985, pl. 44, no. 47); Silchester (May 1916, pl.17, no. 4); Stromberg (M 1995, Taf. 111, no. 1. The two dogs are not in the catalogues of figure-types, see below); Tarragona (Ventura Solsona 1946–47, fig. 59, no. 45); Tongres (Breuer 1929, 4); Valkenburg (Glasbergen 1940–44, Afb. 59, no. 2); (?)Vechten (De Groot 1960, 62, no. 19); Vienna (K07, Taf. 13, no. 2); Vindonissa (K30, Abb.2, no. 8; M 1995, Taf. 106, no. 2, 107, no. 4); Zottegen-Velzeke (Rogge 1972, Abb. 1).

Two large dogs do not appear in the catalogues (K52, Taf. 70, G, and Davies Pryce 1949, pl. 75, no. 11). The one facing to right is shown by Knorr as a bitch, but on two bowls (ML 12201L and la Graufesenque G81, G68) there are no signs of dugs; the one facing to left, catalogued by Oswald as O. 1992, is better drawn by Hermet (pl. 26, no. 19).

The question of whether the mould-maker for the Dr. 29s signed by **Masclus** is the same man is not easily capable of resolution; however, the form of the letters appears to be different, even given that those inscribed below the decoration on Dr. 29 were almost certainly not meant to be read on the bowl.

Ovolo   MM
Borders   cf. GG.
Core   cf. GG.
Tongue   cf. GG
Terminal   Applied centred circle. Often blocked.

This appears to be the same as ovolo GG, with a centred circle added to the tongue. Just one example (Hermet, pl. 77, no. 13 = No. 104). There is another from la Graufesenque (G81/G97 2), but it seems to be a rare variation.

The ovolo appears with other tips: a hollow, seven-petalled rosette (Stanfield 1930, fig. 2, G, signed by **Masclus**, and see remarks for K42, Abb. 1, F in KK above); a six-beaded rosette (la Graufesenque: G47 46, IV, G67, 46 IV, & G75, 50 1–5); finally, a multi-petalled rosette (Stanfield 1930, fig.3, F).

Ovolo   NN
Borders   Single, parallel sides.
Core   Full.
Tongue   Right; plain, shorter than border; the end is forked and turned to the left.
Terminal   Applied circle.

The ovolo is associated with a relatively restricted range of poinçons. Note that the gladiate leaf and the cordate bud (Hermet, pl. 72, no. 8) appear on the Valkenburg bowl (Glasbergen 1940–44, Afb. 60, no. 4). The leaf is also on a Dr. 30 from London (ML 11753G). Another leaf on this bowl (K19, Taf. 52, no. 4), is on a Dr. 29 stamped internally by **Marinus**, who almost certainly bought his moulds in; and it is also on another London Dr. 30 (ML 11820G), which has the small lanceolate leaves appearing on Hermet, pl. 73, no. 10.

The ovolo with a rosette-tipped tongue on a Dr. 30 from Richborough (Davies Pryce 1932, pl. 25, no. 1) looks as if it is related (the two small birds appear together on no. 380). The decorative details do not seem to be on the Dr. 29s from the Hermet/Rey collection, so perhaps the mould-maker specialised in Dr. 30.

Ascribed, but not seen: Hermet, pls. 72, no. 1; 76, no. 6; 78, no. 13.

Ovolo   OO
Borders   Single, parallel sides.
Core   Rather thin, and irregular in shape.
Tongue   Left; plain, alternately vertical and sloped top left to bottom right.
Terminal   Applied small circle, placed to left.

Only one small fragment with this ovolo; other examples, all on Dr. 37, come from: Leicester (Causeway Lane, G. Dannell, report in prep., 11126.01 & GHS); London (Walbrook, 205/4); Verulamium (VCP 2 VI B). The surviving decoration is slight, but is almost certainly early-Flavian.

Ovolo   PP
               Labio
Borders   Single.
Core   Rather thin, slightly chamfered at bottom right.
Tongue   Left (?); plain, very slightly curved to the right.
Terminal   Applied circle, which sometimes overlaps tip of tongue.

Many of the decorative details which appear with this ovolo on Dr. 30 are also on Dr. 29s asssociated with the internal stamp of Labio, from the Hermet/Rey collection. There are very few figure-types and the range of poinçons is limited (Hermet, pls. 72, no. 3; 73, no. 6; 76, nos. 3, 5).

Ovolo   QQ
               Lupus ii
Borders   Single, flared outwards at the top.
Core   Irregular, appears slightly pointed.
Tongue   Left; plain
Terminal   Applied ring.

One example only in the Hermet/Rey collection (Hermet, pl. 69, no. 11). However, the ovolo appears on a Dr. 11 from la Graufesenque with the lunate mould-stamp of **Lupus ii**, and cf. Fiches *et al.* 1978, fig. 13, no. 8.

Ovolo   RR
               Germanus i
Borders   Double.
Core   Slightly curved to right.
Tongue   Right; beaded, shorter than borders.
Terminal   Applied centred, six (?)-petalled rosette, separated from the end of the tongue. This tip is often blocked to a blob.

The ovolo varies in size and shape on individual vessels, which suggests that it was impressed singly. Unfortunately, the stamped vessels, Hermet, pls. 71, no. 12; 72, no. 5; 74, no. 14; 78, no. 17; 78, no. 18; 92, no. 3; 99, no. 3, were not seen, but the illustrations make it likely that they have this ovolo, since only two types are shown on pl. 99 (nos. 37, 38). There is a stamped Dr. 30 from Chichester (Dannell 1989, fig. 14.6, no. 167). Other Dr. 30s with this ovolo come from Augsburg (M 1995, Taf. 68, no. 1); Exeter (Dannell 1991, fig. 17, no. 115); Kempten (K19, Taf. 38, Q); Vertault (Lorimy 1926, 137); Verulamium (Hartley 1972, D31). The ovolo also appears on Déch. 67 (Verulamium 1959, X, VIII (11)) and Knorr 78 (la Graufesenque, 1854–2–3).

Ovolo   RS
               Germanius i
Borders   Double, asymmetrical, flared outwards at top, aligned top right to bottom left.
Core   Pointed.
Tongue   Left; plain.
Terminal   Applied solid, eight or nine-petalled rosette, separated from the end of the tongue. From time to time the tip is very faintly impressed.

One example, with a leaf (Hermet, pl. 8, no. 38), and two trifid motifs (Hermet, pl. 14, nos. 23, 39). Both of these are found on work stamped by **Germanus i** (Hermet, pl. 72, no. 5). One other example has been noted from Colchester (Dannell forthcoming, 1.81M 328).

Ovolo	RT
	Germanus i
Borders	Double, symmetrical.
Core	Tendency to appear pointed.
Tongue	Right; Z-twist cord.
Terminal	Applied (?) trident tip, in the form of a tassel.

Hermet illustrates three Dr. 30s with this ovolo (pl. 79, no. 1 was not seen) which, like RR, is also found on Dr. 37 and Knorr 78. Other Dr. 30s with the ovolo come from: Alès, Vié-Cioutat (M 1995, Taf. 73, no. 2); Artins (Sergent 1956, pl. 2, no. 3); Augst (Furger & Deschler-Erb 1992, Taf. 42, no. 12/32; M 1995, Taf. 75, no. 1; 82, no. 4); Avenches (M 1995, Taf. 77, no. 1); Baden (M 1995, Taf. 74, no. 4); Biesheim (M 1995, Taf. 69, no. 5); London (Dunning 1945, fig. 8, no. 2: the figure is not catalogued); Murviel-lès-Montpellier (Rouquette *et al.* 1989, 146); Northwich (Wild 1972, fig. 13, no. 16); Poitiers-Blossac-Saint-Hilaire (Lombard 1971, 295, no. 18); Rodez (Dausse 1989, pl. 12); Rottweil (K07, Taf. 6, no. 1); Solothurn (K19, Taf. 39, S); Vertault (Lorimy 1926, 137).

Ovolo	SA
	Patricius i
Borders	Double, the outer border is convex, and the two borders often touch at the bottom.
Core	Pear-shaped.
Tongue	Right; plain, slightly angled top left to bottom right.
Terminal	Applied (?) trident, the two external tines are pointed, the central one, square-tipped.

This ovolo is associated with a mould-stamp of **Patricius i**: London (ML 4046G, S476G & S478G) on Dr. 37. The variability of the decorative styles associated with it suggests that the ovolo may have passed to another, as yet unrecognised, workshop. Five other Dr. 30s have been recorded: Geneva (Paunier 1981, no. 106); la Graufesenque (G81 C97 fosse [116]); Leicester (Shires, F280 1321, G. Dannell, report in prep.); London (ML 11954G & 6043G).

Ovolo	SB
	Mo = Mommo?
Borders	Double, the outer border is slightly convex on the left.
Core	Narrow, placed to the right.
Tongue	Right; thickens to bottom.
Terminal	Applied trident; the right tine is almost horizontal.

This ovolo is well connected to a mould-maker who stamped **OFMO**. Stamped and unstamped vessels: la Graufesenque (Hermet, pl. 72, no. 2); Augst (M 1995, Taf. 144, no.

9); Ehl (Helmer 1991, pl.13, no. 6); Fishbourne, (Dannell 1971, fig. 129, no. 43); London (ML 11819G, 11849G, 11859G & 119026L); Moers-Asberg (M 1995, Taf. 146, no. 1); Nijmegen-Hunerberg (Vermeulen 1932, pl. 17, no. 9); Vindonissa (K12, Taf. 18, no. 8, cf. K52, Taf. 77, D); Winchester (WP 1971. 17.609); Wroxeter (Atkinson 1942, pl. 66, no. S29).

Ascribed, but not seen: Hermet, pl. 72, no. 2.

Ovolo	SC
	(Cingius?)-Frontinus?
Borders	Double, the outer flares outwards at top.
Core	Placed to right.
Tongue	Right; plain angled top left to bottom right.
Terminal	Trident, with long tines turned to the right. The tip often impinges on the borders to the right. This tip does not appear to be applied.

The ovolo appears on Dr. 30 with mould-stamps of **Frontinus**: la Graufesenque (mould, M 1995, Taf 66, no. 8); Rocester (B. Dickinson, archive report, see the illustration, M 1995, Taf. 66, no. 6). The decorative details associated with this ovolo are individualistic. In addition to the figures listed, there are a large vine leaf and a large lobed leaf (Hermet, pl. 8, nos. 3, 18) and a trilobe motif (Hermet, pl. 14, no. 42). The ovolo also appears on a Dr. 37 from London (Aldgate) with an unusual, large ivy leaf and a chase of dog and hare (O. 1918 and 2074 types) in a two-zoned design. The same dog, hare, and the Bacchus, O. 565, from no. 445, are all on a Dr. 37 from Vindonissa (K32, Textbild 1, No. 7) with a cursive signature in the decoration, which has been construed as **Cingi Frontini**.

Ascribed, but not seen: Hermet, pl. 69, no. 15.

Ovolo	SD
	Pontus
	Severus iii
Borders	Double, the borders are very convex on the left.
Core	Rather thin, with parallel sides.
Tongue	Right; plain.
Terminal	Applied (?) trident turned to right, the central tine sometimes appears detached.

Two people lay claim to this ovolo: it is known on Dr. 37 with a signature of **Pontus** below the decoration (M 1995, Taf. 166–7); it is also known on both Dr. 30 and Dr. 37 with the mould-stamp of **Severus iii**, die 24a (on Dr. 30, la Graufesenque, M 1995, Taf. 191, nos. 5, 6).

Ovolo	SE
	Memor
	Tetlo
Borders	Double, slightly chamfered at the bottom left.
Core	Thin.
Tongue	Right; plain.
Terminal	Applied trident, turned sharply to the left to tuck under the border.

The impressions tend to suggest that this ovolo was struck

as a pair. It appears on Dr. 37 (cf. Atkinson 1914, pl. 14, no. 74) signed **MIIMORIS** (retrograde) below the decoration, and there is another from la Graufesenque, again signed below the decoration in cursive script, **TIITLON[** (retrograde). The size of the ovolo on bowls is also variable; perhaps it was copied. This limits the certainty of comparative material, but the following Dr. 30s seem to have the larger version: Colchester (Dannell forthcoming, BKCV 88/1064, BKCV 647; May 1930, pl. 17, no. 88); la Graufesenque (G81, G68 & Collection Artières (1)); Leicester (GHS 1975 A77 [43]); London (ML unmarked & 11866G); Neuss (Mary 1967, pl. 18, no. 20); Vechten (Mees 1990, Abb. 10, no. 1; 11, no. 2); Verulamium (Hartley 1972, D36, which has a handle).

Ovolo	SF
	Catterick Racecourse
Borders	Double, inturned at top, large.
Core	Thin, chamfered at the bottom right.
Tongue	Right; plain, thick.
Terminal	Trident with short tines, probably integral with tongue.

An anonymous ovolo which is not well known; there are four other records, all on Dr. 37 (Catterick Racecourse, site 273, 10 & 79, and London ML 3723G & 4627G).

Ovolo	SG
Borders	Double, slightly incurved at top.
Core	Slightly curved to left.
Tongue	Right; plain thick.
Terminal	Trident, turned to right, the left tine longer than the others, all square tipped; apparently integral with tongue.

One example on a small bowl with heavy wreathed festoons used as arcades; for two different sorts of column, see Jacobs 1913, Taf. 1, and Davies Price 1926, fig. 73, S79. Loosely called the Mascvus style' (i.e. **L. Tr- Mascv(l)us**).

Ovolo	SH
Borders	Double, the inner border is placed to the right.
Core	Placed to right, so that it impinges on inner border.
Tongue	Right; plain, thick end turned to right.
Terminal	Trident with short tines turned to right, apparently integral.

One piece with this ovolo: the figure, Hercules, O. 786, is in a heavily wreathed arcade which stands on columns with two rows of fine beads below the capitals.

Ovolo	SI
Borders	Double, outer border flared outwards at the top.
Core	Thin, pear-shaped?
Tongue	Right; plain
Terminal	Trident with short tines turned to right, the central tine attached to that on left, integral.

The way in which the tongue slopes away may be a fault in application, or the result of re-cutting. It is a trait which occurs from time to time with other ovolos with straight tongues. No other example has been noted previously.

Ovolo	SJ
	Sulpicius
Borders	Double, the outer border slightly flared outwards at the top left.
Core	Pear-shaped.
Tongue	Right; plain.
Terminal	Trident with medium-long tines turned to the right. The central tine is attached to that on the left; apparently integral with tongue.

Two examples of an ovolo which is well known on Dr. 37, and carries the mould-stamp of **Sulpicius**: Straubing (Prammer, 1989, Abb. 96); Wilderspool (Dickinson & Hartley 1992, fig. 16, no. 47).

Ovolo	SK
Borders	Double, flared out at the top (?).
Core	Full.
Tongue	Right; plain.
Terminal	Trident, with short tines, just turned to the right; apparently integral with tongue.

Three examples; this looks like the ovolo which is on two Dr. 30s from London (11906G and unmarked), and on Dr. 37s from the Castleford vicus (Site 10, B. Dickinson & B. R. Hartley, report in prep.) and London (ML 6132G).

Ovolo	SL
	Florus iv?
Borders	Double, the outer border looks as if it flares out at the top left.
Core	Placed towards the left.
Tongue	Right; plain.
Terminal	Trident, just turned to the right; applied tip (?).

If the identification of this ovolo is correct, it is the one which is stamped in the mould on Dr. 37 by **Florus iv**: cf. Clausentum (Rogers 1966, fig. 2, no. 39) and le Mas d'Agenais (Bordeaux, Musée d'Aquitaine). Although there are a number of connections for the **Florus** name with Montans (cf. Simpson 1976, 253–7), this ovolo is associated with designs and fabric which come from la Graufesenque (cf. Hartley 1977, 253).

Ovolo	SR
Borders	Double, the outer border flares out at top left, while the inner border is aligned to the right.
Core	Thin, aligned on the inner border, and almost touches it at the bottom
Tongue	Right; plain.
Terminal	Trident, just turned to the right, integral with tongue (?).

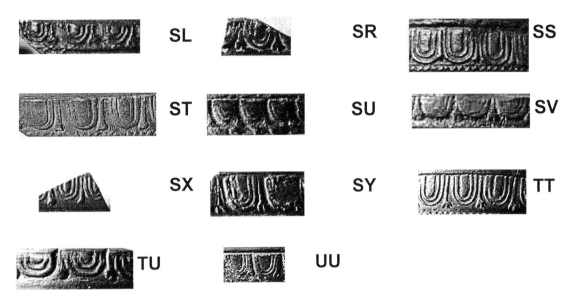

Fig. 3. Ovolos on Dragendorff 30: SL–UU. Scale 1:1. (Photographs by Alain Vernhet and Peter Webster)

The helmet is on a Dr. 37 stamped by **Mercator i** (cf. M 1995, Taf. 129, no. 7 for a clear example), but it is not this ovolo.

Ovolo   SS
Borders   Double, the outer border has sharply carinated sides.
Core   Thinnish, with a square end.
Tongue   Left; plain.
Terminal   Fork (?), applied (?), sharply turned to the left.

Just one example (Hermet, pl. 74, no. 13; note the very crenellated panel borders); two others have been noted: la Graufesenque (G65); Neuss (Mary 1967, Taf. 19, no. 1).

Ovolo   ST
           Crucuro i
Borders   Double, the inner border turns in at the top, and frequently touches the outer border at the bottom.
Core   Long, touching the inner border.
Tongue   Right, sloping slightly top right to bottom left.
Terminal   Probably a blocked trident, integral, turned to the left.

This well-known ovolo appears elsewhere with the mould-stamp of **Crucuro i**: Corseul (Cloastre 1954, 25); Ingold-isthorpe (M 1995, Taf. 55, no. 3); la Graufesenque (Bémont *et al.* 1987, pl. 2). One curious trait is seen on No. 93, and on a Dr. 37 with the ovolo from Bath (RB 301), in which the border under the ovolo alternates quite clearly between zig-zag and beads.

Ovolo   SU
Borders   Double, slightly ovular, with separation of the borders at the bottom?
Core   Short, pointed.

Tongue   Right; plain, attached to the border at the top, but sloping to the right at the end.
Terminal   Small trident tip, apparently integral.

This ovolo has not been recognised previously.

Ovolo   SV
           Biragillus i?
Borders   Double, the outer border is flared outwards at the top left, but curves in at the top right.
Core   Pear-shaped.
Tongue   Right; plain, pointed at top.
Terminal   Trident, turned to right; the centre tine is square-ended, apparently integral. with the tongue.

None of the impressions of this ovolo is very clear.

Ovolo   SX
Borders   Double, chamfered at bottom left.
Core   Narrow
Tongue   Left; plain
Terminal   Small applied trident?

This ovolo may be derived from CG and/or CD. Other examples come from: la Graufesenque (G81–G69) and York (Dickinson & Hartley 1993, nos. 2671, 2673).

Ovolo   SY
           Senilus?
Borders   Double, slightly flaring outwards at top.
Core   Slightly pear-shaped.
Tongue   Right; plain.
Terminal   Trident, turned to right.

It is possible that this is the ovolo which appears with the end of a signature **SENI]LI**? (cf. M 1995, Taf. 182, nos. 6, 7; 183, nos. 1, 2).

Ovolo   TT
             M. Crestio
Borders Double, the outer border is slightly inturned at the
             top.
Core   Thin.
Tongue   Right; plain.
Terminal Four-pronged motif, apparently applied.

Just one example of the ovolo shared by **M. Crestio** (Bregenz, K19, Taf. 28, A) and **Crucuro** (Dr. 37, Hermet, pl. 89, no. 9; Richborough (Davies Pryce 1932, pl. 31, no. 4). The decoration on No. 93 is in fact very similar to that on a vessel from Günzburg (K19, Taf. 29, B), the only difference being a row of four rosettes vertically separating the gladiators. Another related vessel comes from Verulamium (Hartley 1972, D32). It is interesting that the Bregenz vessel has the Mercury, O. 528, which is also on a mould-stamped bowl of **Crucuro** (K19, Taf. 29, no. 3), so the connection between the two bowl makers is fairly proven.

Ovolo   TU
Borders Double, the outer border flat at the bottom.
Core   Short, chamfered on the left.
Tongue   Left; thick.
Terminal Probably a tassel of five filaments, but often
             blocked to look like a trident, or even a blob.

An anonymous ovolo which turns up fairly frequently on Dr. 37 on sites founded in the Flavian-Trajanic period. It seems to be linked to a group of mould-makers who also employed an ovolo with a large trident tip bent sharply under the ovolo to the left (cf. M 1995, Taf. 162, no. 8 for one of the users).

Ovolo   UU
Borders Double, the borders touch on the left.
Core   Chamfered to the left at the bottom.
Tongue   Right; plain (?).
Terminal Small ring applied to left.

One small fragment from the Hermet/Rey collection and just two other certain records: London (Southwark)(Turner & Orton 1979, fig. 6, no. 200; identified from a copy of the original rubbing by Joanna Bird); Silchester (May 1916, pl. 17, no. 1).

Dating the ovolos

The first matter of note is that there appear to be three typological features which seem to be significant for dating: first, tips applied to tongues, other than tridents; secondly, the introduction of tridents as applied tips, and finally the fully fledged, integral, tongue and tip (cf. Oswald & Pryce 1920, 146–50).

In the first group, the fact that the T-1 and T-2 mould-makers of Dr. 29 also used some of their motifs on Dr. 30, suggests that the earliest date for these bowls from the Hermet/Rey collection is likely to be c. AD 55. The related Dr. 29s appear to be from a slightly later group of workshops than those working on the site known as Cluzel 15 (Haalebos 1979) and those represented in the Fosse Malaval (report in prep.). A T-2 Dr. 29 does appear in the Pompeii Hoard (see ovolo EE above), but it is an oddity, and in general, both T-1 and T-2 style bowls are not found much after c. AD 70. Their Dr. 29s occur in the Leaholme fort ditch at Cirencester (B.R. Hartley & B. Dickinson, in Wacher & McWhirr 1982, fig. 44, nos. 40, 41, 42; fig. 45, nos. 44, 49, 51, 52). Two Dr. 30s from this ditch (fig. 46, nos. 55, 56) are clearly in the the style of Hermet/Rey bowls with the FD and GG ovolos. The excavators are of the opinion that 'The accumulated evidence of all sites implies that the Leaholme fort was not finally closed down until the early to mid 70s...', and writing of the samian from the ditch, 'We might also suggest that the vessels were the sole survivors of a consignment of new stock taken into the stores during the early 60s, and such restocking could well equate with a change of unit.' (J.S. Wacher, in Wacher & McWhirr 1982, 65). These remarks need to be borne in mind when assessing the evidence against the Claudian dates which are suggested for the first style of ovolo, from sites like Valkenburg (Glasbergen 1940–44), and for the archaeological context of the 'grande lagène' from la Graufesenque (Labrousse 1968, 517, and see Balsan & Vernhet 1971, 73–108), which has motifs common among the main groups of Dr. 29 and Dr. 30 from the Hermet/Rey collection.

Similar evidence can be seen from York, where there are some parallels with the Leaholme deposit in the samian from the fortress (Dickinson and Hartley 1993). There are a number of Dr. 29s and Dr. 30s which have relationships with material in the Hermet/Rey collection, though the weight of evidence suggests c. AD 65–75 for the York pottery. Moreover, there are Dr. 37s in this deposit, and it is interesting that in the Hermet/Rey collection there are some ovolos which appear on both Dr. 30 and 37. These equate with the first and second styles of ovolo, and are typical of the Pompeii Hoard, where there are large numbers of Dr. 37s with ovolo KK (Atkinson 1914, pls. 7, nos. 39–41; 8; 9) and with ovolo SB (pls. 12–13, nos. 59–63) and ovolo SE (pl. 14).

The third style of ovolo is clearly Flavian, the details on the Dr. 30s with it rarely appearing on Dr. 29. The trident-tipped tongue appears to be a form of reversed 'egg and dart' motif, which overtook the unembellished tongue in popularity on architectural works during the Flavian period (Strong 1994, fig. 1). The fact that the first users of the trident appear to have applied it to the tongue, in a similar manner to rosettes and circles, may have given rise to the variation from architectural detail, since it would have been more distinctive than the dart and easier to locate the sharp end onto the tongue (cf. Blanckenhagen 1940, Taf. 12, no. 38; 35, no. 96, where the ovolo ornament itself is reversed, so that the dart appears impaled on the tongue, and shows its dentations). An alternative possibility is that the potters chose to mimic the *cyma reversa* (Strong 1994, fig. 1), in which there appears to be a tasselled floreate tongue, another popular Flavian architectural motif.

THE FIGURES AND THE USE OF DECORATIVE DETAIL

At this stage of the work with the Hermet/Rey collection it has not been possible to investigate the poinçons which were used to make up the decorative schemes to the point at which statistical analysis can formulate significant groupings. Since Hermet's own catalogue of inanimate details is limited, it did seem useful at least to tabulate the figure-types, using Oswald's (Oswald 1936–37) classification; they are presented in ovolo, figure-type, then site order (Table 2).

Even without more advanced methodology, Table 2 shows that numerous figures were associated with more than one ovolo, and apparently, if the interpretation of ovolo development is correct, across time. This raises some fairly basic issues: first, are the ovolos themselves anything more than decoration, rather than of significance in establishing proprietorial, workshop, or mould-maker groupings? Next, are the types classified by Oswald valid in themselves? This is a very serious problem: thus, where a particular figure-type is identified in conjunction with a given ovolo, it will be necessary to accumulate much more comparative material to be sure that similarly classified types really are the same. A good example of the difficulty can be seen in Oswald's Vulcans, types 70 and 70A, associated with the FD ovolos. Hermet (pl. 75, no. 4, ovolo FDa) shows a projection at the back of the tunic, above the belt, which Oswald ignores in both of his variants; the dagger has a convex pommel, and a striated guard, and the hoop is wreathed. On the Dr. 30 from the Collection Artières (ovolo FDa) the type is very close to O. 70A, the pommel of the dagger is striated and the guard narrow, and probably 'jewelled'; there are ovolo-shaped folds of cloth at the hip, whereas the Hermet type has a single egg-shaped drop. However, these are different again from the Vulcan on no. 361 (ovolo FDb), a larger type (c. 6.0cm, against the other two at c. 5.6cm). The general shape is like O. 70A, but the dagger, with striated pommel, has a broad guard with three rows of 'jewels'. This is probably the Vulcan shown from London (Stanfield 1930, fig. 5, X) and the one from Usk (ovolo FDb, stamped in the mould by **Martialis i**). The London Dr. 30 (ML 11730G, ovolo Fdb) has yet another type of pommel, generally similar to O. 70A, but smaller (it is, unfortunately, broken, but concave, conical, and striated). Clearly there are problems with the drawings, since Oswald is purporting to reproduce some of these as type examples. But the difficulties are more profound. There appear to be multiple variants of a basic type, all used with combinations of other decoration, which seem to be from a single workshop group. Clearly without very careful distinctions in recording, any attempt to form statistical clusters will be vitiated.

The development of a catalogue of inanimate details for Dr. 30 should help to refine this process further, as will conflation with the catalogues which will become available for the other decorated forms. However, it is clear that not all details can have the same factor of reliability in recognition, since most are recorded from bowls, which have been slipped and fired; very small motifs are more subject to variable impression, and to having their finer detail blurred. It is one thing to recognise a five-beaded tendril binding among a group of similarly decorated vessels, where it repeats time and time again, it is quite another to be able to distinguish it from other five-beaded bindings used by other workshops.

These problems reflect upon the use to which samian pottery is put most frequently – that of dating. For Britain, the bulk of the Hermet/Rey collection is associated with the historical period covering the post-Claudian invasion phase through to whatever military disposition is reflected by the York fortress deposit. It straddles the period of the Boudiccan revolt, and, as yet, cannot answer the vexed archaeological question of which particular fortresses and forts were established before, and which after, that revolt. Clearly, the more reliable the evidence for the *floruit* of particular workshops, the nearer will be a solution to that problem, and by extension, others of the same nature.

Equally, the use of statistical clustering, **provided that the underlying data are reliable**, should help identify the development, transitions and decline of workshops, and particularly whether or not 'inheritances' can be traced.

None of these possibilities can be achieved without first getting catalogues of figures and motifs reliably established in formats which will allow easy revision and addition. Imprisoned by the limits of the technology of the past, subsequent scholars have struggled too long with fossilised corpora, piling over-simplified Pelion on ineditable Ossa. Brian Hartley's work with samian potters' stamps has shown a path which this paper seeks to follow.[4]

Notes

1. Carried out under the auspices of English Heritage and the Extra-Mural department of the University of Cardiff.
2. The work would not have been possible without the help of Mlle Annie Philippon and M. R. Taussat, who allowed the material, stored at the Musée Fenaille and the Societé de Belles Letttres d'Aveyron, to be made available.
3. A particular debt is recognised here to Dr Allard Mees, who most kindly made his book available prior to publication by means of both a photocopy and by sending proofs of the plates. During the course of composing this article, various additions were made to his work, and it is hoped that all are reflected here. He also patiently answered a number of queries.
4. In the absence of any more formal programme to collect further examples, the authors would be delighted to receive rubbings of Dr. 30s, with clear impressions of the ovolo, to add to the collection.

Abbreviations

Potters are numbered according to the Leeds 'Index of potters' stamps], with lower-case Roman numerals.

Hermet	Hermet 1934
K07	Knorr 1907
K12	Knorr 1912
K19	Knorr 1919
K30	Knorr 1930
K32	Knorr 1932
K35	Knorr 1935
K42	Knorr 1942
K35	Knorr 1935
K52	Knorr 1952
ML	Museum of London
M 1995	Mees 1995
Narbonne-LN	Narbonne-La Nautique (unpublished material)
O.	Figure types from Oswald 1936–37
Wittkamp Coll.	H. Wittkamp, Katalog Reliefkeramik', 2 edn., privately printed (Beckum)

Table 1. Correlation chart of the Dr.30s from the Hermet/Rey collection with the plates illustrated in Hermet 1934.

BAG	OVOLO	PLATE	BAG	OVOLO	PLATE
124	CC	33.32		RR attrib.	71.12
27	GI	33.37		not seen	72.01
	not seen	35.46		SB attrib.	72.02
	not seen	35.47	392	PP	72.03
	not seen	67.17		RR attrib.	72.05
39	EE	69.01		CA attrib.	72.06
111	DB	69.02		CF attrib.	72.07
253	FDa	69.03	375	NN	72.08
325	SE	69.04	270	FDa	72.09
	FDa attrib.	69.05	78	CF	72.10
175	EF	69.06		no ovolo	72.11
4	BA	69.07	26	GI	72.12
68	JJ	69.08	41	EE	73.01
223	KK	69.09		EE attrib.	73.02
	not seen	69.10	371	FDb	73.03
98	QQ	69.11		FDa/b	73.04
53	JJ	69.12	273	FDa	73.05
1	BA	69.13	391	PP	73.06
188	BB	69.14	342	FDb	73.07
	SC attrib.	69.15	90	FC	73.08
215	KK	70.01	372	NN	73.09
	not seen	70.02	379	NN	73.10
288	FDa	70.03		HA attrib.	73.11
103	LL	70.04		JJ attrib.	73.12
	FA attrib.	70.05		not seen	73.13
	EE attrib.	70.06		FDa/b	73.14
176	EF	70.07		not seen	74.01
	no ovolo	70.08	349	FDb	74.02
	no ovolo	70.09	343	FDb	74.03
35	GI	70.10	422	CH	74.04
44	EE?	70.11		not seen	74.05
	BD attrib.	70.12		FDa/b attrib.	74.06
196	KK	70.13	374	DB	74.07
51	JJ	70.14		CG attrib.	74.08
56	JJ	70.15		not seen	74.09
311	FDb	71.01	165	FG	74.10
319	FDb	71.02		FDa/b attrib.	74.11
307	FDb	71.03	280	FDa	74.12
	HA attrib.	71.04	106	SS	74.13
	DD attrib.	71.05		RR attrib.	74.14
	not seen	71.06		BB attrib.	75.01
	not seen	71.07		BB attrib.	75.02
468	FDa	71.08	287	FDa	75.03
	BD attrib.	71.09		FDa/b	75.04
	RR attrib.	71.10	40	EE	75.05
	no ovolo	71.11		no ovolo	75.06

Note: *Attrib.* refers to Hermet's plates, where there is reasonable confidence in the identification. *Not seen* means that the piece could not be found, nor is Hermet's illustration capable of being assigned.

BAG	OVOLO	PLATE	BAG	OVOLO	PLATE
	Mainz	75.07		RR attrib.	78.17
	not seen	75.08		RR attrib.	78.18
	CG attrib.	75.09		RT attrib.	79.01
139	CG?	75.10	192	FDb	79.02
166	CG	75.11		no ovolo	79.03
105	DD	76.01		no ovolo	79.04
272	FDa	76.02	197	KK	79.05
382	PP	76.03	411	SA	79.06
137	CC	76.04	424	SD	79.07
386	PP	76.05	405	SV?	79.08
	NN attrib.	76.06	413	SA	79.09
	not seen	76.07	330	FDb	79.10
	FDa/b	76.08		RR attrib.	99.03
	not seen	76.09	2	BA	
	GI attrib.	76.10	3	BA	
172	FG	76.11	5	BA	
114	CC	76.12	6	BA	
208	KK	76.13	7	GI	
30	HJ	76.14	9	GI	
131	CC	76.15	10	GI	
184	BB	77.01	11	GG	
57	JJ	77.02	12	CA	
8	GG	77.03	13	CA	
230	BD	77.04	14	CA	
235	BD	77.05	15	CA	
69	JJ	77.06	16	CA	
256	FDa	77.07	17	CA	
	not seen	77.08	18	CA	
	FG attrib.	77.09	19	GJ	
174	FG?	77.10	20	GJ	
232	BD	77.11	21	IIb	
	BD attrib.	77.12	22	IIa	
104	MM	77.13	23	IIa	
	no ovolo	77.14	24	IIa	
	BD attrib.	77.15	25	GI	
185	BB	77.16	29	GI	
	no ovolo	78.01	31	GI	
	no ovolo	78.02	32	GI	
	not seen	78.03	33	GI	
	no ovolo	78.04	34	GI	
	not seen	78.05	36	GI	
	not seen	78.06	37	GI	
	FG attrib.	78.07	38	GI	
126	CC	78.08	42	EE	
	not seen	78.09	43	EE	
	GI attrib.	78.10	45	EE	
	GI attrib.	78.11	46	EE	
86	FC	78.12	47	EE	
	NN attrib.	78.13	48	EE	
	KK attrib.	78.14	49	EE	
28	GI	78.15	50	EE	
	no ovolo	78.16	52	JJ	

BAG	OVOLO	PLATE	BAG	OVOLO	PLATE
54	JJ		120	CC	
55	JJ		121	CC	
58	JJ		122	CC	
59	JJ		123	CC	
60	EE		125	CC	
61	EE		127	CC	
62	EE		128	FB	
63	EE		129	CC	
64	EE		130	CC	
65	FA		132	CC	
66	FA		133	CC	
67	FA		134	CC	
70	JJ		135	CC	
71	JJ		136	CC	
72	JJ		138	CC	
73	JJ		140	CC	
74	JJ		141	CC	
75	JJ		142	?	
76	JJ		143	SV?	
77	JJ		144	SV?	
79	CF		145	SV	
80	CF		146	SR	
81	CF		147	SL	
82	CF		148	SA	
83	CF		149	SY	
84	CF		150	SL	
85	CF		151	SR?	
87	CE		152	CG	
88	SU		153	EE	
89	UU		154	SX	
91	RS		155	SX	
92	BC		156	CG	
93	ST		157	CD	
94	EA		158	CG	
95	FB		159	CG	
96	HI		160	CG	
97	OO		161	CG	
99	HA		162	SX	
100	HH		163	CC?	
101	RR		164	FF?	
102	LL		167	FF	
107	GH		168	FF	
108	SE		169	FF	
109	GA		170	FG	
110	JA		171	FF	
112	CD		173	FG	
113	CC		177	CG	
115	CC?		178	EF	
116	CC		179	EF	
117	CC		180	EF	
118	CG		181	EF	
119	CC		182	EF	

BAG	OVOLO	PLATE	BAG	OVOLO	PLATE
183	DA		247	FDa	
186	BB		248	FDa	
187	BB		249	FDa	
189	BB		250	FDa	
190	FDb		251	FDa	
191	FDb		252	FDa	
193	FDb		254	FDa	
194	FDb		255	FDa	
195	no ovolo		257	FDa	
198	KK		258	FDa	
199	KK		259	FDa	
200	KK		260	FDa	
201	no ovolo		261	FDa	
202	KK		262	FDa	
203	KK		263	FDa	
204	KK		264	FDa	
205	KK		265	FDa	
206	KK		266	FDa	
207	KK		267	FDa	
209	KK		268	FDa	
210	KK		269	FDa	
211	KK		271	FDa	
212	KK		274	FDa	
213	KK		275	FDa	
214	KK		276	FDa	
216	KK		277	FDa	
217	KK		278	FDa	
218	KK		279	KK	
219	KK		281	FDa	
220	KK		282	FDa	
221	KK		283	FDa	
222	KK		284	FDa	
224	KK		285	FDa	
225	KK		286	FDa	
226	KK		289	FDb	
227	BD		290	FDb	
228	BD		291	FDb	
229	BD		292	FDb	
231	BD		293	FDa	
233	BD		294	FDb	
234	BD		295	FDb	
236	BD		296	FDb	
237	BD		297	FDb	
238	BD		298	FDb	
239	BD		299	FDb	
240	BD		300	FDb	
241	BD		301	FDb	
242	BD		302	FDb	
243	BD		303	FDb	
244	BD		304	FDb	
245	BD		305	FDb	
246	no ovolo; Vitalis		306	FDb	

BAG	OVOLO	PLATE	BAG	OVOLO	PLATE
308	FDb		367	FDb	
309	FDb		368	FDb	
310	FDb		369	FDb	
312	FDb		370	FDb	
313	FDb		373	PP	
314	FDb		376	NN	
315	FDb		377	NN	
316	no ovolo		378	NN	
317	FDb		380	NN	
318	FDb		381	NN	
320	AA		383	PP	
321	AA		384	PP	
322	AA		385	DB?	
323	SE		387	PP	
324	SE		388	PP	
326	SE		389	PP	
327	SE		390	PP	
328	SE		393	IA	
329	FDb		394	IA	
331	FDb		395	IA	
332	FDb		396	IA	
333	FDb		397	IA	
334	FDb		398	SA	
335	FDb		399	SA	
336	MISSING		400	SA?	
337	FDb		401	SD	
338	FDb		402	SD	
339	FDb		403	SK	
340	FDb		404	SA	
341	FDb		406	SA	
344	FDb		407	SA	
345	FDb		408	SA	
346	FDb		409	ST	
347	FDb		410	SD	
348	FDb		412	SA	
350	FDb		414	ST/School	
351	FDb		415	no ovolo	
352	FDb		416	SA	
353	FDb		417	IJ	
354	FDb		418	IJ	
355	FDb		419	IJ	
356	FDb		420	IJ	
357	FDb		421	IJ	
358	FDb		423	SI	
359	FDb		425	TU	
360	KK		426	TU	
361	FDb		427	TU	
362	FDb		428	SJ	
363	FDa		429	SJ	
364	FDb		430	SR?	
365	FDb		431	SH	
366	FDb		432	no ovolo	

BAG	OVOLO	PLATE	BAG	OVOLO	PLATE
433	SV?		444	SC	
434	SG		445	SC	
435	TU?		446	SC	
436	TT		447	SC	
437	SB		448	SC	
438	SB		449	no ovolo	
439	SK		452	no ovolo	
440	SF		457	FDb	
441	SX		458	FDa	
442	ST/School		463	SK	
443	SC		467	SC	

Table 2. Figure-types associated with ovolos in the Hermet/Rey Collection – identifiable types

Ovolo		Osw.		Var.	Site and Reference	Mould-stamp *Signature*
AA		1614		TS	322	
BA		2288	A	V	Hermet, Pl. 69.13 =1	
BA		8		TS	Hermet, Pl. 69.7 = 4	
BA		164	A		2	
BA		366			5	
BA		313		TS	4	
BA		133	A	TS	3	
BA		133	A	TS	6	
BB		130			Hermet, Pl. 75.1 (not seen)	
BB	?	924		A	Hermet, Pl. 75.2 (not seen)	
BB		1497	T		Hermet, Pl. 75.1 (not seen)	
BC		2192		V	92	
BD		1013	C	V	234	
BD		1017			234 (or possibly, 1013F)	
BD		435		V	Hermet, Pl. 77.5 = 235	
BD		1016		TS	238	
BD		1017			238	
BD		2180			242	
BD		1043		V	244	
BD		2220		V	245	
BD		2257		V	245	
BD		371	A	TL	Hermet, Pl. 71.9	*SA]BINI.M*
BD		130		V	Hermet, Pl. 71.9	*SABINI.M*
BD		1963	A	TS	Narbonne-la Nautique Fiches et al. 1978, Fig. 15.1	*SABINI.M*
BD		522	A	TS	Hermet, Pl. 71.9	*SA]BINI.M*
BD		371	A		Hermet, Pl. 77.11	*SABINI*
BD		1963		V	Narbonne-la Nautique Fiches et al. 1978, Fig. 15.5	*SA[BINI].M*
BD		1690			Narbonne-la Nautique Fiches et al. 1978, Fig. 15.1	*SABINI.M*
BD		2175			Narbonne-la Nautique Fiches et al. 1978, Fig. 15.3	*SABINI.M*
BD		2175			Narbonne-la Nautique Fiches et al. 1978, Fig. 15.1	*SABINI*
BD		1489		V	Narbonne-la Nautique Fiches et al. 1978, Fig. 15.3	*SABINI*
BD		130		V	Narbonne-la Nautique Fiches et al. 1978, Fig. 15.5	*SA[BINI].M*
BD		1964		V	Narbonne-la Nautique Fiches et al. 1978, Fig. 15.5	*SA[BINI].M*
BD		924	A	TL	la Grauf., G77	
BD		1007		TL	la Grauf., G77	
BD		1008		TL	la Grauf., G77	
CA		434		TS	16	
CA		666		V	16	
CA		1043		V	14	
CA	?	848			la Grauf., LG G69, IV	
CA		1573			la Grauf., LG G69, [60] IV	
CA		878		TS	Hermet, Pl. 72.6 (not seen)	
CC		1013	C	V	113	
CC		1013	G		113	
CC		1737			113	
CC		2232		V	113	
CC		904	A	V	115	
CC		518	A	V	120	
CC		977		V	120	
CC		130			Roanne, K42, Abb.1	*CALUS[*
CC		1020		V	London, ML 11818G	
CC		313			Colchester, Dannell 1996, 1.81 E758	
CC		1021		V	London, ML 11818G	
CC		1963	A	TS	Mainz, K52, Taf. 67A	

Ovolo		Osw.	Var.	Site and Reference	Mould-stamp Signature
CC		1586		Mainz, K52, Taf. 67A	
CC		393		Mainz, K19, Taf. 16. 15a	CJALVS.F
CC		832		Mainz, K19, Taf. 17	CALUS.F
CC		409	V	Mainz, K19, Taf. 17	CALUS.F
CC		390 A		la Grauf., G54 NW 192	
CC		Erot. A(R) A		Mainz, K19, Taf. 17	CALUS.F
CD		103 A		112	
CD		435 A		Augsburg, Roger 1913, Taf.1.1	
CD		546		Augsburg, Roger 1913, Taf.1.1	
CD		1021		Silchester, May 1916, Pl. XVII.9	
CD		965		Colchester, Dannell 1996, MID 2421 (ladder only)	
CD		546		Dammartin-les Pesmes, Gallia, **28**, 360	
CD		411		Dammartin-les Pesmes, Gallia, **28**, 360	
CD		1964		Dammartin-les Pesmes, Gallia, **28**, 360	
CD		1013 A		Gorhambury, Dannell 1990, Fig. 161.11	
CD		1013 B		Gorhambury, Dannell 1990, Fig. 161.11	
CD		882		Gorhambury, Dannell 1990, Fig. 161.11	
CD	?	411		Gorhambury, Dannell 1990, Fig. 161.11	
CD		1013 A		la Grauf., G60 H61 II	
CD		1013 B		la Grauf., G60 H61 II	
CD		1573	V	Verulamium, (Ver 59 XI (29))	
CD		1573	V	Verulamium, (Ver 59 Bldgs. 1&2 X, XI (12))	
CD		2232	V	Verulamium, Ver 59 Bldgs. 1&2 X, XI (12))	
CD		965		Vindonissa, 30.21809 (D. Atkinson, rubbing; man only)	
CD		546		London, ML 11815G	
CD	?	164 A		London, ML 11815G	
CD		1397		Verulamium, "Selfridge 1", Ins. V	
CD		435 A		York, Dickinson & Hartley 1993, 2675	
CD		369	V	Baginton, Hartley 1973, Fig. 13.18	
CF		1970	TS	Hermet, Pl. 72.10 = 78	
CF		2015	TS	Hermet, Pl. 72.7, attrib.	
CF		2156 A		Hermet, Pl. 72.7, attrib.	
CG		895		152	
CG		1370		Hermet, Pl. 74.8, attrib.	
CG		2312		Hermet, Pl. 74.8, attrib.	
CG		2320		Hermet, Pl. 74.8, attrib.	
CG		406	V	Hermet, Pl. 75.10 = 139	
CG		436	V	Hermet, Pl. 75.10 = 139	
CG		666	V	Hermet, Pl. 75.10 − 139	
CG		1489		158	
CG		2260		159	
CG		2147	V	156	
CG		895		152	
CG		2266	V	160	
CG		1013 A		Bingen, Behrens 1920, Taf. 11.2	
CG		1013 B		Bingen, Behrens 1920, Taf. 11.2	
CG		1417		Bingen, Behrens 1920, Taf. 11.2	
CG		1614		Bingen, Behrens 1920, Taf. 11.2	
CG		134	V	la Grauf., G81/F992	
CG		1855	TS	Ver. VCP, B III (23)	
CG		2147	V	Ver. VCP, B III (23)	
CG		435	V	Ver. VCP, B III (23)	
CG		406 A	V	Ver. VCP, B III (23)	

Ovolo		Osw.		Var.	Site and Reference	Mould-stamp *Signature*
CG		895		V	London, ML 12240L	
CG		104		V	London, ML 12240L	
CG		435		V	London, ML 12240L	
CG		406		V	London, ML 12240L	
CG		70	A	V	London, ML 11764G	
CG		164			Cologne, Wittkamp Coll. 60C	
CG		1417		TS	Gadebridge, Dannell 1974, Fig. 93 (lagena)	
CG		882			Gadebridge, Dannell 1974, Fig. 93 (lagena)	
CG		164	A	V	Gadebridge, Dannell 1974, Fig. 93 (lagena)	
CG		435		V	Leicester, (1993 15.90 (269))	
CG		406		V	Leicester, (1993 15.90 (269))	
CG		2175		V	Leicester, (1993 15.90 (269))	
CG		164	A	V	Ribchester, Wild 1988, Fig. 13.142	
CG		2266			Ribchester, Wild 1988, Fig. 13.142	
CG		807	A		la Grauf., G65	
CG		820		V	la Grauf., Coll. Artières	
CG		820		V	la Grauf., G65	
CG		895			Hermet, Pl. 75.9	
CG		895			London, ML 12240L	
CG		436		V	London, ML 12240L	
CH		2032	A		Hermet, Pl. 74.4 = 422	
CH		938	A	V	Hermet, Pl. 74.4 = 422	
CH	?	133			May 1916, Pl. XV.A	
CH		804			May 1916, Pl. XV.A	
CH		501			London, ML 11953G	
CH		1923		V	London, ML 11953G	
DD		134		V	la Grauf., Millau Mus.	
DD		808			la Grauf. G90 39-150 (without wing)	
DD		1013	E	TS	la Grauf., Millau Mus.	
DD		1013	A	V	la Grauf., Millau Mus.	
DD		1013	B	V	la Grauf., Millau Mus.	
DD		1013	F	TS	la Grauf., Millau Mus.	
DD		1573		V	la Grauf., Millau Mus.	
DD		1968		V	la Grauf. Millau Mus., Bémont et al., 1987, Pl. XI, right.	*SABINI MANVS*
EE		2284	A		46	
EE		2284	A		Hermet, Pl. 69.1 = 39	
EE		2145			Hermet, Pl. 69.6 (not seen).	
EE		909	A		Hermet, Pl. 75.5 = 40	
EE		1013	A		Hermet, Pl. 75.5 = 40	
EE		2109			Hermet, Pl. 70.11 = 44	
FA		2191			Davies Pryce 1932, Pl. XXV.2	LVPI
FA		2188			Davies Pryce 1932, Pl. XXV.2	LVPI
FA		2190			Davies Pryce 1932, Pl. XXV.2	LVPI
FA		1935			Narbonne-La Nautique, Mees 1995, Taf. 99.4, same mould as Hermet, Pl. 73.12	LVPI
FA		1968			Narbonne-La Nautique, Mees 1995, Taf. 99.4, same mould as Hermet, Pl. 73.12	LVPI
FA		2071			Narbonne-La Nautique, Mees 1995, Taf. 99.4, same mould as Hermet, Pl. 73.12	LVPI
FA		2180	A		Hermet, Pl. 72.4	LVPI
FA	?	2181			Vindonissa, K52, Taf. 39A	
FA		130	B		Vertault, Hermet, Pl.117.16	LVPI
FA		925			Vertault, Hermet, Pl.117.16	LVPI
FA		1020		V	Oberstimm, Simon 78, Taf. 51. C184	LVPI
FA		1021		V	Oberstimm, Simon 78, Taf. 51. C184	LVPI
FA		1013	A		Oberstimm, Simon 78, Taf. 51. C184	LVPI
FA		1013	B		Oberstimm, Simon 78, Taf. 51. C184	LVPI
FA		435			Oberstimm, Simon 78, Taf. 51. C184	LVPI

Ovolo		Osw.		Var.	Site and Reference	Mould-stamp Signature
FA		1013	A		la Grauf., - Mees & Vernhet, pub. forth.	LVPI
FA		1013	B		la Grauf., - Mees & Vernhet, pub. forth.	LVPI
FA		1013	J		la Grauf., - Mees & Vernhet, pub. forth.	LVPI
FA		1021			la Grauf., - Mees & Vernhet, pub. forth.	LVPI
FA		1043		V	la Grauf., - Mees & Vernhet, pub. forth.	LVPI
FA		1013	H	V	la Grauf., - Mees & Vernhet, pub. forth.	LVPI
FA		2191			la Grauf., - Mees & Vernhet, pub. forth.	LVPI
FA		2188			la Grauf., - Mees & Vernhet, pub. forth.	LVPI
FA		2190			la Grauf., - Mees & Vernhet, pub. forth.	LVPI
FA		2295			la Grauf., G71A 85	
FB		878		TS	Fosse Malaval, Bourgeois pub. forth. (MA 61, temp. ref.)	
FB		1441		TS	Fosse Malaval, Bourgeois pub. forth. (MA 61, temp. ref.)	
FB		1967	A	V	95	
FB		1139	A		95	
FB		1139	A		Fosse Malaval, Bourgeois pub. forth. (MA 25 & 26, temp. refs.)	
FB		1013	A		Fosse Malaval, Bourgeois pub. forth. (MA 27, temp. ref.)	
FB		1013	B		Fosse Malaval, Bourgeois pub. forth. (MA 27, temp. ref.)	
FB		1139	A	V	la Grauf., Coll. Artières, 232	
FDa	?	70	A	V	Kingsholm, Wild 1985, Fig. 21.3	MASCLIN[
FDa		1968			Kingsholm, Wild 1985, Fig. 21.1	MASCLIN[
FDa		1738			Kingsholm, Wild 1985, Fig. 21.1	MASCLIN[
FDa		1924			Kingsholm, Wild 1985, Fig. 21.1	MASCLIN[
FDa		2266		V	255	
FDa		1924		V	Hermet, Pl. 77.7 = 256	
FDa		2288	A	TS	256	
FDa		2175			260	
FDa		925			264	
FDa		1738			271	
FDa		2174			Hermet, Pl. 73.5 = 273	
FDa		131	A		274	
FDa		846			277	
FDa		925			Hermet, Pl. 74.12 = 280	
FDa		1738			Hermet, Pl. 75.3 = 287	
FDa		1968			287	
FDa		2174		TS	Hermet, Pl. 70.3 = 288	
FDa		895			458	
FDa		895			Hermet, Pl. 71.8 = 468	
FDa/b		846			Hermet, Pl. 74.6, attrib.	ALBINI
FDa/b		925		TS	Hermet, Pl. 76.8, attrib.	
FDa/b		393			Hermet, Pl. 74.6, attrib.	
FDa/b		2260			Hermet, Pl. 76.8, attrib.	ALBINI
FDa?		1614			London, Mees 1995, Taf.4.2	ALBINI
FDa		846		TS	Silchester, May 1916, Pl. XVII.2 (same mould as Hermet, Pl. 76.8?)	ALBINI
FDa		2260			Silchester, May 1916, Pl. XVII.2 (same mould as Hermet, Pl. 76.8?)	ALBINI
FDa		1489			Mainz, K19, Taf.5	ALBINI
FDa?		70	A		Martigny, Mees 1995, Taf. 104.2	MASCL[
FDa?	?	103	A		Martigny, Mees 1995, Taf. 104.2	MASCL[
FDa		1489			la Grauf., G81/G 92	
FDa		895			la Grauf., G81/G68	
FDa		1923		V	la Grauf., G47-46 IV	
FDa		1296	B	V	la Grauf., G47-46 IV	
FDa		2260	A		la Grauf., G1950-4	
FDa		925			la Grauf., Box G75-75 1-2	

Ovolo		Osw.		Var.	Site and Reference	Mould-stamp Signature
FDa		131	A	V	la Grauf., Box G75-75 1-2	
FDa		331			London, Leadenhall Court, CB 1298	
FDa		2175			London, Lambert 1915, Fig. 24	*MA*
FDa		2175			Mainz, Esser *et al*., Taf. 38b	*MA*
FDa		70	A	V	London, ML 12216L	
FDa		1007			London, ML 12189L	
FDa		1995		V	Stanfield 1930, Fig. 5X	
FDa		70	A	V	Stanfield 1930, Fig. 5X	
FDa		1992		TS	Stanfield 1930, Fig. 5X	
FDa		2259		V	London, ML 11806G	
FDa?		435			Valkenburg, Glasbergen 1940-44, Afb. 59.2	*JASCL{*
FDa?		406		V	Valkenburg, Glasbergen 1940-44, Afb. 59.2	*JASCL{*
FDa?		895			Valkenburg, Glasbergen 1940-44, Afb. 59.2	*JASCL{*
FDa?		2175			Valkenburg, Glasbergen 1940-44, Afb. 59.2	*JASCL{*
FDa?		1013	G		Vechten, Mees 1995, Taf.4.4	*ALBINI*
FDa		70	A	V	Hermet, Pl. 75.4	
FDa		70	A	V	la Grauf., Coll. Artières (v)	
FDa		79		V	Hermet, Pl. 75.4	
FDa		79		V	la Grauf., Coll. Artières (iii)	
FDa		79		V	la Grauf., Coll. Artières (iv)	
FDa		79		V	la Grauf., Coll. Artières (v)	
FDa		79		V	la Grauf., G66 A 2.1.2	
FDa		131	A	V	Hermet, Pl. 75.4	
FDa		331			London(Southwark), CB 1298	
FDa		1995		V	la Grauf., G66 A 2.1.2	
FDa?		1417		TS	Rottweil, K19, Taf. 98A	*JCLIN*
FDa?		1614			Rottweil, K19, Taf. 98A	*JCLIN*
FDb		406	A		Canterbury, Bird pub. forth. no 647	*MASCLINI[*
FDb		436			Canterbury, Bird pub. forth. no 647	*MASCLINI[*
FDb		2175		V	Canterbury, Bird pub. forth. no 647	*MASCLINI[*
FDb		925			Mainz, Behrens 1915, Abb. 18	*MAS{*
FDb		70	A	V	Boon 1962, Fig. 1	*MARTIALISF*
FDb	?	1573			Hermet, Pl. 79.2 = 192 (Part)	
FDb		1013	F	TS	194	
FDb		2175			252	
FDb		2259		V	306	
FDb		2259		V	312	
FDb		925			329	
FDb		1738			329	
FDb		1924			Hermet, Pl. 79.10 = 330	
FDb		1968		V	Hermet, Pl. 79.10 = 330	
FDb		70			ML 11730G	
FDb		895			Colchester, Dannell 1996, BKC J183,BKC J188, BKC J222	
FDb		880		V	Colchester, Dannell 1996, BKC J183,BKC J188, BKC J222	
FDb		2174		V	338	
FDb		1855		TS	340	
FDb		2147			340	
FDb		2288		V	340	
FDb		1489			344	
FDb		2174		V	350	
FDb		1489			352 (same mould as 344?)	
FDb		70	A	V	361	
FDb		103	A	V	361	
FDb		895			362	
FDb		925			364	

Ovolo	Osw.	Var.	Site and Reference	Mould-stamp Signature
FDb	2259	V	369	
FDb	925		Colchester, Dannell 1996, GBS A1793	
FDb	517	TS	Colchester, Dannell 1996, GBS A1793	
FDb	925		Kreuznach, K52, Taf. 69,B	
FDb	2229		Zwammerdam, Haalebos 1977, Taf. 33.38	
FDb	895		415	
FDb	1013 A		415	
FDb	1013 B		415	
FDb	1489		Entraigues, Jospin 1989, p. 11, 46	MARTIALISF
FDb	1855	V	Entraigues, Jospin 1989, p. 11, 46	MARTIALISF
FDb	2147		Entraigues, Jospin 1989, p. 11, 46	MARTIALISF
FDb	1823		Entraigues, Jospin 1989, p. 11, 46	MARTIALISF
FDb	1924		Entraigues, Jospin 1989, p. 11, 46	MARTIALISF
FDb	1493		Entraigues, Jospin 1989, p. 11, 46	MARTIALISF
Fda?	1417	TS	Rottweil, K19, Taf. 98,A	JCLIN
Fda?	1614		Rottweil, K19, Taf. 98,A	JCLIN
FDb	406		la Grauf., Coll. Artières (i)	
FDb	70	V	Colchester, Dannell 1996, BKC J183,BKC J188, BKC J222	
FDb	70 A	V	la Grauf., Coll. Artières (i)	
FDb	70 A	V	la Grauf., Coll. Artières (ii)	
FDb	103 A	V	la Grauf., Coll. Artières (i)	
FDb	103 A		la Grauf., Coll. Artières (ii)	
FDb	807 A		la Grauf., Coll. Artières (vi)	
FDb	895		la Grauf., Coll. Artières (ii)	
FDb	895		la Grauf., Coll. Artières (vi)	
FDb?	79	V	la Grauf., Coll. Artières 157	
FDb?	103 A		la Grauf., Coll. Artières 157	
FDb?	895		415	MASCLINI[
FDb?	1013 A		415	MASCLINI[
FDb?	1013 B		415	MASCLINI[
FDb?	2174	V	la Grauf., Coll. Artières 157	
FG	1013 A	TS	Hermet, Pl. 74.10 = 165	
FG	1013 B	V	Hermet, Pl. 74.10 = 165	
FG	1737		167	
FG	2072		Hermet, Pl. 76.11 = 172	
FG	1932		Hermet, Pl. 77.10 = 174	
FG	1915	V	la Grauf., G68 I-II [25], [35]	
FG	1932		la Grauf., G68 I-II [25], [35]	
FG	1963		la Grauf., G68 I-II [25], [35]	
FG	2282 A		la Grauf., G68 I-II [25], [35]	
FG	2232 A		la Grauf., G68 I-II [25], [35]	
FG	1368		London, ML 11739G	
FG	1015	TS	London, ML 11802G	
FG	1573		Colchester, May 1930, Pl.XVI.80 and cf. Oswald & Pryce 1920, Pl.X.3)	
FG	103 A	V	Colchester, May 1930, Pl.XVI.80 and cf. Oswald & Pryce 1920, Pl.X.3)	
FG	268	V	Colchester, May 1930, Pl.XVI.80 and cf. Oswald & Pryce 1920, Pl.X.3)	
FG	1573		Usk, Johns 1993, Fig. 92. 52	
FG	268		Usk, Johns 1993, Fig. 92. 52	
FG	1013 G	V	Colchester, Dannell 1996, 1.81 E1194	
FG	1020	V	Colchester, Dannell 1996, 1.81 E1194	
FG	2259	V	Colchester, Dannell 1996, 1.81 E779	
FG	1573		Narbonne-la Nautique, Fiches et al. 1978, Fig. 14.1	SABINI.M
FG	1573		Le Mans, Ribemont 1977, 203	JABIIII
FG	1368		Narbonne-Montfort, Mees 1995, Taf. 168.7	SABINI

Ovolo	Osw.		Var.	Site and Reference	Mould-stamp *Signature*
GG	?	2287		8	
GG		2165	V	11	
GG		2260	∧	11	
GG		1016	A	La Grauf. Fosse Malaval, Bourgeois, pub. forth.	
GG		1013	B V	La Grauf. Fosse Malaval, Bourgeois, pub. forth.	
GG		1020	TL	La Grauf. Fosse Malaval, Bourgeois, pub. forth.	
GG		1021		La Grauf. Fosse Malaval, Bourgeois, pub. forth.	
GG		1043	V	La Grauf. Fosse Malaval, Bourgeois, pub. forth.	
GG		1016		La Grauf. Fosse Malaval, Bourgeois, pub. forth.	
GG		1013	B	Valkenburg, Glasbergen 1940-44, Abb. 59.1	
GG		1020	TL	Valkenburg, Glasbergen 1940-44, Abb. 59.1	
GG		1013	C	Valkenburg, Glasbergen 1940-44, Abb. 59.1	
GG		1013	F	Valkenburg, Glasbergen 1940-44, Abb. 59.1	
GG		1013	G	Valkenburg, Glasbergen 1940-44, Abb. 59.1	
GG		2260	A	Zwammerdam, Haalebos 1977, Taf. 33.39	
GI		1368		7	
GI		2188		29	
GI		2191	A	Hermet, Pl. 72.12 = 26?	*SIICVNDI.M*
GI		2191	A	Hermet, Pl. 72.12 = 26?	*SIICVNDI.M*
GI		1013	A V	Hermet Pl. 33.37 = 27	
GI		1013	B V	Hermet Pl. 33.37 = 27	
GI		1020	TS	28	
GI		1021	V	28	
GI		1586	TS	28	
GI		2188?		29	
GI		889	A	33	
GI		2257	V	10	
GI		1586	V	37	
GI		1970		37	
GI		1442	V	38	
GI		924	A	Fishbourne (1985), FB 85, D1021	
GI		1368		Hofheim, Ritterling 1913, Taf. XXVI.3	
GI		925		Verulamium, Hartley 1972, Fig. 83.D2	
GI		1367		Wiesbaden, Ritterling 1915, Taf. VI	
GI		1586		Hermet, Pl. 76.10	
GI		266	B	Hermet, Pl. 76.10	
GI		2189	V	26	
GI		2192	TS		
HA		975		la Grauf, G75 T 70/2.	
HA		1489		Hermet, Pl. 71.4	
HA		1855		Hermet, Pl. 71.4	
HA		2147		Hermet, Pl. 71.4	
HA		881	V	Hermet, Pl. 71.4	
HA		1968		Hermet, Pl. 71.4	
HA		1370		Hermet, Pl. 71.4	
HI		1016		Fosse Malaval, Bourgeois, pub. forth.	
HI		1017	V	Fosse Malaval, Bourgeois, pub. forth.	
HI		517		Fosse Malaval, Bourgeois, pub. forth.	
IA		925	V	la Grauf., G72-4	
IA		1992		la Grauf., G72-4	
IA		1013	C V	la Grauf., Coll, Rey, 1901-1906, 348	
IA		1935	V	la Grauf., G72-4	
IIa		999		Dickinson 1984, Fig. 71.9	

Ovolo		Osw.		Var.	Site and Reference	Mould-stamp Signature
IIa		1000			Dickinson 1984, Fig. 71.9	
IIa		1682		V	24	
IIb		565		TL	la Grauf,. 'L'	
IIb		134			la Grauf., G54, SE 1-2	
IIb		1794			21	
IIb		1013	F		Gorhambury, (Dannell 1990, Fig. 161.11)	
IIb		1007			Gorhambury, (Dannell 1990, Fig. 161.11)	
IIb		1021			Gorhambury, (Dannell 1990, Fig. 161.11)	
IIb		565		TL	Wroxeter, Atkinson 1942, Pl. 66.S28	
IIb		1042		V	Sint-Michielgestel, Mees 1995, Taf. 41.5	M[
IJ		609			421	
IJ		118		V	420	
IJ		1000			420	
JA		366		V	London, ML (unmarked).	
JJ		1417			Hermet, Pl. 69.12 = 53	
JJ		1970			Hermet, Pl. 69.12 = 53	
JJ		435	A	V	Hermet, Pl. 70.15 = 56	
JJ		435	A	V	Colchester, CPS 1002	
JJ		2147			Colchester, CPS 1002	
JJ		1855		V	Colchester, 1000.21	
JJ		1314			Hermet, Pl. 77.2 = 57	
JJ		1968			58	
JJ		1417			58b	
JJ		1393		V	58b	
JJ		1742	A		Hermet, Pl. 77.6 = 69	
JJ		1932?		V	Hermet, Pl. 77.6 = 69	
JJ		436		V	la Grauf. G54, NE 192	
JJ		2036			la Grauf., G54, NE 1-2	
JJ		925			London, ML 17.926	
JJ		925			Colchester, 32/1964/8	
JJ		2229		V	Exeter, WC 690	
JJ		1968			la Grauf., G54, NW 1-2	
JJ		406	A	V	la Grauf., G54, NE 1-2	
JJ	A	103		V	London (Southwark), Bird & Marsh 1978, Fig. 115.104	
JJ		1314			London (Southwark), Bird & Marsh 1978, Fig. 115.104	
KK		1447		V	Hermet, Pl. 79.5 = 197	
KK		2073		V	Hermet, Pl. 79.5 = 197	
KK		436		V	203	
KK		2271	A	V	203	
KK		1020		V	207	
KK		1013	F	V	207	
KK		1043		V	207	
KK		162		V	Hermet, Pl. 76.13 = 208	
KK		134		V	Hermet, Pl. 76.13 = 208	
KK		2257		V	Hermet, Pl. 76.13 = 208	
KK		2015		TS	210	
KK		899	A		210	
KK		1013	D	TS	217	
KK		938	A		218 (also on the Calvo signed f.37)	
KK		925			221	
KK		Erot.A(L)	A		222	
KK		366		V	222	
KK		666			279	
KK		1007		TL	Hermet, Pl. 78.14 (not seen)	

Ovolo		Osw.		Var.	Site and Reference	Mould-stamp Signature
KK		1008		TL	Hermet, Pl. 78.14 (not seen)	
KK		1013	A		Hermet, Pl. 78.14 (not seen)	
KK		1013	B		Hermet, Pl. 78.14 (not seen)	
KK		666			Hermet, Pl. 78.14 (not seen)	
KK		629			Bingen, Behrens 1920, Taf.11.4	
KK		1573	A		Bingen, Behrens 1920, Taf.11.4	
KK		1296	B		la Grauf., G54, NE 2-3	
KK		463			la Grauf., G54, NE 2-3	
KK		1923		TS	la Grauf., G68, A 68	
KK		436		V	la Grauf., G1901	
KK		2073		V	la Grauf., G54, SE 1-2	
KK		2188	A		la Grauf., G54, NW 1-2	
KK		924	A		la Grauf., G54, SE 1-2	
KK		70		V	la Grauf., (8) G1950-1954	
KK		895			la Grauf., G54,NE 1-2 also on Calvo signed f.37)	
KK		883		V	la Grauf., G54,NE 1-2 (also on Calvo signed f.37, right hand missing)	
KK		1080			la Grauf., 1954	
KK		256		V	la Grauf., 1954	
KK		8		V	Colchester, May 1930, Pl. XVI.85	
KK		895			Colchester, Dannell 1996, GBS B190	
KK		Erot.A(L)	A		Colchester, Dannell 1996, GBS B190	
KK		2073		V	London, ML 11901G, 1937.162	
KK		1923			London, ML 11901G, 1937.162	
KK		895			London, ML 11883G, 1930.92	
KK		2015		TS	London, ML 11905G, 1973.162	
KK		895			Doncaster, Baxtergate 1966, Site DA (17)	
KK		883			Doncaster, Baxtergate 1966, Site DA (17), (right hand missing)	
KK		895			Asciburgium, Vanderhoeven 1974, 606	
KK		162			Asciburgium, Vanderhoeven 1974, 616	
KK		938	A		Asciburgium, Vanderhoeven 1974, 617	
KK		134			Peterborough, Monument 97, D. Mackreth, pub. forth.	
KK		1139	B	TS	York, Dickinson, 1993, 2669	
KK		878		V	York, Dickinson, 1993, 2669	
KK		1573	G		York, Dickinson, 1993, 2669	
KK		1573			London, ML 11740G	
KK		961			la Grauf., 1954, H 18, No. 39	
KK		463		V	la Grauf., 1954, H 18, No. 39	
KK		379			Rottweil, K19, Taf. 96C	
KK		393			Rottweil, K19, Taf. 96C	
KK		1965			Rottweil, K19, Taf. 96C	
KK		548			Rottweil, K19, Taf. 96C	
KK		1765	A		Rottweil, K19, Taf. 96C	
KK		2103		V	Rottweil, K19, Taf. 96C	
KK		2074		V	Rottweil, K19, Taf. 98C	
KK		2015		TS	Burladingen, K19, Taf. 99A	
KK		1671			Burladingen, K19, Taf. 99A	
KK		134		V	Burladingen, K19, Taf. 99G	
KK		1573			Bregenz, K42, Abb. 1A; Martigny, Nijmegen (2), Mees 1995, Taf 15.1-4	CALUS.F
KK		895			Rottweil, K42, Abb. 2A	
KK		379			Rottweil, K42, Abb. 2A	
KK		895			Rottweil, K42, Abb. 2B.	
KK		883			Rottweil, K42, Abb. 2B (right hand missing)	
KK		938	A		Verulamium, 1959 X, XXII, (3)	
KK		895			la Grauf., G1901	

Ovolo		Osw.		Var.	Site and Reference	Mould-stamp *Signature*
KK		925			la Grauf., Coll. Artières	
KK		930		V	la Grauf., G77 S72	
KK		1924			la Grauf., G77 S72	
LL		1573			Vienna, K07, Taf. XIII.2	*MASCLUS.F*
LL		2245			Vienna, K07, Taf. XIII.2	*MASCLUS.F*
LL		1417			Vienna, K07, Taf. XIII.2	*MASCLUS.F*
LL		1614			Vienna, K07, Taf. XIII.2	*MASCLUS.F*
LL		1489			Vienna, K07, Taf. XIII.2	*MASCLUS.F*
LL		2102			Vienna, K07, Taf. XIII.2	*MASCLUS.F*
LL		2045			Vienna, K07, Taf. XIII.2	*MASCLUS.F*
LL		1573			London, Smith 1859, Pl. XXVII.6	*MASCLUS.F*
LL		1614			London, Smith 1859, Pl. XXVII.6	*MASCLUS.F*
LL		2102			London, Smith 1859, Pl. XXVII.6	*MASCLUS.F*
LL		2175			London, Walters 1908, M444	*MA[*
LL		925			Avenches, Mees 1995, Taf. 109.2	*MASCLUS*
LL		2175			Avenches, Mees 1995, Taf. 109.2	*MASCLUS*
LL		2260	A		Augst, Englert 1925, 63	*MASC[*
LL		895			Valkenburg, Glasbergen 1940-44, Afb. 59.2	*]ASCL[*
LL		2175			Valkenburg, Glasbergen 1940-44, Afb. 59.2	*]ASCL[*
LL		406		V	Valkenburg, Glasbergen 1940-44, Afb. 59.2	*]ASCL[*
LL		895			Nuits-Saint-Georges, Mees 1995, Taf. 112.2	*MASCLUS.F*
LL		436		V	Nuits-Saint-Georges, Mees 1995, Taf. 112.2	*MASCLUS.F*
LL		1489			Nuits-Saint-Georges, Mees 1995, Taf. 112.2	*MASCLUS.F*
LL		2260	A		102	
LL		70	A	V	London, ML 12201L	
LL		79			London, ML 1172G	
LL		925			Sheepen, Dannell 1985 , Pl 44.27	
LL		70		V	Silchester, May 1916, Pl. XVII.4	
LL		2260	A		Zottegen-Velzeke, Rogge 1972, Abb. 1	*MASCLUS.F*
LL		2260	A	TS	Narbonne-la Nautique, Fiches et al. 1978, Fig. 12.4	*]VS.F*
LL		925			Neuss, Mary 1967, Taf. 10.13	
LL		70	A	V	Richborough, Pryce 1949, Pl. LXXV.11	*MASCLUS*
LL		103	A	V	Richborough, Pryce 1949, Pl. LXXV.11	*MASCLUS*
NN		1489		TS	Hermet, Pl. 72.8 = 375	
NN		1968			Hermet, Pl. 76.6 (not seen)	
NN		1671	A		Hermet, Pl. 76.6 (not seen)	
NN		1013	F	V	380	
NN		808		TS	Valkenburg, Glasbergen 1940-44, Afb. 60.4	
NN		1963	V		Valkenburg, Glasbergen 1940-44, Afb. 60.4	
PP		2174		V	Hermet, P. 76.5 = 386	
PP		2174		V	391	
RR		704			Hermet, Pl. 71.10 (not seen)	
RR		2398			Hermet, Pl. 71.10 (not seen)	
RR		2311		V	Hermet, Pl. 71.10 (not seen)	
RR		1671		V	Kempten, K19. Taf 38Q	
RR		2015		V	Kempten, K19. Taf 38Q	
RR		704			Hermet, Pl. 71.12 (not seen)	GER*MA*NIF
RR		2398			Hermet, Pl. 71.12 (not seen)	GER*MA*NIF
RR		2309			Hermet, Pl. 71.12 (not seen)	GER*MA*NIF
RR		255		V	Augsburg, Mees 1995, Taf. 68.1	GER*MA*NI.MA
RR		103	A		Augsburg, Mees 1995, Taf. 68.1	GER*MA*NI.MA
RR		79		V	Augsburg, Mees 1995, Taf. 68.1	GER*MA*NI.MA
RR	?	1419			Chichester, Dannell 1989, Fig. 14.6.167	]M*A*NI
RR		1884			Chichester, Dannell 1989, Fig. 14.6.167	]M*A*NI

Ovolo		Osw.		Var.	Site and Reference	Mould-stamp *Signature*
RR		1040			Chichester, Dannell 1989, Fig. 14.6.167	]MANI
RR	?	2175			Exeter, Dannell 1991 Fig. 17.115	[GER]MANIF
RR		2399			Exeter, Dannell 1991 Fig. 17.115	[GER]MANIF
RR		2293			Hermet, Pl. 72.5 (not seen)	GE]RMANI[.MA
RR		2247			Hermet, Pl. 72.5 (not seen)	GE]RMANI[.MA
RR		1013	C	V	Vertault, Lorimy, p. 1926, p. 137	GERMANI
RR		1013	D		Vertault, Lorimy, p. 1926, p. 137	GERMANI
RR		1043		V	Vertault, Lorimy, p. 1926, p. 137	GERMANI
RR		1044		V	Vertault, Lorimy, p. 1926, p. 137	GERMANI
RR		1419			Vertault, Lorimy, p. 1926, p. 137	GERMANI
RR		1870		V	Vertault, Lorimy, p. 1926, p. 137	GERMANI
RR		1870		V	Hermet, Pl. 78.17 (not seen)	
RR		1419			Hermet, Pl. 78.17 (not seen)	
RR		1971			Hermet, Pl. 78.17 (not seen)	
RR		1398			Hermet, Pl. 78.17 (not seen)	
RR		1419			Hermet, Pl. 78.18 (not seen)	GERMANI
RR		1870		V	Hermet, Pl. 78.18 (not seen)	GERMANI
RR		1870			Hermet, Pl. 78.18 (not seen)	GER MANI
RR		70	A		Hermet, Pl. 99.3 (not seen)	]MANI.MA
RS	?	2175			Colchester, Dannell 1996, 1.81 M328	
RT		1700			Hermet, Pl. 79.1 (not seen)	
RT		704			Biesheim, Mees 1995, Taf. 69.5	GERMANI
RT		2404			Biesheim, Mees 1995, Taf. 69.5	GERMANI
RT		704			Rottweil, K07, Taf. VI.1	GERMANI
RT		2398			Rottweil, K07, Taf. VI.1	GERMANI
RT		2398			Baden, Mees 1995, Taf. 74.4	GERMANII
RT		704	C		Artins, Sergent 1956, Pl. II	GERMAN[I
RT		2398			Artins, Sergent 1956, Pl. II	GERMAN[I
RT		2311			Artins, Sergent 1956, Pl. II	GERMAN[I
RT		2320			Artins, Sergent 1956, Pl. II	GERMAN[I
RT		952			Poitiers-Blossac-Saint-Hilaire, Lombard, 1971, 295.18	GE[
RT		594			Poitiers-Blossac-Saint-Hilaire, Lombard, 1971, 295.18	GE[
RT		951			Poitiers-Blossac-Saint-Hilaire, Lombard, 1971, 295.18	GE[
RT		594			Augst, Mees 1995, Taf. 82.4	GERMANIF
RT		1495			Augst, Mees 1995, Taf. 82.4	GERMANIF
RT		1495	A		Augst, Mees 1995, Taf. 82.4	GERMANIF
RT		2175			Augst, Mees 1995, Taf. 82.4	GERMANIF
RT		2403			Augst, Mees 1995, Taf. 82.4	GERMANIF
RT		2320			Augst, Mees 1995, Taf. 82.4	GERMANIF
RT		2404			Augst, Mees 1995, Taf. 82.4	GERMA]NIF
RT		1299	A		Augst, Mees 1995, Taf. 82.4	GERMANIF
RT		2311			Augst, Mees 1995, Taf. 82.4	GERMANIF
RT		1495			Avenches, Mees 1995, Taf. 77.1	GERMANIF
RT		1495	A		Avenches, Mees 1995, Taf. 77.1	GERMANIF
RT		292			Avenches, Mees 1995, Taf. 77.1	GERMANIF
RT		2175			Avenches, Mees 1995, Taf. 77.1	GERMANIF
RT		646			Avenches, Mees 1995, Taf. 77.1	GERMANIF
RT		714		V	Avenches, Mees 1995, Taf. 77.1	GERMANIF
RT		594			Avenches, Mees 1995, Taf. 77.1	GERMANIF
RT		2403			Avenches, Mees 1995, Taf. 77.1	GERMANIF
RT		2404			Avenches, Mees 1995, Taf. 77.1	GERMANIF
RT		1810			Vertault, Lorimy, 1926. 137	GERMANIF
RT		1419			Northwich, Wild 1972, Fig. 13.16	GERMANI
RT		2404			Rodez, Dausse 1989, Pl.12	GERMANIF

Ovolo	Osw.		Var.	Site and Reference	Mould-stamp Signature
RT	1755			Rottweil, K07, Taf. V1.5	GERMANI
RT	1995			Rottweil, K07, Taf. V1.5	GERMANI
RT	1914	B		Rottweil, K07, Taf. V1.5	GERMANI
RT	951			Ales Vie Cioutat, M 1995, Taf. 73.2	GERMANI
RT	967		V	Ales Vie Cioutat, M 1995, Taf. 73.2	GERMANI
RT	955			Ales Vie Cioutat, M 1995, Taf. 73.2	GERMANI
RT	951			Murviel-lès-Montpellier, Rouquette et al. 1989, 146	G[ER]MANIF
RT	967		V	Murviel-lès-Montpellier, Rouquette et al. 1989, 146	G[ER]MANIF
RT	955			Murviel-lès-Montpellier, Rouquette et al. 1989, 146	G[ER]MANIF
RT	704			Hermet, Pl. 71.10	
RT	1495			Hermet, Pl. 99.4	
RT	1495	Λ		Hermet, Pl. 99.4	
RT	2311			Hermet, Pl. 71.10	
RT	2398			Hermet, Pl. 71.10	
RT	2404		TS	Hermet, Pl. 99.4	
SA	395	A		148	
SA	1672		TL	399	
SA	2015		TS	399	
SA	1102		V	412	
SA	814		TS	413	
SA	646			413	
SA	722			413	
SA	597			414	
SA	714		TS	414	
SA	814		TS	416	
SA	646			416	
SA	Erot. A(L)	A		416	
SA	1699		V	404	
SA	1746		V	404	
SA	999			406	
SA	1000			406	
SA	814			407	
SA	2232	A	V	London, ML 6043G.	
SA	1699			London, ML 12225G	
SA	118		TL	Geneva, Paunier 1981, 106	
SA	265		V	Geneva, Paunier 1981, 106	
SA	1738			Leicester, Shires F280 (1321)	
SA	1043		V	Leicester, Shires F280 (1321)	
SA	837		V	la Grauf., G81 c97 fosse [116]	
SA	961			la Grauf., G81 c97 fosse [116]	
SA	961	A		la Grauf., G81 c97 fosse [116]	
SA	1102		V	la Grauf., G81 c97 fosse [116]	
SA	1400		V	la Grauf., G81 c97 fosse [116]	
SB	1013	F		Moers-Asberg, Mees 1995, Taf. 146.1	OFMO
SB	1013	E	V	Moers-Asberg, Mees 1995, Taf. 146.1	OFMO
SB	1417		TS	Vindonissa, K12, Taf. XVIII.8.	OFMO
SB	1614			Vindonissa, K12, Taf. XVIII.8.	OFMO
SB	1968			Vindonissa, K12, Taf. XVIII.8.	OFMO
SB	2074			Nijmegen-Hunnerberg, Vermeulen 1932, Pl. XVII.9	OFMO
SB	2180			Hermet, Pl. 72.2 (not seen)	OFMO
SB	1007			Augst, Mees 1995, Taf. 144.9	OFMO
SB	1008			Augst, Mees 1995, Taf. 144.9	OFMO
SB	895		TS	London, ML 11859G	
SB	80		V	London, ML 11859G	

Ovolo		Osw.		Var.	Site and Reference	Mould-stamp Signature
SB		895		TS	London, ML 11849G	
SB		1015			Fishbourne, Dannell 1971, Fig. 129.43	
SB		1016			Fishbourne, Dannell 1971, Fig. 129.43	
SB		2220			Fishbourne, Dannell 1971, Fig. 129.43	
SB		2180			London, ML 11819G	
SB		517	A		Wroxeter, Atkinson 1942, Pl. 66.S29)	
SC		814		TS	405	
SC		1078		V	444	
SC		565		TS	445	
SC		1738			448	
SC		1755			la Grauf., Mees 1995, Taf. 66.8 (drawn as in the mould)	OFRONTINI
SC		1419		V	la Grauf., Mees 1995, Taf. 66.8 (drawn as in the mould)	OFRONTINI
SC		379			401	
SD		1965		TL	401	
SD		104	B	TS	Hermet, Pl. 79.7 = 424	
SD		548		TS	Hermet, Pl. 79.7 = 424	
SD		1403		TS	la Grauf., Mees 1995, Taf. 191.5	SEVERI
SE		Erot.A(L)	A		323	
SE		379		ts	324	
SE		978		TS	325 (right -hand figure)	
SE		978			326 (pair, but right hand figure a different poincon to 325)	
SE		1043			326	
SE		1397		V	326	
SE		978			327 (pair, but right hand figure a diffrent poincon to 325)	
SE		978		V	327 (pair, but right-hand figure broken)	
SE		704			Vechten, Mees 1990, Abb. 10.1	
SE		878		TS	Vechten, Mees 1990, Abb. 10.1	
SE		1014			London, ML (unmarked)	
SE		1015			London, ML (unmarked)	
SE		369		V	London, ML 11866G	
SE		2258	A		la Grauf., (G81, G68)	
SE		1443		V	Colchester, Dannell 1996, BKC V78/1064	
SE		1013	F		Colchester, Dannell 1996, BKC V78/1064	
SE		1020		V	Colchester, Dannell 1996, BKC V78/1064	
SE		1586		TS	Colchester, Dannell 1996, BKC V647	
SE		1447		V	Colchester, Dannell 1996, BKC V647	
SE		369		V	Verulamium, Hartley 1972, D36 (figure nude, cf. London, ML 11866G, clothed)	
SE		1397			Neuss, Mary 1967, Taf. 18.20	
SE		766	B	V	la Grauf., Coll. Artières	
SF		597		V	440	
SH		597		V	430	
SH		786		V	433	
SJ		1746		TS	429	
SJ		602			429	
SJ		2056		TL	429	
SK		1016			439	
SL		722			147	
SL		786			147	
SR		1208			146	
SR?	?	2407		V	151	
SS		925			la Grauf., G65	
ST	?	999			93	
ST		197	A		la Grauf., Bémont, et al. 1987, Pl. II	
ST		1420		V	la Grauf., Bémont, et al. 1987, Pl. II	

Ovolo	Osw.		Var.	Site and Reference	Mould-stamp Signature
ST	1086	A		la Grauf., Bémont, et al. 1987, Pl. II	
ST	406		V	la Grauf., Bémont, et al. 1987, Pl. II	
ST	435		V	la Grauf., Bémont, et al. 1987, Pl. II	
ST	2072			la Grauf., Bémont, et al. 1987, Pl. II	
ST	1927		V	la Grauf., Bémont, et al. 1987, Pl. II	
ST	134		V	Ingoldisthorpe, Mees 1995, Taf. 55.3	
ST	786			Ingoldisthorpe, Mees 1995, Taf. 55.3	
ST	367		TL	Ingoldisthorpe, Mees 1995, Taf. 55.3	
ST	992		V	442 ('School of')	
ST	1398		V	442 ('School of')	
SV	1161			145	
SV	722			145	
SV	164	A		145	
SX	406		V	la Grauf., G81-G69	
SY	722		TS	149	
SY	646			149	
SY	5			149	
TT	1007		V	436	
TT	1008		V	436	
TT	79			Bregenz, K19, Taf. 28.A	M.CRESTIO
TT	528			Bregenz, K19, Taf. 28.A	M.CRESTIO
TT	1007		V	Verulamium, Hartley 1972, Fig. D32	
TT	1008		V	Verulamium, Hartley 1972, Fig. D32	
TU	1738		TS	425	
TU	1493			425	
TU	609			425	
TU	878			435	
UU	2165	A	V	London (Southwark), Turner & Orton 1979, Fig. 6.200	
UU	517		TS	London (Southwark), Turner & Orton 1979, Fig. 6.200	

Note: Underlined letters in stamps and signatures signify ligatures.

Bibliography

Atkinson, D., 1914 A hoard of samian ware from Pompeii, *J. Roman Stud.*, **4**, 27–64

_____, 1942 *Report on excavations at Wroxeter (the Roman city of Viroconium) in the County of Salop 1923–1927*, Birmingham Archaeol. Soc. (Oxford)

Balsan, L., & Vernhet, A., 1971 Une grande lagène de la Graufesenque, *Gallia*, **29**, 73–108

Behrens, G., 1915 Beiträge zur römischen Keramik, *Mainzer Zeitschrift*, **12–13**, 21–45

_____, 1920 Bingen: Kataloge, *West- und Süddeutscher Altertumssammlungen*, **4**

Bémont, C., Vernhet, A., & Beck, F., 1987 *La Graufesenque, village de potiers gallo-romaine* (Dieppe)

Bird, J., 1995 Illustrated plain and decorated samian, in K. Blockley, P. Blockley, M. Day, S. S. Frere & S. Stow, *Excavations in the Marlowe car park and associated areas*, Archaeol. Canterbury, **5**, 780–92

_____, & Marsh, G., 1978 Decorated samian, in J. Bird, A. Graham, H. Sheldon & P. Townend (eds), *Southwark excavations 1972–74*, London Middlesex Archaeol. Soc. & Surrey Archaeol. Soc., Joint Pub., **1**, 96–102, 200, 262–5

Blanckenhagen, P.-H., 1940 *Flavische Architektur und ihre Dekorationen untersucht am Nervaforum* (Berlin)

Boon, G.C., 1962 Remarks on Roman Usk., *Monmouthshire Antiq.*, **1.2**, 28–33

Breuer, J., 1929 Gobelet Gallo-Romain en terre sigillée provenant de Tongres ou de ses Environs, *Bull. Mus. Royaux d'Art et de Hist.*, **4**, 3–5

Brunsting, H., & Kalee, C.A., 1989 Terra sigillata met reliefversiering, in L.R.P. Ozinga, T.J. Hoekstra, M.D. De Weerd & S.L. Wynia (eds), *Het Romeinse Castellum te Utrecht*, Studies in Prae- en Protohistorie, **3**, 121–38

Cloastre, R., 1954 Marques de potiers sur tessons de céramique sigillée consérves au Musée de Rennes, *Annales de Bretagne*, **61**, 306–27

Dannell, G.B., 1971 The samian pottery, in B. Cunliffe, *Excavations at Fishbourne 1961–1969*, Rep. Res. Comm. Soc. Antiq. London, **27**, 260–300

_____, 1974 The samian, in D.S. Neal, *The excavation of the Roman villa in Gadebridge Park Hemel Hempstead 1963–8*, Rep. Res. Comm. Soc. Antiq. London, **31**, 207–10

_____, 1985 Catalogue of decorated samian, in R. Niblett, *Sheepen: an early Roman industrial site at Camulodunum*, CBA Res. Rep., **57**, 83–91

_____, 1989 The figured samian from the sites, in A. Down, *Chichester excavations 6*, 89–104 (Chichester)

_____, 1990 The decorated samian, in D.S. Neal, A. Wardle & J. Hunn, *Excavation of the Iron Age, Roman and medieval settlement at Gorhambury, St. Albans*, English Heritage Archaeol. Rep., **14**, 197–200

_____, 1991 Decorated samian, in N. Holbrook & P.T. Bidwell, *Roman finds from Exeter*, Exeter Archaeol. Rep., **4**, 46–71

_____, 1995 Further work on the collections of the Abbé Frédéric Hermet and Dieudonné Rey, *Pegasus*, **2**, 24–33

_____, 1996 Petrecvs connected: 30 years on, in J. Bird, M. Hassall & H. Sheldon (eds), *Interpreting Roman London: papers in memory of Hugh Chapman*, 129–33 (Oxford)

_____, forthcoming [Report on South Gaulish samian], in R.P. Symonds

& S. Wade, *Roman pottery from excavations in Colchester 1971–85*, Colchester Archaeol. Rep., **10**

Dausse, L., 1989 Le Jardin des Hespérides, Boulevard Denyd-Puech à Rodez, *Cahiers d'Archéol. Aveyronnaise*, **3**, 55–65

Davies Pryce, T., 1926 (in collaboration with F. Oswald), Terra sigillata or samian ware, in R.E.M. Wheeler, *The Roman fort near Brecon*, Cymmrodorion Soc. Pub., **37** (London)

_____, 1932 The decorated samian, in J.P. Bushe-Fox, *Third report on the excavations of the Roman fort at Richborough, Kent*, Rep. Res. Comm. Soc. Antiq. London, **10**, 94–123

_____, 1949 Decorated samian, in J.P. Bushe-Fox, *Fourth report on the excavations of the Roman fort at Richborough, Kent*, Rep. Res. Comm. Soc. Antiq. London, **16**, 160–83

_____, & Oswald, F., 1928 Roman London: its initial occupation as evidenced by early types of terra sigillata, *Archaeologia*, **78**, 73–102

Dickinson, B.M., 1984 The samian ware, in S.S. Frere, *Verulamium excavations III*, Oxford Univ. Comm. Archaeol., Monograph, **1**, 175–97

_____, & Hartley, B.R., 1992 The samian ware, in J. Hinchliffe, J. Williams & F. Williams, *Excavations at Wilderspool*, Brigantia Monograph Ser., **2**, 31–41

_____, & _____, 1993 Illustrated samian, in J. Monaghan, *Roman pottery from the Fortress: 9, Blake Street*, The Archaeology of York, **16/7**, CBA for York Archaeol. Trust, 745–69

Dunning, G.C., 1945 Two fires of Roman London, *Antiq. J.*, **25**, 48–106

Englert, C., 1925 Die Terra Sigillata-Töpferstempel des Historischen Museums zu Basel, *Anzeiger für schweizerische Altertumskunde*, **27**, 59–63

Esser, K.H., Selzer, W., & Decker, K.V., 1969–70 Die Sammlung Fremersdorf, *Mainzer Zeitschrift*, **63–4**, 137– 57

Fiches, J.-L., 1978 Les coupes Drag. 29 en Languedoc-Roussillon, *Figlina*, **3**, 43–70

_____, Guy, M., & Poncin, L., 1978 Un lot de vases sigillés des premières années du règne de Néron dans l'un des ports de Narbonne, *Archaeonautica*, **2**, 185–219

_____, & Genty, P.-Y., 1980 La céramique sigillée de Ruscino: estampilles et formes estampillées, *Rev. Archéol. de Narbonnaise*, Supp., **7**, 271–301

Furger, A.R., & Deschler-Erb, S. 1992 (eds), *Das Fundmaterial aus der Schichtenfolge beim Augster Theater: typologische und osteologische Untersuchungen zur Grabung Theater-Nordwestecke 1986–87*, Forschungen in Augst, **15**

Glasbergen, W., 1940–44 Pottenbakkersstempels op terra sigillata van Valkenburg Z.H., in A.E. van Giffen, De Romeins castella in den dorpsheuvel te Valkenburg aan den Rijn, *Jaarverslag van de Vereeniging voor Terpenonderzoek*, **25–28**, 206–17

_____, 1948 Terra Sigillata uit Thermenopgraving te Heerlen-Coriovallum, in A.E. van Griffen & W. Glasbergen, Thermen en castella te Heerlen-Coriovallum, *L'Antiquité Classique*, **17**, 237–62

de Groot, J., 1960 Masclus von La Graufesenque, *Germania*, **38**, 55–65

Haalebos, J.K., 1977 *Zwammerdam – Nigrum Pullum: ein Auxiliarkastell am Niedergermanischen Limes*, Cingula, **3**, 119–74

_____, 1979 Primvs, Celadvs und Senicio, *Rei Cretariae Romanae Fautorum Acta*, **19–20**, 121–35

_____, Mees, A.W., & Polak, M., 1991 Über Töpfer und Fabriken verzierter Terra-Sigillata des ersten Jahrhunderts, *Archäol. Korrespondenzblatt*, **21**, 79–91

Hartley, B.R., 1972 The samian ware, in S.S. Frere, *Verulamium excavations I*, Rep. Res. Comm. Soc. Antiq. London, **28**, 216–62

_____ Samian, in Excavations at 'The Lunt' Roman military site, Baginton, Warwickshire, 1968–71: Second interim report, *Birmingham Warwickshire Archaeol. Soc.* **24**, 54–5

_____, 1977 Some wandering potters, in J. Dore & K. Greene (eds), *Roman pottery studies in Britain and beyond*, BAR Supplementary Ser., **30**, 251–61 (Oxford)

Helmer, L., 1991 *La céramique sigillée: 30 ans de recherches archéologiques sur le site d'Ehl-Benfeld* (Hagenau)

Hermet, F., 1934 *La Graufesenque (Condatomago)* (Paris)

Hull, M. R., 1958 *Roman Colchester*, Rep. Res. Comm. Soc. Antiq. London, **20**

Jacobs, J., 1913 Sigillatafunde aus einem römischen Keller zu Bregenz, *Jahrbuch für Altertumskunde*, **6** (1912),172–84

Johns, C. M., 1993 Part III: The decorated samian ware, in W.H. Manning, *Report on the excavations at Usk 1965–1976: the Roman pottery*, 161–203 (Cardiff)

Jospin, J.-P., 1989 Les vases d'Entraigues, in *Archéologie chez vous*, **7**, 10–11

Knorr, R., 1907 *Die verzierten Terra-Sigillata-Gefässe von Rottweil* (Stuttgart)

_____, 1912 Die Terra-Sigillata-Gefässe von Aislingen, *Jahrbuch des historischen Vereins Dillingen*, **25**, 316–92

_____, 1919 *Töpfer und Fabriken verzierter Terra-Sigillata des ersten Jahrhunderts* (Stuttgart)

_____, 1930 Verzierte Sigillata des ersten Jahrhunderts mit Töpfernamen, in *Schumacher Festschrift*, 309–13 (Mainz)

_____, 1932 Terrasigillata der Zeit Vespasians in Rottweil und Pompeji, *Württembergische Vergangenheit*, 29–46 (Stuttgart)

_____, 1935 Römisches aus Risstissen, Unterkirchberg und Strass. Germanisches in Ulm, *Germania*, **19**, 137– 46

_____, 1942 Frühe und späte Sigillata des Calus, *Germania*, **26**, 184–91

_____, 1952 *Terra-Sigillata-Gefässe des ersten Jahrhunderts mit Töpfernamen*, (Stuttgart)

Labrousse, M., 1968 Informations archéologiques, *Gallia*, **26**, 517

Lambert, F., 1915 Recent Roman discoveries in London, *Archaeologia*, **16**, 225–74

Lombard, R., 1971 Inventaire des estampilles de Poitiers (Suite) II – Les produits de la Gaule du Sud, *Rev. Archéol. du Centre*, **10**, 287–302

Lorimy, H., 1926 Inscriptions céramiques gallo-romaines conservées au Musée de Châtillon-sur-Seine, *Bulletin archéologique du Comité des Travaux historiques et scientifiques* (1927), 113–41

Mackreth, D., forthcoming *Monument 97, Orton Longueville, Cambridgeshire: a late pre-Roman Iron Age and early Roman Farmstead*, East Anglian Archaeol.

Mary, G.T., 1967 *Novaesium I: Die südgallische Terra Sigillata aus Neuss*, Limesforschungen, **6** (Berlin)

May, T., 1916 *The pottery found at Silchester* (Reading)

_____, 1922 *The Roman fort of Templeborough near Rotherham* (Rotherham)

_____, 1930 *Catalogue of the Roman pottery in the Colchester and Essex Museum* (Cambridge)

Mees, A.W., 1990 Verzierte Terra Sigillata aus den Ausgrabungen bei Vechten in den Jahren 1920–1927, *Oudheidkundige Mededelingen uit het Rijksmuseum van Oudheiden te Leiden*, **70**, 109–81

_____, 1995 *Modelsignierte Dekorationen auf südgallischer Terra sigillata* (Stuttgart)

Oswald, F., 1936–37 *Index of figure-types on terra sigillata (samian ware)* (Liverpool)

_____, 1948 *The terra sigillata (samian ware) of Margidunum* (Nottingham)

_____, 1952 Decorated samian, in A. Fox, *Roman Exeter (Isca Dumnoniorum): excavations in the war-damaged areas (1945–1947)* (Manchester)

_____, & Davies Pryce, T., 1920 *An introduction to the study of terra sigillata* (London)

Paunier, D., 1981 *La céramique gallo-romaine de Genève* (Geneva)

Prammer, J., 1989 *Das römische Straubing. Ausgrabungen – Schatzfund Gäubodenmuseum*, Bayerische Museen, **11** (München & Zürich)

Ribemont, F., 1977 *Contribution à l'etude du Maine Antique: recherches sur la céramique sigillée dans les cités des Aulerques, Diablintes et Cénomans* (Thèse de 3e. cycle, Histoire de l'Art et Archéologie, Paris 4, 1974) (Paris)

Ricken, H., & Fischer, C. (ed.), 1963 *Die Bilderschüsseln der römischen Töpfer von Rheinzabern* (Bonn)

Rigoir, Y., & Rivet, L., 1994, *De la représentation graphique des sigillées*, S.F.E.C.A.G., Supplément, **1**

Ritterling, E., 1912 *Das frührömische Lager bei Hofheim im Taunus*, Annalen des Vereins für nassauische Altertumskunde und Geschichtsforschung, **40**

_____, 1915 *Das Kastell Wiesbaden. Nach älteren untersuchungen das nassauischen Altertumsverien*, ORL B 31 (Berlin & Leipzig)

Roach Smith, C., 1859 *Illustrations of Roman London* (London)

Rodwell, W., 1982 The samian pottery, in P. Leach, *Ilchester volume 1. Excavations 1974–5*, Western Archaeol. Trust. Monograph, **3**, 129–38

Roger, O., 1913 Bildertypen von Augsburger Sigillaten: III. Folge, *Zeitschrift für Schwaben und Neuburg*, **39**, 26–70

Rogers, G., 1966 Terra sigillata in Southampton Museums, in G. Rogers & L.R. Laing (eds), *Gallo-Roman pottery from Southampton and the distribution of terra nigra in Great Britain*, City Museums Publication, **6**, 3–20

Rogge, M., 1972 Ein signierter Masclus-Becher aus Zottegem-Velzeke (Oost-Vlaanderen), *Helinium*, **12**, 264–8

Rouquette, D., Richard, J.-C., & Soyris, P., 1989 Les estampilles sur céramique sigillée de Murviel-lès-Montpellier (Hérault), *Rev. Archéol. de Narbonnaise*, **22**, 287–310

Sergent, M., 1956 Quelques découvertes à Artins, *Bulletin de la Société*

Archéologique Scientifique et Littérarire de Vendômois, 47–56

Simon, H.-G., 1978 Terra sigillata, in H. Schönberger (ed.), *Kastell Oberstimm. Die Grabungen von 1968 bis 1971*, Limesforschungen, **18**, 227–50 (Berlin)

Simpson, G., 1968 The decorated samian pottery, in B.W. Cunliffe (ed.), *Fifth report on the excavations of the Roman fort at Richborough, Kent*, Rep. Res. Comm. Soc. Antiq. London, **22**, 148–160

————, 1976 Decorated terra sigillata at Montans (Tarn) from the manuscript of Elie Rossignol at Albi, *Britannia*, **7**, 244–73

Stanfield, J.A., 1930 Further examples of Claudian 'terra sigillata' from London, *Antiq. J.*, **10.2**, 114–25

————, 1937 Romano-Gaulish decorated jugs and the work of the potter Sabinus, *J. Roman Stud.*, **27.2**, 168–79

————, 1938 Samian pottery from the Jewry Wall site, in K. K. Kenyon, The Jewry Wall site in Leicester, *Trans. Leicester Lit. Phil. Soc.*, **38**, 24–47

Steiger, R., Schwartz, T., Strobel, R., & Doppler, H., 1977 *Augst, Insula 31: Ausgrabungen und Funde 1960–61*, Forschungen in Augst, **1**

Strong, D., 1994 *Roman museums: selected papers on Roman art and architecture* (London)

Turner, D.J., & Orton, C.R., 1979 Borough High Street, Southwark: excavations in 1962, *Res. Vol. Surrey Archaeol. Soc.*, **7**, 9–11

Ulbert, G., 1959 *Die römischen Donau-Kastelle Aislingen und Burghöfe. Die Funde aus den Jahren 1912 und 1913*, Limesforschungen, **1** (Berlin)

Vanderhoeven, M., 1978 *Terra Sigillata aus Südgallien: Die reliefverzierten Gefässe III*, Funde aus Asciburgium, **7** (Duisburg)

Ventura Solsona, S., 1946–47 Las marcas alfareras de la 'terra sigillata' hallada en Tarragona, *Memorias de los museos arqueológicos provinciales*, **9–10**, 131–65

Vermeulen, W.G.J.R., 1932 *Een Romeinsch grafveld op den Hunerberg te Nijmegen (nit tijd van Tiberius-Nero)* (Paris & Amsterdam)

Wacher, J.S., & McWhirr, A.D., 1982 *Cirencester excavations 1: early Roman occupation at Cirencester*, **1** (Cirencester)

Walters, H.B., 1908 *Catalogue of the Roman pottery in the Department of Antiquities, British Museum* (London)

Weber-Hiden, I., 1987–88 Die Reliefsigillata von Flavia Solva: Ein Überblick. Römisches Österreich, *Jahresschrift der österreichischen Gesellschaft für Archäologie*, **15–16**, 201–37

Wiblé, F., 1981 Forum Claudii Vallensium; la ville romaine de Martigny, *Guides Archéologiques de la Suisse*, **17**

Wild, F., 1972 The samian ware, in G.D.B. Jones, Excavations at Northwich (Condate), *Archaeol. J.*, **127**, 31–77

————, 1985 Samian ware, in H.R. Hurst, (ed.), *Kingsholm. Excavations at Kingsholm Close and other sites with a discussion of the archaeology of the area*, Gloucester Archaeol. Rep., **1**, 56–7, 105–6, 109–11

————, 1988 The samian ware, in B.J.N. Edwards & P.V. Webster (eds), *Ribchester excavations, part 1: excavations within the Roman fort 1970–1980*, 48–58 (Cardiff)

10   Three stamped decorated bowls from Gloucester

Felicity Wild

Comparatively rarely does the reporter on samian ware encounter pieces that are worth publication for their own intrinsic interest. Such pieces include stamped, decorated bowls, which are always worth publishing for the light that they shed on the style of the potter concerned and on his methods of work, as well as for the general use of others working in the field in search of parallels. The bowls published here are from excavations undertaken by Henry Hurst at 10 Eastgate Street, Gloucester. An interim report on the site was published (Hurst 1972, 50–52), but the final report, including the finds, is still awaited. The context from which the pieces came is of no particular significance: all came from contexts containing 2nd-century material. What is of significance is that they are all stamped. All are South Gaulish and are likely to have been products of the potteries at La Graufesenque.

The work of two of the potters, Q. Iulius Habilis and Matugenus, is uncommon. These potters do not appear to have made their own moulds, but to have obtained them from a variety of other sources, which might account for the rarity of their work and the absence of a uniform, recognisable style. The third potter, Iustus, is well-known as a mould-maker and producer of decorated bowls. The present piece adds nothing new to his repertoire.

1. Form 29, with stamp Q.IVL.HABI, die 1a of Q. Iulius Habilis, *c.* AD 70–85.

The upper zone shows a scroll slightly reminiscent of the work of Bassus-Coelus, with a similar leaf-tuft (Knorr 1919, Taf. 13, no. 22). A bowl from Vechten (Knorr 1919, Taf. 13, C) shows its use in a similar scroll. The lower zone is panelled, with a single medallion containing a draped female figure (O.938A), a panel of wavy lines and leaf-tips and a medallion with cupid (O.436). In both medallions, the Nile goose (O.2286) is used as a space-filler. A fourth panel may show a narrow saltire. The parallels appear to point to Calvus, who used O.436 (Knorr 1919, Textbild 13). O.938A (Hermet 1934, pl. 20, no. 131) occurs on a form 30 at La Graufesenque (Hermet 1934, pl. 74, no. 4), with a large rosette-tongued ovolo. The ovolo and type also occur together on a spouted and handled form 37 at La Graufesenque, with the mould-

signature CALVOS and a stamp of Patricius on the handle. A bowl apparently from the same mould was found at Fishbourne (Dannell 1971, fig. 130, no. 49). A similar, though not identical, wreath to that in the upper zone, occurs on a form 29 from Hofheim attributable to Calus/Calvus style (G. Dannell, pers. comm.).

The only other bowl known to have been stamped by Habilis, from Bonn, is in a quite different style. The Bonn bowl is linked to a group of potters including Mommo, Passienus, Pontus, Peregrinus, Iuventus and possibly Frontinus, who all appear to have obtained moulds from a known mould-maker, Potter T12, an anonymous mould-maker identified recently during reassessment of the Hermet Collection at La Graufesenque. The Gloucester bowl shows no affinities with this group and Habilis clearly obtained this mould from a different source. In view of the connections with Calvus, perhaps this potter was providing moulds for Habilis as well as Patricius.

2. Form 29, lower zone only, with stamp OFMATV, die 4a of Matugenus ii of La Graufesenque. *c.* AD 55–70.

Beneath the carination is a horizontal wreath, poorly impressed, probably of the shell (Hermet 1934, pl. 17, no. 8). Below this is a series of striated (?) bifid motifs containing a trefoil bud and the hare (O.2109A; Hermet 1934, pl. 26, no. 73). Spaces are filled with an eight-pointed rosette. The detail of the trefoil bud is not clear, but it may be Hermet 1934, pl. 14, no. 33, used by potters such as Primus (Knorr 1919, Taf. 65, no. 39). A trefoil of similar size, though again the detail is unclear, appears as a horizontal wreath beneath a zone of straight gadroons on a bowl by Matugenus from London (ex Guildhall Museum). The hare is not associated with the work of a particular potter, and no ready parallel appears to be available for the bifid motif.

The style of this bowl is quite different from that of Matugenus' stamped bowls illustrated by Knorr: from Mainz, Aislingen (Knorr 1952, Taf. 38, A and B) and Vindonissa (Knorr 1913, Taf. 18, no. 7). The tendril-binding (Knorr 1919, Taf. 53, no. 8), which occurs on the Vindonissa bowl, links Matugenus with Potter T2, another anonymous mould-maker, who supplied a large group of potters including Ardacus, Felix

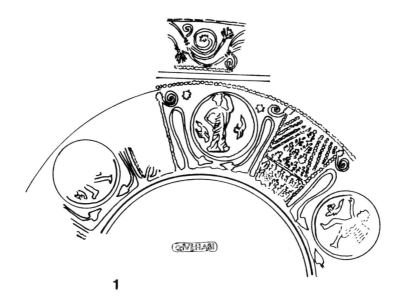

1

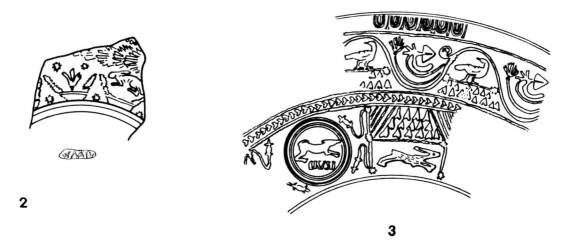

2

3

Fig. 1. Three stamped decorated bowls from Gloucester. Scale 1:2.

and Modestus. Here, Matugenus, too, is using a different source.

3. Form 37. Several sherds of a bowl with a zonal decoration, showing the mould-stamp IIVST, die 15a of Iustus i of La Graufesenque, among the decoration. *c.* AD 75–95.

The upper zone shows a scroll with stirrup-leaf and leaf-tuft in the upper concavities and the bird (O.2247) over leaf-tips in the lower. Beneath a horizontal wreath of small chevron leaves are panels containing Iustus' triple medallion with the hound (slightly larger than O.1965) and name-stamp, and a panel of heart-shaped leaves over the hare (O.2072). M. Alain Vernhet, of the Centre Archéologique de La Graufesenque, has collected and illustrated the motifs occurring at La Graufesenque on bowls by Iustus. His list includes all the decorative motifs used on this bowl and the hound is identical. The hare, however, is smaller than that listed by Vernhet, closer to Oswald's. The bird is not among Vernhet's types, but appears on a bowl in Iustus' style from Catterick.

ACKNOWLEDGEMENTS

In publishing these bowls, I should like to extend my most grateful thanks, firstly, to Henry Hurst, for permission to publish the bowls in advance of the main report; to Malcolm Watkin of Gloucester Museum, for making the sherds available to me, once again, for drawing; to Brian Hartley himself, for providing the stamp identifications along with the other stamps from Gloucester, and, finally, to Geoff Dannell, for discussing with me, if not parallels to the present pieces, then at least other works by the same potters, and the work currently in progress at La Graufesenque in identifying the mould-makers.

Bibliography and abbreviations

O. = figure-types from Oswald, F., *Index of figure-types on terra sigillata ('samian ware')*, University of Liverpool Annals Archaeol. Anthropol., supplement, **23.1–4, 24.1–4** (1936–37)

Dannell, G.B., 1971 The samian pottery, in B. Cunliffe, *Excavations at Fishbourne, 1961–1969, Vol. II: the finds*, Rep. Res. Comm. Soc. Antiq. London, **28**, 260–316

Hermet, F., 1934 *La Graufesenque (Condatomago)* (Paris)

Hurst, H., 1972 Excavations at Gloucester 1968–1971, first interim report, *Antiq. J.*, **52**, 24–69

Knorr, R., 1913 Die Terra-Sigillata-Gefässe von Aislingen, *Jahrbuch des historischen Vereins in Dillingen an der Donau*, **25** (1912)

_____, 1919 *Töpfer und Fabriken verzierter Terra-Sigillata des ersten Jahrhunderts* (Stuttgart)

_____, 1952 *Terra-Sigillata-Gefässe des ersten Jahrhunderts mit Töpfernamen* (Stuttgart)

11   Old wine in new bottles.
Reflections on the organization of the production
of terra sigillata at La Graufesenque

Marinus Polak

As yet little is known about the way in which the manufacture of terra sigillata at La Graufesenque was organized. Although the annual output in the heyday of this production centre must have been counted by hundreds of thousands of vessels (Marichal 1988, 97–8; Vernhet 1991, 37), this branch of the industry is not discussed, or referred to, in the ancient literature. As a consequence, the available sources of information are restricted to the traces of buildings found during excavations at La Graufesenque and to the pottery itself.

Since only a minor part of the kiln site has been investigated, the structure of the settlement is still far from clear. The pottery unearthed at La Graufesenque is a richer source of information. Of particular interest are the so-called 'bordereaux d'enfournement', documents which mainly consist of series of names, sizes and quantities of vessels, preceded by potters' names (fig. 1). So far over two hundred (fragments of) such lists – for which 'docket' seems the best term in English – have been unearthed.

CLASSIFICATION AND DATE

About one quarter of the more than 160 dockets published to date (Marichal 1988; Vernhet & Bémont 1990–1; 1992–3) were found in 1901–6, in excavation trenches lying a maximum of 200 m apart (fig. 2); the documents concerned constitute a relatively homogeneous group. Among the remaining lists only small groups are recognizable at first sight.

To put more order into the collection of dockets those giving two or more names have been selected, 47 in all (Table 1). Of the dozens of potters mentioned in these documents, 47 occur at least twice. The connections between the lists can be visualized by means of a correspondence analysis (fig. 3) – a technique which allows the two-dimensional illustration of complex relationships (cf. Greenacre 1993). The meaning of the axes in the diagrams produced with this method is often difficult to explain, because they summarize several variables. In fig. 3 the horizontal axis may be considered as chronological; the earliest dockets are plotted in the left part of the diagram, and the latest ones to the right. From their position on the vertical axis it is evident that consider-

able differences may exist between more or less contemporaneous documents. The dockets are divisible into three main groups, indicated with the letters A-C (cf. Table 2).

Group A is the largest one, consisting of 28 pieces. With a few exceptions they were unearthed in 1901–6 (fig. 2). Inside group A four subgroups can be distinguished. The first one (A1) consists of two lists differing from the others by the presence of the names Maturus and Vitalis, which also occur in three of the four dockets of group C (Tables 1 and 2); in the case of Vitalis especially two homonymous potters might be involved (cf. Hartley & Dickinson 1978, 240–1, nos. 82–5). One of the dishes of subgroup A1 shows a stamp of Castus; the stamp of the second dish is illegible.

The second subgroup (A2) comprises eighteen dockets, and may be considered as the core of group A. The lists often mention the same names, of which Felix, Masuetos and Tritos are the most frequent. On thirteen dishes a stamp of Castus has been applied, and on two others one of Martialis; the stamps of the remaining vessels are missing.

The five lists of subgroup A3 have much in common with those of A2. Four have been written on dishes of Castus, and the fifth one on a plate of Germanus. The dockets of subgroup A3 differ from the ones mentioned earlier by the presence of the name Verecundos, which otherwise only occurs in the lists of the subgroups A4 and B1.

Subgroup A4 consists of three dockets occupying a relatively marginal position within group A. As opposed to most of the other documents of group A they have all been written on plates. One of these still has its stamp, reading TERTIVS.F. Each of the lists includes one name which also occurs in group B: Paullinus, Tabos and Verecundos.

The documents of group A can be dated to the third quarter of the 1st century AD, on account of the names mentioned and of the stamps related to them. To judge by their position in fig. 3 the vessels of Martialis are probably older than those of Castus, Germanus and Tertius. Several of the names of this group (such as Agedilios, Albanos, Albinos, Castos, Cervesa, Felix, Masuetos, Privatos and Tertius) are also known from stamps, while others (such as Agios, Cornutos, Deprosagijos, Malciu and Summacos) appear only in the dockets.

Fig. 1. Composition of a kiln load (V1 below), written ante cocturam *on a Drag. 15/17 stamped* OF.RVFI, *found at La Graufesenque in 1991. Scale 1:1.*

Group B comprises fifteen dockets, and is in several aspects less homogeneous than group A, as the considerable spread in fig. 3 illustrates. Two pieces were found in 1991, eight in 1965–81, two in 1953–4, two in 1901–3 and one probably in 1880–6 (fig. 2). This group contains both dishes and plates, with stamps of Calvus, Logirnus, Modestus, Rufinus, Cosius Rufinus and Senilis. From the stamps it appears that the documents date from the end of the reign of Nero and the Flavian period.

The main link between the eleven lists of subgroup B1 and those of group A is constituted by the name of Verecundos, occurring in seven dockets. Of the other names known from group A only those of Albanos and Privatos occur more than once in subgroup B1.

The lists of subgoup B2 are united by the presence of the name of Callistus, which is otherwise only mentioned in one of the dockets of subgroup B1. Of the potters belonging to group B, some (including Cresces, Iucundus, Meθillus and Primulus) are known from stamps, and others (such as Agillius, Callistus, Stepanos and Vales) are not.

The latest group of dockets (C) consists of four examples found close to each other in 1950–2 (fig. 2). To judge by the coarse rouletting in the internal bases of the plates on which they have been written, they must date from the late 1st and early 2nd centuries AD. The group has only a few names in common with the others. Vitalis and Maturus also occur in group A, and Urbanos in group B; in the case of Vitalis two potters with the same name may be concerned (cf. above), but for the others this seems less likely. Most of the potters mentioned in this group of documents are not known from stamps. Criciro could be identical with Crucuro, and Vastus and Vebrullus with the potters who stamped VAXTI and OF.VEBR.

SOME ASPECTS OF THE CONTENTS

The character of the dockets is shown by the first lines of some of them, mentioning the phrase *furnus oneratus* or, in Gaulish, *tuθos luxtos* (Marichal 1988, 99–100). Apparently these documents comprise an enumeration of the vessels delivered by various potters to be fired in the same kiln.

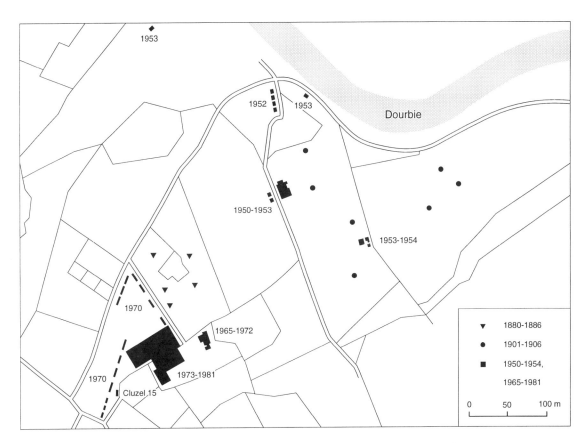

Fig. 2. Location of the excavations at La Graufesenque (after a drawing by A. Vernhet).

Table 1. Survey of the names mentioned in two or more of the analyzed dockets. ‡Names occurring in stamps. M1–112: Marichal 1988, nos. 1–112; V1: Vernhet & Bémont 1990–1; V2: Bémont & Vernhet 1992–3.

Name		Name
Agedilios		Agedilios
Agillius		Agillius
Agios		Agios
Albanos		Albanos
Albinos		Albinos
Amandinus		Amandinus
Augustalis		Augustalis
Callistus		Callistus
Calvus ‡		Calvus ‡
Castos		Castos
Castus ‡		Castus ‡
Cervesa		Cervesa
Cintusmus		Cintusmus
Cornutos		Cornutos
Cotutos		Cotutos
Cresces		Cresces
Deprosagijos		Deprosagijos
Felix		Felix
Galus		Galus
Iucundus		Iucundus
Lousios		Lousios
Malciu		Malciu
Martialis ‡		Martialis ‡
Masuetos		Masuetos
Maturus		Maturus
Meθilos		Meθilos
Melus		Melus
Montanos		Montanos
Paullinus		Paullinus
Primigenios		Primigenios
Primulus		Primulus
Privatos		Privatos
Scota		Scota
Secundanus		Secundanus
Secundinus		Secundinus
Secundos		Secundos
Stepanos		Stepanos
Summacos		Summacos
Tabos		Tabos
Tertius		Tertius
Tetio		Tetio
Tritos		Tritos
Urbanos		Urbanos
Vales		Vales
Vebrullus		Vebrullus
Verecundos		Verecundos
Vindulus		Vindulus
Vitalis		Vitalis

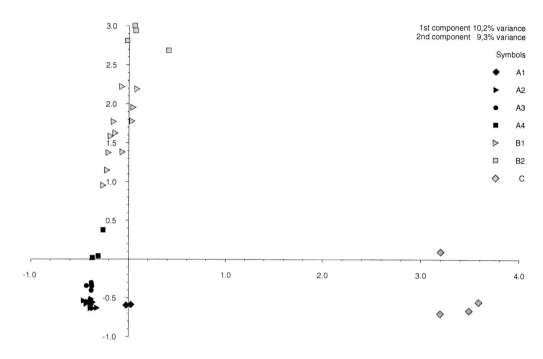

Fig. 3. Result of a correspondence analysis of 47 dockets from La Graufesenque (cf. Table 1).

docket	group	x	y
M1	A3	-0,38139	-0,40526
M2	A1	0,02552	0,58669
M3	A2	-0,39683	-0,59013
M4	A2	-0,39884	-0,55016
M5	A2	-0,38900	-0,59433
M6	A1	-0,02279	-0,59388
M7	A3	-0,37689	-0,35226
M8	A2	-0,38663	-0,57346
M9	A2	-0,39610	-0,54172
M10	A2	-0,38900	-0,59433
M11	A2	-0,32949	-0,62969
M12	A2	-0,42169	-0,55437
M13	A2	-0,39475	-0,53854
M14	A2	-0,42679	-0,55825
M15	A2	-0,39881	-0,56264
M16	A3	-0,37841	-0,32737
M17	A2	-0,39937	-0,63502
M19	A2	-0,36960	-0,63628
M20	A3	-0,38027	-0,30409
M22	A2	-0,38657	-0,56342
M23	A2	-0,38842	-0,51497
M27	B1	-0,26737	0,95411
M28	A2	-0,46763	-0,53707
M30	A4	-0,30961	0,04345
M32	B1	-0,16249	1,77296
M35	A4	-0,25904	0,37773
M46	B1	-0,22890	1,14906
M47	B1	-0,07874	2,21994
M53	B1	0,07512	2,19083
M55	B2	0,40733	2,68896
M66	B2	-0,01860	2,81260
M74	B1	-0,21446	1,37365
M75	C	3,49073	-0,65948
M76	C	3,58744	-0,54993
M77	C	3,20300	0,10210
M81	C	3,19902	-0,69895
M85	A2	-0,37083	-0,55698
M86	B1	-0,19337	1,58531
M87	B2	0,06785	2,94128
M89	A3	-0,43109	-0,34510
M93	A2	-0,44238	-0,57788
M94	B1	0,02546	1,77946
M95	B1	-0,14571	1,62501
M97	A4	-0,36893	0,01973
M112	B2	0,05785	3,00307
V1	B1	0,03577	1,95336
V2	B1	-0,07266	1,38164

Table 2. Survey of 47 dockets from La Graufesenque, with their position in fig. 3.
M1–112: Marichal 1988, nos. 1–112;
V1: Vernhet & Bémont 1990–1;
V2: Bémont & Vernhet 1992–3.

The most obvious supposition is that the dockets have been drawn up by or on behalf of the producers of the dishes and plates on which they have been written. It is not unlikely that they were responsible for the loads of sigillata concerned. In this context it may be revealing that the finds of 1901–6 not only comprise lists on vessels of Castus and Germanus, but also kiln construction parts signed with their names (Hermet 1934, pl. 116, nos. 13 and 15).

If Castus was really charged with firing the vessels mentioned in the lists written on his dishes, the potters referred to there may not have belonged to his *officina*. At least it is hard to imagine that he – and many others with him – would keep such detailed records just for his own use. It is much more likely that he only registered how many vessels other producers had entrusted to him, to be able to calculate the losses in case of an accident. From this perspective it is not surprising that the kiln operator – as the producer responsible for the firing of the kiln will be called here for convenience – normally does not occur in the lists himself.

Several dockets contain 'anonymous' lots of sigillata, i.e. vessels which are not preceded by a potters' name. When such lots have been noted halfway down a list, it may be assumed that they belong to the last mentioned potter. A few lists, however, start with 'anonymous' vessels. So far they have been assigned to the kiln operator (Hermet 1934, 302; Marichal 1988, 105–6), but it may be asked whether that is justified, since the dockets concerned may constitute a sequel to another list, and the 'anonymous' vessels may, therefore, have been produced by a potter unknown to us.

If it is true that the dockets (normally) only contain products of potters other than the kiln operator, the producers who are not otherwise known from stamps have not signed their vessels with the name of the latter. This conclusion is supported by the fact that Deprosagijos, for example, is mentioned on dishes of both Castus and Martialis. A second argument is supplied by a number of dishes which have been signed *ante cocturam* with a name not corresponding with the stamp applied to them: Cotto on a dish of Regenus (Oswald 1931, 260), Iuperus (?) on a dish of Masculus, and Virillis on a dish of Cocus (Marichal 1988, nos. 206 and 208). These examples justify the assumption that the person mentioned in the stamp is not always the actual producer of the vessel. Who is the employer and who the employee may differ from case to case.

The wording of several dockets suggests that potters sometimes co-operated in producing one or more lots. In one of the lists of group A 4500 *catili* of *Tritos duci Deprosagi toni Felixx* are mentioned, and at least 1650 *paraxidi* of *Vindulus duci Cosoj* (Marichal 1988, no. 12). Although we cannot exclude the possibility that records of this kind mean that each of the potters named has delivered the amount of vessels mentioned at the kiln, such co-operative ventures seem the most likely explanation of the phrases used.

At first sight it seems legitimate to conclude from the dockets that some potters specialized in certain forms. Albanos, for example, delivered almost exclusively *pannas*, Deprosagijos mainly *catili* and *paraxidi*, Felix *catili*, Masuetos *acitabli*

and *paraxidi*, Privatos *acitabli* and *licuias*, Summacos *catili* and Tritos *acitabli*, *licuias* and *paraxidi* (cf. Marichal 1988, 245–9). However, this division may simply result from the law of supply and demand.

In the dockets of the earliest group the vessels are enumerated in a more or less fixed order. This might well mirror the way in which the kiln was loaded (cf. Marichal 1988, 103). Inside the lists three sections can be distinguished. The first one mainly consists of *canastri*, *mortari* and *pannas*, usually in this order. This section may also contain *vinaria*, *atramitari*, *inbratari* and *broci*. In dockets where *canastri* are absent, the first section regularly includes *catinos* or small numbers of *catili*; this could be an argument to consider not only *catinos*, but also *canastri* and small numbers of *catili* as plates (cf. Oxé 1925, 81–2). If the first section also contains *licuias*, they do not occur elsewhere.

The second section includes mainly *catili*, *paraxidi* and *licuias*. The *catili* nearly always precede the *paraxidi*; the place of the *licuias* varies. The *pultari* also seem to belong in this section. If *mortari* are mentioned, only small numbers are concerned, and they are specified as *uxedi*.

The third and last section normally only consists of *acitabli*. In a few dockets small lots of other forms are listed here, which may have served to fill in the last holes in the kiln.

The uniformity of the composition of the kiln loads drawn up in the dockets of group A may be illustrated clearly by means of a correspondence analysis (Table 3 and fig. 4). The horizontal axis in this case expresses the contrast between dockets with many (on the left) and few (on the right) *licuias*. The vertical axis reflects the difference between lists with many *mortari* and *acitabli* (above) and those with many *pannas* and *canastri* (below). The dockets of group A, plotted around and above the horizontal axis, can be separated into examples with many *liciuas* and few *catili* and *paraxidi* on the one hand (to the left of the vertical axis) and examples with little or no *licuias* on the other (to the right of the vertical axis). The difference is thus mainly to be found in the vessels from the second section. The three sections account for approximately similar proportions of the load in most dockets, the first section comprising about 8%, the second 60% and the third 32%. The two most recent lists in this diagram (V1 and V2) differ from the others by high percentages of *canastri* and *pannas*; the order in which the vessels are enumerated in these dockets equally deviates from the pattern described for the oldest lists.

The similarities and dissimilarities in the composition of the individual loads might indicate that each kiln operator employed a limited number of fixed loading patterns to arrange the vessels in his kiln. For those potters who did not dispose of a kiln of their own this could mean that they had to turn to several kiln operators to have their entire range of vessels fired.

CONCLUSION

The dockets found at La Graufesenque constitute a rich source of information which has not yet been fully exploited.

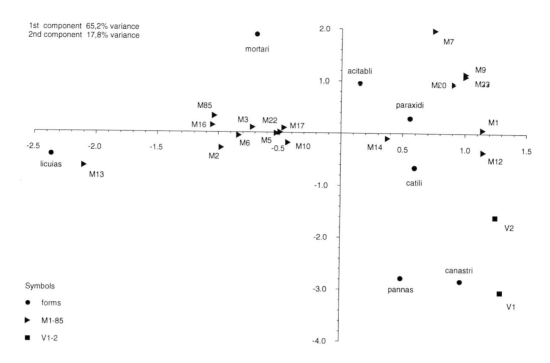

Fig. 4. Result of a correspondence analysis of 19 more or less complete dockets from La Graufesenque and of the seven most frequent types of vessel (cf. Table 3). M1–85: Marichal 1988, nos. 1–85; V1: Vernhet & Bémont 1990–1; V2: Bémont & Vernhet 1992–3.

docket	total	acitabli	canastri	catili	licuias	mortari	pannas	paraxidi
M1	27945	9500	1110	7660			1025	8150
M2	28693	8000	635	5900	8000	328	770	4700
M3	29825	9000	390	5500	7200	225	850	6200
M5	28420	8500	100	7100	6100	405	1000	5000
M6	29110	8500	510	6440	7420	790	850	4600
M7	29915	18050	210	6450		705	1000	3300
M9	23205	9000	790	6150		665	80	6400
M10	30350	9000	710	7170	6200	460	1000	5500
M12	25380	8000	500	7450			1900	7450
M13	27930	7500	380	3500	11900	600	1500	2550
M14	25070	8000	300	6330	2300	490	1700	5850
M16	29855	9000	230	4550	7700	945	1380	4300
M17	29790	9500	540	6450	6000	600	1000	5300
M20	30120	10000		8850	330	1085	865	8500
M22	33845	8500		7165	7450	300	1200	9150
M23	27735	9000		6255	300	280	650	11000
M85	29740	8500		3200	7600	940		6050
V1	19925	3600	1000	7325			2700	2950
V2	26390	5700	1030	8350			2500	6800

Table 3. Survey of the dockets illustrated in fig. 4, with the most frequent types of vessel. M1–85: Marichal 1988, nos. 1–85; V1: Vernhet & Bémont 1990–1; V2: Bémont &Vernhet 1992–3.

The hypotheses presented here barely surpass the level of speculation, and need to be tested by means of a more thorough analysis. At this stage only preliminary inferences may be drawn. The less external evidence there is to support such inferences, the more care must be taken in putting weight upon them.

The least daring conclusion is that many potters at La Graufesenque contracted out the firing of their products. This may also be deduced from the contents of the 'Fosse de Cirratus', a rubbish deposit containing thousands of vessels from the same kiln load, deformed by overheating (*Gallia*, **41** (1983), 478–9). Among the wasters, dated to *c.* AD 40, was a pile of fused cups of forms Ritt. 5 and Drag. 27g with stamps of both Anextlatus and Apronius. Other deposits, such as the 'Fosse de Gallicanus' (*c.* AD 55/60), 'Cluzel 15' (*c.* AD 60/ 65), a deposit cut in 1953–4 (late Flavian) and the one beside

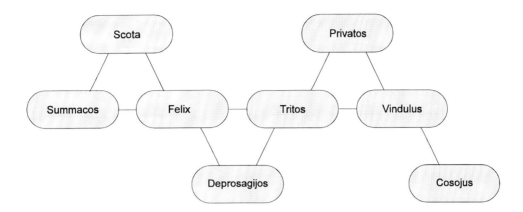

Fig. 5. The relations between eight potters as they occur in the dockets from La Graufesenque.

the 'Grand Four' (*c.* AD 80–120/130) show a similar pattern (*Gallia*, **30** (1972), 475–6; *Gallia*, **32** (1974), 458–9; *Gallia*, **38** (1980), 465; Vernhet 1981; Bémont 1987; Haalebos 1979; Haalebos *et al.* 1991, 82–3).

From the dockets found so far it appears that several potters have turned to more than one kiln operator. In many cases a potter may have switched from one operator to another, without delivering his products to several potters at the same time; Malciu, for example, may have turned to Castus first, and to Germanus only later. But in other cases it is not impossible that a potter simultaneously supplied different kiln operators with his products. Tritos, for example, delivered almost exclusively *licuias, acitabli* and *paraxidi* to Castus, but *catili* to Martialis. The explanation might be that Castus already had a few regular suppliers of *catili*: Felix, Scota and Summacos. And if the Felix mentioned in the dockets is the same man as the Felix named in several stamps, he must have delivered his cups and bowls of form Drag. 29 to other kiln operators than Castus, as he is registered in Castus's dockets only as a supplier of *catili*.

If it is correct that potters who are mentioned together as suppliers of a lot of vessels did join forces in producing them, the variety of links suggests that temporary rather than permanent co-operations were involved. Of the fifteen potters mentioned jointly with another, eight occur in different com-

binations (fig. 5). Since Deprosagijos occurs both with Felix and Tritos it seems unlikely that the potters mentioned together with either Felix or Tritos should be considered as their employees.

Bibliography

Bémont, C., 1987 La fosse Malaval 1 (La Graufesenque). Traitement numérique, *Rei Cretariae Romanae Fautorum Acta*, **25/26**, 331–42

_____, & Vernhet, A., 1992–3 La fournée des nones d'octobre, *Annales de Pegasus*, **2**, 19–21

Greenacre, M. J., 1993 *Correspondence analysis in practice*

Haalebos, J. K., 1979 PRIMVS, CELADVS und SENICIO, *Rei Cretariae Romanae Fautorum Acta*, **19/20**, 121–35

_____, Mees, A. W., & Polak, M., 1991 Über Töpfer und Fabriken verzierter Terra-Sigillata des ersten Jahrhunderts, *Archäologisches Korrespondenzblatt*, **21**, 79–91

Hartley, B. R., & Dickinson, B., 1978 The samian stamps, in Down, A., *Chichester excavations III*, 234–41

Hermet, F., 1934 *La Graufesenque (Condatomago)* (Paris)

Marichal, R., 1988 *Les graffites de la Graufesenque*, Gallia Supplément, **47** (Paris)

Oswald, F., 1931 *Index of potters' stamps on terra sigillata ('samian ware')* (Margidunum)

Oxé, A., 1925 Die Töpferrechnungen von der Graufesenque, *Bonner Jahrbücher*, **130**, 38–99

Vernhet, A., 1981 Un four de la Graufesenque (Aveyron): la cuisson des vases sigillés, *Gallia*, **39**, 25–43

_____, 1991 *La Graufesenque. Céramiques gallo-romaines*

_____, & Bémont, C., 1990–1 Un nouveau compte de potiers de la Graufesenque portant mention de flamines, *Annales de Pegasus* (1993), 53–6

12   Un vase moulé de Montans au décor volontairement effacé

Jean-Louis Tilhard

Cette courte note a pour but de signaler deux tessons d'un même vase de céramique sigillée moulée, original et inédit (apparemment un *hapax*), qui suscite quelques interrogations sur des pratiques ouvrières dans les ateliers de sigillée et sur la commercialisation de certaines productions.

Ces tessons ont été trouvés voice une dizaine d'années par Monsieur J. Cubelier de Beynac sur une parcelle de terrain lui appartenant, au lieu-dit Lécussan, sur la commune de Moirax (Lot-et-Garonne, France) (fig. 1); ils font partie d'un modeste mobilier recueilli en surface, après des travaux agricoles, sur un site gallo-romain,[1] mobilier qui comprenait, outre des fragments de tuiles à rebords bien caractéristiques, quelques tessons de poterie commune et de sigillée (parmi ces derniers, des tessons lisses et quelques décors caractéristiques de Montans, fin 1er/début 2ème siècle ap. J.-C.), qui ne seront pas présentés ici, car ils ne présentent pas d'intérêt céramologique exceptionnel. La prospection de surface n'a pas apporté d'éléments permettant de caractériser le site qui a fourni les tessons; il s'agit d'un établissement rural non défini, situé à proximité de la Garonne, sur une hauteur qui domine une courbe du fleuve, à quelques kilomètres au sud de la ville d'Agen, ancienne capitale de la cité des Nitiobroges.

Monsieur Cubelier de Beynac m'avait soumis ce mobilier peu après sa découverte et j'avais été intrigué par les deux fragments qui sont présentés ici.[2] Avant comme depuis cette date, je n'avais et n'ai rien vu de semblable dans les collections ou les ensembles de céramique sigillée que j'ai pu observer non plus que dans les publications, et il m'a donc paru utile de les porter à la connaissance de la communauté des céramologues[3] par cette notule.

Les deux tessons qui nous occupent (fig. 2) appartiennent tous les deux au même vase hémisphérique de type Drag. 37, à décor moulé, mais ils ne sont pas jointifs. Le vernis en est rouge orangé assez sombre, peu brillant mais bien adhérent; la pâte est beige jaunâtre; l'aspect général du support est bien caractéristique des productions de Montans.[4] Le premier tesson a conservé la majeure partie du bord au-dessus de la frise d'oves dont le séparent quelques sillons peu profonds; c'est une bande lisse, légèrement bombée, terminée par une lèvre arrondie extérieurement dont manque le bord. Le vase présente un sillon interne (à 1,5 cm environ sous le bord de la lèvre) comme c'est fréquemment le cas sur les Drag. 37 de Montans.[5] Le deuxième tesson comprend une petite partie du bord, et sous la même frise d'oves, la majeure partie de la panse, qui devrait correspondre aux deux tiers ou aux trois quarts de la zone décorée; il manque donc seulement la partie inférieure de la vasque et le pied du vase. La très petite portion de circonférence conservée par le bord du premier de ces tessons ne permet pas de restituer avec suffisamment de précision le diamètre du vase; la courbure du reste de la panse paraît correspondre à un petit ou moyen module.

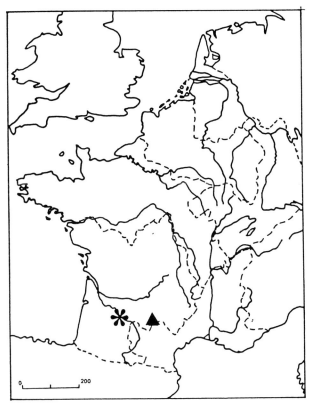

Fig. 1. Carte de localisation approximative de Lécussan (Moirax, Lot-et-Garonne; figuré par un astérisque), par rapport à Montans (Tarn; figuré par un triangle), dans le cadre des provinces gauloises d'époque flavienne.

L'originalité de notre vase réside dans l'absence de décor moulé sous la frise d'oves; ceux-ci sont composés de deux arceaux bordant le cœur et d'un bâtonnet à droite, confondu avec l'arceau extérieur et muni d'un pendentif légèrement renflé et dévié à gauche. Ce type d'oves est bien attesté sur les produits de Montans, en particulier sur les vases signés d'*Attillus*.[6] Sous les oves, la surface lisse de la panse, inhabituelle à cette place, présente une succession de facettes horizontales de quelques millimètres de largeur, qui correspondent aux traces laissées par un outil utilisé pour façonner la surface courbe du vase (ou du moule), et remplacent le décor à relief que l'on s'attendrait à y trouver. La base du vase n'étant pas conservée, il n'est pas possible de dire si toute la surface habituellement décorée était lisse, ou si une zone inférieure décorée en relief réapparaissait sous ces facettes (celà semble toutefois peu probable).

On doit se demander tout d'abord si le moule qui a produit ce vase comportait cette zone lisse (non décorée volon-tairement ou par oubli, ou effacée). Il est cependant difficile d'admettre qu'un moule ne présentant qu'une frise d'oves ait pu être cuit, et utilisé ensuite pour la production de vases. D'autre part, un examen minutieux des tessons permet de penser que l'effacement du décor a eu lieu sur le vase et non sur le moule; en effet, la base du pendentif des oves a été légèrement tronquée par la plus haute des facettes (fig. 2) et il apparaît donc que celles-ci ont été faites après l'impression des oves.

Ceci pourrait cependant correspondre à un moule dont le décor aurait été effacée sous les oves. Mais, sur nos tessons, la frise d'oves est en léger relief, séparée par un ressaut de la surface lisse de la panse, qui se trouve donc en retrait (celà apparaît en coupe, fig. 2, à gauche). Si la zone lisse avait été faite dans le moule sous les oves, en effaçant le reste du décor,

les facettes devaient être plus profondes que la bande portant la frise d'oves, et devraient donc nous apparaître, sur le vase qui a été tiré de ce moule, en relief par rapport aux oves; ce qui n'est pas le cas. En outre les facettes, aux arêtes bien nettes, correspondent mieux à la finition d'une surface convexe (celle du vase), qu'à celle d'une surface concave (celle du moule).

C'est donc sur le vase, après démoulage, et avant cuisson, que le décor a été soigneusement effacé sous les oves; l'extré-mité du pendentif des oves a été touchée lors de cette opéra-tion, qui a laissé la frise d'oves en légère surélévation par rapport au reste de la panse.

Alors que des décors empâtés, parfois à peine discernables, sont fréquents sur les vases moulés de Montans, particu-lièrement sur les productions tardives,[7] il s'agit là d'un cas bien différent, puisque les oves sont très nets, ce qui correspond à une volonté délibérée d'effacer le décor sous les oves, en conservant ceux-ci. Il est probable que toute la partie décorée a subi cette opération (mais on ne peut en être totalement certain en l'absence de la base du décor). Le vase a ensuite été engobé et cuit comme les autres production 'normales'.

Nous sommes maintenant amené à nous interroger sur les raisons qui ont conduit le potier fabricant ou finisseur de ce vase à en effacer le décor. Deux explications peuvent être présentées:

1° – Il est possible qu'un accident au démoulage ou après celui-ci (impression défectueuse du décor ou d'une partie du décor, choc ou accident quelconque ayant endommagé le décor) ait conduit le potier à effacer la zone décorée en reprenant le vase au tour (éventuellement au moment de la finition) avec un outil utilisé habituellement pour le tournassage; cette opé-ration, simple et d'une exécution rapide, transformait le vase décoré défectueux en vaisselle quasi-lisse, et évitait de jeter au rebut un vase qui avait occupé et immobilisé le moule; le potier aurait voulu en quelque sorte ne pas perdre sa produc-tion qui représentait un certain travail, et compléter ainsi eventuellement sa fournée.

On pourra facilement objecter à cette hypothèse que nombre de vases moulés commercialisés présentent des défauts dans le décor (traces diverses, décors mal imprimés, empâtements divers) sans pour autant avoir été lissés de cette manière, et que la perte représentée par la mise au rebut de ce vase était très probablement minime, voire négligeable, par rapport à la fournée en préparation.

2° – L'autre explication envisageable est anecdotique: il s'agirait de la fantaisie 'gratuite' d'un potier, décidant de lisser un décor sans raison particulière; mais c'est une aberration en ce qui concerne la rentabilité de l'opération: ce vase ne pouvait probablement pas s'écouler comme un vase moulé, et son élaboration avait demandé plus de temps qu'un vase lisse.

On peut d'ailleurs dans les deux cas se demander pourquoi le potier n'a pas effacé aussi les oves, sans pouvoir apporter de réponse satisfaisante à cette question. Dans le premier, la frise d'oves n'étant pas affectée par un éventuel accident qui

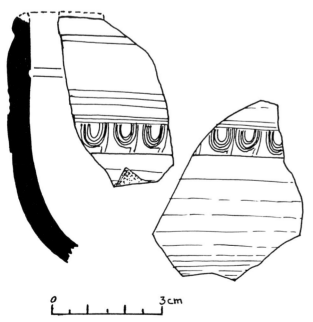

Fig. 2. Deux tessons de Drag. 37 trouvés à Lécussan (Moirax, Lot-et-Garonne). Échelle 1:1.

aurait touché le reste de la panse, le potier aurait voulu la conserver comme élément décoratif (nous n'avons pas trouvé d'élément de comparaison éventuel avec d'autres catégories de vaisselles contemporaines, sauf avec des productions de céramique commune présentant une zone de décor à la roulette sur le haut de la panse). Dans le deuxième cas, on ne peut fournir d'explication autre qu'une nouvelle fantaisie.

Quelles que soient des motivations qui aient amené un ouvrier à lisser ce vase moulé, il est évident que celui-ci a été traité comme une production 'normale', cuit et ensuite commercialisé (c'est à dire sans avoir été éliminé après le défournement, ni ensuite par des marchands éventuels); à Lécussan-Moirax, il se trouve en effet à une distance d'environ une centaine de kilomètres de son lieu de fabrication, dans la zone de grande diffusion des productions de Montans (on sait qu'elle correspond au bassin de la Garonne et à ses marges),[8] et il a apparemment suivi un circuit de distribution jusqu'aux environs d'*Aginnum*/Agen. Mais, il nous est impossible de connaître les conditions dans lesquelles il a été vendu (comme vase lisse, comme vase moulé, comme deuxième ou troisième choix? en admettant qu'il ait bien été vendu, car toute autre hypothèse relevant de l'anecdote est permise), ni ce qui a amené son propriétaire a en faire l'aquisition; il est vrai que notre ignorance dans ce domaine n'est pas moindre pour les autres vases sigillés conformes aux normes.

Quant-à la période à laquelle ce vase a été produit (et diffusé), on ne peut la fixer que d'après des critères céramologiques, puisque le contexte stratigraphique est inconnu. La forme légèrement bombée du bord, assez court et nettement vertical, est une caractéristique des Drag. 37 relativement précoces et disparait au 2ème siècle où les bords deviennent généralement plats, plus larges et plus évasés. Les oves d'*Attillus* sont par ailleurs datables du dernier quart du 1er siècle,[9] et c'est probablement à ce moment (approximativement la période flavienne) qu'il faut situer notre vase.

On voit donc que ce vase fragmentaire pose un certain nombre de questions auxquelles on ne peut apporter de réponses précises, au moins dans l'état actuel de nos connaissances. Illustratif de la fantaisie d'un travailleur d'officine, il s'inscrit en dehors des schémas d'une production strictement organisée et standardisée, qui aurait dû entraîner son élimination avant cuisson ou avant commercialisation. Son caractère d'exception, voire d'aberration, interdit cependant de voir en lui autre chose qu'une simple curiosité anecdotique, sans signification particulière, en marge d'une production contemporaine de grandes séries d'objets standardisés.

Notes

1. Lieu-dit Lécussan, commune de Moirax (Lot-et Garonne), parcelle cadastrale n°33, section B dite de Poncillon, première feuille. Il n'est pas nécessaire ici de donner les coordonnées Lambert du site.
2. Je remercie bien cordialement Monsieur Cubelier de Beynac de m'avoir communiqué ces tessons et autorisé à les étudier.
3. Il est possible que des éléments semblables existent dans des publications dont je n'ai pas connaissance, mais si c'est le cas, ils constituent cependant des raretés, en particulier dans le domaine des sigillées d'Aquitaine.
4. Il ne me paraît pas utile de donner ici les références à un code de couleurs, toujours plus ou moins subjectives, alors que l'attribution des tessons à Montans ne fait pas de doute.
5. Il suffira de signaler quelques exemplaires munis de sillon(s) interne(s) sur le lieu de production: Martin 1986, 65, fig. 7, et 66, fig. 8, n°.10, 12, 13; et sur les lieux de consommation: Tilhard 1977, pls. 8 et 34, n°. 54, avec mêmes oves, et divers autres; Martin *et al.* 1993, 423, figs. 279/A I J, 280/D N R, 281/A B et 282/A O.
6. Martin 1986, fig. 8, n°. 11, 12, 14, 15 (style d'Attillus); Labrousse 1975, 70, Drag. 37 signé ATTILLI dans le décor; Simpson 1976, n°.7, 19, 28; Fouet 1969, 214, figs. 95, n°.98, et 97, n°.1449; Tilhard 1977, n°. 30, 39–40, 54, 55, 60; Martin *et al.* 1993, 423, figs. 278/O, 279/E et 280/A.
7. Dont il n'est pas nécessaire pour notre propos de fournir de références.
8. Marsh 1981, 200–11; Martin 1986, 70, fig. 10.
9. Martin 1986, 66, fig. 8, n°. 11–17; Martin *et al.* 1993, 424, fig. 280 A (datation 80–100).

Bibliographie

Fouet, G., 1969 *La villa gallo-romaine de Montmaurin*, Supplément à Gallia, **20**
Labrousse, M., 1975 Céramiques et potiers de Montans, *Les Dossiers d'Archéologie*, **9**, 59–70
Marsh, G., 1981 London's samian supply and its relationship to the development of the Gallic samian industry, dans Anderson, A. C., et Anderson, A. S., *Roman pottery research in Britain and north-west Europe*, Brit. Archaeol. Rep. Int. Ser., **123.1**, 173–238
Martin, T., 1986 Montans, dans Bémont, C., et Jacob, J. P., *La terre sigillée gallo-romaine*, Documents d'Archéologie Française, **6**, 58–71
————, Rousse, D., & Vernhet, A., 1993 Les céramiques sigillées de la collection Fité de Hoste, dans Cauuet, B., Domergue, C., *et al.*, *Un centre sidérurgique de la Montagne Noire, le domaine des Forges (les Martys, Aude)*, Supplément à Revue Archéologique de Narbonnaise, **27**
Simpson, G., 1976 Decorated terra sigillata at Montans (Tarn) from the manuscript of Elie Rossignol at Albi, *Britannia*, **7**, 244–73
Tilhard, J-L., 1977 *La céramique sigillée du Musée de Saintes, II: les vases à décor moulé*

13   Lezoux – La Graufesenque et la Romanisation

Hugues Vertet

Brian Hartley a fouillé à Lezoux avec moi pendant plusieurs années (Hartley & Vertet 1968), et nous nous sommes tous deux beaucoup intéressés à la Graufesenque. Aussi suis-je heureux de participer aux hommages rendus à ce grand archéologue avec qui j'ai eu, et j'espère avoir encore, le plaisir de travailler. De là voudrais-je signaler ici que s'ouvre un champ de recherches nouveau et plus vaste à partir de toutes les découvertes et de toutes les études qui ont été réalisées sur ces deux grands centres gaulois de production de céramique (Bet & Vernhet 1994; Vertet 1994).

Lezoux et la Graufesenque[1] sont comme les enfants de la même famille italienne.[2] Il y a beaucoup de ressemblances mais ils ne sont pas jumeaux. Leur croissance et leur vie sont différentes. Ils se sont développés dans la même province administrative: l'Aquitaine, mais l'un au sud et l'autre au nord. Ils n'ont pas eu les mêmes structures de production, leur histoire ne concorde pas, leurs produits et leurs sigillées, au premier abord analogues, ne se superposent que rarement et par épisodes.

Comparer deux milieux éloignés où se fabriquaient en masse des objets analogues, de peu de valeur, nous permettrait, me semble-t-il, d'examiner à quel critère correspondait une demande d'objets nouveaux qui se développe dans les régions conquises de l'occident romain et, de là, d'entrer plus avant dans le processus de romanisation du petit peuple de la Gaule.

LEZOUX

Située à 30 kilomètres de la capitale des Arvernes, cette fabrique est au centre de la Gaule, au bord de la vaste plaine alluviale de l'Allier qui coule vers le nord. Elle s'est implantée dans une région sans très grandes villas, semble-t-il. Un réseau de voies terrestres faciles et variées la met en relation avec Clermont-Ferrand et Lyon, autant qu'avec le Massif Central et avec le sud et le nord de la Gaule. La rivière, flottable, sert aussi à écouler ses productions vers l'Atlantique autant que vers le nord, avec une rupture de charge vers Nevers.

Au début du premier siècle, dès l'époque de Tibère, Lezoux produit des assiettes, des tasses, qui sont des copies de vaisselle italique. On y fabrique aussi des calices (Dr. 11). Certains décors représentent des scènes de chasse. Les poinçons sont surmoulés sur ceux des vases de Marcus Perennius, potier d'Arezzo, et leur arrangement est identique. A cette influence italique directe s'ajoutent des gobelets de type Aco, à surface rouge, rarement revêtus de glaçure plombifère. Leurs modèles viennent de Lyon ou de la vallée du Rhône mais ils n'en ont pas la finesse (Lasfargues et al. 1960; 1967). Des vases carénés (Dr. 29) sont inspirés de la Graufesenque, mais avec un pied original (Bet & Montineri 1989; Vertet 1967a). De curieux vases en anneaux surmontés de sangliers trouvent leurs modèles seulement au Proche-Orient. On y trouve aussi d'autres produits inspirés de la tradition locale, comme la 'Terra Nigra' ou des vaisselles italiques comme des cruches à engobe rouge ou blanc. Ainsi sommes-nous 50 ans après la conquête dans un carrefour d'influences remarquables (Vertet 1971a; 1971b). Les productions avaient pu se diffuser jusqu'en Grande-Bretagne, en Germanie (Vertet 1968), en Suisse, etc. Tous ces facteurs laisseraient supposer une extension rapide notamment de la sigillée dont la demande est si forte alors.

Mais celle-ci ne continue pas sur ce bel élan. Les Arvernes avaient adopté la pratique du moule et du tour rapide, mais non les argiles calcaires (Picon & Vertet 1970) ni la vitrification de l'engobe qui paraissent avoir produit le succès de la Graufesenque. On peut s'en étonner puisque ces connaissances existaient dans les ateliers de Lyon, par exemple dans les ateliers de la Muette, et que les relations de Lezoux avec la métropole des Gaules semblent avoir été suivies.

En fait, la fabrication de la sigillée diminue et se réduit chez les Arvernes. On imite à partir des années 30 ou 40 et de façon maladroite les vases de la Graufesenque qui poursuit un très fort développement. Les poinçons-matrices tibériens ont disparu. Ils sont peu nombreux, les décors répétitifs, ce dont Titos est un témoin (Piboule et al. 1981). Les vaisselles lisses sont rarement estampillées. Cette décadence tient-elle seulement à une cause technique? D'autres facteurs encore inconnus sont-ils en cause? Il y aurait lieu ici à des recherches.

A la fin du 1er et au début du 2e siècle, la situation se renverse. Lezoux connaît un renouveau autant dans les décors que dans les techniques, avec des potiers comme Libertus et Butrio. Le vernis vitrifié et les pâtes calcaires apparaissent. La

Graufesenque cède sa place de tête. Pendant tout le 2e et le début du 3e siècle, Lezoux devient la fabrique la plus importante de la Gaule. Au 3e et au 4e siècle la production de sigillée existe encore mais sa diffusion est mal connue pour le moment (Picon *et al.* 1969–70).

Dans le centre de la Gaule, sur le plan de la terre sigillée, Lezoux garde toujours la place de tête. La qualité des argiles, des engobes, des techniques, la variété des décors, la standardisation des formes sont toujours remarquables. Ses moules, ses poinçons-matrices et les modèles de ses formes lisses et moulées se diffusent dans la région. Cela crée un style particulier de sigillée qui semble un label d'exportation. On l'a retrouvé dès Tibère dans l'atelier de Coulanges à 100 km à vol d'oiseau (Vertet 1965) et à partir de Trajan dans toutes les fabriques. De là, les créations régionales de moindre qualité ne se vendent guère au loin. Ajoutons que la durée de la fabrication de la sigillée dépasse à Lezoux celle de tous les autres centres de la région.

Des ateliers périphériques fort actifs se sont développés dans la même région que Lezoux (Vertet 1980a). Ils parsèment le bassin de l'Allier et débordent sur celui de la Loire chez les Eduens. Cet environnement dynamique est spécifique car il s'y trouve une vie autonome et des productions originales sur plusieurs plans. Il serait important d'en développer l'étude; en voici les principaux exemples connus:

— Saint-Rémy-en-Rollat a donné des copies en terre blanche de calices, imités de l'orfèvrerie et des vases à glaçure plombifère, puis semble s'orienter vers la sigillée et les figurines.
— Vichy a réussi la meilleure qualité de glaçures et les ateliers de la gare se sont augmentés d'ateliers situés de l'autre côté de l'Allier au 2e siècle.
— Saint-Bonnet-Yzeure a perfectionné pendant le 1er siècle la fabrication de céramiques indigènes, a fourni quelques gobelets de type Aco à glaçure et produit des statuettes très originales, comme de grands bustes féminins portant des torques à tête de serpent (de Vigan *et al.* 1980).
— Toulon-sur-Allier a créé au 2e siècle et peut-être jusqu'au 3e, un type de sigillée influencé par les traditions indigènes et avec Saint-Pourçain-sur-Besbre, des figurines en terre blanche que Lezoux ne produit que rarement et en quelques exemplaires.
— Coulanges se spécialise au 2e siècle dans les jattes en terre blanche souvent estampillées sur le rebord, après avoir produit des sigillées, puis de la vaisselle commune de bonne qualité.
— Les Martres-de-Veyre ont produit beaucoup de sigillée avec des moules de Lezoux. Ajoutons que parmi les spécificités de ces différents ateliers, les reliefs d'applique à surface noire ou à glaçure rouge paraissent différents à Vichy et à Lezoux. Dans ce dernier centre, des techniques comme le moulage au plâtre apparaissent puis disparaissent rapidement sans se diffuser ailleurs (Vertet 1969). Toutes ces fabriques ne sont certes pas étudiées et elles peuvent réserver des surprises. Même si elles ont des relations

d'échange, elles ne sont point superposables dans leurs installations, leurs évolutions, leurs productions.

Le dynamisme de cette économie potière se marque par l'adaptation aux événements. Pendant la période de récession de la sigillée du 1er siècle, les ateliers arvernes développent d'autres productions. Elles mettent sur un vaste marché de la belle céramique commune, des statuettes en terre cuite, des vases et figurines à glaçure plombifère, à surface micacée, des parois fines, etc. Au moment où la production de sigillée redevient florissante, une restructuration se produit, marquée par d'importants changements en bien des domaines. Une standardisation des formes lisses et moulées s'installe. Les vases à glaçure plombifère disparaissent, les lampes, apparaissent puis se réduisent à quelques exemplaires. Adaptation à une production plus efficace? à un marché autre? à un goût qui a évolué?

LA GRAUFESENQUE

Cette fabrique est située au bord sud de la province d'Aquitaine, dans l'espace ouvert par le confluent du Tarn et de la Dourbie, au pied des plateaux des Causses. Les voies de communication sont plus rares qu'autour de Lezoux. Le Tarn est moins porteur de marchandises que l'Allier. Les vallées sont encaissées. Les Cévennes constituaient un obstacle vers l'est. Les routes permettent d'aller, à 60 km à Rodez, chef-lieu des Rutènes. Le Causse du Larzac est un passage privilégié vers le sud. Les relations sont malcommodes avec Lyon, mais faciles avec Arles, Fos, Nîmes et Narbonne, la 'Rome française', distante de 200 km. Ces obstacles n'empêchent pas une commercialisation très active.

Les premières productions, imitations assez grossières des céramiques campaniennes et arétines précoces, datent des deux dernières décennies avant notre ère et semblent précéder celles de Lezoux. Lorsque la production des céramiques sigillées se développe, surtant entre 20 et 120 de notre ère, elle réduit considérablement la production locale des céramiques non-sigillées, qui reprendra après 120, avec des pâtes orangées ou craquelées bleutées.[3]

L'histoire de la Graufesenque est plus linéaire que celle de Lezoux. Les vases à glaçure rouge demeurent ici la production principale, sans les aléas qui caractérisent les fabriques arvernes. Les ateliers périphériques ne sont que six ou sept, alors que 30 ont déjà été reconnus autour de Lezoux. Ils apparaissent plus comme des succursales que comme des ateliers originaux. Leurs produits sont souvent indiscernables de ceux de la maison-mère. Ainsi, au Rozier, sur vingt potiers, dix-neuf sont communs à Millau.

Les structures d'habitations, de temples, découvertes à La Graufesenque nous donnent l'idée d'une organisation inconnue encore à Lezoux. Tout a-t-il été détruit par les installations mérovingiennes ou médiévales? Les constructions en torchis ont-elles fondu dans le climat pluvieux? N'ont-elles jamais existé? Rien ne décèle, jusqu'à présent, chez les Arvernes, une agglomération analogue à celle trouvée dans les ateliers rutènes. Les célèbres graffiti de la Graufesenque témoignent de personnages, de location d'esclaves, d'une comptabilité serrée (Marichal 1988). A-t-elle existé en Auvergne? Sous quelle forme? Seuls deux ou trois petits tessons portent des traces de chiffres. A-t-elle été portée sur des documents périssables comme le bois? Nous ne le savons pas encore.

Les milieux socio-économiques qui entourent ces fabriques seront aussi à comparer. La façon dont elles se sont insérées dans leur contexte pourrait expliquer une partie de leurs différences. Ont-elles été parachutées dans les campagnes gauloises? Des ateliers urbains comme celui de la Muette à Lyon (Lasfargues *et al.* 1986), ceux de Rodez ou de Clermont-Ferrand ont-ils été des étapes intermédiares? Des vestiges de potiers précédents, datés de l'indépendance existent-ils près des producteurs de sigillée? Un seul four de la Tène a été découvert à Lezoux jusqu'à maintenant, et aucun dans les installations périphériques arvernes. Dans le centre de la Gaule, plusieurs fabriques paraissent nées 'ex-nihilo', sur le trajet de routes ou de rivières. Les choix qui ont présidé à leur implantation ne tiennent peut-être point seulement à la qualité des argiles. De riches Gaulois ou de riches Romains seraient-ils intervenus dans la création de certains ateliers du début de notre ère? Une liste alphabétique d'ouvriers trouvée à Yzeure pourrait indiquer que dès le début de l'installation, une gestion à la romaine y fut appliquée.[4]

Contexte General

L'attrait méditerranéen

L'étude de ces deux centres ne peut se faire sans examiner toutes leurs productions et sans les inclure dans le contexte général de la Gaule et de l'Empire romain qui imprégnait même les pauvres gens. Le processus qui a amené en Gaule les influences grecques et romaines avait débuté bien avant la conquête. Les monnayages, les importations d'objets divers, l'architecture des villes, etc., en sont des preuves. Les récentes fouilles de Bibracte soulignent par exemple combien la Gaule était tournée vers Rome avant l'arrivée de ses soldats (Goudineau & Peyre 1993).

Ce mouvement a été accéléré quand les Romains s'y sont installés et s'est poursuivi pendant des siècles. Mais c'est de façon inégale qu'il a touché les régions, les milieux, et, dans ces milieux, les individus, et à l'intèrieur des individus, des zones diverses de leur esprit. Nous devons inscrire Lezoux et la Graufesenque dans ce processus complexe, commencé bien avant leur fondation. Ils sont deux témoins privilégiés de l'influence méditerranéenne sur le peuple pour trois raisons au moins: par la masse de documents qu'ils apportent, parce qu'ils s'inscrivent dans des lieux précis et sur de longues périodes bien datées, et parce qu'ils impliquent des fabricants et des consommateurs populaires dans un feed-back constant.

On doit rappeler aussi que sur bien des points, la Gaule, l'Italie et d'autres régions de l'Empire romain se trouvaient au moment de la conquête à un niveau de technicité analogue. Il n'y avait pas les hiatus énormes que nous rencontrons dans les rapports modernes entre pays développés et pays du Tiers-Monde. Les Romains pouvaient apprendre des Gaulois des méthodes de tonnellerie, d'émaillage, de charcuterie, par exemple, et leur apporter des perfectionnements dans le tour, le moulage, les modèles, le vernis, l'utilisation d'argile et la cuisson. Ils apportaient des techniques plus performantes, mais aussi une rationalisation de la production, un savoir de gestion, le tout à un niveau d'intégration possible. Cet état de choses permettait d'installer rapidement des fabriques avec des ouvriers locaux attentifs, ingénieux et performants.

Ont-ils utilisé les potiers en activité? Ce n'est pas sûr. De tels artisans sont connus comme traditionalistes et leur capacité de renouvellement est minime. Il se peut que la main d'oeuvre des nouveaux ateliers ne le sait pas intégrés. Ils ont probablement continué leur production traditionnelle fort utile. On la retrouve, évoluant plus ou moins vite, pendant que la sigillée prenait un essor rapide.

Les estampilles nous apportent des listes de noms latins: Primus, Secondus, ou romanisés: Illiomarus, Sacrillos, qui marquent un recrutement indigène. Capables de productions nouvelles, ce personnel tenait à conformer les produits aux besoins d'une clientèle qui avait la même culture et le même niveau de vie que lui (Vertet 1974). Elle était largement touchée par les colporteurs et les marchés grâce au développement des routes et des transports et le choix des clients influençait la production. Par exemple, tous les moules de statuettes existaient dans les ateliers, mais l'archéologie montre que les sujets qui se vendaient bien étaient fabriqués en bien plus grand nombre que les autres (Rabeisen & Vertet 1986, introduction).

Les images

Ainsi se créa rapidement une mode gallo-romaine dans les produits céramiques. Mais il est toujours important de ne pas se contenter de dire: 'C'était une mode!' mais de se demander 'Pourquoi et comment cette mode s'est-elle répandue dans un milieu populaire à ce moment, à cette époque? Pourquoi a-t-elle disparu au 3e ou 4e siécle dans l'Occident méditerranéen?' Les raisons populaires sont souvent plus complexes que celles des couches aisées, dont nous saisissons mieux l'engouement intéressé pour une Gaule romaine qui pouvait les enrichir.

L'enthousiasme des Gaulois pour la sigillée, ses formes et ses décors, pour les statuettes, les *oscilla*, les lampes, pose question. Sur quoi reposait l'attrait de la nouveauté, à quels besoins et à quels désirs symboliques correspondaient ces objets peu utiles dans la vie pratique (Vertet 1986b; Demarolle 1986)? C'est une production de demi-luxe qui conquiert le marché, comme cela se produisit avec l'huile, le vin, les fruits dans la production agricoles (Colloque de Pisa, 1981).

Cette avalanche d'images véhiculées par la céramique attire l'attention. Elles viennent de la culture méditerranéenne et sont multipliées en quantitié énorme par des potiers Rutènes et Arvernes, de façon légèrement différente. Voici quelques questions, observations et suggestions sur lesquelles il serait possible, je pense, d'engager des recherches:

A   Pourquoi trouvons nous plus de vases décorés sur la sigillée gauloise que sur celle d'Italie, alors que les sujets représentés n'appartiennent pas à la tradition indigène gauloise? Pourquoi les potiers ont-ils choisi certains sujets et non d'autres dans le vaste répertoire que diffusait la bimbeloterie commerciale italique? Quel sens et quelle valeur attribuaient les Gaulois des campagnes aux personnages mythologiques, représentés sur les objets qu'ils achetaient? En connaissaient-ils les pouvoirs et les aventures et comment? Pourquoi les figurines, dont le rôle essentiel est d'être des images, se répandent-elles si rapidement non seulement en Gaule, mais en Grande Bretagne, en Suisse, en Germanie? Pourquoi les sujets les plus répandus ne correspondent-ils point aux images de pierre et de bronze les plus fréquentes (Vertet 1985b)?

B   Au début du 1er siècle, la Graufesenque et Lezoux ont quelques poinçons matrices identiques, dont actuellement on recherche le parcours. Puis, ni le répertoire décoratif, ni le style des deux grandes fabriques ne deviennent superposables. Continuer à comparer avec minutie tous les sujets des deux ateliers serait sans doute fructueux pour notre propos.

C   On notera que dans leurs deux productions, il est rare que le décor soit narratif comme dans l'art grec ou romain. Il tient de l'art indigène qui aime surtout meubler harmonieusement des surfaces. Plus précisément, un style répétitif et stylisé réapparaît sur la sigillée dans les périodes de récession, en fin de production, ou même au milieu du 2e siècle. Ainsi, à Toulon-sur-Allier certains potiers s'éloignent-ils du style installé par Lezoux, par une émergence de l'art des campagnes.[5] Un art populaire restait donc vivant pendant la Gaule romaine, au milieu de styles plus directement inspirés par l'art d'Italie, et ce sont les potiers qui nous en ont laissé des traces.

D   Les répertoires des sujets représentés sur la sigillée, les reliefs d'applique, les lampes, les *oscilla*, les figurines... sont différents. Ils sont certes souvent surmoulés sur des motifs importés, mais on remarquera que quelques uns comme Marsyas ou Achille, passent d'un relief de gourde à la sigillée, d'autres, de la sigillée aux lampes. Dans ces fabrications en grande série, les exceptions deviennent significatives.

E   Les retouches minimes sur les poinçons-matrices, sur les lampes, sur les statuettes sont loin d'être indifférentes. Ainsi, dans le répertoire d'un décorateur de sigillée, le même personnage apparaît avec trois attributs différents, ailleurs, un cocher devient un Admète, sur des séries de figurines, les serpents du caducée de Mercure sortent de terre et s'enroulent autour d'un autel,[6] une draperie devient une eau qui coule (Vertet 1990b), une nourrice change de tête (Vertet 1980b) ou bien porte tantôt un tantôt deux bébés (Vertet 1989b), etc.

F   La fréquence des sujets selon les répertoires sera une source de comparaison utile. Elle nous renvoie à des aspects plus larges de la politique impériale. Rome avait fait de la religion un lien de l'Empire. L'empereur était divinisé, et tous les dieux de la Gaule étaient devenus des distributeurs des largesses de Rome, comme le souligne P. M. Duval. Mais cette stratégie habile avait tendance à transférer au politique les pulsions religieuses. Les monnaies avec leurs devises et les visages impériaux, les sculptures et les peintures, les temples, les capitoles, le travail d'intégration des cultes de tradition celtique, correspondait plus à une stratégie qu'à l'expression spontanée des peurs et des protections divines. Le sentiment populaire reste trop éloigné semble-t-il de cette problématique pour s'en satisfaire. Il conserve ses divinités protectrices traditionnelles. Un désir certain d'images se fait jour à cette époque. Lorsque par une heureuse coïncidence, les images proposées correspondent aux besoins, comme la jeune fille nue et la nourrice, elles sont adoptées au niveau des ateliers céramiques. Leur succès rend ces deux figurines les plus souvent moulées et les mieux vendues, avec un succès qu'elles ne rencontrent pas dans les matérieux onéreux comme la pierre ou le bronze. Elles représentent, pense-t-on, une permanence des dévotions à l'eau et à la Terre-mère, proches des besoins immédiats des pètites gens (Vertet 1974).

Ce sont des formes importées détournées de leur sens initial qui coexistent dans la piété populaire avec les divinités éblouissantes de la Rome Eternelle. De la même façon, les images à double ou triple sens coexistent très bien à la même époque, comme le berger qui ramène sa brebis fait partie des bergeries augustéennes, il représente le fidèle apportant son offrande à Jupiter Dolichénus, et le Christ ramenant la brebis perdue pour les premiers chrétiens.

Ces approches diverses nous montrent que les potiers de la Graufesenque et de Lezoux portent témoignage d'un double aspect que présente le peuple gaulois conquis par Rome. Ils adoptent certes les images des dieux des vainqueurs, mais, en même temps ils dévoilent la persistance des croyances populaires traditionnelles en pleine évolution. Elles apparaissent sous une forme nouvelle qui comporte l'introduction de l'image. C'est un phénomène culturel notable.

Nous avons donc à démêler ce qui est de l'admiration, de la tentation, de l'appropriation, de la transformation des sujets par les artisans. Ils choisissent des sujets signifiants. Ils expriment l'émergence des besoins auxquels le peuple désire donner un langage de formes qui garde sa mémoire. L'invisible devient visible[7] et prend allure humaine et commerciale en argile. Ce processus évolue dans le milieu artisanal et dans sa clientèle. La créativité se manifeste dans l'usage complexe de ces images mais nous ne le saisissons pas, ou à peine (Vertet 1967b; 1988).

CONCLUSION

De très nombreux travaux ont étudié et continuent d'étudier la romanisation à partir du développement urbain, du tracé des routes, de la construction des temples, des grandes villas, réalisés sur des impulsions du pouvoir politique ou par des gens aisés. De là, on a déduit la situation des pauvres gens. Serait-il possible, plus qu'on ne l'a fait, de prendre la question par l'autre extrémité et d'analyser les réactions des artisans et des consommateurs de biens peu onéreux, en remontant vers le pouvoir? (Drinkwater 1990; Drinkwater & Vertet 1992).

La comparaison entre les ateliers de la Graufesenque et de Lezoux pourrait nous aider dans cette approche difficile. Mais elle ne devrait pas porter sur les productions seules, mais sur tout ce que nous savons des environnements différents, des influences diverses, des techniques, des formes et des images, et aussi sur ce qui a été accepté, développé, transformé ou refusé des apports étrangers. Elle nous introduirait dans la diversité de la romanisation au niveau du quotidien.

Le sujet est notable. Ce sont deux centres de production d'objets qui concernent les principaux aspects de la vie: la cuisine et la consommation, l'éclairage et la religion, le décor de la maison et la tombe, etc. Au sud et au nord du Massif central, ils répondent à un besoin analogue dans une période de mutation de civilisation. Pour avancer dans ce programme, il nous faut certes encore de nombreux travaux d'archéologie et d'analyse. Mais ne serait-il pas utile d'essayer de réunir des spécialistes divers, c'est à dire tous ceux qui pourraient observer les facettes différentes de ce fait de société remarquable?[8]

Car est intervenue ici un chaîne compliquée d'acteurs où les hommes, les cultures, les contraintes géographiques jouent leur part. C'est sur ce vaste projet que je voudrais attirer l'attention de tous nos collègues; et je suis heureux de le signaler dans les *Mélanges* offerts à notre ami Brian Hartley, dont les intérêts historiques et archéologiques sont si largement ouverts.

Notes

1. Une nombreuse bibliographie existe sur ces deux fabriques. On en trouve une bonne partie dans Bémont & Jacob 1986. Sur la Graufesenque, on consultera les derniers travaux de A. Vernhet et son bilan des ateliers du Sud de la Gaule (Vernhet 1986); sur Lezoux, Vertet 1985a; 1986a; 1989a.
2. Déchelette 1904 l'avait déja souligné. Les fouilles et les études l'ont confirmé largement: Vertet 1962a; 1963.
3. M. Vernhet a eu la grande amabilité de nous confirmer et de développer oralement son excellent article paru dans les D.A.F. sur les ateliers du Sud de la Gaule (Vernhet 1986).
4. C'est l'opinion du professeur Robert Marichal; Vertet 1990a.
5. On notera le même processus sur des gobelets d'Aco de la vallée du Pô.
6. Vertet 1962b. Un phénomène analogue est signalé par Benabou 1976.
7. On peut rapprocher ce phénomène, certes avec prudence, de ce que dit Vernant (1982).
8. Pour aborder un fait social aussi complexe, des géographes, historiens, éthnologues, psycho-sociologues, spécialistes d'onomastique et de langue gauloise autant que de l'histoire de l'art et des statistiques, etc. seraient certainement bien utiles.

Bibliographie

Bémont, C., & Jacob, J-P. (eds), 1986 *La terre sigillée gallo-romaine. Lieux de production du Haut Empire: implantations, produits, relations*, Documents Archéol. Française, **6**

Benabou, M., 1976 *La résistance africaine à la romanisation* (Maspéro)

Bet, P., Delage, R., & Vernhet, A., 1994 Lezoux et Millau, confrontation d'idées et de données, in SFECAG 1994, 43–62

————, & Montineri, D., 1989 La sigillée moulée tibério-claudienne du site de la ZAC de l'enclos de Lezoux, in SFECAG 1989, 55–69

Colloque de Pisa, 1981 *Società romana e produzione schiavistica*, Actes du Colloque de Pisa, 1979 (3 vols., Bari)

Déchelette, J., 1904 *Les vases céramiques ornés de la Gaule romaine* (Paris)

Demarolle, J., 1986 Céramique et religion en Gaule romaine, in Haase, W., & Temporini, H. (eds), *Aufstieg und Niedergang der römischen Welt*, **2** (Berlin)

Drinkwater, J., 1990 For better or worse? Towards an assessment of the economic and social consequences of the Roman conquest of Gaul, in Blagg, T.F.C., & Millett, M. (eds), *The early Roman Empire in the west*, 210–19 (Oxford)

————, & Vertet, H., 1992 'Opportunity' or 'opposition' in Roman Gaul?, in Wood, M., & Queiroga, F. (eds), *Current research on the Romanization of the western provinces*, Tempus reparatum/BAR Internat. Ser., **575**, 25–8 (Oxford)

de Vigan, C., Connier, Y., & Vertet, H., 1980 Quatre séries de figurines – bustes, paons, coqs, édicules – découvertes dans l'atelier de Saint Bonnet, Yzeure, *Recherches sur les ateliers de potiers de la Gaule Centrale*, **1**, 231–57 (Éditions Sites, Le Blanc Mesnil)

Goudineau, C., & Peyre, C., 1993 *Bibracte et les Eduens*, Collection 'Les hauts lieux de l'histoire'

Hartley, B., & Vertet, H., 1968 Fouilles de Lezoux 1967 – le chantier Audouart, *Rev. Archéol. Centre*, **7**

Lasfargues, A., Lasfargues, J., & Vertet, H., 1960 Observations sur les gobelets d'Aco de l'atelier de la Muette (Lyon), *Rev. Archéol. Centre*, **1**, 35–44

————, ————, & ————, 1967 Les frises supérieures des gobelets lyonnais de type Aco, *Rev. Archéol. Est*, **18**, 198–203

————, ————, & ————, 1986 L'atelier de potiers augustéens à Lyon: la fouille de sauvetage de 1976, *Notes d'Epigraphie et d'Archéologie Lyonnaises*, 61–80

Marichal, R., 1988 *Les graffites de la Graufesenque*, Gallia Suppl., **47** (Paris)

Piboule, A., Senechal, R., & Vertet, H., 1981 *Les potiers de Lezoux de 1er. siècle: Titos* (Éditions Sites, Le Blanc Mesnil)

Picon, M., Meille, E., & Vertet, H., 1969–70 Quelques observations techniques sur les sigillées de 4. siècle à Lezoux, *Rei Cretariae Romanae Fautorum Acta*, **12–13**, 125–9

————, & Vertet, H., 1970 La composition des premières sigillées de Lezoux et le problème des céramiques calcaires, *Rev. Archéol. Est*, **21**, 207–18

Rabeisen, E., & Vertet, H., 1986 *Les figurines gallo-romaines en terre cuite d'Alésia*, Centre de Recherches sur les Techniques gallo-romaines (Dijon)

SFECAG 1989 Société Française de l'Étude de Céramique Antique en Gaule, *Actes du Congrès de Lezoux, 1989* (Marseille)

————, 1994 Société Française de l'Étude de Céramique Antique en Gaule, *Actes du Congrès de Millau, 1994* (Marseille)

Vernant, J.P., 1982 Les problèmes de l'image dans la Grèce ancienne, Colloque 'De la figuration des dieux aux catégories de l'image', *Recherches et Documents du Centre Thomas More*

Vernhet, A., 1986 *passim*, in Les ateliers du sud de la France, in Bémont & Jacob 1986, 31–120

Vertet, H., 1962a Les vases caliciformes gallo-romaines de Roanne et la chronologie de la terre sigillée de Lezoux au début du 1er siècle, *Gallia*, **20**, 350–80

————, 1962b Remarques sur l'aspect et les attributs du Mercure gallo-romain populaire dans le centre de la Gaule, Mélanges offerts à Albert Grenier, 3, *Collection Latomus*, **58**, 332–47 (Bruxelles)

————, 1963 Influence des céramiques arétines sur les céramiques du centre de la Gaule au début du 1er siècle, *Bull. Soc. Nationale Antiq. France*, 88–90

————, 1965 Vases sigillés moulés du 1. siècle, *Congrès National des Sociétés des Savantes, Clermont Ferrand*, 105–19

————, 1967a Céramique sigillée tibérienne à Lezoux, *Rev. Archéol.*, **1**, 255–93

————, 1967b Pendentif en terre sigillée trouvé à Lezoux, un nouveau Jupiter à l'anguipède?, *Rev. Archéol. Centre*, **6**, 305–10

————, 1968 Vase caliciforme de Lezoux à Trèves, *Rev. Archéol. Est*, **19**, 267–74

————, 1969 Observations sur les vases à médaillons d'applique de la vallée du Rhône, *Gallia*, **27**, 93–133

————, 1971a Remarques sur les rapports entre les ateliers céramiques de Lezoux, de la vallée de l'Allier, de la Graufesenque et ceux de Lyon, *Acta Rei Cretariae Romanae Fautorum*, **13**, 92–111

————, 1971b Remarques sur les rapports entre les ateliers céramiques de Lezoux, de la vallée de l'Allier, de la Graufesenque et ceux de Lyon, *Actes du Congrès National des Sociétés Savantes, Toulouse*, 191–210

————, 1974 Pauvres potiers, pauvre misère, *Dossiers Archéol.*, **6**, 85–9

_____, 1980a Carte des ateliers de potiers de la Gaule Centrale, *Recherches sur les ateliers de potiers de la Gaule Centrale*, **1**, 13–41 (Éditions Sites, Le Blanc Mesnil)

_____, 1980b Bricolage et changement de tête sur quelques statuettes en argile gallo-romaines, *Recherches sur les ateliers de potiers de la Gaule centrale*, **1**, 179–230 (Éditions Sites, Le Blanc Mesnil)

_____, 1985a Recherches sur les potiers de la Gaule centrale, *Mélanges offerts à Pierre-François Fournier*, 15–37

_____, 1985b Religion populaire et rapport au pouvoir d'après les statuettes d'argile arvernes sous l'Empire romain, *Archéologie et rapports sociaux en Gaule. Table Ronde du Centre Nationale de la Recherche Scientifique* (1984), 72–122 (Paris)

_____, 1986a *passim*, in Les ateliers du centre de la France, in Bémont & Jacob 1986, 121–72

_____, 1986b Recherches sur les traumatismes historiques créés par la conquête de la Gaule et la romanisation, *Colloque Archéologie et Médecine,* *7 Rencontres Internationales d'Archéologie et d'Histoire, Antibes, Octobre 1986*, 319–39

_____, 1988 Recherches sur le sens des figurines en terre blanche gallo-romaines, *Actes du Colloque 'Le monde des images en Gaule et dans les provinces voisines'*, 229–41 (Éditions Errance)

_____, 1989a Recherches sur les ateliers de potiers de la Gaule Centrale, résultats, problèmes, projets, in SFECAG 1989, 11–19

_____, 1989b Observations sur les figurines de nourrices en argile gallo-romaines fabriquées dans les ateliers de potiers du centre de la Gaule, à la lumière des découvertes récentes, 169–76 (Saint Dié des Vosges)

_____, 1990a Observations sur la sociologie et l'économie des ateliers de potiers gallo-romains de la Gaule Centrale, *Bull. Soc. Nationale Antiq. de France*, 127–36

_____, 1990b La draperie des Vénus en terre blanche des ateliers arvernes au 2. siècle, *Mélanges Pierre Lévêque, 4: Religion*, 405–17 (1990-)

_____, 1994 Observations, in SFECAG 1994, 61–2, 171–2

14   A collection of samian from the legionary works-depot at Holt

Margaret Ward

The works-depot of Legio XX Valeria Victrix at Holt, Clwyd, lies 7½ miles south of the legionary fortress of Chester. The depot has been discussed by Grimes 1930 (hereafter Grimes), Thompson 1965, Petch 1969 and Carrington 1994, and its tile and pottery production have been considered by Greene 1977, McWhirr 1979, Stephens 1984, Swan 1984 and 1992, and Jones 1994. Part of the site, which covers 20 acres (8 ha), still reveals a spread of Roman tile and brick lying on the surface. During a recent brief visit to Hilly Field east of Old Chester Lane (SJ 406 545; fig. 1), the writer picked up a tegula stamped LE[...] retrograde (Grimes, fig. 59, type 29), a chip of Grimes' ansate type 18, a pierced revetment tile (Grimes, 135, no. 4) and overfired brick *c.* 2½" (6.5cm) thick. Along with numerous tile fragments, these were recovered from the area east and southeast of the 'Barracks'. Geophysical survey of the site has long been advocated (Petch 1969, 43; Jones 1994, 46) and excavation and preservation have been strongly recommended (Swan 1984, 154; 1992, 28). Although at present Hilly Field is pasture grazed by cattle, damage is still being caused to the Roman buildings in the Wall Lock field by deep ploughing. The excavations by T.A. Acton in 1907–1915 were only partial and some of the site was already destroyed (Grimes, 12, 14–15). Rescue excavation should be seen as an urgent priority.

The author once recommended the reconsideration of the samian from Holt published by Grimes (Bulmer 1980, 50). Reference was made there (and in Jones 1994, 46) to samian collected recently by Mr. G. Bevan. It seems appropriate here to identify the man and his activity. Between 1969 and 1981, Geoffrey Bevan of Wrexham made frequent visits to the site, saw the threat to the archaeological remains caused by every ploughing, and noted the structural damage. His records state that the site remained much as it had done since about 1923, when the dumps of excavated material containing a considerable quantity of discarded pottery and tiles were shovelled back into the abandoned trenches or spread over the fields by the farmer owners. He also noted that Roman artefacts were tipped on Old Chester Lane which passes through the site, when repairs to the surface were called for. He himself made a collection which included 53 stamped tiles and much pottery. There was little metalwork or coins such as others

have found there in recent years. This may indicate the scope of his interest as much as the limitations of his monocular vision. After ploughing in 1975 the farmer gave permission for the removal 'by shallow excavation' of finds in the area south of the Barracks from a track inside the hedge at the south end of the Wall Lock (fig. 1, area IX). He noted that Acton's hut had been moved here from its original position according to the O.S. map of 1914 and suggested that the farmer had emptied from it onto the track the last of Acton's excavated artefacts. He noted that at least one sherd of Holt Ware in this group joined another from the Barracks (area I).

Mr Bevan himself was an excellent draughtsman and a great character, a veteran of World War II with many memories of life during the first war. In the second war he volunteered as a lorry driver for the British army in Italy, and it was there he developed an interest in the Romans. He continued his interest in archaeology after retiring as a draughtsman from the Denbighshire County Architect's Department, helping as a volunteer from 1972 in the Grosvenor Museum's Excavations Section, Chester (Carrington 1983). He had been the only one present at excavations at Ffrith in the 1960s to make notes on where the finds came from (Blockley 1989, 139). Although he did not note stratigraphical details, his geographical zoning at Holt is important because it provides at least some information on provenance, unlike Acton's records (Grimes, 16). In 1978, Mr. Bevan asked the present writer to look at his samian collection from Holt, but (as well as having only one eye) he was deaf and our communications were sometimes confusing. Shortly before he died in 1983, he donated all his finds to the Grosvenor Museum, Chester, were they are now stored along with his records and a lengthy typescript. Valuable contents include original drawings by E.F. Davies (see Grimes, 2), copies of additional photographs of Acton's excavations, and Bevan's own observations. One notebook, for instance, records that during the drought of 1976 blocks of local sandstone were seen in the bed and west bank at a location on a bend of the River Dee just downstream from the site. Although not located precisely, this area lies upstream from a crossing suggested tentatively by Jones 1991, 76.

Despite the very small size of the sample, a summary of Bevan's samian collection and its visual representation (figs. 2 and 3) will show how Grimes' published material, discussed thereafter, is complemented. There was a total of 144 sherds, recovered in or around the living quarters ('Barracks'), workshops and kilns. Of these 101 sherds came from the Barracks areas (fig. 1, areas I, II/A, VIII) and 69 of these came from the ploughed Wall Lock. Owing to their survival on the surface of agricultural land, almost all the samian ware consisted of badly abraded fragments. It seemed that this small collection would add little to Grimes' classic work. It soon became apparent that Grimes' illustrations were far from reliable. For instance, a rubbing of his fig. 51, no. 170 revealed a beadrow, Rogers A2, and ovolo B223 as used by Cinnamus, while no. 126 should represent the distinctive use of Rogers ovolo B213 (Libertus-Butrio).

As work continued on Bevan's seemingly dull and scrappy collection, it was clear that elements of the same decoration were repeated in Grimes' report and that sherds located on the surface in the 1970s belonged or probably belonged to bowls excavated 60 years before. This inter-connection of sherds was noted also in a collection of unpublished material from Holt in the National Museum of Wales, Cardiff, which P.V. Webster kindly rubbed for the writer. A quick survey of 162 decorated sherds revealed that 41% was S.G., 57% C.G. and 2% E.G. Some sherds proved to have been published already by Grimes (fig. 5, no. 17). However, several new sherds belonged to Grimes' bowls, some adjoining other finds (e.g. figs. 4, no. 9, 5, no. 15). This unique feature, of sherds interconnected in collections separated so far in time, may owe much to re-excavation. However, some sherds which may have

belonged to Grimes' bowls (nos. 7, 9, 15 and 17 here and an unillustrated sherd in the same style of Drusus i (I) as Grimes, fig. 42, nos. 92 and 99) were all found south of the Barracks in an area (VIII) not excavated by Acton. If not dredged to the surface by deep ploughing, these sherds may represent the spreading of excavated finds over the fields as noted above. It is possible that other sherds probably belonging to Grimes' bowls were part of the backfilling of his trenches elsewhere on the site (nos. 5, 12, 14 and 16). Any reburied material may have remained in the area of the site from which it was originally excavated, but this must remain speculative.

In addition to these collections, the writer tried to locate three large and significant pieces said to be from Holt. These were bowls in the styles of Vegetus, Docilis and Cinnamus which were seen, rubbed and identified by Dr. G. Simpson in the Council Offices, Prestatyn in 1956. The bowls were labelled only 'Holt. Given by the widow of Col. R.H. Linaker, FSA'. I traced them as far as Clwyd County Record Office in Hawarden, where in 1994 I had an appointment to see a box listed in their inventory as 'Holt Roman Pottery', only to be told that the box was missing.

In Bevan's collection, a maximum of 142 vessels was composed of 143 sherds (excluding one which was missing in 1994; see below). Some sherds may well have belonged to the same vessel, but it was impossible to calculate minimum numbers based on such a large quantity of scraps, all fragmentary and most in very poor condition. Statistical analysis proved difficult and unreliable. Only the slightest traces of any potters' stamps survived, abraded almost beyond visibility on two basal fragments of plainware, one of Flavian-Trajanic origin and the other early 2nd-century. S.G. ware was predomi-

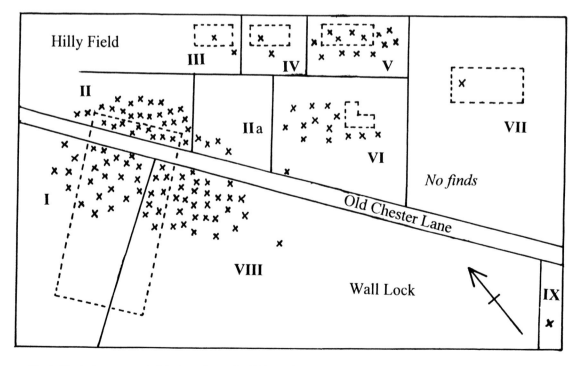

Fig. 1. Sketch plan, not to scale, following a diagram by G. Bevan showing the provenance of 133 samian sherds found up to May 1976, according to Bevan's zoning of Grimes' buildings, I–IX (X was used for unprovenanced material).

	18 and 18R	18 or 18/31	18R or 18/31R	18/31	18/31R	18/31 or 31	18/31R or 31R	31R	dish	
SG	12	2	1		1				2	= 18
CG	1	1		2	5	1	2	1	3	= 16
Total	13	3	1	2	6	1	2	1	5	= 34

	C.11	23	27	33	35	45	cup	ind.	encl.	67	30	30 or 37	37	**Total**
SG	1	1	5				2	18	1	2	3		18	**69**
CG			2	2	1	*	1	16			1	2	32	**73**
Total	1	1	7	2	1	*	3	34	1	2	4	2	50	**142**

* sherd missing in 1994

Fig. 2. Table summarising the samian forms in Bevan's collection.

nant among the sherds recovered from the Barracks (areas I and II), while C.G. ware was preponderant in the material collected from the industrial area of Hilly Field to the east. Five sherds of Antonine date were from the Barracks areas and the other two were from the heart of the industrial activity, the kilns and drying sheds (areas VI, VII). In all, eleven sherds (8%) showed signs of burning; seven out of eight burnt sherds from the Wall Lock came from Barracks areas I and II. None were of Trajanic-Hadrianic date, but this may reflect simply the mistaking of burnt sherds for overfired Les Martres ware. Two burnt sherds, one of Antonine date, were recovered from the area of the double-flue kiln and drying shed (VI). A single dish which was found in the area of the main kiln-plant (VII) and was produced *c.* AD 160–200, bore no signs of having been burnt.

In all, 69 vessels (consisting of 70 sherds) were produced in South Gaul and formed 49%, while 73 vessels (51%) originated in Central Gaul. There were no East Gaulish products. All the S.G. ware originated after *c.* AD 70. One or two fragments, including fig. 4, no. 1, could possibly have represented form Dr. 29 which was popular up to *c.* AD 85. However, form 37 was the more likely even for these sherds. Although it was possible only to say with any certainty that twenty vessels originated after *c.* AD 80, it is likely that the great bulk of the material was Domitianic-Trajanic. The S.G. ware composed 40% of all the moulded vessels and around 55% of the plain samian. Excluding indeterminate sherds, 54% of the collection was moulded ware (47% of the S.G. assemblage and 60% of the C.G. assemblage). This may be compared with much lower proportions at sites in Chester (e.g. Bulmer 1980a, 87). At Holt, all these proportions have been affected by the unusually numerous moulded bowls from Les Martres-de-Veyre. 48% of the C.G. bowls were probably produced by the Trajanic-Hadrianic potters, of which 39% probably came from Les Martres itself. In all, around 30% of all the C.G. ware in this collection may have originated at Les Martres, and half of this was moulded ware. The original moulds were certainly used at Les Martres in the Trajanic period, but following the exodus of potters to Lezoux, bowls were produced from them there in the Hadrianic period (Hartley 1977, 254). Thus nos.

9 and 10 seem to be bowls produced from moulds of Potter X–13, a potter known to have supplied moulds to Donnaucus in the Trajanic period at Les Martres. No. 10 appears to have been a bowl produced at Lezoux after the exodus. Again, whereas no. 11 in the style of Potter X–9 originated at Les Martres, two fragments (both from area VIII; not illustrated) may represent the Lezoux phase of production from moulds of X-9 (cf. Dickinson 1990, 226, no. 45; Dickinson 1993, 92). Since very little Les Martres ware has been recorded on Hadrian's Wall sites, the supply to Britain is thought to have terminated by 120 or so. The dating of subsequent exports from Lezoux is considered below.

Around 30 sherds were dated to the Hadrianic-early Antonine period and formed 41% of the C.G. ware. Of these, at least eight decorated bowls could have been Hadrianic products (some not illustrated; see fig. 6). This production (35%) of the identifiable C.G. bowls is very high compared with only 17% by Antonine potters. The fragments of Antonine origin, plain and decorated, formed no more than 11% of the C.G. total, but this figure may reflect uncertainties in the precise dating of battered fragments, particularly from the dish forms. Three bowl fragments bore recognisable decoration seemingly of Antonine date. One sherd, no. 17, was in the style of Criciro v, taken to work largely in the Antonine period; this was found south of the Barracks (area VIII). Another, no. 18 which was recovered from the Barracks area I, bore decoration which was very badly abraded and only just recognisable as probably Antonine. One sherd amongst the unlocated material of 1968 included so tiny and battered a fragment of ovolo that positive identification was impossible even though later 2nd-century origin was suspected. In addition to these, only one plainware sherd was firmly dated after *c.* AD 160 and in the range *c.* 160–200. This came from a deep dish of the late C.G. form Dr. 31R and was recovered from the area of the main kiln-plant (VII). The writer in 1978 recorded in Bevan's collection a sherd from a C.G. mortarium of form Dr. 45, dated *c.* 170–200. This was probably the latest vessel represented in the collection. It was said to have been found in the area of the workshops (V), but by 1994 it was missing.

Owing to the abraded condition of all the sherds and to the scarcity of footrings recovered, it is impossible to comment on evidence of wear in use. At least one sherd, from South Gaul, showed repair-work (no. 4). Found in the western area of the Barracks (I), there is now no trace of a rivet through a drilled, round hole. The success of the repair is unclear; there is evidence of attempted drilling below it. From the eastern part of the Barracks (II) came a rimsherd of a C.G. dish probably produced *c.* AD 120–150 with a dove-tailed rivet-hole cut through it; again no rivet has survived. It is also unclear how successful the repair was on an unpublished Holt sherd in the style of Austrus noted as showing a rivet-hole (NMW 25.1/u/n, with the same sea-bull as Grimes fig. 42, no. 97). The writer has noted elsewhere the use of bronze and lead repair-work on samian vessels (Ward 1989, 154; Ward 1993, 19–20). Brian Hartley (1954, 10–12) has discussed bronze-working at both Heronbridge and Holt. There was at least one riveted bowl at Heronbridge, although the nature of that repair is not recorded (Hartley 1952, fig. 6, no. 9; Hartley & Kaine 1954, fig. 9, no. 9 appears to represent another).

We may now consider Grimes' published material. His note (p. 49) on the striking predominance of late 1st- to early 2nd-century decoration over the Flavian still holds good. No exclusively pre-Flavian plain forms were represented. Among the stamped vessels, only one dish of form Dr. 18 by Ingenuus ii was firmly pre-Flavian in origin (*c.* AD 50–65); another of the same form by Rufus iii was dated *c.* 65–90. Among the moulded bowls, there was only one bowl of form Dr. 29, manufactured before *c.* AD 85 but probably Flavian. At least four 29s were noted in the NMW uunpublished Holt collection, but all seemed Flavian. Grimes illustrates around thirteen bowls of form 37 which were of purely Flavian origin,

including no. 70 which bears the name of M. Crestio (*c.* AD 75–95). The majority of the S.G. bowls was probably produced *c.* 80/90–110. Grimes (p. 101) assigned his fig. 36, no. 25 and 28 in L. Cosius' style to the late Flavian period; L. Cosius probably worked slightly later, *c.* 90–110. As usual, moulded bowls form a large part of the assemblage from South Gaul. The 88 S.G. vessels formed 51% of Grimes' decorated ware. The large proportion of S.G. ware also noted in Bevan's collection is reflected by the stamped samian. Of the 64 stamped and signed vessels (59 of them plainware) recorded from Holt in the Leeds catalogue, 27 were from South Gaul (42%). All were from La Graufesenque, which did not export after *c.* 110, and the bulk of the stamps originated after *c.* AD 80. A histogram, fig. 8, gives an instant impression of their range in date of production, but the small size of the sample renders it statistically unreliable. Comparison may be made with a histogram illustrating the entire Bevan collection (fig. 3), but here the material was far less specifically datable. These graphs should be used only as a visual aid to summarise the material at a glance.

It may be significant that the 27 S.G. stamps probably represented the work of only 20 potters. At least four, and probably five, potters were each represented by two stamps from the same die on the same form of vessel. One or two other potters were represented by stamps from different dies and on different forms of vessel. While this cannot be thought to provide evidence of a samian shop as has been suggested at sites such as Castleford, the recurrence of vessels of the same period stamped by potters using the same dies suggests the arrival of contemporary batches. A similar occurrence was noted at Piercebridge, where batches arrived from Lezoux in the Antonine period (Ward 1993). All the Holt examples were produced at La Graufesenque *c.* 70–95 or *c.* 80/85–110. It is

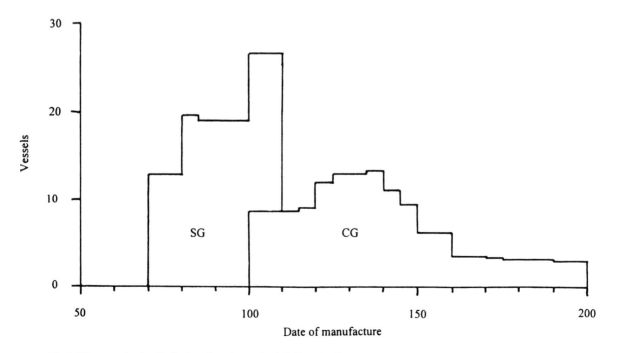

Fig. 3. Histogram showing distributions of samian per decade in Bevan's collection (maximum 143 vessels against date of manufacture).

noteworthy that the remaining 37 stamps of 2nd-century origin represented the work of 37 different potters.

Grimes' statement (p. 98) that the Domitianic-Hadrianic decorated bowls outnumbered the remainder by two to one is also fairly accurate, although there are a few more bowls of Trajanic-Hadrianic origin than he suspected. Concerning the Trajanic material, Pryce & Birley (1935, 74) listed eighteen bowls from Les Martres-de-Veyre at Holt. From these we may subtract at least one (Grimes no. 102) as Hadrianic, but note that no. 105 may represent two bowls and add perhaps ten to thirteen more (nos. 97, 103, 109, 110?, 111, 116, 118, 122, 123, 136?, 141, 162 and 173?). However, without published descriptions of fabrics it is difficult to say how much originated from moulds used at Trajanic Les Martres and how much at Hadrianic Lezoux. To judge from Bevan's collection, most of the bowls were probably produced at Les Martres. Of Grimes' 82 C.G. bowls, 40% were probably produced by the potters working at Trajanic Les Martres and Hadrianic Lezoux, an exceptionally large proportion reflected in the other Holt collections. At sites where occupation is steady in the earlier Roman period, there is frequently a gap here in the samian sample (cf. Marsh 1981, fig. 11.8; Bulmer 1980, 17). The proportion of Les Martres stamps among those of 2nd-century and later date even at Chester (10.9%: Dickinson & Hartley 1971, 129) is dwarfed by the proportion at Holt. Here ten stamped vessels in the Leeds catalogue were from Les Martres, forming 32% of 31 C.G. stamps on plainware and 27% of all the 2nd-century and later stamped and signed vessels. Six of the stamps were of Trajanic origin, three Trajanic-Hadrianic and one Hadrianic-early Antonine. The Trajanic material thus formed 19% of the C.G. stamps on plainware. These figures represent an outstandingly high proportion of plainware from Les Martres, for the quantity of moulded bowls exported to Britain from Les Martres was markedly higher than its plainware.

Thompson (1965, 59) suggested that Grimes' dating of the Holt samian was too early and he suspected more Antonine material. It is now clear that many of the Lezoux bowls were indeed produced rather later in the 2nd century than Grimes suggested (fig. 6). Attianus ii, for instance, who stamped Grimes fig. 46, no. 121, was not a Trajanic-Hadrianic potter but worked in the Hadrianic-early Antonine period. P.V. Webster has pointed out to me that dates of manufacture also should be pushed forward in contemporary samian reports such as Brecon (Pryce 1926), and it may be significant that Pryce himself was involved with the Holt report (Grimes, 98 footnote). It is now clear that there is a very large proportion (c. 35–40%) of the C.G. bowls which were produced by potters working in the Hadrianic to early Antonine period. These are the potters whose work is little represented in Antonine Scotland (see Hartley 1972, table IV), where only a few products of such potters as Drusus ii (II) are recorded (Dickinson 1984, 183). Miss B.M. Dickinson has pointed out (pers. comm.) that there is very little Lezoux ware on the line of the Stanegate which preceded the Hadrianic frontier. She draws the conclusion that although there certainly were potters working at Lezoux c. 120, their products were not reaching

Britain until c. 125. At Holt, the Hadrianic and Hadrianic-early Antonine bowls included three with stamps of Geminus iii, Sacer ii and Attianus ii, all making moulds at Lezoux in the period c. 125–145 (Leeds catalogue). In all the collections, the Lezoux group of Sacer-Attianus and subsequently Criciro v seems particularly well-represented. Of these, Grimes' nos. 149 and 154 may belong to the same bowl in the style of Sacer ii, a suggestion made by Mrs J. Bird and supported by examination of their fabric by P.V. Webster. In addition to this group, the unpublished NMW material included samian by such potters as Cettus, a contemporary of Criciro but one who worked at Les Martres. Contemporary at Lezoux was Tetturo, now known to have worked before 160 (see S&S, 274 on this Holt bowl, whose rubbing shows an ovolo much smaller than Rogers B143). Among the 31 plainware stamps from Central Gaul listed for Holt in the Leeds catalogue, twelve (39%) are datable to the Hadrianic-early Antonine period (including the four Les Martres stamps whose range falls largely in this period). Adding to these the stamped or signed decorated bowls, 41% was of Hadrianic-early Antonine origin. Furthermore, another five stamps not attributed to specific potters are thought likely to have been contemporary products.

There were a few more decorated bowls of purely Antonine date than Grimes noted (p. 50), but still these are thought to represent only about 12 vessels. Including those probably in the style of Criciro v, these formed 14% of the C.G. and E.G. bowls. This is a very small proportion compared with groups from Chester (cf. Bulmer 1980, fig. 3). Grimes' nos. 140, 163 and 169 seem to be in the early style of the Cinnamus ii – Cerialis ii group which was current from c. 135 to the earlier Antonine period. To these three Miss B.M. Dickinson suggests adding no. 159 (listed by Rogers 1977, 249, as Albucius). In the unpublished NMW collection at least two examples were seen of the early Cinnamus group's style and two with either their ovolo, Rogers B144 or B143. One plain dish of form 18/31 (R) was stamped by Cinnamus ii, c. 140–160. Two other plainware stamps by other potters were dated c. 140–160 and 140–165, and another probably by Patricius ii was of early to mid-Antonine origin. There were also two decorated bowls in Cinnamus' later style of c. 150–175 (Grimes nos. 124 and 170). Although it now seems that Grimes no. 159 may not be Albucius' style (see above), Rogers' attribution of no. 167 to that potter still stands. Dr. G. Simpson has dated Albucius' work as c. 140–170 (S & S, 258). Miss Dickinson tells me that in the Leeds catalogue Albucius ii is considered to have worked c. 150–175/180. His plainware occurs in such late deposits as the Wroxeter Gutter, and his use of the later forms 31R, 79, 80, Tg and Tx is more frequent than his use of the earlier dish and cup forms. Grimes published only one decorated C.G. bowl which can be dated firmly after c. 160: no. 161, apparently in the style of Paternus v (II), dated c. 160–195 in the Leeds catalogue; the terminal date of exportation from Lezoux is discussed elsewhere (see Ward 1993). Rogers (1977, 249) has noted all the latest samian at Holt as arriving probably after 160. However, it might be safer to say, concerning the C.G. moulded bowls, after 150. Not in evidence are the products of prolific late potters such as Casurius ii and

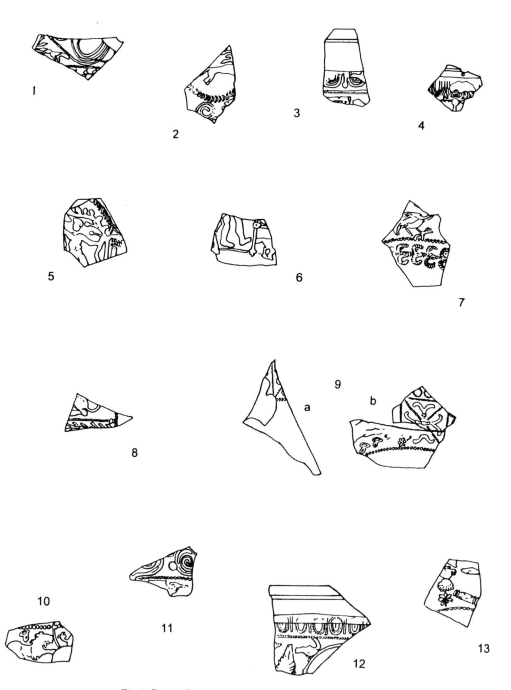

Fig. 4. Decorated samian sherds in Bevan's collection, all at 1:2.

1. *V 1039. S.G. Dr. 37? Probably* c. *AD 70–85.*

2. *V 1471. S.G. Dr. 37. Flavian, and probably* c. *AD 70–90.*

3. *II 332. S.G. Dr. 37. Rimsherd with ovolo used by L. Cosius and part of a festoon; cf. Knorr 1912, Taf. 18, no. 1.* c. *AD 90–110.*

4. *I 3237. S.G. Dr. 30. Ovolo used by the* amici cognatique Germani? *Domitianic-Trajanic. The plain band bears a broken rivet-hole, with further drilling below.*

5. *IV–V 398. S.G. Dr. 37. Probably the same bowl as Grimes, fig. 38, no. 54. Domitianic-Trajanic.*

6. *II 2302. S.G. Dr. 37. Cf. Grimes, fig. 36, no. 25 etc. Domitianic-Trajanic.*

7. *VIII 755. C.G. Dr. 37. Style of Potter X–2 from Les Martres-de-Veyre; cf. Grimes, fig. 42, no. 101. Trajanic.*

8. *VI 1852. C.G. Dr. 37. Style of the Potter of the Rosette? Soft fabric, but presumably Trajanic.*

9. *VIII 754. C.G. Dr. 37. Joined Grimes, fig. 42, no. 95 and two unpublished sherds (NMW 25.1/u/n), (b) drawn from rubbings. Style of Potter X–13?, from Les Martres. Trajanic.*

10. *II 2036. C.G. Dr. 37. Style of Potter X–13, probably from Lezoux and Hadrianic.*

11. *VI 1736. C.G. Dr. 37 with surfaces abraded away. Style of Potter X–9, from Les Martres. Trajanic.*

12. *X 51. C. G. Dr. 37. Rogers B213, used at Lezoux by Libertus and Butrio, and with the other motifs on Grimes, fig. 46, nos. 126 and 128 – same bowl?* c. *AD 115–140, probably Hadrianic.*

13. *I 541. C.G. Dr. 37. Not firmly attributable to Butrio, but probably Hadrianic.*

Do(v)eccus i (II), although in the unpublished NMW collection at least one sherd (no. 25.1/682) may have represented Casurius' work. Only one Lezoux stamp in the Leeds catalogue was *c.* 160–200, that on a dish form 31R of Marcellinus ii of Lezoux (Grimes, 123, stamp 23).

Of the samian from East Gaul, two decorated vessels from early workshops are suggested from Grimes' illustrations: no. 134 features a cupid used at La Madeleine (Ricken 1934, Taf. 7, no. 85) and is probably of Hadrianic-early Antonine date. Grimes' no. 131 was probably from an earlier 2nd-century factory in East Gaul, where similar rosette-friezes were used at Chémery, La Madeleine and in the Argonne; the dating of these early E.G. factories was discussed by the writer in a report on a major collection from Piercebridge which awaits publication twelve years on (Ward forthcoming). There was also one stamped cup of form 27 not attributable to a specific workshop or potter within the Hadrianic or early Antonine workshops and one other plainware stamp on a dish form 31R by Iuvenis ii of Rheinzabern, dated *c.* 160–200. One stamped bowl of Ianus II was also represented (Grimes fig. 44, no. 108). This sherd has been examined by P.V. Webster who thought it likely to be a product of Rheinzabern rather than of Heiligenberg, where Ianus ii worked *c.* 135/140–150. If indeed from Rheinzabern, it will have been produced *c.* 150–180/190 but it probably would not have reached Britain before *c.* 160. This sherd was one of two decorated E.G. vessels noted by Rogers (1977, 249). The second, no. 171, was uni-

dentified by Grimes and attributed by Rogers only to a potter of Rheinzabern. A rubbing by P.V. Webster of a sherd in the NMW unpublished Holt collection, no. 25.1/746, shows the same decoration, but again indistinctly. The leaf is probably Ricken & Fischer 1963, P61, and the ovolo may be their E 17. These motifs were used by many different potters at Rheinzabern, but both were used notably by B[elsus?] F Attoni who worked in the later 2nd to early 3rd century. This bowl cannot be attributed or dated any more specifically, but it may be the latest samian vessel recorded from Holt. There were no vessels likely to represent late production at Rheinzabern and Trier such as are found in Chester (Bulmer 1980a, 51, 58).

Grimes was selective in his publication of the plain samian. He says (p. 98) that the plain forms reflected the evidence of the decorated ware. Fig. 7 summarises the information as published, but clearly no statistical analysis can be based on such vague figures. Certainly there was a very large number of fragments of the dish forms 18, 18/31 and 31 (and presumably their rouletted versions), whatever their precise form. The range of forms is extended by Bevan's collection (fig. 2) and comparative information is provided by fig. 9, which shows the fairly limited range of forms whose stamps are recorded for Holt in the Leeds catalogue. Grimes' illustrations certainly included late forms such as a dish of form Dr. 32 which was produced after *c.* 160 and was probably East Gaulish. There was also more than one deep dish said to be of E. G. form Ludowici Sb (Grimes, 120). Without inspec-

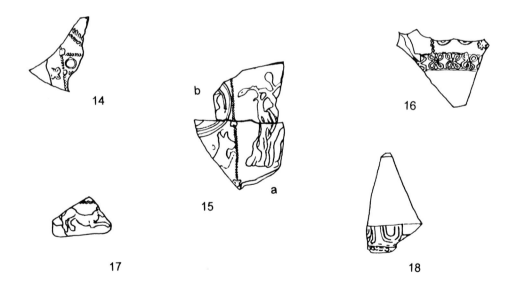

Fig. 5. Decorated samian sherds in Bevan's collection, all at 1:2.

14. *V 2226. C.G. Dr. 37. Probably the same bowl as Grimes, fig. 51, no. 168 with ovolo Rogers B15?, known for Attianus ii. c. AD 120/125–145.*

15. *VIII N 1934. C.G. Dr. 37. Poor moulding. Style of Drusus ii (II) or Attianus ii? Probably same vessel as Grimes, fig. 48, no. 137 with ovolo Rogers B61 (known for Drusus ii). Joins NMW 25.1/901, (b) drawn from a rubbing. c. AD 125–145.*

16. *II 2309. C.G. Dr. 37. Grimes, fig. 50, no. 165 seems the same vessel, by the Quintilianus i group. c AD 125–150.*

17. *VIII 2890. C.G. Dr. 37. Panther, shorter than Oswald 1518. Possibly the same bowl as Grimes, fig. 51, no. 172 (NMW 25.1/433g includes this panther) with ovolo Rogers B52 and F8 but not a dot-rosette as drawn there; motifs used by Criciro v. c. AD 135–170.*

18. *I 2439. C.G. Dr. 37. Ovolo Rogers B223? used by several potters including Cinnamus, above traces possibly of Casurius' beadrow A3 rather than Pugnus' guideline. Probably Antonine.*

GRIMES COLLECTION			BEVAN COLLECTION
Date	vessels		vessels
65–80	1	(Dr. 29)	
70 00/100	c 13	(including M Crestio	3
70–110	c 29	(many c. 80–110)	
80–110	c 38+		10
90–110	c 6	(3 in L. Cosius' style)	1 (L. Cosius' style)
TOTAL	**87**		**TOTAL 14**
Trajanic	1	X–2	1
	3	Potter of Rosette	1
	6	Drusus i (I)	
	1	Drusus i or X–12/13	1
	2	Igocatus	
	1	Igocatus or Austrus	
	*1	X–11	1
	*1	X–11/12	
	*1	X–12	
	*2	X–12/13	
	*3	X–13	3
	1	X–8	
		X–9 (Les Martres)	1
	8	(Les Martres potters)	1
Trajanic-Hadrianic		X–8 or X–9 (Lezoux?)	1
		X–9 (Lezoux?)	1
	1	X–13 or a Drusus	
	1	X–13 or Attianus ii	
Hadrianic	1	X–14	
	2	Libertus/Butrio	1
		Butrio	1
	2	Geminus iii	
	2	Austrus	
	4	Drusus ii	1
Hadrianic-early Ant.	1	Vegetus iii/Quintilianus i	
	3	Quintilianus i group	1
	4	Sacer ii	
	2	Sacer/Attianus group	1
	4	Attianus ii or related	1
	2	X–6 and Large S Potter	1
	1	X–6/Tittius/Pugnus ii	
	1	Docilis i	
	1	Tetturo	
E.G.	2	early E.G. workshop	
Hadrianic-Antonine		X–7 group/Pugnus/Cinnamus	1
	3	Criciro v	1
	4	early Cinnamus ii group	
	**8	ind.	2
Antonine		Pugnus/Cinnamus/Casurius	1
	2	later Cinnamus ii	
	1	Albucius ii	
	1	Paternus v (II)	
E.G.	1	Ianu(s) ii, at Rheinzabern?	
E.G.	1	Rheinzabern (BF Attoni?)	
TOTAL	**86**		**TOTAL 23**

* Taken here to be Les Martres.
** At least 2 were Antonine

Fig. 6. Summary of the decorated samian in Grimes' and Bevan's collections (maximum nos. of vessels).

tion of the fabric, one suspects that this represents the C.G. form Dr. 31R, but at any rate the form was produced after *c.* 160. As in Bevan's collection, there was at least one mortarium of form Dr. 45 (Grimes, 121). Whether from Central or East Gaul, this must have been produced after *c.* 170.

We may now consider the dating of legionary activity at Holt itself. Along with the coin evidence from the site which has been studied by Dr. D. Shotter and which will be discussed in detail elsewhere (see Appendix), the samian ware provides an external source of information in dating the occupation. The writer once suggested that along with other ceramic evidence the samian might indicate occupation of the site beginning before AD 100 (Bulmer 1980, 50). Reviewing the samian ware both published and unpublished has confirmed that impression. However, the coin and samian evidence seem to diverge concerning the earliest occupation of the site. Although the samian, stamped and unstamped, does not suggest any pre-Flavian occupation at Holt, Dr. D. Shotter

	C.11	C.15	15/17	18 etc	18/31 etc	31 etc	27	32	33	35	36	44	45	46	67	78	29	30/R	37
SG	*		7	85	82		*		*	*	*					1	1		86
CG	*	*			36	30?	*		*			*		2	*			2	81
EG					?			*					1?						4
Total	*	*	7	85	118	30	*	*	*	*	*	*	1?	2	*	1	1	2	171

* = present, but numbers unspecified

Fig. 7. Summary of the samian forms from Holt as published by Grimes.

notes that the coin evidence may be taken as supportive of activity ending in the first years of the Flavian period before a period of abandonment. The presence of an early fort has been suggested recently in the area of Holt (Mason 1988, 179) and perhaps at Farndon (Jones 1991, 77).

The evidence of the stamped and the decorated samian – its large proportion of the late Domitianic-Trajanic material, the scarcity of form 29 and the absence of all except one Neronian vessel – could well support the beginning of occupation at Holt soon after the general disappearance of form 29 from the market. This, together with the coin evidence reviewed by Dr. Shotter and summarised here in the Appendix, might point to the foundation of Holt following the arrival of Legio XX Valeria Victrix at Chester, which probably occurred shortly after AD 87 and the withdrawal from Scotland. This may indicate slightly earlier foundation than the end of the 1st century (cf. Jones 1994, 44).

The proportion of Trajanic-Hadrianic samian at Holt is exceptionally great. In the Trajanic period on sites believed to have been occupied steadily in the earlier Roman period (cf. Bulmer 1980, 17; Marsh 1981, fig. 11.8), there is frequently a gap in the samian sample. As noted above, very little Les Martres ware reached Hadrian's Wall sites; this implies cessation of the supply by 120 or so. Miss B.M. Dickinson has pointed out the great scarcity of Lezoux ware on the Stanegate (see above). If Lezoux products were not reaching Britain until c. 125, then there seems to have been a period in the early 120s when most of the samian in use in Britain presumably was from Les Martres, with some La Graufesenque ware surviving in use. Clearly Holt was receiving large imports of samian in the Trajanic and Hadrianic periods. It has been suggested that the production of Holt pottery may have ended in the 120s and c. 125–130 (G. Dunn and A. Jones, in Carrington 1994, 43 and 45 respectively), when the Twentieth Legion moved up to Hadrian's Wall and was largely absent from Chester. However, the Hadrianic assemblage at Holt obviously contrasts with the situation at Chester as a quick glance at Marsh 1981, fig. 11.8, reveals. On many sites excavated in Chester, the samian of Hadrianic manufacture seems overwhelmed by the ensuing bulk of Antonine material (cf. Bulmer 1980, fig. 3). It may be wise in the future to check this Hadrianic material at Chester, since at Holt the evidence of the stamped and decorated samian strongly affirms a high level of activity continuing well into the Hadrianic period at least. Rogers (1977, 247) noted that 'apart from a number of somewhat later sherds, the most recent fragments are in the early CINNAMVS style.' One may argue rather that the numerous vessels of the early Cinnamus group, combined with the many

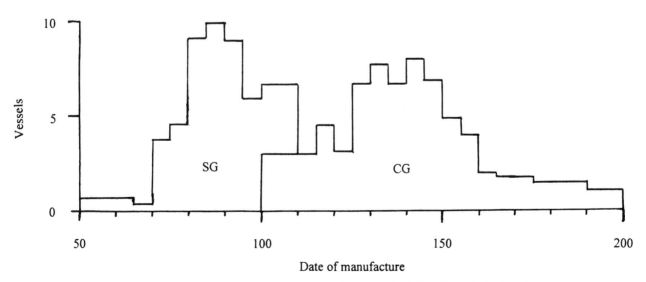

Fig. 8. Histogram showing distributions of signed and stamped samian per decade from Holt in the Leeds catalogue (maximum 64 vessels against date of manufacture).

products of contemporary potters known to have worked into the very early Antonine period, could indicate a fairly high level of activity continuing a little past AD 135. We may note the samian of very closely similar date in pit B I 3 at Alcester (Hartley *et al.* 1994, 106). This included the styles probably of Libertus/Butrio, Quintilianus, the Sacer group, and the Cerialis ii – Cinnamus ii group (*c.* 135–170). The stamped plainware was of Hadrianic-early Antonine origin, of which one stamp dated *c.* 135–160 was on dish form 31 by Criciro. One unstamped dish Dr. 18/31 was worn and one Dr. 18/31R was riveted. Although this material from a pit represents a fairly closely dated group compared with the accumulation of material at Holt, it may be significant that this material at Alcester suggested a date *c.* 145–155 for the filling of the pit. On the basis of the samian evidence, one can only speculate how far past 135 activity may have continued at Holt.

It is clearly important not to look at the samian in isolation. Dr. Shotter notes that the declining coin-loss from Hadrian's time onwards is more marked that at most other sites in the north-west. He suggests that this is indicative of little organised activity after the mid-130s. Noted above are a very few samian vessels (three of them stamped) which must be dated to the mid-Antonine period or later. Contemporary with these are the consular tile-stamps of AD 167 which have been discovered in Chester and elsewhere (Hassall 1978, 476; Philpott 1994). However, these stamps have not yet been noted at Holt itself and Philpott (1994, 10) has suggested another source of production. At any rate some late samian is to be expected if there was any residential occupation in the late 2nd or 3rd century. The presence of a few late sherds in all the collections from Holt suggests that this was so. Dr. Shotter notes as significant the complete absence of the usually common coins of Septimius Severus (Appendix, period X). In contrast, the presence of a single coin of Gordian III (AD 238–244, period XII) at a time of low coin-loss might be sufficient evidence upon which to argue for some kind of activity in the 230s/240s. The coin evidence combines with the scarcity of late samian noted above to suggest that from the later 2nd century into the early 3rd occupation was much reduced. It seems that tiles were being produced there up to the mid-3rd century, accompanied by at least an intermittent military presence (see Grimes, fig. 59, no. 25 and 12–13; Hassall 1979, 262; Swan 1992, 27). For this later period of tile production at Holt, contemporary archaeological evidence in the Chester fortress is informative. However, this evidence remains to be considered in a later paper.

Appendix

Table of chronological distribution of 70 coins by period, summarised by Dr D. Shotter from his report

			%
I	(–AD41)	4	5.71
II	(41–54)	1	1.43
III	(54–68)	1	1.43
IV	(68–96)	23	32.86
V	(96–117)	14	20.00
VI	(117–138)	8	11.43
VII	(138–161)	1	1.43
VIII	(161–180)	3	4.28
IX	(180–192)	1	1.43
X	(192-222)	–	–
XI	(222-235)	–	–
XII	(235–259)	1	1.43
XIII	(259–275)	3	4.28
XIV	(275–294)	2	2.86
XV	(294–324)	–	–
XVI	(324–330)	–	–
XVII	(330–346)	7	10.00
XVIII	(346–364)	–	–
XIX	(364–378)	–	–
XX	(378–388)	–	–
XXI	(388–)	1	1.43

Acknowledgements

The writer wishes to thank the Grosvenor Museum, Chester, and in particular Dan Robinson for allowing publication of Mr. Bevan's collection and free access to all his records. The Department of Archaeology and Numismatics of the National Museum of Wales, Cardiff and in particular Richard Brewer and Evan Chapman are thanked for making their collections available for study. I should like to thank Brenda Dickinson and David Shotter for contributing so helpfully and promptly their detailed lists of the samian stamps and coins respectively. It is hoped that these, together with Dr. Shotter's analysis of the coin evidence, will be published in full in another paper by the writer. Dr. Shotter records his thanks to

	15/18	18	18R	18/31 etc	18/31 etc	18/31R etc	18/31	31R	27	27g	33	33 or	37	**Total**
SG	1	11	1			1			6	5	1		1	27
CG				9	1	2	3	1	9		5	1	3	34
EG								1	1				1	3
Total	1	11	1	9	1	3	3	2	16	5	6	1	5	64

Fig. 9. Summary of the stamped and signed samian vessels by form, in the Leeds catalogue records for Holt.

Edward Besly at the NMW, Dr. Caroline Earwood of Clwyd-Powys Archaeological Trust, and Dan Robinson of the Grosvenor Museum. The writer is grateful to Joanna Bird for her moral support throughout and for making many detailed comments on the material; to Peter Webster for his help and patience in rubbing some of Grimes' bowls and almost all the unpublished sherds in the NMW collection; to Dr. Grace Simpson for providing copies of her rubbings and helpful comments as always; and to my family for their patience, in particular Simon Ward for his support as well as for references to archaeology in Chester.

I should like to thank Brian Hartley for all his help and kindness over many years. As Brian attended the King's School, Chester and excavated at Heronbridge just downstream from Holt, a paper on the Holt samian seems a suitable offering. This idea proved more realistic than something on the '*Titanic*' which our then 5-year-old son Christopher would have liked me to contribute in return for Brian's encouragement of his interest in that subject.

Abbreviations and Conventions

S.G., C.G., E.G. = South Gaulish, Central Gaulish, East Gaulish wares

Potters' names are given according to the forthcoming Leeds catalogue of stamps, followed where applicable by the number given in Stanfield & Simpson 1990: e.g. Paternus v (II)

NMW no. 25.1/... = National Museum of Wales accession no. for sherds from Holt

Grimes = Grimes 1930

Oswald followed by a number = type no. from Oswald 1936–37

Rogers = motif no. from Rogers 1974

S & S = Stanfield & Simpson 1990

Bibliography

Blockley, K., 1989 Excavations on the Romano-British settlement at Ffrith, Clwyd, 1967–9, *J. Fintshire Hist. Soc.*, **32**, 135–65

Bulmer, M., 1980 An introduction to Roman samian ware, with special reference to collections in Chester and the north-west, *J. Chester Archaeol. Soc.*, **62** (1979), 5–72

_____, 1980a Samian, in Mason, D.J.P., *Excavations at Chester, 11–15 Castle Street and neighbouring sites 1974–8, a possible Roman posting house (mansio)*, Grosvenor Museum Archaeol. Excav. Survey Rep., **2**

Carrington, P., 1983 Obituary, Mr Geoffrey Bevan, *Cheshire Archaeol. Bull.*, **9**, 113

_____, (ed.) 1994 *English Heritage book of Chester* (London)

Dickinson, B.M., 1984 The samian ware, in Frere, S., *Verulamium excavations volume III*, 175–99 (Oxford)

_____, 1990 The samian ware, in McCarthy, M.R., *A Roman, Anglian and medieval site at Blackfriars St., Carlisle*, Cumberland Westmorland Antiq. Archaeol. Soc. Res. Ser., **4**, 213–36

_____, 1993 The samian ware, in Zienkiewicz, J.D., Excavations in the *scamnum tribunorum* at Caerleon: the Legionary Museum site 1983–5, *Britannia*, **24**, 87–98

_____, & Hartley, K.F., 1971 The evidence of potters' stamps on samian ware and on mortaria for the trading connections of Roman York, in Butler, R.M. (ed.), *Soldier and civilian in Roman Yorkshire: essays to commemorate the nineteenth centenary of the foundation of York*, 127–42 (Leicester)

Greene, K., 1977 Legionary pottery, and the significance of Holt, in Dore, J., & Greene, K. (eds), *Roman pottery studies in Britain and beyond*, BAR Suppl. Ser., **30**, 113–32 (Oxford)

Grimes, W.F., 1930 *Holt, Denbighshire: the works-depot of the twentieth legion at Castle Lyons*, Y Cymmrodor, **41**

Hartley, B.R., 1952 Excavations at Heronbridge 1947–48, *J. Chester Archaeol. Soc.*, **39**, 3–20

_____, 1954 Bronze-worker's hearth, *J. Chester Archaeol. Soc.*, **41**, 1–14

_____, 1972 The Roman occupation of Scotland: the evidence of the samian ware, *Britannia*, **3**, 1–55

_____, & Kaine, K.F., 1954 Roman dock and buildings, *J. Chester Archaeol. Soc.*, **41**, 15–37

_____, Pengelly, H., & Dickinson, B., 1994 Samian ware, in Cracknell, S., & Mahany, C., *Roman Alcester: southern extramural area 1964–1966 excavations part 2: finds and discussion*, CBA Res. Rep., **97**, 93–119

Hassall, M.W.C., 1978 in Hassall, M.W.C., & Tomlin, R.S.O., Roman Britain in 1977: inscriptions, *Britannia*, **9**, 473–85

_____, 1979, Military tile-stamps from Britain, in McWhirr, A. (ed.), *Roman brick and tile*, BAR International Ser., **68**, 261–6 (Oxford)

Jones, A., 1994 Roman ceramics in their regional context, in Carrington, P., *From flints to flower pots, current research in the Dee-Mersey region*, 42–50 (Chester)

Jones, G.D.B., 1991 Farndon, an archaeological opportunity, *Manchester Archaeol. Bull.*, **6**, 75–7

Knorr, R., 1912 *Südgallische Terra-Sigillata-Gefässe von Rottweil* (Stuttgart)

Marsh, G., 1981 London's samian supply and its relationship to the development of the Gallic samian industry, in Anderson, A.C., & Anderson, A.S. (eds), *Roman pottery research in Britain and north-west Europe: papers presented to Graham Webster*, BAR International Ser., **123**, 173–238 (Oxford)

Mason, D.J.P., 1988 'Prata legionis' in Britain, *Britannia*, **19**, 163–89

McWhirr, A., 1979 Origins of legionary tile-stamping in Britain, in McWhirr, A. (ed.), *Roman brick and tile*, BAR International Ser., **68**, 253–9 (Oxford)

Oswald, F., 1936 *Index of figure types on terra sigillata (samian ware)*, suppl. to Annals Archaeol. Anthropol. Univ. Liverpool, **23.1–4**, **24.1–4**

Petch, D.F., 1969 Works-depot, in Nash-Williams, V.E., rev. M.G. Jarrett, *The Roman frontier in Wales*, 2 edn, 42–4 (Cardiff)

Philpott, R.A., 1994 A recent group of Twentieth Legion tiles from Tarbock, Merseyside, *Archaeology north-west, the bulletin of CBA north-west*, **7**, 8–10

Pryce, T.D., 1926 Terra sigillata, in Wheeler, R.E.M., *The Roman fort near Brecon*, Y Cymmrodor, **37**, 122–213

_____, & Birley, E., 1935 The first Roman occupation of Scotland, *J. Roman Stud.*, **25**, 59–80

Ricken, H., 1934 Die Bilderschüsseln der Kastelle Saalburg und Zugmantel, *Saalburg Jahrbuch*, **8**, 130–82

_____, & Fischer, C. (ed.), 1963 *Die Bilderschüsseln der römischen Töpfer von Rheinzabern. Textband* (Bonn)

Rogers, G.B., 1974 *Poteries sigillées de la Gaule Centrale, I: les motifs non figurés*, Gallia Suppl., **28** (Paris)

_____, 1977 A group of wasters from Central Gaul, in Dore, J., & Greene, K. (eds), *Roman pottery studies in Britain and beyond*, BAR Suppl. Ser., **30**, 245–250 (Oxford)

Stanfield, J.A., & Simpson, G., 1990 *Les potiers de la Gaule centrale* (2 (French) edn.), Revue Archéologique Sites, **37** (Gonfaron)

Stephens, G.R., 1984 Roman Holt: personnel, production and water supply, *Trans. Denbighshire Hist. Soc.*, **33**, 81–92

Swan, V.G., 1984 *The pottery kilns of Roman Britain*, RCHM Suppl. Ser., **5** (London)

_____, 1992 Legio VI and its men: African legionaries in Britain, *J. Roman Pottery Stud.*, **5**, 1–33

Thompson, F.H., 1965 *Roman Cheshire*, Cheshire Community Council History of Cheshire, **2** (Chester)

Ward, M., 1989 The samian ware, in Blockley, K., *Prestatyn 1984–5, an Iron Age farmstead and Romano-British industrial settlement in north Wales*, BAR Brit. Ser., **210**, 139–54 (Oxford)

_____, 1993 A summary of the samian ware from excavations at Piercebridge, *J. Roman Pottery Stud.*, **6**, 15–22

_____, forthcoming The samian, in Large, S., & Scott, P.R. (ed. A Fitzpatrick), *Excavations at Piercebridge, Co. Durham*

15 An unusual decorated jar from Northamptonshire

Graham Webster

When I was appointed the first full-time curator of the Grosvenor Museum, Chester, in 1948, there was, I soon discovered, a local archaeologist known from the shape of his rather large moustache as Walrus Williams. He had been excavating on a site which is still enigmatic, known as Heronbridge, a few miles south of Chester. Among the local help he had secured was Brian Hartley, then a senior scholar at the Kings School. It did not take me long before I realised that he was very bright and I managed to persuade him to join the summer school at Great Casterton, Rutland, organised by Maurice Barley of Nottingham University and directed by Dr Philip Corder (Corder 1950; 1954; 1961). Brian was there for several seasons and I have remained in touch with him and his first wife, Kay, ever since. This early link was briefly indicated in his paper in my own *Festschrift* (Hartley 1981).

My brief contribution is an unusual decorated globular jar, pieces of which were found in the excavation of a Romano-British villa near Bozeat, Northants., by the Bozeat Historical and Archaeological Society under the direction of David Mallows. Unfortunately only fragments were recovered, but sufficient to allow a reconstruction (fig. 1). The fabric of this vessel is an orange-brown[1] and the colour-coat a dark chocolate brown. Around the central area there is a series of mythi-

cal figures produced from a mould. The form itself approximates to form Déchelette 66.

On the three fragments found there are five figures and the lower part of the legs and feet and part of a gown of two more. All the identifiable figures except the drunken Bacchus and attendants at right are found on moulds of Bémont's group GM 11, in the style of Libertus (Bémont 1977, fig. 17 and pls. 5–14). The Bacchus group is on another black-slipped 66 from Sèvres signed by Libertus (Stanfield & Simpson 1958, pl. 51, no. 602). The other figures on the main sherd are a man in a tunic carrying a folded cloth over his arm, a caryatid and an Apollo with his right arm raised and the left resting on his lyre; there is a male mask at the top of the frieze (Bémont 1977, fig. 17, respectively nos. 44, 87, 15 (the Apollo is better illustrated on the Sèvres jar noted above) and probably 102). Sherd a) has a seated Vulcan with his tongs (Bémont 1977, fig. 17, no. 13) and the caryatid repeated. Sherd b) has the caryatid again, and the two incomplete figures: the robed figure may be Bémont 1977, fig. 11, no. 79, while the booted feet could belong to the warrior on a form Déchelette 64 in Libertus style (Stanfield & Simpson 1958, pl. 52, no. 612.

Libertus regularly made samian with a deliberate black slip which is usually brownish and rather uneven in thickness, and

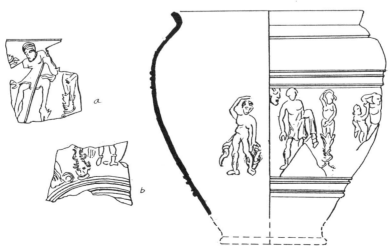

Fig. 1. Decorated jar found near Bozeat, Northants. Scale 1:2.

a range of moulded jar and beaker forms. He was active at
Lezoux *c.* AD 125–145.

ACKNOWLEDGEMENTS

I would like to thank Grace Simpson and Joanna Bird for their
helpful comments.

Note

1.   The description follows Brown, A. Z., *Pottery colour chart for use in de-
      scribing earthenware pottery* (undated).

Bibliography

Bémont, C., 1977 *Moules de gobelets ornés de la Gaule Centrale au Musée des
       Antiquités Nationales*, Gallia Supp., **33** (Paris)
Corder, P., 1950 *The Roman town and villa at Great Casterton, Rutland*
_____, 1954 *The Roman town and villa at Great Casterton, Rutland, second
       interim report for 1951–53*
_____, 1961 *The Roman town and villa at Great Casterton, Rutland, third interim
       report for 1954–58*
Hartley, B. R., 1981 The early military occupation of Lincoln and Chester,
       in Anderson, A. C., & Anderson, A. S. (eds), *Roman pottery research in Britain
       and north-west Europe. Papers presented to Graham Webster*, Brit. Archaeol.
       Rep. Internat. Ser., **123**, 239–47 (Oxford)

16 Zur Verwertbarkeit von Reliefsigillaten des 2. und 3. Jahrhunderts

Ingeborg Huld-Zetsche

EINLEITUNG

In den vergangenen Jahrzehnten und besonders in den letzten Jahren hat sich immer mehr die Erkenntnis gefestigt, daß ein gewisser Prozentsatz an Modeln für Reliefsigillaten von nachfolgenden Töpfern weiterbenutzt wurde. Dies gilt für die Töpfereien von Trier,[1] Rheinzabern,[2] Blickweiler und Eschweiler Hof[3] und mutmaßlich für weitere, z.B. Lavoye und La Madeleine.[4]

Das gesamte Ausmaß der sich daraus ergebenden „späten Ausformungen" ist bisher nirgends erfaßt; auch die Bearbeitung der Trierer Werkstätten I und II ergab für diejenigen Formschüsseln, die ihre Hersteller langfristig überlebten, nur vorläufige Zahlen: Rund 30% wurden für die Werkstatt II mit ihrem ursprünglichen Bestand von 900 Formschüsseln errechnet, wobei dieser Zahl eine sehr vorsichtige Einschätzung zugrunde liegt und sie wahrscheinlich noch höher anzusetzen ist.[5]

In dieser Situation, die ganz klar eine große Beeinträchtigung unserer Datierungsmöglichkeiten mit Reliefsigillaten bedeutet, stellt sich natürlicherweise die Frage, ob unsere Bemühungen für eine gründliche Aufarbeitung dieser Scherbengattung noch einen Sinn haben.

Ich möchte dazu einige Überlegungen zusammenfassen.

DIE ANTIKE ENTWICKLUNG

Gut zu übersehen sind die Verhältnisse in den Töpfereien von Trier. Seit der Mitte des 2. Jahrhunderts hatten sich die Sigillata-Töpfer auf eine Massenproduktion ihrer Waren umgestellt. Dies geht aus den hohen Gesamtzahlen ihrer Model hervor (z.B. der Werkstatt II und des DEXTER).[6] Aber auch die Serien mit identischer Dekoration, die ich als „Tagesproduktion" bezeichnet habe, sprechen für eine sehr gezielte Vermehrung der Produktionsmittel.[7] Es kommt hinzu, daß im Laufe der Zeit die Qualität der Sigillata sichtbar gemindert wurde: Am Ende des 2.Jahrhunderts sind die Bilderschüsseln überwiegend orangefarben, was durch niedrige Brenntemperaturen erreicht wurde, d.h. also durch Einsparung von Holz[8] und Brennzeit, und die niedrigen Standringe werden nicht mehr so niedrig und fein herausgedreht wie noch zur

Mitte des 2. Jahrhunderts.[9] Am deutlichsten wird die „Massenproduktion" in der Zeit zwischen 230 und 260, wo sowohl eine veränderte Tonqualität[10] als auch sehr nachlässiges Ausformen des Reliefs und sehr grob geformte Standringe immer zusammen auftreten.[11]

Insgesamt läßt sich aus diesen Merkmalen einer verschlechterten Qualität die Einstellung der Töpfer ablesen: Massenproduktion und Verdienst waren vorrangig, der Stolz auf eine handwerklich gute Töpferware spielte keine Rolle.

Mit dieser Einstellung geht aber auch die Verwendung alter, nicht zerbrochener Model konform: Modische Neuheiten waren den Bildprogrammen nicht mehr abzugewinnen, Tonqualität und Art der Ausformung (Ränder, Standringe, Wandung, Farbe, Oberfläche) gab allen Schüsseln zusätzlich ein einheitliches Aussehen. Händlern und Käufern war eine Unterscheidung zwischen „alten" und „modernen" Dekorationen aufgrund der simplen Aufreihung wiederholter, überwiegend abgeformter Motive praktisch gar nicht möglich. Die Tatsache eines gewissen Anteils an „späten Ausformungen" in den großen Lieferungen fiel nicht auf; weder Töpfer noch Händler oder Verbraucher hatten damit ein Problem.

NEUE FORSCHUNGSAUFGABEN

Probleme ergaben sich allerdings für die Archäologen, die sich bisher auf die Bestimmung des Reliefs und seine vermeintliche Datierung nach dem jeweiligen Töpfer verlassen haben. Es gilt demnach, die Unsicherheiten und Grenzen in unseren chronologischen Vorstellungen zwischen 160 und 260 n.Chr. zu erkennen und darüber hinaus neue Wege bei der Erforschung von Reliefsigillaten dieser Zeit zu finden.

FORMSCHÜSSEL-CHRONOLOGIEN

Unerläßlich ist zunächst das Erarbeiten von Formschüssel-Chronologien. Erst wenn die Entstehungszeit des Models resp. der Bilderschüssel-Dekoration bekannt ist, kann eingeschätzt werden, ab wann frühestens die gefundene Bilderschüssel verkauft worden sein kann, und erst dann wird man – aufgrund der Fundkomplexe und/oder der Sigillataqualität – eine Aussage treffen können, ob es sich womöglich um eine spätere Ausformung handelt.[12]

Formschüssel-Chronologien sind gleichbedeutend mit den Arbeitszeiten der Töpfer, die die Formschüsseln hergestellt haben. Man kann sie am besten durch genauen Punzen-Vergleich erreichen; wenn der Töpfer einzelne beschädigte Punzen benutzte, ist das Nacheinander der Dekorationsserien am leichtesten zu erkennen.

Kann man aber eine relative Abfolge der Töpfer und ihrer Dekorationsserien angeben, so ist diese etwa gleichbedeutend mit dem Wert einer Münzreihe: Wenn an einem Fundort die Dekorationen einer ganzen Töpfergruppe fehlen, so ist zu folgern, daß ihre Produkte noch gar nicht auf dem Markt waren.[13] Für einzelne Reliefsigillaten ergäbe sich wenigstens ein *terminus post quem*, d.h. eine Scherbe mit der Dekoration eines Töpfers, der z.B. erst um 220 begonnen hat, kann jedenfalls nicht vor diesem Zeitpunkt entstanden sein.

STANDRINGE UND SIGILLATAQUALITÄT

Mit Hilfe der Formschüssel-Chronologien bzw. der datierten Fundkomplexe muß die Entwicklung der Standringformen an den Schüsseln Drag. 37 gefestigt werden. Seitdem wir das Beispiel des „Massenfundes" aus der Trierer Töpferei kennen, wo innerhalb einer Werkstatt alle Bilderschüsseln mit der gleichen Standringform versehen wurden,[14] dürfen wir wohl voraussetzen, daß entsprechend in allen Betrieben bestimmte Formen vorherrschend waren. Dabei ist von Töpferei- oder eindeutigen Depotfunden auszugehen, d.h. von Fundkomplexen, die sich auf eine äußerst kurze Entstehungszeit zurückführen lassen.[15] Für Trierer Reliefsigillaten konnte inzwischen eine Unterscheidung in drei Gruppen erfolgen;[16] dies müßte für große Töpfereien wie Lezoux und Rheinzabern ebenfalls erarbeitet werden. Standringe zur Schüssel Drag. 37 sind nun einmal jeweils nach der Ausformung neu angedreht worden, und sie belehren uns besser über den Zeitpunkt der Entstehung als die Dekoration selbst. Angesichts dieser Tatsache sollte die Forschung sich darauf einstellen, daß eine systematische Aufarbeitung von Standringformen mit der Chance einhergeht, besser datieren zu können. Nur bedingt sind die glatten Ränder und ihre Lippenbildung für chronologische Fragen verwertbar. Sehr hohe Ränder (6–9cm) wurden in Trier erst im zweiten Drittel des 3. Jahrhunderts hergestellt. Allerdings gab es in dieser späten Phase gleichzeitig niedrige Ränder.[17]

Insgesamt wird bei der Bestimmung von Reliefschüsseln die Sigillataqualität zu beachten sein; Dickwandigkeit, schlechte Ausprägung des Reliefs und eine rauhe Oberfläche gehen oft Hand in Hand und sind dann ein chronologisches Indiz.

VERGLEICH MIT GLATTEN SIGILLATEN

Der von mir eingeschlagene Weg, über Sigillataqualität zeitgleiche oder spätere Ausformungen zu erkennen, hat unter anderem auch eine Chance, wenn man glatte Sigillaten von Relieftöpfern in die Untersuchung einbeziehen kann. Bekanntlich entfällt das Problem später Ausformungen bei Näpfen und Tellern, die nur einen Namensstempel tragen, d.h. wir gehen davon aus, daß diese Geschirre zu Lebzeiten des namentlich genannten Töpfers entstanden sind. Zumindest bei den Töpfern, die sowohl reliefverzierte als auch glatte Sigillaten im Programm hatten, lassen sich also die Waren bezüglich ihrer Qualität vergleichen.[18]

Um wenigstens beispielhaft etwas anführen zu können, habe ich aus dem Bestand des Frankfurter Museums für Vor- und Frühgeschichte die glatten Sigillaten der Trierer Töpfer AFER, DVBITATVS, MAI.IAAVS und TORDILO zusammengestellt. Mit den Originalen vor Augen ist es beruhigend zu sehen, daß die Waren eines jeden Töpfers in sich einheitlich sind, auch wenn – wie bei TORDILO – rote und orangefarbene Sigillaten nebeneinander produziert wurden: Sie sind jedenfalls in den Oberflächen und im Bruch gleich. Reliefsigillaten mit den Dekorationen dieser Töpfer haben nun entweder die gleiche Qualität oder sie unterscheiden sich so deutlich, daß sie als spätere Produktion gut zu erkennen sind.

Eine zusätzliche Möglichkeit, vor allem bei den Trierer Sigillaten, sind natürlich chemische Analysen.[19] Die Töpfer in Trier hatten kein anstehendes großes Tonlager zur Verfügung wie die Rheinzaberner Töpfer und bezogen ihre Tone im Laufe der Zeit wohl von verschiedenen Tonlagern; eine allmähliche Reduzierung bestimmter Arbeitsgänge kam hinzu. Insofern gibt es bei Tonanalysen teilweise gravierende Unterschiede, die durchaus als chronologische Differenzen interpretiert werden dürfen.

Um den vorgeschlagenen Vergleich mit gestempelten glatten Sigillaten zu erleichtern, wären entsprechende systematisch durchgeführte Tonanalysen die Voraussetzung.

LISTE MIT „SPÄTEREN AUSFORMUNGEN"

Wenn in dieser Weise die Unterschiede der äußeren Form und der Tone beachtet und erkannt werden, ist auch die Bestimmung von „späteren Ausformungen" möglich. Und ein letzter Schritt ist schließlich die Aufzählung und Festlegung aller Dekorationen, deren Formschüssel nachweislich von späteren Töpfern benutzt wurde.[20] Auch wenn eine ziemlich vollständige und deshalb brauchbare Liste erst nach mühsamer Vorarbeit zu erreichen ist, wird sie dann die grundlegende Basis für unsere Datierung mit Reliefsigillaten sein.

ZUSAMMENFASSUNG

Wir können zusammenfassen, daß wir gegenwärtig für ein festes Chronologiesystem der Rheinzaberner und Trierer Reliefsigillaten wenig gesicherte Grundlagen haben. Unsicherheiten über die Entstehung von Formschüssel-Serien – besonders in Rheinzabern – und zusätzlich die bisher kaum beachtete Möglichkeit, daß das Reliefprodukt gar nicht vom Originaltöpfer, sondern aus späterer Zeit stammt, haben unsere Bestimmungen und Datierungen teilweise fehlgeleitet.

Im Grunde genommen sind wir darauf angewiesen, ein völlig neues Forschungsprogramm in Angriff zu nehmen. Erst nach konsequenter Beachtung der genannten Punkte wird man auf lange Sicht sagen können, daß die Reliefsigillaten des späten 2. und des 3. Jahrhunderts sehr wohl für eine kurzfristige Datierung herangezogen werden können.

WIRTSCHAFTSHISTORISCHE AUSWERTUNG

Abgesehen von diesem vordringlichen Anliegen, die Grundlagen unserer Datierung zu verbessern, gibt es aber noch einen weiteren Aspekt bei der Auswertung von Reliefsigillaten, der nicht vergessen werden sollte: Reliefsigillaten eignen sich immer noch am besten für das Nachzeichnen der antiken Wirtschaftsgeschichte. Zu der Tatsache, daß Keramik im Boden nicht vergangen ist wie Metall oder organische Stoffe, kommt hinzu, daß der Reiz an „Bilderschüsseln" für Sammler und Hobby-Archäologen schon immer besonders hoch war und wir daher in Sammlungen und Museen eine hohe Zahl an Reliefsigillaten aufbewahrt finden. Die Gefahr, daß hier die Materialbasis zu gering wäre, besteht also nicht. Keineswegs beeinträchtigt wird eine wirtschaftshistorische Auswertung durch das Vorkommen „später Ausformungen" – im Gegenteil, sie gewähren uns interessante Einblicke in die Arbeitsweise der Betriebe. Fragen nach Umfang und Produktivität einzelner Werkstätten, nach Absatzmärkten, nach dem Anwachsen des Handels und dem Qualitätsabfall der Waren können theoretisch am besten durch Reliefsigillaten beantwortet werden. Voraussetzung ist allerdings auch hier, daß mit einer umfangreichen, systematischen Neubearbeitung der mittelkaiserlichen Reliefsigillaten begonnen wird.

Anmerkungen
1. Huld-Zetsche 1971a; 1972, 62–5; 1978; 1993, 52–6.
2. F. Reutti, Tonverarbeitende Industrie im römischen Rheinzabern, *Germania*, **61** (1983), 33–69 bes. 55 Anm. 39; Bittner 1986, 254 f.; Simon & Köhler 1992, 91 f.; I. Huld-Zetsche & B. Steidl, Die beiden neuen Geschirrdepots von Echzell und Langenhain, *Münstersche Beiträge zur antiken Handelsgeschichte*, **13** (1994), 47–59.
3. Petit 1989. Nach Autopsie der publizierten Sigillaten aus Bliesbruck handelt es sich durchgehend um Sigillataqualitäten, die sich von denjenigen aus der Mitte des 2. Jahrhunderts deutlich absetzen.
4. In den Beständen des Frankfurter Museums für Vor- und Frühgeschichte gibt es Reliefsigillaten aus Lavoye und La Madeleine von sehr unterschiedlicher Qualität; dickwandige, orangefarbene Scherben sind teilweise aus Schichten der 2. Hälfte des 2. Jahrhunderts belegt, wurden aber auch irrtümlich der 1. Hälfte des 2. Jahrhunderts zugewiesen, vgl. Fischer 1973, Abb. 74, 6–7 und Abb.76, 15.
5. Huld-Zetsche 1993, 56.
6. Für die Werkstatt II vgl. Huld-Zetsche 1993, 22–7. Für den Trierer Töpfer DEXTER liegen bisher keine genauen Zahlen vor, doch hatte er mit Sicherheit mehrere hundert eigene Model zur Verfügung; allein 50 davon waren noch im Trierer „Massenfund" vorhanden.
7. Huld-Zetsche 1993, 24.
8. Freundlicher Hinweis von F. K. Bittner.
9. Huld-Zetsche 1993, 47–52, und Taf. 96–101.
10. Die optisch erkennbare schlechtere Qualität wird durch Tonanalysen bestätigt: Huld-Zetsche 1978, 331–4; Huld-Zetsche 1993, Beitrag von

G. Schneider, 65–8; Huld-Zetsche & Steidl, Kapitel Tonanalysen (Anm. 2).
11. Huld-Zetsche, 1978, 324–8; Huld-Zetsche 1993, 54–5.
12. Für die Trierer Töpfereien ist das Neben- und Nacheinander der Reliefsigillata-Töpfer ungefähr bekannt (Huld-Zetsche 1971b, 235, Abb. 1); inzwischen waren Korrekturen möglich, und es werden sicher noch einige folgen. Besonders schwierig ist aber die Rheinzaberner Formschüssel-Chronologie, weil jeweils viele Töpfer nebeneinander Model produzierten und sich die zeitlichen Überschneidungen kaum erfassen lassen. An den bisherigen Einteilungen muß dringlich gearbeitet werden. Zudem wird zur Datierung fast nur auf die Formschüssel-Chronologie von H. Bernhard (1981) Bezug genommen. Ohne Beachtung der Möglichkeiten später Ausformungen enthält diese Handhabung eine Fehlerquelle.
13. In dieser Weise arbeitete H.-G.Simon, und erfolgreich war es vor allem in den Fällen, wo die Töpfer der letzten Gruppe nach Bernhard fehlten, vgl. Simon & Köhler 1992, 88 ff.
14. Huld-Zetsche 1972, 85–6, Taf. 45, H.W.U.585.
15. Zum Thema „Geschirrdepots" hat vor allem M. Rhodes einen sehr verdienstvollen Beitrag geliefert (Roman pottery lost en route from the kiln site to the user. A gazetteer, *J. Roman Pottery Stud.*, **2** (1989), 44–58), der nun ständig ergänzt werden müßte, vgl. Huld-Zetsche & Steidl (Anm. 2).
16. Huld-Zetsche 1993, 49–51; die „mittlere" Gruppe der Standringe wird vor allem durch das Geschirrdepot von Echzell vertreten, ebd. Taf. 101.
17. Huld-Zetsche 1993, 55; Simon & Köhler 1992, 93.
18. In Trier sind das 16 Töpfer, vgl. Huld-Zetsche 1993, 55, Anm.199, und M.Frey, Die römischen Terra-sigillata-Stempel aus Trier, Beiheft **15** der *Trierer Zeitschrift* (1993). – Die Zahl der Rheinzaberner Töpfer liegt wesentlich höher und ist anhand der publizierten Stempel für beide Waren (Ludowici Kat. V und VI) zu erschließen.
19. Vgl. Anm. 10.
20. Ein Anfang ist gemacht mit den Trierer Werkstätten I und II, wo in den Katalogen zu den Dekorationen der Vermerk „spätere Ausformung möglich" auf länger benutzte Model verweist.

Literaturabkürzungen

Bernhard, H., 1981 Zur Diskussion um die Chronologie Rheinzaberner Relieftöpfer, *Germania*, **59**, 79–93

Bittner, F.K., 1986 Zur Fortsetzung der Diskussion um die Chronologie der Rheinzaberner Relieftöpfer, *Bayerische Vorgeschichtsblätter*, **51**, 233–59

Fischer, U., 1973 Grabungen im römischen Steinkastell von Heddernheim 1957–1959, *Schriften des Frankfurter Museum für Vor- und Frühgeschichte*, **2**

Huld-Zetsche, I., 1971a Glatte Sigillaten des 'Massenfundes' aus Trier, *Rei Cretariae Romanae Fautorum Acta*, **13**, 21–39

_____, 1971b Zum Forschungsstand über Trierer Reliefsigillaten, *Trierer Zeitschrift*, **34**, 233–45

_____, 1972 *Trierer Reliefsigillata. Werkstatt I*, Materialien zur römisch-germanischen Keramik, **9** (Bonn)

_____, 1978 Spät ausgeformte römische Bilderschüsseln, *Bonner Jahrbuch*, **178**, 315–34

_____, 1993 *Trierer Reliefsigillata. Werkstatt II*, Materialien zur römisch-germanischen Keramik, **12** (Bonn)

Petit, J.-P., 1989 La commercialisation de la céramique sigillée dans la bourgade gallo-romaine de Bliesbruck (Moselle) au milieu du 3e siècle après J.-C. Révélation d'une production tardive de vases ornés des potiers AVITUS, L.A.L. et L.AT.AT. de Blickweiler et Eschweiler-Hof, *Jahrbuch des Römisch-Germanischen Zentralmuseums Mainz*, **36**, 473–519

Simon, H.-G., & Köhler, H-J., 1992 *Ein Geschirrdepot des 3. Jahrhunderts. Grabungen im Lagerdorf des Kastells Langenhain*, Materialien zur römisch-germanischen Keramik, **11** (Bonn)

17   A decorated samian dish from the London waterfront

Joanna Bird

It is 25 years since I carried a very large box of samian from W.F. Grimes' Walbrook excavations by train from London to Leeds, to work under Brian Hartley's supervision.[1] During the next two weeks I learned more than I would have believed possible, but what most influenced and impressed me was Brian's facility for seeing the potters as individuals, recognising their idiosyncrasies despite their mass-production methods. This was also the occasion of my first meeting with the late potters of East Gaul, an acquaintance which has grown, through chance and choice, in the intervening years. Something on their work seemed appropriate here, and it is offered to Brian with affection and gratitude.

The samian dish which forms the subject of this paper, no. 1 in the catalogue below, was found during excavation of the London waterfront at Billingsgate Lorry Park by the Museum of London's Department of Urban Archaeology in 1982.[2] Three pieces were recovered, two of them together; the small base sherd with the barbotine animal – probably a horse or sea-horse – was found in a different layer but the very tip of the ear is present on one of the other sherds, enabling them to be joined and completing the profile of the vessel. The dish is unusual for its form and, more particularly, for the barbotine decoration which has been applied to the floor. The search for samian dishes with similar decoration has so far produced only nine other examples, seven of which have figures of animals or birds and one a floral motif.

Catalogue

1. London, Billingsgate Lorry Park (figs. 1, 2). Dish, Dr. 36 variant with beaded outer lip. The rim is decorated with a wreath of paired barbotine scrolls; the floor has a rouletted circle, an inner wreath of overlapping barbotine leaves applied over an incised circle, and a barbotine animal, probably a horse or sea-horse, in the centre (Brigham 1990, Table 6, Phase III.1; J. Bird, Museum of London Archaeology Service archive report, BIG82.6555 & 7502).

2. Winchester, St. George's Street (fig. 2). Dish base with low footring. The floor has a pair of incised circles and the figure

of an animal, probably a lion, in the centre (Dannell 1964, 81 and fig. 23, no. 7).

3. Rheinzabern (fig. 3). Dish, Dr. 36 variant with beaded outer lip; the inner lip is also beaded and there is an offset at the junction of wall and floor. The rim is decorated with an elaborate barbotine running scroll; the floor has a wreath of paired barbotine leaves applied over an incised circle, and a barbotine hare in the centre (Hirte 1984, 81–2 and Abb. 25; Ludowici 1905, 250, fig. 26, shows part of this dish but not the hare; Historisches Museum der Pfalz, Speyer, Sammlung Ludowici).

4. Rheinzabern (fig. 2). Dish, Lud. Tb. Approximately one-third of the base with a rouletted circle and part of a hare. The hare is included in Ludowici's catalogue of potters' stamps and marks but described 'Kein Stempel. Bild ausgearbeitet aus dem Grund des Tellerbodens' and is probably barbotine, therefore (Ludowici 1905, 93, M19, no. 4080).

5. Friedberg (not illustrated). Dish with barbotine cockerel (Hirte 1984, 81 note 84, citing Anthes 1914).

6. Rheinzabern (fig. 2). Dish base with an incised circle on the floor and a central barbotine bird (F. Reutti, pers. comm.; site ref. Rhz.79/142).

7. London (fig. 2). Dish base with the barbotine figure of a bird in the centre of the floor (Stanfield 1936, 114 and fig. 7, no. 24, A and B).

8. Mainz (not illustrated). Dish with barbotine bird (Hirte 1984, 81 note 84, citing Anthes 1914).

9. Silchester, Insula III (fig. 2). Large dish base with an incised circle on the floor. The central barbotine motif is too incomplete to be identified: possibly the tail and wing-tip of a bird (Reading Museum 1995.81.1652).

10. Rheinzabern (fig. 4). Dish, Dr. 36 variant with beaded outer lip. The rim is decorated with paired barbotine scrolls

facing inwards round an inner border of curved single leaves. The floor has a rouletted circle round an incised one, with a large central barbotine flower. The flower is daisy-like, with nineteen petals rather unevenly arranged around a plain central boss; each petal has a dot at the base and a neatly defined rib (Hirte 1984, 80 and Abb. 24; Historisches Museum der Pfalz, Speyer, Sammlung Ludowici).

DISCUSSION

The fabric of the Billingsgate dish is hard and fine, a light reddish-orange in colour; the slip is orange-red, shiny but slightly rough on the surface, with a faint iridescence overlying it. Both fabric and slip are characteristic of the factory at Rheinzabern, as are the fabric and slip of the Silchester dish (no. 9), while nos. 3, 4, 6 and 10 were actually recovered there. Unfortunately neither the London piece published by Stanfield (no. 7) nor the piece from Winchester (no. 2) could be located for examination, but both these and the examples from Friedberg and Mainz (nos. 5 and 8) fall within the

known distribution area for Rheinzabern ware, and it is probable that all the dishes were made there. The production of a small quantity of a rare form at a major factory was not unusual: while the samian industry was characterised by standardisation of form and by mass-production of both plain wares and mould-made decorated vessels, there is evidence that several of the potteries experimented with unusual forms which occur only rarely as site finds (e.g. Stanfield 1929; 1936) and are often only encountered at the kiln-site, as is the case with some of the South Gaulish forms illustrated by Hermet (1934).

Where the profile is complete (nos. 1, 3 and 10) the form of the dishes is a variant of Dragendorff form 36; the outer lip is bordered by a heavy bead which is not present on the original type but which occurs on a plain Rheinzabern form of closely similar profile, Ludowici To'.[3] While Dr. 36 is normally ornamented on the rim with a band of simple barbotine leaves, the rims of these three dishes carry much more elaborate decoration consisting of a running scroll or a wreath of scroll motifs. Of the other more fragmentary examples, the

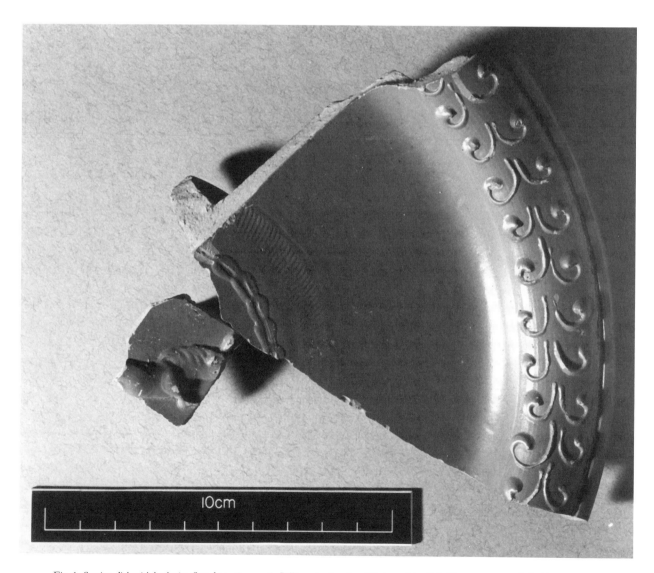

Fig. 1. Samian dish with barbotine floor decoration: no. 1, Billingsgate, London. (Photograph by Eric Hunter, courtesy of Guildford Museum)

piece from Winchester (no. 2) has a lower and rather more elegantly turned footring, but the shallow profile of the body could belong to a Dr. 36. The example from London (no. 6) was described by Stanfield as 'a large dish possibly allied to Dragendorff form 31' (1936, 114), but a Dr. 31 of the date likely for these pots would normally have a marked upwards 'kick' in the interior, and the surviving profile is close to the

Billingsgate piece. Ludowici describes no. 4 as his form Tb (1905, 93); the other pieces are all unidentified dish fragments. F. Reutti considers (pers. comm.) that no. 7 is perhaps more likely to be a Dr. 32 than a Dr. 36, though the bases of some Rheinzabern Dr. 32 dishes are also close in profile to the vessel from Billingsgate (e.g. Oswald & Pryce 1920, pl. 63, no. 7).

The more complete vessels – three out of the ten – do

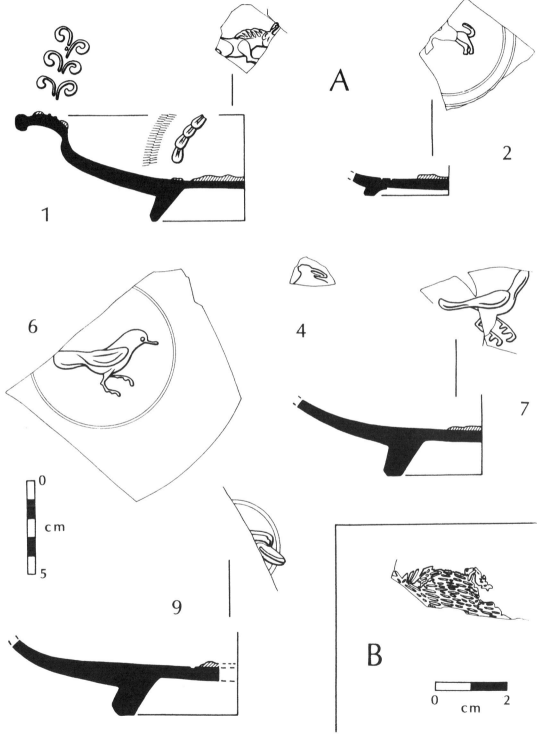

Fig. 2. **A**: *samian dishes with barbotine floor decoration. No. 1, Billingsgate, London; no. 2, Winchester (after Dannell 1964);*
no. 4, Rheinzabern (after Ludowici 1905); no. 6, Rheinzabern (after a colour photograph, courtesy of F. Reutti); no. 7, London (after Stanfield 1936);
no. 9, Silchester. **B**: *boar stamp on samian dish, Billingsgate, London. Scale: A, all 1:2; B, 1:1.*

Fig. 3. Samian dish with barbotine floor decoration: no. 3, Rheinzabern (detail at right). Rim diam. 275mm. (Photographs courtesy of F. Reutti)

suggest that the Dr. 36 variant was preferred, probably so as to combine the barbotine decoration on the floor with that on the rim. Rim fragments of other examples of Dr. 36 or Dr. 36 variants with unusually elaborate rim decoration have been noted from Britain. One from Southwark, London, has three bands of little S-scrolls on the rim, an internal wall/floor offset, as no. 3 above, and a rouletted circle on the floor (Stanfield 1929, 140 and fig. 9, no. 44), while one from London is decorated in cream as well as self-coloured barbotine with a scroll of grapes and vine tendrils sheltering a pheasant-like bird (Stanfield 1929, 140 and fig. 9, no. 45). A dish from Old Ford, London, combines the profile of form Curle 15 (what survives of the angular lower wall is also close to Lud. Tb) with the simple rim of a normal Dr. 36 and an internal wall/floor offset; the barbotine rim decoration consists of a wreath of short scrolls between bands of comma-shaped motifs (Bird 1984, 30 and fig. 6, no. 36).[4] A more complete example of Dr. 36 has a simple rim carrying elaborate barbotine scrolls with heart-shaped leaves and tendrils, an internal wall/floor offset, and a rouletted circle on the floor enclosing a series of inscribed concentric circles in place of a barbotine motif (de la Bédoyère 1988, fig. 41). With such a small and fragmentary group, however, it is clearly not possible at present to say whether the barbotine floor decoration was confined to any specific form or forms, or whether more elaborate rim decoration was regularly associated with additional ornament on the floor.

Barbotine decoration is produced by piping or trailing soft clay onto the surface of the pot, and it was introduced into the samian repertoire in Italy and South Gaul in the second half of the 1st century AD. It continued in use for a limited range of forms throughout the 2nd century, but at the end of the 2nd century or in the early 3rd its use was greatly extended by potters working at Rheinzabern. They introduced a wide range of jar and beaker forms decorated in this way, and also applied the technique to forms which had previously been left

plain, such as Dr. 43 mortaria and bowls of form Dr. 44 (Lud. SMb etc.). It was even used occasionally to ornament the deep rims of mould-decorated bowls of form Dr. 37 with motifs such as scrolls, leaves, a hare, a dolphin and a splendid chained guard-dog (Ludowici 1905, 251, fig. 34; Ludowici & Ricken 1948, Taf. 113, no. 1b, Taf. 135, no. 5b, Taf. 209, no. 17; May 1916, pl. 36, no 15; Oswald & Pryce 1920, pl. 29, no. 10). The skill of these potters was considerable: barbotine technique leaves little room for error or correction, and some of the ornament produced is of the highest standard. The majority of the vessels were decorated with heart-shaped leaves and tendrils, but figured vessels were also produced. On these, the main themes were hunting scenes variously showing hunters, bears, hounds, deer, hares, boar and occasionally lions, usually set among tendrils, leaves and berries; birds, including long-tailed species such as pheasants or peacocks, similarly set among foliage; and, more rarely, fish (e.g. Ludowici 1905, 243–54, figs. 1–42; Roller 1965, Abb. 7). Horses are uncommon, but one is shown on a Lud. SMc from Rheinzabern (Oswald & Pryce 1920, pl. 62, no. 1), and a beaker sherd from Rheinzabern also carries what is probably a horse, to judge from the shape of its head (unpublished; photograph courtesy of F. Reutti).

Where barbotine decoration was being introduced so extensively, it is perhaps not surprising that potters experimented with decorating the floors of flat dishes. It is highly unlikely that the motifs were seen as an alternative to potters' stamps, but the use of stamps may have suggested the position of the ornament. In fact, although the floors of most plain samian forms bore potters' stamps or marks, it is a characteristic of Dr. 36 that it is not normally stamped, perhaps because only a small number of potters specialised in the barbotine decoration and their work could easily be identified when a kiln was unloaded. Some stamped examples of Dr. 36 were produced in the later period at both Trier and Rheinzabern (Huld-Zetsche 1971, Abb. 11, Typ 10b; Reutti

1983, 55) but they are not common. The stamps impressed on plain samian usually consist of the potters' names but other motifs, such as palmettes and rosettes, occur throughout the history of the industry. Rosettes in particular were in use at Lezoux in the Antonine period and at some of the East Gaulish potteries, including Rheinzabern, in the Antonine period and later, and may have suggested the large daisy design of no. 10. More significantly, Ludowici lists several animal stamps which were used at Rheinzabern instead of potters' names: they include a bear or boar, M11; a dog, M36; fish, M10, M18, M27 and M37; and an eagle, M28. They are recorded on a range of bowl and dish forms, including Dr. 31, Dr. 32 and Lud. Tb (Ludowici 1905; 1908; 1912; 1927). An incomplete boar stamp within a rouletted circle (fig. 2, B) was also present among the Billingsgate material, impressed on a dish, probably of form Lud. Tb, from Phase III.1 (J. Bird, Museum of London Archaeology Service archive report, BIG82.6691).

The inspiration for decorating the floor of the vessel with raised ornament may in fact have come from outside the immediate samian industry. The earlier series of African Red Slip Ware forms to carry appliqué motifs was manufactured mainly during the first half of the 3rd century (Hayes 1972, 211–14). They occur as extremely rare finds in the German provinces, but among these finds are two sherds from Trier of a dish decorated round the floor with appliqué figures of a bull and, probably, a lion (Hayes 1972, 59, form 40; Walters 1974, 155, no. 8 and pl. 38). It is conceivable that a Rheinzabern potter may have seen such a dish and imitated it in barbotine. Other contemporary influences are also possible, such as the use of relief motifs on the floors of silver vessels, sometimes associated with decorated rims (Strong 1966, 172–3 and pls. 48B and 49). While the relationship between late samian and fine silver may seem rather remote, the sharing of ideas among craftsmen in different materials at this period

is demonstrated by the close links in both form and decoration between 3rd-century facet-decorated hemispherical cups produced in cut glass, incised samian and punch-impressed silver (Bird 1993, 4).

None of the dishes with barbotine floor decoration comes from a closely dated context. The central sherd of the Billingsgate dish came from Phase III.1 of the waterfront, a low embankment of later 3rd-century date which sealed the earlier quay and contained redeposited pottery of the early to mid-3rd century (Brigham 1990, 106, 162). However, it is probable that the late East Gaulish samian from this site originally formed part of the much larger group of Trier and Rheinzabern wares, dated c. AD 235–245, from the adjacent St. Magnus House/New Fresh Wharf site (Bird 1986). No. 6, the dish from Rheinzabern with the bird motif, came from an area dated generally to the first half of the 3rd century (Reutti 1983, Beilage 3; F. Reutti, pers. comm.). A date in the first half of the 3rd century, and probably within the second quarter, is therefore likely for this group of dishes. This dating receives some support from the adoption of Lud. To' and the bead-rimmed Dr. 36 variant by Romano-British potters making copies of current samian forms from c. AD 240 onwards (e.g. Young 1977, forms C49–50), in particular the Stanground potter active in the early to mid-3rd century who clearly based some of his eccentric repertoire on contemporary Rheinzabern forms (Dannell 1973, fig. 1, no. 1a). This small group of dishes shows that, despite the relatively poor quality of contemporary moulded samian, lively and attractive barbotine ware was still being produced by the Rheinzabern potters.

ACKNOWLEDGEMENTS

I am most grateful to Fridolin Reutti of Rheinzabern, who has generously provided information, photographs and the

Fig. 4. Samian dish with barbotine floor decoration: no. 10, Rheinzabern (detail at right). Rim diam. 270mm. (Photographs courtesy of F. Reutti)

references to Hartwig Hirte's unpublished 1984 thesis. I would
also like to thank David Bird and Brenda Dickinson, who have
read and commented on the text. The Billingsgate dish was
kindly made available for publication by Roberta Tomber,
Museum of London Archaeology Service; I am also indebted
for information to Geoff Dannell, Hartwig Hirte, Helen Rees
(Historical Resources Centre, Winchester), Alison Parnum
(Reading Museum), Jenny Hall (Museum of London) and
Michael Rhodes (Torre Abbey Museum, Torquay). Mary
Alexander at Guildford Museum kindly arranged for Eric
Hunter to photograph the Billingsgate dish.

Notes

1. The final report on the Walbrook excavations is being prepared for
   publication by John Shepherd, Museum of London.
2. The results of the waterfront excavation are discussed in Brigham 1990.
   The Museum of London's archaeologists were however denied access
   to much of the Billingsgate site, and large amounts of unrecorded
   material were trucked away and dumped (J. Schofield, in de la Bédoyère
   1986, 4). An important collection of samian was retrieved from the
   dumps by the late Christopher St. John Breen for the Dartford &
   District Archaeological Group and published by Guy de la Bédoyère
   (1986); it is now held by the Group as a study collection.
3. The various samian forms noted in the discussion are illustrated in
   Oswald & Pryce 1920.
4. This was identified in the original report as a Trier product, but the
   elaborate barbotine and the form would be more appropriate for
   Rheinzabern.

Bibliography

Anthes, E., 1914 Sigillata mit Innenverzierung, *Römisch-Germanisches Korres-pondenzblatt*, **7**, 26–7
Bird, J., 1984 The samian, in Mills, P.S., Excavations at Roman Road/Parnell Road, Old Ford, London E.3, *Trans. London Middlesex Archaeol. Soc.*, **35**, 29–30
_____, 1986 Samian wares, in Miller, L., Schofield, J., & Rhodes, M., *The Roman quay at St. Magnus House, London. Excavations at New Fresh Wharf, Lower Thames Street, London 1974–78* (ed. T. Dyson), London Middlesex Archaeol. Soc. Special Paper, **8**, 139–85 (London)
_____, 1993 3rd-century samian ware in Britain, *J. Roman Pottery Stud.*, **6**, 1–14
Brigham, T., 1990 The late Roman waterfront in London, *Britannia*, **21**, 99–183

Dannell, G.B., 1964 Samian ware, in Cunliffe, B., *Winchester excavations 1949–1960, volume 1*, 76–82, 179 (Winchester)
_____, 1973 The potter Indixivixus, in Detsicas, A. (ed.), *Current research in Romano-British coarse pottery*, Counc. Brit. Archaeol. Res. Rep., **10**, 139–42 (London)
de la Bédoyère, G., 1986 *The Roman site at Billingsgate Lorry Park, London. A catalogue of the samian and other finds*, Brit. Archaeol. Rep. Brit. Ser., **154** (Oxford)
_____, 1988 *Samian ware*, Shire Archaeology, **55** (Princes Risborough)
Hayes, J.W., 1972 *Late Roman pottery* (London)
Hermet, F., 1934 *La Graufesenque (Condatomago)* (Paris; reprint Marseille, 1979)
Hirte, H., 1984 *Untersuchungen zur barbotineverzierten Terra Sigillata in Rheinzabern*, unpublished thesis, Department of Classical Archaeology, University of Mannheim
Huld-Zetsche, I., 1971 Glatte Sigillaten des 'Massenfundes' aus Trier, *Rei Cretariae Romanae Fautorum Acta*, **13**, 21–39
Ludowici, W., 1905 *Stempel-Bilder römischer Töpfer aus meinen Ausgrabungen in Rheinzabern 1901–1905 nebst dem II Teil der Stempelnamen [Katalog II]* (Munich)
_____, 1908 *Urnen-Gräber römischer Töpfer in Rheinzabern und III Folge dort gefundener Stempelnamen und Stempelbilder bei meinen Ausgrabungen 1905–1908 [Katalog III]* (Munich)
_____, 1912 *Römische Ziegelgräber. Katalog IV meiner Ausgrabungen in Rheinzabern 1908–1912. Stempelnamen, Stempelbilder, Urnengräber* (Munich)
_____, 1927 *Katalog V. Stempelnamen und Bilder römischer Töpfer, Legionsziegelstempel, Formen von Sigillata- und anderen Gefässen aus meinen Ausgrabungen in Rheinzabern 1901-1914* (Munich)
_____, & Ricken, H. (ed.), 1948 *Katalog VI meiner Ausgrabungen in Rheinzabern 1901–1914. Die Bilderschüsseln der römischen Töpfer von Rheinzabern: Tafelband* (Speyer)
May, T., 1916 *The pottery found at Silchester* (Reading)
Oswald, F., & Pryce, T. Davies, 1920 *An introduction to the study of terra sigillata treated from a chronological standpoint* (London)
Reutti, F., 1983 Tonverarbeitende Industrie im römischen Rheinzabern. Vorbericht für die Grabungen der Jahre 1978–1981, *Germania*, **61**, 33–69
Roller, O., 1965 *Die römischen Terra-Sigillata-Töpfereien von Rheinzabern* (Limes-Museum Aalen)
Stanfield, J.A., 1929 Unusual forms of terra sigillata, *Archaeol. J.*, **86**, 113–51
_____, 1936 Unusual forms of terra sigillata: second series, *Archaeol. J.*, **93**, 101–12
Strong, D.E., 1966 *Greek and Roman gold and silver plate* (London)
Walters, V.J., 1974 *The cult of Mithras in the Roman provinces of Gaul*, Études Préliminaires aux Religions Orientales dans l'Empire Romain, **41** (Leiden)
Young, C.J., 1977 *The Roman pottery industry of the Oxford region*, Brit. Archaeol. Rep., **43** (Oxford)

18 Die Datierung der Rheinzaberner Reliefsigillata

Klaus Kortüm und Allard Mees

EINFÜHRUNG

In den Arbeiten von Brian Hartley spielen 'Dated Sites' eine Schlüsselrolle. Mit ihrer Hilfe gelingt es ihm die Chronologie vor allem der südgallischen und der mittelgallischen Sigillata in den Griff zu kriegen. Eine wesentliche Stütze sind dabei die durch die britische Forschung erschlossenen historischen Okkupationslinien. Blicken wir auf den Kontinent und hier insbesondere auf den Großbetrieb von Rheinzabern, so muß man festhalten, daß 'Dated Sites' im klassischen Sinne mit Material aus dieser Töpferei trotz der umfangreichen Grabungstätigkeit der letzten Jahre rar geblieben sind. In der für die Frage der Datierung der Rheinzaberner Reliefsigillata relevanten Zeit ab der Mitte des 2. Jhs. sind die historischen Abfolgen weitgehend zum Stillstand gekommen. Das ist einer der Gründe, warum die Forschung zur Rheinzaberner Chronologie teilweise andere Ansätze verfolgt hat.

FORSCHUNGSSTAND

Die wesentlichen Bemühungen gehen von der von Ricken unbegründet gelassenen Abfolge der Töpfer in seinem Tafelband aus und versuchen mit Hilfe verschiedener mathematischer Verfahren dem 'Geheimnis' dieser Abfolge auf die Spur zu kommen.[1] Ausgangspunkt sind dabei die von den verschiedenen Töpfern gemeinsam benutzten Punzen, die zu Gruppenbildungen genutzt werden.[2] Darauf bauen dann die chronologischen Überlegungen auf.

Zu einer einfachen linearen Abfolge, die der von Ricken ungefähr entspricht, kommt man z.B., wenn man – wie jüngst geschehen – die Rheinzaberner Dekorationsserien ('Töpfer') einer Seriation unterwirft. Konfrontiert man die daraus resultierende Abfolge mit geschlossenen Fundvergesellschaftungen, so zeigt sich, daß sich die Gruppierung der Töpfer darin zwar im Großen und Ganzen widerspiegelt, aber im Detail vereinzelt Widersprüche bestehen.[3] Dies gilt gleichermaßen für andere Gruppierungsversuche.[4]

Ein Grund mag darin liegen, daß die Gruppierung mittels Punzenvergesellschaftungen selbst im idealen Falle nur die Chronologie der *Modelherstellung* erschließt, die Fundver-

gesellschaftungen aber auf den *Umlaufzeiten der Ausformungen* beruhen. Zwischen beiden Polen der Datierung muß aber keine lineare Beziehungen bestehen.

Hinzu kommt, daß bei einer Punzenseriation durch blockweise Punzenweitergabe innerhalb des Produktionszentrums Verzerrungen entstehen können. Ein Beispiel ist die Serie Reginus I, deren Punzen z.T. durch die ('späten') Dekorateure 61 (Marcellus II) und 62 (Augustalis) übernommen wurden und deshalb in einer produktionsinternen Seriation als 'zu jung' eingeordnet wird.[5] Auch mehrere unabhängig arbeitende Töpfergruppen führen zu Problemen. Daher stehen Chronologien auf der Grundlage von Punzengruppierungen unter starkem methodischem Vorbehalt.

Im folgenden soll deswegen der Versuch unternommen werden, das Vorkommen von Ausformungen in geschlossenen Fundkomplexen unabhängig von der Rheinzaberner Produktionsstruktur zu analysieren.

DATENVORLAGE

Dazu dient eine Sammlung von Fundvergesellschaftungen aus dem gesamten Verbreitungsgebiet Rheinzaberns. Bevorzugt wurden solche Komplexe aufgenommen, die absolut datiert sind oder bei denen man davon ausgehen kann, daß es sich um zeitlich eng umgrenzte Materialhorizonte handelt. Diese Sammlung umfaßt zur Zeit 40 *features*.[6] Zur Gliederung des Materials wurde zunächst eine Seriation[7] durchgeführt, die auf den Häufigkeitsangaben der Ausformungen eines Formschüsselherstellers in den Fundkomplexen basiert. Die resultierende Matrix zeigt Abb. 1.

Während der Arbeit an der Tabelle erwies sich, daß neben dem Inhalt der Fundkomplexe auch der stark unterschiedliche Umfang für die Anordnung der Zeilen und Spalten wichtig ist. Die Einheiten mit großen Werten bestimmen die Mittelwerte der Zeilen und Spalten nämlich in so erheblicher Weise, daß die Unterschiede zwischen den kleineren *features* relativ weniger Bedeutung erlangen, was aus archäologischer Sicht nicht gerechtfertigt ist. Dies schränkt die Aussagekraft dieser Häufigkeitsseriation von Seiten der Statistik ein.

Eine Korrespondenzanalyse,[8] die am selben Datenmaterial

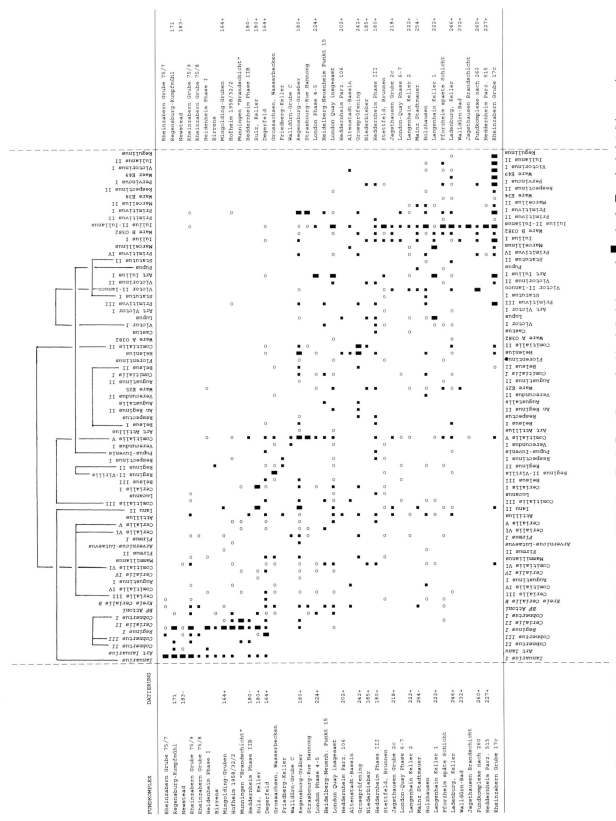

Abb. 1. Seriation von Fundkomplexen mit Rheinzaberner Reliefsigillata. Für die Darstellung wurden folgende Symbole verwendet: ■ = häufig; ▪ = durchschnittlich; ○ = selten.

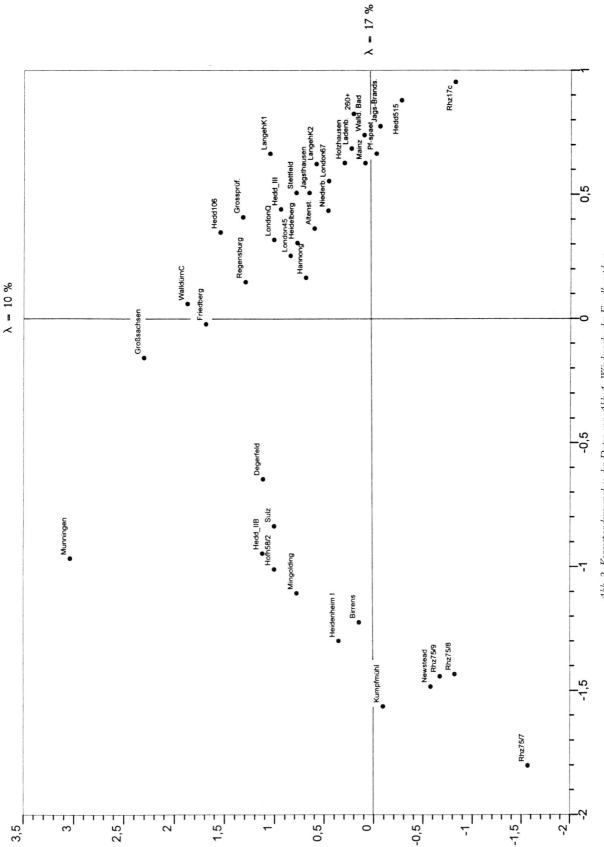

Abb. 2. Korrespondenzanalyse der Daten von Abb. 1. Wiedergabe der Fundkomplexe.

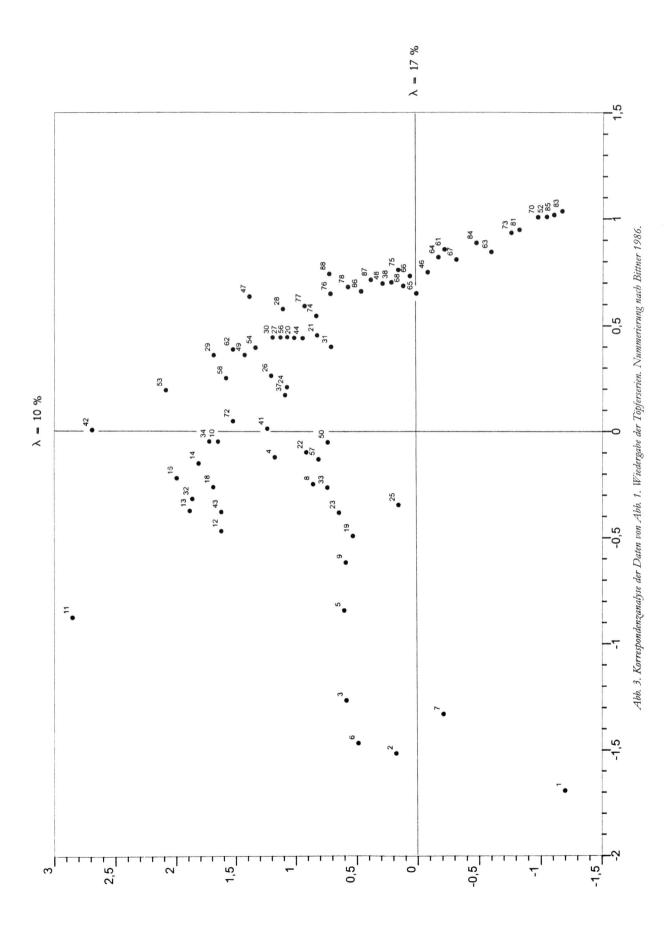

Abb. 3. Korrespondenzanalyse der Daten von Abb. 1. Wiedergabe der Töpferserien. Nummerierung nach Bittner 1986.

durchgeführt wurde, scheint die Bedenken zu bestätigen (Abb. 2). Die größten Fundkomplexe (Rhz. 75/7–9, Rhz. Gr. 17c) befinden sich bei den extremen Werten der 1. Komponente (x-Achse).

Deutlich wird aber auch etwas Anderes: die starke Gruppierung sämtlicher Fundkomplexe an den äußeren Werten der 1. Komponente. Offensichtlich sind die Daten entlang der Zeitachse nicht gleichmäßig verteilt. Es scheint vielmehr so zu sein, daß sowohl aus der Anfangszeit wie vom Ende der Reliefsigillataproduktion Rheinzaberns verstärkt Materialhorizonte vorliegen. Hier dürften historische Gegebenheiten eine Rolle spielen. Für die Entstehung der Fundkomplexe auf der linken Seite der 1. Komponente werden z.T. die Markomannenkriege als Erklärung herangezogen. Die Bildung der Fundkomplexe rechts wird meistens mit den Vorgängen der Germaneneinfälle im mittleren Drittel des 3. Jhs. in Zusammenhang gebracht.[9] Diese dichothomische Verteilung ist für eine Seriation nicht gerade förderlich.

Um das Problem der sehr unheitlichen Mengen in den Fundkomplexen zu umgehen, wurde eine Anwesenheits/Abwesenheits-Seriation durchgeführt (Abb. 4). Daß die großen *Units* in diesem Verfahren nicht zu stark dominieren, wird durch das Resultat bestätigt: sie befinden sich nicht mehr an den Ecken der Matrix. Zugleich ist die Streuung der Variablen geringer als bei der Seriation mit den Häufigkeitswerten. Die mutmaßliche chronologische Reihenfolge der Fundkomplexe – erkennbar an den absoluten Daten[10] – wurde nicht im negativen Sinne beeinflußt. Die resultierende Abfolge der Töpfer ist in beiden Fällen ähnlich. Verschiebungen über mehr als 10 Positionen hinweg sind in den beiden Matrizen selten. Größere Abweichungen sind bei den Serien Attillus, Primitivus I + III, Pupus-Iuvenis, Reginus-Virilis, Belsus I, Iulius I, Castus und Victor I festzustellen.

Bei den Korrespondenzanalysen dieser Datensammlungen ist die Qualität der resultierenden Parabeln unterschiedlich. Die Häufigkeitsdaten (Abbn. 2 und 3) erbringen eine viel flachere Parabel als die Anwesenheitsdaten (Abbn. 5 und 6) weil die Gegensätze zwischen den einzelnen Fundkomplexen durch die Häufigkeit verschärft werden.[11]

Zur Auswertung

In allen Verfahren wird eine deutliche Diagonale in der Seriation (Abbn. 1 u. 4) bzw. eine Parabel in der Korrespondenzanalyse (Abbn. 2, 3, 5 und 6) erreicht. Dies scheint auf einen kontinuierlichen Wandel in der Zusammensetzung der Reliefsigillata in den 'Dated Sites' zu deuten. 'Spätausformungen'[12] spielen offensichtlich keine entscheidende Rolle in der Rheinzaberner Reliefsigillataproduktion, denn dann wären z.B. die Diagonalen nicht so ausgeprägt. Das gilt auch für die Häufigkeitsseriation, wenn man die Schwerpunkte beachtet.

Bei der Streuung der älteren Töpfer in den späten Fundkomplexen ist zu bedenken, daß diese auch residuale Stücke enthalten dürften. Insbesondere bei Funden aus Schichten oder Kellereinfüllungen ist damit zu rechnen, daß auch sekundär umgelagertes Altmaterial enthalten ist. Ohne eingehende Fundkritik lassen sich diese Stücke aber nicht *a priori* aussondern und selbst dann wird man wohl nur selten die für eine mathematische Verarbeitung wünschenswerte Eindeutigkeit erlangen.[13]

Die Chance, daß die vollständige Umlaufzeit einer Ware in den obigen Matrizen erfaßt ist, wird bei den häufig auftretenden Töpfern natürlich größer als bei den selten gefundenen Produkten. Berücksichtigt man ferner, daß im vorliegenden Fall die Fundkomplexe mit Produkten aus der mittleren Produktionszeit Rheinzaberns weitgehend zu fehlen scheinen, so ist damit zu rechnen, daß bei einer Reihe von kleineren Dekorationsserien nur Stücke aus der Anlauf- oder Auslaufzeit ihrer Produktion erfaßt sind, oder gar nur residuale Stücke. Deshalb können Waren in der Tabelle als 'zu früh' oder 'zu spät' eingeordnet sein. Bei größeren Serien ist denkbar, daß die Schwerpunkte falsch wiedergegeben sind. Dies hat natürlich auch Einfluß auf die Reihenfolge der Fundkomplexe.

Ein weiterer Vorbehalt hinsichtlich der Aussagekraft der Seriationen ist, daß die Fundkomplexe heterogen sind. Neben Gesamtreihen von Fundplätzen mit mehr oder weniger genau bekanntem Anfang bzw. Ende (z.B. Newstead, Holzhausen, Degerfeld) gibt es Vergesellschaftungen mit Depotcharakter (Langenhain, Großsachsen) oder Einfüllungen von Baustrukturen wie Kellern, Brunnen oder Gruben (Rheinzabern, Pforzheim, Ladenburg, Stettfeld usw.). Theoretisch könnte man sicher viele Argumente dafür vorbringen, daß der Befund auf die Zusammensetzung der Funde Einfluß genommen hat. Ob jedoch tatsächlich Verzerrungen eingetreten sind, läßt sich letztlich nur dann zuverlässig beurteilen, wenn man die Chronologie sowie die Produktionsverhältnisse kennen würde. Da genau diese Frage aber erst Gegenstand der Untersuchung ist, bleibt in diesem Punkt momentan nur ein *non liquet*.

Eine Stabilisierung der Matrizen könnte erzielt werden, wenn man mehrere Töpferserien zusammenfügen würde. Hier bieten sich in erster Linie diejenigen Serien an, die die gleichen Modelsignaturen (Stempel) zeigen, aber durch Ricken voneinander getrennt wurden (Tabelle 1).[14] Bei einer verdichteten Matrix dürften sich leichter Schwerpunkte ausbilden und die Zufälligkeiten eines Fundkomplexes zu einer Art statistischem Rauschen herabsinken. Insofern könnte man dies auch auf alle Dekorationsserien eines Töpfers ausdehnen. Beschränkt man sich auf die Stempel, so ergibt sich, daß die Stempelkopplungen in 3 von 11 Fällen zehn Positionen der Häufigkeitstabelle überspringen.[15] Bei der Anwesenheitsmatrix ist die Summe der Abweichungen höher.

Auch die Randstempel könnte man in die Untersuchung mit einbeziehen. Die Modeldekorateure, die über gleichnamige Ausformer miteinander verknüft sind, gruppieren sich mit der Ausnahme von Comitialis I ganz links in den Seriationsmatrizen (Abbn. 1 und 4).[18] Sie sind *kursiv* wiedergegeben. Die Gleichzeitigkeit mehrerer Modelhersteller, die durch die Randstempel der Ausformer nahegelegt wird, läßt sich also auch über die datierten Fundkomplexe nachweisen.

Ein Mehr an Fundkomplexen oder weniger Töpfer wären auch deswegen wünschenswert, weil in der vorliegenden Matrix die Zahl der Fundkomplexe gegenüber der großen Zahl zu datierender Töpfer deutlich zurückbleibt. Das führt dazu, daß seltene Serien in der Tabelle entweder gar nicht

Dekorationsserie	Ludowici-*Die*					Zusatzstempel
Belsus I	a					
Belsus II	a					
Cerialis III		c	d			Consta et Ni
Cerialis V		c		c		
Cerialis VI		c				
Cobnertus I	b	c				
Cobnertus II	a	c				
Cobnertus III	a					*Martinus*
Comitialis II	a					Ioventi
Comitialis III	b					*Costio*
Comitialis V	a					Latinni
Comitialis VI	b		d	e	h g	
Ianu I	x					
Ianu II	x					
Lucanus I	x					
Lucanus II/E 8	x ([16])					
Marcellus I	x					
Marcellus II	x					
Pervincus I	a	b	c	d	e	
Pervincus II/E 31		? ([17])				
Pupus	x					
Pupus-Iuvenis	x					Iuvenis
Reginus II			d	e	g	
Reginus II-Viril			d	e		Virilis
Statutus I	x					
Statutus II	x					
Victor I	x					
Victor II-Ianuco	x					
Victor III	x					
Victorinus II	a	b	d			
Victorinus III	a					

*Tabelle 1: Dekorationsserien mit Stempelverbindungen. Graffiti sind **kursiv** wiedergegeben.*

auftauchen (die Tabelle umfaßt 72 der 89 Rheinzaberner Dekorationsserien), oder nur in 2 oder 3 Fundkomplexen. Neu hinzukommende Fundkomplexe können demnach die Reihenfolge der kleinen Modelhersteller noch erheblich ändern.

Bei dieser Ausgangslage wird man datierende Aussagen vor allem in Hinblick auf die Großserien treffen können. Hierzu zählen Ianus I, Reginus I, Cobnertus I-III, Cerialis I-V, Comitialis I-VI, Primitivus I-IV, Iulius I, Iulius II-Iulianus I und Victor.

Mit allem Vorbehalt schlagen wir folgende Daten für die **Haupt**umlaufzeiten dieser Waren vor:

Ianus I, Reginus I, Cobnertus I-III: 150/160–190/200
Cerialis I-V: 160/170 – 220/230
Comitialis I-VI: 170/180 – 230/240
Primitivus I-VI, Iulius I: 190/200 – 250/260
Iulius II, Victor: 220/230 – 260/270

Die Struktur der Datenbasis bringt es mit sich, daß für das Enddatum in der Regel mehr Anhaltspunkte zur Verfügung stehen als für den Anfang. Gerade das Enddatum einer Um-

laufzeit ist aber naturgemäß unscharf und kann gar nicht präzise bestimmt werden.[19] Die Anfangsdatierungen dürften sich dagegen bei verbesserter Datenbasis zuverlässiger bestimmen lassen als heute. Die kleineren Töpferserien sind zur Zeit höchstens nur relativ, d.h. als eher früh, mittel oder spät einzuordnen. Dabei dürfte die Anordnung der Töpfer (natürlich auch die der Fundkomplexe) in der Häufigkeitsseriation aus archäologischer Sicht der Vorzug gegenüber der Anwesenheits/Abwesenheits-Seriation gegeben werden, da diese u.a. die archäologischen Unwägbarkeiten (insbesondere die Residualität) eher berücksichtigt.

Wendet man seinen Blick der Datierung der Fundkomplexe zu, so läßt sich aus den Tabellen erkennen, daß grundsätzlich mit einer heterogenen Zusammensetzung der Reliefsigillata zu rechnen ist. Die Zeithorizonte unterscheiden sich weniger aufgrund des Vorkommens bestimmter Töpfer, sondern vielmehr in ihrem Gesamtbild. Insofern sollte in Zukunft bei Datierungsfragen der Definition von Materialhorizonten der Vorzug vor der Einzeldatierung bestimmter Töpfer gegeben werden. Nur dann ist die für die historisch-archäologische Auswertung nötige Genauigkeit zu erzielen.

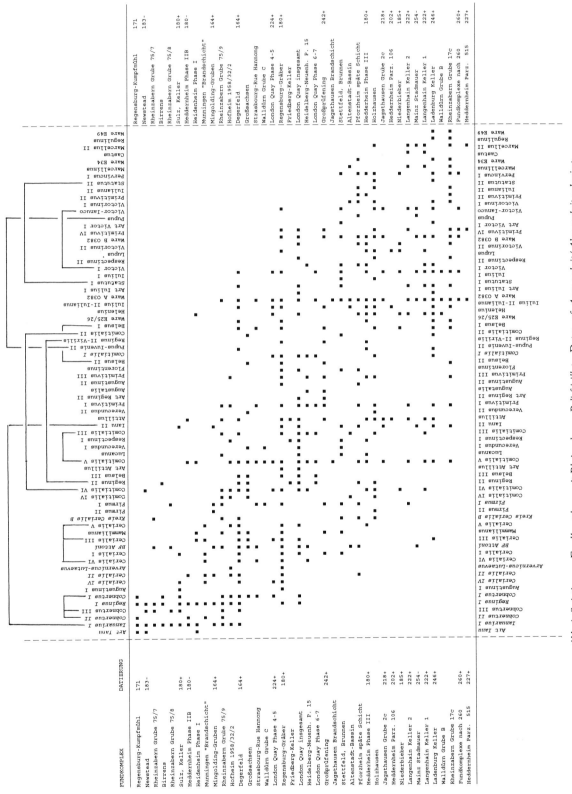

Abb. 4. Seriation von Fundkomplexen mit Rheinzaberner Reliefsigillata. Daten auf Anwesenheit/Abwesenheit reduziert.

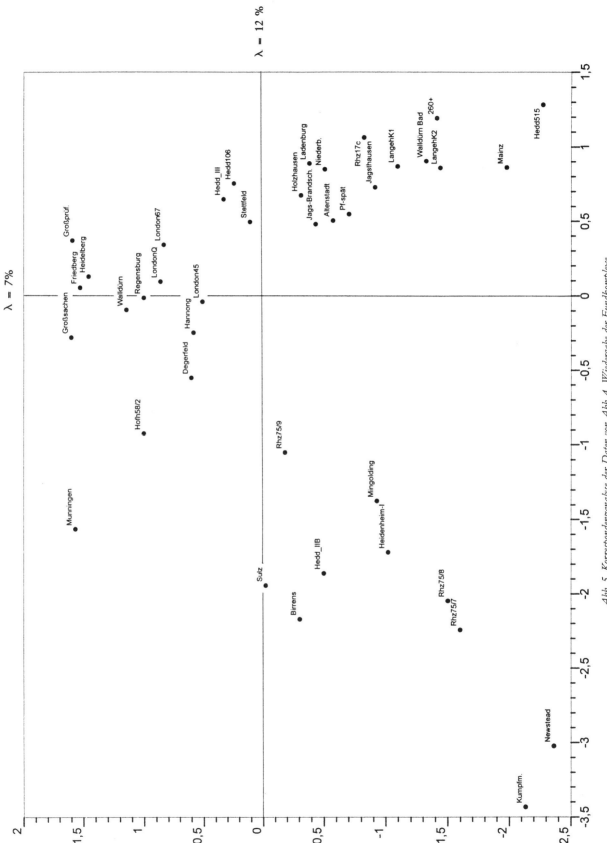

Abb. 5. Korrespondenzanalyse der Daten von Abb. 4. Wiedergabe der Fundkomplexe.

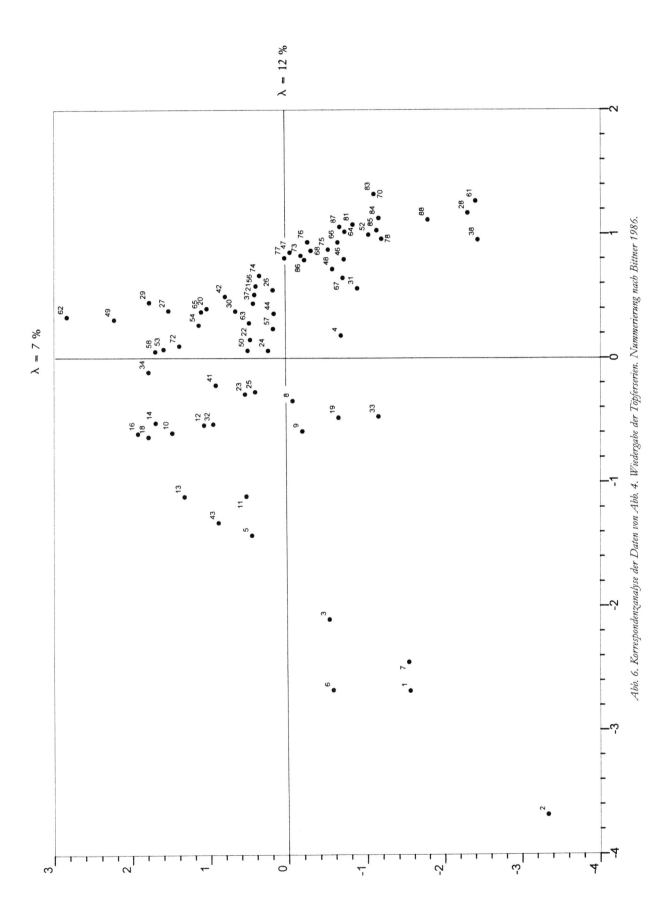

Abb. 6. Korrespondenzanalyse der Daten von Abb. 4. Wiedergabe der Töpferserien. Nummerierung nach Bittner 1986.

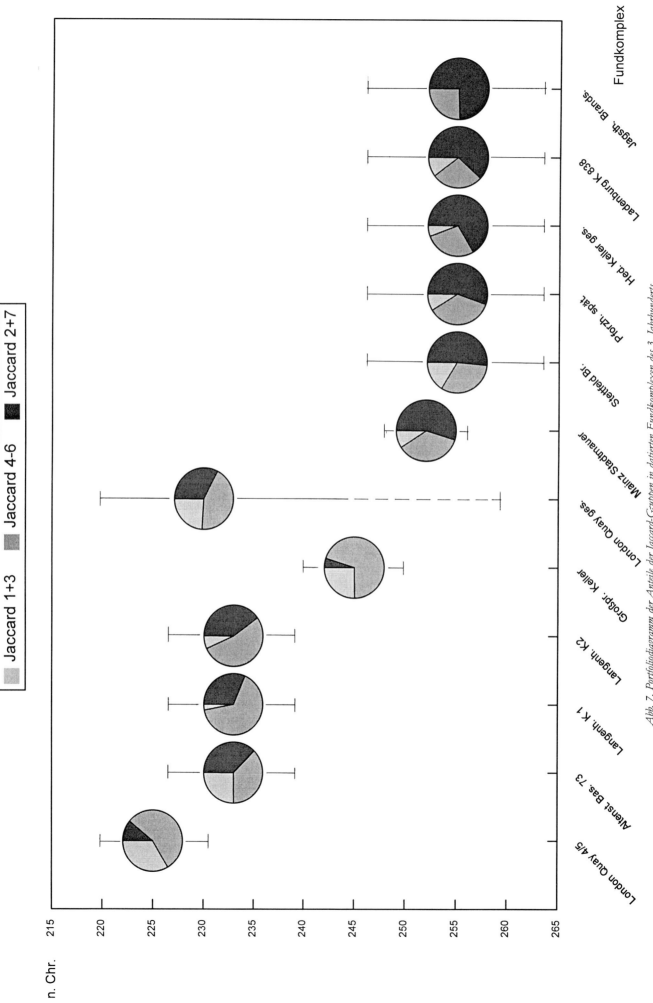

Abb. 7. Portfoliodiagramm der Anteile der Jaccard-Gruppen in datierten Fundkomplexen des 3. Jahrhunderts.

Dabei müßten verstärkt auch die übrigen Formen der Fein-keramik Berücksichtigung finden. Eine Bevorzugung der Reliefsigillata (auch gerade bei Veröffentlichungen von Fundkomplexen !), wie sie in der Vergangenheit häufig statt-fand, ist sicher nicht berechtigt.[20]

REGIONALITÄT

Die eingangs genannten Untersuchungen der Punzenver-gesellschaftungen haben gezeigt, daß in Rheinzabern mehrere Gruppen von Töpferserien bzw. Punzenfamilien unterschie-den werden können. Diese lassen sich in drei bzw. vier große Gruppen einteilen, was besonders anschaulich in einer Kor-respondenzanalyse der Punzen zu Tage tritt. (Dies sind die Jaccard-Gruppen 1 und 3, 4 bis 6, 2 und 7.)[21] Trägt man den Anteil dieser Großgruppen der Korrespondenzanalyse in den Fundkomplexen zusammen mit der mutmaßlichen Datierung auf – was für das 3. Jh. in Abb. 4 geschehen ist – so erkennt man, daß die Punzenfamilien in den archäologischen Hori-zonten von 233 n.Chr. und 260 n.Chr. (die mit den Ger-maneneinfällen in Verbindung gebracht werden) unterschied-lich vertreten zu sein scheinen.[22] Dies wird in den Matrizen der Seriationen durch die große Anzahl von Modellherstellern nicht in dem Maße deutlich. Die Schwierigkeit dieser Betrach-tung besteht darin, daß auf Punzengruppierungen zurück-gegriffen wurde, was anfänglich ja in Bezug auf die Datier-ungen der Töpfer bewußt vermieden wurde, da keineswegs bewiesen ist, daß es sich um homogene ('gleichzeitige') Werk-stattkreise handelt. Auch haben die Aussagen nur dann ihre Gültigkeit, wenn die angenommenen präzisen Datierungen stimmen, was nicht als gesichert gelten kann, und daß der Inhalt der Fundkomplexe auch repräsentativ für die Zeit ist.

In diesem Zusammenhang ist ein Blick auf den Fund-komplex Großprüfening wichtig. Auffällig ist nämlich, daß dieser zu der angenommenen Datierung von 244 n. Chr. nicht so recht paßt. Die Zusammensetzung ähnelt viel eher älteren Fundkomplexen als solchen der Mitte des 3. Jhs. Die Seriatio-nen deuten gleiches an. Hierin äußert sich möglicherweise der Einfluß einer regional unterschiedlichen Verbreitung der Sigil-lataserien. Eine Untersuchung zur Zusammensetzung der Funde aus Siedlungen von Großbritannien bis zum Schwar-zen Meer hat ergeben, daß regionale Großräume feststellbar sind, in denen sich die Zusammensetzung der Rheinzaberner Reliefsigillaten stark ähnelt, die untereinander aber deutliche Unterschiede aufweisen. Diese Räume sind das nördliche Obergermanien mit Germania Inferior und Britannien, das südliche Obergermanien und Rätien sowie der Donauraum.[23] Diese Gebiete sind auch als kulturhistorische Räume und als 'Keramikprovinzen' anderer Manufakturen bekannt. Ob die Unterschiede daher rühren, daß Rheinzabern auf unter-schiedliche Konkurrenzsituationen traf, oder ob hier schon von der Manufaktur aus unterschiedlich beliefert wurde, bliebe zu klären. Bei der Datierung von Rheinzaberner Sigil-laten muß jedenfalls in Zukunft verstärkt der regionale Markt berücksichtigt werden. Momentan beruhen unsere chrono-logischen Vorstellungen in hohem – vielleicht in zu hohem – Maße auf den Verhältnissen des nördlichen Verbreitungs-gebietes.[24]

Anmerkungen

1. Ludowici u. Ricken 1948.
2. Bernhard 1981; Bittner 1986; Mees 1993, Abb. 3.
3. Mees 1994, Liste 1.
4. Bernhard 1981; Zanier 1993.
5. Mees 1993, Tabelle 2–3.
6. Wir danken an dieser Stelle allen Kollegen, die uns uneigennützig ihr oft noch unpubliziertes Material überlassen haben. Siehe für die Daten: Altenstadt-Bassin: Schönberger u. Simon 1983, 193, FK 47; Degerfeld: Simon 1968, 23; Friedberg, Keller: Wagner 1987/1988, Abb. 6; Fund-komplexe nach 260 n.Chr.: Mees 1994, Liste 1; Großprüfening: Fischer 1990, 35 mit Anmerkung 133; Großsachen, Wasserbecken: Hagendorn 1991; Heddernheim, Parzellen: Nuber 1969, 145–6; Heddernheim, Phase IIB und III: Fischer 1973, 208; Heidelberg-Neuenheim, Fund-punkt 15: unpubliziert, Mitteilung M. Kemkes; Heidenheim, Phase I: Heiligmann 1990, 185; Hofheim, Grube 1958/32/2: Mees 1994, Liste 1; Holzhausen: Pferdehirt 1976; Jagsthausen, Brandschicht: Kortüm 1988, 333f.; Jagsthausen, Grube 2c: Kortüm, unpubliziert; Ladenburg, Keller: unpubliziert, Mitteilung H. Kaiser; Langenhain, Keller 1 und 2: Simon u. Köhler 1992; London Quay: Bird 1986, 139 und persön-liche Mitteilung; Mainz, Stadtmauer: nach freundlicher Mitteilung A. Heising; Mingolding: Fischer 1990, 270ff; Munningen: Simon 1976, 50; Newstead: Hartley 1972, Appendix VII; Niederbieber: Oelmann 1914. Die Dekorationen Taf. 8, 24.27.29.30.31.32.34 wurden bestimmt; Pforzheim späte Schicht: Kortüm 1995; Regensburg, Kumpfmühl: Faber 1994, 191ff; Regensburg, Gräberfeld: Schnurbein 1977; Rheinzabern, Grube 17c: Bittner 1986, 250; Rheinzabern, Grube 75/7–9: Gimber 1993, 135ff; Stettfeld: Knötzele 1993; Strasbourg, Rue Hannong: unpubliziert, Mitteilung G. Kuhnle-Aubrey; Sulz, Keller 7: Schaub 1993, 83; Walldürn, Grube B und C: Weinrich-Kemkes 1993.
7. Mit Hilfe des Bonner Archaeological Statistics Package, Version 4.5.
8. Zum Verfahren s. Greenacre 1993.
9. Wenn diese Verknüpfungen auch z.T. durch Münzdatierungen nahe-gelegt werden, so bleibt doch zu bedenken, daß sie in aller Regel spekulativ sind und keinesfalls als vorgegebene Datierungen verwendet werden können. Auf der anderen Seite sollten historische Ereignis-horizonte gerade an deutlichen Gruppenbildungen erkennbar sein, da eine allein dem Zufall verpflichtete Genese der Fundkomplexe eine ausgeglichene Abfolge ergäbe.
10. Meist geben Münzen einen *tpq* für die Ablagerung des Fundensembles, gelegentlich sind es auch Dendrodaten oder solche der Epigraphik (z.B. Bad Walldürn, 232+). In einigen Fällen ist das Ende der Ablagerung eines Fundkomplexes ungefähr bekannt, der Anfang aber nicht (z.B. Newstead, 183+).
11. Greenacre 1984, 226ff.
12. Bittner 1986, 254; Huld-Zetsche 1993, 62.
13. Sehr aufschlußreich sind hier die Ausführungen von A. Schaub (Schaub 1993, 85ff.) zum Keller in Sulz. Er konnte durch eingehende Analyse feststellen, daß von den zeitlich mit dem Brand parallelen Stücken sowohl kleine wie auch große Bruchstücke bzw. Einzelstücke vorliegen, von Altstücken aber nur kleine Scherben existieren (Resi-dualität betrifft hier im übrigen keine Rheinzaberner Töpfer). Für die Zukunft könnte man sich deswegen überlegen, ob man statt der Anzahl nicht ein Maß für die Größe der Scherben verwendet. Dann würden sich bei hinreichend großer Datenmenge die residualen Stücke sicher eindeutiger von den dem aktuellen Umlauf entstammenden Stücken unterscheiden lassen.
14. Hier dürften vor allem stilistische Kriterien ausschlaggebend gewesen sein. Ganz durchschaubar ist die Arbeitsweise von Ricken auch in diesem Punkt nicht.
15. Durch Nichtvertretensein von Töpfern in der Matrix sind einige Stempelkopplungen nicht beurteilbar.
16. Bittner 1986, 236, Abb. 1.
17. Bittner 1986, 236, Anmerkung 8.
18. Zu den Randstempeln Mees 1994, Liste 1.
19. Man kann im Grunde nur Wahrscheinlichkeitsangaben machen wie: Bis 220 n. Chr. sind 95% der Ware xy aus dem Umlauf verschwunden usw.
20. Eine analoge Betrachtung der Fundkomplexe mit glatter Sigillata hat ergeben, daß sich die Reihenfolge der Fundkomplexe bei beiden

Gattungen weitgehend entsprechen. Einer integralen Betrachtung allen Materials steht leider die angeführte Publikationslage im Wege.

21. Mees 1993, Abb. 3; Mees 1994, Fig. 4a.

22. Dabei wurde Reginus I zu 1 gezählt, die übrigen residualen Serien zu der nächstliegenden Großgruppe.

23. Mees 1994, Fig. 9. Mittlerweile hat sich das Bild auf breiterer Datenbasis verdeutlicht.

24. Manuskriptschluß: Juli 1994.

Literatur

Bernhard, H., 1981 Zur Diskussion um die Chronologie der Rheinzaberner Relieftöpfer, *Germania*, **59**, 79–93

Bird, J., 1986 Samian wares, in Dyson, T. (Hrsg.), *The Roman quay at St. Magnus House, London*, London and Middlesex Archaeological Society Special Paper, **8**, 139–185 (London)

Bittner, F.-K. 1986 Zur Fortsetzung der Diskussion um die Chronologie der Rheinzaberner Relieftöpfer, *Bayerische Vorgeschichtsblätter*, **51**, 233–59.

Fischer, Th., 1990 *Das Umland des römischen Regensburg*, Münchener Beiträge zur Vor- und Frühgeschichte, **42** (München)

Gimber, M., 1993 *Das Atelier des IANVS in Rheinzabern* (Karlsruhe)

Greenacre, M., 1984 *Theory and applications of correspondence analysis* (London)
_____, 1993 *Correspondence analysis in practice* (London)

Hagendorn, A., 1991 *Das Wasserbecken der römischen Villa von Großsachsen, Gemeinde Hirschberg* (Magisterarbeit, Freiburg)

Hartley, B. R., 1972 The Roman occupation of Scotland: the evidence of samian ware, *Britannia*, **3**, 1–55

Heiligmann, J., 1990 *Der Alb-Limes*, Forschungen und Berichte zur Vor- und Frühgeschichte in Baden-Württemberg, **35** (Stuttgart)

Huld-Zetsche, I., 1993 *Trierer Reliefsigillata Werkstatt II*, Materialien zur Römisch-Germanischen Keramik, **12** (Bonn)

Knötzele, P., 1993 *Terra Sigillata aus Stettfeld (Grabungen 1974–1987)* (Magisterarbeit, Freiburg)

Kortüm, K., 1988 Ein archäologischer Aufschluß im Kastellvicus von Jagsthausen, Kreis Heilbronn, *Fundberichte aus Baden-Württemberg*, **13**, 325–49

_____, 1995 *Portus-Pforzheim. Untersuchungen zur Archäologie und Geschichte in römischer Zeit*, Quellen und Studien zur Geschichte der Stadt Pforzheim, **3** (Pforzheim)

Mees, A. W., 1993 Zur Gruppenbildung Rheinzaberner Modellhersteller und Ausformer, *Jahresberichte aus Augst und Kaiseraugst*, **14**, 227–55.

_____, 1994 Potiers et moulistes. Observations sur la chronologie, les structures et la commercialisation des ateliers de terre sigillée décorée, *Société Française d'Étude de la Céramique Antique en Gaule, Actes du Congrès de Millau 1994*, 19–41 (Marseille)

_____, Organisation, Verbreitung und Chronologie der Rheinzaberner Relieftöpfer (in Vorbereitung)

Nuber, H. U., 1969 Zum Ende der reliefverzierten Terra-Sigillata-Herstellung in Rheinzabern, *Mitteilungen des Historischen Vereins der Pfalz*, **67**, 136–47

Oelmann, F., 1914 *Die Keramik des Kastells Niederbieber*, Materialien zur Römisch-Germanischen Keramik, **1** (Frankfurt)

Ludowici, W., & Ricken, H. (ed.), 1942 *Die Bilderschüsseln der römischen Töpfer von Rheinzabern: Tafelband* (Speyer)

Robertson, W. S., 1951 A method for chronologically ordering archaeological deposits, *American Antiquity*, **4**, 293–301.

Schaub, A., 1993 *Bebauung und Chronologie einer Parzelle des römischen Vicus von Sulz am Neckar* (Magisterarbeit, Freiburg)

von Schnurbein, S., 1977 *Das römische Gräberfeld von Regensburg*, Archäologische Forschungen in Castra Regina-Regensburg I, Materialhefte zur bayerischen Vorgeschichte, Reihe A31 (Kallmünz/Opf)

Schönberger, H., & Simon, H.-G., 1983 *Die Kastelle in Altenstadt*, Limesforschungen, **22** (Berlin)

Simon, H.-G., 1968 Das Kleinkastell Degerfeld in Butzbach, Kr. Friedberg (Hessen). Datierung und Funde, *Saalburg Jahrbuch*, **25**, 5–60

_____, 1976 Terra sigillata Bilderschüsseln und Töpferstempel auf glatter Ware, in Baatz, D., Das Kastell Munningen im Nördlinger Ries, *Saalburg Jahrbuch*, **23**, 37–53.

_____, & Köhler, H.-J., 1992 *Ein Geschirrdepot des 3. Jahrhunderts. Grabungen im Lagerdorf des Kastells Langenhain*, Materialien zur Römisch-Germanischen Keramik, **11** (Bonn)

Wagner, P., 1987–88, Untersuchungen am Keller einer Villa rustica in Friedberg-Bauernheim, Wetteraukreis, *Fundberichte aus Hessen*, **27/28**, 99–121.

Weinrich-Kemkes, S., 1993 Zwei Metalldepots aus dem römischen Vicus von Walldürn, Neckar-Odenwald-Kreis, *Fundberichte Baden-Württemberg*, **18**, 253–324.

Zanier, W., 1992 *Das römische Kastell Ellingen*, Limesforschungen, **23** (Mainz)

19   Samian from the City of Lincoln: a question of status?

Margaret J. Darling

INTRODUCTION

Most research on pottery includes an element devoted to examining the pottery from a site for evidence towards an assessment of trading connections, economy and status. Samian is viewed as the ceramic status symbol for the period up to the mid-3rd century. Thus, if samian occurs on a rural site, certain conclusions are drawn. But samian vessels are multi-purpose, and although predominantly tableware, where do samian mortaria fit in, and why do they not appear until the later 2nd century? At the other end of the scale from mortaria sit the decorated vessels.

Remembering a certain missing stamped coarseware mortarium which was finally located serving as a fruit bowl in the site hut, it seems likely that the occasional complete bowl of form 29, 30 or 37 may well have temporarily served a similar purpose for a samian specialist, before being returned to the museum for display. Was this their use in the Roman world? While we can imagine vegetables being served in an elegant form 29, is it not conceivable that for many owners these were the samian vessels above all that demonstrated status, which commonly delights in display – are these not the display cabinet vessels as seems to be the case with some later Roman glass?

Regarding financial value, the relative prices of just two samian vessels appear to be given by graffiti from the Continent, a decorated form 37 of Cinnamus bearing the price of 20 *asses* (Noll 1972), while a plain vessel of the plate form Ludowici Ta' is priced at 12 *asses* (Kovacsovics 1987; I am grateful to Chris Going for drawing my attention to these graffiti, and to Brenda Dickinson for the references). The only clear standard we have for assessing these prices is a soldier's pay, and for the period in question this could have been still at the rate under Domitian of 300 *denarii*, assuming no increase under Commodus, or perhaps increased to the 450 *denarii* paid by Septimius Severus (Watson 1969, 91). The daily rate therefore ranged between 13 to 20 *asses*. If we assume the higher figure, a Cinnamus bowl would cost a day's pay, a relatively substantial cost. Given that the decorated bowl is nearly twice the cost of the plain vessel, clearly it is of interest to determine what is the normal ratio of decorated to plain samian

vessels, so that the higher status assemblages can be identified.

THE LINCOLN SITES

Identifying differences between sites is important when dealing with the pottery from a city. A check through the samian in the City of Lincoln Archaeology Unit archive revealed substantial variations between sites in the percentages of decorated samian vessels, a pattern which clearly warranted investigation. This study of the samian draws on that archive, where the standard measure is sherd count; all samian vessels are individually dated, an essential prerequisite for analysis. The archive is viewed as a mechanism to provide a 'window' into the data, so that anomalies and differences between sites can be seen quickly at a basic level and, should these appear of interest, further investigation can be instituted, involving full quantification. Sherd count seems entirely adequate for the present purpose in view of the sample sizes, and the lack of evidence for differential fragmentation between sites.

For the purpose of publishing recent excavations, the city has been divided into three topographical areas, the upper city encompassing the legionary fortress and the original *colonia* (mostly unavailable for excavation due to the cathedral, castle and other historic buildings), the lower city representing the extended *colonia*, and the Wigford suburb, which stretches to the south of the river along the main roads, the Fosse Way and Ermine Street. Since work is still in progress on the samian from the city, this investigation is confined principally to the first area for publication, the Wigford suburb (Jones & Vince forthcoming), and some larger sites from elsewhere in the city (fig. 1).

Wigford sites

The ten sites in the Wigford suburb are of diverse chronology and character, and some produced only small samples. They can be broadly divided into three groups. The more southerly group includes Monson Street (M82) in the area of the early cemetery which has produced legionary and later tombstones, and the adjacent St. Mary's Guildhall south of

169

the junction of Ermine Street and the Fosse Way (SMG82). To the north lie sites at St. Mark's Station (Z86 and ZE87) and St. Mark's Church (SM76), the latter the largest site, with strip buildings fronting onto the main road. Approximately 100m north of these is the site of Holmes Grainwarehouse (HG72) by the Brayford Pool (Darling & Jones 1988), where Iron Age pottery occurred together with early Roman occupation. A highly unusual assemblage with a large proportion of samian and later fine wares came from the site of Brayford Wharf East (BWE82) on the edge of the Brayford, which largely comprised successive dumps of rubbish, as did St. Benedict's Square (SB85) further north.

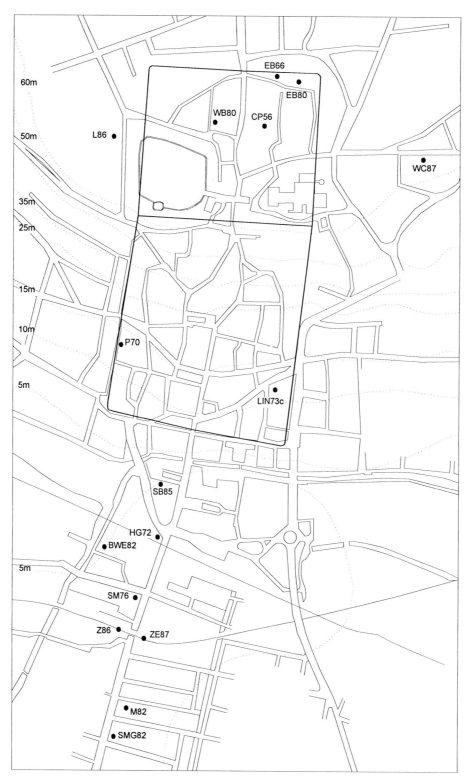

Fig. 1. Map of Lincoln showing sites mentioned in the text.

Chronologically the sites split into three different groups: (1) those sites starting with 1st-century occupation: the Brayford site, HG72 and the southern sites, M82 and SMG82; (2) the sites of the St. Mark's area where occupation appears to have started at the earliest in the mid- to late 2nd century (although dumps at ZE87 contain earlier 2nd-century samian) but where the dating profile suggests they did not continue uniformly into the later 4th century: SM76 and Z86, together with the Brayford site BWE82; and finally (3) the site at St. Benedict's Square, SB85, where the dumps contain the highest proportion of East Gaulish samian, but which is unfortunately the smallest sample.

Clearly, the most useful are sites where occupation was relatively even and continuous throughout the samian importation period. Only three of the sites come even near this specification, Monson Street (M82), St. Mary's Guildhall (SMG82), and the Holmes Grainwarehouse site (HG72), although the latter has very low quantities of samian for the 3rd century. The main difficulty was the paucity of evidence for 1st-century samian, since Holmes Grainwarehouse accounted for 77% of the South Gaulish samian from the Wigford sites, but had exceptionally high proportions of decorated wares of all periods and thus seemed unlikely to give a true picture. This site is excluded from the following analysis (although the ratios of plain to decorated wares are shown). The investigation was therefore extended with the objective of obtaining more reliable data from other sites for the 1st century.

Other city sites

The other sites are mainly from the upper city. The largest is that of Cottesford Place (CP56), excavations by Dennis Petch in 1956-58 on the site of the public baths (final report in prep.).

While this produced 36% South Gaulish wares, much of the samian came from the rubbish dumps after the abandonment of the baths in the 3rd century. There are two sites located in the same area of the north defences on East Bight, EB66 (Darling 1984) and EB80, with 40-50% South Gaulish wares, but with only small quantities of later East Gaulish samian. An extra-mural site immediately outside the west defences, The Lawn (L86) also had a sizeable South Gaulish group at 30%, while excavations close to the Mint Wall in the centre of the fortress and colonia at West Bight (WB80) produced 24% South Gaulish. The final upper city site is Winnowsty Cottages (WC87), an extra-mural site lying beyond the east defences, which produced no South Gaulish wares. The absence of early occupation on this site may be due to its location further from the fortress.

Two lower city sites were also examined. The Park (P70), excavations across the west defences of the lower colonia in the area of a gate (Colyer 1975; final report forthcoming), which produced a very large samian assemblage, over 2400 sherds, most of which derived from earlier rubbish dumps used to heighten the rampart in the 4th century, the main emphasis being on mid- to later 2nd-century samian. The other site, adjacent to the defences of the lower colonia on the east side, Silver Street (LIN73C), directed by Professor John Wacher, had a more even chronological distribution of samian.

Differences based on sources

The chart (fig. 2) of the sources of samian for the two main areas (The Park and Silver Street sites are included with the upper city sites; HG72 is excluded) shows the nature of the sample, the city sites providing the evidence for South Gaulish wares, while East Gaulish wares are best represented by the

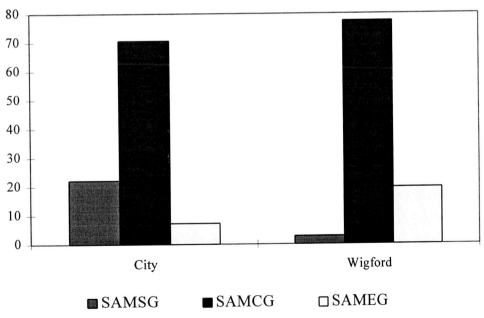

Fig. 2. Sources of samian from sites in the city and the Wigford suburb.

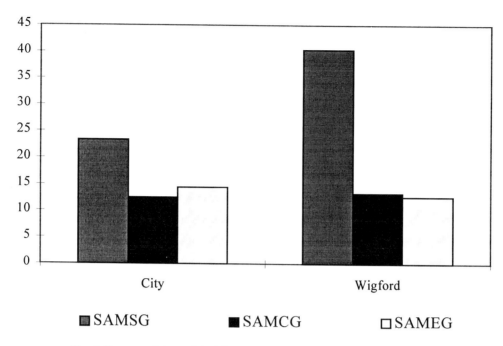

Fig. 3. Percentages of decorated sherds by source from sites in the city and the Wigford suburb.

Wigford sites. The total samples from each broad area were: city 5633 sherds, Wigford 2183 sherds. On the assumption that the differences seen between the percentages of decorated sherds from different sites had a chronological basis, the first examination of these percentages was on the basis of fabric.

The results over all the sites are shown on fig. 3. Clearly the high percentage of decorated South Gaulish samian from the Wigford sites arises partly from the small sample (only 62 sherds; the HG72 site is excluded), but investigation has shown that when South Gaulish sherds occur in considerably later dumps on those sites, decorated sherds predominate. Do the decorated vessels have a longer life? The only sample worth considering from Wigford is that from Monson Street, where the decorated South Gaulish sherds accounted for 27%, not substantially higher than the 23% noted for the city sites. The chart however indicates that there is a chronological basis, the percentage of decorated sherds declining from a peak in the South Gaulish wares.

The percentages of decorated wares vary considerably between sites, so that there are overlaps as illustrated by fig. 4 (the small sample of South Gaulish wares from Wigford is excluded).

The differences derive from site specific problems, as with the two adjacent sites of EB66 and EB80 on the north defences. The assemblage from EB66 has consistently lower percentages of decorated wares, 12.2% South Gaulish compared with 24.9% from EB80, 14.5 Central Gaulish against 25.5%, and 11% against 16.7% of East Gaulish. This may be due to the extent of deposits yielding South Gaulish wares being smaller at EB66, while the bulk of the Central Gaulish wares from that site came from rampart layers predominantly of ashy material, conceivably moved from a specific rubbish

dump, and certainly a different source to that used for the rampart in EB80. The character and content of the rampart layers varied between the two trenches on this site, demonstrating the difficulties in dealing with the pottery from excavations across defences (Darling 1984, 48).

Despite the overlaps, it is clear that an assemblage dominated by Central Gaulish wares can be expected to yield a lower percentage of decorated vessels than one predominantly of South Gaulish samian. Differences between Central and East Gaulish are more difficult to assess, and are perhaps best approached on sites with larger quantities of later East Gaulish samian.

Chronological changes

The next question follows naturally – did the decline in decorated wares occur immediately Central Gaulish potters took over the market or was it gradual? To investigate the closer dating of such changes, the dates of all the samian from the various sites was converted to numeric dates where necessary, and the resulting data put through a program called Plotdate written and kindly adapted by Paul Tyers (Tyers 1994). This spreads the values (in this case, sherd counts) chronologically. Ratios of plain to decorated wares were calculated from this data, and are plotted as culmulative columns for Wigford and for the city sites (fig. 5). Wigford, where occupation was more concentrated in the later 2nd and 3rd centuries, is the more satisfying chart, showing the increasing quantities of plain wares through the 2nd century, peaking at *c.* AD180. The city sites, with a higher proportion of South Gaulish wares and lower Central Gaulish presence, are more complex, but the chart also shows the plain wares becoming commoner through the 2nd century, again peaking at *c.* AD180.

Site specific difficulties obviously affect the results. In Wigford, for instance, the site at St. Mary's Guildhall (SMG82) has an exceptionally high proportion of plain wares in the twenty-year bracket from AD180, forcing the culmulative column higher than might be expected. But in the same area, the peculiarity of Holmes Grainwarehouse with its unusually low ratios may even up the results. Turning to the city sites, East Bight 1966 (EB66) has low ratios of plain to decorated for the later 2nd century, depressing the peaks, but high ratios for the earlier 2nd century. Similarly West Bight (WB80) has a high ratio for the later 1st century.

The later East Gaulish wares are much more difficult to evaluate. Many of these sherds have broad dating, and while the results suggest that decorated wares were becoming more common, it is less clear cut. The sample overall is only 821 sherds, 10% of the total samian. Similar research is needed on sites with good samples of East Gaulish samian, preferably geographically spread to determine whether decorated wares were marketed more widely. It is possible that the range reaching Lincoln might differ from that nearer the port of entry, and perhaps the decorated vessels, presumably of higher cost and profit to the merchant, travelled further.

Since it is clear that the crucial period of change is the later 2nd century, the period of the twenty-year brackets AD140-180 is examined in more detail. The sample sizes are city 2533 sherds and Wigford (excluding HG72) 1637 sherds. The main sites accounting for 62% of the samian of this period are Cottesford Place in the upper city (CP56: 12.4%), The Park in the lower city (P70: 27.6%), and St. Marks Church in Wigford (SM76: 21.7%).

When the values are charted, fig. 6, both the Wigford and city sites show lower values for the period *c.* AD140, but the

later two periods are very similar in size, quantities from the Wigford sites slightly increasing in the last period, while those from the city sites show a small decrease.

The values of the decorated sherds were totalled, and the percentages calculated for each area for an overall view, and to avoid site specific abnormalities. These percentages of the decorated sherd values are charted on fig. 7, and they show a progressive decline in the numbers of decorated sherds on the Wigford sites, while the percentages for the city sites start slightly lower, retain that level for the middle period, but decline in the last period. The higher proportion of decorated sherds from Wigford for the first period may derive from dumps of refuse used to raise the levels of some of the site rather than be indicative of higher status. Since the overall quantities involved change little over the three periods, the decline in decorated sherds from the Central Gaulish potters in both areas seems proven as occurring in that final period, the peak of Central Gaulish importation.

Can the spatial differences be interpreted as indicative of varying status? The bulk of the samian from The Park (P70) derived from rampart layers, much deposited in the 4th century remodelling of the defences, but containing mostly late 2nd- to 3rd-century pottery. The peculiarity of the pottery assemblage has a mirror image in that of the glass assemblage, and the large deposit of animal bone is interpreted as a consistent group from wholesale butchery. The evidence suggests that in order to heighten the rampart during the remodelling work, large rubbish dumps were used, seemingly a secondary deposition of primary rubbish dumps. These seem unlikely to have come from far away, and there is no reason to believe they are not typical of the rubbish generated by that area of the city.

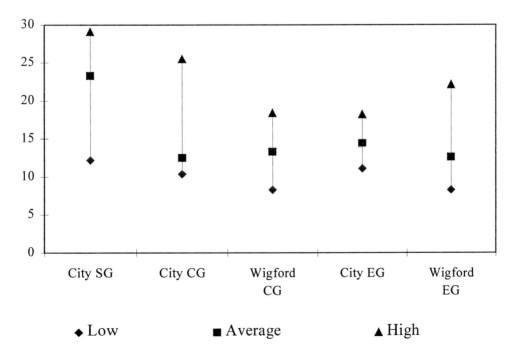

Fig. 4. Ranges by source of percentages of decorated sherds from the city and the Wigford suburb.

Much of the samian from the Cottesford Place bath-house (CP56) came from rubbish dumped into the derelict building in the 3rd century, and again, this is likely to be typical refuse from the upper city. Equally there is no evidence to suggest the samian from the Wigford site of St. Marks Church (SM76) is other than rubbish from occupation in that area.

The figures show that the residents in the city were using and throwing away more decorated samian than the occupiers of the strip-buildings running south along Ermine Street. While it is a modern supposition that higher status occupation would have been located within the defences, this analysis suggests that, given difficulties due to the chronological

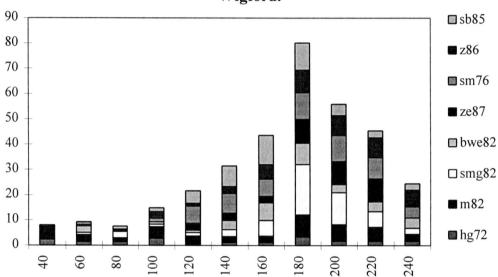

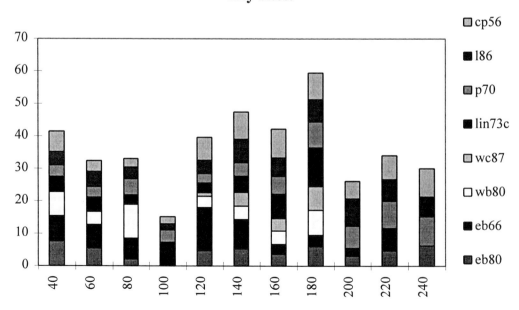

Fig. 5. Histograms of the ratios of plain to decorated sherds from the city and the Wigford suburb.

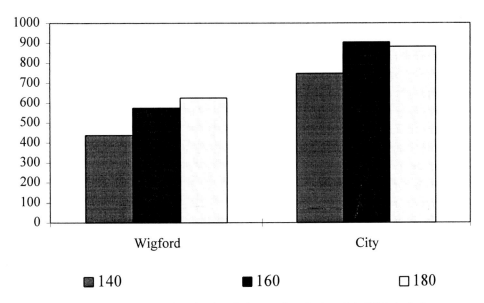

Fig. 6. Sample sizes for the mid- to later 2nd century from the city and the Wigford suburb.

changes, the ratio of plain to decorated samian can be used as a status indicator. It is essential that the samian is securely related back to the site depositional evidence, and that samples of reasonable size are available.

SUMMARY OF THE LINCOLN EVIDENCE

So far as Lincoln is concerned, it seems clear that the character of the samian coming into the city changed chronologically, the Central Gaulish wares including decreasing numbers of decorated vessels over a period of time, culminating in the highest ratio of plain to decorated in the late 2nd century. The percentages of decorated (and the ratios of plain to decorated) for the South Gaulish wares may well be peculiar to the city, given its origin as a legionary fortress. On the data available from Lincoln, a case can be argued that the mainly higher ratios of plain to decorated wares for the Wigford suburb, largely composed of low-status strip buildings, arises from the lower status of the suburb's occupiers in relation to that of people living in the upper city and, bearing in mind the site of The Park, the lower city. It is proposed therefore that the percentage of decorated samian can be used as an indicator of status.

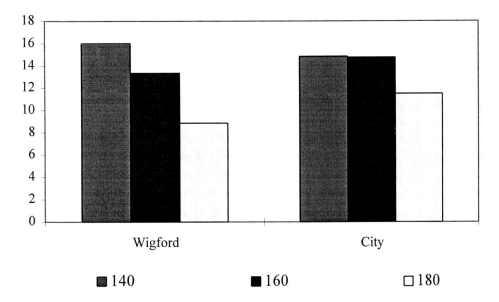

Fig. 7. Percentages of decorated sherds for the mid- to later 2nd century from the city and the Wigford suburb.

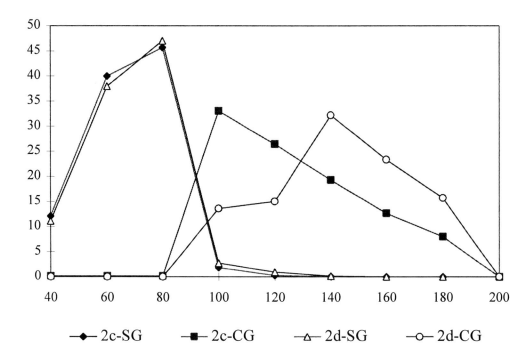

Fig. 8. Plotdate graph of the samian by source from Verulamium Insula XIV, Periods IIC and IID.

THE EVIDENCE FROM OTHER SITES

New analysis work produces a dilemma – once you have results, with what can you compare them? Do they conform to a trend seen elsewhere? As data from other sites become available, these interim Lincoln results can be seen in context. Figures have been published from Usk legionary fortress, indicating percentages of decorated to plain of 30% for the predominantly South Gaulish assemblage (Tyers 1993, 127), broadly akin to those from Verulamium Insula XIV (Hartley 1972). The small quantity of South Gaulish samian from New Fresh Wharf in London contained over 29% decorated sherds, while in the much larger sample of Central Gaulish wares the percentage of decorated sherds had dropped to 11%, and the later East Gaulish sherds included 18% decorated (Bird 1986). But since this material mostly came from the filling of the Roman quay, it can hardly be regarded as a normal assemblage.

A site with more potential for this investigation is the Verulamium Insula XIV (Frere 1972). A scan of the samian reported by Brian Hartley indicates that that large assemblage, over 2,600 vessels reported, produces a pattern. The site assemblage starts in Periods I to IIB with high percentages of almost solely South Gaulish decorated wares, between 28-30%, confirming the generally higher percentages of decorated vessels from South Gaul. Examination has therefore concentrated on Periods IIC and IID, with almost equal quantities of South Gaulish to Central Gaulish in Period IIC, and a predominance of Central Gaulish in the final Period IID.

A plot of the percentage by date of all the samian from these two periods by source (fig. 8) shows the largely residual South Gaulish assemblages to have virtually identical dating

profiles; the Central Gaulish wares from Period IIC have a strong Trajanic emphasis, while in the succeeding Period IID, the peak has moved to the early Antonine period. The analysis suggested that these two periods might produce useful results, particularly bearing on the wares from Les Martres-de-Veyre.

When the percentage of decorated vessels irrespective of source is plotted by date, the resulting curves are very similar, going from a peak of over 40% c. AD60 to the start of a decline c. AD100, ending with percentages of between 7 and 12% at c. AD180. The figures were then examined for the percentages of decorated vessels by source (fig. 9). This shows the South Gaulish vessels maintaining a fairly consistent level until the late South Gaulish vessels occur, their very paucity producing aberrant figures. The Central Gaulish starts c. AD100 with a similar level, but declines thereafter, to end in Period IID at below 7% at c. AD180. This low percentage may be due to the smaller size of the sample of later samian. The relatively high percentages for c. AD100 would seem to indicate that the ratio of decorated to plain vessels from Les Martres-de-Veyre was close to that from South Gaul.

CONCLUSIONS

It is apparent from the analysis above that there was a progressive decline in the ratio of decorated to plain samian vessels once the Central Gaulish potters took over the market, although it is possible that this did not start until the flood of imports from Lezoux after c. AD125. The results from the Lincoln sites show the lowest level dated c. AD180, when approximately only 11% of the samian vessels were decorated. Despite the differences between sherd count (from Lincoln

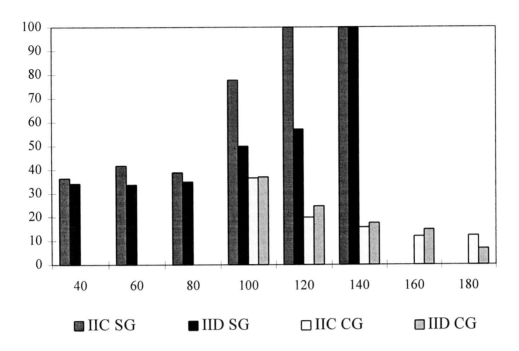

Fig. 9. Percentages of decorated vessels by source from Verulamium Insula XIV, Periods IIC and IID.

sites) and vessel count (from Verulamium), the results are consistent. Whether this decline continued with the East Gaulish wares is uncertain. The identified vessels from the defensive site at Caister-on-Sea amounted to 474 vessels, of which over 67% were from East Gaul (Darling & Gurney 1993). On a vessel count basis, the percentage of decorated East Gaulish vessels was 12%, but this comes from a coastal defensive site, possibly initially supplied by the *Classis Britannica*, and can hardly be viewed as a normal assemblage. Since the foundation of the site can be dated to the 3rd century, the Central Gaulish decorated vessels accounted for a seemingly high 22% of all Central Gaulish wares, and the East Gaulish assemblage is notable for a high proportion of mortaria (Darling & Gurney 1993, 155). Other sites with good samples of later East Gaulish samian are needed to explore this further.

Given that there appears to be a chronological decline in the quantity of decorated vessels, the question of status based on the percentage of decorated vessels will need to be carefully examined, taking into account the date range of the vessels. To explore this further, assemblages from varying types of site are needed, such as military sites, both early and later, and early villa sites and seemingly lower status rural sites. The examination of the ratios of decorated to plain samian from different areas of a city may produce useful information about status, and differences between the upper and lower city of Lincoln will be investigated more fully once the database is complete.

It is a pleasure and a privilege to offer this small contribution to Brian Hartley, whose kindness has been unfailing over the years, and much appreciated. However much you explore data using computer aids, it is the material evidence itself which is paramount, and it is only because of the sound foundation laid by him that such questions as those above can be posed.

ACKNOWLEDGEMENTS

Finally I must extend my thanks to Brenda Dickinson and Joanna Bird, without whose samian reports, care and attention to dating and help this paper would have been impossible; the responsibility for this manipulation of their data lies with the author.

Bibliography
Bird, J., 1986 Samian wares, in Miller, L., Schofield, J., & Rhodes,M., *The Roman quay at St. Magnus House, London*, London Middlesex Archaeol. Soc. Special Paper, **8**, 139-85
Colyer, C., 1975 Excavations at Lincoln 1970-1972: the western defences of the lower town. An interim report, *Antiq. J*, **55**, 227-66.
Darling, M.J., 1984 *Roman pottery from the upper defences*. The Archaeology of Lincoln, **XVI-2**.
_____, & Gurney, D., 1993. *Caister-on-Sea. Excavations by Charles Green, 1951-55*, East Anglian Archaeol., **60**
_____, & Jones, M.J., 1988 Early settlement at Lincoln, *Britannia*, **19**, 1-58
Hartley, B.R., 1972 The Samian ware, in Frere, S. S., *Verulamium excavations, vol. I*, Rep. Res. Comm. Soc. Antiq. London, **28**, 216-62
Jones, M.J., & Vince, A.G. (eds.), forthcoming The archaeology of Wigford and the Brayford Pool, *Lincoln Archaeol. Studies*, **2**
Kovacsovics, W. K., 1987 As XII – Eine Preisangabe auf einem Sigillatateller aus Salzburg, *Germania*, **65**, 222-5
Noll, R., 1972 Eine Sigillataschussel mit Eigentumsvermerk und Preisangabe aus Flavia Solva, *Germania*, **50**, 148-52.
Tyers, P.A., 1993 The plain samian, in Manning, W. H. (ed.), *Report on the excavations at Usk 1965-1976: the Roman pottery*, 127-60
_____, 1994 *Plotdate*
Watson, G.R., 1969 *The Roman soldier* (London)

20   Expert systems in sigillata and numismatic studies

George Rogers

An earlier version of this paper was originally published in the French journal *Sites*, **45** (April 1991), 28–32. *Sites* is published by the Association Française d'Archéologie Métropolitaine, rue des Écoles, Gonfaron (Var). I have taken the opportunity of revising the original paper in an English translation on the occasion of this *hommage* to our friend Brian.

Let us start from the following premise: 'Expert systems are made by experts to be used by non-experts'. This is of course a gross simplification; on the one hand, it is not usually the expert himself who creates the expert system, and on the other hand, certain expert systems are intended to be used by experts. DENDRAL is an expert system used to identify organic molecules from the fragments left after the bombardment of a specimen in a mass-spectrometer. This system has been 'fed' for many years with the expertise of numerous chemists in the field, and in fact works so well that it now exceeds the knowledge of the individual chemists. We may think also of PROSPECTOR, an expert system in the field of geology, which from the information stored in it and from prospection data suggests the possible presence of minerals. It is credited with the discovery of an unknown deposit of molybdenum in Canada.[1]

These examples are of course exceptions: for the moment, it is difficult to envisage an expert system capable of making such discoveries in the field of archaeology. Let us now return to the beginning and discuss expert systems created by experts for the use of non-experts.

EXPERTS AND EXPERTISE

Personally, I don't much like the word 'expert' in this context. I prefer the use of the word 'expertise'; everyone has some, in one field or another. This expertise may be very wide, or very deep, or both at the same time. For example, a numismatist may have wide knowledge of antiquity and a deep knowledge of the coinage of Constantine and his family. This is normal, and depends on the training he has received and his subsequent numismatic work. The same is true for a botanist, who by his education has a good knowledge of the entire veg-etable kingdom. However, if he has not specialised in mycology, there is a serious risk that he will be stumped when faced with a common bluestalk mushroom. And yet this same botanist is a true expert in orchids, of world-wide reputation.

THE EXPERT SYSTEM – THE USER'S POINT OF VIEW

To remain with the botanical analogy, anyone who has fought with a flora to try to identify a plant has already used an expert system. A flora corresponds well to our definition, for it was created by an expert (or rather a long line of experts) for the use of non-experts. Note also the following characteristics:

— Some familiarity with the subject is supposed (I still remember my early battles to identify my first flower by means of a flora – the flower in question was a primrose, to make things easy).

— It is the expert system that asks the questions: 'How many petals does the flower have ?'.

— An experienced user can go directly to a given point by volunteering information to the expert system: 'It belongs to the cabbage family'.

— Most of the time the expert system works in a dichotomic or binary mode: 'Is the flower symmetric – yes/no ?', although often a multiple choice may be offered by the system: 'How many stamens does the flower have ?'.

— The system operates on facts and rules. The user presents facts in response to the questions of the system, but the system uses rules stored in its memory to navigate through the system: 'If the flower has four petals **and** the petals are heavily folded **then** the plant belongs to the poppy family'.

— This particular system, the flora, is not computerised, but there is no reason why it should not be. Much time could thus be saved in traversing the knowledge tree. On the other hand, its use in the field is more problematical, considering the size of the computer at the present moment. That will certainly come, and there now exist pocket computers capable of doing this, except perhaps for the memory required to store the rule base.

— The dichotomic flora has a rigid structure. If we reply correctly to all the questions, we will probably obtain an identification, but there is no place for error. If a piece of data is missing or anomalous (remember the four-leafed clover) we may well come to an incorrect conclusion. The choice is either to persist in the hope of finding the correct path at one of the branches, or return to the field to find less anomalous examples. The flora implemented on a computer, if it has been programmed to do it, can continue to search by itself for possible avenues, and to ask questions in consequence.

— The flora also contains the notion of 'fuzzy' data, particularly if the floral group is subject to hybridization. An expert system on a computer may be programmed to include a confidence level, thus allowing the machine to reply: 'It is variety A with 60% of confidence, variety B with 30% of confidence, or variety C with 10% of confidence'.

The flora that we have examined therefore corresponds quite well to an expert system. In fact, it conforms to the type referred to as based on facts and rules. Other forms exist which we will not consider here. Further details may be found in the bibliography.

THE APPLICATION OF SUCH A SYSTEM TO ARCHAEOLOGY

Let us now look at some possible applications of expert systems to archaeology. We will examine successively the case of decorated terra sigillata from Central Gaul, and then the case of Roman numismatics, two fields in which I have worked for many years. Finally, I shall make some observations on other fields with which I am much less familiar.

Decorated Terra Sigillata

The problem is the identification of a fragment of Central Gaulish sigillata and its attribution to a known potter. Having first made a rubbing of the sherd in question (and eventually a drawing) the specialist will probably proceed in the following way:

1. He identifies the figure types with the help of Oswald's *Index* (Oswald 1936–37).

2. He identifies the decorative details with the help of the catalogue that I published in 1974 (Rogers 1974).

3. He carefully notes the names of the potters having used each motif.

4. Usually, after having followed steps 1 to 3 above, the name of one (or more) potter appears with a higher frequency in the lists.

5. The sherd is now compared with the plates of the book by Stanfield & Simpson (1958), to try to establish a positive identification.

6. If there are too many disparities between the sherd and the plates of Stanfield & Simpson, the next potter on the list is selected and we start again.

For many years, I have taught this method of identification to numerous persons, students and others, at Lezoux. The results are excellent: apart from a few rare cases where the person is totally impermeable to the notion of 'style' (in the archaeological sense, not the artistic), most sherds are identified without difficulty. It should be noted however that for the first attempts we use easily identified potters; also there still remains a relatively high proportion of sherds where even the specialist is in difficulty.

The essentially mechanical nature of steps 1 to 4 suggests that they should be quite simple to automate. On the other hand, step 5 to 6 are, and will probably remain, the domain of the human specialist.

However, the usual type of expert system seems to me to be very badly adapted to this kind of work. We know that on the moulded vases from Lezoux there are several hundred figure types and about a thousand decorative details. These stamps were used by several hundred potters between the early 2nd century and about AD 260. The expert systems actually in use work with only a few hundred rules, and even if future systems are able to work with several thousand, the user interface may well be more of a hindrance than a help.

On the other hand, it would be quite easy to create a system to help in the identification of the stamps with programming methods that have been perfectly well understood for many years:

1. Using a scanner, an image of each poinçon is created for each type in the Oswald and Rogers catalogues.

2. A corresponding database is created, where each image is associated with a list of attributes describing each stamp:

Human, animal, mythological.

Standing, seated, lying down, walking, running, jumping.

Facing, from behind, to the right, to the left.

Etc.

3. The user is interrogated to obtain a description of the motif to be identified by means of a simple interface. When the number of possibilities is reduced to a reasonable quantity, they are displayed on the screen, individually or by groups, until the user recognises the poinçon and informs the system.

4. The system holds this identification in memory and moves on to the identification of the next stamp.

5. When all the poinçons have been identified, the system itself counts the number of potters having used the identified stamps and prints it out in the form of a summary list, starting with the most well-represented potter:

10 of the 14 poinçons were used by CINNAMVS.
5 of the 14 poinçons were used by ALBVCIVS.
3 of the 14 poinçons were used by PATERNVS.
2 of the 14 poinçons were used by BELSA.

6. It is now up to the user to confirm the identification by reference to the plates of Stanfield & Simpson.

This system could be built today with no great difficulty; even the storage needed for the images is no longer a problem. Many parts of this system exist already, for instance a database associating stamp and potter. To complete the system it would be enough to digitalise the images using a scanner and to create the database for the attributes.

Numismatics

Like many other fields, numismatics can be either pure or applied. Pure numismatics is essentially a work of attribution, seriation, and dating. The efforts of many generations of numismatists have made numismatics one of the best-structured domains of all the humanistic disciplines. For all series of coins there exist detailed catalogues, from the first coins, through those of Greece and Rome, mediaeval and modern times, down to the coins of necessity of the first World War.

Just for Roman coinages, for example, we have the catalogue of Crawford for the Republic (Crawford 1974), and the ten volumes of the *Roman Imperial coinage* (the last volume was completed in 1994) for the Empire (Mattingly & Sydenham 1923–94). We have therefore a complete coverage from the earliest coinages of the Republic to those of the last emperors of the West.

Applied numismatics is the identification of coins found on sites or in hoards, the compilation of catalogues of these finds, and their use for dating the various phases of archaeological sites, but also attempts to understand the circulation of coinage on the site, the region, and the province, and in the case of Rome, the entire Empire (Reece 1973).

It is difficult and painful work, for the coins are frequently in a dreadful state of conservation. I am persuaded that it is here that computers can intervene usefully.

How therefore does a specialist go about identifying a coin presented to him by an archaeological colleague with the words: 'We found this in the construction level of a Roman villa. Can you identify it ?'

The numismatist will usually go through the following steps:

1. He weighs the coin and makes a drawing or cast in plaster.

2. If necessary, he cleans it.

3. He notes the metal and the diameter of the coin, as well as several other parameters (die axis, type of flan, thickness, provenance, find-spot, etc.).

4. By now, he probably has a good idea of the denomination of the coin, particularly if it is Roman, where the number of possibilities is, even so, limited. My own experience is that it is possible to teach the essentials of the Roman monetary system in a couple of hours of practical work if a good selection of material is available.

5. Having decided, for example, that the coin is a *dupondius* of the Roman imperial period, the numismatist first tries to identify the emperor. Fortunately the coin portraits are very characteristic, at least in the early period, and even reduced to a silhouette, there is usually little difficulty in identifying the emperor using a series of imperial portraits, as in the book by Klawens (1963) for example.

6. Having (hopefully) identified the emperor (let's say Marcus Aurelius), and read a few letters of the inscriptions, the numismatist gets out his *Roman Imperial coinage,* volume **3**, and goes through the painful motions of reviewing the totality of the *dupondii* of that emperor.

7. With a little luck, and after a couple of hours work, the coin is at last identified.

The stages susceptible of being computerised are 4, 6, and 7.

At first sight, an expert system seems to be a good solution for automating step 4, for that allows us to determine the denomination of the coin. This is certainly true, but we have already noted that the number of possibilities is quite limited, and that two hours of practice are enough to train the apprentice numismatist in the denominations of Roman numismatics.

Nevertheless, there remain many traps that must be avoided; there are coins of the late 3rd and 4th centuries which may easily be confused with the medium-sized coins of earlier times. We may think of the large silvered coins of the reform of Diocletian, or the coins with the bull of the Emperor Julian. This might make it interesting to construct an expert system.[2]

But the major problem remains steps 6 and 7, for, as we have already seen, to search for the legends of Marcus in the usual reference works is a long and fastidious work, particularly if the start of the legend has not survived, thus making the use of the indices of the RIC particularly difficult. If it is impossible to identify the emperor with certitude, the problem becomes even more complex; how many different coin types did the Roman State strike between the start of the coinage until the end of the Western Empire ? I doubt very much if anyone has ever tried to count them, for even this task would be long and tedious, but let us say perhaps one or two hundred thousand as a rough guess. It is obvious that here, an expert system can be of no use.

So what can we do? I believe that there are two possible solutions, one simple, the other of greater difficulty.

The first solution consists quite simply of computerizing the indices of the RIC:

— A first index would contain the obverse and reverse legends, together with the volume and the page or pages on which that legend is to be found. A rapid calculation shows that for the *RIC*, a database of about 10,000 lines of say 50 characters each should suffice, giving a file of about 500,000 characters, a perfectly reasonable figure for today's computers.

— A second index would contain the reverse types (and the obverse type too, when it is other than the head of the emperor). It is very difficult to estimate the size of such a database, but it would certainly be very much larger than that containing the legends.

It is clear that the two databases should be split up by RIC volume to accelerate searching (for example, it would be useless to search for a *sestertius* in the volumes for the later Empire).

Note that this solution could be set up immediately; the only problem is the time needed to do it. I have in fact already created a partial database for obverse and reverse legends; as an example, RIC **3** takes up 1472 lines and 57764 characters. It took about two weeks of part-time typing. Searching is rapid; on an IBM compatible, 486 machine, the RIC **3** file can be searched so rapidly that the result seems to be displayed instantaneously.

A more onerous solution would be to create an enormous database holding a complete description of each known coin type. For the moment, it is difficult to imagine the creation of such a database as the time taken to type all this information would be particularly restrictive. The task could be simplified by the use of a scanner and an optical character reader, but the amount of checking and correction required could take a lot of time. Nevertheless, I believe that it is possible at the moment to undertake the creation of more modest databases for particular projects. For instance, some years ago, I undertook to make a database for all the known coins of Augustus, including the Greek series (this was before the publication of *Roman provincial coinage*: Burnett *et al.* 1992). This database also comprises about half a million characters, and needed several months of part-time typing.

EXPERT SYSTEMS IN OTHER FIELDS OF ARCHAEOLOGY

We have examined the cases of terra sigillata and numismatic studies, and my conclusion, rather pessimistic, is that there are very few occasions where an expert system would be useful in such studies. We do not need expert systems; we **badly** need machine-readable files which can be searched in a short time, and we **do** need automated systems to help us to identify decorative elements.

There are, however, many other fields in archaeology which do not contain such vast amounts of material, but which are nevertheless very complex and difficult to exploit by a non-expert. I am thinking particularly of certain categories of object found in excavations which pose serious problems of identification and dating for archaeologists in the field. They are found in small quantities on most sites; what we usually call 'small finds', *fibulae* and beads for example (a major site near Fréjus produced about 50 coins, but only one bead and not a single *fibula*). Specialists in such fields are rather rare (compared to coins and sigillata) and therefore the field archaeologist is confronted with problems of identification in a documentation spread over hundreds of often inaccessible papers, not counting the financial problems of acquiring such documentation, to be used perhaps once or twice a year.

It seems to me that it is perhaps here that an expert system can render great service in the absence of a human expert, and it is to be hoped that these persons might care to undertake the same kind of analysis in their own fields that I have attempted here.

Notes

1. A reading list in expert systems where descriptions of these systems (and others) may be found would include the following works. Alty & Coombs 1984 is an excellent introduction to expert systems, and good descriptions of several operational expert systems are given in Harmon & King 1985, Michie 1982 and Weiss & Kulikowski 1984. Brough & Alexander 1986 is an expert system for palaeontology written in PROLOG, and several examples of expert systems of various types written in Turbo Prolog are given in Townsend 1988.

   Persons with a reading knowledge of French will be able to appreciate Gardin *et al.* 1987, one of the rare books entirely devoted to expert systems in humanistic research, including archaeology. Despite the title, the average reader will find this book rather difficult to digest, being an exploration of leading edge technology by experts in archaeology and computer science. Human factors specialists in particular will appreciate (p. 163):
   'Ask your question'
   "spb (amphore, amph18, non(provenance(ile-cos)).nil),);"
   This user interface could be improved.

2. This points out one of the problems of producing useable expert systems; either the problem is so complex as to be unmanageable, or, as the case here, completely trivial.

Bibliography

Alty, J.L. & Coombs, M.J., 1984 *Expert systems, concepts and examples* (Manchester)

Brough, D.R., & Alexander, I.F., 1986 The fossil expert system, in *Expert Systems*, **3**.2

Burnett, A., Amandry, M., & Père Pau Ripollès, 1992 *Roman provincial coinage*, **1** (London and Paris)

Crawford, M. H. 1974 *Roman Republican coinage* (Cambridge)

Gardin, J. C. *et al.*, 1987 *Systèmes expertes et sciences humaines* (Eyrolles, Paris)

Harmon, P., & King, D., 1985 *Expert systems: artificial intelligence in business* (New York)

Klawans, Z. H., 1963 *Reading and dating Roman imperial coins* (Racine, Wisconsin)

Mattingly, H., & Sydenham, E. A., 1923–94 *Roman imperial coinage* (10 vols., London)

Michie, D. (ed.), 1982 *Introductory readings in expert systems* (New York)

Oswald, F., 1936–37 *Index of figure-types on terra sigillata ('samian ware')*, Annals Archaeol. Anthropol. Suppl., **23**.1–4, **24**.1–4 (Liverpool)

Reece, R., 1973 Roman coinage in the Western Empire, *Britannia*, **4**, 227–51

Rogers, G.B., 1974 *Poteries sigillées de la Gaule Centrale, 1: les motifs non figurés*, Gallia Suppl., **28** (Paris)

Stanfield, J.A., & Simpson, G., 1958 *Central Gaulish potters* (London)

Townsend, C., 1988 *Turbo Prolog applications* (Sybex, Paris)

Weiss, S.M., & Kulikowski, C.A., 1984 *A practical guide to designing expert systems* (New Jersey)

21   Un dépôt pré-flavien à Tongeren (Belgique)

M. Vanderhoeven

L'Institut pour le Patrimoine Archéologique de la Communauté flamande entreprend depuis 1986 d'importantes fouilles archéologiques à Tongeren. Elles ont pour objectif une connaissance plus précise et plus large du passé romain de la ville.

Quatre siècles de présence romaine dans la capitale de la *Civitas Tungrorum* ont imposé aux structures urbaines de nombreuses mutations. Ainsi, les recherches effectuées sur un terrain d'environ 0,5 ha. de surface situé dans le secteur est de la ville ont donné de nouveaux aperçus sur l'évolution de l'habitat dans ce secteur (fig. 1).

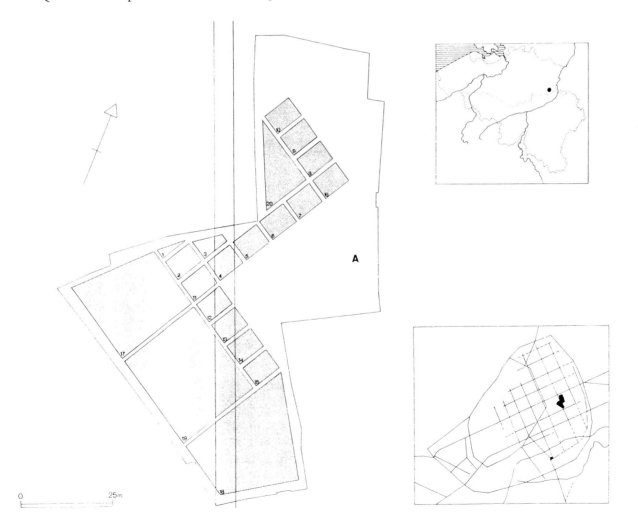

Fig. 1. Tongeren. Situation du secteur fouillé et du puits (A). D'après Vanderhoeven et al. 1992, fig. 1.

183

Neuf niveaux d'habitations successifs au moins ont été identifiés dont sept font apparaître des constructions en bois et deux des constructions en pierre. On y distingue sept étages chronologiques depuis le règne d'Auguste (*c.* 10 av. J.-C.) jusque dans le 3e s. (*c.* 250 ap. J.-C.). Une couche d'incendie bien nette est visible partout. Elle comporte de nombreux fragments d'argile calcinée et des décombres provenant de la destruction de la ville. Elle a été mise en rapport avec la révolte des Bataves en 69/70 et forme une rupture stratigraphique. Le matériel le plus ancien de cette zone peut être comparé avec celui du camp d'Oberaden (10–8 av. J.-C.).

De la deuxième période, nous connaissons les restes d'habitations à deux travées, l'une pour l'habitat et l'autre pour l'étable, du type Alphen-Ekeren et datant de l'époque tibérienne. Ces habitations ont fait place, sous le règne de Claude, à d'autres dont les structures sont plus conformes au plan habituel des habitations urbaines en zone romanisée. Ce sont ces habitations qui, après avoir subi des transformations sous Néron, furent incendiées en 69/70.

Le matériel que nous présentons dans cet article provient d'un puits creusé à l'époque Claudienne (fig. 2). Il donne un bon aperçu de la céramique en usage à Tongeren à l'époque pré-flavienne.

INVENTAIRE DU MATÉRIEL (figs. 3–6)

L'inventaire des pièces ci-après est volontairement laconique; les descriptions sont limitées aux éléments que les dessins ne font pas apparaître.

1. Fragment de bord d'un gobelet en céramique brune, paroi lisse.
   (94.TO.023.619)
2. Fragment de bord d'une urne en céramique brun clair.
   (94.TO.023.620.1)
3. Fragment de paroi d'une urne en céramique grise, décorée d'une bande de pastilles de couleur blanche.
   (94.TO.023.620.2)
4. Fragment d'une coupe sigillée Drag. 29.
   (94.TO.023.621.1)
5. Fragment d'une coupe sigillée Drag. 29.
   (94.TO.023.621.2)
6. Fragment de fond d'une assiette en terre sigillée marquée du sigle OF AQVITAN.
   (94.TO.023.621.3)
7. Fragment de bord d'un gobelet en terra nigra, céramique gris clair.
   (94.TO.023.621.5)

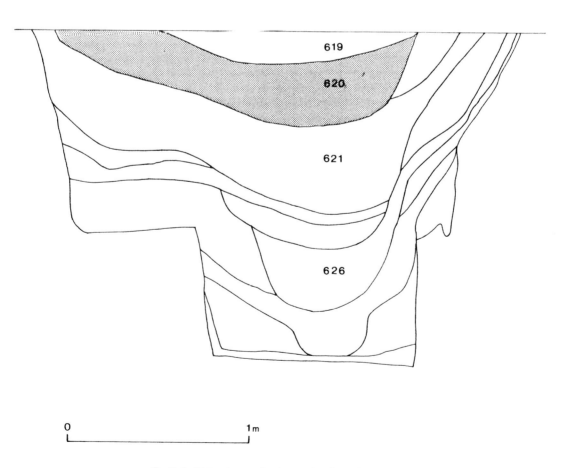

Fig. 2. Profil du puits avec situation stratigraphique du matériel.

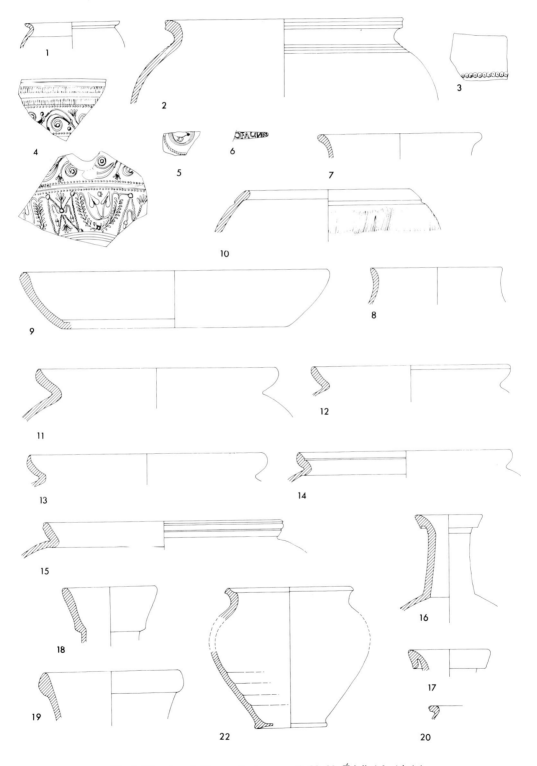

Fig. 3. Céramique de l'époque néronienne, nos. 1–20, 22. Échelle 1:3; sigle 1:1.

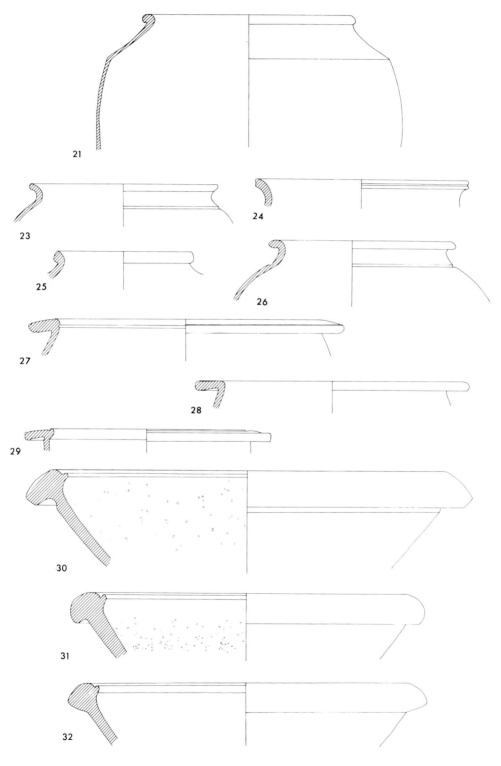

Fig. 4. Céramique de l'époque néronienne, nos. 21, 23–32. Échelle 1:3.

8. Fragment de bord d'un gobelet en terra nigra, céramique brun clair.
(94.TO.023.621.6)

9. Fragment d'une assiette en terra nigra, céramique brune.
(94.TO.023.621.7)

10. Fragment de bord d'une 'kurkurne', céramique gris brun, décorée au peigne.
(94.TO.023.621.8)

11. Fragment de bord d'un gobelet en céramique brun clair.
(94.TO.023.621.15)

12. Fragment de bord d'un gobelet en céramique brun clair.
(94.TO.023.621.16)

13. Fragment de bord d'un gobelet en céramique brun clair.
(94.TO.023.621.17)

14. Fragment de bord d'un gobelet en céramique brun clair.
(94.TO.023.621.18)

15. Fragment de bord d'un gobelet en céramique brune, particules dorées en surface.
(94.TO.023.621.19)

16. Goulot d'une cruche en céramique jaunâtre.
(94.TO.023.621.20)

17. Lèvre d'une cruche en céramique jaune clair.
(94.TO.023.621.21)

18. Lèvre d'une cruche en céramique grise.
(94.TO.023.621.22)

19. Lèvre d'une cruche-amphore en céramique jaune clair.
(94.TO.023.621.23)

20. Lèvre d'une cruche-amphore en céramique jaune clair.
(94.TO.023.621.24)

21. Plusieurs fragments d'une urne en céramique grise, rugueuse.
(94.TO.023.621.13)

22. Plusieurs fragments d'une urne en céramique grise, rugueuse.
(94.TO.023.621.14)

23. Plusieurs fragments d'une urne en céramique grise, rugueuse.
(94.TO.023.621.25)

24. Fragment de bord d'une urne en céramique grise, rugueuse.
(94.TO.023.621.26)

25. Fragment de bord d'une urne en céramique gris clair, rugueuse.
(94.TO.023.621.27)

26. Fragment de bord d'une urne en céramique gris clair, rugueuse.
(94.TO.023.621.28)

27. Fragment de bord d'une urne à bord horizontal en céramique gris foncé, rugueuse.
(94.TO.023.621.29)

28. Fragment de bord d'une urne à bord horizontal en céramique gris foncé, rugueuse.
(94.TO.023.621.30)

29. Fragment d'une urne à bord horizontal en céramique gris foncé, rugueuse.
(94.TO.023.621.31)

30. Fragment de bord d'un mortier en céramique jaune, rugueuse.
(94.TO.023.621.32)

31. Fragment de bord d'un mortier en céramique grise, rugueuse.
(94.TO.023.621.33)

32. Fragment de bord d'un mortier en céramique jaune, rugueuse.
(94.TO.023.621.34)

33. Fragment de bord d'un mortier en céramique jaune, rugueuse.
(94.TO.023.621.35)

34. Fragment de bord d'un couvercle en céramique grise, rugueuse.
(94.TO.023.621.9)

35. Fragment de bord d'un couvercle en céramique gris foncé, rugueuse.
(94.TO.023.621.10)

36. Fragment de bord d'un couvercle en céramique gris foncé, rugueuse.
(94.TO.023.621.11)

37. Fragment de bord d'un couvercle en céramique gris foncé, rugueuse.
(94.TO.023.621.12)

38. Petite écuelle en céramique brun clair, rugueuse.
(94.TO.023.621.4)

39. Fragment de bord d'une tasse sigillée Ha. 11.
(94.TO.023.626.1)

40. Assiette sigillée Ha. 2 avec sigle central ACA.
(94.TO.023.626.13)

41. Tasse sigillée Drag. 27 avec sigle MACCAR.
(94.TO.023.626.12)

42. Coupe en terra nigra, céramique grise, couverte brillante noire. Sigle radial ALIATV.
(94.TO.023.626.10)

43. Coupe en terra nigra, céramique grise, couverte brillante noire. Sigle radial ALIATV.
(94.TO.023.626.11)

44. Plat en terra nigra, céramique gris clair, couverte noire. Trois sigles radiaux ME.
(94.TO.023.626.6)

45. Plat en terra nigra, céramique gris clair, couverte noire avec nuages gris. Trois sigles radiaux ACVT.
(94.TO.023.626.8)

46. Plat en terra nigra, céramique gris clair, couverte noire avec nuages gris. Trois sigles radiaux OANNOM.
(94.TO.023.626.7)

47. Plat en terra nigra, céramique gris clair, couverte noire. Trois sigles radiaux illisibles.
(94.TO.023.626.9)

48. Fragment de bord d'un gobelet en céramique jaunâtre.
(94.TO.023.626.1)

49. Col de cruche en céramique brun-jaune, rugueuse.
(94.TO.023.626.3)

50. Petite urne en céramique gris clair, rugueuse.
(94.TO.023.626.14)

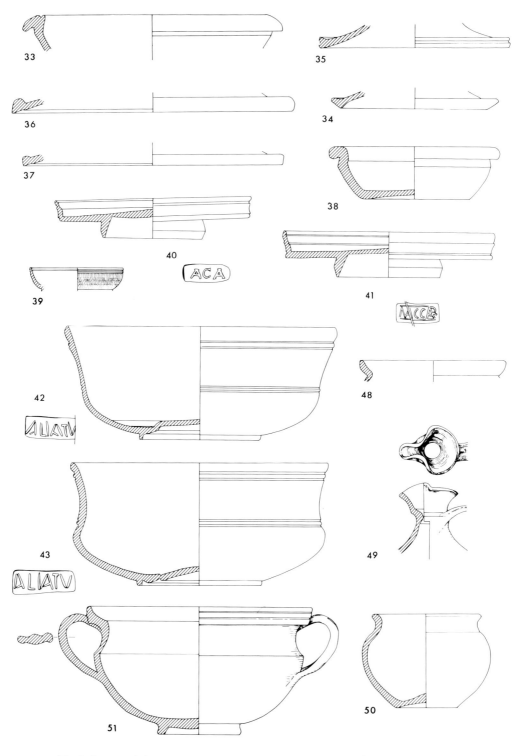

Fig. 5. Céramique de l'époque néronienne et claudienne, nos. 33–43, 48–51. Échelle 1:3; sigles 1:1.

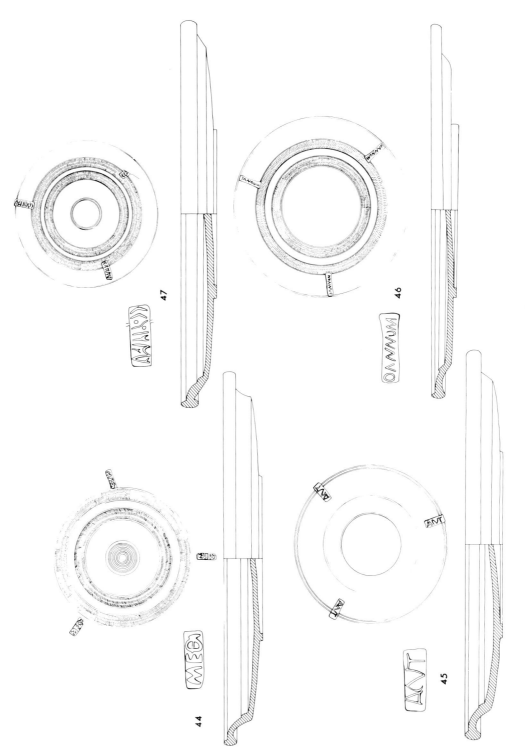

Fig. 6. Céramique de l'époque claudienne, nos. 44-47. Échelle: 1/3; sigles 1:1.

51. Calice en céramique jaune brune, rugueuse.
    (94.TO.023.626.4)

INTERPRÉTATION DES TROUVAILLES

La fosse que nous présentons a été creusée au moment où les fermes à deux travées de l'époque tibérienne ont été remplacées, à l'époque claudienne, par de grandes maisons d'habitations (Vanderhoeven *et al.* 1992, 128).

Il faut souligner la découverte, sur le fond de la fosse, d'un service composé de deux coupes (fig. 5, nos. 42–43) et de quatre plats en terra nigra (fig. 6, nos. 44–47) accompagnés de deux assiettes en terra sigillata (fig. 5, nos. 40–41), d'une petite urne (fig. 5, no. 50) et d'un calice (fig. 5, no. 51). Le fragment de bord d'un gobelet (fig. 5, no. 48) et le goulot d'une cruche peuvent également appartenir à l'époque claudienne (fig. 5, no. 49). Le fragment d'une tasse en terre sigillée, forme Ha.11 (fig. 5, no. 39) peut être considéré comme intrusive et provenir d'un contexte plus ancien.

Les maisons furent transformées au cours du règne de Néron (Vanderhoeven *et al.* 1992, 97) et le puits fut, à ce moment, rempli de déchets divers (figs. 3, nos. 1–22 ; 4, nos. 21–32 ; 5, nos. 33–38). Ce matériel était accompagné de nombreux fragments de paroi d'amphores et de dolia ainsi que de nombreux fragments d'os d'animaux.

En 69/70, le puits déjà comblé fut recouvert d'une importante couche de décombres provenant des maisons incendiées dans cette partie de la ville.

REMERCIEMENTS

Nous tenons à remercier le Prof. Dr. G. de Boe, Directeur de l'Institut pour le Patrimonie archéologique, pour l'autorisation qu'il nous a donnée de faire connaître cette trouvaille avant l'étude de l'ensemble de la fouille. Que MM. P. Becker, A. Vanderhoeven et G. Vynckier soient remerciés pour leur aide; les dessins sont de la main de Mmes B. Pauly et M. Willaert.

Liste des publications se rapportant au secteur fouillé

Vanderhoeven, A., van de Konijnenburg, R., & de Boe, G., 1987 Het Oudheidkundig bodemonderzoek aan de Kielenstraat te Tongeren, Interimverslag 1986, *Archaeologia Belgica*, **3**, 127–38

————, Vynckier, G., & Vynckier, P., 1991a Het Oudheidkundig bodemonderzoek aan de Kielenstraat te Tongeren, Interimverslag 1987, *Archeologie in Vlaanderen*, **1**, 107–24

————, & ————, 1991b Het project 'Stadsonderzoek' te Tongeren. De oudste (?) bewoning, *Archeologie in Limburg*, **47**, 1–7

————, ————, Ervynck, A., & Cooremans, B., 1992 Het Oudheidkundig bodemonderzoek aan de Kielenstraat te Tongeren (prov. Limburg), Interimverslag 1990–1993, Deel 1, De voor-Flavische bewoning, *Archeologie in Vlaanderen*, **2**, 89–146

22   Where did Cen, Reditas and Sace produce pots?
A summary of the range and distribution
of Romano-British stamped wares

Val Rigby

INTRODUCTION

The *corpus* of potters' stamps on Roman coarse wares developed accidentally alongside that of Gallo-Belgic imports from 1968 because some stamps recorded as Gallo-Belgic fine wares were found not to be so: it appeared a good idea however to maintain them in a separate list. As with all *corpora*, the immediate aim was to provide a tool to further research by building up a life history of a potter through detailed accumulated knowledge of each die used, so that eventually all but the most fragmentary and abraded stamps could be identified and dated. Distribution patterns of such specific products would then illustrate something of growth and change in the Romano-British pottery industry. Speculation on economic and social change would be underpinned by a few facts - so much for the intention.

The definition of what constitutes a Roman coarse ware is only the first of several problems encountered during its compilation. By custom, it has become confined to fabrics typically included in the coarse pottery section of Roman pottery reports, and hence excludes stamps on mortaria as well as known or deduced imported fine wares, specifically samian and Gallo-Belgic imports, i.e. terra nigra, terra rubra, mica-coated and black eggshell wares. Each of these classes now has its own *corpus* of stamps, and it is noteworthy that they are in detail mutually exclusive. Some common names do occur in more than one list, but they are in parallel, for style- and die-links are absent.

The coarse ware *corpus* now comprises 447 stamped vessels, 31 far too fragmentary or abraded for classification, from 101 sites lying principally south and east of the Fosse Way, with a particular concentration in the east Midlands into East Anglia. It is not comprehensive, since two groups excluded in the beginning for various reasons which seemed significant at the time have not been studied; they are stamps on Oxfordshire products (Young 1977) and 'Caerleon Ware' (Boon 1966). To include them will raise the total above 500 but still a rather meagre total when compared to the equivalent mortarium *corpus*, in which stamps of the potter Sollus of Verulamium totalled at least 70 examples in 1986 (Hartley 1986, 238, no. 14).

The main divisions are the same as those for Gallo-Belgic imports, that is Names, Copies and Marks. Names are in alphabetical order, and provide the most reliable results. There are only 40 clearly cut, literate and easily recorded names, approximately 10% of decipherable stamps: it is a much lower proportion than, for example, Gallo-Belgic imports where Names comprise over 60%. Most letters were cut in a cursive rather than in the formal epigraphic style of inscriptions more commonly used by samian and Gallo-Belgic die-cutters. The shortage of Names is unfortunate because they are most easily recorded and retrieved, and can be more reliably consolidated to provide evidence of the scope and chronology of a potter's working life.

Where recognisable, cursive letters too were mainly used in Copies. They are grouped according to the initial and any subsequent recognisable letter, but 'style' is a significant factor, and one which is almost impossible to define simply and impose uniformly. They are the most difficult to record since it is not possible to be sure which way up to read them; moreover, they typically include so many poorly shaped cursive letters that they cannot be fully transcribed with any degree of certainty. As a result, when dealing with fragments and abraded impressions, die-links can be missed until a complete stamp is available. It is virtually impossible to group them into the output of individual potters or workshop groups, except by relying on probability using die-style, vessel-form, fabric and provenance.

Marks are grouped by motif, repeated single motifs and then combinations, and finally by 'style'. They cause similar limitations on deciphering and interpretation as Copies (see below). The general use of cursive letters has almost certainly meant that the number of recognisable and repeated Names is artificially depressed and that of Copies and Marks inflated in the record.

The final limitation is the shortage of archaeologically attested kilns where stamped vessels were made. No workshops using Name dies have been located. At Keston, Kent, there is a die or poinçon for a Copy and one for a Mark, but no vessels stamped with them were found; conversely, eight platters had been stamped with different Marks, but the dies were not located (Philp 1991, 157–8, 279–80). Marks were used at West Stow (West 1989) and Wherstead, Suffolk (Plouviez, report in preparation) and Wiggonholt, Sussex (Evans 1974); Rushden (Woods & Hastings 1984) and Ecton, Northants. (Johnstone 1969), and Hacheston, Suffolk, are strong probables. The outlines of a marketing pattern can be discerned only for West Stow and Wiggonholt. On typological grounds it appears that Keston and Rushden are the earliest, for close copies of Gallo-Belgic platters and beakers were included in the repertoire so that a pre-Flavian date is likely; the remainder were active sometime between AD 80 and 180.

A few stamps have been recorded on platters and cups in grog-tempered wares; however, none has been found in a definite pre-conquest context. For example, in the King Harry Lane Cemetery, Verulamium, Herts. only two from a total of 120 platters are stamped and they occurred in graves outside any enclosure, and were therefore assigned to Pottery Period 3, the Claudio-Neronian period (Stead & Rigby 1989, 157). One out of four locally made platters in a burial at Baldock, Herts. associated with Claudio-Neronian samian was stamped with a mark (Stead & Rigby 1986, 73, fig. 32).

Despite the limitations, some progress has been made and specific examples have been chosen from the *corpus* to illustrate the possibilities. Different types of distribution pattern occur, probably as a result of insufficient data, and it is assumed that they will change as more stamps emerge. Local is here defined as being within 30km (acf – as the crow flies), or a return journey in a day for a cart.

REGIONAL DISTRIBUTION

There is a group of fifteen stamps bearing at least four different Names found on nine sites in northern Britain. As read, the complete names are Cen, Sace and Red(i)tas, with a fourth beginning SO.., or ending ..OS; there are also two illegible stamps, a fragment and a complete impression (fig. 1 and Appendix 1). An obvious die-style division can be made: Cen and Sace, and the SO.. fragment could have been cut by the same hand, but Reditas is different. The stamps occur on a platter-form which is characterised by a markedly domed base and a convex wall profile with a sharply inturned and carinated lip (Gillam 1957, no. 337). The bases of the remaining stamps conform. Where recorded the fabrics are similar, coarse sand-tempered grey wares with darker grey or black surfaces. The forms and fabrics are sufficiently similar to suggest manufacture in related workshops, possibly at the same pottery. The dating evidence suggests production in the Flavian-Trajanic period (Appendix 1).

This is one of the most convincing and extensive regional groups in Britain, yet it cannot be attributed to any specific sources, and illustrates graphically how much remains to be discovered about Romano-British pottery production and distribution. Four names have been recorded at Doncaster, the remaining finds are on sites more or less directly connected to Doncaster with land or river routes making it an obvious candidate for one or more workshop (fig. 1). Production could have been begun somewhat earlier, in the late 1st century, since

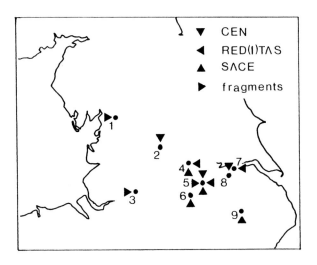

Fig. 1. Cen, Reditas and Sace stamps, with their distribution. Scale: 1:1.
1. *Burrow in Lonsdale, Cumbria;* ***2.*** *Ilkley, West Yorks.;* ***3.*** *Manchester;* ***4.*** *Castleford, West Yorks.;* ***5.*** *Doncaster, South Yorks.;*
6. *Templeborough, South Yorks.;* ***7.*** *Old Winteringham, Lincs.;* ***8.*** *Dragonby, Lincs.;* ***9.*** *Lincoln*

large-scale pottery manufacture is certainly known there from the 2nd century AD, and included stamped mortaria and stamp-decorated vessels which were distributed throughout northern Britain as far as Scotland. The platter form is commonly represented in a variety of different fabrics in assemblages from sites around the Humber estuary, implying a regional connection: recorded sites include Roxby, a probable kiln working in the 2nd century, Winterton and Thealby on the south bank, Brough-on-Humber, North Cave, Malton, Langton and Rudston to the north, and York. Predicting sources of supply from distribution patterns may be an interesting exercise but it is doomed to disappointment since it is the pattern of archaeological activity which is being illustrated rather than the distribution of Romano-British pottery.

Names are scarce in the *corpus*, so that it can be considered as exceptional for one-third to be concentrated on a few sites in northern Britain. With the exception of Dragonby and Castleford, the stamps were found at forts, adjacent to forts, or in areas deduced to be forts, associated with the occupation of northern Britain in the period from AD 70 to the construction of Hadrian's Wall. There is no evidence that Cen, Reditas or Sace were military potters but a greater degree of literacy may have prevailed amongst sections of the population closely connected with the Roman army, if not serving in it: when dealing with such a bureacracy, literacy must have proved of inestimable value. In the absence of a native British tradition for marking an individual's products the idea was adopted from imported products; moreover, many of the potters or die-cutters, or both, could have been immigrants.

REGIONAL DISTRIBUTION WITH OUTLIERS

West Stow is only one of two potteries producing vessels stamped with Marks with any recorded distribution pattern (fig. 2; West 1989). Locally, at less than 12km distance (acf) to the south, Dies 4/11, 4/11' and four others have been found at Pakenham, Suffolk (Plouviez *et al.,* report in preparation). The stamps at Pakenham illustrate nicely one of the problems discussed above. Fragmentary impressions of West Stow Dies 4 and 11 published separately have now proved to be opposite ends of the same die, Die 4/11, which was however re-used after being broken, and is now designated as Die 4/11'. At a rather greater distance, 20–30kms (acf) to the north, Die 5 occurs at Brandon, Suffolk, and Die 6 at Hockwold-cum-Wilton, Norfolk (the provenances are transposed in West 1989, 88). Further afield to the north-west, and beyond the famed 30km return cart journey, another stamp from Die 4/11 is recorded at Grandford, Cambs. (Potter 1982, fig. 29, no. 184). Beyond this local distribution, one die-link has been established with Colchester, Die 16, and using diestyle, form and fabric range, West Stow potters appear to have supplied nine other stamped vessels from a recorded total of 82, at least 12% (Symonds & Wade, forthcoming). The West Stow pottery therefore may have been a significant regional supplier to the more westerly areas of East Anglia, with a seeming product distinction between the north and the south

if the dies are significant. Its stamped products apparently did not reach Londinium and its environs, probably the largest market in the province, despite the absence of any obvious extra difficulty compared to Colchester. However, Die 5 is recorded at Doncaster, considerably beyond the geographical region to the north. Such evidence for local, regional and inter-regional distribution is fine, but why Doncaster, where are the remaining stamped West Stow products in the intervening areas, and why not London?

One factor in the Doncaster connection may be traced to the supposition that no trader ever wants to move empty space, and pots are a cheap and non-perishable make-weight cargo. East Anglia is typically considered as the bread-basket for the Roman army in northern Britain, and presumably much grain was transported by ship. Both formal and casual arrangements for space-fillers and return cargoes may have been made, with West Stow pots, and others, being included. Certainly northern pots were brought into East Anglia, for North Lincolnshire, Dales, East Yorks. and Huntcliff Wares have been found in some numbers, and their opportunistic inclusion as part of return cargoes seems likely. Since Londinium and its suburbs also required quantities of foodstuffs, the 'return load' effect should also be present in the ceramic assemblage.

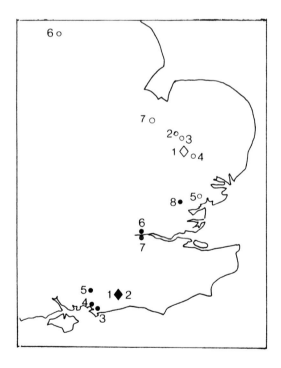

Fig. 2. Current distribution of stamped products of the West Stow and Wiggonholt kilns.

Open symbols: *1. West Stow kilns, Suffolk; 2. Hockwold-cum-Wilton, Norfolk; 3. Brandon, Suffolk; 4. Pakenham, Suffolk; 5. Colchester, Essex; 6. Doncaster, South Yorkshire; 7. Grandford, Cambs.*

Filled symbols: *1. Wiggonholt, West Sussex; 2. Hardham Camp, Pulborough, West Sussex; 3. Chichester, West Sussex; 4. Fishbourne, West Sussex; 5. Elsted, West Sussex; 6. Londinium; 7. Southwark; 8. Braintree, Essex*

LINKED REGIONAL CONCENTRATIONS

Six stamps found at Wiggonholt are clearly related to seven found at the adjacent site of Hardham Camp, Pulborough, and considered to be products of the same pottery (Evans 1974, fig. 9, nos. 17–21; Winbolt 1927, 11). The dies are completely or partially bordered, two are double-line, and the remainder single-line, the motifs are restricted to I, V and X, and the combinations suggest five die-style groupings.

Stamped vessels made at Wiggonholt/Hardham have been found at Chichester, Fishbourne and Elsted, West Sussex, Londinium and Southwark, and Braintree, Essex (Down, report in press). The Sussex-London connection was first identified with the Aldgate/Pulborough samian potter, and now is reinforced with trade in coarse wares (Evans 1974, 144). The platter forms and the fabrics are very similar, easily falling within the definition of products of a single workshop (fig. 3): six other platters, stamped with different dies, from Chichester, Fishbourne, London and Southwark were probably made at the same source. Why was there such a close connection? Besides the return load factor, political considerations may have intervened, with Cogidubnus providing the connection (Down, report in press). The Braintree find is an oddity. The form is different in detail, much closer to a Gallo-Belgic prototype, with internal moulding and a slight foot-ring, which may indicate that it is the earliest product, and that the potter moved or the die was transferred from Essex to Sussex.

The Braintree find emphasises the problem of serendipity and chance. The London-Sussex connection had been established before its discovery. There was also a noticeable difference between the two most extensive lists of stamped coarse ware vessels, those of London and Colchester, which suggested that these major markets were supplied from separate regional sources with the obvious exception of imports and functionally specialist wares like mortaria. In the 1st and 2nd centuries AD London looked to the west, to Catuvellaunian and Atrebatic regions, while Colchester and the Trinovantian region relied on East Anglia. The Braintree find upsets this neat picture, an accidental find which could easily have slipped through the net, its information strictly fortuitous.

As a single find, it is difficult to see how it affects the original hypothesis. The major differences between the stamp lists of London and Colchester remain. Perhaps Braintree Roman settlement was in the London catchment area, rather than that of Colchester: it lies roughly the same distance from both. If not regional and tribal, then perhaps the explanation is chronological. There may be sufficiently marked precise dating differences within the existing samples from London and Colchester to maximise differences and mask similarities in their sources of Romano-British coarse pottery.

WIDESPREAD SPORADIC

A rather unexpected die-link connects a pair of bowls with deep flanged rims in parchment ware from a grave in Winchester and a cup in micaceous red-ware from Gloucester (Collis 1978, fig. 61, 5–6; Rawes 1972). The die is almost literate and to aid recording, the stamp has been transcribed as Attixius (Appendix 2). Whether it is a Name or a Copy it is still a rarity in Britain; it is the only recorded instance where a die has been used on two such different coarse fabrics found on distant sites. Moreover, stamped vessels in pale- or parchment-coloured fabrics are rare, comprising just 8% of the *corpus*.

Three stamps made with one die found in two different locations is not an adequate database to deduce source; however, certain points can be made. Even when unstamped, the bowl-form with its wide and deep flange is rare in southern Britain, and so was either only an occasional product of Romano-British potteries or alternatively, was imported. A third example has been found in a burial at Neatham stamped with a similar, but different die (Millett & Graham 1987, fig. 50, no. 26). Its treatment in both the Winchester and Neatham pottery reports demonstrates that the form was considered as non-local. The Farnham potteries, including Alice Holt, were the main suppliers of coarse wares to Neatham, and the bowl is outside the form and fabric repertoire there (Millet & Graham 1987, 77).

The Attixius workshop, whether located in Britain or Gaul, had to have access to clays from which micaceous oxidised and parchment wares could be produced, and had to be located in an area able to supply both Gloucester and Winches-

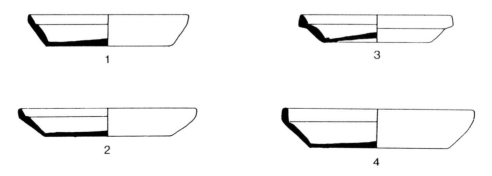

Fig. 3. Platter-forms stamped with dies related to Wiggonholt/Hardham. Scale: 1:4.
1. *Hardham Camp;* **2.** *Fishbourne;* **3.** *Braintree;* **4.** *Southwark.*

ter. Alternatively, the die, if not the potter, moved between two different kiln sites, one where potters specialised in micaceous oxidised wares, and the other, in parchment wares.

Gloucester had a flourishing pottery industry in the later 1st and 2nd centuries. The cup was found on the site where mica-coated vessels were made, and the micaceous red fabric falls within the definition of Gloucester products. It is the only stamped vessel; there was no tradition for stamping Gloucester products or for making parchment wares (Rawes 1972; Timby 1991).

The fabric could also be defined as 'Caerleon Ware', and here the use of maker's stamps, Names and Copies, was a fairly common practice, although no name or die-links have been established from existing published records which are not complete (Boon 1966, fig. 64). Some products, principally mortaria, were distributed to Gloucester, Cirencester and other sites on the east bank of the Severn estuary (Boon 1966, fig. 4). Whether Caerleon or Gloucester is preferred as the more likely source of the red cup, two production centres were almost certainly involved.

There is one known Roman pottery fairly close to Neatham and Winchester where stamped vessels were produced and bowls with deep flanged rims in parchment ware may have been produced, and that is Wiggonholt/Hardham, West Sussex (see above). The connection is tenuous. The recorded stamps are Marks in no way related to Attixius. Only one flanged rim was found, illustrated upside down and wrongly interpreted as a dish rim both here, and also at Angmering villa; finally, the grey and orange wares are much coarser in texture than the Gloucester cup (Evans 1974, fig. 10, no. 32; Scott 1938, fig. 24, no. 2). But it remains perhaps the strongest possibility. Others are the Verulamium Region and Oxfordshire potteries because of the significance of parchment wares in their output, and their widespread distribution networks in the 2nd century. Following this line of argument, the New Forest potteries are yet another candidate. In the late Roman period parchment wares were an important component of their output, so that bowls with deep flanged rims may have been part of a 2nd-century phase of production in that area.

CONCLUSION

The prevalence of Marks and shortage of Names compared with Gallo-Belgic imports may have implications for assessing the standard of literacy in Britain and Gaul, but they may also demonstrate that pottery making was organised differently in the two provinces. Large firms mass-producing fine wares for wide distribution in the western Empire were more likely to include literate and skilled die-cutters amongst their large labour-force of slaves and labourers. Individual potters making coarse wares in small workshops for restricted local or regional markets were less likely to have access to such skills unless working closely with the military. The latter scenario seems more applicable to coarse ware production in Britain in the 1st and 2nd centuries AD.

There are so many unsolved questions about these stamps, the most significant being the most basic for they are fundamental to estimating how regularly any die was used - why were they used and by whom? The re-use of West Stow Die 4/11 suggests that dies were significant and not easily replaced yet Dies 5 and 6 are so similar they could easily be confused. They may have belonged to the same potter in which case the difference of an additional vertical stroke did not matter. Some die-styles would have been readily distinguishable from the rest by the potters concerned, but it is unlikely that a customer could remember any significant differences. A pot-merchant or market trader could have gained the expertise to do so if it was advantageous.

Assuming that dies were used for quality and quantity control at source to distinguish the products of individual potters when communal production and firing took place, then West Stow Die 5 could have been used to stamp hundreds of vessels over a comparatively short period in one year. Careful packing of the kiln might mean that only the top vessel of each pile needed the maker's stamp rather than all, thus greatly reducing the number of stamped vessels produced, but the original total would still be greatly in excess of recorded examples.

Briefly surveying the *corpus*, a minimum of 300 different dies are represented, averaging less than 2 stamps per die, which can in no way be representative of output. The maximum number of impressions recorded is seven, West Stow, Die 5 (West 1989). Excluding those from known kiln sites, the maximum number from the consuming end of the market is five, all found at Colchester, and most probably Neronian-early Flavian in date, and either Gaulish imports, or made there (Symonds & Wade, forthcoming). The comparable totals for recognised major mortarium producers in Britain are in excess of 50 stamps impressed from two or three dies. Major samian potters used many dies, many of which are more common in Britain than any die in the coarse ware *corpus*. There may be unique factors involved which adversely affected the recovery of stamped Romano-British coarse wares and over-rode any advantages of proximity to markets. The problem may be exacerbated by an apparent tendency to hoard samian, either complete or broken vessels, or both.

The period when stamped vessels were most common is the 100 to 150 years from the Claudian to the Antonine periods, the time when the archaeological sample is probably considered to be most complete and hence most representative. It can be argued however that the acute shortage of stamps on coarse wares indicates that the archaeological sample for the best represented Romano-British period is too small to be reliable and there are still enormous gaps in the material evidence for the whole Romano-British sequence. As far as research is concerned, not only is too little known of where Roman pottery was produced, but too little has been recovered from settlements where it was used, with the result that serendipity exerts too great an effect on the results of research.

APPENDIX 1

i. Stamps of the
CEN/REDITAS/SACE workshops (fig. 1)

CEN(...)   the complete stamp appears to be an abbrevia-
                         tion, possibly Centus or Centismus
Die   Cen 1A1
Position   central on upper surface
Form   platter Gillam type 337
Fabric 1   dark grey-black coarse-grained, quartz sand-
                         tempered matrix; metallic burnished surface
                         inner surface, matt exterior
Fabric 2   orange-brown sand-tempered ware
Decoration   none on upper surface

Sites and contexts
Doncaster (2)   1) unpublished, record no. XD 3 (Site DE), al-
                         most complete
                         2) Buckland & Magilton 1986, fig. 40, 300
Ilkley (1)   Hartley 1966, fig. 10, no. 31); from the demo-
                         lition layers sealing buildings of the first fort,
                         or makeup for the Antonine building phase
Dragonby (1)   Stead 1976, 178; found in the upper layers of
                         Kiln 3, but the fabric is different to that of the
                         kiln products

REDTAS   possibly Reditas or Redetas
Die   Reditas 1A1
Position   central on upper surface
Form   platter Gillam type 337
Fabric   as Cen above
Decoration   none on upper surface

Sites and contexts
Castleford (1)   unpublished, record no. 198
Doncaster (1)   unpublished, record no. XD6 (Church Street
                         1967)
Old Winteringham (1)   Stead 1976, fig. 92, no. 1; residual in its context.
                         The form occurred in a Flavian-Trajanic con-
                         text (Stead 1976, fig. 76, no. 51)

SACE   an abbreviation, possibly of Sacerus
Die   Sace 1A1
Position   central on upper surface
Form   platter Gillam form 337
Fabric   as Cen above
Decoration   none recorded

Sites and contexts
Castleford (1)   unpublished, record no. 418
Doncaster (1)   unpublished, record no. XD4(DS/IT)
Lincoln (1)   Darling & Jones 1988, cf. fig. 8, no. 81, from
                         'The Lawns' site
Templeborough (1)   May 1922, 120, where the fabric is described
                         as 'clay hard grey, coated with black bitumen'

Die   Sace 1A2
Position   central on upper surface
Form   platter, variant unknown
Fabric   as Cen above
Decoration   none recorded

Sites and contexts
Lincoln (1)   Darling & Jones 1988, fig. 8, no. 81; not strati-
                         fied, but considered to belong to the occupa-
                         tion of the fortress

ii. Fragment from unidentified name

SO[...] or [...]OS or CO[...]
Position   central on upper surface
Form   platter without foot-ring, variant unknown
Fabric   coarse-grained quartz sand-tempered ware;
                         grey core, orange surfaces, matt exterior, bur-
                         nished interior. Probably an oxidised version of
                         the usual Cen-group fabric.

Sites and contexts
Doncaster (1)   unpublished, record no. XD2 (DT/RC)

iii. Unidentified fragments

1. Burrow in Lonsdale, Cumbria (Hildyard 1955, fig. 6, no. 4)
Position   central on upper surface
Form   platter Gillam type 337
Fabric   as Cen above
Decoration   bordered sunburst wreath, radial single-strand
                         comb-impressed stamps
Context   no useful information

2. Manchester (Jones & Grealey 1974, fig. 38, no. 156)
Position   central on upper surface
Form   platter Gillam type 337
Decoration   wreath as no. 1 above

APPENDIX 2

a) Stamps of the potter ATTIXIVS

Die   Attixius 1A1
Position   central inside bowl
Form   bowl with deep flanged rim
Fabric   parchment ware, off-white, tempered with
                         quartz sand

Sites and contexts
Winchester (2)   a pair of bowls stamped with same die in a cre-
                         mation burial found at Nuns Walk (Collis 1978,
                         fig. 61, nos. 5–6). The original date of *c.*AD 50
                         has been revised for the publication to late
                         Flavian-Hadrianic, presumably *c.*AD 85–125.

Die   Attixius 1A1
Position   central
Form   cup or small bowl
Fabric   fine-grained micaceous red ware

Sites and contexts
Gloucester (1)   one example found on the College of Art site,
                         where pottery production occurred from the
                         late 1st century to the mid-2nd century (Rawes
                         1972).

b) *VIVIXIIAI*

Die	not the same die as Attixius 1A1, but closely related, possibly indicating the same production centre
Position	central
Form	bowl with deep flange
Fabric	Creamy pink matrix tempered with fine quartz sand and with red grog inclusions; burnished finish

Sites and contexts

Neatham	one example found in cremation burial 5 with 20 other vessels, grouped in three discrete areas of the grave (Millett & Graham 1987, 58–60). The samian has been dated *c.*AD 130–165, with a *t.p.q.* of AD 140, which has an effect on the published date of the Nuns Walk, Winchester burial.

Postcript (21st August 1995)

Since submitting this text in February my lament that the archaeological sample is too small to be reliable has received an added boost. Mention of two additional stamps has to be made.

Information kindly provided by the Carlisle Archaeological Unit adds Carlisle to the distribution of Reditas stamps, thus reinforcing the connection with the early military dispositions in the north. In the circumstances one can only turn to prediction and state that in the fullness of time Reditas, Cen or Sace will also be found at Corbridge, South Shields, Newstead and Camelon, i.e. wherever in northern Britain terra nigra platters of Camulodunum form 16 have already been identified, while conversely many imported terra nigra platters will come to light in south Yorkshire.

Stamps found in Leicester in 1976 which I examined for the first time in June 1995 introduce Leicester as a complicating factor in the Sussex-London axis (material from excavations kindly submitted by the Archaeological Field Unit of Leicestershire Musuems, Arts and Records Service). The die is different from those included in the distribution map in my paper, but it is represented in the London assemblage, while the fabric and typological details place it in the Sussex-London group. It appears to be an even more unlikely outlier than the Braintree find although its discovery in an excavation was perhaps less archaeologically fortitous.

Bibliography

Boon, G. C., 1966 'Legionary' Ware at Caerleon? *Archaeol. Cambrensis,* **115,** 45–66
Buckland, P. C., & Magilton, J. R., 1986 *Archaeology of Doncaster I, the Roman civil settlement,* BAR British Ser., **148** (Oxford)
Collis, J., 1978 *Winchester excavations vol. II 1949–1960*
Darling, M. J., & Jones, M. J., 1988 Early Settlement at Lincoln, *Britannia,* **19,** 1–57
Evans, K. J., 1974 Excavations on a Romano-British site, Wiggonholt, 1964, *Sussex Archaeol. Collect.,* **112,** 97–151
Gillam, J. P., 1957 Types of Roman coarse pottery vessels in Northern Britain, *Archaeol. Aeliana,* 4 ser., **35,** 180–251
Hartley, B. R., 1966 The Roman fort at Ilkley, excavation of 1962, *Proc. Leeds Philosophical Literary Soc.,* **12.2,** 23–72
Hartley, K. F., 1986 Mortarium stamps, in Stead & Rigby 1986, 237–8
Hildyard, E. J. W., 1955 Excavations at Burrow in Lonsdale 1952–53, *Trans. Cumberland Westmorland Antiq. Archaeol. Soc.,* new ser., **54**
Johnstone, D. E., 1969 Romano-British pottery kilns near Northampton, *Antiq. J.,* **49,** 75–97
Jones, G. D. B., & Grealey, S., 1966 *Roman Manchester* (Manchester)
May, T., 1922 *The Roman fort of Templeborough near Rotherham*
Millett, M., & Graham, D., 1987 *Excavations on the Romano-British small town at Neatham, Hampshire 1969–1979,* Hampshire Field Club Monograph, **3**
Philp, B. J., *et al.,* 1991 *The Roman villa site at Keston, Kent. First report (excavations 1968–1978)*
Potter, T. W., 1982 The Romano-British village at Grandford, March, Cambridgeshire, *British Museum Occas. Papers,* **35**
Rawes, B., 1972 Roman pottery kilns at Gloucester, *Trans. Bristol Gloucester Archaeol. Soc.,* **91,** 18–59
Scott, L., 1938 The Roman villa at Angmering, *Sussex Archaeol. Collect.,* **79,** 3–44
Stead, I. M., 1976 *Excavations at Winterton and other Roman sites in North Lincs.,* DoE Archaeol. Rep., **9**
————, & Rigby, V., 1986 *Baldock: the excavation of a Roman and pre-Roman settlement 1968–72,* Britannia Monograph Ser., **7**
————, & ————, 1989 *Verulamium: the King Harry Lane Site,* English Heritage Archaeol. Rep., **12**
Symonds, R. P., & Wade, S., forthcoming *Roman pottery from excavations in Colchester, 1971–8,* Colchester Archaeol. Rep., **10**
Timby, J., 1991 The Berkeley Street pottery kilns, Gloucester, *J. Roman Pottery Stud.,* **4,** 19–32
Winbolt, S. E., 1927 Excavations at Hardham Camp, Pulborough, April 1926, *Sussex Archaeol. Collect.,* **68,** 89–132
West, S., 1989 *West Stow, Suffolk: the prehistoric and Romano-British occupations,* East Anglian Archaeol. Rep., **48**
Woods, P. J., & Hastings B. C., 1984 *Rushden: the early fine wares* (Rushden)
Young, C. J., 1977 *The Roman pottery industry of the Oxford region,* BAR, **43** (Oxford)

23 The incidence of stamped mortaria in the Roman Empire, with special reference to imports to Britain

Kay Hartley, with illustrations by Malcolm Stroud

I am delighted to have this opportunity to express my appreciation of the never-failing encouragement and help given by Brian throughout the years. He has always taken a lively interest in the stamps on mortaria and this paper would no doubt have benefited from his advice. The object of this paper is to correct some past errors and to draw attention to the perhaps surprising distribution of stamped mortaria, and indeed of coarse ware mortaria in general, which may not be universally appreciated.

INTRODUCTION

In 1960, with the help of an initial grant of £35 from the Central Research Fund of London University, I first visited France to look at stamped mortaria. This was prompted by queries arising from mortaria found in Britain. It was increasingly necessary to know more about those in northern and central France than was afforded by the published lists in CIL and *Pro Nervia* I-V. The particular objective was to seek out mortaria which had stamps identical to those found in Britain. Stamps were known to be rare in Germany but that was regarded as exceptional; mortaria there were required only by the army and were accordingly made in military depots, where they were not normally stamped. It had long been evident that Britain had many stamped mortaria and it seemed eminently reasonable to believe that France, occupied earlier and with a more Romanized culture, would have many more. So obvious did this seem that it took many visits to various parts of France before I could accept fully that this was far from being true; the opposite was, in fact, nearer to the truth!

THE POTTERS OF THE VERULAMIUM REGION – ALBINUS, MATUGENUS *ET AL.*

The most pressing reason for my visit was to seek evidence of any activity on the Continent of that most common of potters in Britain, Albinus, for whom more than 400 mortaria are now known.[1] I was also looking for Matugenus, Sollus, Q. Rutilius Ripanus and others who produced similar mortaria

and who are very important for the Flavian period (Castle 1972; 1976; Frere 1972; 1984; Saunders & Havercroft 1977). Philip Suggett had excavated at Brockley Hill for some years and was certain that Matugenus, Melus, and many other potters worked there, but this was still strongly contested (Suggett 1953; 1954; 1955).

One mortarium found in London has one stamp reading MATVGENV, while the other can be restored to ALBINI.FI, indicating that Matugenus was the son of Albinus. Stamps from different dies on a mortarium from Holditch, Staffs., await completion of the name in the nominative case but probably have a similar reading. The homogeneity of the fabrics and forms used by Albinus, Matugenus and other potters mentioned above indicated production in the same area. The fabrics used by Castus and G. Attius Marinus were similar to the above and kilns and undoubted wasters belonging to them were found at Radlett in the 19th century (Page 1898).

If Suggett's claims were true, there was every indication of a large-scale pottery industry, covering a wide area, an industry of prime importance for Britain in the Flavian and Trajanic periods, and not only for mortaria. This production area, now known as the 'Verulamium region', stretches from Verulamium to Brockley Hill and includes kiln-sites at Radlett, Brockley Hill, Bricket Wood, sites at Verulamium itself and probably elsewhere (Saunders & Havercroft 1977; Anthony 1968; Corder 1941).

It had been generally believed that these potters worked in Gaul and exported mortaria to Britain. The link with Radlett had been missed because there was a tendency to consider stamps without reference to other attributes of the vessel i.e. its fabric, form etc. The numbers of stamps present at Brockley Hill were enough to suggest that Suggett was right. His publication of the die of Matugenus in 1955 (Suggett 1955, 62; RIB **2**, 2409.22) was fairly conclusive, but as an old find in a private collection it was not universally accepted. Because I made a point of examining every available stamped mortarium, as a matter of course, I did notice similarities and differences in fabric, albeit on a rudimentary scale at first.[2] I expected large numbers of stamped mortaria in Gaul, but either none by these potters, or their stamps on mortaria in a different fabric indicating that they had worked in Gaul before coming to Britain.

The belief that these mortaria were imported may seem extraordinary now, but there were several reasons for it. Albinus and Ripanus often used counterstamps, indicating workshops at *Lugdunum* or *Lugudunum*. This alone made Lyons a prime favourite for the production centre and *Lugdunum Batavorum* in the Netherlands another candidate. A stamp reading LVGDVNENSIS from Saintes (CIL XIII.3, 10006, I, republished in Santrot & Santrot 1979, no. 196, drawing 7) was frequently quoted in connexion with Albinus but examination of this mortarium showed nothing in common with ours, whose stamps never have this reading anyway. It appears to be a one-off and probably from some fairly local source. The mortaria at Lyons were not accessible and I have still not seen them but examination of other mortaria was enough to settle that question. Nowhere in France, not even at Vienne, only 28km from Lyons, did I find any other stamp beginning in LVGD or LVGVDV, and no other is published. Brockley Hill, however, was identified with *Sulloniacae* in the Antonine Itinerary and there was no evidence for a *Lugdunum* anywhere in the area. There is now a possible candidate at Bricket Wood, where counterstamps reading LVGD.F (G represented by a laterally inverted D) were found at a kiln used by Oastrius, AD55–75/80 (Saunders & Havercroft 1977).

The lettering and borders of some of the stamps of Matugenus, Sollus etc. are among the finest on mortarium stamps anywhere and it was considered unlikely that potters in Britain had produced them. One theory was that they were made by Gaulish samian potters who exported to Britain, e.g. Matugenus, a name appearing on both samian and mortaria. Certainly potters who made other stamped ware sometimes

stamped mortaria, but possible examples of Gaulish samian potters doing this are, at best, extremely rare.[3]

Finally, the kilns at Brockley Hill were not of the standard expected of such potters and were not accepted as kilns by everyone. The problems about Brockley Hill sorted themselves out eventually, thanks mainly to Philip Suggett and to Stephen Castle who continued his work. Certainly I found no evidence of these potters on the Continent. One single fragment is now known from Nijmegen with a counterstamp reading FECIT, from a die attributable to Moricamulus (Bogaers & Haalebos 1980, 85, fig. 30, no. 5: not seen, fabric assumed to be from the Verulamium region; Frere 1972, nos. 29–30; 1984, nos. 88–89). This all confirmed what was clear from the beginning, because if such common potters had been stamping mortaria on the Continent, examples would already have been recorded in CIL. The question of where these potters came from remains unanswered. The only clue so far, and an enigmatic one, lies in two fragments probably from the same vessel with a stamp of Albinus, found at Colchester and soundly attributed on fabric to production there (Frere & Wilkes 1989, 239, nos. 1–2; Symonds & Wade forthcoming, 199, S.15 and fig. 4.25, no. 15).

Q. Valerius Veranius[4] (figs. 1–2)

My second reason for going to France was to examine as many as possible of the twelve mortaria of Q.Valerius Veranius which were then published. I began at Bavay, whose large collection of stamps, published in *Pro Nervia*, included at least four of his (Darche 1924, 262–3),[5] and where he was believed to have worked. Darche published stamps from two dies, one interpreted by him as Q. VALERIVS/VERANIV (three examples) (fig. 1, no. 1), and the other giving a slightly abbre-

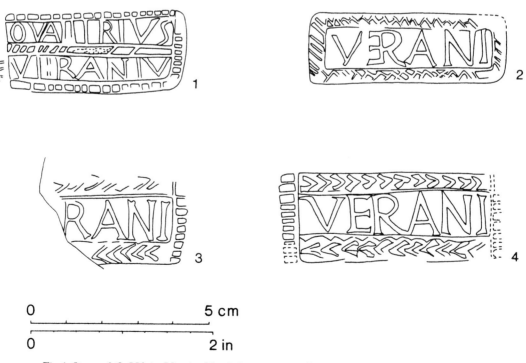

Fig. 1. Stamps of Q. Valerius Veranius. Nos. *1–3*, stamps seen at Bavay, no. *4* from Richborough. Scale 1:1.

viated *cognomen,* VERANI with ER ligatured (as fig. 1, no. 2). In the collections at Bavay I found nine of his mortaria: four with stamps generally similar to fig. 1, no. 1 (119 28.2.12, Sablière L; 1018/913 21/12/23, Sablière M; 1782 7/8/21, Sablière L; and N232); four with stamps identical to fig. 1, no. 2 (5730/738 Sablière M; 4832 16/2/25 Sablière M; 1055/1914 Sablière L; and N112); and the single stamp fig. 1, no. 3 (747/ 5837 Sablière M; Carmelez 1981, pl. 51, no. 35). Eight of the nine were recorded as from the sand quarries (Sablières) just outside Bavay; the ninth (N232) is likely to be a local find.

Some later writers have followed Darche in reading the stamp fig. 1, no. 1 as Q VALERIVS/VERANIV. None of these four stamps are perfect impressions but careful rubbings suggest that they all read Q VAIIIRIVS/VIIRANIV, with Q registered as O, VA very close together rather than ligatured, and LE represented by III, though the final I is broken on one stamp giving some similarity to the cross-bars of an E. In the lower line, E is also represented by II, a common enough occurrence in mortarium stamps. They appear to be from two dies giving identical readings but differing slightly in size. The discovery of clearer impressions will resolve these difficulties.

Two additional stamps appear to have been found since 1975: **i.** under VERANVS (*sic*) in Carmelez 1990 (66, and pl. iv, no. 15; 70Z1707, Sud du *forum,* Bavay); the illustration gives VERANI, with blind A and reversed N. If this drawing is correct it indicates a new die as there is no example of a reversed N in any of the ten die-types of Q. Valerius Veranius known to me, including fig. 1, nos. 2–3, which give *cognomen* only; **ii.** under Quintus Valerius Veranius, Carmelez illustrates a two-line stamp (1990, pl. 4, no. 9; 71Z861 Sud du *forum*), read as Q VALERIVS/VERANIVS with a raised central division (Carmelez 1990, 64). This is nearest to stamps published from Cirencester, Richborough and elsewhere (Wacher & McWhirr 1982, 147, M1; Cunliffe 1968, pl. 89, no. 92) but these never have any central division so that this appears to be from a second new die recorded since 1975.[6]

Only one of the stamps which I saw, [VE]RANI (747/5837 Sablière M; fig. 1, no. 3; Carmelez 1981, pl. 1, no. 35), is from a die represented in Britain (fig. 1, no. 4, from Richborough, and on 22 other mortaria in Britain). This appears still to be true. The converse seems also to be true: no stamp from any other die-type represented at Bavay has been recorded from any other site further away than nearby Haussy. This suggests that these dies were used for only a short time and that the distribution of the mortaria stamped with them (now ten) was very local.

RIM-PROFILES: GILLAM FORM 238

Veranius produced some rim-profiles which are variants from the Gillam 238 form, but those associated with Bavay stamps 1–2 (fig. 1) differ markedly from the norm. Fig. 1, no. 3, was the only one of his stamps seen in 1960 and 1975 which was on a mortarium identical in form and fabric to his mortaria in Britain, i.e. a typical Gillam 238. In 1975 I also examined a large quantity of unstamped mortarium rims and only one

rim-sherd came from a Gillam form 238. Given the distributions of the stamps from the different dies, together with differences in rim-form and fabric, I came to the conclusion that the one stamped fragment which accorded with ours, and the fragment with a broken stamp of Q. Valerius Suriacus, were probably from the same region as our Gillam 238 mortaria and that that region was unlikely to be at or close to Bavay.

FABRIC

Similar clays were available on both sides of the English Channel giving rise to mortaria in fairly fine-textured fabrics, ranging from cream to pale brown in colour with variously sorted inclusions composed mostly of quartz with some red and black iron-rich material and sometimes calcareous material. The trituration grit is commonly flint with some admixture of quartz. Mortaria found and undoubtedly made at Colchester at different periods during the Roman occupation show that superficial differences can be chronological, due to differing techniques and perhaps to minor differences in the sources of the clay. Attribution to different sources in Kent, Essex, East Anglia, or adjacent parts of France would be impossible with only macroscopic examination and at least difficult with geochemical analysis, if fabric were the sole determining factor.

That said, the fabric norm at Bavay is a definite brown and the above stamps, fig. 1, nos.1–2, are on mortaria in this fabric, but no. 3, widely represented in Britain, and a stamp of Q. Valerius Suriacus (Carmelez 1981, pl. 1, no. 1; die as Cunliffe 1968, no. 63), are on mortaria of Gillam type 238, in cream fabric with pinkish core, and are in every way typical of their mortaria in Britain. Veranius did, however, often produce a pale brownish fabric and it might not be impossible for that fabric to have been produced at Bavay.

MORTARIUM PRODUCTION AT BAVAY

When I last examined the collection in 1975 I saw a maximum of 440 stamped mortaria; Carmelez 1990, 55, indicates a total of 658 and 25 more stamps are drawn in Carmelez 1994, 113, pl. 12. An estimate of 700–800 in 1996 seems reasonable. The large numbers of identical stamps and the occasional overfired or distorted sherds attest local production and kilns have, indeed, been found in the Sablières, though few if any of the old records link mortaria to individual kilns. This high total can therefore be assumed to include kiln-waste as well as pottery in use at *Bagacum* and its immediate vicinity. Only two of the stamped mortaria which I saw can be attributed with complete certainty to potteries elsewhere.[7] It may, therefore, seem rash to claim that these two mortaria of Q. Valerius Veranius and Q. Valerius Suriacus and the single unstamped sherd were not made locally, but they certainly show up as exceptional in the collection.

Certain deductions can be made from the collection without considering such factors as the date of individual potters working there or the overall period of production. The evidence to date indicates that Q. Valerius Veranius began stamp-

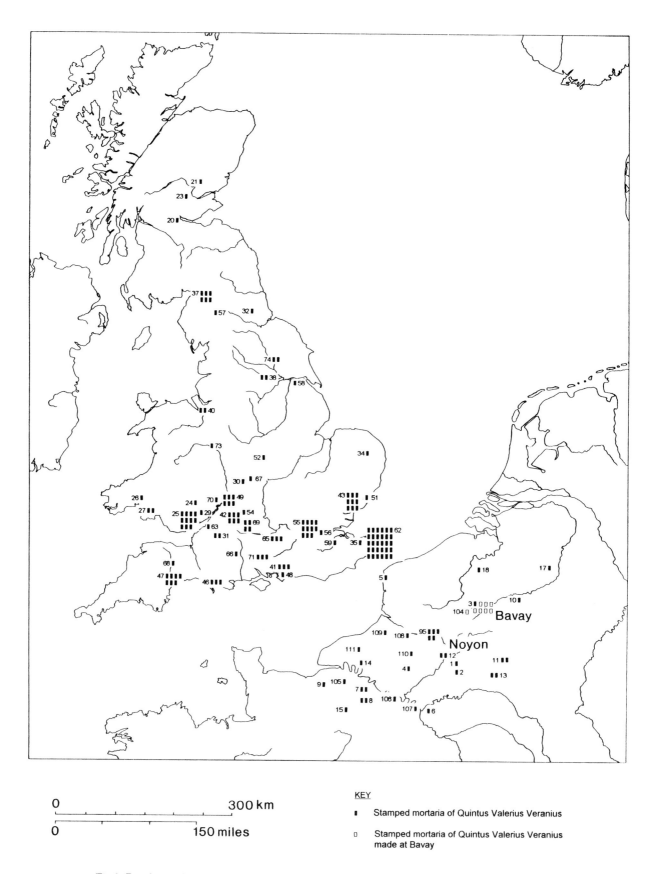

KEY

■   Stamped mortaria of Quintus Valerius Veranius

□   Stamped mortaria of Quintus Valerius Veranius
    made at Bavay

*Fig. 2. Distribution of mortaria stamped by Q. Valerius Veranius; a further open symbol should now be added for Bavay.
For key to place-names see pp. 214–15.*

ing mortaria at Bavay and that his early products were distributed only locally. There is not enough evidence to show that he and Q. Valerius Suriacus began their production of Gillam form 238 at Bavay using a variant fabric and, in the case of the former, different dies, but it is not impossible. Given the vast collection at Bavay and the minimal representation of Gillam form 238 (two stamped mortaria and one unstamped sherd) there is every reason to believe that the major production of these potters and of this form was elsewhere.

PRODUCTION ELSEWHERE

In view of the heavy distribution of Gillam 238 mortaria in Britain compared to their sparsity on the Continent it was not unreasonable in 1973–1977 to suggest that Q. Valerius Veranius and others who made this form could have had a subsidiary workshop in Kent, but it was certainly unwise (Hartley 1973, 40; 1977, 13). It is much easier to float an idea than to erase it! Better understanding of the distribution of imported mortaria in general as well as that of indigenous products has long made it clear that these were imports (see below). Also it has long been evident that there was only minimal production of mortaria in Kent in the 1st century (Pollard 1988). I was able to make such a suggestion only because of the similarity of some clays in Kent to those on the opposite side of the Channel; even then it was reasonably clear that they did not work in East Anglia or the Surrey/Sussex area, which have comparable clays. I have for some years described Gillam 238s as imports but from a site other than Bavay, located in northern France (see below).

OTHER POTTERS STAMPING FORM GILLAM 238 (fig. 3)[8]

Q. Valerius Veranius was of course not the only potter to make Gillam form 238, he was just the most important. One hundred and thirty-seven of his mortaria are recorded from Britain and 34 from the Continent.[9] The following eleven potters (including Vassonus) also specialised in this form; 115 of their mortaria have been found in Britain, and 25 on the Continent:

	Britain	Continent
Cacumattus and related potter Vassonus	14	2
Cassarius	13	2
Gracilis	16	0
T.IV.AF	3	2
C. Iulius Priscus (not Privatus as often suggested)	8	4
Litugenus II	25	2
Lossa	2	1
Orbissa	4	4
Q. Valerius Esunertus	9	3
Q. Valerius Suriacus	7	4
Unidentified	14	1
TOTAL	**115**	**25**
Q. Valerius Veranius	137	34[9]
GRAND TOTAL	**252**	**59**

This makes a grand total of 252 stamped mortaria of form Gillam 238 and its variants in Britain and 59 from the Continent. Even now only 34 mortaria of Q. Valerius Veranius with stamps from the dies represented in Britain have been recorded from the Continent. Litugenus II is now recorded at Amiens and Vendeuil-Caply (Piton & Delebarre 1993, fig. 27, no.16. LITVGIINOS, ?Vichy, in CIL XIII.3, 10006, 44 is a different potter). Until recently all such potters other than Q. Valerius Veranius were represented on the Continent by seven mortaria: Cacumattus (1); Orbissa (3), and Q. Valerius Suriacus (3).

NOYON (OISE)

For some time I believed that the main source for Gillam 238s was likely to be in the Pas-de-Calais but this can now be discounted, because one pottery producing such mortaria has now been located, at Noyon (Oise) (Ben Redjeb 1992a). The site at Noyon has suffered from modern development and no kilns were found, but wasters and fragments from kilns demolished in antiquity are reported (Ben Redjeb 1992a, 56). The excavator published six mortarium stamps, a paltry number for a site of such potential. They are clearly identifiable as Cacumattus, Q.Valerius Veranius (2) and C.Iulius Priscus (3) (misinterpreted in the report). The three mortaria of Cacumattus and Veranius, who are relatively common potters, cannot be regarded as adequate evidence that they worked on the site, though it is suggestive. The three mortaria of Priscus are a different matter. He is an uncommon potter, unrecorded on the Continent at the time of these excavations but now recorded at Rouen (information Y-M. Adrian). We have eight stamps in Britain which can be attributed to him, but none which gives the end of his name, and his *cognomen* has previously been described as PRI[...], Privatus or Priscus. His name is now certain and his single die gives the reading OFCIVLPRISC, with F inside O, I inside C and PRI ligatured, probably followed by SC ligatured (Ben Redjeb 1992a, fig. 34; see Cunliffe 1968, pl. 88, no. 28, for the most complete example in Britain). This should be interpreted as '*Officina* of C. Iulius Priscus' (genitive case understood). The term *officina* was rarely used in mortarium stamps and Cacumattus is one of the few other potters who used it; it is interesting that in some dies he also placed the F inside the O. The rarity of his work together with the considerable evidence for mortarium production on the site provide good reason to believe that Priscus worked at Noyon. All twelve potters who specialised in the Gillam 238 form are securely dated within the period AD65–100 (Holbrook & Bidwell 1991 and Cunliffe 1968, among others).

At Noyon there are mortaria of more than one period, mostly forms which were never stamped. In the two reports (Ben Redjeb 1992a; 1992b), the excavator illustrates a total of 51 rim-profiles and records nearly 100 rim-sherds in contexts linked to the 'boucherie.' These numbers might appear of less consequence on a British site but many visits to France seeking both stamped and unstamped mortaria, together with examination of published reports, suggests that a site with the numbers indicated is likely to be a production site.

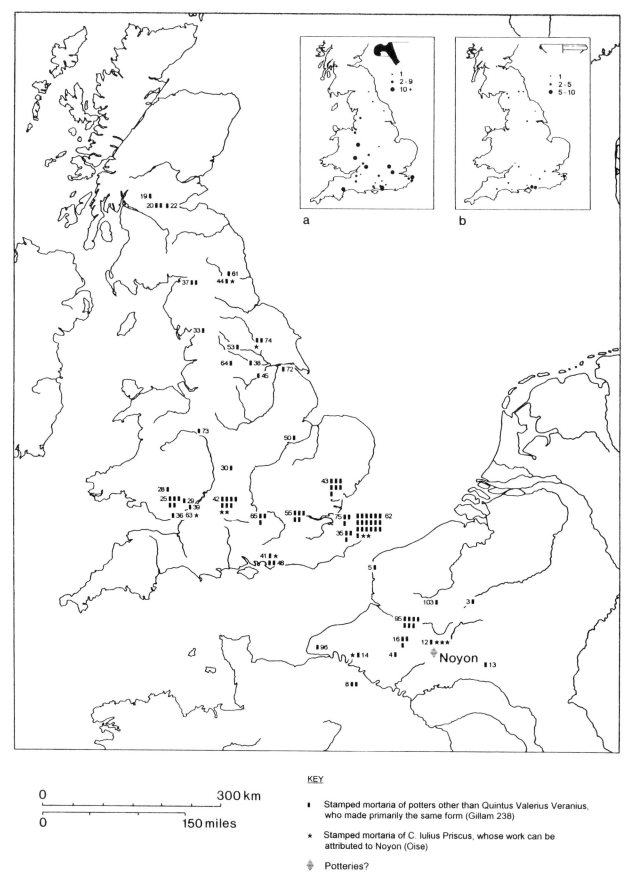

KEY

■   Stamped mortaria of potters other than Quintus Valerius Veranius, who made primarily the same form (Gillam 238)

★   Stamped mortaria of C. Iulius Priscus, whose work can be attributed to Noyon (Oise)

Potteries?

*Fig. 3. Distribution of mortaria stamped by potters other than Q. Valerius Veranius, who worked in the same tradition, including C. Iulius Priscus, who can be attributed to Noyon, and unidentified stamps. Inset **a** and **b**: distribution in Britain of unstamped types Bushe-Fox 22–30 and Gillam 255 respectively. For key to place-names see pp. 214–15.*

This is a preliminary estimate prior to seeing the finds, but enough are published to suggest that the following types were made there: **Bushe-Fox 22–30** (Ben Redjeb 1992a, 62, fig. 22, nos. 3, 6, 8–9; 1992b, 80, fig. 5, nos. 125–128); **Gillam 255** (Ben Redjeb 1992b, fig. 5, nos. 129–131); variants of **Gillam 272** (Ben Redjeb 1992b, fig. 5, nos. 133–134, 137–141, 144–

148, 150–151, 153), and similar mortaria with upright bead (Ben Redjeb 1992b, fig. 5, nos.135–136, 142–143, 149, 152). The possibility of production of these widely differing forms at identical sources has long been appreciated but, given the wide source area for the type of fabric and trituration grit, it could not be regarded as certain. Now, however, Peter Rush

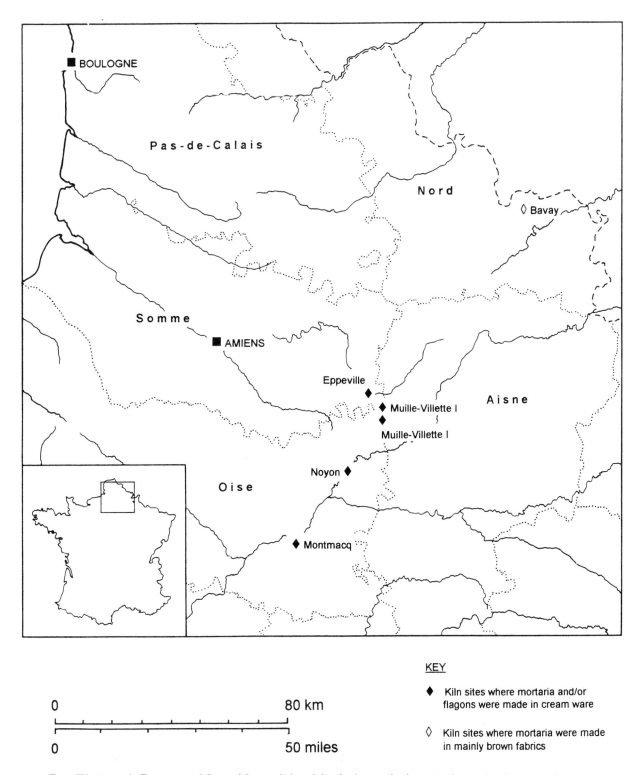

Fig.4. Kiln-sites in the Departments of Oise and Somme which are believed to have produced mortaria that may have been exported to Britain.

using neutron activation analysis has both confirmed the common production area of Gallo-Belgic mortaria and states that Gillam 238 mortaria cannot be differentiated from the other forms attributed to Gallia Belgica in terms of fabric, either by visual inspection or by neutron activation analysis (Rush 1993, 104, 194 and elsewhere). The Noyon variants of Gillam 272 are likely to resemble Colchester in fabric and in trituration grit. Many Rhineland Gillam 272 mortaria are easy to identify from the packed, tiny, quartz trituration grit and its method of application (Richardson 1986, 110–12, nos. 1.69–1.72 and 1.78–1.80); the trituration grit may be of crucial importance in distinguishing collared mortaria made in the north of France and in the Rhineland since the fabric can be visually similar. Fig. 3, insets (a) and (b), indicate the distribution in Britain of Bushe-Fox 22–30 and Gillam 255 respectively. None of these unstamped types are closely or very securely dated, though Bushe-Fox 22–30 is believed to have begun as early as AD70+ (Holbrook & Bidwell 1991), Gillam 255 appears in Antonine contexts and Gillam 272 within the period AD140–300. Careful assessment of the variants of these types from closely dated contexts could make it possible to date some of them more closely. It is surprising that Bushe-Fox 22–30, which appears to overlap Gillam 238 in date, should be produced on the same site.

It has for some time been realised that all of the above mortaria were imported from Gallia Belgica (Holbrook & Bidwell 1991, 195, TC20–21; 198–205, TC22–TC53), but the potteries involved were not expected to be so far inland. Ben Redjeb comments that Noyon was an industrial complex and mentions its good location for communication by road with Amiens and Boulogne, and hence Great Britain. The possibility of river transport is also worth considering. The activity there of C. Iulius Priscus is sufficient in itself to indicate that pottery was imported into Britain from Noyon. The distribution in France of mortaria stamped by the Gillam 238 potters and especially the number recorded from Amiens (twelve) would certainly fit with production at Noyon. Stephane Dubois suspects that up to 80% of the pottery in use at Amiens from at least the mid-1st to the 2nd century was from Noyon (pers. comm.).

Further work is clearly necessary to define the area of production covered by potteries working in the same tradition as those at Noyon. M. Dubois has kindly supplied the information used to make up fig. 4, which shows other known pottery-producing sites at Eppeville (Somme), Muille-Villette I (Oise; producing Gillam 255) and Muille-Villette II, and Montmacq (Oise). These were producing mortaria in similar fabrics and are likely to be part of the same important industrial complex; there may well be others.[10] The pottery from these sites is still awaiting any detailed examination and publication and it should be stressed that production of the Gillam 238 mortaria can as yet be associated only with Noyon. Flagons were frequently produced in the same potteries as mortaria, and flagons produced at Noyon and at most if not all of the other sites mentioned above would have been imported into Britain along with the mortaria; other pottery may well

have been involved in the trade. Flagons similar to those found in Britain were being produced nearer to the Channel, e.g. in the Pas-de-Calais at Bourlon (pers. comm., Dr P. Tyers), but there is little or no evidence of mortarium production at this or any other kilns in this area (Tuffreau-Libre 1977)

DISTRIBUTION OF STAMPED MORTARIA OF GROUP I (III) (figs. 5 & 6)

Ben Redjeb (1992a; 1992b) provides no evidence that any Group I mortaria were made at Noyon. It should be noted that Group I, as published in Hartley, K. F., 1977, conflated at least three different types: **i** (Holbrook & Bidwell 1991, 195, TC8–18) never stamped and in distinctive fabrics, whose distribution and constituents would fit with production in central France (Williams 1993, 424, 'Fabric 13'); **ii** the Atisii potteries at Aoste (Isère), which produced mainly two basic types, Gillam 236 and mortaria approximating to Group I, 1A-E (Hartley, K. F., 1977, fig. 2.1), though no stamped Aoste mortaria of this second form are recorded from Britain; **iii** deeply hooked mortaria approximating to Group I, 1A-E (Hartley, K. F., 1977; Manning 1993, 399, fig. 185, nos. 7–10. Only category (iii) is considered here. Many of these were stamped, but only once; some were unstamped. In fabric and trituration grit they are generally similar to Gillam type 238, and they probably came from more than one source, in the area between Tongeren and the River Iton in Normandy. Bavay is a possible source for Verecundus I and Martialis I but apart from two mortaria of Verecundus at Bavay they are associated with cream fabric rather than the brown one typical there.[11] Q. Valerius Se(...) was by far the most important potter stamping Group I (iii) mortaria, but eleven others are known. All are securely dated within the period AD50–85.

	Britain	Continent
Boriedo[12]	1	0
Buc(c)us	4	0
C.LE?	2	0
Fronto[12]	2	0
Martialis 1	2	3
Mottius Bollus	4	0
Orgil	4	0
Paullus 1	4	0
Prasso	3	0
Verecundus 1	1	3
Summacus 1[13]	6	2
Unidentified	6	1
TOTALS	**39**	**9**
Q. Valerius Se(...)	44	3
GRAND TOTALS	**83**	**12**

The stamped mortaria of Group I, type iii total 83 in Britain and twelve on the Continent. Unidentified stamps could include four mortaria of Q. Valerius Se(...) from Britain and one from Boulogne.

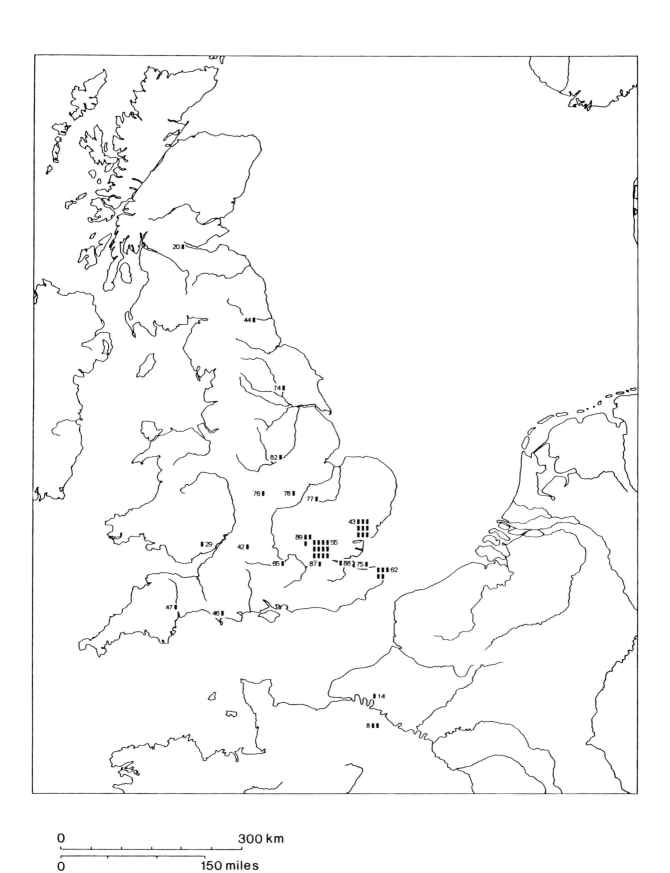

Fig. 5. Distribution of mortaria stamped by Q. Valerius Se(...). For key to place names see pp. 214–15.

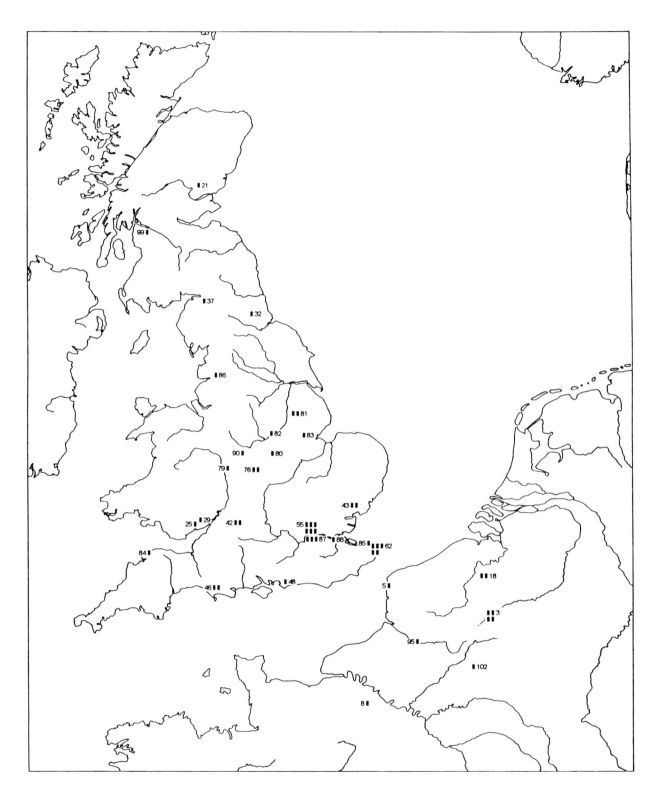

Fig. 6. Distribution of stamped mortaria of potters other than Q. Valerius Se(....), who made primarily Group I (iii) mortaria. For key to place-names see pp. 214–15.

DISTRIBUTION OF MORTARIA IMPORTED INTO BRITAIN FROM GALLIA BELGICA

The stamped mortaria of Groups I (iii) and II in Britain far outnumber those on the Continent. Further excavation will certainly alter these figures but it is unlikely to change the proportions. The numbers on the Continent are in fact ludicrously small, especially for Group I (iii).

The distribution in Britain of all mortaria imported from Gallia Belgica, both stamped and unstamped (figs. 2, 3, 5 and 6), show clear points of similarity except that the latter are probably less common than the stamped types in the north of England and in Scotland. The main concentrations are in the coastal areas approaching the Thames estuary, in the London area and in south-west England and south Wales, which they no doubt reached by coastal traffic. There are some smaller clusters of the stamped mortaria in north-east England and Scotland which suggest delivery at the Humber, Tyne and Forth; the Severn may also have been used. The midlands, north Wales, and southern Scotland have few in comparison; north-west England also has few except for Carlisle, which perhaps received some of its stamped mortaria via the Tyne.

This appears to be a normal distribution pattern for imports from northern France (Richardson & Tyers 1984, 140, fig. 3). It is notably different from the distribution patterns of British workshops but has most in common with Colchester, which must have used coastal traffic for dispersal to north-east England and Scotland (Hull 1963, 114, fig. 62). Mortaria recovered from the sea include three of Cassarius found together in Oaze Deep in the Thames estuary, one of Q. Valerius Se... and one of Prasso. Though poorly documented, these, especially the Cassarius mortaria, are likely to be from shipwrecks. There is nothing in the distribution of Group I (iii) mortaria in Britain to suggest that they were not imports, even though some of the potters have never been recorded on the Continent. The distribution of Group I (iii), Group II (Gillam 238), Bushe-Fox type 22–30 and Gillam 255 surely indicates that some potteries in northern France were heavily geared to trade with Britain until at least the late 2nd century. All this despite the huge quantities of mortaria made in Britain in the Verulamium region, the midlands and elsewhere.

DISTRIBUTION OF MORTARIA FROM SOLLER, KR. DÜREN (fig. 7)

Fig. 7 shows stamped mortaria of Verecundus II whose workshop was at Soller, Kr. Düren in Lower Germany (Haupt 1984). Verecundus II specialised to a considerable extent in producing huge mortaria which were probably targeted at a specialised market. His mortaria are very characteristic and many unstamped fragments can be attributed to him with certainty (see inset map (a) for this distribution in Britain). Inset map (b) gives the distribution in Britain of collared mortaria of form Gillam 272, attributable to the Rhineland (including Soller). The Rhine would have been used for transport. Gillam 272 mortaria were imported from the Antonine

period perhaps until the end of the 3rd century (Richardson 1986, 110–12, nos. 1.69–1.72 and 1.78–1.80), but the flanged mortaria stamped by Verecundus II are certainly not later than the early 3rd century. The distribution of Rhineland mortaria is generally similar to that of the mortaria from northern France. London is known to have been a delivery point for Rhineland mortaria in the second half of the 2nd and first half of the 3rd centuries, probably along with East Gaulish samian (Richardson 1986). Mortaria of Verecundus II are also commoner in Britain than elsewhere but collared mortaria are very common in the Rhineland.

Not all mortaria which are believed to have been imported have this type of distribution. Some distinctive, mostly unstamped, mortaria which are undoubtedly Neronian-Flavian predominate in south-west England and south Wales with only outliers elsewhere at sites of easy access from the coast (Holbrook & Bidwell 1991, 194, fig. 77). Their source is uncertain but the fine wares associated with them at Exeter are attributed to Spain. Two of the recorded examples are stamped by an otherwise unknown potter Lesbius.

THE INCIDENCE OF STAMPED MORTARIA IN THE ROMAN EMPIRE (fig. 8)

I suggest in what follows that all coarseware mortaria, not just stamped ones, are less common in many parts of the Roman Empire than might be expected. Stamps give a useful clue to manufacture and distribution patterns, and low numbers of stamps indicate either largescale use of unstamped mortaria or the minimum use of any coarseware mortaria.

Stamped mortaria are being found all the time, and even my records for Britain are not complete but they should include 90–95% of those found. Obviously my records for elsewhere in the Roman Empire are less complete, but published information has been supplemented by visits to France, Belgium, Holland and Germany. Friends and colleagues, too numerous to list, have given me details of mortaria I would, in many instances, have missed. I am especially grateful to the late Professor J. E. Bogaers and to M. Vanderhoeven who in the 1970s kindly gave me access to their records of stamped mortaria in Holland and Belgium, respectively. Consequently, although my records for sites outside Britain varies from one area to another, it probably includes 90% for Holland and at least 70%–80% for the rest of the Empire.

On visits to the Continent I have consistently found fewer stamped mortaria than in Britain. They appear to have been common only in limited areas of the Empire. It was possible to waste days in France looking for non-existent stamps. The significance of this was obscured in northern France because, with the fortunate exception of Bavay, whole collections had been destroyed in one or other of the two world wars, so that stamps of Q. Valerius Veranius from Arlaines, Reims (two examples), and elsewhere, recorded in CIL, no longer existed. When M. Vertet found a stamped mortarium at Lezoux I took the opportunity of asking how frequently stamped mortaria were found in France and was interested that he should consider them rare; this certainly agreed with my findings. All the

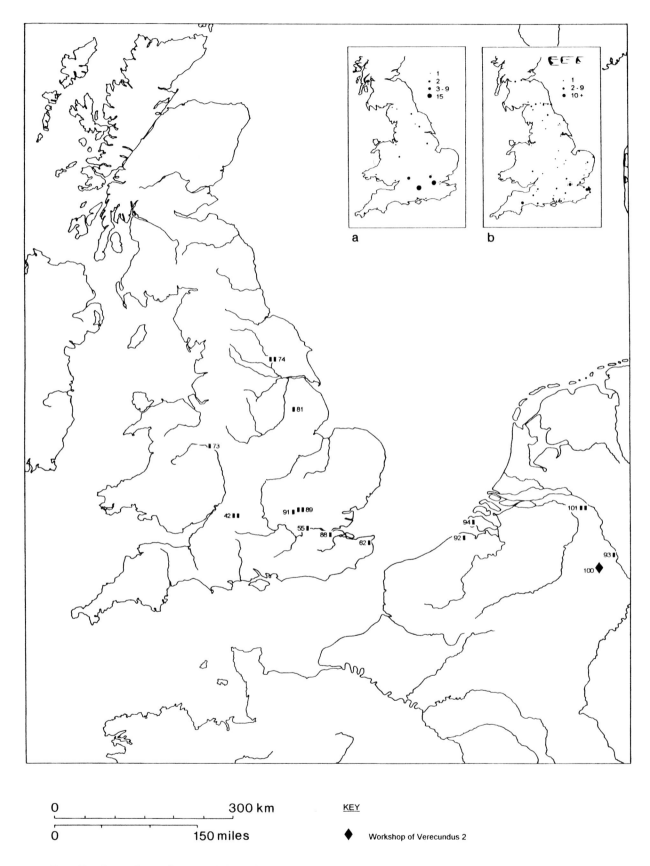

0 _____ 300 km

0 _____ 150 miles

KEY

◆   Workshop of Verecundus 2

*Fig. 7. Distribution of stamped mortaria of Verecundus II of Soller, Kr. Düren. Inset **a**: distribution in Britain of unstamped sherds attributable to Verecundus II; inset **b**: distribution of collared mortaria attributable to the Rhineland. For key to place-names, see pp. 214–15.*

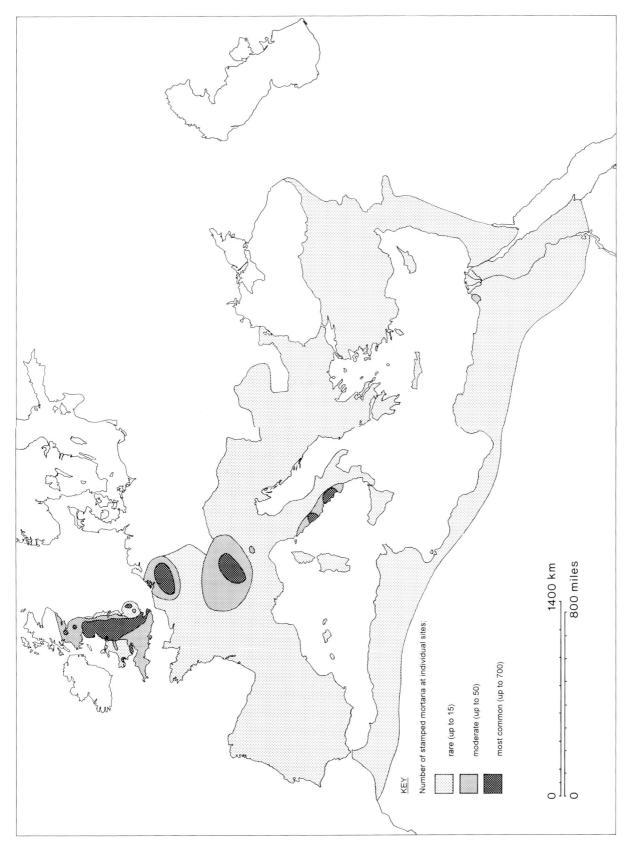

KEY

Number of stamped mortaria at individual sites;

rare (up to 15)

moderate (up to 50)

most common (up to 700)

1400 km

800 miles

0

0

Fig. 8. Incidence of stamped mortaria in the Roman Empire. [17]

information I have been able to assemble for France tends in the same direction (and see Dubois forthcoming, on the small total for Amiens). Some areas have a fair number but with the exception of Bavay, and perhaps Coulanges and Aoste, for which totals are unknown, they are nowhere near as common as in most of Roman Britain; all three sites have associated production areas.

After Britain, the two areas of the Empire which have the largest numbers are Bavay plus Belgium, and Switzerland. It is there that my totals will be most out of date but this is unlikely to alter the relative proportions of stamped mortaria used in different parts of the Empire. Outside Britain and these areas they range from unknown to rare and moderate and I can offer no explanation why they should predominate where they do.

TOTALS OF STAMPED MORTARIA FROM DIFFERENT COUNTRIES OR AREAS, WITH INDIVIDUAL TOTALS FOR A VARIED RANGE OF SITES

These will often be underestimates but they should approximate to the truth. Greek stamps on mortaria produced in Syria are included.[14] * indicates sites where numbers are known to be inflated to a greater or lesser degree by kiln-waste. For British sites in **bold** print, see the concluding remarks below.

GERMANY and AUSTRIA		250±*
Hofheim	3+	
Mainz	5+	
Neuss	6+	
Xanten	5+	
Magdalensburg	32	
Trier	3	
BALKANS and GREECE		110
ASIA MINOR		13
NEAR EAST		320*
AFRICA		71 (45 in Egypt)
Alexandria	17	
Sidi Khrebish (Berenice)	15	
Cherchel	2	
Carthage	4	
MEDITERRANEAN ISLANDS		13
ITALY		172
Pompeii	84	
Rome	37	
SPAIN and PORTUGAL		17
FRANCE		2826±*

(inc. 1000 estimated for Coulanges* & Aoste* (Isère), for which total numbers are unknown to me)

Bavay	700–800*	
Evreux	11	
Rouen	7	

Amiens	23
Vannes	5
Corseul	6
Orléans	7
Poitiers	9
Rezé	9
Alésia	20–39
Autun	40–93
Lyon + Trion	9+
Vichy	25
Vienne	54
St Romain-en-Gal	28
Vaison-la-Romaine	5
Annecy	24
Fréjus	9
Rodez	5
La Graufesenque	2
Aîme (Savoie)	7
Les Bolards	31±
Strasbourg	4

SWITZERLAND		850+
Augst	92	
Bern (Engehalbinsel)	100+	
Aventicum	300–400*	
Vidy	42+*	
Vindonissa	35+	
Chur	33	
NETHERLANDS		197
Arentsburg	35	
Halder, St Michielsgestel	26*	
Nijmegen+De Holdeurn	34	
Herkenbergh, nr. Meersen	12	
Venlo	9	
BELGIUM		616
Anthée	23	
Liberchies	78	
Amay	51*	
Braives	82	
Taviers	14	
Vervoz	36	
Tongeren	115	
BRITAIN		10,000±*
ENGLAND		
Binchester	34	
Corbridge	631	
South Shields	25	
Ambleside	20	
Carlisle	196	
Ribchester	60	
Castleford	75	
York	136	
High Cross	28	
Leicester	350	
Caistor St. Edmunds	79	

Chelmsford	35
Great Chesterford	17
Colchester	833+*
London+Southwark	700+
Richborough	124
Verulamium	288+*
Canterbury	88+*
Silchester	**33**
Tiddington, Warks.	**17**
Bath	**13**
Cirencester	**56**
Gloucester	**38***
Dorchester, Dorset	**5**
Kenchester	**8**
Exeter	**25**
Shepton Mallet*	**8***
Winchester	**6**
Clausentum (Southampton)	22

WALES

Segontium (Caernarvon)	10
Brecon Gaer	10
Caerhun	14
Loughor, West Glam.	11
Usk	25
Caerleon	135+
Caersws	23
Caerwent	50+
Carmarthen	44

SCOTLAND

Balmuildy	30
Rough Castle	27
Camelon	74
Strageath	24
Cramond	8
Mumrills	37
Cardean	4
Bar Hill	21
Ardoch	12
Newstead	70
Birrens	16
Inveresk	24
Bearsden	38*

The total of 10,000+ stamped mortaria from Britain and 5,455+ from the rest of the Empire leaves us with the interesting situation that Britain, the furthest outpost of the Empire, had considerably more stamped mortaria than all other parts of the Empire put together. If 6,000 were posited for the rest of the Empire to allow for the less efficient recording it still leaves Britain with approaching twice as many! Up to 2,500 of the British total and more than 1,500 of the total for elsewhere are likely to be kiln-waste but the reduced figures 7,500 and 4,500 show a similar contrast. Totals and distribution obviously depend on the amount of excavation, publication and access to publication, and more stamps are being found daily but the evidence is surely sufficient to offset any such shortcomings.

CONCLUDING REMARKS

The distribution of stamped mortaria gives some indication of the areas where the practice of stamping them was common but provides no obvious information on the usage of mortaria which were never stamped. Much quantification would be necessary to illustrate this accurately but details already available indicate the situation fairly clearly.

Some of the areas with intermediate numbers of stamps (15–70) have many unstamped mortaria. Dr J. K. Haalebos has kindly informed me that there were only three stamped mortaria in more than 2,500 mortarium rim-sherds, found during seven years of excavation in the *canabae* of *Legio X Gemina* at Nijmegen. This sort of proportion is especially applicable to sites in the Netherlands and Germany. On some sites in Britain also, relatively low numbers of stamped mortaria are clearly linked to local production of unstamped mortaria. Chester with 72–90 stamped mortaria is one example (others perhaps less obvious are Lincoln, York and even Carlisle). Compared to Nijmegen (34), the total appears large but for Britain 72–90 is very moderate for a site of such importance where so much excavation has taken place. Unstamped mortaria are, however, common and were produced locally.

The whole of south-west England and southern England west of London (i.e. sites in bold print) stands out in Britain as an area with low numbers of stamped mortaria. The reason here is different. Relatively few stamped, and in the 1st and 2nd centuries not even many unstamped, mortaria were made there. Instead of using mortaria from British sources, they continued after AD100 to rely quite heavily on imports of Bushe-Fox 22–30 (fig. 3, inset (a)), Gillam 255 (fig. 3, inset (b)), and Gillam 272, (fig. 7, inset (c)). The distribution of stamps in that area has, therefore, much in common with the distribution in France and provides something of a contrast with the midlands and north of England. It has been suggested to me that this area had in fact relatively few mortaria (stamped or unstamped) in the 1st and 2nd centuries (pers. comm., V. Swan). This would increase the similarity to adjacent areas in France.

There is no obvious reason why one should be able to extrapolate from the distribution of stamped to the distribution of unstamped coarseware mortaria, but the evidence available certainly suggests that if the areas on fig. 8 which have large numbers and moderate numbers of stamped mortaria are combined, they cover, with few exceptions, those parts of the Roman Empire where coarseware mortaria, stamped or unstamped, were in commonest use.[15]

Others have commented on the relative rarity of mortaria in some parts of the Empire (Reece 1988, 38). Peter Webster has long maintained that mortaria are under-represented in Wales. At Whitton, a rural site in South Glamorgan, he states that mortaria formed less than 1% of all pottery found and suggests that some wide-mouthed bowls characteristic of south Wales might have been used as mixing bowls, which was clearly one function of mortaria. There is, however, no evidence of the wear which would result if they had been used for grinding or pulverizing (Webster 1981, 113–14). The wear so often evident on coarseware mortaria leaves no doubt whatever that they were used for these purposes. The small numbers of mortaria are again pointed out in three groups from Usk: numbers of mortaria in totals of kitchen vessels, 5:57; 2:33 and 4:34 (Webster 1993, 233 and 360).

These proportions may represent uncommonness in Britain, but they are higher than those in many parts of the Empire. In deposits of recently examined pottery at Mons Claudianus in Egypt, 2–3 mortaria (Italian) were found in at least eight tonnes of pottery; and at Caesarea Maritima, two mortaria (Syrian) were recovered from c.20 kilos of pottery (R. Tomber, pers. comm.). J.A. Riley lists only 31 mortarium fragments from all periods at Sidi Khrebish (Riley 1979, 419–42). Cherchel, Carthage and Sabratha present a similar picture though Alexandria has at least seventeen stamped mortaria.

The distribution of unstamped mortaria in France is uncertain but numbers appear to be low in many areas. The following numbers of sherds were recorded from excavations in the 1980s at Beaurieux, Les Grèves (Aisne): Ceramic Phase 3 (Augustan to early Tiberian) 0:4683; Ceramic Phase 4 (later Tiberian to AD100 and possibly very early 2nd century) 1:6386; and Ceramic Phase 6 (3rd to early 4th century) 48:2950. In all there were 72 mortarium sherds in a total of c.24,000 pottery sherds found on the site (S. Willis, in Haselgrove & Lowther, forthcoming).[16] The Beaurieux figures do not indicate much use of coarseware mortaria in the 1st century at this site and their rarity in most parts of northern France in this period tends to support this, especially when contrasted with their commonness in many parts of Britain.

Variation in the usage of pottery mortaria does not necessarily indicate differing diets as is sometimes suggested. It may rather pose the problem of just why they were so common in some areas and what was used elsewhere for the same purposes; how far 'commonness' is linked with a military presence and why? Few data are available on stone mortars but they do not seem to be common enough to fill the gap. In his *De genere vasorum vel poculorum XV,* Nonius Marcellus defines a 'mortarium' as a vessel 'in which are ground those things which are to be pulverised'. Any suitable pottery vessel could be used as a mixing bowl, but any used as a 'mortarium' would show wear. Literary sources in general suggest that they could be made of wood, stone or metal and specific reference to pottery mortaria is in fact rare. Wooden ones would be a solution but none has yet been found or recognized.

Key to placenames (figs. 2, 3, 5–7)

1	Ambleny (Aisne)
2	Arlaines (Aisne)
3	Bavay (Nord)
4	Beauvais (Oise)
5	Boulogne (Pas-de-Calais)
6	Chelles (Seine et Marne)
7	Condé-sur-Iton, Evreux
8	Evreux (Eure)
9	Lisieux (Calvados)
10	Mettet, Luxembourg
11	Nanteuil (Ardennes)
12	Noyon (Oise)
13	Reims (Marne)
14	Rouen (Seine-Maritime)
15	Rugles (Eure)
16	Vendeuil-Caply (Oise)
17	Tongeren, Belgium
18	Velzeke-Ruddershove, Belgium
19	Bochastle, Scotland
20	Camelon, Scotland
21	Cardean, Scotland
22	Mumrills, Scotland
23	Strageath, Scotland
24	Abergavenny, Wales
25	Caerleon, Wales
26	Carmarthen, Wales
27	Loughor, Wales
28	Penydarren Park, Glamorgan, Wales
29	Usk, Wales
30	Alcester, Warks.
31	Bath
32	Binchester, Durham
33	Burrow-in-Lonsdale, Lancs.
34	Caistor St. Edmunds, Norwich
35	Canterbury
36	Cardiff
37	Carlisle
38	Castleford, Yorks.
39	Chepstow, Gwent, Wales
40	Chester
41	Chichester
42	Cirencester
43	Colchester
44	Corbridge
45	Doncaster
46	Dorchester, Dorset
47	Exeter
48	Fishbourne, Sussex
49	Gloucester
50	Great Casterton, Rutland
51	Harwich
52	High Cross, Leics.
53	Ilkley
54	Lechlade, Glos.
55	London
56	Lower Warbank, Kent
57	Old Penrith
58	Old Winteringham, Lincs.
59	Maidstone
60	Manchester
61	Red House Fort, nr. Corbridge, Northumberland
62	Richborough
63	Sea Mills, Devon
64	Slack, West Yorks.
65	Silchester
66	Stockton, Wilts.

67   Tiddington, Warks.
68   Tiverton, Devon
69   Wanborough, Wilts.
70   Weston-under-Penyard, Hereford & Worcester
71   Winchester
72   Winterton, Lincs.
73   Wroxeter
74   York
75   Oaze Deep, Thames Estuary
76   The Lunt, Baginton, Warks.
77   Godmanchester, Cambs.
78   Kettering, Northants.
79   Kinver, Staffs. (Greensforge)
80   Leicester
81   Lincoln
82   Broxtowe, Notts.
83   Old Sleaford, Lincs.
84   Martinhoe, Devon
85   Minnis Bay, Birchington, Kent
86   Ribchester, Lancs.
87   Southwark
88   Springhead, Kent
89   *Verulamium*
90   Wall, Staffs.
91   Gorhambury, Herts.
92   Aardenburg, Netherlands
93   Cologne
94   Middelburg, Netherlands
95   Amiens (Somme)
96   Saint-Romain-de-Colbosc (Seine-Maritime)
97   Catterick, Yorks.
98   Aldborough, Yorks.
99   Barochan, Scotland
100   Soller, Kr. Düren
101   Xanten
102   Roucy (Aisne)
103   Bourlon (Pas-de-Calais)
104   Haussy (Nord)
105   Brionne (Eure)
106   Les Mureaux (Yvelines)
107   Paris
108   Crouy-Saint-Pierre (Somme)
109   Blangy-sur-Bresle (Somme)
110   Villers-Vicomte (Oise)
111   La Vâtine (Seine Maritime)

ACKNOWLEDGEMENTS

Thanks are due to Yves-Marie Adrian, Paul Arthur, the late E.B. Birley, the late Professor J. E. Bogaers, Stephane Dubois, Iva Curk, Brenda Dickinson, Dr J. Evans, Dr J. K. Haalebos, Dr Richard Reece, Valery Rigby, J. A. Riley, Vivien G. Swan, Dr Roberta Tomber, Dr P. Tyers, M. Vanderhoeven, Alain Vernhet, Peter V. Webster, Helmut Wittkamp, Dr S. L. Wynia, Dr Robin Symonds and indeed to all people who have ever sent me details of stamps, who are too numerous to thank individually.

Notes

1.   Probably most of the imported Gillam 238 mortaria were stamped and these never had more than one stamp; the number of such mortaria represented by stamps in any given group is therefore always clear. Most mortaria stamped in Britain and elsewhere, like most of those of Albinus, carried two stamps, one to each side of the spout, and a count of stamps alone can be misleading. It is normally clear how many vessels are involved in any group, but in very large kiln groups and in assessing the numbers of an individual potter's mortaria from, for example, London, various means may be needed to estimate the number of mortaria represented. Although more work is needed for precision, '400 mortaria' refers in this instance to vessels rather than to the number of stamps which, counted individually, would be considerably larger. All numbers in this paper refer to numbers of vessels rather than numbers of stamps.

2.   Weathered surfaces, museum dust and artificial lighting make examination of fabric difficult at the best of times. Although it is not always necessary, reliable fabric examination can only be made from a 'fresh' break because the broken edges are weathered as well as the surfaces, and both differ from the interior of the fabric.

3.   Possible examples are a mortarium stamp found at Lezoux by M. Hugues Vertet, which is not from any known samian die; also two stamps of Rauracus at Lavoye, not from any known die of the samian potter of that name who may have worked there before migrating to Westerndorf (Chenet & Gaudron 1955, 36; Hartley, B.R., 1977, 256).

4.   All comments concerning Q. Valerius Veranius include his two or more *cognomen* stamps reading Veranius, unless otherwise stated. The term Gillam 238 (Gillam 1970) is used throughout in preference to Group II (Hartley, K. F., 1977). There is no Gillam equivalent to Group I or to Bushe-Fox 22–30.

5.   More recent attempts to publish the mortarium stamps from Bavay have been made by Gricourt 1967; Terrisse 1969; Carmelez 1980; 1981; 1982; 1990; 1994. Darche 1924, 262–3 is referred to here because it was then the only publication available. Unfortunately, copies of F.E.A.P. (Carmelez) are extremely rare in Britain making it impossible to cross-check adequately with the most recent catalogue.

6.   Carmelez 1990, pl. 4, nos. 9 and 15 (71Z861 and 70Z1707 Sud du *Forum*) are not represented on fig. 2 because further information is needed concerning form and fabric before assigning them to the certain Bavay products or to those less likely to have been made there. However, as both stamps are from dies unrepresented outside Bavay and its immediate locality, there should probably be two extra blank symbols at Bavay.

7.   G. Atisius Gratus, no. 2040/335, and G. Atisius (…), no. 5960, both made at Aoste (Isère). Two others, stamped G. ATISIVS (4762 and 9z or 97/735) are not typical Aoste exports and need further checking. Brariatus and Adiutor are known to have had workshops elsewhere but this does not preclude activity at Bavay.

8.   A larger number of potters were listed in Group II in Hartley, K. F., 1977, 6–8. It is occasionally difficult to decide whether a potter should be attributed to Group I or Group II, sometimes because the examples are fragmentary. In this paper the potters in Group II (i.e. Gillam 238) have been more carefully sifted. Orbissa and Q. Valerius Esunertus fit least satisfactorily, but they fit better into Group II than Group I. A few potters, including Q. Valerius Veranius and Orbissa, did occasionally produce variant profiles (see also note 13). Some rare potters whose full names are still unknown, e.g. ALB[...] and RVF[...] are included in Group II as unidentified potters and none of these are known from the Continent. ALB[...] is, incidentally, a different potter from the Albinus who worked in the Verulamium region.

9.   This total excludes the eight mortaria from Bavay, seen in 1975, which had stamps as fig. 1, nos. 1–2, plus Carmelez 1990, pl. 4, nos. 9 and 15, plus one from Haussy (Nord), all of which are believed to be early work of Q. Valerius Veranius, made at Bavay.

10. I am indebted to M. Stephane Dubois for information about mortaria found at Amiens and some other sites in the Departments of Oise and Somme, and to M. Dubois and M. Eric Binet for permission to publish these details before publication of their report.

11. Martialis 1 and Verecundus 1: many mortaria are stamped with these names but only those associated with two die-types (Hobley 1973, fig. 14, no. 3; De Laet & Nenquin 1953, fig. 4, nos. 4–5 (Martialis); Gould

1966–7, fig. 9, no.70 (Verecundus)) are included here because these are always on the appropriate rim-profile. Dies associated with other profiles may well belong to other potters because these are common names; there were at least two and probably more potters named Verecundus on the Continent and up to five Romano-British potters named Martialis excluding this Gallo-Belgic man. At no time have I ever suggested that Martialis 1 and Verecundus 1 worked in Britain (as indicated in Carmelez 1990, 72).

12. For further details concerning Group I potters, Boriedo and Fronto, see Hanson forthcoming.

13. Three mortaria with stamps reading SVMMA FE from Baden (Switzerland), Les Bolards and Suèvres are not on fig. 6. The distribution for this die differs markedly from that of the other dies and the mortaria concerned have much in common with the products of the Aoste potteries although he is not recorded there. There is a possibility that Summacus began working at Aoste but later moved to northern France, but it must be stressed that further evidence is needed to clarify his activity. Some of the work of Q. Valerius Se(...) shares these characteristics.

14. The practice of stamping mortaria ceased in most if not all parts of Britain in the 2nd century; there is no question of it continuing beyond the early 3rd century at the latest. It is unlikely that it continued later in France, Belgium, Holland, Germany or Italy. It may have ended earlier in some areas, and this could be a contributory factor to the smaller numbers of stamps on the Continent. Mortarium production attributed to Ras-el-Bassit in Syria is regarded as late 3rd-century and 4th-century (Hayes 1967; Blakely *et al.* 1992; Vallerin 1994). These potters probably derived their potting tradition from Dacia and Moesia etc., with which they have much in common, rather than from Italy. Their mortaria were extremely tough and probably survived a long time in use. The late dating consistently given to them would carry more conviction if the details of residuality and redeposition were accessible, but the 3rd-century dating of Justinianus in Pannonia also supports a late use of the practice of stamping in some of the more eastern parts of the Empire (Curk 1976; Bjelajac 1994, 146).

15. Simitthus in north-west Tunisia could perhaps be an exception to this, having a large number of unstamped mortaria for a site in Africa, but no stamped mortaria (Vegas 1994, figs. 165–7).

16. I am indebted to to Dr Haselgrove, University of Durham and to Dr Steven Willis, the author of the pottery report, for permission to quote these details before publication.

17. A total of 23 stamped mortaria is now known for Amiens, which should, therefore, be in the moderate zone. This does not, however, affect the argument since this total is extremely small for such a site after very extensive excavation (Dubois forthcoming). Similarly Magdalensburg should be in the moderate category with its total of 31 stamped mortaria (Zabehlicky-Scheffenegger 1996).

Bibliography and abbreviations

CIL: *Corpus Inscriptionum Latinarum*, 1863– (cited by volume and number)
RIB 2: R. G. Collingwood & R. P. Wright, *The Roman inscriptions of Britain, vol. 2: inscriptions on material other than stone* (eds S. S. Frere & R. S. O. Tomlin), seven fascicules, 1990–95 (cited by item number)

Anthony, I.E., 1968 Excavations in Verulam Hills Field, St. Albans, 1963–4, *Hertfordshire Archaeol.*, **1**, 9–50

Ben Redjeb, T., 1992a Une agglomération secondaire des Viromanduens: Noyon (Oise), *Revue Archéologique de Picardie*, **1/2**, 37–74

————, 1992b La céramique gallo-romaine de l'îlot des 'Deux-Bornes' (fouilles 1985) à Noyon (Oise), *Revue Archéologique de Picardie*, **1/2**, 75–82

Binet, E., forthcoming [*L'habitat privé en milieu urbain: les fouilles du Palais des Sports à Amiens*]

Bjelajac, L., 1994 Mortaria in the Moesia Danube Valley, *Revue de l'Institut Archéologique, nouvelle série*, **43–4** (1992–3), 139–48

Blakely, J.A., Brinkmann, R., & Vitaliano, C.J., 1992 Roman mortaria and basins from a sequence at Caesarea: fabrics and sources, in Vann 1992, 194–213

Bogaers, J.E., & Haalebos, J.K., 1980 Opgravingen in de Romeinse Legioen-svestingen te Nijmegen, III (Canisiuscollege, Hoge Veld, 1975–1977), *Oudheidkundige Mededelingen uit het Rijksmuseum van Oudheden te Leiden*, **61**, 39–111

Bushe-Fox, J.P., 1913 *Excavations on the site of the Roman town at Wroxeter, Shropshire, in 1912*, Rep. Res. Comm. Soc. Antiq. London, **1** (Oxford)

Carmelez, J.C., 1980 Les pelves du Musée de Bavay, *Fouilles et études, Archéologie et pédogogie: Lycée de Bavay*, **2**, 29–63

————, 1981 Les pelves du Musée de Bavay, *Fouilles et études, Archéologie et pédogogie: Lycée de Bavay*, **3**, 41–83

————, 1982 Les pelves du Musée de Bavay, *Fouilles et études, Archéologie et pédogogie: Lycée de Bavay*, **4**, 54–86

————, 1990 Complément au répertoire des marques sur pelves et mortiers du Musée de Bavay, *Fouilles et études, Archéologie et pédogogie: Lycée de Bavay*, **12**, 55–78

————, 1994 Un entrepôt de céramique détruit à la fin du IIè siècle à Bavay. Etude de synthèse et bilan, *Fouilles et études, Archéologie et pédogogie: Lycée de Bavay*, **14**, 79–152

Castle, S.A., 1972 A kiln of the potter Doinus, *Archaeol. J.*, **129**, 69–88

————, 1976 Roman pottery from Brockley Hill, Middlesex, 1966 and 1972–74, *Trans. London Middlesex Archaeol. Soc.*, **27**, 206–27

Chenet, G., & Gaudron, G., 1955 *La céramique sigillée d'Argonne des IIe et IIIe siècles*, Gallia Supplément, **6** (Paris)

Corder, P., 1941 A Roman pottery of the Hadrian-Antonine period at Verulamium, *Antiq. J.*, **21**, 271–98

Cunliffe, B. W. (ed.), 1968 *Fifth report on the excavations at the Roman fort at Richborough, Kent*, Rep. Res. Comm. Soc. Antiq. London, **23** (Oxford)

Curk, I.M., 1976 *Poetovio I* (Ljubljana)

Darche, P., 1924 Les marques de Potiers à Bavay, *Pro Nervia*, **2.4**, 257–72

De Laet, S.J., & Nenquin, J., 1953 Een gallo-romeinse vicus te Velzeke-Ruddershove, *Kultureel Jahrboek voor de Provincie Oostvlaanderen*, 3–57

Detsicas, A.(ed.), 1973 *Current research in Romano-British coarse pottery*, Counc. Brit. Archaeol. Res. Rep., **10** (London)

Dore, J., & Greene, K. (eds), 1977 *Roman pottery studies in Britain and beyond*, Brit. Archaeol. Rep. Suppl. Ser., **30** (Oxford)

Dubois, S., forthcoming [La céramique à Amiens aux 1er-2e siècles – les mortiers estampillés] in Binet forthcoming

Dyson, T. (ed.), 1986, *The Roman quay at St Magnus House, London*, London Middlesex Archaeol. Soc. Special Paper, **8**

Frere, S.S., 1972 *Verulamium excavations, volume I*, Rep. Res. Comm. Soc. Antiq. London, **28** (Oxford)

————, 1984 *Verulamium excavations, volume III*, Oxford Univ. Comm. Archaeol. Monograph Ser., **1** (Oxford)

————, & Wilkes, J.J., 1989 *Strageath*, Britannia Monograph Ser., **9** (London)

Gillam, J.P., 1970 *Types of Roman coarse pottery vessels in northern Britain*, 3 edn. (Newcastle upon Tyne)

Gould, J., 1966 Excavations at Wall, Staffs., 1964–6, on the site of the Roman forts, *South Staffordshire Archaeol. Hist. Soc.*, **8**, 1–40

Gricourt, J., 1969 À propos d'une marque sur pelve découverte à Lewarde (Nord): notes sur la fabrication et le commerce de ce type de poterie à Bavai, *Revue du Nord*, **49** (1967), 703–14

Hanson, W.S., forthcoming *Elginhaugh: a Flavian fort and its annexe*, Britannia Monograph Ser. (London)

Hartley, K. F., 1973 The marketing and distribution of mortaria, in Detsicas 1973, 39–51

————, 1977 Two major potteries in the first centuries A.D., in Dore & Greene 1977, 5–17

Hartley, B.R., 1977 Some wandering potters, in Dore & Greene 1977, 251–61

Haselgrove, C.C., & Lowther, P.C., forthcoming [Beaurieux excavation report]

Haupt, D., 1984 Römischer Töpfereibezirk bei Soller, Kreis Düren, Beitrage zur Archäologie des römischen Rheinlands, 4, *Rheinische Ausgrabungen*, **23**, 391–476

Hayes, J.W., 1967 North Syrian mortaria, *Hesperia, J. Amer. School Classical Stud. Athens*, **36.4**, 337–47

Hobley, B., 1973 Excavations at the 'The Lunt' Roman military site, Baginton, Warwickshire, 1968–71, *Trans. Birmingham Warwickshire Archaeol. Soc.*, **85** (1972), 7–92

Holbrook, N., & Bidwell, P. T., 1991 *Roman finds from Exeter*, Exeter Archaeol. Rep., **4** (Exeter)

Hull, M. R., 1963 *The Roman potters' kilns of Colchester*, Rep. Res. Comm. Soc. Antiq. London, **21** (Oxford)

Jarrett, M. G., & Wrathmell, S., 1981 *Whitton: an Iron Age and Roman farmstead in South Glamorgan* (Cardiff)

Lloyd, J. A. (ed.), 1979 *Excavations at Sidi Khrebish, Benghazi (Berenice), volume II* (Tripoli)

Manning, W. H. (ed.), 1993 *Report on the excavations at Usk 1965–76: the Roman pottery* (Cardiff)

Page, W., 1898 Notes on a Romano-British pottery lately found at Radlett, Herts, *Proc. Soc. Antiq. London,* 2 Ser., **17**, 261–71

Piton, D. (ed.), 1993 *Vendeuil-Caply* Nord-Ouest Archéologie, **5** (1992–3) (Berck-sur-Mer)

_____, & Delebarre, V., 1993 La céramique gallo-romaine de Vendeuil-Caply, in Piton 1993, 267–339

Pollard, R.J., 1988 *The Roman pottery of Kent*, Kent Archaeol. Soc. Monograph Ser., **5** (Maidstone)

Rakob, F. (ed.), 1994 *Simitthus II, der Tempelberg und das römischen Lager*, Band 2 (Mainz)

Reece, R., 1988 *My Roman Britain* (Dorchester)

Richardson, B., 1986 Pottery, in Dyson 1986, 96–139

_____, & Tyers, P.A., 1984 North Gaulish pottery in Britain. *Britannia*, **15**, 133–41

Riley, J.A., 1979 The coarse pottery from Berenice, in Lloyd 1979, 91–465

Rush, P.S., 1993 *The economics of Roman mortaria: ceramic production and distribution in southern Roman Britain*, unpublished thesis, Department of Archaeological Sciences, University of Bradford

Santrot, M. H., & Santrot, J., 1979 *Céramiques communes gallo-romaines d'Aquitaine*, Centre de Recherches Interdisciplinaires d'Archéologie Analytique, E.R.A.584 (Paris)

Saunders, C., & Havercroft, A.B., 1977 A kiln of the potter Oastrius and related excavations at Little Munden Farm, Bricket Wood, *Verulamium Museum Occas. Paper*, **1**, *Hertfordshire Archaeol.*, **5**, 109–56

Suggett, P.G., 1953 Report on the excavations at Brockley Hill, August and September, 1951, *Trans. London Middlesex Archaeol. Soc.*, new ser., **11.2**, 173–188

_____, 1954 Excavations at Brockley Hill, March 1952 to May 1953, *Trans. London Middlesex Archaeol. Soc.*, new ser., **11.3**, 253–76

_____, 1955 The Moxom Collection, *Trans. London Middlesex Archaeol. Soc.*, **18.1**, 60–4

Symonds, R.P., & Wade, S., forthcoming *Roman pottery from excavations in Colchester, 1971–86* (eds P. Bidwell & A. Croom), Colchester Archaeol. Rep., **10**

Terrisse, J-R., 1969 Les sigles de Bavay sur mortaria, amphores, dolia et tegulae, *Ogam*, **12.2–3** (1960), 158–68

Tuffreau-Libre, M., 1977 La céramique de l'officine gallo-romaine du Pont-Rouge à Bourlon, *Bulletin de la Commission Départementale des Monuments Historiques du Pas-de-Calais*, **10.1**

Vallerin, M., 1994 *Pelves* estampillés de Bassit, *Syria*, **71**, 171–204

Vann, R. L., 1992 *Caesarea Papers. Straton's Tower, Herod's Harbour, and Roman and Byzantine Caesarea* (Ann Arbor)

Vegas, M., 1994 La céramique du 'camp' à Simitthus, in Rakob 1994, 142–247

Wacher, J., & McWhirr, A., 1982 *Early Roman occupation at Cirencester* (Cirencester)

Webster, P.V., 1981 The coarse pottery, in Jarret & Wrathmell 1981

_____, 1993 The post-fortress coarsewares, in Manning 1993, 227–361

Williams, D.F., 1993 The petrology of mortarium fabrics 5, 6, 11 and 13, in Manning 1993, 424–5

Zabehlicky-Scheffenegger, S., 1996 Rote Reibschüsseln: eine Sonderform der Mortaria vom Magdalensberg, *Rei Cretariae Romanae Fautorum Acta*, **33**, 157–69 (Abingdon)

24   Early Roman amphorae from Le Mans

Patrick Galliou

Like most major French towns, Le Mans has, in recent years, undergone extensive urban renovation works which brought to light – and eventually destroyed – substantial and prominent monuments and structures of *Suindinum*, the *civitas* capital of the *Aulerci Cenomani*. Among these, the fascinating wooden structures, well dated to the first three decades of the first century AD, unearthed on the site of the former convent of Les Filles-Dieu, are of particular interest, as they once again underline the continuity of native architectural techniques during Roman times, and this even in major urban centres.[1]

Such urban districts usually offer archaeologists large assemblages of Roman pottery, from thick-bodied containers to fine tablewares, and it therefore comes as no surprise that Les Filles-Dieu, among masses of other contemporary products, should have yielded a small group of amphorae (fig. 1), used to bring such foreign delicacies as wine, olive-oil, and fish-sauces from the Mediterranean world to the kitchens of the newly Romanized province of *Lugdunensis*.[2]

Though they clearly belong to the mainstream of southern imports into Northern Gaul and offer no typological *unicum* or outstanding stamp, the Filles-Dieu amphorae will hopefully help to illustrate the variations in trading patterns within the Roman Empire, which, in a neighbouring domain, have been so well documented by Brian Hartley's highly perceptive analyses of the evolution and distribution of samian ware. Without the rock-firm chronology of individual potters and distinctive styles he has so carefully put together over the years, much of our pottery research would indeed be lame, and amphora studies to some extent a matter of guesswork.

SPANISH AMPHORAE

Wine amphorae from southern Spain

Two body sherds, in a rough sandy fabric, grey-green in colour, and provided with a solid conical spike, certainly belong to the Peacock 15/Haltern 70/Callender 9 class, produced in *Baetica*, in the Guadalquivir valley, between -50 and +50, and widely exported towards the northern provinces between the last decades of the 1st century BC and the reign of Claudius.[3]

Tituli picti appearing on some of the amphorae from the Port-Vendres II wreck show that at least some of them contained *defrutum*, a sweet liquid obtained by boiling down the must, which was used to mellow wines and to preserve olives.[4] Most, however, were used to carry the wines of the Baetican vineyards, well documented by both Latin literature and provincial archaeology.[5]

Oil amphorae from southern Spain

Two fragmented amphorae,[6] in the same sandy fabric as the Peacock 15 described above, belong to another Baetican class of containers (Peacock 24/Dressel 25/Oberaden 83/Haltern 71), probably slightly earlier than the following type (Peacock 25, see below). Such amphorae were used to carry oil from the Guadalquivir valley[7] and commonly occur in Rome, on the German *Limes*,[8] in Gaul[9] and Britain,[10] in Augustan/Tiberian contexts.

Another fragment (rim, collar and handles), in the same sandy fabric, belongs to the later class of Baetican oil amphorae, namely the ubiquitous Peacock 25/Dressel 20. Made in the same region as the above between the early decades of the 1st century AD and the end of the 3rd century AD,[11] they were massively exported to Rome[12] and the provinces.[13] The profile of the rim, however, tends to show that the Le Mans amphora belongs to one of the earliest, pre-Neronian sub-types.[14]

Fish-products amphorae from southern Spain

Besides olive-oil and wine, the province of Baetica was reputed, throughout the Roman Empire, for the quality of its fish preserves and sauces,[15] and kilns making the amphorae used to trade these products[16] have indeed been identified near Cadiz and Algeciras.[17]

Three amphorae from Les Filles-Dieu, though pertaining to that general series, should however be classified in one of its sub-classes, called Peacock 16, characterized by different body and rim profiles. It is very likely, on account of their fabric[18] and some of their typological idiosyncrasies,[19] that they

220 PATRICK GALLIOU

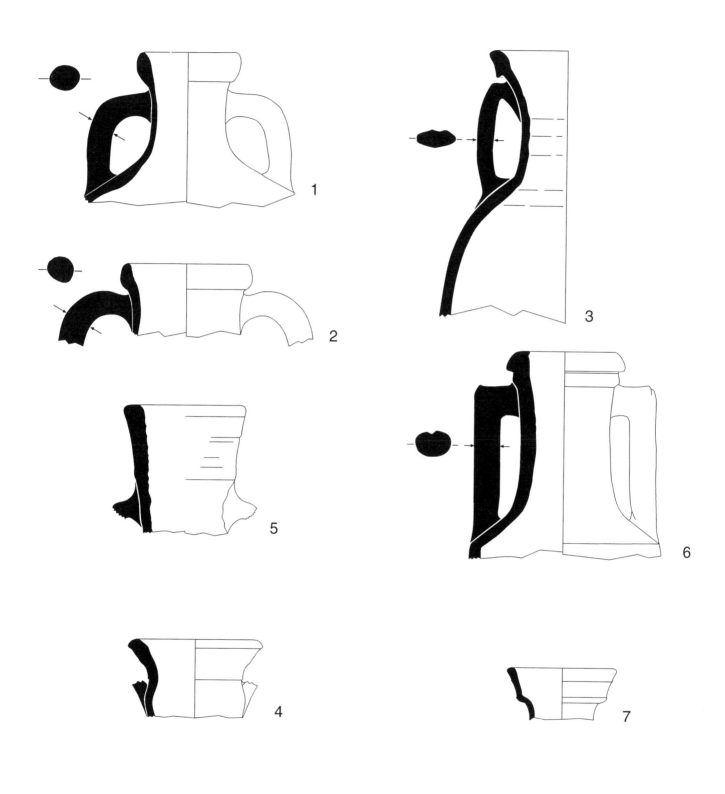

*Fig. 1. Early amphorae from Le Mans. **1.** Peacock 24; **2.** Peacock 25; **3.** Peacock 16; **4.** Peacock 17; **5.** Peacock 6; **6.** Peacock 10; **7.** Peacock 29. Scale 1:5.*

were produced in the same areas – and perhaps even in the same kilns – as the other Baetican amphorae described above, from the late 1st century BC to the early 1st century AD. One of them has two graffiti, a retrograde F on the lower part of the collar and CLE on the upper part of the body.

Three additional vessels belong to the very common class known as Peacock 17/Beltrán 1, made in the same region as the previous type to carry similar products,[20] and widely distributed in the western Roman provinces from the late 1st century BC to the early 2nd century AD.[21] The neighbouring *civitas* capital of *Iuliomagus Andecavorum* (Angers), for instance, has produced at least fifteen such amphorae, though Peacock type 16 amphorae are curiously absent from the urban sites excavated so far.[22]

Wine amphorae from north-eastern Spain

The bulk of the Les Filles-Dieu amphorae is however composed of vessels made on the territory of the *Leetani*, in the north of *Tarraconensis*, as containers for the local wines.[23] These come in two major typological classes, Peacock 6/Pascual I and Peacock 10/Dressel 2–4, which, in north-western France, generally appear in late 1st century BC/early 1st century AD contexts.[24] Though amphorae of the same type were produced in a variety of sites throughout Italy and the western provinces of the Roman Empire,[25] the fabrics of the Le Mans containers[26] and the stamps they sometimes bear are so clearly of Catalonian types as to dispel any doubt as to their geographical origin.

Eleven fragments of the distinctive rounded handles and high vertical rims of Peacock 6/Pascual I amphorae are present in the Les Filles-Dieu assemblage, together with at least twelve spikes, five of which are stamped. All of these elements are in fabric 2, as defined by D. F. Williams.[27] One spike, much discoloured and fissured by heavy heating, contains a lump of glassy material and was clearly reused in some 'industrial' context.

The five stamps (fig. 2, nos. 1–5) may be analysed as follows:

AS: this oval-shaped stamp (18 × 19mm) should almost certainly be completed as VAS. It appears on Peacock 6/Pascual I amphorae kept in Badalona Museum as well as on various Catalan and South Gaulish sites.[28]

M ?: incomplete stamp, which could perhaps be read M. This might be attributed to the Torre Llauder (Mataro) kiln.[29]

N: small square stamp (11mm), impressed obliquely. This mark is not attested in the Catalan kilns, but appears on Leetanian Peacock 10/Dressel 2–4 amphorae from the La Chrétienne-H wreck.[30]

SLL: oval-shaped stamp (21 × 18mm), impressed obliquely. Though very common in Catalonia, at Sant Miquel, Can Cabot and in the Caldes de Montbui museum,[31] it apparently does not appear in Mediterranean wrecks.

TF ?: circular stamp (17mm). The reading is uncertain and the mark cannot so far be attributed to any precise Catalan source.

Besides these highly idiosyncratic Peacock 6/Pascual I containers, the Les Filles-Dieu assemblage also contains three fragments of Peacock 10/Dressel 2–4 amphorae, together with three spikes. Most appear in the characteristic Catalan fabric defined by A. Tchernia.[32] Four of these fragments are stamped (fig. 2, nos. 6–9):

A: small square stamp (9mm), impressed on the lower part of the body of an amphora in sandy fabric, quite different from the ordinary Catalan types. This stamp, though not attested on the production sites, appears on Catalan Peacock 10/Dressel 2–4 amphorae from wrecks.[33]

?: fragmentary stamp, on the spike of a Peacock 10/Dressel 2–4 amphora in the Catalan fabric.

F: retrograde oval-shaped stamp (18 × 13mm), on the spike of a Peacock 10/Dressel 2–4 amphora in the Catalan fabric. Numerous examples are known from the production area (in Badalona museum),[34] various wrecks and southern Gaulish sites.[35]

C. F. PE: rectangular stamp (29 × 14mm), on the spike of a Peacock 10/Dressel 2–4 amphora in the Catalan fabric. Though so far unknown on the production sites, this stamp appears on Spanish Peacock 10/Dressel 2–4 amphorae from the Diano Marina wreck.[36]

GAULISH AMPHORAE

More than fifty amphora kilns have been so far identified in France.[37] Located mostly in *Narbonensis*,[38] they generally produced flat-based containers used for the trading of local wines. Only one fragment from the Les Filles-Dieu assemblage may however be attributed to the Peacock 29/Gauloise 3 type, produced at Corneilhan (Hérault) and Velaux (Bouches-du-Rhône) particularly during the 1st century AD. Besides these, one of the Peacock 10/Dressel 2–4 amphorae from Les Filles-Dieu, in an orange-buff fabric, may well come from one of the Gaulish production centres listed by F. Laubenheimer rather than from *Tarraconensis*, though only chemical analysis would tell.

UNPROVENANCED AMPHORA

A body sherd in a greenish fabric with fairly large brown nodules is impressed with a circular stamp (31mm), probably reading ANT (fig. 2, no. 10). Though this is attributed to southern Spain by Callender,[39] there is still some degree of doubt as to the precise shape and origin of the Le Mans amphora.

AMPHORAE AND LONG-DISTANCE TRADE

Amphorae, as '*an important form of trade packaging in the ancient world*',[40] are a major instrument in the evaluation and quantification of the movements of certain foodstuffs within (and sometimes without) the Roman Empire. Thus, the small assemblage from Les Filles-Dieu, with its overwhelming

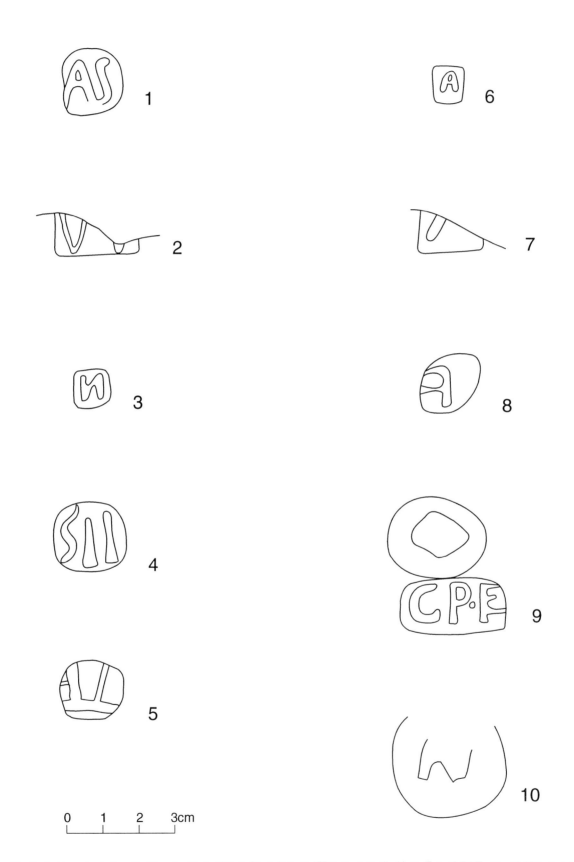

Fig. 2. Amphora stamps from Le Mans. 1. AS; 2. M(?); 3. N; 4. SLL; 5. TF(?); 6. A; 7. illegible; 8. F; 9. C.F.PE.; 10. ANT(?). Scale 1:2.

proportion of Spanish containers, should help us understand how such commodities as Baetican wine, oil and marine products, together with the wines of *Tarraconensis* and, to a much lesser extent *Narbonensis*, reached *Suindinum* in the first three decades of the 1st century AD.

It is of course tempting to imagine that Baetican products were dispatched to *Lugdunensis* and further north, to still unconquered *Britannia*, by the Atlantic maritime route circling the Spanish peninsula. Though this may appear as the shortest line to the North, the investigation of Baetican imports in Galicia[41] and the Astures[42] has had very disappointing results, and it is most likely that Baetican commodities were sent to Narbonne and the mouths of the Rhône, which gave access to major land and river routes towards Atlantic Gaul and Britain on the one hand, eastern Gaul and the German *Limes* on the other.[43] The same routes were certainly used by the wines from northern *Tarraconensis* traded in Peacock 6/ Pascual I and Peacock 10/Dressel 2–4 amphorae along the Atlantic seaboard, Britain, and the Rhône-Saône-Rhine axis.[44] The containers described above may then have reached *Suindinum* by the sea route, branching off into the Loire and the Sarthe, or, alternatively, by the Rhône route, goods being offloaded at Lyon and transported overland to Roanne, whence they could be shipped down the Loire and up the Sarthe.

Quantification of this assemblage clearly shows that wine was the main commodity brought to *Suindinum* in the early decades of the 1st century AD (77%), this probably following on a tradition established in the late La Tène communities of north-western France.[45] Customers were however now offered a wider variety of vintages, from *Baetica* (6%),[46] *Tarraconensis* (88%) and *Narbonensis* (6%), Italian imports declining correspondingly.[47] Fish-products rank second in the assemblage (14%) and, together with Baetican oil (7%), may well indicate slight changes in the diet of native communities, as complex processes of pre-Romanization[48] or Romanization[49] began transforming some of their tastes and habits. Though admittedly small in number,[50] the Les Filles-Dieu amphorae thus provide an interesting glimpse into the economic life of early *Suindinum* and the array of imports offered for sale on its markets and in its shops. Besides, as quantifications by content and origin roughly correspond to those available for other contemporary sites of western Gaul[51] and differ fairly widely from what is known in other western provinces,[52] it is quite likely that they do point to major underlying economic trends, diversely affecting the various regions of the Roman West. Much more work on the attribution and quantification of amphorae from urban and rural sites needs however to be done before satisfactory conclusions on the subject can be reached. Tomorrow, then, to fresh Woods and Vessels new.

Notes

1. The site has not been yet fully published. For a preview: J. Guilleux *et al.* 1983, 81.
2. The 43 fragments analysed below were presented for study by the excavator, Mlle F. Goupil. We cannot be certain that there has not been a selection of particularly distinctive amphora elements.
3. Colls *et al.* 1977, 38–8; Siraudeau 1988, 183–4, in particular.
4. Cato, *de Agricultura* 7.4; Colls *et al.* 1977, 87.
5. Colls *et al.* 1977, 129–34.
6. The rim, collar and handles have been partly preserved in both fragments.
7. The bibliography devoted to Baetican oil is huge. Among many titles: Tchernia 1964, 419–49; Beltrán Lloris 1970, 464–92; Ponsich 1979; Remesal Rodríguez 1986; 1992, 105–13.
8. Beltrán Lloris, 1970, 466–9.
9. Siraudeau 1988, 187.
10. Williams & Peacock 1983, 263–80.
11. Zevi 1967, 234–8. Production continued during the later Roman Empire, Baetican oil being then exported in Dressel 23 amphorae: Remesal Rodríguez 1991, 355–61.
12. The Monte Testaccio in the suburbs of Rome is probably entirely made up of discarded Peacock 25/Dressel 20 amphorae; cf. Rodríguez Almeida 1984.
13. Cf. for instance, among many others, Thévenot 1950, 65–75; Rouquette 1970, 319–30; Colls *et al.* 1977, 134–9; Martin-Kilcher 1983, 337–47; Remesal Rodríguez 1989, 351–60.
14. Cf. Peacock & Williams 1986, fig. 65, no. 3 (before AD 50); Guénoche & Tchernia 1977, 241–59.
15. See Pliny, *Hist. Nat.* XXXI, 93–4; Martial, *Epigrams* XIII, 102–3, etc. The literary and archaeological evidence is brought together in Ponsich & Tarradell 1965. These industries actually extended into Lusitania (cf. Edmondson 1987), Galicia and the Astures (cf. Fernández Ochoa & Martínez Maganto 1994, 115–34; Fernández Ochoa 1994) and further north into western Gaul (cf. Sanquer & Galliou 1972, 199–223).
16. Zevi 1966, 214–7, showed that the *tituli picti* appearing on amphorae of Dressel types 7–13 implied that these vessels contained marine products from southern Spain.
17. Peacock 1974, 232–43.
18. It is very similar to that of the Baetican wine and oil amphorae described above.
19. Three of them certainly belong to the A variety (Peacock & Williams 1986, 118), some of which were made in the kilns of Algeciras, Cerro de los Mártires and Puerto Real (Peacock & Williams 1986, 73), though apparently in different fabrics.
20. Cf. Beltrán Lloris 1970, 415–7.
21. For example, Ettlinger 1977, 16.
22. Siraudeau 1988, 184–5.
23. The Leetanian vineyards are well documented by both Pliny, *Hist. Nat.* XIV, 71, and Martial, *Epigrams* XIII, 118. On the wine production of Tarraconensis and trading patterns, see in particular: Pascual Guasch 1962, 334–45; 1977, 47–96; Tchernia 1971, 38–85; Miro 1983; 1985, 455–61; 1987, 249–67; Corsi-Sciallano & Liou 1985; Gallion 1991, 99–105; Revilla Calvo & Carreras Monfort 1993, 53–92.
24. Galliou 1987, 381.
25. **Peacock 6/Pascual 1**: *Aspiran* (Hérault), Genty & Fiches 1978, 71–92; *Corneilhan* (Hérault), Laubenheimer & Widemann 1977, 59–82; *Montans* (Tarn), Labrousse 1976, 496. **Peacock 10/Dressel 2–4**: *Italy*, Peacock 1977, 262–9; Hesnard 1977, 157–68; *Switzerland*, Martin-Kilcher *et al.* 1987, 113; *France*, Laubenheimer 1986, 175–87 (Crouzilles, Indre-et-Loire); 1989, 118–23; Becker 1986, 147–50; *? Great-Britain*, Castle 1978, 383–92. It should also be stressed that this form ultimately derives from Greek prototypes made on the Aegean island of Kos.
26. **Peacock 10/Dressel 2–4**: Tchernia 1971; **Peacock 6/Pascual I**: Williams 1981.
27. Williams 1981.
28. Miro 1982–3, 234 and map 7.
29. Pascual Guasch 1977, 61–4; Miro 1982–3, 230.
30. Corsi-Sciallano & Liou 1985, 83 and fig. 71.
31. Pascual Guasch 1977, 41, 50, 58, figs. 9, no. 17, 10, no. 16, 12, no. 12, and 13.
32. Tchernia 1971.
33. Corsi-Sciallano & Liou 1985, 78, 95.
34. Pascual Guasch 1977, fig. 13, nos. 16, 17.
35. Miro 1982–3, 234 and map 9.
36. Corsi-Sciallano & Liou 1985, 98, fig. 80, no. 1, and 164.
37. Laubenheimer 1989.
38. Laubenheimer 1985.
39. Callender 1985, no. 85.

40. Peacock & Williams 1986, 2.
41. Cf. Naveiro 1991, 63–73.
42. Carreras forthcoming.
43. Cf. among many others, Bonnard 1913; Rougé 1966; Peacock 1978, 49–51; Chic 1981, 223–49; Roman 1983.
44. Cf. in particular: *Atlantic seaboard*, Laubenheimer & Watier 1991, 5–39; Galliou 1987; 1991; *Britain*, Williams 1981, 79–81; Revilla Calvo & Carreras Monfort 1993; *Rhône-Saône-Rhine axis*, Becker *et al.* 1986, 65–89; Remesal & Revilla 1991, 389–439; Revilla Calvo & Carreras Monfort 1993.
45. Galliou 1982.
46. If we admit that some Peacock 15/Haltern 70 amphorae carried wine and *defrutum*, cf. above.
47. Tchernia 1987, 135.
48. This is the case of the oil amphorae shipped to Britain in the pre-conquest period; cf. Williams & Peacock 1983.
49. Cf. for example the Peacock 16 amphora in one of the graves of the Augustan period at Goeblingen-Nospelt (Luxemburg); Thill 1967, no. B12.
50. The quantification problems sketched by Peacock & Williams 1986, 18–19, will be left aside here.
51. For example, Laubenheimer & Watier 1991.
52. See Martin-Kilcher 1990, 175–204.

Bibliography

Becker, C., 1986 Note sur un lot d'amphores régionales du 1er siècle après J.C. à Lyon, *Figlina*, **7** 147–50

————, Constantin, C., Desbat, A., Jacquin, L., & Lascoux, J.-P., Le dépôt d'amphores augustéen de la rue Favorite à Lyon, *Figlina*, **7**, 65–89

Beltrán Lloris, M., 1970 *Las ánforas romanas en España* (Zaragoza)

Blázquez, J.M., & Remesal, J. (eds), 1983 *Producción y comercio del aceite en la antigüedad. II congreso* (Madrid)

Bonnard, L., 1913 *La navigation intérieure de la Gaule à l'époque gallo-romaine* (Paris)

Callender, M.H., 1965 *Roman amphorae* (London)

Carreras, C., forthcoming El comercio en Asturia a través de las ánforas, *Los finisterres atlánticos en la antigüedad, Gijón, 10–12 July 1995*

Castle, S.A., 1978 Amphorae from Brockley Hill, 1975, *Britannia*, **9**, 389–92

Chic, G., 1981 Rutas comerciales de las ánforas olearias hispanas en el occidente romano, *Habis*, **12**, 223–49

Colls, D., Etienne, R., Lequémont, R., Liou, B., & Mayet, F., 1977 *L'épave Port-Vendres II et le commerce de la Bétique à l'époque de Claude*, Archaeonautica, **1** (Paris)

Corsi-Sciallano, M., & Liou, B., 1985 *Les épaves de Tarraconaise à chargement d'amphores Dressel 2–4*, Archaeonautica, **5** (Paris)

Edmondson, J.C., 1987 *Two industries in Roman Lusitania: mining and garum production* (Oxford)

Ettlinger, E., 1977 Aspects of amphora typology – seen from the north, in *Méthodes classiques et méthodes formelles dans l'étude des amphores*, Collections de l'École Française de Rome, **32**, 9–16

Fernández Ochoa, C., 1994 *Una industria de salazones de época romana en la Plaza del Marqués* (Gijón)

————, & Martínez Maganto, J., 1994 Las industrias de salazón en el norte de la Península Ibérica en la época romana. Nuevas aportaciones, *Archivo Español de Arqueología*, **67**, 115–34

Galliou, P., 1982 *Les amphores tardo-républicaines découvertes dans l'ouest de la France* (Brest)

————, 1987 Les amphores Pascual 1 et le commerce antique au 1er siècle de notre ère, in *Mélanges offertes au Docteur J-B Colbert de Beaulieu* (Paris)

————, 1991 Les amphores Pascual 1 et Dressel 2–4 de Tarraconaise découvertes dans le nord-ouest de la Gaule et les importations de vins espagnols au Haut-Empire, *Leetania*, **6**, 99–105

Genty, P.Y., & Fiches J.-L., 1978 L'atelier de potiers gallo-romains d'Aspiran (Hérault). Synthèse de travaux de 1971 à 1978, *Figlina*, **3**, 71–92

Guénoche, A., & Tchernia, A., 1977 Essai de construction d'un modèle descriptif des amphores Dr. 20, in *Méthodes classiques et méthodes formelles dans l'étude des amphores*, Collections de l'École Française de Rome, **32**, 241–59

Guilleux, J., Lambert, C., & Rioufreyt, J., 1983 La période gallo-romaine, in *La Sarthe, des origines à nos jours* (Saint-Jean-d'Angely)

Hesnard, A., 1977 Note sur un atelier d'amphores Dr. 1 et Dr. 2–4 près de Terracine, *Mélanges de l'École Française de Rome*, **89**, 157–68

Labrousse, M. 1976 Informations archéologiques, *Gallia*, **34**

Laubenheimer, F., 1985 *La production des amphores en Gaule Narbonnaise* (Paris)

————, 1986 La production de deux ateliers du bassin de la Loire moyenne, *Revue Archéologique du Centre de la France*, **25.2**, 175–87

————, 1989, Les amphores gauloises sous l'Empire: recherches nouvelles sur leur production et leur chronologie, in *Anfore romane e storia economica: un decennio di ricerche. Atti del colloquio de Siena, 22–24 maggio 1986*, 118–83

————, & Watier, B., 1991 Les amphores des Allées de Tourny à Bordeaux, *Aquitania*, **9**, 5–39

————, & Widemann, F., 1977 L'atelier de Corneilhan (Hérault), *Revue d'Archéometrie*, **1**, 59–82

Martin-Kilcher, S., 1983 Les amphores à huile de Bétique (Dressel 20 et 23) d'Augst (*Colonia Augusta Rauricorum*) et Kaiseraugust (*Castrum Rauracense*), in Blázquez & Remesal 1983, 337–47

————, 1990 Le vin et la Suisse romaine, in Chevallier, R. (ed.), *Archéologie de la vigne et du vin*, 175–204 (Tours)

————, Maggetti, M., & Galetti, G., 1987 Fabrikation von Weinamphorae der Form Dressel 2–4 in Augusta Rauricorum, *Jahrbuch der Schweizerischen Gesellschaft für Ur- und Frühgeschichte*, **70**

Miro, J., 1982–3 La prioduccio d'amfores al Maresme: una sintesi, *Laietania*, **2–3**

————, 1983 La producción de ánforas romanas en Catalunya (Oxford)

————, 1985 Vi català a França (seglesi 1 a.C. – 1 d.C.). Una sintesi preliminar, in *El vi a l'antiguitat. Economia, produccio i comerç al Mediterrani Occidental*, 455–61 (Barcelona)

————, 1987 El litoral catalán: navegación, materiales arqueológicos submarinos e interpretación comercial en época antigua, in *VI Congreso Internacional de arqueología submarina, Cartagena 1982*, 249–67

Naveiro, J., 1991 *El comercio antiguo en el noroeste peninsular* (La Coruña)

————, 1977 Las ánforas de la Layetania, in *Méthodes classiques et méthodes formelles dans l'étude des amphores*, Collections de l'École Française de Rome, **32**, 47–96

Peacock, D.P.S., 1974 Amphorae and the Baetican fish industry, *Antiq. J.*, **54**, 232–43

————, 1977 Recent discoveries of Roman amphora kilns in Italy, *Antiq. J.*, **57**, 262–9

————, 1978 The Rhine and the problem of Gaulish wine in Roman Britain, in Du Plat Taylor, J., & Cleere, H. (eds), *Roman shipping and trade: Britain and the Rhine provinces*, CBA Res. Rep., **24**, 49–51

————, & Williams, D.F., 1986 *Amphorae and the Roman economy* (London and New York)

Ponsich, M., 1979 *Implantation rurale antique sur le Bas-Guadalquivir* (Paris)

————, & Tarradell, M., 1965 *Garum et industries antiques de salaison dans la Méditerranée occidentale* (Paris)

Remesal, J., & Revilla, V., 1991 Weinamphoren aus Hispania Citeror und Gallia Narbonensis in Deutschland und Holland, *Fundberichte aus Baden-Württemberg*, **16**, 389–439

Remesal Rodríguez, J., 1986 *La annona militaris y la exportación del aceite bético a Germania* (Madrid)

————, 1989 Die Stempel auf Amphoren des Typs Dressel 20 aus Worms, *Archäologisches Korrespondenzblatt*, **19**, 351–60

————, 1991 El aceite bético durante el Bajo Imperio, in *Arte, sociedad, economía y religión durante el Bajo Imperio y la antigüedad tardía. Homenaje al Profesor Dr. D. José Blázquez Martínez*, Antigüedad Cristiana, **8**, 355–61

————, 1992 *Instrumentum domesticum* e storia economico: le anfore Dressel 20, *Rivista Internazionale per la Storia Economica e Sociale dell'Antichità*, **11**, 105–13

Revilla Clavo, V., & Carreras Monfort, C., 1993 El vino de la Tarraconense en Britannia, *Münsterische Beiträge zur antiken Handelgeschichte*, **12.2**, 53–92

Rodríguez Almeida, E., 1984 *Il Monte Testaccio: ambiente, storia, materiali* (Rome)

Roman, Y., 1983 *De Narbonne à Bordeaux, un axe économique du premier siècle av.J.-C.* (Lyon)

Rougé, J., 1966 *Recherches sur l'organisation du commerce maritime en Méditerranée sous l'Empire romain* (Paris)

Rouquette, D., 1970 Marques sur amphores à huile du Département de l'Hérault, *Revue des Études Ligures*, **36**, 319–30

Sanquer, R., & Galliou, P., 1972 *Garum*, sel et salaisons en Armorique gallo-romaine, *Gallia*, **30**, 199–223

Siraudeau, J., 1988 *Amphores romaines des sites angevins et leur contexte archéologique* (Angers)

Tchernia, A., 1964 Amphores et marques d'amphores de Bétique à Pompei et Stabies, *Mélanges de l'École Française à Rome*, **77**, 419–49

————, 1971 Les amphores vinaires de Tarraconaise et leur exportation au début de l'Empire, *Archivo Español de Arqueología*, **44**, 38–85

————, 1986 *Le vin de l'Italie romaine* (Rome)

Thévenot, E., 1950 L'importation de produits espagnols chez les Eduens et les Lingons à la fin du IIe siècle de notre ère, d'après les marques d'amphores, *Revue Archéologique de l'Est*, **1.2** (April-June 1950), 65–75

Thill, G., 1967 Die Keramik aus vier spätlatenezeitlichen Brandgräbern von Goeblingen-Nospelt, *Hemecht*, **19**, 199–213

Williams, D.F., 1981 The Roman amphora trade with Late Iron Age Britain, in Howard, H., & Morris, E.L. (eds), *Production and distribution: a ceramic viewpoint*, BAR Int. Ser., **120**, 123–32 (Oxford)

————, 1987 The amphorae, in *Romano-British industries in Purbeck*, 79–81 (Dorchester)

————, & Peacock, D.P.S., 1983 The importation of olive-oil in Roman Britain, in Blázquez & Remesal 1983, 263–80

Zevi, F., 1966 Appunti sulle anfore romane, *Archeologica Classica*, **18**, 207–47

————, 1967, Review of M. H. Callender, Roman amphorae, in *J. Roman Stud.*, **57**, 234–8

25   Pottery production at Corbridge in the late 1st century

J. N. Dore

INTRODUCTION

It is a pleasure and a privilege to contribute a paper to a volume in Brian's honour, on a site the refinement of whose chronology he has influenced crucially on a number of occasions.

Only a small amount of the coarseware from Corbridge has ever been published. I am currently engaged in cataloguing, for English Heritage, the whole collection. In the course of this I have become aware (or rather more aware, since my suspicions had been aroused during the examination of material for the site report, Bishop & Dore 1989) that a significant proportion of the early material could be classified into a small number of distinctive and consistent forms and fabrics. Their characteristics, the quantities in which they occur at Corbridge, and the sparseness of their distribution on other sites of the same period suggest that they may have been produced at the Corbridge site.

FORMS (fig. 3)

I have classified the material into two bowl/dish and six jar forms. The codes used are the Museum type-series codes which I have been allocating during cataloguing. The full code scheme consists of four parts:

1) C or F (= Coarse or Fine)
2) AM (= amphora)
   FL (= flagon)
   BK (= beaker)
   JA (= jar)
   BO (= bowl or dish)
   M (= mortarium)
   OT (= other)
3) A three-figure numeric code (in the series 000–999). This is the main number code within each vessel class
4) A two-figure numeric code (in the series 00–99). This is designed to allow subdivision or re-allocation of types, or insertion of new types.

   Individual vessels also have a discrete Museum catalogue number beginning CO.

Thus, the full code for e.g. BO 1 below is C BO 001 00. For the sake of brevity the shortened code is used here since the first and fourth parts are not, in this instance, significant.

Bowls and Dishes

BO 1

This form falls within the class known as 'carinated bowl with reeded rim', which is always thought of as being quintessentially Flavian. It was affectionately known by John Gillam as the 'Scotty Dog' form since the sectional profile of the rim resembles the head of a scotty dog. The vessels have a certain elegance and though the lines are soft, the features, and particularly the rim, are distinctive. In examples in which enough survives, there is an unelaborate foot. The carination is never highly articulated. The sectional profile of the upper wall is slightly curved and its general trend is inclined outwards at about 10 degrees from the vertical; in a few examples the upper wall is more or less vertical, but there are no examples in which it is inward leaning (demonstrating what John Gillam used to call, borrowing shipbuilding terminology, 'tumble-home'). In sectional profile the rim is an undulating, down-turned flange whose upper face is not so much reeded as moulded, appearing as a gentle ridge between shallow valleys.

BO 14

This is the dish accompaniment to the bowl BO 1. Its wall leans out at an angle of *c.* 15 degrees from the vertical, and is slightly curved in sectional profile. Its base is flat in most examples (where sufficient survives to judge), but raised in some, such as CO 15735. The rim is a short, thick flange with certain variable characteristics: in most examples it is more or less horizontal, but in a few, such as CO 15735, it is up-tilted; the outer face of the rim is mostly plain, occasionally grooved as in CO 7752 and CO 5321. Most importantly the upper face of the rim is treated in one of two ways:

a) it is moulded in exactly the same way as BO 1;
b) it is grooved with two narrow channels separated by a broad, flat topped ridge.

The link between BO 1 and 14 is clearly demonstrated by the common and highly distinctive treatment of the rim exhibited in variant a). One could perhaps make a case for variant b) being an attribute defining a different form, one outside this BO 1 - BO 14 grouping, but there are, I think, sufficient other shared attributes (of shape and manufacturing technique) to regard it as a variant within the group.

Jars

JA 1
A high shouldered jar with a small, fine everted rim, the inner face of which is often slightly relieved, possibly to provide a seating for a lid. A more complete example than those shown here which was illustrated in Richmond & Gillam 1953 (no. 2: all the sherds of this cannot now be found) shows a narrow base.

JA 3
A high shouldered jar. A short, outswept rim with a back-cut face springs either directly from the shoulder or, as in the illustrated example, sits atop a barely developed neck. One example (CO 3989) has rudimentary rustication.

JA 4
Similar to JA 3, the rim being generally longer. There is often a single groove on the shoulder.

JA 6
High shouldered jar with developed neck and articulated shoulder. The outer face of the rim is gently curved, the inner face is relieved possibly to locate a lid.

JA 7
As JA 6 except that the rim is more upright with less projection

JA 8
As JA 6 except that the outer face of the rim is relieved or grooved.

It is important to realise the inter-relatedness of these jar forms. There are formal links between the different forms which suggest a closeness which goes beyond mere derivation from the common ceramic tradition of the era. JA 6, 7 and 8 are quite clearly related. JA 3 and 4 are simply, in formal terms, the JA 6/7/8 group without the developed neck; enough forms of JA 3 and 4 exist in which a neck is barely present to show this to be so. The greatest formal separation occurs between JA 1 and the rest, but again, sufficient examples of JA 1 exist in which there is a hint of development between the base of the rim and the shoulder (as in CO 5708 = Richmond & Gillam 1953, no.2) and the outer surface of the rim is on the point of being articulated as two faces rather than a continuous curve to suggest links with JA 3 and 4. In short, the jar types as defined represent snapshots, as it were, from a formal continuum, rather than entirely discrete entities.

Diameters

BO 1: Range: 18 - 39 cms
       Mode: 22–25 cms
BO 14: Range: 23 - 37 cms
       Mode: 27
JA 1: Range: 12.5 - 18 cms
       Mode: 15–18 cms
JA 3: 15 - 17 cms
JA 4: 14 - 16 cms
JA 6: c. 17 cms
JA 7: 10.5 - 15 cms
JA 8: 13 - 16 cms

FABRICS

There are three basic fabrics:

Fabric 1 (228 examples)

The palette of available colours is essentially pale yellow (7.5YR 8/4 or 10YR 8/3), pink (5YR 8/4) or red (2.5YR 6/8). There is often a different coloured core and body and core combinations can be any of the six possible from this three-colour set.

The inclusions are sub-rounded grains of quartz and rounded iron-rich grains. In the majority of examples the frequency is common rather than abundant (defined as being 10–30% of the area of the fresh break examined under the microscope, which was occupied by inclusions, and estimated by comparison with standard charts, e.g. Terry & Chilingar 1955). In all except the larger examples of BO 14 the sizing of the inclusions is as follows: quartz: main fraction c. 0.2mm, max 1.0mm; iron-rich: 0.5–1.0mm, occasionally 1.0–2.0mm. In all the examples of BO 1 and all except the larger examples of BO 14 the iron-rich grains form only a small proportion of the inclusion suite. In JA 1 and the larger examples of BO 14 the iron-rich grains form a higher proportion of the suite, to the extent that they outweigh the quartz in some examples of JA 1. In the larger examples of BO 14 the inclusion suite is also generally coarser (i.e. main fraction c. 0.5mm, max 1.0mm).

In all examples in this fabric the surface treatment is unsophisticated, but there are slight variations between forms. In BO 1 all surfaces are wiped and the lower part of the lower wall is knife trimmed. In BO 14, where it can be seen in the more complete examples, the interior floor is mostly completely untreated, neither smoothed nor wiped but simply pressed more or less flat, like a pastry lining when pressed into a pie dish. The rim, inner wall and the top of the outer wall are wiped. The lower part of the exterior wall and the underside of the base are knife-trimmed and show extensive scoring where the blade dragged grains of temper. One example of JA 3 and three examples of JA 4 show rustication (JA 3: CO 3989, very rudimentary; JA 4: CO 2976, 3948, 4228, low relief).

It is in this fabric that sherds of what could be termed 'near waster' status occur, all examples of JA 1. Five sherds show clear evidence of overcooking: biscuity, slightly porous texture, dark orange and grey 'scorch' marks on the surface. One sherd (CO 17508), in addition to the biscuit texture, shows distortion and a hint of spalling.

Fabric 2 (70 examples)

Body colour is pale grey (8/0) or medium grey (6/8) with a darker surface. Inclusion frequency is common (see fabric 1 for definition). Quartz is the main component (though it has to be said that the dark body colour makes detection of iron-rich grains extremely difficult) and grain size is as follows: main fraction c. 0.2mm, max 1.0mm. All of the forms occur in this fabric except JA 1. The highest incidence is for JA 4, JA 7 (which occurs exclusively in this fabric) and JA 8. A high proportion of the examples of JA 4 have a well burnished outer surface.

Fabric 3 (8 examples)

Either pale grey with a black core or black with a black core with thin pale grey margins. In either case the colour bands are sharply defined. The surface is dark grey or black. As with fabric 2 the iron-rich inclusions are barely visible. The quartz is finer and sparser than in fabric 1: main fraction 0.2mm or finer. Surfaces are wiped and knife-trimmed on the exterior. The overall impression is that vessels in fabric 3 are finer than those of the other two fabrics both in terms of execution and fabric texture. JA 6 and 8 occur in this fabric and there are single examples of BO 1 and 14.

Fabrics	1	2	3	Total
Forms				
BO 1	96	5	1	102
BO 14	45	2	1	48
JA 1	62	0	0	62
JA 3	14	4	0	18
JA 4	8	19	0	27
JA 6	3	5	3	11
JA 7	0	18	0	18
JA 8	0	17	3	20
Total	228	70	8	306

Fig. 1. Form vs. fabric.

DATING AT CORBRIDGE

Current thinking divides the history of Corbridge into the following phases (taken from Bishop & Dore 1989, 140):

Phase 1:   c. AD 86–103
Phase 2:   c. AD 105–122
Phase 3:   c. AD 122–139

Phase 4a: c. AD 139–158
Phase 4b: c. AD 158–163
Phase PF: Post Fort

From the 306 catalogued vessels 53 occurred in contexts which can be assigned to phases with at least some degree of confidence. These assignments have been derived from the following sources:

1) Bishop & Dore 1989. The index on p. 307 ff. lists all the finds groups which could be reliably phased at the time of preparing the publication.

2) Richmond & Gillam 1953; 1955.

3) A further examination of entries in the Finds Books. This yielded a small number of additional contexts which could be assigned to early phases. In these cases the descriptions of the context as recorded in the Finds Book have been reproduced verbatim in the catalogue, and followed by some attempt at interpretation.

Fig. 2 summarises this information. Numbers refer to occurrences. Where a context could only be assigned to a range of phases (e.g. 1–2) the occurrences have been placed under the latest phase of the range.

Phase:	1	2	3	4	PF
Form					
BO 1	5	5	3	3	1
BO 14	2	2	1	3	1
JA 1	1	2		2	1
JA 3		1		1	1
JA 4		2		2	
JA 6		2		1	
JA 7		2		3	1
JA 8		2	1		

Fig. 2. Dating summary.

From the above it will be seen that BO 1 and 14 and JA 1 can be associated with the earliest Roman phase of the site's history, whereas JA 3, 4, 6, 7 and 8 can be placed no earlier than phase 2.

DISTRIBUTION OUTSIDE CORBRIDGE

In searching through the published record one finds few examples on other sites which are sufficiently similar to justify suggesting that they originated from the same production as the Corbridge vessels. The three sites which consistently produce the closest parallels for the Corbridge vessels are Vindolanda, Carlisle and Old Penrith.

Vindolanda

BO 1: Hird 1977, nos. 74, 224, 374
BO 14: Hird 1977, nos. 19, 73, 489, 176

JA 1: Hird 1977, no. 262
JA 4: Birley & Birley 1938, no. 47
JA 8: Hird 1977, no. 459

There are examples of BO 1 & 14 from contexts of phase II, currently dated to *c.* AD 92–97.

Carlisle

BO 1: Taylor 1991, nos. 137, 143, 237
BO 14: Taylor 1991, no. 225
JA 3: (Annetwel Street unpublished)
JA 4: Taylor 1990, fig. 196, no. 21; 1991, no. 173

None of this material occurs in contexts earlier than phase 5, i.e. *c.* AD 105.

Old Penrith

BO 14: Austen 1991, no. 459
JA 4: Austen 1991, no. 295, 297, 300

Residual in context.

CONCLUSIONS

In making our case for on-site production of this material in the late 1st century the evidence favours certain forms over others. The best evidence is the presence of sherds of material all of which can be classed as 'near waster', and one of which, CO 17508, should, I think, be regarded as a true waster. These sherds are all examples of JA 1 in Fabric 1, and we can therefore, I think, regard the case for this form+fabric combination as conclusively proved. By virtue of the common fabric we **should** be able to extend the proof to the two other forms which occur almost exclusively in Fabric 1 (i.e. BO 1 & 14). Taken alone, however, the fabric might not suffice; my definition of fabric 1 as a 'real' fabric, i.e. one resulting from a single production grouping, may not, after all, be sufficiently rigorous. The combination of evidence is more conclusive: numerous occurrences of a limited range of well defined forms (reinforced, in the case of BO 1 and 14, by the strong cross-links provided by the distinctive rim characteristic), in what appears to be a common fabric, potentially all from a single phase (phase 1). This, surely, suggests in the strongest terms that BO 1 and 14 were produced at Corbridge at the same time as JA 1.

The evidence for JA 3–8 is weaker. They occur in smaller numbers, mostly in fabrics two and three (i.e. fabrics not supported by waster evidence). Formally they can be related to JA 1 but since their possible date range is wider (i.e. phases 1–2) they are not necessarily contemporary. While the evidence is suggestive, the case for their production at Corbridge must, I think, remain open for the time being.

THE CATALOGUE

Because of the long history of excavation and publication at Corbridge, there is a large amount of reference information linked to the finds. I have standardised the organisation and presentation of this as follows (reading from the top left to the bottom right of a hypothetical vessel containing entries for every class of information):

Information	*Entries in which present*
Museum catalogue number (e.g. CO 2432)	all
Information (other than finds group) written on sherd(s) (e.g. 'COR 48 DRAWN 26 AH 48'); reported verbatim, in quotes	some
Finds group code (e.g. IX59: figures indicate year of excavation; an asterisk '*' indicates year of excavation unknown)	most
Region of the site where the vessel was recovered (e.g. TEMPLE III or XI A/B1: Roman numerals usually indicate a site number, followed by a trench code: see Bishop & Dore 1989, figs. 3 and 4 for site trench locations)	most
Verbatim context description taken from the relevant Finds Book (where contexts give additional phase information not contained in Bishop & Dore 1989), followed by interpretation where necessary; all enclosed in brackets	some
Any additional catalogue references (e.g. Cat 87/ 60: this refers to the working catalogue assembled in 1987 for the 1989 publication)	some
Site phase: see section on dating for the derivation of this; phase assignments which are unaccompanied by references were derived from Bishop & Dore 1989.	some

BO 1

CO 2432 IX59 XI A/B1 Cat 87/ 60
CO 2433 HO65 XI U7 Cat 87/ 3 Phase: 2–3 ?
CO 2433 HO65 XI U7 Cat 87/ 3 Phase: 2–3 ?
CO 2436 DV59 XI B1 Cat 87/ 25
CO 2437 5471 (same vessel) GE59 BG70 XI D1 E3 Cat 87/ 47
      Phase: 4b
CO 2440 QO64 XLIV C Cat 87/241 Phase: 2
CO 3275 LU66 XI SR RM7 N ('Baulk between NE/NW square.
      Depth approx. 5ft': this is certainly deep enough to be early.)
      Phase: 1–2 ?
CO 3393 IF71 XI SR RM10 SE ('Pit. Depth 82ins': possibly early.)
      Phase: 1 ?
CO 3440 HO71 XI SR RM5 NW ('Fill of wattle and daub burnt
      plaster and clay. Depth 53ins': this could be the destruction at
      the end of 1b, particularly as a post trench of phase 2 from the
      same trench is described as cut into this kind of material.) Phase:
      1 ?
CO 3918 BC70 XI E2 Phase: 4–PF
CO 4039 ZJ59 XI D1
CO 4040 FS60 XI B3
CO 4042 HV63 XI ER K
CO 4044 4049 LA60 WEST COMPOUND *Illustrated*

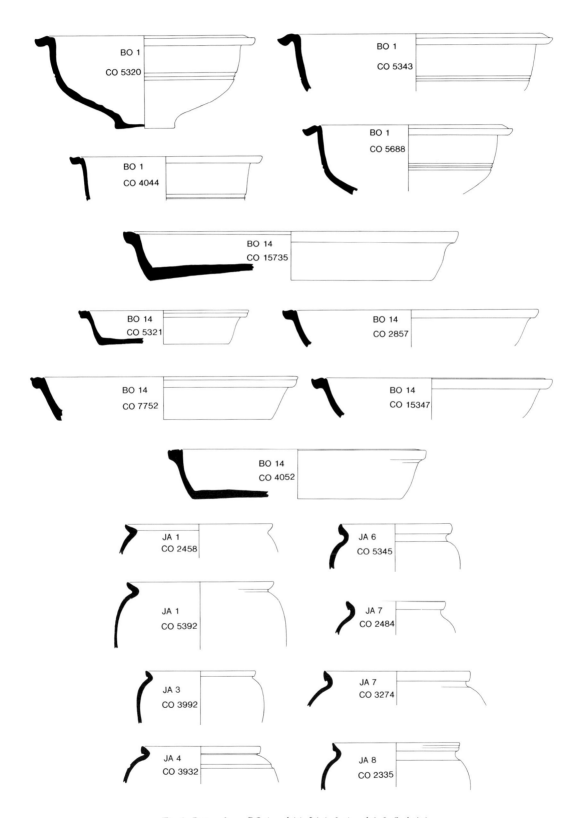

Fig. 3. Pottery forms BO 1 and 14, JA 1, 3, 4 and 6–8. Scale 1:4.

CO 4051 JT60 WEST COMPOUND
CO 4053
CO 4056 GQ59 XI D1
CO 4057 IU60 WEST COMPOUND
CO 4062 IZ59 XI C1
CO 4064 DD59 XI B1
CO 4168 AT59 XI NE (NR RM0)
CO 4222 IZ65 XI SR RM9 NW Phase: 1
CO 4712 IR68 TEMPLE III B6
CO 4800 LX68 TEMPLE III B6
CO 5186 LS60 WEST COMPOUND
CO 5207 CO61 XI E1
CO 5208 EN59 XI B1 ('E/W trench running alongside N side of
    square at depth 3ft 6ins': this should be a partition trench in
    the east range of the Phase I store building. See Bishop & Dore
    fig. 21, component 16.) Phase: 1
CO 5320 BG70 XI E3 Cat 87/130 Phase: 4b *Illustrated*
CO 5343 DC70 XI E0 Cat 87/129 Phase: 4a *Illustrated*
CO 5608 KQ52 TEMPLE I/II Phase: 1b
CO 5688 17013 (same vessel) 'COR 48 DRAWN 26 AH 48' AH48
    AY48 XII B. Published: Richmond & Gillam 1953, no. 26.
    Phase: 2 *Illustrated*
CO 10380 18448 (same vessel) 'From box labelled CORBRIDGE
    1938 40T Upper levels and bag labelled 20N L3' (5688),
    'Corbridge from box labelled Corbridge 1938 40T Upper lev-
    els and bag labelled 20N' (17013)
CO 5690 'CF 48 COR DRAWN 25'. Published: Richmond & Gillam
    1953, no. 25. Phase: 2
CO 5691 'COR C 48 DRAWN 28 27' AH48 XII B. Published:
    Richmond & Gillam 1953, no. 27. Phase: 2
CO 5709 'COR DRAWN 53/46 K 48'. Published: Richmond &
    Gillam 1953, no 46. Phase: 3
CO 6096 AK53 XI
CO 6110 XI *
CO 6158 XC *
CO 7734 YA *
CO 7736 TG *
CO 7741 WS *
CO 7743 XZ *
CO 7745 WS *
CO 7747 XI *
CO 7750 VT *
CO 10373
CO 12242 'XI E C'
CO 15295
CO 15296
CO 15299
CO 15301
CO 15305
CO 15316
CO 15318
CO 15323
CO 15327
CO 15329
CO 15332
CO 15333
CO 15335
CO 15337
CO 15340
CO 15344
CO 15346
CO 15349 'EA 13'
CO 15352

CO 15353
CO 15354
CO 15355
CO 15359
CO 15362
CO 15363
CO 15364
CO 15367
CO 15368
CO 15369
CO 15371
CO 15372
CO 15417
CO 15419
CO 16079 BT59 XI WR RM8
CO 16779 WC47
CO 16784 'N of XII 7/47 LIII'
CO 16870 AY48 XII B
CO 16981 BB48 XII B
CO 16996 HH48
CO 17014 BG48 XII A/B
CO 17018 'Drawn 23' AH48 XII B
CO 17021 AX49 N OF GRANARIES
CO 17095 '3 B 48' 'Drawn'
CO 17265 AR51 N OF GRANARIES F
CO 17345 EW52 XI CENTRE
CO 17346 EW52 XI CENTRE
CO 17586 'BT C 37/50'
CO 17591 'CF C37/50'
CO 17592 'CF C37/50'
CO 18353 DL59 XI B1
CO 18540 KZ58 XI NW
CO 18541 KJ58 XI NW
CO 18672 DT57 XI NE

BO 14
CO 2418 DZ62 XI D4 Cat 87/ 84 Phase: 4a-PF
CO 2419 LF66 XI SR RM7 N Cat 87/124 Phase: 1–4
CO 2421 FL59 XI WR RM8 Cat 87/299 Phase: PF2
CO 2857 NQ68 XII E2 Phase: 4b *Illustrated*
CO 3397 IF71 XI SR RM10 SE ('Pit Depth 82ins': possibly early)
    Phase: 1 ?
CO 4041 HT59 XI D3
CO 4043 JO59 XI C1
CO 4046 AK61 XI C4
CO 4047 KQ59 XI C1 ('Cutting into west face, lowest occupation
    level - with food bones and mussel shell': there seem to have
    been two occupation levels visible in the section.) Phase: 1–2?
CO 4052 4065 5181 5201 (same vessel) DD59 DD59 XI B1 *Illus-
    trated*
CO 4063 GO61 XI B4
CO 5152 AA80
CO 5321 CP61 DP61 DU61 XI E1 Cat 87/ 67 Phase: 4 *Illustrated*
CO 5468 FW62 XI A6 Phase: PF
CO 5693 'COR C 48 DRAWN no 48' C48 XII B. Published: Rich-
    mond & Gillam 1953, no. 48. Phase: 3
CO 5732 GA54 XX 1A. Published: Richmond & Gillam 1955, no.
    1. See also Richmond & Gillam 1955, fig. 3 (which shows the
    actual findspot on section) Phase: 1
CO 7746 WS *
CO 7748 7749 7752 15314 (same vessel) WS * *Illustrated*
CO 7751 VZ *
CO 7753 WS *

CO 12211 SQ *
CO 15298 'XXXIII'
CO 15306
CO 15322
CO 15347 'XXXIII' *Illustrated*
CO 15420
CO 15735 *Illustrated*
CO 15861 IG55 TEMPLE III
CO 15864 IQ55 TEMPLE III
CO 16921 BV48 XII C
CO 16992 AR48 XII
CO 17015 'K 48'
CO 17022 BS49 N OF GRANARIES
CO 17083 'K 48'
CO 17090 DC48 XII
CO 17093 CF48 XII B
CO 17101 CF48 XII B
CO 17565 'BE 37/50'
CO 18496 AZ56 XX A
CO 18899 DZ58 XI NW
CO 18949 HF56 XI ('Broad N-S sleeper trench running from large
 E/W sleeper trench': Possibly from one of the Phase 2 barracks
 in the retentura.) Phase: 2 ?

JA 1

CO 2458 GP59 XI D1 Cat 87/ 41 *Illustrated*
CO 2459 CE59 XI B1 Cat 87/ 22 Phase: 4a
CO 2966 JY58 XI ER N SE ('Very wet dark brown subsoil. Traces
 of burning. Loose cobbles': this should be early). Phase: 1–2 ?
CO 3028 HP58 XI ER N NW
CO 3303 BH63 XI C5 Phase: PF
CO 3984 GA59 XI A1
CO 3988 KS60 WEST COMPOUND
CO 3990 KY59 XI B/C1
CO 3991 KX59 XI B/C1
CO 3995 GQ60 XI C3
CO 3997 DX59 XI A1
CO 3998 JE59 XI C1
CO 3999 LD59 XI C/D1
CO 4002 JH62 XI Z1
CO 4003 FT62 XI B6
CO 4007 KX59 XI B/C1
CO 4008 DV61 XI E1
CO 4009 FE62 XI A62
CO 4010 JV60 XI B3
CO 4090 KY59 XI B/C1
CO 4676 PJ67 TEMPLE III C1
CO 5203 HB60 XI NC NE
CO 5392 GU59 XI A1 Cat 87/ 51 *Illustrated*
CO 5466 CE59 XI B1 Phase: 4a
CO 5708 'COR Site XXXIX DRAWN 53/2 AJ 37/50' AJ37 Pub-
 lished: Richmond & Gillam 1953, no. 2. Phase: 1
CO 5710 17715 (same vessel) 'U' 'AM48 DRAWN 17' AM48 XII
 A Published: Richmond & Gillam 1953, no. 17 (The published
 drawing is not really accurate). Phase: 2
CO 6162 TG *
CO 7718 WS *
CO 7719 WS *
CO 7722 VT *
CO 7723
CO 10397 possible waster
CO 12286 ST * possible waster
CO 14377 AB57 XI NE possible waster

CO 14421 AJ57 XI WR RM3
CO 16003 KD58 XI NR RM0
CO 16124 PK61 XI N
CO 16742 'TI 47' possible waster
CO 16743 'TI 47'
CO 16749 'TI 47'
CO 16778 'CORBRIDGE T I 47'
CO 16976 DC48 XII
CO 16983 CD48 XII A
CO 17000 CY48 W GRANARY
CO 17004 AY48 XII B
CO 17007 CF48 XII B
CO 17011 BE48 XII B
CO 17058 GE50 N OF GRANARIES probable waster
CO 17084 CF48 XII B
CO 17086 DC48 XII
CO 17088 'Drawn 16' CF48 XII B
CO 17089 'X48'
CO 17098 CF48 XII B
CO 17259 GH51 ?
CO 17352 HC52 XI SE
CO 17353 HN52 XI 1G
CO 17582 'CF C37/50'
CO 17793
CO 18445 '= 1911 no 31' WS * possible waster
CO 18580 HU55 XI
CO 19306 IF80
COR 80 IF 381

JA 3

CO 2495 GE59 XI D1 Cat 87/ 43
CO 2497 CP61 XI E1 Cat 87/ 65 Phase: 4
CO 2919 IH68 XII W2
CO 3123 EF65 XI SR RM9 NW
CO 3369 FW71 XX N
CO 3459 FW71 XX N
CO 3627 AD64 XI X6
CO 3797 FB70 XXXIX N 1
CO 3989 LO60 WEST COMPOUND Rudimentary rustication
CO 3992 FB63 XI ER K *Illustrated*
CO 3993 ED63 XI ER K
CO 4004 FC63 XI ER K
CO 4664 OX67 TEMPLE III B2 ('Within wall corner, dark grey soil,
 soot and ash, from a little lower down than OC67 which is *c.*
 67ins down': the 'wall corner' belongs to a building of PF1; the
 depth places the context at the right level to be early; the de-
 scription might suggest something asociated with the first
 rampart in this area, which is thought to belong to phase 2)
 Phase: 1–2? (but see caveat in Bishop & Dore 1989, 88, para.4).
CO 5407 JX64 XLIV C Cat 87/220 Phase: PF
CO 12421
CO 16860 'L 48'
CO 17258 GH51 ?
CO 18588 BC55 XX 2B

JA 4

CO 2976 GY68 XII E1 Low relief rustication ('From within grey
 material containing ochre plaster fragments. From depth of 4ft
 9ins at SW corner.': this could be the destruction at the end of
 phase 1b) Phase: 1 ?
CO 3279 IH66 XI SR RM7 SW ('5ft 9ins': This is certainly deep
 enough to be early) Phase: 1–2 ?
CO 3328 DZ70 XXXIX N 2

CO 3853 IR62 XI Z1
CO 3922 BO70 XI E2 Phase: 4
CO 3931 DL59 XI B1
CO 3932 LB60 XI B2 *Illustrated*
CO 3946 ZJ59 XI D1
CO 3948 DA59 XI A1 Low relief rustication
CO 3952 DV59 XI B1
CO 3971 GK70 XI E3 Phase: 4a ?
CO 3978 DD59 XI B1
CO 4226 DK65 XI SR RM9 NW
CO 4228 DK65 XI SR RM9 NW Low relief rustication
CO 4231 DK65 XI SR RM9 NW
CO 7715 YR *
CO 7717 WS *
CO 8281 SL *
CO 8309 VT *
CO 12212 SQ *
CO 14353 CA73 STREET 1 E
CO 14379 AB57 XI NE
CO 15421
CO 16987 AZ48 XII C
CO 17009 CY48 W GRANARY
CO 18544 JV58 XI NW SW
CO 18603 AU55 XX 2A

JA 6
CO 2485 IX59 XI A/B1 Cat 87/ 58
CO 3811 HL69 TEMPLE III S
CO 3910 BI70 XI E2 Phase: 4
CO 3933 GQ59 XI D1
CO 3979 FG60 XI D2
CO 4651 OC67 TEMPLE III B2 ('Within wall corner, dark grey soil, soot and ash from c 67 ins down': the 'wall corner' belongs to a building of PF1; the depth places the context at the right level to be early; the description might suggest something asociated with the first rampart in this area, which is thought to belong to phase 2) Phase: 1–2 ? (but see caveat in Bishop & Dore 1989, 88, para.4)
CO 4652 OC67 TEMPLE III B2 (see CO 4651 above); Phase: 1–2 ?
CO 5345 DZ59 XI A1 Cat 87/ 27 *Illustrated*
CO 8293 WT *
CO 17251 GH51 ?
CO 17780

JA 7
CO 2483 CU61 XI E1 Cat 87/ 30 Phase: 4a
CO 2484 GE59 XI D1 Cat 87/ 42 *Illustrated*
CO 2484 GE59 XI D1 Cat 87/ 42
CO 3274 DC66 XI SR RM7 NW Phase: PF1 *Illustrated*
CO 3429 FV71 XX N
CO 3433 EN71 XI SR RM10 NW
CO 3642 LA60 WEST COMPOUND
CO 3938 KM59 XI A2 ('Lowest occupation layer (over gravel overlain by sand)': there seem to have been two occupation levels visible in the section) Phase: 1–2 ?
CO 3962 GV62 XI C6
CO 3973 FC61 XI E1
CO 4104 FA68 XII W1 Phase: 2–4
CO 4132 BQ68 XII W3
CO 4649 OO67 TEMPLE III B2 ('Within wall corner grey sandy soil with soot ash and bands of clay from c 72ins down': the 'wall corner' belongs to a building of PF1; the depth places the

context at the right level to be early; the description might suggest something asociated with the first rampart in this area, which is thought to belong to phase 2) Phase: 1–2 ? (but see caveat in Bishop & Dore 1989, 88, para. 4)
CO 5459 LE66 XI SR RM7 N Phase: 1–4
CO 9527 'DS' XI *
CO 16216 'XII II 47'
CO 17646 '37/50 AE'
CO 17887 'C37/39s/II4'

JA 8
CO 2335 EQ66 XI SR RM7 SW ('In mixed clay soil sand material at a depth of 4ft 6ins': this is certainly deep enough to be early). Phase: 1–2 ? *Illustrated*
CO 5711 'COR DRAWN 39 G 48' Published: Richmond & Gillam 1953, no. 39. Phase: 3
CO 8219 US *
CO 8302 SL *
CO 9427
CO 12159 'C '38 40T L6'
CO 12180 'From tray labelled TOPSOIL 19–33–35'
CO 12678 SK *
CO 12814 SK *
CO 12815 SK *
CO 12818 SK *
CO 12876 SK *
CO 14392 AB57 XI NE
CO 15971 CK58 XI ER N SW
CO 17252 GH51 ?
CO 17364 KQ52 TEMPLE I/II Phase: 1–2
CO 17420 TO35
CO 17613 '37/50 AL'
CO 17621 'AE'
CO 18602 CG55 XX 2C

ACKNOWLEDGEMENT

I am grateful to English Heritage for allowing me to publish this material, and to their Curator at Corbridge, Georgina Plowright, for much valuable assistance.

Bibliography
Austen, P.S., 1991 *Bewcastle and Old Penrith, a Roman outpost fort and a frontier vicus, excavations 1977–78* (Kendal)
Birley, E., & Birley, M., 1938 Fourth report on excavations at Chesterholm-Vindolanda, *Archaeol. Aeliana*, **15**, 222–37 (Newcastle)
Bishop, M. C., & Dore, J. N., 1989 *Corbridge, excavations of the Roman fort and town, 1947–80* (London)
Gillam, J. P., 1970 *Types of Roman coarse pottery vessels in northern Britain* (Newcastle)
Hird, L., 1977 *A report on the pottery found in the pre-Hadrianic levels at Vindolanda during the excavations of 1972–1975* (Bardon Mill)
McCarthy, M.R., 1990 *A Roman, Anglian & medieval site at Blackfriars Street Carlisle* (Kendal)
Richmond, I.A., & Gillam, J.P., 1953 Buildings of the first and second centuries north of the Granaries at Corbridge, *Archaeol. Aeliana*, **31**, 205–53 (Newcastle)
_____, & _____, 1955 Some excavations at Corbridge 1952–54, *Archaeol. Aeliana*, **33**, 218–52 (Newcastle)
Taylor, J., 1990 Part three: the pottery, in McCarthy 1990, 197–301
_____, 1991 *The Roman pottery from Castle Street, Carlisle: excavations 1981–2*, Cumberland Westmorland Antiq. Archaeol. Soc. Res. Ser., **5** (Carlisle)
Terry, R.D., & Chilingar, G.V., 1955 Summary of 'Concerning some additional aids in studying sedimentary formations' by M.S. Shvetsov, *Sedimentary Petrology*, **25.23**, 229–34

26   Une enfance de Dionysos:
moule d'applique de la collection Constancias

Colette Bémont

La récente publication du mobilier céramique gallo-romain de la collection Constancias acquis par J. Déchelette en 1899 et 1900 pour le musée de Roanne (Bémont 1994) a révélé la présence d'un moule de médaillon incomplet et apparemment inédit. Faute, peut-être, d'informations suffisantes sur sa provenance Déchelette ne l'a fait figurer ni dans le catalogue des moules et reliefs d'applique de Lezoux, ni parmi les médaillons de la vallée du Rhône. Et aucune des études spécialisées ultérieures auxquelles je me suis référée[1] ne mentionne l'objet ou un positif qui en serait issu.

DESCRIPTION (fig. 1)

Fragment d'un moule circulaire (Inv. Roanne 1614; Catalogue no. 123), collection Constancias.
Diam. total: 7,5 cm; diam. du décor: 6,7 cm
Pâte granuleuse, beige rosé micacée. Manquent sur le côté droit du moule presque la moitié de la bordure et une petite partie du décor.

Le tableau est encadré d'un tore bordé intérieurement d'un listel. La scène figurée[2] comprend trois personnages. A gauche: un homme de profil à droite, assis, apparemment courbé, semble tenir dans sa main droite, posée sur son genou gauche surélevé, les pieds d'un petit personnage nu, debout de face, le bras droit levé et plié. A droite: une femme de trois-quarts dos, le torse nu et enveloppée à partir du bas des hanches d'une draperie nouée sur le ventre, se penche, tend les bras vers le petit personnage et le touche, ou le tient à la hauteur de la hanche gauche. En bas du décor, un objet circulaire et creux, posé en biais sur la tranche, est placé sous le pied gauche de l'homme et lui sert d'appui. Au centre devant les jambes de la femme, un petit quadrupède de profil à gauche, dressé sur ses pattes arrière, prend appui de ses pattes avant sur l'objet circulaire.

Fig. 1. Moule de Roanne: à gauche la face décorée, à droite l'empreinte du décor (clichés Musée des Antiquités Nationales). Échelle 1:1.

Entre la tête de l'animal et le bras gauche de la femme, sur le fond du médaillon, un graffite avant cuisson en capitales a été lu NE.[3]

Le climat de la scène est suggéré, au premier abord, par la femme et l'animal. Le costume de la première, réduit à une draperie et à une parure (un bracelet au bras gauche)[4] fait d'elle avec la plus grande vraisemblance une divinité, Venus ou nymphe. Le corps du quadrupède est pansu et râblé, le cou, vigoureusement arqué, et l'absence de la queue, cachée par les jambes de la femme, n'aide pas l'identification. La tête – petite, ronde, aux courtes oreilles couchées – et l'attitude générale de l'animal, malgré l'allure anormalement massive et trapue du corps, incitent cependant à reconnaître un félin. De petite taille, si l'on admet quelque proportion ou hiérarchie entre les éléments de la scène: ce pourrait être une panthère. Si cette hypothèse est étayée par d'autres éléments, nous reconnaîtrons peut-être là un épisode légendaire ou une représentation cultuelle se rapportant à Dionysos, dieu traditionnellement associé à ce fauve.

L'interprétation tend à se confirmer quand on observe les deux autres personnages: moins faciles à identifier au premier coup d'oeil, ils paraissent à l'examen compatibles avec nos suppositions. L'homme assis se trouve privé par la cassure du moule de la totalité du tronc et de l'arrière de la tête. On distingue néanmoins les plis d'une étoffe glissant d'une cuisse sur l'autre – qui suggèrent une courte tunique, ou un pan de tissu – et le large front chauve et la barbe, qui font du personnage un vieillard.[5] Ces caractères, dans la version romaine du cortège de Dionysos, sont propres au vieux Silène.[6] La taille du petit personnage est susceptible de diverses justifications;[7] l'explication qui se présente la première à l'esprit est pourtant qu'il s'agit d'un enfant. Et, malgré un traitement sommaire du relief, le modelé assez mou et peu athlétique du corps tend à accréditer une telle lecture. Ce pourrait être le jeune Dionysos, qui selon la tradition fut pendant un temps entouré des soins d'un groupe de nymphes et du vieux Silène.

Des comparaisons avec des panneaux sculptés dionysiaques donnent, malgré des différences, la clé de cette composition. Quatre reliefs appartenant à des sarcophages d'enfants, datés entre la fin du règne de Trajan et le milieu du IIe s. (Turcan 1966, pls. 3 a, 8 b, 17 a; Simon 1962)[8] et dispersés entre différents musées,[9] illustrent des épisodes de l'enfance de Dionysos, durant le séjour du jeune dieu dans la contrée mythique de Nysa: le bain, l'allaitement par des nymphes nourrices et surtout l'habillage lié à sa consécration comme *mystès* (fig. 2). Les exemples de cette cérémonie analysés très soigneusement dans l'ouvrage de R. Turcan présentent d'incontestables ressemblances avec le médaillon: la composition générale dont l'enfant debout, de face, occupe le centre, entre des personnages tournés vers lui; l'attitude de l'homme assis à gauche, penché vers l'avant et, selon les cas, touchant ou tenant solidement les pieds de l'enfant;[10] le choix des participants: silènes ou satyres et nymphes. En outre le vêtement liturgique du petit Dionysos des sarcophages: la nébride nouée sur l'épaule droite, permet d'interpréter la bande épaisse et fruste qui traverse obliquement le torse de l'enfant du médaillon.

La structure du décor sur céramique diffère pourtant des exemples lapidaires. La scène est simplifiée: sur un fond vide, à la réserve d'un léger relief (un drapé ?) derrière l'épaule et la tête de Silène, elle ne comporte dans son état actuel que deux assistants, une nymphe et Silène, au lieu de trois[11] ou quatre personnages. De plus une substitution est opérée entre satyre et Silène: ce dernier, sur le médaillon, occupe la place et s'acquitte de la fonction du satyre des quatre sarcophages.[12] Ce raccourci ne résulte pas d'une simple manipulation plastique mais présente une certaine logique: sur les sarcophages l'enfant pose la main droite sur la tête du satyre penché, tandis que Silène, assis dans la partie droite du tableau – c'est à dire à la gauche du petit dieu – remet à ce dernier une branche épaisse, lisse et terminée par une touffe de rameaux feuillus, qu'il entoure parfois en même temps d'une bandelette (sarcophages de Rome et Princeton). Or le Dionysos du médaillon, représenté dans l'attitude classique que prêtent souvent reliefs et rondes bosses au dieu juvénile,[13] tient déjà dans son poing droit levé, le bras étant plié à angle droit, un objet peu discernable, mais terminé par une sorte de pomme et qu'on ne peut guère interpréter que comme un thyrse, bien que la hampe ait été estompée[14] (probablement lors du moulage du médaillon-prototype). Notons aussi que le socle rocheux ou l'autel, sur lequel il se dresse d'ordinaire est escamoté par le genou de Silène. Il semble donc que ce schéma décoratif économique corresponde à un moment de la cérémonie

Fig. 2. Le sarcophage de Munich (d'après Matz 1968–75, 3, Beilage 89)

légèrement différent de celui qu'ont fixé certains sculpteurs, voire à une autre tradition quant au rôle et à l'attitude de chaque personnage.

Le geste de la nymphe, inédit sur les sarcophages, n'est pas très explicite; peut-être mêt-elle la dernière main à l'ordonnance du costume, ou s'apprête-t-elle à ajuster la *mitrè* sur la tête du dieu (rôle dévolu à une femme placée à gauche sur les sarcophages de Munich et du musée Capitolin). En tout cas la tête du petit personnage mesure quelques millimètres et l'éclat qui a sauté dans le moule à la hauteur de l'épaule gauche de l'enfant ne permet de juger ni de l'état de sa coiffure ni, à l'arrière plan, du mouvement de la main droite que la nymphe lève à ce niveau. Autres particularités: la présence de la panthère et celle de l'objet circulaire sur lequel elle s'appuie. L'animal ne joue pas apparemment un rôle fonctionnel et contribue plutôt, du fait son association fréquente et exclusive avec le dieu ou son cortège, à identifier la scène. L'objet circulaire, de taille très modeste et réduit à une bordure épaisse ou à un étroit morceau de paroi, ne saurait guère être un bouclier.[15] Doit-on y reconnaître un vase renversé – bassin de la toilette de l'enfant ou vase à vin? La première de ces deux hypothèses me paraît actuellement la plus vraisemblable: l'absence d'anses et la simplicité de la forme conviennent peu à un canthare et semblent exclure la référence allusive aux représentations de l'animal en train de laper le vin s'écoulant du vase renversé. En revanche un large bassin hémisphérique est destiné à l'eau du bain dans les scènes associées à l'habillage sur les sarcophages du musée Capitolin et de Munich.[16]

Les petites variations observées sur les sarcophages prouvent le caractère légèrement fluctuant du rendu de cette scène, mais témoignent d'une remarquable constance dans son organisation globale. Le décor du médaillon en revanche diffère nettement de ce carton. Justifié sans doute par la taille du champ disponible,[17] le raccourci implique un choix original des personnages, une mise en scène particulière et l'adaptation au moins de l'attitude de la nymphe à la courbure du cadre, c'est à dire un carton distinct de celui des panneaux sculptés. Une recherche bibliographique ne m'a pas permis jusqu'à présent de trouver la reproduction de ce nouveau modèle sur d'autres supports – mosaïques, peintures, camées, céramiques arrétines, vases de bronze ou d'argent, médaillons sur situles de plomb.[18] Le seul autre objet signalé comme portant un exemple de la même scène: le camée de Laurent de Médicis, ne conserve que deux officiants, mais il s'agit du satyre et de Silène, ils sont assis et occupent leurs places habituelles. De toutes façons ce bijou, tenu maintenant pour une copie réalisée au XVe s. à Florence d'après un relief de sarcophage (Matz 1968–75, **3**, 219), ne saurait donner lieu à aucun rapprochement.

Un fait paraît en tout cas évident: la réduction du nombre des personnages confère à chacun des assistants une plus grande importance. La femme en particulier, en sortant de l'arrière plan, semble du même coup échapper au rôle de comparse, sinon de figurante, qui était dévolu aux nymphes des sarcophages. S'agit-il encore d'une de ces nourrices anonymes ou avons-nous affaire à une autre éducatrice? On pense évidemment à celle qui inventa les rites mystiques et,

la première, revêtit l'enfant de l'habit dionysiaque. Nonnos, au Ve s., dans les *Dionysiaques* en fait une sorte d'allégorie en la nommant Mystis. Quel qu'ait pu être ailleurs ou auparavant le nom qui la désigne,[19] cette figure a été identifiée sur des monuments du Ier s.:[20] un panneau de la Farnésine et une plaque Campana, comme l'associée privilégiée de Silène lors de la consécration d'un jeune initié devant lequel on découvre le van. R. Turcan, qui a proposé de la reconnaître également dans la vieille femme représentée entre autres sur le sarcophage de Munich au second plan, derrière le jeune Bacchus chevauchant un bouc,[21] ainsi que dans d'autres scènes du cycle bacchique, insiste sur le rôle spécifique de la vieille nourrice ou prêtresse. Pour tentante qu'elle soit, notre hypothèse se heurte donc à une objection: si cette nourrice mystagogue se présente obligatoirement sous les traits d'une femme *agée*, il est difficile de l'identifier avec la nymphe du médaillon. Il resterait toutefois à démontrer le caractère contraignant de cette convention, quelle que soit la date ou l'origine des représentations du thiase ou de la légende bacchique. La femme de la Farnésine et celle de la plaque Campana ne présentent pas de signes particulièrement évidents de décrépitude. Mais on peut admettre qu'il s'agit là d'une scène d'initiation type, plus que d'un épisode anecdotique et légendaire: on comprendra dans ces conditions la banalisation ou l'idéalisation du personnage féminin. En revanche, et sous réserve d'inventaire, il existe au moins un exemple contemporain de notre moule, ou antérieur à celui-ci, où le petit dieu est clairement mis en cause dans une scène des rites d'initiation. Sur la mosaïque d'El-Jem c'est une jeune femme, tenant une branche effeuillée et le van mystique qui, en compagnie de Silène juché sur son âne, suit le jeune Dionysos Mystes chevauchant un lion. Et l'on s'accorde actuellement pour reconnaître dans cette mystagogue Mystis,[22] ou du moins son équivalent dans la seconde moitié du IIe s. Admettre, comme c'est le cas, que l'identité de la fonction implique celle du personnage, oblige à supposer, quelles que soient les causes (diversité des traditions mythologiques, provincialisme, affaiblissement de l'intérêt pour l'aspect anecdotique du récit...), des variations dans l'iconographie de l'initiatrice du dieu. Et l'identification de la femme du médaillon retrouve dès lors une certaine vraisemblance.

Le graffite ne se prête encore à aucune interprétation satisfaisante. La lecture la plus simple est NE, mais le ductus un peu irrégulier de la première lettre, qui présente une première haste oblique permet d'hésiter entre N, AN en ligature et AI.[23] La barre supérieure de l'E, déborde légèrement à gauche et n'exclut pas une ligature TE. Mais aucune des hypothèses fondées sur ces lectures[24] ne semble évoquer le nom, ou le début du nom, de l'un ou l'autre des acteurs, inscrit sur le médaillon comme il advient assez fréquemment.[25] S'agit-il de la marque du fabricant? Les signatures connues et illustrées sur des échantillons de la vallée du Rhône[26] se rencontrent en général à la périphérie du champ décoré, non au centre. Dernière hypothèse à laquelle je me tiendrai provisoirement: l'inscription primitive – nom propre ou fragment de texte? – est incomplètement conservée, et une partie indéterminée de celle-ci se trouvait dans la section disparue du moule.

Appartenant à une collection constituée à Lezoux, ce petit objet pose un dernier problème: celui de son origine. En effet les reliefs actuellement attribués aux ateliers ledosiens sont le plus souvent dépourvus de cadre et leur encombrement se limite à la surface irrégulière occupée par les personnages ou éléments divers qui les composent. Certaines séries affectent bien une forme géométrique, mais elles sont quadrangulaires. En revanche les médaillons de la vallée du Rhône comportent tous, comme le nôtre, un encadrement circulaire: en général un tore (par exemple les médaillons signés Felix), ou une couronne de feuillage. Le moule de Roanne a-t-il été produit à Lezoux et représente-t-il une rareté dans la tradition locale des décors appliqués ? Est-il venu de l'extérieur ? Il pourrait témoigner alors de la diversité des sources d'approvisionnement de Constancias. Mais quel atelier s'intéressant à la technique de l'applique, sinon Lezoux, fut assez connu et exploré avant 1842 pour fournir dès cette époque des outils de potiers?[27] Il pourrait, plutôt, contribuer à prouver des échanges au IIe ou au IIIe s. entre les artisans de Lezoux et ceux d'autres centres de production.

Compte tenu de son caractère insolite et des pratiques contestables de certains collectionneurs de XIXe s.[28] le moule a fait l'objet au Laboratoire de recherche des musées de France d'études physico-chimiques. Les mesures de thermo-luminescence confirment l'authenticité de l'objet, donc l'intérêt iconographique de cette nouvelle version de la scène d'"investiture". Par ailleurs cette méthode permet également de proposer pour la période de cuisson une fourchette assez large (1650 ans + - 154 ans, c'est à dire entre 191 et 499 ap. J.-C.), mais compatible avec la datation qu'on attribuait stylistiquement à la production de l'ensemble des vases à médaillons d'applique dits de la vallée du Rhône (IIe s. – cours du IIIe) et qu' A. Desbat a confirmée et précisée sur des bases archéologiques: du début du IIe au IVe s. avec une production maximale à la fin du IIe et au début du IIIe s.[29] Par ailleurs les ressemblances observées entre la composition de la pâte et celle de l'argile de quelques moules de vases provenant de Lezoux et présumés sensiblement contemporains ne sont pas actuellement suffisantes pour permettre de conclure à une origine commune. Seules des comparaisons avec d'autres échantillons, en particulier des médaillons de la vallée du Rhône, pourront permettre de faire progresser l'enquête.

Remerciements

Je remercie G. Becquart, conservateur du musée J. Déchelette, qui a bien voulu me confier cet objet, ainsi que G. Querré et A. Bouquillon, qui se sont chargés, au LRMF, des mesures de thermoluminscence et de l'étude de la pâte du moule.

Notes

1. Consulter en particulier le corpus d'A. Audin et P. Wuilleumier (Wuilleumier & Audin 1952), le recensement dû à A. Desbat (Desbat 1980–81) et sa bibliographie. Depuis 1980 voir A. Desbat *et al.*, Vases à médaillons d'appliques inédits de Lyon et de Martigues (Bouches-du-Rhône), *Revue Archéologique de Narbonnaise*, **16**, 1983, 395–403; L. Rivet, Anciens et nouveaux médaillons d'applique d'Istres et de Marseille, *Société Française d'Étude de la Céramique Antique en Gaule, Actes du Congrès d'Orange*, 1988, 75–80; A. Desbat, L'atelier de médaillons d'applique de Saint-Péray, *Archéologia*, **255**, mars 1990, 56–9.

2. La description est faite selon l'usage d'après l'épreuve en relief, inversée par rapport au décor imprimé en creux dans le moule.

3. Cf. la p. 13 de l'inventaire manuscrit conservé au musée de Roanne.

4. Malgré le reflet paraissant sur la photographie, la coiffure ne comporte aucun ornement. La chevelure serrée en rouleau autour du visage et nouée en chignon bas sur la nuque ressemble malgré la raideur de l'exécution à celle des nymphes du sarcophage de Munich. Et la draperie présente une incontestable analogie avec le vêtement des nourrices baignant le petit Dionysos sur les sarcophages de Munich et du musée Capitolin.

5. La vigueur du bras et des jambes ne prouve que le peu de réalisme du style.

6. Outre la ressemblance des traits physiques on constate qu'un morceau d'étoffe enveloppe souvent les cuisses de Silène assis (Turcan 1966, pls. 3a, 8b, 17a).

7. Ce pourrait être la figuration d'un être humain par rapport à celles de dieux ou de certains personnages mythologiques (cf. la création de l'homme par Prométhée, Renach 1912, **1**, 105, nos. 322 et 433), ou encore la représentation d'une statue de culte.

8. = Matz 1968–75, 30, 200, 201, 202; Gaspari 1986, Dionysos/Bacchus nos. 163–166.

9. Vienne (Kunsthistorisches Museum), Rome (Capitole), Munich et Princeton.

10. Dans certains des cas (Princeton et musée du Capitole) il semble le chausser de bottines à revers dentés (*embades*) ou vérifier l'ajustement des chaussures (Turcan 1966, 413, 414).
    Cette interprétation est reprise dans les notices du *Lexicon Iconographicum Mythologiae Classicae*.

11. Le fragment de Vienne, mutilé derrière Silène, ne comporte qu'une femme. Mais la remarquable similitude des quatre reliefs incite à supposer que sa composition initiale comprenait également une assistante à droite.

12. La confusion des rôles exclut qu'il puisse s'agir d'une simple inversion des places liée à la technique du moulage.

13. Cette attitude correspond par exemple au type AI.2A du classement des bronzes figurés (Manfrini-Aragno 1987).

14. Un examen à la loupe permet de distinguer sous le bras à l'aplomb de la main un petit trait vertical.

15. Outre que l'objet serait anormalement petit, on voit mal comment justifier une allusion aux Corybantes dont l'intervention se situe selon la tradition après la première éducation de l'enfant chez les nymphes et dans la demeure d'Athamas.

16. Le même récipient, associé au bain de l'enfant, se retrouve sur d'autres sarcophages, sans la scène d'habillage (cf., par exemple, Matz 1968–75, **3**, Beilage 90, à Baltimore).

17. Il ne faut pas cependant oublier que certains médaillons, même de taille assez modeste, étaient encombrés d'une foule de personnages.

18. Je remercie Mmes A. Barbet, M. Blanchard, H. Guiraud et S. Tassinari et M. F. Baratte de l'aide qu'ils m'ont apportée durant cette enquête.

19. Voir, par exemple, dans les Hymnes orphiques (Diehl, XLVIII, 4) la nourrice Hipta à laquelle le van mystique est assigné comme attribut et qui apparaît comme l'initiatrice par excellence du jeune Dionysos.

20. Pour les commentaires de ces reliefs voir Turcan 1966, 383, nos. 6 et 7.

21. Turcan 1966, 408 et 409.

22. Cf. par exemple le commentaire de G. Chrétien dans l'introduction à l'Edition Budé des livres IX et X des *Dionysiaques* (Paris, 1985, 21).

23. Cet A présumé ne présente à l'examen ni barre ni trait oblique ou vertical et on ne peut exclure que le petit point apparent sur les photos soit un simple défaut dans une pâte assez granuleuse.

24. NE, AIE, AITE, ANE, ANTE....

25. La référence à une épithète de Bacchus comme *Antheus*, à supposer qu'elle se justifie dans ce contexte, impliquerait qu'on apporte une correction à l'orthographe d'un mot dont la lecture ANTE est déjà très conjecturale. S'il s'agit du nom de la femme, l'absence d'autres références ne permet pas de le reconnaître.

26. Ont été conservés selon les cas tantôt le nom plus ou moins mutilé du créateur du modèle, tantôt la formule complète 'cera + le nom (au génitif)'. Voir Desbat 1980–81, 169 et 170; Desbat *et al.* (*op. cit.*, note 1).

27. La date de la mort de V. Constancias (1848) représente le terme possible de sa quête, que la tradition fait d'ordinaire débuter vers 1820 et durer jusqu'en 1842. Mais le site de Lezoux fit l'objet au moins de ramassages, sinon de fouilles sauvages, à partir de 1773/1780.

28. Voir en dernier lieu Bémont 1993, 87–98.

29. Desbat 1980–81, 49–57, 175–182.

Bibliographie

Audin, A., & Vertet, H., 1972 Médaillons d'applique à sujets religieux des vallées du Rhône et de l'Allier, *Gallia*, **30**, 235–58

Bémont, C., 1993 Les poinçons-matrices des ateliers du Centre: état des recensements, *Antiquités Nationales*, **25**, 87–98

————, 1994 *La collection Constancias, céramiques gallo-romaines de Lezoux au musée de Roanne* (Roanne)

Desbat, A., 1980–81 *Les médaillons d'applique des fouilles récentes de Lyon,* Figlina, **5–6**

Gaspari, C., 1986 Dionysos/Bacchus, *Lexicon Iconographicum Mythologiae Classicae*, **3.1**, 540–66

Manfrini-Aragno, I., 1987 *Bacchus dans les bronzes hellénistiques et romains. Les artisans et leur répertoire*, Cahiers d'Archéologie romande, **34** (Lausanne)

Matz, F., 1968–75 *Die Dionysischen Sarkophage*, **1–4** (Berlin)

Reinach, S., 1912 *Répertoire de reliefs grecs et romains*, **1–3** (Paris)

Simon, E., 1962 Dionysischer Sarkophag in Princeton, *Mitteilungen des Deutschen Archäologischen Instituts, Römische Abteilung*, **69**, 136–58

Turcan, R., 1966 *Les sarcophages romains à représentations dionysiaques, essai de chronologie et d'histoire religieuse*, Bibliothèque des Écoles Françaises d'Athènes et de Rome, **210** (Paris)

Wuilleumier, P., & Audin, A., 1952 *Les médaillons d'applique gallo-romains de la vallée du Rhône* (Paris)

27 From Katendrecht back to Nijmegen: a group of pottery moulds and relief-tablets from Ulpia Noviomagus

J. K. Haalebos and L. Swinkels

In 1961 a remarkable group of finds was obtained by the Rijksmuseum van Oudheden at Leiden and published in the next year by its conservator, W.C. Braat.[1] It consisted of a so-called Hemmoorer bucket of a yellow copper alloy and a series of pottery moulds and relief-tablets (figs. 2–3, nos.1–4). The findspot was more than remarkable: according to the antique dealer, from whom the objects had been purchased, the whole collection had been brought up by a sand-dredger in the neighbourhood of Katendrecht near Rotterdam. Braat rightly expressed his doubts of the accuracy of this indication: 'Man weiss jedoch nie wie viel man auf solche Angaben eines Antikenhändlers vertrauen kann. Auch werden die Händler selbst oft von den Baggerleuten irre geführt.' In his view, in any case, four of the six objects offered to him were of exceptional interest on their own: two tablets with representations of an animal frieze and of the goddess Minerva, and two moulds, one of which illustrated the history of Kleobis and Biton (Herodotus I, 31). More usual were two vessels which he considered to be candlesticks or lamps.[2]

In 1977 a study was made of the legionary pottery at Nijmegen, the so called (Nijmegen-)Holdeurn Ware, and it was pointed out that this military pottery had not only been produced in the kilns of De Holdeurn near to Berg en Dal (municipality of Groesbeek), 5km to the east of Nijmegen, but probably also on the Hunerberg next to the fortress of Legio X Gemina at Nijmegen.[3] Pottery production in the Flavian *canabae* of Legio X Gemina has been proved in recent years by the find of two kiln sites.[4] Before these discoveries one of the more important indications of Roman pottery activities in the neighbourhood of the fortress was an old find in the collections of the Provinciaal Museum G.M. Kam at Nijmegen, a white tablet (fig. 1) which may perhaps be regarded as a mould for pottery decoration and which had been described as follows: 'It was found in the '20s on the south side of the Sterreschansweg, probably to the W of the houses nos 30 and 32. The negative design consists of two friezes. On the lower half is a hunting scene with a running dog and a tiger addorsed; a tree stands between the animals and at both ends of the scene. Daniëls' remark that the figures on it strongly recall those on terra sigillata must apply to this sec-

Fig. 1. Nijmegen-Hunerberg. White pipe-clay tablet for pottery decoration, found in the canabae *of Legio X Gemina. Scale 2:3. (Photo P. Bersch)*

tion, though there are no exact parallels. The upper half is of a totally different character. The motifs are not at all like those on terra sigillata, but seem rather to be inspired by monumental sculpture. The frieze is formed by a heap of weapons and other militaria such as cuirasses, oval and hexagonal shields, *peltae*, greaves, spears, bows and a standard with boars. The whole thing is strongly reminiscent of reliefs like those on the triumphal arch in Orange, for example. As unusual as the design is the shape of the tablet. Though it has survived pretty well complete, there are no finished edges. The whole thing looks as though a ball of clay was flattened with a paddle and the sides were left as they were. So, in places the tablet failed to contain the whole scheme of decoration, and for example only half a cuirass appears on the right hand side of the upper frieze. It seems as though the mould was made by somewhat arbitrarily pressing clay against an existing object. The resulting design – in surprisingly high relief – was certainly not complete in itself and required neatening up before it could have been applied to a vessel or to a stucco wall.'[5]

Apparent parallels to this odd tablet were difficult to find. The closest to it was the relief with the animals 'from Katendrecht' (fig. 2, no.1), but because of the suspect find spot it was not taken into consideration. Connections between Nijmegen and the area of Katendrecht, in Roman times far outside the civilised world, were not clear.

In 1994 the man who had actually found the ceramic objects 'from Katendrecht' reported to the Provinciaal Museum G.M. Kam with the story of the discovery and with other finds which he had kept in his possession all these years. He also produced an old photograph that showed pieces from his collection and the relief-tablets purchased by the Rijksmuseum at Leiden. This confirmed his account, that all the

objects belonged together. They had been found during building activities on the south side of the Weurtseweg in the western part of the city of Nijmegen in 1959 in a pit measuring 80 × 80 × 40 cm. The findspot is within the territory of the Roman town of Ulpia Noviomagus. The whole collection comprises 25 pieces: two relief-tablets, five moulds, sixteen pottery vessels or sherds and two strange objects in the form of flat mushrooms in coarse brick-like pottery, probably rubbing stones or pounders.[6] All the objects could have been deposited at the same time. The pottery suggests a date for the deposit in the second half of the 2nd century.[7]

Since 1961 the Rijksmuseum van Oudheden possesses two moulds and two tablets from this collection (figs. 2 and 3, nos. 1–4):[8]

1. The rectangular relief-strip (13.5 × 3.3 × 1.2 cm) of white clay, mentioned above, with an animal frieze, consisting of two lions attacking an ass. The left-hand side is broken away. The tablet has been fired at a fairly high temperature and its unusually high and sharp relief shows no sign of wear. In the long sides grooves are to be seen, which must have been caused by the cutting of the tablet with a knife or some other implement. The preserved right-hand side is slightly concave. The back is uneven, but an attempt has been made to smooth the surface. In style the animals represented resemble those of the Nijmegen tablet (fig. 1) and so find their inspiration in the terra sigillata of South or Central Gaul.

2. Rectangular plaque (13.9 × 6.5 × 1 cm) of the same material as no. 1 with the representation of a standing Minerva with spear and shield. More clearly than on the preceding piece there are traces to been seen of an orange-brown clay on the edges of the figure. The edges of the tablet have been made

Fig. 2. Nijmegen-West. Pottery tablets and a mould of white clay, found in the town of Ulpia Noviomagus, south of the modern Weurtseweg. Scale 1:2. (Photo R. Gras)

in the same way as those of the animal frieze. The clay used in moulding this relief must have been relatively dry, to judge from the cracks in the uplifted right arm of the goddess.

3. Mould with the negative shape of an egg. The block (8.7 × 7 × 4.5 cm) is markedly thick and heavy. The concavity of the egg is no deeper than 2.3 cm. The mould has been made of a white clay, which is however not as bright as that used for the two reliefs. On the sides of the block marks have been incised, which suggest the possibility that the form is part of a bipartite mould. The bottom is more or less straight, but has not received a final smoothing.

4. Mould for a medallion (8.5 × 6.8 cm), made of a light grey-brown clay and formed by pressing a lump of clay against an exsisting medallion. In the forming of the mould the clay has bulged out over the rim of the positive roundel. So apparently the model was not part of a (metal) vessel, neither was it fixed on another support. The surface of the image is curved, more than one would expect for the wall of a normal pot. The relief taken from this mould could therefore easily be applied to the wall of a jar or jug. The back has been shaped and in places smoothed by the fingers of the craftsman. At the bottom right some faint scratches[9] are to be noticed, which Braat has read as MA and interpreted as the initials of the maker.

As has already been established by H. Brunsting, the medallion depicts the story of Kleobis and Biton. Several lines of text have been added to the scene. Braat proposed the

reading NATIS [FV]IT DIGNA in the third line.[10] Both scene and text are discussed more fully below under no. 5.

Three more moulds have now been obtained by the Provinciaal Museum Kam (fig. 3, nos. 5–7):[11]

5. A round mould with the same scene as no. 4, but slightly different in form and dimensions (8.2 × 7.1 cm). As with no. 4 the back is rounded and shows traces of finishing. No. 5 is thicker and somewhat more curved. This mould shows traces of burning (see also no. 7).

The story of Kleobis and Biton is told by Herodotus (I, 31), who relates how the priestess of the goddess Hera at Argos, on the occasion of a religious festival, had to be driven to the sanctuary in the countryside in a carriage drawn by oxen. When the animals did not arrive in time, her sons Kleobis and Biton took their place under the yoke. On arrival at the sanctuary, she prayed to Hera and asked the goddess to bestow on her sons what is the best for man. In fulfilment of this prayer they quietly passed away in their sleep, having laid themselves down in the sanctuary after the festival had ended.

The Nijmegen medallions show the priestess, named Kydippe in later sources,[12] standing before the temple of Hera. In her left hand she holds a torch and her right hand is raised upwards in prayer. The temple has a prostyle portico of only two columns and stands on a high podium accessible by a flight of four steps. A tall acroterium above the pediment probably represents the statue of a god or goddess. In front of the temple an altar has been erected, on top of which a fire

Fig. 3. Nijmegen-West. Pottery moulds of grey-brown clay, found in the town of Ulpia Noviomagus. Scale 1:2. (Photo R. Gras).

is burning. Kleobis and Biton are lying naked in the fore-ground, one at full length, the other sunk down sideways on his knees. To the right a woman turns away, apparently over-come by grief. Thus the medallions seem to depict three successive stages in the story: the prayer by Kydippe, the boys asleep in the sanctuary and the discovery of their unexpected death.

Representations of Kleobis and Biton in ancient art are rare.[13] In Greek literature sculptures are mentioned in Delphi,[14] Argos[15] and Cyzicus on the coast of Asia Minor.[16] Apart from the two famous statues at Delphi,[17] the representations still extant are of Roman date. An early imperial altar in Rome, two Augustan glass paste intaglios in Berlin and two bronze coins of Plautilla and Julia Domna minted in Argos show the boys pulling the carriage, on which their mother is standing.[18] A paste intaglio from the Titelberg in Luxemburg has the same motif.[19] Finally, the scene appears on a relief from Rome and now in Venice (fig. 4), the interpretation of which has been contested for a long time.[20] However, K. Fittschen has con-vincingly argued that it most probably served to close the grave of two children: by means of the scenes on the relief their untimely death was equalled to the fate of Kleobis and Biton.[21] On account of its style the relief is dated to the years AD 160–170. Apart from the carriage with Kydippe being pulled by her sons the relief also shows the events in the sanctuary of Hera and the apotheosis of the boys. In the central scene the mother, holding two torches, stands in front of the temple, while Kleobis and Biton are lying asleep at her feet.[22]

Fig. 4. Rome. Central part of a relief with the representation of Kydippe standing before the temple of Hera (now in Museo Archeologico in Venice). (Photo Deutsches Archäologisches Institut Rome neg. no. 68.5093).

The Nijmegen medallions present the only parallel to this scene and depict the same moments of the story. Because of its specific function, the boys in the Venice relief have very youthful looks. In accordance with tradition, in the medalli-ons they are represented as strong and muscular young men. Two pairs of tiny figures visible on the sides of the central altar may finally refer to the protagonists of the story.

Partly above and partly in front of Kydippe seven lines of text have been added to the scene. Doubt attends every let-ter, and even the second line, read by Braat as 'NATIS FVIT DIGNA', [23] seems to be far from certain.

6. A more or less conical mould for the head of a dog or a wolf (3.9 × 3.8–5.5cm). In the rim the pointed ears of the animal are to be discerned. The inside shows some clear fissu-res, which have probably been caused by pressing too-dry clay with too much force on the positive from which the mould has been taken. A remarkable difference from the first two moulds exists in the finishing of the outside of the form. This was not smoothed by fingers but cut with a knife, as was the flat base.

7. A smaller mould 2.2cm high, of similar form to no. 6, for a bearded head with a remarkable rounded forehead. The oval upper surface measures 4.0 × 3.5cm, the base 3.3 × 2.8cm. There are some black traces of burning, which are probably due to the modern use of the mould by the finder for casting lead.

Although no pottery wasters were recorded with the find, the whole group may be considered as the property of a pot-ter. The animal frieze and the plaque mould of Daniëls from the Hunerberg can be parallelled in pottery.[24] In a pottery bowl (probably of the type Stuart 210) found with the moulds and the other objects, remains of a strange (for the Netherlands) orange-brown clay have been preserved.[24a] Traces of the same clay seem to be present on the Minerva tablet and may indi-cate the possibility that the relief was used in making new moulds. The white fabric suggests the possibility that the reliefs and the mould no. 3 were imported from Cologne, where such a clay, unknown in the Netherlands, was easily obtained. However there is some evidence that white pipe-clay was imported to Nijmegen and used by the potters on the Hunerberg.[25]

The round moulds with the story of Kleobis and Biton recall the terra sigillata with applied medallions from the Rhône area. The Provinciaal Museum Kam has two exam-ples of this pottery, an indented beaker[26] and a jug with three handles.[27] The decoration on these vessels consists of a Mer-cury, combating gladiators, a *quadriga*, a dog and a deer. His-torical or mythological scenes, as on the Nijmegen moulds, are well known from the terra sigillata medallions, which display the same habit of putting long, sometimes metrical texts in the decoration.[28] There is no reason to suppose the production of terra sigillata at Nijmegen. Applied moulded decoration however is not restricted to terra sigillata but can be found on Central Gaulish colour-coated ware, as is dem-onstrated by a beaker from the *canabae* of Legio X Gemina at

Fig. 5. Paris, rue de l'Abbé de l'Epée. Fragment of a stucco relief from a wallpainting. After Eristov &Marquis 1991, 259, fig. 8.

Nijmegen,[29] on glazed pottery from the same area,[30] on fine white ware from Cologne (fig. 7)[31] and on hard grey ware in Trier, where a fragment of a mould for a medallion is also known.[32] Hand-modelled figures (including Mercury) have been found on the walls of vessels in the Nijmegen legionary ware (Nijmegen-Holdeurn Ware). So it is not surprising to find indications of the production of pottery reliefs at Nijmegen and one can imagine a local potter copying his designs from samian vessels from the Rhône and importing moulds from Cologne, unless he was able to make them himself with imported clay.

On the other hand there remains the possibility that the Nijmegen finds are the remains of the workshop of a wall-painter and stucco-worker, as has been considered for the mould-tablet from the *canabae* (fig. 1). This possibility is supported by a recent find of a fragment of a stucco-relief with a scroll and animals (fig. 5)[33] and by the large number of small pots – called amphora stoppers or candle sticks – which would be useful on the table of a painter, rather than in the hands of a potter.

Whatever the purpose of the moulds of the medallion of Kleobis and Biton will have been, their origin is clear. A frag-

ment of a medallion with the same representation has been found at Lyon (fig. 6).[34] It shows Kydippe before the altar and the left-hand one of her sons at her feet. The boy on the Lyon medallion is somewhat larger than in the Nijmegen mould, 34mm against 31mm. So we can safely suppose that the Nijmegen roundel has been made by *surmoulage* of a medallion imported from the Rhône area.

The popularity of these vessels can also be demonstrated by one of the finds mentioned above, the white plaque from Cologne. The decoration on this round plaque (fig. 7), with a diameter of 12.5cm, has been described by Klein[35] as follows: 'Auf derselben erblickt man in Flachrelief links im Hintergrund ein Thor mit zwei hohen gewölbten Eingängen, davor einen Mann stehend auf einem niedrigen, von zwei Pferden gezogenen Triumfwagen, die ein Diener führt; zur Seite der Pferde ein dieselben anbellender Hund. Hinter dem Wagen schreitet eine Person mit langem bis auf die Füsse reichenden, flatternde Gewande einher, in der hoch erhobenen Rechten einen Kranz haltend, um ihn die Triumphiren-den aufs Haupt zu setzen.' The inscription at the bottom of the medallion had Klein at a loss and he ended his commentary on it with the words: 'Die Deutung dieser Worte mögen Kundigere versuchen.'

His reading of the text was:

FELIX.VIEN[...]DEIVSFI[...]
FCASI[....]E[.]A[.]V[.]

In 1984 Desbat published a beautiful indented beaker from Lyon with the same scene, but with more details in a far larger roundel (diam. 16cm). One can imagine that the Cologne tablet is a descendant of this medallion in a somewhat coarse version after two or more generations of remoulding. If the tablet is not a reworked form of the Lyon original, we have to assume two nearly identical reliefs in the Gaulish pottery repertoire. The vessel from Lyon makes the scene perfectly clear (fig. 8): the naked man on the chariot appears to be a fully dressed lady with a *corona muralis*, the tutelary genius of the town of *Vienna* (Vienne), as is indicated by the inscrip-

Fig. 6. Fragment of an applied medallion with Kydippe before an altar and one of her sons at her feet, found at Lyon. After Desbat 1981, 136, R 001. Scale 1:1.

Fig. 7a,b. Roundel of white pipeclay with the representation of a triumphal procession, found at Cologne.
a (top), after Klein 1889, 85; b (bottom), photo courtesy of Rheinisches Landesmusuem Bonn. Scale a, 1:1; b, approximately 2:3.

Fig. 8. Medallion on an indented beaker, found at Lyon and representing the tutelary Genius of Vienna. After Desbat 1984, 397, figs. 3 and 4. Scale 1:2.

tion. The servant in front of the horses is characterised as the god Mercury by his rod or *caduceus*. The figure after the chariot with the long garment has wings (which can with hindsight be discerned in the rim of the tablet from Cologne) and must be identified as a Victory. The whole scene may be summarised as the triumphal entrance into the city of the town goddess of *Vienna*, as is proved by the inscriptions:

a. In the gateway:[36]

VIEN(na)
FLOR(cntia)
FELIX

b. At the bottom of the medallion:

[FELIX.VI]ENNA.POTENS.FLORE(ntia)[37]
[SVO] PRINCIPE SALVO

i.e. 'the town of Vienna, Prosperous, Mighty and Flourishing because of (? or: under) the Good Fortune of her Emperor'.

The restoration of the first line of inscription *b.* proposed by Desbat, is now confirmed by the piece from Cologne, where the missing words FELIX.VIEN[NA] are well preserved. The second line causes a problem. Desbat found here some traces that reminded him of a letter O and proposed here to restore

SVO, 'bien que cette formule soit peu classique'. The drawing of the Cologne medallion is quite clear on this point and gives FCASP[RINCI]PE [S]A[L]V[O] and suggests a possible beginning [IM]P CAES, but even with this interpretation the formulation is far from classic. There is however little reason to cast doubt on the reading of the first letter as F; the horizontal bars can clearly be seen.[38]

ACKNOWLEDGEMENTS

The authors wish to thank A. Desbat (Lyon) for his kind support and U. Heimberg and U. von Prittwitz und Gaffron for the photos of the Cologne plaque and for the opportunity to study the collection of medallions at the Rheinisches Landesmuseum Bonn. G. Schnieder (Freie Universität Berlin) contributed the analysis of the clay in one of the pottery vessels from Nijmegen.

Notes
1. Braat 1962, 96–103.
2. Stuart 1962, type 151 A.
3. Haalebos & Thijssen 1971, 101–29.
4. Haalebos 1994, 23–9.
5. Daniëls 1955, 130; Provinciaal Museum Kam inv. no. B.B.IX.29.
6. They are wheel made and clearly unused. Diam. 8.5 and 11 cm. A similar object in the Provinciaal Museum G.M. Kam forms part of a collection of sherds from Wijchen (no inventory number). Cf. also Hull 1963, 108–9, fig. 50, no. 3; Hull suggests that such objects might have been used to force the clay into a mould for decorated samian and to ensure a smooth finish to the interior.
7. Mainly by the presence of bowls in coarse granular fabric, types Stuart 1962, 210 and 211, and of a white smooth walled flagon Stuart 111, neither of which would have appeared before the middle of the 2nd century.
8. Inv. nos. h 1961.3.2–5.
9. Described with some exaggeration by Braat as 'ziemlich deutlich'.
10. Braat 1962, 103. In fact, these words can be discerned in the second line of the text (see below).
11. Inv. nos. 1994.5.5 ff.
12. *Anthologia Palatina* III, 18; Plutarch, *Mulieres erudiendas esse* fr. 133 (Sandbach); Hyginus, *Fabulae* 254; and Servius, *Scholium ad Vergilii Georgica*, III, 132.
13. EAA II, 1959, 713–714, s.v. Cleobi e Bitone (C. Caprino); LIMC III/1, 1986, 119–120, s.v. Biton et Kleobis (P.E. Arias).
14. Herodotus I, 31.
15. Pausanias II, 20, 3; Pollux VII, 16.
16. *Anthologia Palatina,* III, 18.
17. Boardman 1978, 24, fig. 70. The traditional identification, founded on the restored inscription (cf. van Groningen 1959, 18) is doubted by Vatin (1982), who interprets the statues as representing the Dioscuri.
18. LIMC III/1, 1986, 119–120, nos. 5 and 7–9.
19. Weiler 1980, 225, no. 58.
20. LIMC III/1, 1986, 120, no. 10.
21. Fittschen 1970. Cf. Koch/Sichtermann 1982, 82–3.
22. Fittschen 1970, fig. 10.
23. Braat 1962, 103.
24. Haalebos 1995, 148, 156, Abb. 9, no. 3.
24a. G. Schneider (Berlin) has kindly analysed the clay, which matches (with about 20% iron oxide with silicium and aluminium) the composition of an unburnt red ochre. Its origin could not be determined.
25. Haalebos 1995, 147, 153, Abb. 5, no. 16.
26. Mestwerdt 1909, 8–9 and fig. 3; Brunsting 1937, 36; 1969, 27, fig. 14, mentioned also by Wuilleumier & Audin 1952, 16 and note 33. The *quadriga* in one of the medallions on this beaker is also known from a sherd found in Frankfurt-Heddernheim (Germany), cf. Fischer 1963, 391–2 with fig. 1.

27. Mestwerdt 1908, 14–16 and fig. 4; Hubrecht & Gerhartl-Witteveen 1986, 5, no. 5; cf. also Wuilleumier & Audin 1952, pl. 8, no.196 a.
28. Cf. Déchelette 1904, 2, 279–81, no. 80 (Atalanta and Hippomedon/ Hippomenes) and 290–2, no. 101 (combat between Hercules and Mars after the dead of Cycnus). The same pieces are illustrated by Wuilleumier & Audin 1952, 22–3, no. 1 and 30–31, no. 16.
29. Not published, but cf. Symonds 1992, fig. 4, no. 50 (Group 3).
30. Corocher 1994, 96–7, and figs. 20–1.
31. Klein 1889, 85–6, no. 3254; Wuilleumier & Audin 1952, 16.
32. Lehner 1896, 251 and pl. 9, no. 12.
33. Eristov & Marquis 1991, 259, fig. 8; cf. also Eristov 1994, 221, 223–4.
34. Desbat 1980–81, 136–7, R 001.
35. Klein 1889, 85–6.
36. Faint traces of the same words can be discerned on the Cologne tablet (R.L.B. inv. no. 3254), which was inspected in the Rheinisches Landesmuseum at Bonn by courtesy of U. Heimberg on 17.3.1995.
37. Without too much imagination the end of the first line on the Cologne tablet can now be restored as [P]O<u>TENS</u> FLOR[E].

Bibliography and abbreviations

Boardman, J., 1978 *Greek sculpture. The archaic period* (London)

Braat, W.C., 1962 Ein römischer Messingeimer vom Hemmoorer Typ und einige Begleitfunde, *Oudheidkundige Mededelingen uit het Rijksmuseum van Oudheden te Leiden*, 43, 96–103

Brunsting, H., 1969 *400 jaar Romeinse bezetting van Nijmegen* (3 edn, Nijmegen)
_____, 1937 Het grafveld onder Hees. Een bijdrage tot de kennis van Ulpia Noviomagus, *Archaeologisch-historische bijdragen*, 4 (Amsterdam)

Corocher, J., 1994 Un vase à médaillons d'applique trouvé à Vichy, *Revue archéologique*, 1994/1, 81–98

Daniëls, M.P.M., [1955] *Noviomagus, Romeins Nijmegen* (Nijmegen)

Déchelette, J., 1904 *Les vases céramiques ornés de la Gaule romaine (Narbonnaise, Aquitaine et Lyonnaise)*, 1–2 (Paris)

Desbat, A., 1980–81 Vases à médaillon d'applique des fouilles récentes de Lyon, *Figlina*, 5–6, 1–203
_____, Jouanaud, J.L., & Blanchard, L. 1983 Vases à médaillons d'applique inédits de Lyon et de Martigues (B.-du-R.), *Revue archéologique de Narbonnaise*, 16, 395–403

EAA: *Enciclopedia dell'arte antica*, 1958 (Roma)

Eristov, H., 1994 Un temoignage de loyalisme impériale dans un décor peint?, *Gallia*, 51, 217–32

_____, & Marquis, P., 1991 Peintures et stucs de la rue de l'Abbé de l'Epée à Paris, *Kölner Jahrbuch für Vor- und Frühgeschichte*, 24, 255–60

Fischer, U., 1963 Médaillon d'applique aus Heddernheim, *Germania*, 41, 391–2

Fittschen, K., 1970 Zum Kleobis- und Biton-Relief in Venedig, *Jahrbuch des Deutschen Archäologischen Instituts*, 85, 171–93

Groningen, B.A. van, 1959 *Herodotus' Historiën met inleiding en commentaar* (Leiden)

Haalebos, J.K., 1994 Opgravingen op het terrein van het voormalige Canisius-college te Nijmegen, 1993, *Jaarboek Numaga*, 41, 145–56
_____, 1995 Nijmegener Legionskeramik: Töpferzentrum oder einzelne Töpfereien?, *Rei Cretariae Romanae Fautorum Acta*, 33, 145–56
_____, & Thijssen, J.R.A.M., 1977 Some remarks on the legionary pottery ('Holdeurn ware') from Nijmegen, in Beek, B.L. van, Brandt, R.W., & Groenman-van Waateringe, W. (eds), Ex Horreo, *Cingula*, 4, 101–13 (Amsterdam)

Hubrecht, A.V. M., & Gerhartl-Witteveen, A.M., 1986 *Rijksmuseum G.M. Kam, museum van Romeins Nijmegen* (Rijswijk)

Hull, M. R., 1963 *The Roman potters' kilns of Colchester*, Rep. Res. Comm. Soc. Antiq. London, 21

Klein, J., 1889 Die kleineren inschriftlichen Denkmäler des Bonner Provinzialmuseums, *Bonner Jahrbücher*, 87, 60–86

Koch, G., & Sichtermann, H., 1982 *Römische Sarkophage* (München)

Lehner, H., 1896 Die römische Stadtbefestigung von Trier, *Westdeutsche Zeitschrift für Geschichte und Kunst*, 15, 211–66

LIMC: Ackermann, H.C., et al. (eds), 1981– *Lexicon Iconographicum Mythologiae Classicae* (Zürich/München)

Mestwerdt, G., 1908 Nymwegen. Römisches Gefäss mit 3 Medaillonbildern, *Römisch-germanisches Korrespondenzblatt*, 1, 14–16
_____, 1909 Nymwegen. Zweites römisches Gefäss mit 3 Medaillonbildern, *Römisch-germanisches Korrespondenzblatt*, 2.1, 8–9

Stuart, P., 1962 Gewoon aardewerk uit de Romeinse legerplaats en de bijbehorende grafvelden te Nijmegen, *Oudheidkundige Mededelingen uit het Rijksmuseum van Oudheden te Leiden 43*, supplement (reprint: *Beschrijving van de verzamelingen in het Rijksmuseum G.M. Kam*, 8, 1977)

Symonds, R.P., 1992 *Rhenish Wares. Fine dark coloured pottery from Gaul and Germany* (Oxford)

Vatin, C., 1982 Monuments votifs de Delphes, V, Les couroi d'Argos, *Bulletin de Correspondence Hellénique* 106, 509–25

Weiller, R., 1980 Intailles antiques découvertes au Grand-Duché de Luxembourg (Luxembourg)

Wuilleumier, P., & Audin, A., 1952 *Les médaillons d'applique gallo-romains de la vallée du Rhône* (Paris)

28   Second-century pottery from Caerleon derived from metal and samian prototypes

Janet and Peter Webster

Any comparison between the pottery assemblages of legionary sites and those of non-legionary establishments is likely to highlight the extent to which the former contain plentiful examples of vessels which are generally considered to be 'imitations' of originals in other materials. Here we wish to examine the range of such vessels from just one site, the legionary fortress at Caerleon (with its civilian settlement), to look at the vessels 'imitated' and to question whether the potters of Caerleon were merely imitators or something more creative. The study is largely restricted to the 2nd century as it is to this period that the most plentiful evidence belongs.

We shall make frequent reference to 'Caerleon Ware', the oxidised and slipped pottery produced at or near Caerleon in the Hadrianic and Antonine period. Here we shall adopt the restricted definition proposed by George Boon in his study of Caerleon pottery (Boon 1966) but it must be remembered that 'Caerleon Ware' is just one of a variety of wares produced for (but not necessarily by) the legion at Caerleon throughout much of the period of its occupation of the site. The vessels discussed here will not, therefore, be limited to any one fabric but they can all be considered to be local in manufacture. They will first be considered in terms of the vessel forms from which they are apparently derived.

METAL FORMS

Vessels which can be securely derived from metal prototypes are scarce among the Caerleon assemblage. It is difficult to separate vessels directly derived from metalwork from those derived from pottery or glass versions of metal shapes. Here we have only catalogued pottery vessels which seem to have positive affinities with metal vessels. On the whole we have assumed that where, as for instance in the case of the samian form 27, there exists a metal prototype to a common samian form, it is the latter, not the former which formed the inspiration for the Caerleon potters.

1. Handled flagon in light orange Caerleon Ware with an orange slip. There is burnishing on the rim externally and below the neck cordon. The neck has been burnished vertically. The 'thumb-stop' at the top of the handle suggests derivation from metal jugs where thumb-stops are commonly used across a range of different forms: cf., for example, Tassinari 1975, pl. 29, no. 151; den Boesterd 1956, pl. 12, no. 277; Tassinari 1975, pl. 35, nos. 180, 183. The cordon on the neck may also be derived from a metal vessel; den Boesterd discusses two bronze jugs from Nijmegen, of similar overall form to the Caerleon piece, each of which features what she describes as a rather narrow, slightly projecting rib round the neck (den Boesterd 1956, 82–3, nos. 291, 292, pl. 12). She dates these vessels from the end of the 1st century AD to the 3rd century.

It has been noted (Webster 1993) that the Caerleon piece belongs to a class which appears elsewhere in pottery and derivation from a vessel which is, itself, a metal derivative cannot be entirely ruled out.

However, our vessel may be compared with several continental examples in bronze, not only with regard to its overall form: cf. Tassinari 1975, 66–7, nos. 171, 172, pl. 33, but also, perhaps, in its decorative detail, cf. Tassinari 1975, 65–6, no. 170, pl. 32 and Boucher & Tassinari 1976, 147, no. 190. Each of these two bronze jugs has a band of decoration round its neck, consisting of a row of stylised leaves or tendrils, bordered above and below by a raised beaded band; to this the wavy line ornament above the cordon of the Caerleon vessel may be related.

Bronze jugs such as these may, in turn, be derived from a precious metal prototype, for the gilded silver decorated jugs from Boscoreale have such a decorated cordon around the neck (Baratte 1986, 22–3, 63, 64, 82).

A bronze jug from Welshpool, Montgomeryshire, one of several bronze vessels packed into a cauldron and buried with other items, perhaps in the later 2nd century (Boon 1961), should be noted here. Of the same overall form as the vessels under discussion, the Welshpool jug has a raised rib round the neck decorated with what is described as 'a simplified *cymatium*'. Boon was of the opinion that the piece, which signs of wear suggest was old when it was deposited, was of Italian manufacture and not later than Flavian date (Boon 1961, 20–2, fig. 4.1, pls. 5a, 6). It was, perhaps, a vessel such as this which provided the inspiration for the pottery jug under discussion.

Amphitheatre: Wheeler & Wheeler 1928, no. 55.

2. Flagon neck in orange fabric with plentiful mica dusting externally. The surface treatment strongly suggests that the vessel was intended to resemble a metal piece. The trefoil mouth of the vessel is consistent with derivation from a metal type but is by no means diagnostic since the feature is common on pottery jugs, too. The vessel has a pronounced rib round the neck. The incidence of cordons on the necks of bronze jugs is discussed above (no.1) but the rib on the Mill Street piece is, perhaps, closer to the pronounced rib which may occur on a provincial series of bronze vessels, of 2nd and 3rd century date, and exemplified by a jug from near Lyon discussed by Boucher & Tassinari (1976, 151–2, no. 193). These, however, are very squat vessels with a wide, low body and with the spouted mouth and handle cast in one piece and separately applied to the vessel. The Caerleon jug is not of this form. But other metal vessels of more conventionally jug-like form worthy of mention here are a bronze example, from the Musée des Antiquités Nationales, Paris (Tassinari 1975, 70, no. 185, pl. 35), which has a stout cordon encircling the neck at the mid-point and the mouth fashioned into a rudimentary trefoil opening, and the fine silver jug from Chaourse (Baratte & Painter 1989, 113–14, no. 50) embellished with a stout, decorated, gilded rib encircling the neck close to its mid-point. Painter suggests a 2nd- rather than 3rd-century date for the Chaourse piece.

Mill Street excavations (Webster, in Evans forthcoming). Excavation code, 79.161.957. Unstratified.

3. Flagon neck in light orange fabric with slight indication of a surface wash over a slightly granular finish. The vessel was burnished below the neck. This would probably not qualify as 'Caerleon Ware' according to the Boon definition but is clearly a local product and presumably by the Caerleon Ware potters.

Pinched neck flagons of this general type need not be derived from anything more specific than a potter's whim. However, in this case, the handle includes what would appear to be an imitation thumb-stop at the junction of handle and neck. This 'thumb-stop' is likely to be derived from metal vessels where its use was widespread. Its incidence on bronze vessels of a variety of forms is cited in the discussion of no. 1, above.

Prysg Field: Nash-Williams 1932, no. 115.

4. Lipped jug in hard orange Caerleon Ware with a darker slip. Derivation from a metal prototype is by no means certain but the jug may be compared with a series of smaller bronze vessels of similar form discussed by den Boesterd (1956, 67–9, nos. 232–9, pls. 10, 16, particularly no. 236; see also Radnóti 1938, pl. 13, no. 72, and Eggers 1951, Type 125, Taf. 11). Eggers illustrates a number of these jugs from Britain (1966, 137–9, Abb. 37b, 38a, 39a) including one from Hauxton, Cam-

bridge, which comes closer to the Caerleon vessel in size (Liversidge 1958, 8–9, fig. 1). But it must be noted that the handles of the bronze vessels of this series rise prominently above the rim of the vessel at the rear of the mouth, in contrast with that of the pottery vessel described here.

Hospital: Murray Threipland 1969, period 2a, no. 8.

5. A very similar jug to no. 4 above, but with a slightly different rim profile. It is in a somewhat granular orange-buff fabric, burnished and with an orange slip below the level of the base of the handle. It is thus on the fringe of the Caerleon Ware definition.

Amphitheatre: Wheeler & Wheeler 1928, no. 57.

6. Flask in light orange Caerleon Ware with a faint light orange-buff surface wash. The similarity with the so-called 'unguent flasks' often found in pottery is obvious. But it is, perhaps, also worth noting here the similarity to small bronze unguent flasks of the type with a high foot ring, low, bulbous body and slender neck with a heavy vertical rim, discussed, for example, by den Boesterd (1956, 86, nos. 303–4, pl. 12), Tassinari (1975, 75–6, no. 206, pl. 39) and Radnóti (1938, pl. 53, no. 5). Such bronze flasks are often equipped with cast loops below the rim to hold a chain by means of which they could be attached to a bath-set.

Prysg Field: Nash-Williams 1932, no. 129.

7. Flask in orange-buff fabric with a smooth but unslipped surface. The slim pulley-wheel rim is unusual. For discussion of the general type see no. 6 above.

Hospital: Murray Threipland 1969, period 3a, no. 6.

8. Handled jar in orange Caerleon Ware with a darker slip. In overall shape the vessel has some affinities with large bronze jugs of the type with a wide, high body and a wide neck and mouth, exemplified by Tassinari's no. 164 from the Musée des Antiquités Nationales, Paris (1975, 63–4, nos. 164 (with replacement, though antique, handle) and 165, pl. 31); the shoulder groove and the thick rim to the mouth may indicate some relationship with the more slender necked large bronze jugs exemplified by Tassinari's nos. 171 and 172 from the M.A.N. (1975, 66–7, pl. 33).

The handle of the pottery vessel, where it emerges from the rim, is decorated with twin face-masks, moulded each from the same mould and looking upwards and outwards, away from the mouth of the vessel. The face-mask is a common embellishment on the handle of a metal vessel. Frequently it serves as an escutcheon at the base of a handle (den Boesterd 1956, pls. 10–12, nos. 225a, 226a, 236b, 260a, 263, 273a, 277a, 278, 279, 282a, 284–6 and 291). They serve, too, to ornament the tops of handles to bronze jugs where they more normally look inwards, over the vessel mouth, as, for example, on handles from the M.A.N. (Tassinari 1975, 68, no. 178, pl. 34) and from Nijmegen (den Boesterd 1956, 79, no. 281, pl. 12) but the outward looking face-mask occurs also, Radnóti illustrating a fine example from Sisak (1938, pl. 53, no. 1; see also his pl. 14, no. 82).

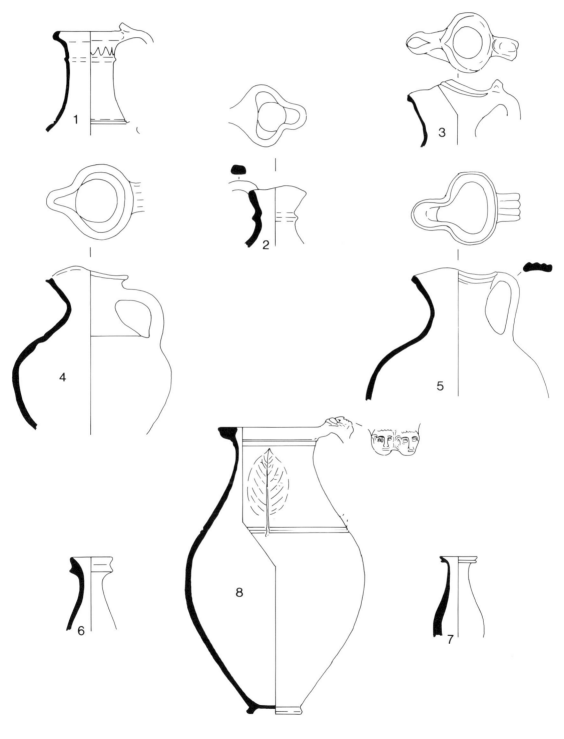

Fig. 1. Pottery from Caerleon, nos. 1–8. Scale 1:4.

The impressed motif of a plum or apple leaf which decorates the neck of the pottery vessel seems, in the form in which it occurs, to be without parallel in any material. The use of the leaf motif to decorate the body of metal vessels is common. Examples range from the high quality silver drinking cups of the 1st century AD (Strong 1966, 135–6, pl. 33A, from Casa del Menandro, Pompeii, pl. 33B, from Alesia; Baratte 1986, 53, from Boscoreale; Toynbee 1964, 302–3, pl. 70b, from Hockwold-cum-Wilton, Norfolk) to less elegant but equally flamboyant enamelled bronze 'saucepans' (Moore 1978, 320–1, fig. 2, nos. 2, 3). Leaves were commonly used, too, as practical embellishments to metal vessels where the suitability of their shape to form escutcheons or thumb-stops was exploited (den Boesterd 1956, pls. 11–12, nos. 257a, 258, 268a, 270, 296, 299 and nos. 296, 297 for example). Although a derivation from some such source cannot be excluded here, the connection is very remote and it seems more likely that the leaf on the Caerleon pottery jar reflects the artistic whim of its potter.

Amphitheatre: Wheeler & Wheeler 1928, no. 54; Boon 1966, fig. 2, no. 3.

8a. (Not illustrated) A small fragment from the top of a jug handle in orange-red Caerleon Ware with traces of a red slip. The outward facing mask has been identified as Silenus. See the discussion under no. 8 above of the possible derivation from metal prototypes of such face masks on pottery jug handles.

Jenkins Field III: Boon 1966, 61, pl. 3, no. 4.

9. Bowl in pinkish-buff fabric with a band of decoration encircling the vessel a little below the rim. This has been achieved with cut lines slashing across a treble corrugation. The vessel closely resembles the body of the so-called Gödåker type of bronze 'saucepan' and, in this case at least, there seems little doubt that it is from just such a vessel that the pottery bowl is derived.

The bronze 'saucepan' of Gödåker type is characterised by the bulging walls of its round bowl and its flaring foot; it is equipped with a handle. Examples of the type are discussed by den Boesterd (1956, 10–11, nos. 25–29, pl. 2) and Tassinari (1975, 29–32, nos. 13–18, pls. 3–5). It is thought to have been manufactured in both Italy and Gaul from the later 1st century AD. An example is known from Caerleon. It was recovered during excavations on the site of the Legionary Museum (Boon 1984, 403–7, fig. 13; Zienkiewicz 1993, 40, 106, no. 1) from a well infilled by the end of the 1st century AD.

The pottery vessel has its point of maximum girth higher than that of the bronze 'saucepan' from Caerleon and in that it more nearly resembles den Boesterd's (1956) no. 29 and Tassinari's (1975) no. 15 than its bronze neighbour. There is no reason to suppose that it was ever equipped with a handle.

A plain or a decorated band, incorporating leaf or palisade ornament, may encircle the bronze 'saucepan' a little way below the rim (Tassinari 1975, 29–30, no. 13, pl. 3; 30–31, no. 15, pl. 4; 31–2, no. 18, pl. 5). The leaf ornament has been variously identified and is discussed by den Boesterd (1956, 10) and Boon (1984, 405). The decoration of the pottery vessel

from Caerleon is a very much simplified rendition of such ornament and adds nothing to their discussions.

Jenkins Field: Nash-Williams 1929, no. 38. The closely similar vessel, no. 39 has not been located.

Metal-derived forms: discussion

Obviously the techniques of manufacture employed to produce a metal vessel are very different from those used to produce a pottery vessel, even without considering the variation of 'fabric' (the differences between precious metal and humble alloy, fine ware and coarse ware etc.) within each sphere. Each medium allowed its craftsman to exploit different properties of the material he was using to produce different functional and decorative features from those which could be produced in another medium. Thus if a potter took as his model a metal vessel he would be unlikely to replicate it exactly, especially for mass production. Figure-moulded handles which occur frequently on otherwise plain bronze jugs, for example, might be expected to be a refinement which the potter would choose to omit, and hinged lids which were commonly used on bronze jugs, often being the only evidence for such vessels recovered from a site, were presumably as much beyond the capacity of the Roman potter as they are beyond 20th-century technology (how useful they would be on ceramic tea-pots today!). Close copying of metal forms by the potters serving the Caerleon market is not, therefore, to be expected. The pottery vessels discussed in the catalogue above, however, display features which are not those of pottery, but which can be linked with possible metal prototypes. These pots, few though they are, and the analogies which they have with metal vessels, serve to show that more is evidenced here than a common repertoire of functional shapes for vessels regardless of their fabric.

Few pottery vessels have been included in this section of the catalogue; only, in fact, those where affinities with metal vessels seem secure or noteworthy. Undoubtedly there are other pots from the site for which a metal derivation could and/or should be assumed.

The majority of the metal vessels with which analogies have been suggested are *either* of 1st-century AD manufacture and/or currency and Italian origin, *or* are developments from 1st-century Italian vessels, a little later and, sometimes, of provincial manufacture. But there seems to be little evidence for the copying of distinctively provincial metal vessels which may, of course, have been too late in their evolution for the potters concerned. Copies of the provincial series of bronze jugs with low, wide body, narrow neck and separately made handle and mouth (e.g. Tassinari 1975, 69–70, nos. 180, 183, pl. 35; the type is evidenced at Caerleon), would be readily recognisable for example; the type was common in the 2nd and 3rd centuries but the beginning of the series is not capable of close dating.

It may be argued that the majority of metal vessels cited are of types which are not known to have been in use at Caerleon and that many are of too early a currency for the site or for the potters. Certainly the representation of bronze vessels from Caerleon is not extensive (Webster 1995) and, with a few exceptions, is made up of fragmentary pieces only; it contains, however, a substantial proportion of 1st- and 1st/2nd-century material. Three factors need to be borne in mind here. Firstly, it is now widely accepted that the army on campaign was equipped with metal vessels and utensils, the result of which must have been, and indeed was, the spread of quality metal vessels, some of very high quality, to the fringes of the Empire; certainly, the evidence of the bronze vessels from the legionary fortress at Usk supports this (Manning *et al.* 1995). Secondly, metal vessels, at least of non-precious metal, are much more durable in use than ceramic ones and, therefore, have a considerably longer functional life-span, far outlasting changes in fashion and style and there must have been a greater incentive to continue to use what was, after all, a more costly item, albeit out of date. Thirdly, as has recently been discussed with reference to the metal finds from Usk, the Roman army had an admirably efficient system for recycling scrap metal and there are few sites which produce more than a few handles, escutcheons or lids, the remnant of what must have been a more extensive assemblage of bronze tableware. The jug from Welshpool, referred to above, may be cited as evidence of an Italianate vessel still current in Wales in the mid-2nd century; no doubt it was not an isolated phenomenon, and the Gödåker style pottery bowl can be linked with the bronze Gödåker vessel from the Legionary Museum site, although it is unlikely to have been a copy of that vessel. Given these examples, the evidence for 1st-century AD bronze tableware from Usk and the known, albeit scant, assemblage of bronze vessels and fragments from Caerleon, there seems little doubt that there was 1st-century metal material available to the Caerleon potters for copying in the 2nd century.

The final question which must be asked is why the Caerleon potters chose to copy metal vessels when manufacturing their products. A number of possible reasons suggest themselves (but none is more convincing than another). As has been pointed out, metal vessels were used by the army on campaign and there may, as a result, have been a tradition among the military of using metal tableware, particularly vessels to do with the serving of liquid. Certainly, by the early 2nd century, metal vessels which came into the country with the army of conquest will have been wearing out. Many will no longer have been replaceable in their exact form and purchasers may have turned to or accepted cheaper, locally made and, therefore, more readily available substitutes. Indeed, in the case of some of the vessels discussed above it would seem as if the potter himself had no great familiarity with the vessels he was imitating but was perhaps working from memory or according to descriptions given by his client.

THE PROBLEM OF THE HEMISPHERICAL BOWLS

Listed below are five vessels, all classifiable as 'hemispherical bowls'. In the past, derivation from samian forms has been claimed for this group. However, for chronological reasons, such claims seem improbable. We would not regard derivation from metal prototypes as at all certain but they are published here so that such a possibility can be reviewed for the first time.

The smaller bowls were derived from Ritterling form 8 by Nash-Williams and Boon but the pre-Flavian date of this samian form makes it an unlikely original for something produced in Caerleon Ware in the 2nd century. Some of the large bowls have some resemblance to the samian form 31 and its East Gaulish equivalents and samian influence here cannot be discounted. However, clear derivatives of form 31 are very rare in Caerleon ware and imitation of obscure variants, therefore, unlikely.

Hemispherical bowls are, of course, a common metal vessel form. A range of vessels may be cited, from silver examples from Boscoreale (Baratte 1986, 22, far left) through to bronze ones from Pannonia (Radnóti 1938, pl. 12, no. 60; pl. 38, no. 1); they may occur with or without a foot-ring (Kraskovská 1978, 81, fig. 14, nos. 7–9, for example).

Vessels such as a bronze 'deep platter' from Nijmegen with a suggested late 1st/early 2nd-century AD date and parallels from the Casa del Menandro, Pompeii (den Boesterd 1956, 32, no. 85, pl. 4), may have been the inspiration for bowls such as our nos. 13–14, or they might perhaps have been scaled down versions of such bronze bowls as those discussed by den Boesterd from Doorwerth and Nijmegen (1956, 52–3, nos. 172–173, pl. 8) of 1st-century AD date and Campanian manufacture. But the shape is such a basic and simple one that the ancestry of the pottery vessels must remain uncertain.

Small drinking cups of simple bowl shape are known among the repertoire of metal vessel shapes but their origins are as uncertain as those of the small pottery cups under discussion here (our nos. 10–11). Two plain hemispherical bronze cups from Nijmegen described by den Boesterd (1956, 33–4, nos. 93, 94, pl. 4), dated by analogy with other examples to the early 3rd century AD or later, are compared by her with terra sigillata cups of the Hofheim/Ritterling 8 form but the absence of a comparable vessel in bronze contemporary with the Ritterling 8 form is noted by her. Nor are such cups confined to everyday materials. An example in silver from the Graincourt-les-Havrincourt assemblage is discussed by Baratte (Baratte & Painter 1989, 145, no. 91). The type is dated by him to the 3rd century AD and reference made to a number of other instances of 3rd-century examples.

10. Shallow cup in light orange Caerleon ware with a red slip. Prysg Field: unstratified.

11. Cup in light orange Caerleon Ware with a red slip. Prysg Field: Nash-Williams 1932, no. 416.

12. Hemispherical bowl in Caerleon Ware. Prysg Field: Nash-Williams 1932, nos. 127–9. Not certainly identified in the museum collection.

13. Bowl in pink-buff fabric with a mica-dusted surface. Prysg Field: Nash-Williams 1932, no. 202.

14. Hemispherical bowl in orange Caerleon Ware with a red slip. Prysg Field: Nash-Williams 1932, no. 125.

SAMIAN FORMS

These are considered in the numerical order of form, starting with the Dragendorff/Déchelette/Walters series.

Form 18/31. This is one of the more popular of the Caerleon Ware forms. The Caerleon version is fairly close to the samian original. Differences may well be due to the fact that the Caerleon pieces were made without the aid of such sophisticated formers as was samian plainware (cf. Csysz 1982). Certainly on this form, the centre floor only rarely rises and there is a marked variation of footring and overall size, which is all suggestive of individually thrown vessels. One feature frequently found on the Caerleon examples but not on the samian original is a marked step at the wall/floor junction. We have illustrated a number of vessels to show the range of sizes and other minor variations.

15. Dish in light orange with an orange slip. This vessel seems close to the samian form but the step at the wall/floor junction and the free-formed foot may be noted.
    Prysg Field: Nash-Williams 1932, no. 205.

16. Dish in light orange fabric with traces of orange slip. A more rounded profile than no. 15 above.
    Prysg Field: Nash-Williams 1932, no. 207.

17. Dish in orange Caerleon Ware with an orange-red slip. A variant of no. 16 above.
    Prysg Field: Nash-Williams 1932, no. 205.

18. Dish in orange-buff Caerleon Ware. An angular version of the form.
    Museum Street: Murray Threipland 1965, fig. 5, no. 13.

19. Dish in orange-buff Caerleon Ware with an orange-red slip. The size would be sufficient for form 18/31R but there is no rouletting on the floor.
    Prysg Field: Nash Williams 1932, no. 209.

20. Dish or bowl base in orange Caerleon Ware with a darker slip. The central kick and rather bowl-like proportions suggest that this may be one of the few Caerleon Ware vessels derived from the samian form 31.
    Cambria House, Mill Street (Webster, in Evans forthcoming). Site code 82.389.

21. Dish in orange fabric with an orange-red slip. This is one of several vessels which have an added internal groove at the rim (see also Wheeler & Wheeler 1928, no. 37; there is another example among unpublished material from the Prysg).
    Prysg Field, Barrack 7, centurion's quarters, stone phase.

Form 27. This is a highly recognisable form, but possibly less common than the published examples suggest. Most, but not all examples are in Caerleon Ware. Variations of size again abound. The rim bead tends to be defined by a groove rather than a true bead. The internal groove or ledge at the same point on the samian form is missing. Footrings show marked variation.

22. Cup in buff fabric with a light orange surface and traces of mica-dusting both internally and externally. The contrast of rounded upper profile and straight lower one would be very unusual in the samian form.
    Hospital: Murray Threipland 1969, period 2, no. 13.

23. Cup in buff, slightly sandy Caerleon Ware with traces of a pink surface.
    Hospital: Murray Threipland 1969, period 2a, no. 11.

24. Cup in light orange fabric. No slip survives but this was probably slipped Caerleon Ware. The shape is quite close to the samian form, but the profile shows none of the sharp angles. The footstand goes only part-way towards a samian form.
    Vicus culvert, Bear House Field I, Museum Acc. no. 54.389A.

25. Cup in Caerleon Ware; a very flattened profile.
    Fortress Baths: Zienkiewicz 1986, fig. 36, no. 10.

26. Cup in pink-buff fabric.
    Jenkins Field: Nash-Williams 1929, no. 59.

27. Cup in Caerleon Ware; almost wide enough to class as a dish.
    Prysg Field: Nash-Williams 1932, nos. 212, 213. Neither vessel has been located.

Form 31. This form appears rarely in Caerleon ware, but there are a few vessels which seem likely to be derived from it, rather than the earlier form 18/31. The chronological significance of this will be discussed below. A probable vessel of this form is illustrated as no. 20 above.

Form 33. This is one of the more interesting of Caerleon productions. It does occur in Caerleon Ware versions fairly close to the samian original (cf. no. 28 below), but it also occurs in more freely interpreted versions in the same fabric (nos. 30–32). Vessels virtually identical in form to the Caerleon ware examples but in a much coarser fabric also occur (our no. 29). Such vessels reinforce the view, implicit in the Nash-Williams reports, that the fine slipped or burnished and oxidised pottery which we now call 'Caerleon Ware' (and he called 'Legionary Ware') is only one of a variety of fabrics produced near and for the fortress at Caerleon. There is no reason to suppose that the potters who produced the coarser versions of form 33 were not the same ones as produced the Caerleon Ware vessels.

28. Cup in light orange Caerleon Ware with an orange-red slip. The vessel has the internal groove at the rim of the samian form but lacks any external groove. It is also more flared than most samian 33s.
    Vicus culvert, Bear House Field I, Museum Acc. no. 54.389A.

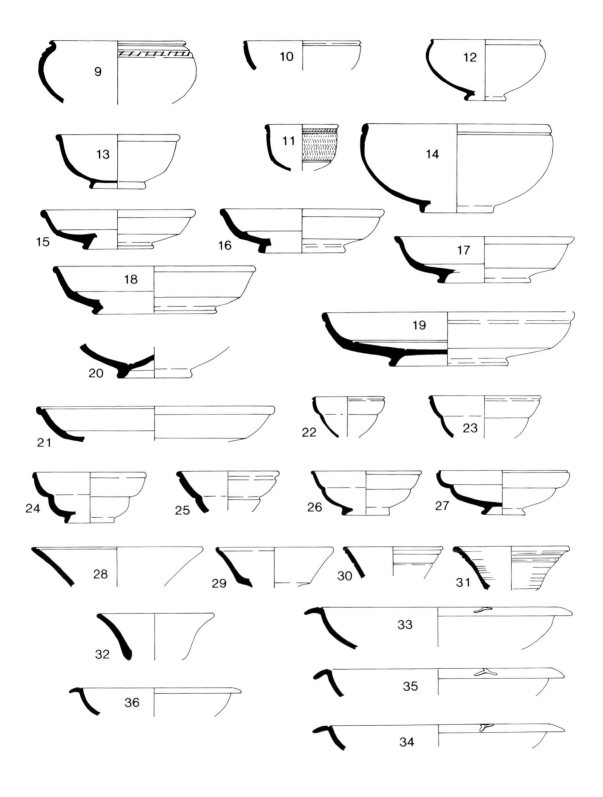

Fig. 2. Pottery from Caerleon, nos. 9–34. Scale 1:4.

29. Cup in coarse orange fabric with a filler of quartz-like sand and what appears to be ground clay. The vessel is sufficiently close to Caerleon Ware forms for it to be almost certain that it is a product of the same industry, but this vessel is unlikely ever to have been slipped.
   Prysg Field: unstratified.

30. Cup in a fabric which now appears orange to grey with a grey slip. Presumably it was intended to be oxidised but has become partially reduced either in firing or subsequently. The multiple grooves externally suggest that the potter intended a variation on the samian form 33 theme.
   Vicus culvert, Bear House Field I, Museum Acc. no. 54.389A.

31. Cup in light orange fabric with a red colour coat. Grooves and facets formed by burnishing have produced a vessel some way removed from the samian form.
   Vicus culvert, Bear House Field I, Museum Acc. no. 54.389A.

32. Cup in orange fabric with a red slip. The curvilinear shape, the result of free throwing on the wheel, is typical of many Caerleon 'form 33' types.
   Prysg Field: unstratified.

Form 36. Of the cup and dish 'set', forms 35 and 36, only the dish seems to have inspired many local versions. The closest to the samian original are Caerleon Ware vessels such as our nos. 33–5, where the trailed barbotine leaf decoration of the samian vessel is imitated. The imitation is, however, of poor quality and very palsied, perhaps because the local clay did not lend itself to such work, but more likely because the Caerleon potters did not use a sufficiently refined clay to make the thick but fluid slip necessary for such an operation. Perhaps for this reason, vessels inspired by form 36, but without the trailed decoration, are also commonly found. The Caerleon vessels fall into three distinct categories:

Nos. 33–35 have thin flanges, vestigial barbotine decoration and a groove at the flange and internal wall junction.

33. Dish in light orange-buff fabric. The orange-red slip survives internally.
   Prysg Field: Nash-Williams 1932, no. 133.

34. Dish in light orange fabric with a deep red slip.
   Prysg Field: Nash-Williams 1932, no. 135 or 136 (cf. no. 39 below).

35. Dish in light orange fabric with an orange slip.
   Prysg Field: unstratified.

36. Dish in light orange-buff fabric, very abraded.
   Prysg Field: probably Nash-Williams 1932, no. 137 but no barbotine was observed on the fragment examined.

Nos. 37–41 have more solid rims than nos. 33–35 above and are generally wide shallow dishes. Barbotine appears to have been optional.

37. Dish in orange-buff fabric with a red slip.
   Prysg Field: Nash-Williams 1932, no. 134.

38. Dish in light orange fabric with a red slip.
   Prysg Field: possibly Nash-Williams 1932, no. 132.

39. Dish in light orange fabric with a red slip.
   Prysg Field: possibly Nash-Williams 1932, no. 135 or 136 (cf. no. 34 above).

40. Dish in orange fabric with slight traces of slip.
   Prysg Field: unstratified.

41. Dish in light orange fabric with a red slip.
   From Prysg Field: no codes survive on this piece.

No. 42 appears to be a looser interpretation of the samian form 35/36 theme.

42. Bowl in orange-buff fabric with faint traces of orange-red slip. It is bright orange internally and may have been burnt.
   Vicus culvert, Bear House Field I, Mus. Acc. No. 54.389A.

Form 37. Vessels at Caerleon derived from form 37 make an interesting and varied collection. Most common is a Caerleon Ware bowl clearly designed to suggest the samian original (our nos. 43–47) but using barbotine splotches, some in vaguely animate shapes, to substitute for the moulded figures. There are also a number of other hemispherical bowls in Caerleon Ware which may owe something to form 37 (e.g. our nos. 48–50). The rather poor attempts at decoration on Caerleon Ware versions of this form contrast with two, probably 1st-century, moulded vessels from the Prysg (Nash Williams 1932, nos. 184 and 451) the white slip of which make them most likely to be the product of the same local kilns as produced the earliest Caerleon mortaria (cf. Zienkiewicz 1992, 92–5) in the later 1st or early 2nd century.

43. Bowl in light red Caerleon Ware with some red slip.
   Prysg Field: Nash-Williams 1932, no. 185.

44. Bowl in light orange Caerleon Ware with a burnished surface and orange-red slip.
   Amphitheatre: Wheeler & Wheeler 1928, no. 35.

45. Bowl in orange fabric with a faint slip.
   Prysg Field: probably Nash-Williams 1932, no. 194.

46. Bowl in orange fabric with no surviving slip.
   Prysg Field: unstratified.

47. Bowl in light orange fabric with faint traces of red slip.
   Prysg Field: Nash-Williams 1932, no. 190.

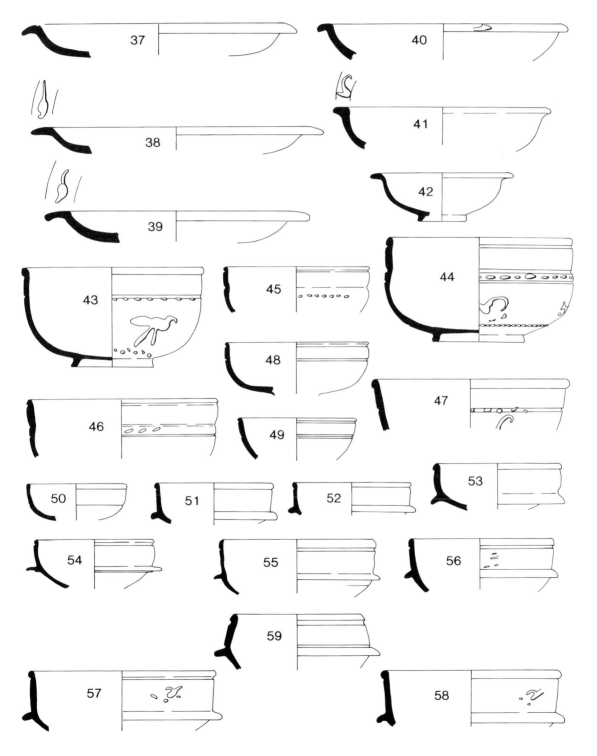

Fig. 3. Pottery from Caerleon, nos. 35–58. Scale 1:4.

Nos. 48–50 are small bowls, the zonal arrangement of which seems to link them loosely with form 37.

48. Bowl in buff to pink-buff fabric with a pink-red slip in places.
 Prysg Field: Barrack 7(35)S.

49. Bowl in light orange micaceous fabric with a red slip.
 Prysg Field: unstratified.

50. Cup in orange fabric with an orange-red slip. The external lines seem to link this with form 37 but there are also links with bowls such as no. 10 above.
 Prysg Field: unstratified.

Forms 38, 44, 81 and their variants. This range of samian forms, all of which are likely to have been related to the flanged bowl form 38, have been grouped together here. Caerleon vessels range from those which are reasonably close to samian originals to free interpretations. In particular, barbotine decoration appears on forms which would be undecorated if in samian.

Nos. 51–55 are all likely to be derived from the samian form 38.

51. Bowl in light orange with an orange-red slip.
 Prysg Field: Nash-Williams 1932, no. 174.

52. Bowl in light orange-buff fabric with some evidence of slip remaining in the grooves.
 Prysg Field: Nash-Williams 1932, no. 176.

53. Bowl in light orange fabric with a slip which is orange internally and maroon externally.
 Prysg Field: Barrack 7(9)S+.

54. Bowl in buff fabric.
 Prysg Field: Nash-Williams 1932, no. 175. Not located.

55. Bowl in orange-buff Caerleon Ware.
 Prysg Field: Nash-Williams 1932, no. 173.

Nos. 56–58 are generally similar to nos. 51–55 but with barbotine decoration above the flange.

56. Bowl in light orange-buff fabric with an orange-red slip.
 Prysg Field: Barrack 7(38)S3.

57. Bowl in light orange fabric. No slip survives.
 Prysg Field: Nash-Williams 1932, no. 179.

58. Bowl in light orange with an orange-red slip.
 Prysg Field: Nash-Williams 1932, no. 177.

Nos. 59–60 appear to be freer interpretations of form 38.

59. Bowl in Caerleon Ware.
 Fortress Baths: Zienkiewicz 1986, fig. 36, no. 12.

60. Bowl in orange-buff Caerleon Ware with a darker slip.
 Fortress Baths: Zienkiewicz 1986, fig. 24, group 14, no. 12.

No. 61 is likely to be derived from form 44, although the barbotine is a Caerleon addition.

61. Bowl in orange-buff Caerleon Ware with an orange slip.
 Amphitheatre: Wheeler & Wheeler 1928, no. 36.

Nos. 62–67 appear to be related to form 81 and particularly to its variant Ludowici Sn. It has been suggested elsewhere that the barbotine decorated vessels such as our no. 67 may be related to the East Gaulish products Ludowici SMb and SMc (Webster 1993, 259) but the Rheinzabern dating appears to be against this (we are grateful to Dr Allard Mees for confirming this from the Rheinzabern records).

62. Bowl in orange fabric with an orange-red slip.
 Prysg Field: Barrack 7(39)S.

63. Bowl in light orange-buff fabric with no signs of slip.
 Mill Street (Webster, in Evans forthcoming), site code 79.001.

64. Bowl in light orange fabric with a slip which appears orange internally and orange-brown externally.
 Prysg Field: possibly Nash-Williams 1932, no. 181, although no barbotine is evident on the piece examined.

65. Bowl in orange fabric with an orange slip darkened internally and below the flange externally.
 Prysg Field: Nash-Williams 1932, no. 182.

66. Bowl in light orange fabric with an orange-red slip.
 Prysg Field: Barrack 3(4)S.

67. Bowl in orange Caerleon Ware with a maroon slip.
 Prysg Field: Nash-Williams 1932, no. 177.

Curle 11. Caerleon yields a number of vessels which show some influence from the samian form Curle 11. These vary from vessels such as our no. 68 which are clear imitations of the samian form to vessels which might as easily be classified as 'mortar-like bowls'.

68. Flanged bowl in light orange fabric with a mottled slip. The effect was achieved by slipping the vessel in creamy white, then dabbing on red slip possibly with a sponge. In form, this is one of the closest imitations of samian ware achieved by the Caerleon potters. The technique seems more appropriate to the late 1st or early 2nd-century potters supplying Caerleon rather than the 'Caerleon Ware' industry.
 Quay: Boon 1978, fig. 12, no. 1.
The vessels published as nos. 69–74 all seem to show some

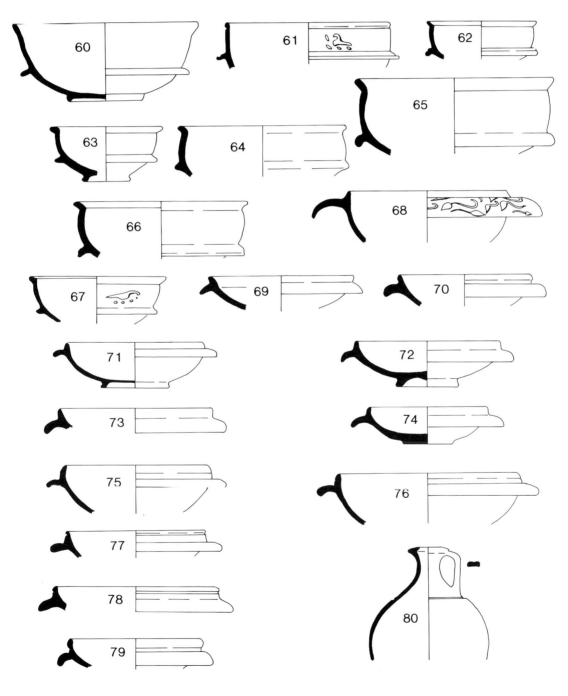

Fig. 4. Pottery from Caerleon, nos. 59–80. Scale 1:4.

inspiration from Curle 11. They are offered as a typological sequence based on the size of flange and the angle of the rim above the flange.

69. Dish in orange fabric with traces of a red slip.
   Prysg Field: unstratified.

70. Dish or bowl in orange fabric, burnished and with an orange slip.
   Prysg Field: unstratified.

71. Bowl in orange Caerleon Ware with an orange-red slip.
   Prysg Field: Nash-Williams 1932, no. 144.

72. Dish in Caerleon Ware.
   Amphitheatre: Wheeler & Wheeler 1928, no. 38. Not located.

73. Dish in light orange fabric with traces of slip.
   Prysg Field: unstratified.

74. Dish in a slightly granular and micaceous orange fabric. The fabric is more 'sandy' than most Caerleon ware and was probably never slipped.
   Vicus culvert, Bear House Field, Museum Acc. no. 54–389A.

Nos. 75–79 all have some sort of groove or line on the upper rim. Although the position of the flange is higher than one would expect on form 38, some influence from that samian form may be suggested and an Antonine rather than earlier date may be more likely.

75. Bowl in orange Caerleon Ware with an orange-red slip.
   Prysg Field: Nash-Williams 1932, no. 148.

76. Bowl in light orange Caerleon Ware with a dark red slip.
   Prysg Field: Nash-Williams 1932, no. 147.

77. Bowl in orange fabric with slight traces of slip.
   Prysg Field: unstratified.

78. Bowl in orange-buff Caerleon Ware with traces of red slip.
   Museum Street: Murray Threipland 1965, fig. 5, no. 10.

79. Bowl in orange-buff Caerleon Ware with a burnished orange surface.
   Museum Street: Murray Threipland 1965, fig. 5, no. 11.

Other
A flagon from the Amphitheatre seems likely to be derived from the samian flagon form, Oswald & Pryce, pl. 83, no. 2.

80. Flagon in orange-buff Caerleon Ware with a burnished surface and orange slip. The neck has been burnished vertically.
   Amphitheatre: Wheeler 1928, no. 56.

Samian-derived forms: discussion

The great majority of the vessels discussed above are either in Caerleon Ware or the related but unslipped (and sometimes coarser) local oxidised fabric. All these seem to belong to the same period and to the same source. It is, therefore, worth considering the samian forms from which the Caerleon vessels are derived and their likely date. Stratigraphically, most Caerleon excavators have placed Caerleon Ware in the Hadrianic-Antonine period. Boon, on the basis of the single imitation of a glass pillar-moulded bowl (Nash-Williams 1929, no. 126), suggested that the ware cannot have started after the mid-Trajanic period and this is broadly supported by recent excavation (cf. Zienkiewicz 1992, 94–6). There is, however, some disagreement on the duration of the industry. Greep would favour production into at least the late 2nd century (Zienkiewicz 1986, 56). In the report on the Usk pottery a date c.AD160–70 was suggested (Webster 1993, 256). We see no reason to alter the latter suggestion, but it is worth amplifying the evidence.

Among the vessels discussed above the most common forms are those of the first half of the 2nd century. Vessels derived from forms 18/31, 27 and Curle 11 are reasonably numerous. Form 38, but more particularly its variants 44 and 81, were also popular. All this suggests production into the middle of the 2nd century.

However, vessels derived from securely late 2nd-century samian forms seem absent. Despite the fact that the Caerleon Ware potters produced large numbers of mortaria, they never imitated the later 2nd-century samian mortaria. We should, perhaps, not press this particular argument too far in view of the absence of samian mortarium forms from the fortress (cf. Webster 1990; 1992; the samian mortaria are, however, represented in the civil settlement). Even if form 45, in particular, seems to have been little used by the military, the same is not true of other later 2nd-century forms such as 79/80 and 31/31R. But local vessels derived directly from forms 79/80 are also missing. Perhaps most telling is the evidence of the dish/bowl sequence 18/31 and 31. The former is well represented, the latter rare. Although Form 31 and its larger (and probably slightly later) version with internal rouletted circle, 31R, are among the commonest of later samian forms, no certain Caerleon Ware derivatives of 31R have been noted. It, therefore, seems highly unlikely that Caerleon Ware production survived long into the currency of forms 79/80 and 31/31R. An end-date of c.AD160/170 seems reasonable on the evidence.

GENERAL DISCUSSION

The main purpose of this article is to discuss samian and metal derivatives among the pottery of Caerleon. It should, however, be noted in passing that the Caerleon potters sometimes turned elsewhere for inspiration. The apparently unique pottery version of a glass pillar-moulded bowl (Nash-Williams 1929, no. 126) has already been mentioned. It may reasonably be regarded as a one-off item such as one might expect in the vicinity of kilns. It is suggested in the case of metal-derived forms that 'imitation' may, in part, have taken place when the metal forms themselves became scarcer through old age. Is this another example of the same phenomenon?

Whatever the purpose of the pillar-moulded bowl in Caerleon ware, there can be little doubt about the rough-cast beakers produced in large numbers by the same makers. These are clearly derived from rough-cast ware produced in northern Gaul and particularly the Argonne (cf. Anderson 1981; Symonds 1990). This ware is fairly well represented in Britain from the later 1st century until the mid-2nd (cf. Gillam 1970, types 72–3, 75). However, it is rare in 2nd-century Caerleon and there can be little doubt that this is because the Caerleon Ware potters discovered that they could produce a cheaper or more serviceable version of the same thing. The Caerleon product is generally coarser than its Gaulish competitor, but it was obviously extremely popular locally, as the numbers recovered from the Baths show (Zienkiewicz 1986, fig. 28). One assumes that local production, coupled with a fabric and finish which is less fine, enabled the Caerleon ware producers to undercut the competition and, indeed, flood the market for small fineware beakers.

Why produce derived forms?

It is easier to detail the Caerleon vessels derived from pieces in other materials than to determine why they were produced. A number of possibilities seem to present themselves:

a) that the vessels are direct imitations of originals in other materials produced as cheap substitutes to undercut more expensive alternatives;

b) that they filled a gap in the market produced by an inadequate supply of the alternatives;

c) that vessels in other materials served as an inspiration for local vessels rather than as a model for direct copying.

It seems possible that all three explanations can be advanced for aspects of the Caerleon production.

We have already suggested that the rough-cast beakers in Caerleon ware were intended as substitutes for an imported product and, given the difference in quality, there seems little doubt that the Caerleon versions must have been both cheaper and (obviously) more easily obtainable. They can probably be regarded as direct imitations.

Gaps in the market are less easy to determine. The apparently early date of the metal forms from which Caerleon pottery vessels are derived has led us to suggest that, to some extent, as traditional metal forms wore out or became unavailable, they may have been replaced in other materials. We may also note that many observers have postulated a dip in samian supplies to Britain as the main export centre shifted from South to Central Gaul (cf. Marsh 1981). This Trajanic 'dip' in supplies comes just as Caerleon Ware appears and it is perhaps not too fanciful to see part of its early production as a response to inadequate samian supply.

Analysis of the samian forms actually found within the fortress (cf. Webster 1990; 1992) shows a restricted range of forms in use. It is from this that the Caerleon samian-derived assemblage comes. We may infer a cast of mind which equated certain samian and metal forms with specific functions. If this is the case, then production of local pottery substitutes for temporarily unavailable samian (or metal) vessels seems reasonable.

Such argument does, not, however, account for all the products of the local kilns, or indeed all vessels derived from samian or metal prototypes. Later Hadrianic and Antonine samian appears to have been plentiful and there is no reason to suppose that it was not readily available. Despite this, the Caerleon potteries appear to have continued to produce samian-derived forms. The number of extant vessels derived from either samian or metalwork does not seem to be sufficient to allow us to suggest production throughout the manufacturing period on a scale sufficient to provide plentiful cheap alternatives. We need some other explanation. It may well be that both purchaser and potter found a number of the samian and metal shapes visually pleasing and that they, therefore, served as the basis for forms inspired by, but not slavishly following the originals. The result would be a vessel which was designed to form an alternative to the piece from which it was derived, but was not necessarily intended to be compared directly with it. We should perhaps remember that only archaeologists have an obsession with the minutiae of form and that the man in the street makes his judgement on more general grounds of appearance and potential utility. There is every reason to suppose that the man in the Caerleon *contubernium* was no different in this respect from his modern counterpart. We may conclude that the Caerleon potters were not mere imitators. Instead they seem to have taken a limited range of samian and metal forms and used them as a starting point for vessels which often owe as much to the potter's own ability in manipulating his material as they do to the work of other craftsmen.

APPENDIX:

PUBLISHED VESSELS FROM THE PRYSG FIELD

The Nash-Williams publication of the Prysg Field excavations (1932) is notable for collections of vessels which are grouped under single illustrations. In no case does Nash-Williams state which vessel in the group he has illustrated. It is, however, possible in most cases to work this out using the pots themselves and the published information, but it is not possible simply from the published report. Where vessels in such groups have been used above, we have tried to identify the exact Nash-Williams number when possible. It needs to be noted, therefore, that the appearance of a publication number after a Prysg pot does not necessarily imply that the vessel is *illustrated* in Nash-Williams 1932.

Postcript

Late in 1996, a pottery kiln was discovered at Abernat Farm, about a mile east of Caerleon. This is clearly one of a group of kilns in the vicinity making Caerleon Ware, including some of the forms illustrated here. This is the first Caerleon Ware kiln discovered and confirms the local origin of the fabric.

ACKNOWLEDGEMENTS

We would like to thank the staff of the National Museum of Wales, and especially Richard Brewer, Susan Fox and David Zienkiewicz, for assistance in compiling this article.

Bibliography

Anderson, A.C., 1981 Some continental beakers of the first and second centuries AD, in Anderson & Anderson 1981, 321–48

_____, & Anderson, A.S. (eds), 1981 *Roman pottery research in Britain and north-west Europe*, British Archaeol. Rep. Internat. Ser., **123** (Oxford)

Baratte, F., 1986 *Le trésor d'orfèvrerie romaine de Boscoreale* (Paris)

_____, & Painter K. 1989 *Trésors d'orfèvrerie gallo-romains* (Paris)

Boon, G.C., 1961 Roman antiquities at Welshpool, *Antiq. J.*, **41**, 13–31

_____, 1966 Legionary ware at Caerleon?, *Archaeol. Cambrensis*, **115**, 45–66

_____, 1978 Excavations on the site of a Roman quay at Caerleon and its significance, *Cambrian Archaeol. Assoc. Monographs Collect.*, **1**, 1–24 (Cardiff)

_____, 1984 A trulleus from Caerleon with a stamp of the First Cavalry Regiment of Thracians, *Antiq. J.*, **64**, 403–7

Boucher, S., & Tassinari, S., 1976 *Bronzes antiques du Musée de la civilisation gallo-romaine à Lyon I. Inscriptions, statuaires, vaiselles* (Lyon)

Czysz, W., 1982 Der Sigillata-Geschirrfund von Cambodunum-Kempten. Ein Beitrag zur Technologie und Handelskunde mittelkaiserzeitlicher Keramik, *Bericht der Römisch-Germanischen Kommission*, **63**, 282–350

den Boesterd, M.H.P., 1956 *Description of the collections in the Rijksmuseum G.M.Kam at Nijmegen, V. The bronze vessels* (Nijmegen)

Eggers, H.J., 1951 *Der römische Import in freien Germanien* (Hamburg)

_____, 1966 Römische Bronzegefässe in Britannien, *Jahrbuch des Römisch-Germanischen Zentralmuseums Mainz*, **13**, 67–164

Evans, E., forthcoming [Report on excavations in Mill Street, Caerleon]

Gillam, J.P., 1970 *Types of Roman coarse pottery vessels in northern Britain*, 3 edn. (Newcastle upon Tyne)

Kraskovská, L., 1978 *Roman bronze vessels from Slovakia*, British Archaeol. Rep. Internat. Ser., **44** (Oxford)

Liversidge, J., 1958 Roman discoveries from Hauxton, *Proc. Cambridge Antiq. Soc.*, **51**, 7–17

Manning, W.H., Price, J., & Webster, J., 1995 *Report on the excavations at Usk 1965–1976. The Roman small finds* (Cardiff)

Marsh, G., 1981 London's samian supply and its relationship to the Gallic samian industry, in Anderson & Anderson 1981, 173–238

Moore, C.N., 1978 An enamelled skillet-handle from Brough-on-Fosse and the distribution of similar vessels, *Britannia*, **9**, 319–27

Murray Threipland, L., 1965 Caerleon: Museum Street site 1965, *Archaeol. Cambrensis*, **114**, 130–45

_____, 1969 The Hall, Caerleon 1964: excavations on the site of the legionary hospital, *Archaeol. Cambrensis*, **118**, 86–123

Nash-Williams, V.E., 1929 The Roman legionary fortress at Caerleon in Monmouthshire. Report on excavations carried out in 1926, *Archaeol. Cambrensis*, **84**, 237–307

_____, 1932 The Roman legionary fortress at Caerleon in Monmouthshire. Report on excavations carried out in the Prysg Field 1927–29. Part III, *Archaeol. Cambrensis*, **87**, 265–349

Oswald, F., & Pryce, T.D., 1920 *An introduction to the study of terra sigillata* (London)

Strong, D.E., 1966 *Greek and Roman gold and silver plate* (London)

Symonds, R.P., 1990 The problem of roughcast beakers and related wares, *J. Roman Pottery Stud.*, **3**, 1–17

Tassinari, S., 1975 *La vaisselle de bronze, romaine et provinciale, au Musée des Antiquités Nationales*, Gallia Suppl., **29** (Paris)

Toynbee, J.M.C., 1964 *Art in Britain under the Romans* (Oxford)

Radnóti, A., 1938 *Die römischen Bronzegefässe von Pannonien*, Dissertationes Pannonicae, **2.6**

Webster, J., 1995 Archive list of bronze vessels from Caerleon, lodged in the Roman Legionary Museum, Caerleon

Webster, P. V. 1990 The Caerleon samian project, *Archaeology in Wales*, **30**, 17–18

_____, 1992 The Caerleon samian project 1991–1992, *Archaeology in Wales*, **32**, 45–6

_____, 1993 The post-fortress coarse-wares, in Manning, W.H. (ed.), *Report on the excavations at Usk 1965–1976. The Roman pottery*, 225–361 (Cardiff)

Wheeler, R.E.M., & Wheeler, T.V., 1928 The Roman amphitheatre at Caerleon, *Archaeologia*, **78**, 111–218

Zienkiewicz, J.D. 1986 *The legionary fortress baths at Caerleon, II. The finds* (Cardiff)

_____, 1992 Pottery from excavations on the site of the Roman Legionary Museum, Caerleon 1983–5, *J. Roman Pottery Stud.*, **5**, 81–109

_____, 1993 Excavations in the *Scamnum Tribunorum* at Caerleon: the Legionary Museum site 1983–5, *Britannia*, **24**, 27–140

29   Hoards of Roman coins found in Britain: the search and the byways

Anne S. Robertson

INTRODUCTION

As long ago as 1903 Sir George Macdonald discussed the two main reasons for the concealment of hoards of coins – *custodiae causa* and *metus causa*, with specific reference to the *Trinummus* and the *Aulularia* of Plautus. He concluded:

> 'These examples from Plautus bring me to a point that is, in my opinion, quite fatal to the view that *custodiae causa* can account for anything other than a very small proportion of the hoards that come to light from time to time ... Such money as was buried *custodiae causa* would surely be dug up again in ninety-nine cases out of a hundred ... We are thus left with the alternative of *metus causa*.

Sir George Macdonald continued:

> 'I said that the instinct to bury treasure underground in times of danger was a most natural one ... I suppose everybody will agree that there never was a more "human" man than Mr. Samuel Pepys. His diary for the early days of June, 1667, reflects the alarm caused throughout London and all over England by the Dutch raid on the Thames ... "I presently resolved of my father's and wife's going into the country; and at two hours' warning, they did go by the coach this day with about £1,300 in gold in their night bag ... I did, about noon, resolve to send Mr. Gibson away after my wife with another 1,000 pieces, under colour of an express to Sir Jeremy Smith." The money was duly buried in the garden. Under dates, Oct. 10th, 11th, 12th, of the same year, you will find details as to the troubles he encountered in digging it up again.' (Macdonald 1903)

HOARDS OF ROMAN COINS FOUND IN BRITAIN:
THE SEARCH

There have now been recorded about 1800 hoards of Roman coins found in Britain, plus about 200 other finds of coins which may have been hoards (Robertson forthcoming). The earliest contemporary accounts of such discoveries were searched for in libraries, museums, newspapers and other sources. The co-operation of museum officials was also gratefully received in the process of tracking down Romano-British coin hoards found long ago, or not so long ago, which were, or are, partly or wholly preserved in museums. Thus became possible the examination of about 300 Romano-British coin hoards which are wholly or partly represented in museums in Britain. Consultation also took place with other archaeologists in their special fields of expertise, including the distinguished recipient of the present tribute Brian Hartley.

The search for actual records of discoveries of hoards of Roman coins found in Britain is only the first stage of an investigation and/or interpretation of their significance. The partnership of recording and interpretation was in existence as early as the *Anglo-Saxon Chronicle*:

> 'The writer of the *Anglo-Saxon Chronicle*, when he recorded under the year 418 that the Romans collected all the hoards of coins that were in Britain and hid some in the earth and carried some with them to Gaul, can only have been led to this statement by a knowledge of the frequent discovery of such hoards in Alfred's time, as in our own, or by a long tradition of their discovery' (Brooke 1932, 1f.).

(a) The historical evidence of Romano-British coin hoards

Two main reasons for the concealment of Romano-British coin hoards have been proposed. One was some violent interruption of the even tenor of Romano-British life through war, civil war, piracy, brigandage, or the like. The second reason was a devaluation of a familiar currency, which instead of being handed over to officialdom for undervalued replacement, or for melting down, was withheld and consigned to various resting places in the hope of eventual revaluation and reinstatement. An uncertain number of hoards deposited for the first reason were not recovered but remained hidden until revealed in recent times (Carson 1976; Jarrett 1983; Kent 1960; Reece 1973; Sutherland 1956). Hoards set aside for the second reason may have been abandoned when it became clear, finally, that the currency of which they were composed had become valueless.

(b) The numismatic evidence
of Romano-British coin hoards

(i) Purely numismatic, i.e. evidence as a corpus of Roman coins, regardless of provenance.

The total number of Roman coins certainly recovered, and examined, from Romano-British coin hoards is not far short of one million. This offers a very rich numismatic resource, with rare potential for continuing study of an emperor's coin output, in different metals, sequence of issues and use of reverse types and mints.

(ii) As Romano-British currency

The chronological arrangement of Romano-British coin hoards highlights the introduction, distribution and circulation of Roman coins in Britain (Robertson 1974; and forthcoming). What can, it is hoped, be agreed, is that coins deliberately incorporated in a Romano-British hoard must, in most cases, have been extracted for saving out of coins current in Britain, or at least acceptable as currency or money.

(c) The archaeological evidence
of Romano-British coin hoards

(i) Containers (coarse ware pots: fig. 1)

Throughout the whole time-span of the Roman occupation of Britain, coin hoards were most commonly stored in coarse ware pots, wooden boxes and money bags. The two last have seldom been discovered intact, but the chronological distribution of their remains, or vestigia, ranges from Claudius to Honorius. Coarse ware pots, on the other hand, have proved virtually indestructible. They have been recorded as containers of about 600 Romano-British hoards.

The coarse ware pots serving as containers of Romano-British coin hoards were mostly jars, cooking pots, beakers or flagons, varying in size with the size of the hoards, but usually having a fairly narrow neck. At least five pots had had a slot cut in the base, neck or shoulder, in the manner of a modern 'piggy bank'. A sixth pot had a hole cut in the bottom which was later plugged with lead. The dates of the 'money box' hoards range from the reign of Antoninus Pius, AD 138–61, to that of Constantine II Augustus (AD 337–61). There seems to have been a timeless awareness in Roman Britain that money was more likely to stay saved if extraction from its container was rendered much more difficult than insertion.

(ii) Containers (samian ware)

Only two Romano-British hoards are recorded as having certainly been contained in vessels of samian ware. It is, at first sight, surprising that they were, apparently, so rarely employed for that purpose. The reason was, no doubt, the simple one that samian ware usually took the form of shallow platters, wide-mouthed cups, or open bowls, whose shapes made them quite unsuitable for holding coins safely.

(iii) Containers of glass, silver, bronze, lead or pewter

(iv) Perishable containers

Containers of what might be called 'organic', 'vegetable', or other perishable material, partly because their very survival invites astonishment ... The recorded evidence for their presence has often been fragmentary in the extreme (like shreds or threads of material), or even ghostly, in the form of a cluster of coins retaining the shape of a bag.

(v) Multiple containers

A minority of Romano-British hoards were accommodated in two or more containers. These were usually but not always coarse ware pots, varying from two to five in number. Owners of late 1st or 2nd century hoards, or of 3rd century hoards down to Gallienus, appear to have been content, as it were, with one or two pots. These were the periods when good quality silver coins could readily be acquired for hoarding, in small bulk, but of intrinsic value. Thereafter, hoards of later 3rd century *antoniniani* and early to mid-4th century AE often took the form of large numbers of coins, which required more than one pot to hold them.

In a very few hoards, phases of the saving process have been distinguished. For example the Gosbecks, Colchester 1983 hoard ending with Aurelian was preserved in three pots, in which distinct sequences of coin layers could be detected. Moreover, although all three pots seem to have belonged to one and the same deposit, one of the pots contained the earliest part of the hoard. In another of the pots, 'the finest coins were concentrated in the upper part of the pot ... the fine coins which had presumably been separate, being added at the end.' In another hoard, from Appleford, 1954, to Constantius II Augustus or later, one of the two pots, the smaller, contained the earlier part of the hoard, and may have been buried before the other larger pot with the later part of the hoard, although both belonged to the same owner.

HOARDS OF ROMAN COINS FOUND IN BRITAIN:
THE BYWAYS

(a) The coins

Those Romano-Britons who owned, and subsequently, lost hoards of Roman coins were able to select for saving purposes coins already circulating in their area, or coins newly introduced into Britain from elsewhere. In general, such hoards mirror the rise and fall of denominations, for example the *denarius* vis à vis the *antoninianus*, and also the presence of less common denominations, for example the gold double *aureus* and silver *quinarii* (half-*denarius*).

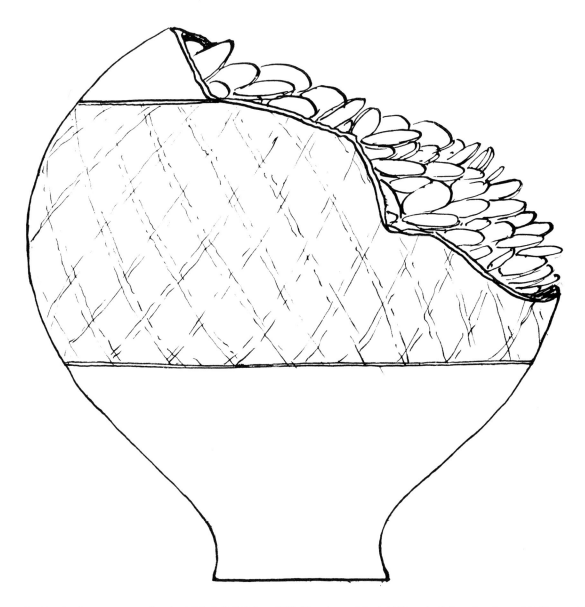

Fig. 1. Coin hoard and pottery container found at Mildenhall, Suffolk, c. 1832. The coins surviving in 1953 consisted of one denarius and 1285 antoniniani, the latest dated c. AD 270 (Robertson 1954). Drawn by Henry Andrews, Curator of Moyse's Hall Museum, Bury St. Edmunds, in 1936. Scale 1:1.

Romano-British hoards also encompass coins generally regarded as intrinsically rare issues. There are admittedly 'rarities' of somewhat dubious standing, like 'silver coin of Julius Caesar which are esteemed a great curiosity, being in the highest state of perfection' from the Chelvey, 1806 hoard. Nevertheless recently identified examples exist of an *aureus* of Julius Caesar in a gold Claudian hoard, and of *denarii* of Julius Caesar in a hoard ending with Gaius. The comparatively rare coinages of transitory or little-known imperial ladies had, and have their own attraction, not least for the portraiture. More surprising is the fleeting appearance of scarce *antoniniani* of Macrianus and Quietus, minted at Antioch, and possibly Emesa, in AD 260. Still more unexpected is the inclusion of an *antoninianus* of Pacatian in a hoard found in 1986 at Stevenage, Hertfordshire, and ending in the AD 260s, with coins of Postumus. Pacatian was a short-lived usurper of AD 248–9, in the Balkans, supported by elements of the Roman army,

CONCORDIA MILITVM. His coins were probably minted at Viminacium on the Danube. So far, the Stevenage *antoninianus* is the only coin of Pacatian recorded from Britain.

There were times and circumstances which tolerated, if not encouraged the manufacture and circulation of irregular (or 'barbarous') copies of official Roman coins. Such impersonators in Romano-British hoards are primarily subjects for inclusion in a study of Romano-British currency. They also form one manifestation of a phenomenon widespread throughout the Roman Empire.

(b) The passage of time

The early recorders of Romano-British coin hoards have bequeathed to later researchers many examples of careful inquiry into the circumstances of discovery, and the details of the coins found. An unsurpassed example is the account of the Antonine hoard found at Auburn, East Yorkshire, in 1570/1. The writer was prepared to go himself to the spot as soon as he heard of the find. He at least got details from local informants, recovered as many of the coins as he could, slightly cleaned them, and reported his discovery to the Queen's representative. Exactly the same general principles are or should be followed today.

Care has even been taken to have discoveries of Romano-British coin hoards confirmed by finders, or eye-witnesses. Perhaps the most engaging eye-witness was Mr. Hotham, foreman when the Cowlam (Yorkshire) hoard was found, 1858, in ploughing. Forty-six years later, Mr. Hotham, then a veteran of 78, was invited, at a meeting of the East Riding Antiquarian Society, to confirm the circumstances of the discovery. The twelve lads present, he said 'all wanted some (coins) in their pockets ... You should have seen the lads reaching ower the pankin, and scramping the money in ... They said "We'll nivver work na mair".' The lads were not the first, nor will they be the last, to exaggerate the value of ancient coins.

Early records show that containers and associated objects found with Romano-British coin hoards have often been carefully sought for further study, and/or preserved by removal to a place of safety or even to museums. One of the most praiseworthy efforts to deal with an associated object was that of ensuring that the Royston, *c.* 1833 skeleton 'was carefully taken up by Mr. Deck, practical chemist of Huntingdon'.

Exceptions were a few containers, associated objects and even coins, which were put to somewhat bizarre after-use. Two bronze containers were turned into 17th-century brewing vessels. A lady purchaser of *antoniniani* from the Aberyswyth 1880/1 hoard 'made bracelets, chains, ear-rings, and sleeve-links of the coins. She died from blood poisoning, the result, it was said, and quite truly, of continually removing the verdigris from the coins.' Coins from another hoard were attached to watch-chains. At least two Romano-British hoards of AE coins were recycled as English trade tokens.

The greatest pains, however, were more often taken by earlier recorders to recover and to list coins from Romano-British hoards, in the light of then current knowledge and standards.

It was anticipated that records of Romano-British coin hoards would preserve many 'period pieces'. The Great Stainland, *c.* 1714 hoard fell 'into the hands of an exciseman. He carried the coins into the north whence he never returned.' The Victorian interest in archaeology is strikingly illustrated by the treatment of the Bourton, *c.* 1895 villa hoard, which was found the day before an expected visit by the Cotswold Field Club. The hoard was quickly covered over again by the excavator, G. Witts. The next day, at the end of his discourse on the villa, he 'said, in a casual way, "Let's see if we can find anything." He took up a pickaxe and immediately found the coins.'

It was also anticipated that there would be confirmation of the wise saying: 'Certain researches are possible only at certain epochs' (Ferguson 1896, 176). What was not so fully anticipated was the evidence that certain *discoveries* are at times only made possible by fortuitous circumstances entirely unrelated to the study of the discoveries concerned.

Striking examples are the large number of Romano-British coin hoards discovered during railway excavations in the 19th century, and by the use of metal detectors in the 20th century.

'I warn you that in a little while others will find their past in you and your times' – Author unknown

Bibliography

Brooke, G.C., 1932 *English coins*

Carson, R.A.G., 1976 Gold and silver coin hoards and the end of Roman Britain, *British Museum Yearbook*, **1**, 68–82

Ferguson, J., 1896 Valedictory presidential address, *Trans. Glasgow Archaeol. Soc.* new ser., **2** (1981–6), 176

Jarrett, M.G., 1983 Magnus Maximus and the end of Roman Britain, *Trans. Hon. Soc. Cymmrodorion*, 1983, 22–35

Kent, J.P.C., 1960 From Roman Britain to Saxon England, in Dolley, R.H.M. (ed.), *Anglo-Saxon coins*, 1–22

Macdonald, G., 1903 Coin finds and how to interpret them, *Proc. Royal Philosophical Soc., Glasgow, 11 March, 1903*, 4–21

Reece, R., 1973 Roman coinage in the western empire, *Britannia*, **4**, 227–51

Robertson, A. S., 1954 *Numis. Chron.*, 40–52

_____, 1974 Romano-British coin hoards; their numismatic, archaeological and historical significance, in Casey, J., & Reece, R. (eds), *Coins and the archaeologist*, Brit. Archaeol. Rep., **4**, 12–36 (Oxford)

_____, forthcoming *Romano-British coin hoards*

Sutherland, C.H.V., 1956 Coinage in Britain in the fifth and sixth centuries, a reassessment of the problems, in Harden, D.B. (ed.), *Dark Age Britain: studies presented to E T Leeds*, 1–10

30   Do brooches have ritual associations?

Grace Simpson and Beatrice Blance

Although brooches are far less numerous than samian pot-sherds, they are just as widely distributed, and are equally rarely found in datable contexts. It is a pleasure to contribute this paper in appreciation of Brian Hartley's work on chronology and ceramics.

In the Late Hallstatt burial mound at Hochdorf, near Stuttgart in Germany, pairs of brooches were found along the inner side of the grave chamber walls. This suggested to the excavators that the brooches were used to secure hangings (Planck 1985, 79–105, 130–161). In prehistoric and Roman Britain, brooches were regularly deposited in graves. Finds from sites such as King Harry Lane at St Albans show that one or two brooches were placed in a grave after cremation had taken place, perhaps to secure a cloth containing the ashes. Some graves contained three or four brooches. Evidence from King Harry Lane dispels the notion that pairs of brooches are exclusively associated with female burials. Brooches are found elsewhere in apparently ritual contexts, such as in a votive pit at Chelmsford (Wickenden 1992, 71–3), or poked into the wall of a little shrine at Nornour (Butcher 1993, 10–12), or pushed into a deep hole and rammed down with soil as was the Collingwood type Riii trumpet brooch found at Crickley Hill in Gloucestershire (Philip Dixon, pers. comm.). The recurring association of certain types of brooch with temple sites decided the writers to check this impression and to review the dating evidence so far as it exists.

This study would not have been possible without M. R. Hull's 50 years of dedicated research on brooches in Britain. His work, currently being edited and revised by us, records some 10,000 brooches and it is to be published under the title *Brooches from pre-Roman and Roman Britain* (forthcoming). The list of temples was extended from those in Hull's *Corpus* to include some more recently excavated sites, bringing the total to 28 sites. These were then roughly divided into an eastern and northern group, and a western group, as follows:

Eastern and northern sites

Baldock, Herts. Hints of religious activity at the north-east corner of Site A were two miniature axes, a spear, and a ritual rattle. In the filling of a 3rd-century well, A13, were 44 early spearheads and bolt-heads (Stead & Rigby 1986, 146–9).

Brigstock, Northants. Circular and polygonal shrines. Several horse and rider statuettes and other votive objects (Greenfield 1963; Taylor, M. V., 1963; Wheeler, H., 1981).

Chelmsford, Essex. A votive pit containing brooches, none later than AD 100, and most a good deal earlier, located outside a later octagonal temple (Wickenden 1992).

Coventina's Well, Carrawburgh, Northumberland. A spring with votive deposits (Allason-Jones & McKay 1985).

Corbridge, Site 16, Northumberland. A circular building which contained a sculptured panel depicting a seated female holding a sceptre with Fortune or Abundance beside her, and a horse-and-rider brooch, the most northerly known (Forster & Knowles 1910, 229–32).

Farley Heath, Surrey. Inadequately published rectangular temple, excavated by S. E. Winbolt. An embossed bronze strip was found in 1848 (Winbolt 1927; Goodchild 1947).

Frilford, Berks/Oxon. Rectangular temple complex. Miniature shield and sword found (Bradford & Goodchild 1939).

Harlow, Essex. Celtic shrine with large coin deposit, overlain by Romano-British square temple. A helmeted head of Minerva and other votive objects were found (France & Gobel 1985; Bartlett 1988; Haselgrove 1989).

Hockwold-cum-Wilton, Norfolk. Two temple sites, Leylands Farm and Sawbench, and possibly a third near the site of the treasure of silver cups. At Leylands Farm, a crown and five diadems were found together with *ad locutio* and horse-and-rider brooches. Probably a temple to Mars, who was a fertility god and protector and healer (Gurney 1957; Johns 1986).

Kate's Cabin, Water Newton, Cambs. Possibly a shrine. Unpublished: fifteen brooches in Hull forthcoming (Greenfield 1958).

Lowbury Hill, Berks. Michael Fulford (report in prep.), suggests that there was a temple in a corner of the enclosure excavated by Donald Atkinson. Late Iron Age pottery is contemporary with early brooches. There were votive bracelets, finger rings, and coins (Atkinson 1916).

Poole's Cavern, Derbys. Ritually damaged votive objects from a watery grotto (Bramwell 1983).

Redhill, Notts. The site overlooks the river Soar near its confluence with the Trent (Hawkes & Jacobsthal 1945; Hildyard 1946). Important Celtic and Roman finds.

Springhead, Kent. At least five temples. Pits of votive character underlie the Roman levels, strongly suggesting an earlier important religious sanctuary: excavations by the late W. S. Penn (Harker 1980 for refs).

Thetford, Fison Way, Norfolk. A succession of round temples within a ritual enclosure which was greatly enlarged about AD 50, with nine rows of fences between the inner and outer ditches. Presumably the site was destroyed by the Romans, following Boudicca's rebellion, about AD 61–3 (Gregory 1991). The much later Thetford treasure associated with the worship of the woodland god Faunus was found nearby (Johns & Potter 1983).

Thistleton, Rutland/Leics. A rectangular temple overlying a round temple excavated but unpublished by Ernest Greenfield (*J. Roman Stud.*, **52**, 171–2). There is a dedication to Mars Rigonemetus.

Woodeaton, Oxon. An early Iron Age shrine, continuing through the Roman period. Many votive objects indicate the worship of Minerva, Venus and Mars (Kirk 1951; Goodchild & Kirk 1954).

WESTERN SITES

Butcomb, Somerset. Pre-Roman and late Roman temple site (Fowler 1969–71).

Chedworth, Glos. A temple complex with fragments of sculpture portraying pagan gods, and an inscription to Mars-Lenus (RIB, no. 126; Webster 1983).

Cold Kitchen Hill, Wilts. An exposed hilltop which appears to have been a sanctuary site, with finds of miniature axes and spears, *ad locutio* brooches, antlers, etc. (Cunnington 1934, 115ff; Hull & Hawkes 1987, 43).

Hayling Island, Hants. Round temple within a courtyard, over an Iron Age shrine. Many votive objects (Downey, King & Soffe 1977; 1978; 1979).

Lamyatt Beacon, Somerset. 3rd-century stone-built temple, and an earlier shrine, associated with brooches, 21 miniature pots, six bronze figurines representing Mercury, Minerva, Mars, Hercules and a genius or priest. Several antler burials (Leach 1986).

Lydney Park, Glos. Pre-Roman votive deposits below a stone-built rectangular temple with associated buildings. Dedication to Mars-Nodens. Other deities, and many votive objects (Wheeler & Wheeler 1932; Casey 1981, 1982).

Maiden Castle, Dorset. A round temple, Site L, beginning in the 1st century, and continuing into the 4th century, with a marble of Diana and hind, and two antlers. A rectangular stone temple, Site B, late 4th century, continuing into the 5th, with finds suggesting an earlier foundation; bronze plaque of Minerva (Wheeler, R.E.M., 1943).

Nettleton, Wilts. A succession of superimposed shrines situated beside a running stream, and in use from Flavian times until the 4th century. Dedications to Apollo, Rosmerta and Silvanus, and statues of Diana and Mercury (Wedlake 1982).

Nornour, Isles of Scilly. Round building with benches and central table. Twenty miniature pots, thirteen Romano-Gaulish white clay female figurines, and other votive objects. Mr Hull was led to believe that this was a manufacturing site for brooches, but this clearly is not the case (Dudley 1968; Butcher 1993).

Uley, West Hill, Glos. Prehistoric, Romano-British and post-Roman religious site. Cult of Mercury, with many votive deposits and lead curses (Woodward & Leach 1993).

Wycomb, Glos. Temple and theatre excavated 1863–4 (McWhirr 1986). A bronze of Mars, and hooded figures (*cucullati*), and hoodless deities, in relief (Rawes 1976).

Mr Hull listed over 600 of the 905 brooches recorded from these temple sites. This does not exhaust the list of temple sites: others will be referred to in the text, and some 251 brooches have been reported since his death in 1976.

Tables 1 and 2 show the distribution of all these brooches, classified according to Hull's typology. Nine brooches, not among the types listed in these tables, include a pelta-shaped brooch Type 236 from Woodeaton, a cruciform brooch Type 225 from Springhead, and two with scalloped edges Type 240 from Nornour.

Hull Types 1–4 : La Tène Brooches

Forty are recorded from temple sites, 28 of them from sites in the western area, including 22 from Cold Kitchen Hill, seven from Woodeaton and four from Maiden Castle. Four examples of the Upavon type, Hull's Group L, probably of the 4th century BC, each lack a pin mechanism. Presumably they were votive objects, and one of them is from the temple area at Woodeaton, Hull 7029 (Hull & Hawkes 1987, 58–61, 66; Hattatt 1987, 18–19, no. 733).

Hull Types 9–20: Nauheim and Derivative Types

Some of the commonest types found on temple sites: 127 are recorded, of which 85 were found on eastern sites, but particularly large numbers were at three sites, 29 at Woodeaton, 25 at Cold Kitchen Hill, and 22 at Lowbury Hill. The Thetford temple site, in the east, has one true Nauheim, see fig. 1, no. 1, and ten fragments, all of iron (Gregory 1991, 123, fig. 113, no. 21). Simpson (1979, 332–5, 338) discussed the general dating of Nauheim derivatives and quoted Hull, who recorded 520 examples in Britain, 89 of them from temple sites:

> 'Generally speaking Nauheim derivatives are pre-Roman (Meare and Glastonbury Lake Villages), but they continued after AD 43 in considerable numbers and are found across England as far north as Northamptonshire and Lincolnshire...'

Four brooches from northern England and four from Scotland were probably the personal possessions of captives

Table 1

Hull Types	Description	Eastern Sites			Western Sites			Grand total
		Hull	Other	Total	Hull	Other	Total	
1–4	La Tene	10	2	12	22	6	28	40
9–20	Nauheim & Derivatives	61	24	85	28	14	42	127
21–3	Langton Down	6	4	10	–	2	2	12
25–8	Rosette	4	3	7	1	1	2	9
29–36	Fantail	4	1	5	1	1	2	7
37–9	Aesica	6	3	9	–	1	1	10
40–44	Eye	2	1	3	1	–	1	4
46–59	Aucissa	6	3	9	7	3	10	19
60–79	Hod Hill	18	16	34	3	25	28	62
89–93	Colchester	46	31	77	2	9	11	88
94	Dolphin	11	–	11	–	1	1	12
95–103	Polden Hill	15	3	18	11	13	24	42
104–43	T-derivatives & SW Types	27	4	31	105	9	114	145
144–5	Sawfish	8	2	10	2	1	3	13
147–50	Lamberton Moor	2	3	5	4	6	10	15
153–70	Trumpet Head	18	4	22	9	7	16	38
171–9	Knee	4	–	4	9	3	12	16
180–83	Enamelled bow	1	1	2	7	–	7	9
184–90 193–8	Sheath footed & proto crossbow	6	–	6	1	2	3	9
191–2	Crossbow	2	1	3	–	7	7	10
				363			324	687

Table 2

Hull Types	Description	Eastern Sites			Western Sites			Grand total
		Hull	Other	Total	Hull	Other	Total	
200	Dragonesque	–	–	–	–	1	1	1
203–23 247+168	Animals, etc.	7	2	9	3	6	9	18
204	Horse-and-rider	2	9	11	1	11	12	23
224	Early disc	–	2	2	–	–	–	2
226–8 229–33	Diamond shaped & lantern-like	8	2	10	44	1	45	55
249A&B	Embossed disc	2	–	2	5	1	6	8
249C	*ad locutio*	–	8	8	4	1	5	13
250 252–60 262–8 279	Disc Enamelled disc Disc with lugs Scalloped star	15	11	26	28	11	39	65
270–71	Disc with stone	6	4	10	2	3	5	15
273–7	Weapons, sandal, fusiform, axe, dagger, shield	–	–	–	12	6	18	18
				78			140	218

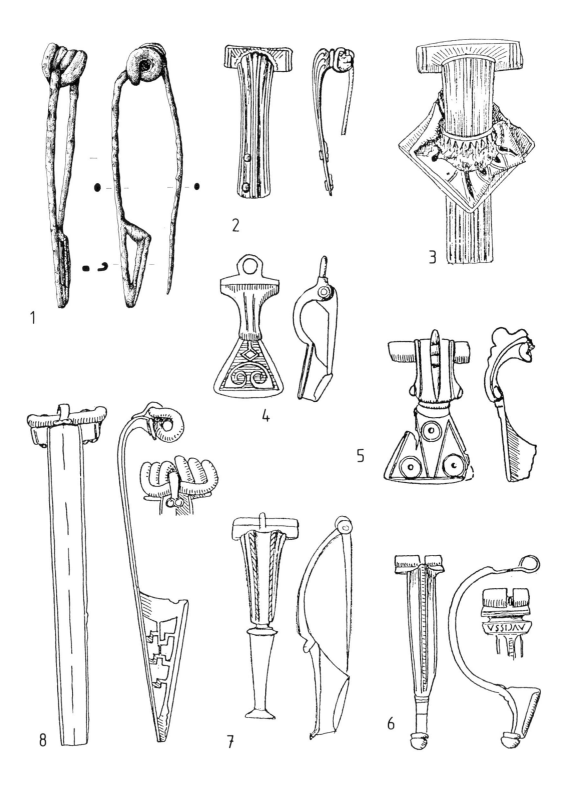

Fig. 1. **1.** *Type 9, Thetford;* **2.** *Type 21B, Lydney Park;* **3.** *Type 26A, Baldock;* **4.** *Type 36, Thistleton;* **5.** *Type 37, Kate's Cabin;*
6. *Type 51B, Harlow;* **7.** *Type 60, Cold Kitchen Hill;* **8.** *Type 89, Upper Deal. Scale 1:1.*

or refugees, as were probably the seven found at Usk and the three at Caerleon (Simpson 1979, 338).

Hull Type 200: The Dragonesque Brooch

Only one brooch of this type was found on a temple site: Site L at Maiden Castle.

Hull Types 21–44: Langton Down, Rosette, Fantail, Aesica and Eye Brooches

The total number found on temple sites is small, only 42, of which 29 are from eastern sites.

Langton Down: Types 21–23. Twelve examples are known, ten of them from the eastern area, two of which were found by metal detectors at the Thetford temple (Gregory 1991, fig. 114, nos. 29, 30).

At Lydney Park a Langton Down, Hull 4265 (see fig. 1, no. 2) was found on the surface of the prehistoric layer under the stone-built temple (Wheeler & Wheeler 1932, 71).

According to Donald Mackreth:

'The floruit of the Langton Down brooch lies essentially in the first part of the 1st century AD. However it is far from clear whether most examples in Britain should be regarded as having arrived after AD 43, …while most dated examples in Britain cannot be shown to be pre-Roman, the manufacturing period would seem to have ended by the time of the conquest' (Mackreth 1985, 22).

On the Continent, the earliest well-dated examples are from the Lindenhof, near Zurich, founded about 22 BC (Ettlinger 1973, 79).

Rosette Brooches: Types 25–28. Nine are recorded from temple sites, seven of them from the eastern area; see fig. 1, no. 3 from Baldock. Mr Mackreth sees these as forerunners of the Aesica brooches which he dates to the middle of the 1st century AD. This places the various Rosette brooches as being contemporary with the Langton Downs. Certainly Rosette brooches were already present in Phase I, dated AD 1–40, at the King Harry Lane cemetery, and they were still being placed in graves in Phase 3, dated AD 40–60 (Stead & Rigby 1989).

Fantails: Types 29–36. These are represented by seven examples at temple sites; see fig. 1, no.4 from Thistleton. At King Harry Lane cemetery a Fantail brooch was found with a Rosette brooch in grave 353 belonging to phase 2 and dated to AD 30–55 (Stead & Rigby 1989).

Aesica brooches: Types 37–39. Ten are known from temple sites, nine of them in the eastern area; see fig. 1, no. 5 from Kate's Cabin. Mackreth (1982, 313–4) suggests that '…the beginning of the Aesica type should fall in the middle years of the 1st century AD, and most probably before AD 50'. He considers that the type was made in southern England and, in his opinion, the earliest seems to be the one from Wadden Hill,

Stoke Abbott, Dorset, a Roman fort abandoned by AD 60. The Aesica brooch with a rearward facing hook found at the Thetford temple provides a similar date (Mackreth, in Gregory 1991, 124, fig. 114, no. 28).

Eye brooches: Types 40–44. These are poorly represented on temple sites: only four have been recorded. Hull redated them in the *Corpus*, after his work in *Camulodunum* (Hawkes & Hull 1947), and he placed them earlier, and is thus in agreement with Ulbert (1959, 64–5), that they date from the Augustan to Claudian periods.

Hull Types 46–79: Aucissa and Hod Hill Brooches

Of the 81 brooches found on temple sites, 62 are of the Hod Hill type; see fig. 1, no. 7 from Cold Kitchen Hill. Such brooches are well represented on the Continent (Feugère 1985, types 21–23; Ulbert 1959, Taf. 15), and they arrived in Britain with the Roman army in AD 43. Two Aucissa brooches were lost during the demolition of the Thetford temple in AD 61–63 (Gregory 1991, 126–7). In the King Harry Lane cemetery Aucissa brooches are found with Colchesters, Langton Downs, Rosettes and Fantails in graves of phases 2 and 3. In Britain, Aucissa brooches (see fig. 1, no. 6 from Harlow) can be dated to the Claudio-Neronian periods.

The type site for Hod Hill brooches is a Roman fort, within a prehistoric hillfort, evacuated in AD 51 (Richmond 1968, 119). Brailsford (1962, 9) dated the brooches from the site to the Claudian period. Three Hod Hill brooches were found at the Thetford temple site, demolished in AD 61–63 (Gregory 1991, 126–8), and Mackreth comments that no fully developed Hod Hill has yet been published from an assured pre-conquest context. He considers that their distribution in Britain shows that they were in common use up to about AD 60. Whatever that usage was, it did not include any part of the ritual at the King Harry Lane cemetery, for no Hod Hills have been published from that site, although a brooch in grave 153 may be a rare Hod Hill type (Type 73) which seems to owe its inspiration to the Rosette brooch.

Hull Types 89–93: Colchester Brooches and Derivatives

Type 89 is the continental form, and only one has been recorded from a temple site, at Springhead, Hull 9356. Types 90–93 have been further classified into Colchester A brooches, Types 90–91, which are one-piece brooches (see fig. 2, 9 from Lydney Park) and Colchester B, Types 92–93, which are two-piece brooches (see fig. 2, no. 10 from Woodeaton). From these two groups come 88 at temple sites, 77 of them from the eastern area. This distribution mirrors what Hull had found for the type in general, which he describes as being on the south-east side of the Fosse Way, with 'trails' down to Maiden Castle or into Wales or the Severn valley, possibly lost by the followers of Caratacus.

In his chapter in *Camulodunum* in 1947, Hull suggested that none of the Colchester type brooches need be dated before the early years of the 1st century AD (Hawkes & Hull 1947,

309). But, writing some 25 years later in his *Corpus*, he puts forward a date as early as Julius Caesar's incursions for a Type 89 Colchester continental brooch in grave 1 at Upper Deal in Kent (see fig. 1, no. 8: Bushe-Fox 1925, pl. 13, no. 7). A Type 90A brooch was found with a Rosette brooch in grave 397 at King Harry Lane, and another in grave 202: both of these graves belong to phase 1, AD 1–40, and match a Type 90A in Grave 2 at Upper Deal (Bushe-Fox 1925, pl. 13, no. 9). Hull concluded that brooches of Type 90 could be dated to the early Augustan period, that is from 23 BC. Brooches of Types 91 and 92 continue into the early years of the 1st century, with centres of manufacture in Hertfordshire, Essex and Kent, and eight of these were found at the Thetford, Fison Way, temple. Mr Mackreth suggests that the production of Colchesters and their derivatives came to an end as a result of Boudicca's defeat in AD 60–61 (Mackreth, in Gregory 1991, 123). The King Harry Lane cemetery was in use between AD 1–60, and Colchester brooches there are predominantly of Type A. One of the latest is probably a Colchester B of Type 92 in grave 316, attributed to phase 3; but the general lack of Colchester B brooches at the cemetery is noteworthy.

Mr Hull considered that Type 93 brooches, which are two-piece brooches, continued in use beyond AD 65, even as late as AD 80. He based this conclusion on the high incidence of these brooches at Camulodunum, but our examination of this evidence shows that these brooches are either unstratified finds in old collections or are residual. Their distribution pattern, to which Hull did not refer, is very similar to that of Type 92. There seems to be no reason, therefore, to place these brooches any later than the destruction of Camulodunum by Boudicca, and we agree with Mackreth's assessment that their manufacture would have ceased even earlier.

Hull Type 94: The Dolphin Brooch

Twelve examples are known from temple sites, eleven of them in the south-east (see fig. 2, no. 11 from Thistleton). Dolphin brooches are often confused with Polden Hill brooches, but Hull distinguished the Dolphin as being of two pieces, with a spring made separately and attached to the head of the bow by a single hook, his Type 94A. A few later Dolphins may be hinged, his Type 94B. In Hull's opinion the Dolphin must have been developed about the time when the Colchester brooch was changing from a one- to a two-piece brooch. He dates it to the Claudian period because it is well represented at Camulodunum and in the Santon Hoard. It may be earlier at Bagendon. None was recorded at King Harry Lane.

Hull Types 95–103: Polden Hill Brooches

Forty-two have been found in the temple sites. They are fairly evenly distributed across the country. The Polden Hill brooch has an axial bar through the spring, anchored in the discs at either end of the crossbar (see fig. 2, no. 12 from Wycomb). Hinged Poldens are rare. Although a common type, few occur in good datable contexts. Typically they are in post-conquest and pre-Flavian levels, AD 43–70. The Polden Hill Hoard

contained a brooch of Type 98 and one of Type 100C. Brailsford (1975, 34) concluded that the evidence of all the datable elements in the hoard concurred in giving a date to the hoard of about the middle of the 1st century AD.

Hull Types 104–143: T-Derivative 104–7 and South-Western T-Brooches 108–143

The long crossbar gives these brooches, which are derived from the Polden Hill series, their characteristic shape. Fig. 2, no. 13 is a Type 107 from Cold Kitchen Hill. They are found predominantly in the western area: 114 examples as opposed to 31 from temples in the east. The figure for western sites is, however, inflated by 91 examples from Nornour in the Isles of Scilly. Two of Type 116 were found at Hod Hill which was evacuated by AD 51, and a Type 119 was found at Waddon Hill, evacuated by about AD 60. A brooch of Type 104 from Caerleon was in a deposit dated not later than Flavian, i.e. late 1st century. The dating evidence for some other types, such as 109 and 110, shows that they were in use between AD 70 and 150.

Hull Types 144–145: Sawfish Brooches

This distinctive little brooch (see fig. 2, no. 14 from Woodeaton) is represented by only thirteen examples from temple sites, ten of them from the eastern area. Examples from Broxtowe near Nottingham, Strutt's Park, Derby (unpublished), and Newstead (Curle 1911), indicate a date from the middle of the 1st century into the early 2nd century for its use.

Hull Types 147–150: Lamberton Moor or Headstud Brooches

Fifteen examples are known from temple sites, ten of them from the western area. This distribution contrasts with that of the Sawfish brooches, but the numbers are probably too small to be significant. They are characterised by a stud, often lost, at the head of the bow and, like trumpet brooches, they have a distinctive foot.

Two similar Lamberton Moors (see fig. 3, no. 15) and a Backworth brooch were found at the Red House baths, near Corbridge (Daniels 1959, 156–7, not illustrated). This site is earlier than the earliest fort at Corbridge, had a short occupation, and is contemporary with a nearby Agricolan supply base. Brian Hartley, describing the samian from the baths wrote:

'...none need have been made earlier than AD 80, none necessarily later than AD 85' (Hanson *et al.* 1979, 1).

Two early Lamberton Moor brooches were also found in the nearby Agricolan supply base. An example from a votive pit at Chelmsford was dated before AD 100 (Wickenden 1992, 24). The latest example of the type is from Balmuildy on the Antonine Wall, abandoned about AD 163 (Hartley 1972, 38–40).

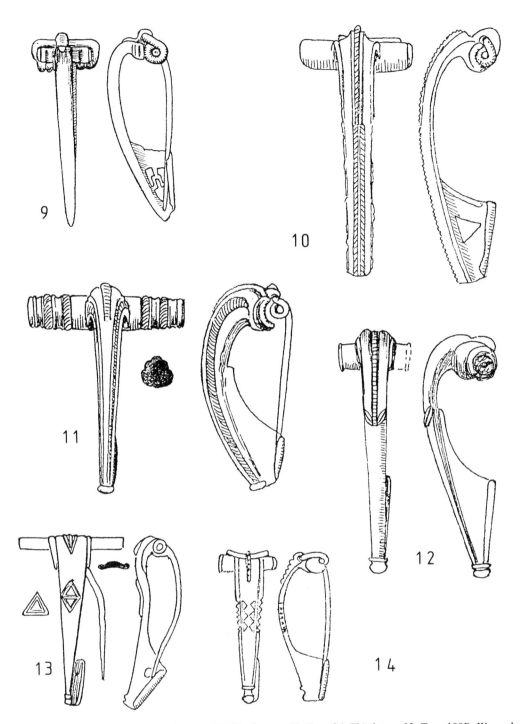

*Fig. 2. **9.** Type 90D, Lydney Park; **10.** Type 92, Woodeaton; **11.** Type 94, Thistleton; **12.** Type 100B, Wycomb; **13.** Type 107, Cold Kitchen Hill; **14.** Type 144, Woodeaton. Scale 1:1.*

Hull Types 153–170: Trumpet-Headed Brooches including the Backworth Type

Thirty-eight are recorded from temple sites, 22 of them in the eastern area. These ornate brooches began, according to Boon & Savory (1975, 57–60), between AD 25–50. This dating allowed for a direct chronological development from the pre-Roman Aylesford type, Hull Type 20, which was coming to an end around AD 25. These brooches continued in use into the 2nd century. In Hull's opinion the Backworths, Lamberton Moors and Aesica brooches were contemporary, and were all native British types of pre-Roman origin. They represent a flowering of Celtic ornament in the Roman period (see fig. 3, no. 16 from Poole's Cavern).

Hull Types 171–179: Knee Brooches

This brooch marks a change in fashion. Previously, brooches had mainly been worn by women, but from this time onwards they were in widespread use by the military and administrative orders.

Characteristics of Knee brooches are their short bow and

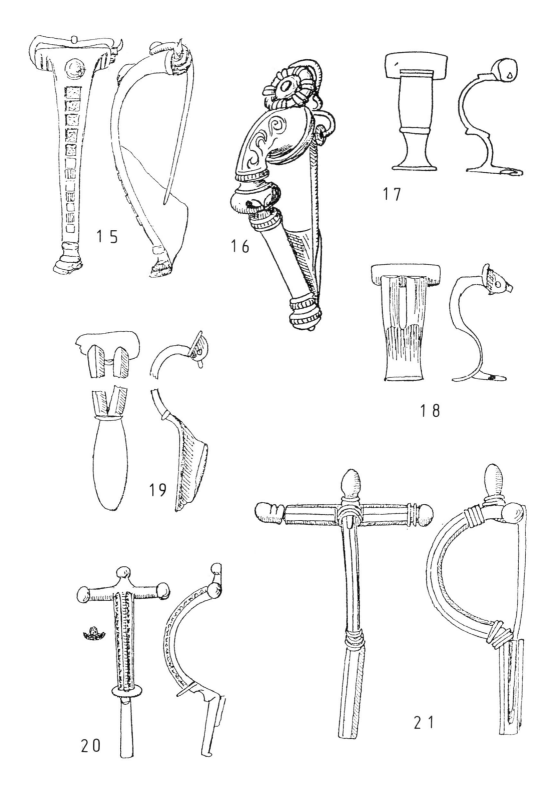

Fig. 3. 15. Type 148B, Red House baths; 16. Type 153B, Poole's Cavern; 17. Type 175A, Woodeaton; 18. Type 175, Nornour; 19. Type 187B, Nornour; 20. Type 190, Springhead; 21. Type 191B, Woodeaton. Scale 1:1.

long horizontal catchplate for securing thicker folds of material (see fig. 3, no. 17 from Woodeaton). Sixteen have been found at temple sites, mostly in the western area. Of particular interest is Type 175B, a British type which has a divided bow: only ten are known, of which six are from temple sites in the south-west: four at Nornour (see fig. 3, no. 18) and one each at Woodeaton and Uley.

Knee brooches originated in Germany in the 2nd century AD (Hattatt 1987, 261–2). Over a hundred were found at the Saalburg and Zugmantel (Boehme 1972). Eastwards, they were found at Dura-Europos, abandoned AD 265 (Toll 1949, pl. 11). They were in use from the late 2nd century until the mid-3rd century.

Hull Types 180–183: Enamelled Bow Brooches

Seven of the nine brooches found on temple sites come from Nornour in the Isles of Scilly.

Hull Types 184–189, 194 and 195: Sheath-Footed Brooches

So named after their characteristic catchplate for the pin. They are not common on temple sites: only nine are recorded, of which six are from eastern sites. Sheath-footed brooches originated in southern Russia and were brought to north-western Europe by Germanic tribes. They begin about the time of the principate of Marcus Aurelius, AD 161–180, and continue into the 3rd century. A sheath-footed brooch with a divided bow found at Nornour, Hull 7934 (see fig. 3, no. 19, Type 187B) has good parallels at Dura-Europos (Toll 1949, pl. 14).

Hull Types 190–192: Proto-Crossbows and Crossbows

These are also types associated with the military and with administrators. Over 200 have been recorded in Britain, but only four proto-crossbows and ten crossbows are recorded from temple sites in our survey. Five of the crossbows were found at Lydney Park (see fig. 4, no. 22) but Uley and Woodeaton have each produced two examples, and three of the proto-crossbows also come from these two sites.

Small early forms of crossbows are illustrated on fig. 3, nos. 20 and 21 from Springhead and Woodeaton. They match those called 'Vorformen' or prototypes at the Saalburg and Zugmantel around AD 200 (Böhme 1972, 764–9, 813–21). During the 3rd century these prototypes replaced all other brooches in military contexts and, by AD 300 at the latest, they were replaced by crossbow brooches, Type 192, which continue through the 4th century to the early 5th century (Keller 1971, 32–41).

In the angle of the buildings at the temple complex at Pagans Hill, Chew Stoke in Somerset, one arm from a proto-crossbow, Hull 1920, was found (Rahtz & Harris 1958). The temple sites of Nornour, Woodeaton, Lydney Park and Uley are noteworthy for their numbers of military type brooches, Types 171–195, compared with the other temple sites in our survey.

Hull Types 203, 205–223, 247: Animals

Eighteen such brooches have been found at temple sites, and this includes the trumpet-fly brooch, Type 168, from Farley Heath. No one kind of animal predominates, and one or two examples of horses, stags, dogs, hares, birds and insects, have turned up at nearly a dozen of the temple sites: Hockwold, Carrawburgh, Hayling Island, Nettleton, Uley, Nornour, Springhead, Thistleton, Farley Heath, Cold Kitchen Hill and Woodeaton. On the continent, Riha dates such brooches to the 2nd century AD (Riha 1979, 203).

Hull Type 204: Horse-and-rider Brooches

Twenty-three have been found at eight temple sites: eight from Hockwold (see fig. 4, no. 23) five from Lamyatt Beacon, three from Hayling Island, two each from Woodeaton and Cold Kitchen Hill, and one each at Nornour, Nettleton, Corbridge Site 16 (Forster & Knowles 1911, 186–8), and the Haddenham religious complex near Cambridge (Ferris 1985; Evans 1984).

Mr Ferris has shown that the 52 known in Britain are mainly in East Anglia, and he includes five sites with what appear to be ritual deposits or offerings: Lode and March in Cambridgeshire; Brampton in Norfolk; Lackford and Undley in Suffolk. Thirty-eight of the 52 known horse-and-rider brooches, therefore, come from temple or probable ritual sites.

The exact form of the British brooches is unknown on the Continent: the few horse-and-rider brooches found there are quite different (see Osterburken, ORL 2, 1895, pl. 6, no. 18; Lerat & Blind 1956, pl. 17, no. 298).

We agree with Mr Mackreth who dates the general phenomenon of enamelled animal brooches to:

> '...the 2nd century running into the 3rd and this range should cover both manufacture and survival in use' (Mackreth, in Ferris 1985, 8)

Hull Type 224: Early Disc Brooches with a Glass Centre

Although relatively scarce in Britain, there are three from temple sites: Baldock, Chelmsford (Wickenden 1992, no. 25; see fig. 4, no. 24) and Hayling Island. The last named has a very close parallel at Hofheim near Wiesbaden (Ritterling 1913, pl. 10, no. 253). Another early disc brooch set with glass accompanied an infant burial at King Harry Lane, grave 68, and in the same grave were two Langton Downs and a Rosette brooch. This grave belonged to phase 3, AD 40–60, and also indicates a mid-1st century date for these brooches.

Hull Types 226–233: Diamond Shapes 226–8, Lantern Like 229–33

The diamond shapes are more common, with 35 examples, 26 of them from Nornour, while the remainder were found scattered mostly over eastern sites (see fig. 4, no. 25 from Harlow). Of the twenty lantern-like brooches only two were

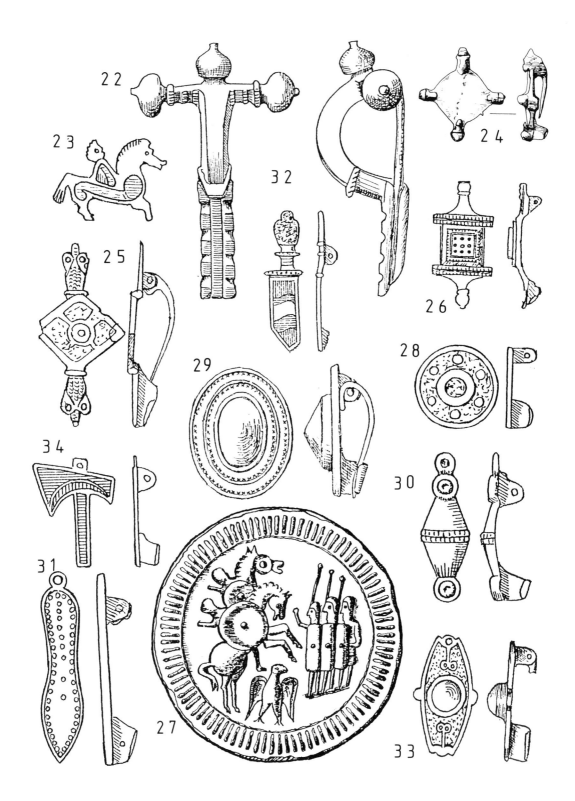

Fig. 4. **22.** *Type 192, Lydney Park;* **23.** *Type 204, Hockwold;* **24.** *Type 224, Chelmsford;* **25.** *Type 228, Harlow;*
26. *Type 230, Chedworth;* **27.** *Type 249C, Wiggonholt (scale 2:1);* **28.** *Type 252, Pagans Hill;* **29.** *Type 271A, Lowbury Hill;*
30. *Type 273, Nornour;* **31.** *Type 275, Normour;* **32.** *Type 274B, Normour;* **33.** *Type 277, Lydney Park;* **34.** *Type 274, South Shields.*
Scale 1:1.

not found at Nornour, and they came from Chedworth (see fig. 4, no. 26) and Farley Heath. Generally, they are 2nd century in date.

Hull Types 249A and B: Embossed Disc Brooches

Eight of both varieties have been found on temple sites, two from the eastern area and six from the western. Hull regarded these as being British-Celtic in origin and he dated them to the 1st century but continuing into the 2nd century AD. Over 60 examples were recorded by him.

Hull Type 249C: The Ad Locutio Embossed Disc Brooches

These come at the end of the series. Thirteen have been found on temple sites, but Hockwold and Cold Kitchen Hill account for eleven of them. One was in Coventina's Well, and another was at Wycomb. The reconstruction of the design of the Wiggonholt brooch, correcting the original drawings of those at Cold Kitchen Hill, is shown on fig. 4, no. 27 (Goodchild 1941).

The finest and best preserved is a stray find from Lackford in Suffolk, and Hattatt suggested that there had been two centres of manufacture and distribution, one in East Anglia and the other on the Wiltshire-Dorset border (Hattatt & Webster 1985, 434; Hattatt 1985, 177–8). The type seems to be more common on temple sites than anywhere else. The *ad locutio* is taken from a coin of Hadrian of AD 117–138.

Two other embossed disc brooches classified by Hull as Type 249C come from temple sites. One from Chedworth has a unique decoration of seven heads around a stone setting. The other, from Nornour, bears an embossed human head.

Hull Types 250–268 and 279: Disc Brooches

Sixty-five were found on temple sites, many of them from Nornour. Mostly of British manufacture, and widely distributed, many are old finds and good dating evidence is usually lacking. A rare example of dating evidence comes from Pagans Hill, Chew Stoke, Somerset, a religious complex, where an enamel disc brooch (see fig. 4, no. 28) Type 252B, Hull 1918, was found three quarters of the way down a 56 feet deep well which, on coin evidence, ceased to be used after the first quarter of the 4th century AD (Rahtz & Harris 1958).

On the other hand, emperors, such as Antoninus Pius (138–161), Septimius Severus (193–211) and Caracalla (198–217), are shown wearing their military cloaks fastened with domed disc brooches (British Museum sculptures no. 1463, 1916, 1917).

Hull Types 270 and 271: with a Central Raised Stone Setting

Brooches of Type 270 are circular and those of Type 271 are oval (see fig. 4, no. 29 from Lowbury Hill). Fifteen were found on eleven of the temple sites: Nornour, Uley and Cold Kitchen Hill are those in the western area. Since the total listed by Hull is 89, these represent a significant proportion. None was found in Scotland. Ten (over 10% of the total) were found in Silchester. Few have any useful dating context.

They are rare on the Continent, but a Type 270 was found at the Saalburg and a Type 271 at Zugmantel; both are *Limes* forts which were overrun about AD 260. All are of British manufacture and there is no good evidence to date them later than the middle of the 3rd century. Indeed Mackreth suggests that '...all purely British brooches had ceased to be made by AD 250' (Mackreth 1992, 60).

Hull Types 273–277: Miniature Axes, Daggers, Shields, Fusiform Missiles and Sandals

Eighteen, all from the western area, but this distribution is distorted by the finds from Nornour of eight sandal brooches, four fusiform missiles and a dagger brooch (see fig. 4, nos. 30, 31, 32). A similar dagger, an axe, and a fusiform missile were found at the Nettleton shrine. Miniature weapons were not confined to brooches: a miniature axe and spear were found at Baldock, and a miniature axe at Brigstock. At Kirmington in South Humberside a miniature gladiator's helmet, an axe and four miniature shields were found. A bronze shield brooch comes from the probable shrine at Gestingthorpe in Essex (see also fig. 4, no. 33 from Lydney Park). Sarnia Butcher notes similar shield brooches from Caerwent, Newhaven and Straubing (Butcher 1985).

Few people would quibble with the notion that miniature weapons are votive, and brooches form but a small part of this inventory. The subject is too wide to examine here in any detail, but we can, however, note that four other axe brooches, very similar to the one from Nettleton shrine are known in England from Camerton, South Shields in County Durham (see fig. 4, no. 34), in East Anglia, and at the Wanborough temple in Surrey. This last was found in the immediate vicinity of the temple there (O'Connell & Bird 1994, fig. 33, no. 48).

All are enamelled, and Hattatt suggested that they are a native British adaptation (Hattatt 1989, 168). He dated axe brooches '...mainly to the second half of the 2nd century AD' (Hattatt 1987, 220). With regard to the fusiform missiles and the sandals, Hull could only date them as '...probably 2nd century'.

None of the shield brooches has a dated context and they are generally considered to be of 2nd century date, but Ian Stead points out that such a date is later than the context in which that shape of shield was in use (Stead 1991, 26).

DISCUSSION

Not all temple sites have yielded brooches, but at well-excavated sites such as Chelmsford, Hayling Island or Nettleton, it has been shown that brooches occur regularly in votive deposits and are not the result of casual loss. Similar deposits are known on the Continent. At Tremblois, some 200 iron penannular brooches were found together to the south of the temple entrance (Paris 1960). At the sanctuary of Les Bolards

at Nuits-Saint-George many brooches, which would not have
+been out of place at Springhead, Thetford, or the King Harry
Lane cemetery, occurred in deposits (Fauduet & Pommeret
1985).

Some brooch types are not found at temple sites. In our
survey, for example, no brooches of the sunwheel type, Hull
Type 266B, were noted except for one of a rare variety at
Nornour (Green 1983, 168–75). The wheel brooch is associated with the Celtic Jupiter.

Another brooch type lacking from our survey is the cock
or hen, although one was found with a burial at Lancing Down
temple (Smith 1848). At Milton Keynes, beside a pool, there
was a sacrificial burial of a cock associated with a curious
carved oak wheel symbol (Williams & Hart 1990). The cock
is one of the attributes of Mercury, a Roman god who was
associated with native British gods. At Nettleton, Mercury is
associated with Rosmerta, as also at the sanctuary complex
at Genainville (Mitard 1993). At the settlement and temple
site of Cottenham in Cambridgeshire fragments of statues of
Mercury, Luna and Sol have been found, and Sol appears to
be wearing a disc brooch (Taylor 1985, fig. 13). Tacitus records
that '...Agricola gave private encouragement and official assistance to the building of temples' (*Agricola* 21), and his predecessors may have done the same, as for example for the final
phase at Thetford, Fison Way.

A pre-Roman continental cult of the Cernunnos is associated with antlers, and a silver coin depicting the god wearing antlers was found at Petersfield in Hampshire (Boon 1982).
Burials with antlers are known at shrines such as Lamyatt
Beacon, where there is a whole pantheon of gods.

A peculiarly British cult is represented by horse-and-rider
portrayals, whether in the form of brooches or statuettes. At
Brigstock several such statuettes were found (Greenfield 1963;
Taylor, M.V., 1963; Wheeler, H., 1981). At Lamyatt Beacon
horse-and-rider brooches were associated with Mars,
Hercules, Mercury and Minerva. Mr Hull records two disc
brooches from Cavenham Heath in Suffolk, a site which also
produced bronze head-dresses (Layard 1925). At Willingham
Fen the remarkable head-dresses and sceptres associated with
the Commodus-Hercules cult, and buried in a wooden box,
may have come from the temple complex at Haddenham
which yielded a horse-and-rider brooch and a hare brooch
(Evans 1984). Regalia and a few brooches are stratified at the
Wanborough temple (O'Connell & Bird 1994).

Another remarkable ritual deposit containing brooches
was the shaft at Jordan Hill, near Weymouth, Dorset, which
contained layers of deposited bird remains (Warne 1844).
Deep shafts are discussed by Richard Bradley (1990, 175).
Anne Ross and Richard Feachem have drawn attention to
several pits at Newstead, the fillings of which were ritual rather
than casual (Ross & Feachem 1976). At Ashill in Norfolk a
ritual pit of Flavian date also contained brooches (Gregory
1977). Anne Ross lists 58 possible ritual sites in Britain, but
concludes:

'...we cannot hope to offer full interpretations or explanations for
all the strange and baffling features of these shafts and pits...'
(Ross 1968).

The evidence indicates that the origin of the custom of
placing brooches in votive deposits is pre-Roman, but it continued throughout Roman times. How long it continued we
cannot be sure, since in pagan Anglo-Saxon times brooches
are found mostly in cemeteries. The custom was still known,
however, to the 8th or 9th century Irish writer of 'The Voyage of Mael Dúin'. He describes how Mael Dúin and his com-
panions reached a small island with snowy white houses within
a fortress whose ramparts almost reached the clouds of
heaven. Around the inside of the largest white house hung
rows of objects. One row consisted of big swords with gold
and silver hilts, another of big gold and silver collars, but the
third row was of gold and silver brooches with their pins in
the wall (Downey *et al.* 1978, 10; Jackson 1971, 154).

ACKNOWLEDGEMENTS

Acknowledgments for permission to reproduce fig. 1, no. 1,
are noted with thanks to Norfolk Museums Service (it is illustrated in Gregory 1991/92, fig. 113, no. 21), and for fig. 4,
no. 24, with thanks to N. P. Wickenden and Chelmsford Museums Service (it is illustrated in Wickenden 1992, no. 25).

Abbreviations
RIB   Collingwood, R.G., & Wright, R.P. (eds), *The Roman inscriptions of
        Britain, vol. 1: inscriptions on stone* (Oxford, 1965)
ORL   Fabricius, E. (ed.), *Der obergermanisch-raetische Limes des Römerreiches*

Bibliography
Allason-Jones, L., & McKay, B., 1985 *Coventina's Well: a shrine on Hadrian's
    Wall* (Chesters Museum)
_____, & Miket, R., 1984 *Catalogue of small finds from South Shields Roman
    fort*, Soc. Antiq. Newcastle upon Tyne Monograph Ser., **2**
Atkinson, D., 1916 *The Romano-British site on Lowbury Hill, Berkshire* (Read-
    ing)
Bartlett, R., 1988 Harlow Celtic temple, *Current Archaeol.*, **112**,163–8
Böhme, A., 1972 Die Fibeln der Kastelle Saalburg und Zugmantel, *Saalburg
    Jahrbuch*, **29**
Boon, G.C., 1982 A coin with the head of Cernunnos, *Seaby Coin and Medal
    Bull.*, **769**, 276–82
_____, & Savory, H.N., 1975 A silver trumpet-brooch with relief deco-
    ration, parcel-gilt, from Carmarthen, *Antiq. J.*, **55**, 41–61
Bradford, J.S.P., & Goodchild, R.G., 1939 Excavations at Frilford, Berkshire,
    1937–8, *Oxoniensia*, **4**, 1–70
Bradley, R., 1990 *The passage of arms* (Cambridge)
Brailsford, J.W., 1962 *Antiquities from Hod Hill in the Durden Collection* (British
    Museum, London)
_____, 1975 The Polden Hill hoard, Somerset, *Proc. Prehist. Soc.*, **41**, 222–
    34
Bramwell, D., *et al.*, 1983 Excavations at Poole's Cavern, Buxton, *Derbyshire
    Archaeol. J.*, **103**, 47–74
Bushe-Fox, J.P., 1925 *Excavation of the Late-Celtic urn-field at Swarling, Kent*, Rep.
    Res. Comm. Soc. Antiq. London, **5**
Butcher, S., 1985 Roman brooches, in Draper, J., *Excavations by Mr H.P. Cooper
    on the Roman site at Hill Farm, Gestingthorpe, Essex*, East Anglian Archaeol.
    Rep., **25**
_____, 1993 *Nornour*, rev. edn, Isles of Scilly Museum Publication, **7**
Casey, P.J., 1981; 1982 Excavations at Lydney Park, Glos., *Archaeol. Reports
    for 1980, 1981*, Univ. Durham & Newcastle upon Tyne
Cunnington, M.E., 1934 *Catalogue of antiquities in the Museum of the Wiltshire
    Archaeol. & Natur. Hist. Soc. at Devizes*, **2**
Curle, J., 1911 *A Roman frontier post and its people; the fort at Newstead in the Parish
    of Melrose* (Glasgow)
Daniels, C.M., 1959 The Roman bath house at Red House, Beaufront, near
    Corbridge, *Archaeol. Aeliana*, 4 ser., **37**, 85–176

Downey, R., King, A., & Soffe, G., 1977; 1978; 1979 Interim reports on the excavations on Hayling Island (London)

Dudley, D., 1968 Excavations on Nornour in the Isles of Scilly, 1962–6, *Archaeol. J.*, **124**, 1–64

Ettlinger, E., 1973 *Die römischen Fibeln in der Schweiz* (Berne)

Evans, C., 1984 A shrine provenance for the Willingham Fen hoard, *Antiquity*, **58**, 212–14

Fauduet, I., & Pommeret, C., 1985 Les fibules du sanctuaire des Bolards à Nuits-Saint-George (Côte d'or), *Revue Archéol. Est et Centre-Est*, **36**, 63–116

Ferris, I.M., 1985 Horse-and-rider brooches in Britain: a new example from Rocester, Staffs, *Trans. South Staffordshire Archaeol. Hist. Soc.*, **26**, 1–10

Feugère, M., 1985 *Les fibules en Gaule Méridionale de la conquête à la fin du V siècle après J.-C.*, Revue Archéol. de Narbonnaise, Suppl., **12**

Forster, R.H., & Knowles, W.H., 1910; 1911 Corstopitum: excavations in 1909, 1910, *Archaeol. Aeliana*, 3 ser., **6**, 205–72; **7**, 143–267

Fowler, P., 1969–71 Fieldwork and excavation in the Butcomb area, *Trans. Univ. Bristol Spelaeological Soc.*, **12**, 169–94

France, N.E., & Gobel, B.M., 1985 *The Romano-British temple at Harlow, Essex*, West Essex Archaeol. Group

Goodchild, R.G., 1941 Romano-British disc-brooches derived from Hadrianic coin-types, *Antiq. J.*, **21**, 1–8

_____, 1947 The Farley Heath sceptre, *Antiq. J.*, **27**, 83–4

_____, & Kirk, J., 1954 The Romano-Celtic temple at Woodeaton, *Oxoniensia*, **19**, 15–37

Green, M., 1983 The Roman wheel-brooch from Lakenheath, Suffolk, and a note on the typology of wheel-brooches, *Bull. Board Celtic Stud.*, **30**, 168–75

Greenfield, E., 1958 'Durobrivae', *J. Roman Stud.*, **48**, 139–40

_____, 1963 The Romano-British shrines at Brigstock, Northants., *Antiq. J.*, **43**, 228–63

Gregory, T., 1977 *The enclosure at Ashill*, East Anglian Rep., **5**

_____, 1991/1992 *Excavations at Thetford, 1980–82, Fison Way*, East Anglian Archaeol. Rep., **53**

Gurney, D., 1986 Leylands Farm, Hockwold-cum-Witton, *East Anglian Archaeol. Rep.*, **31**, 49–104

Hanson, W.S., *et al.*, 1979 The Agricolan supply base at Red House, Corbridge, *Archaeol. Aeliana*, 5 ser., **7**, 1–98

Harker, S., 1980 Springhead; a brief reappraisal, in Rodwell, W. (ed.), *Temples, churches and religion in Roman Britain*, Brit. Archaeol. Rep., Brit. Ser., **77**, 285–8

Hartley, B.R., 1972 The Roman occupations of Scotland: the evidence of samian ware, *Britannia*, **3**, 1–55

Haselgrove, C., 1989 Iron Age coin deposition at Harlow Temple, *Oxford J. Archaeol.*, **8**, 73–88

Hattatt, R.A., 1985 *Iron Age and Roman brooches* (Oxford)

_____, 1987 *Brooches of antiquity* (Oxford)

_____, 1989 *Ancient brooches and other artefacts* (Oxford)

_____, & Webster, G., 1985 New light on *ad locutio* repoussé disc brooches, *Antiq. J.*, **65**, 433–7

Hawkes, C.F.C., & Hull, M.R., 1947 *Camulodunum*, Rep. Res. Comm. Soc. Antiq. London, **14**

_____, & Jacobsthal, P., 1945 A Celtic bird-brooch from Red Hill, near Long Eaton, Notts, *Antiq. J.*, **25**, 117–24

Hildyard, E.J.W., 1946 Romano-British fibulae from Red Hill, *Nottingham Archaeol. Soc. Rep.*, **10** (1945), 8–10

Hull, M.R., & Hawkes, C.F.C., 1987 *Corpus of ancient brooches: Britain: pre-Roman bow brooches*, Brit. Archaeol. Rep., Brit. Ser., **168**

_____, Simpson, G., Blance, B., Butcher, S., & Hattatt, R.A., *Brooches from pre-Roman and Roman Britain*, forthcoming

Jackson, K.H., 1971 *A Celtic miscellany: translations from the Celtic literatures* (London)

Johns, C., 1986 The Roman silver cups from Hockwold, Norfolk, *Archaeologia*, **108**, 1–13

_____, & Potter, T., 1983 *The Thetford treasure* (British Museum, London)

Keller, E., 1971 [Late Roman crossbow brooches in South Bavaria], *Münchner Beiträge zur Vor- und Frühgeschichte*, **14**, 26–55

Kirk, J., 1951 Bronzes from Woodeaton, *Oxoniensia*, **14**, 1–45

Layard, N., 1925 Bronze crowns and a bronze headdress from a Roman site at Cavenham Heath, Suffolk, *Antiq. J.*, **5**, 258–65

Leech, R., 1986 The excavations of a Romano-Celtic temple and a later cemetery on Lamyatt Beacon, Somerset, *Britannia*, **17**, 258–328

Mackreth, D.F., 1982 Two brooches from Stonea, Cambs. and Bicester, Oxon., and the origin of the Aesica brooch, *Britannia*, **13**, 310–15

_____, 1985 Brooches (from the Southern Fen Edge), in Taylor, A., 1985, 13–29

_____, 1992 Roman brooches from Gastard, Corsham, Wilts, *Wiltshire Archaeol. Mag.*, **85**, 51–62

McWhirr, A., 1986 *Roman Gloucestershire* (Gloucester County Library)

Mitard, P.-H., 1993 *Le sanctuaire gallo-romain de Genainville (Val-d'Oise)* (Guiry-en-Vexin)

O'Connell, M.G., & Bird, J., 1994 The Roman temple at Wanborough, excavation 1985–1986, *Surrey Archaeol. Collect.*, **82**, 1–168

Paris, R., 1960 Un temple celtique et gallo-romain en forêt de Châtillon-sur-Seine (Côte d'Or), *Revue Archéol. Est et Centre-Est*, **11**, 164–75

Planck, D. (ed.), 1985 *Der Keltenfürst von Hochdorf: Katalog der Ausstellung* (Stuttgart)

Rahtz, P., & Harris, L.G., 1958 The temple well and other buildings at Pagans Hill, Chew Stoke, N. Somerset, *Proc. Somerset Archaeol. Natur. Hist. Soc.*, **101–2**, 15–51

Rawes, B., 1976 The Wycomb site, Andoversford 1969–70, *Glevensis*, **10**, 23–9

Richmond, I.A., 1968 *Hod Hill: excavations carried out between 1951 and 1958* (British Museum, London)

Riha, E., 1979 *Die römischen Fibeln aus Augst und Kaiseraugst*, Forschungen in Augst, **3**

Ritterling, E., 1913 *Das frührömische Lager bei Hofheim im Taunus*, Nassauische Annalen, **40**

Ross, A., 1968 Shafts, pits, wells – sanctuaries of the Belgic Britons?, in Coles, J.M., & Simpson, D.D.A. (eds), *Studies in ancient Europe*, 255–85 (Leicester)

_____, & Feachem, R., 1976 Ritual rubbish?: the Newstead pits, in Megaw, J.V.S. (ed.), *To illustrate the monuments* (London)

Simpson, G., Hawkes, C.F.C., & Hull, M.R., 1979 Some British and Iberian penannular brooches and other early types in the Rhineland and the *decumates agri*, *Antiq. J.*, **59**, 319–42

Smith, C.R., 1848 Roman remains at Lancing, *Collectanea Antiqua*, **1**, 92–4

Stead, I.M., 1991 Many more Iron Age shields from Britain, *Antiq. J.*, **71**, 1–35

_____, & Rigby, V., 1986 *Baldock: the excavation of a Roman and pre-Roman settlement, 1968–72*, Britannia Monograph Ser., **7**, London

_____, & _____, 1989 *Verulamium: the King Harry Lane site*, English Heritage Archaeol. Rep., **12**

Taylor, A., 1985 Prehistoric, Roman, Saxon and medieval artefacts from the Southern Fen Edge, *Proc. Cambridge Antiq. Soc.*, **74**, 1–52

Taylor, M. V., 1963 Statuettes of horsemen and horses and other votive objects from Brigstock, Northants., *Antiq. J.*, **43**, 264–8

Toll, N.P., 1949 The fibulae, in *Final report IV: the excavations at Dura-Europos* (Yale)

Ulbert, G., 1959 *Die römischen Donau-Kastelle Aislingen und Burghöfe*, Limes-forschungen, **1**

Warne, C., 1844 Roman remains at Preston near Weymouth (Jordan Hill), *Gentlemens Magazine*, **21**, 185–7

Webster, G., 1983 The function of Chedworth Roman 'villa', *Trans. Bristol Gloucestershire Archaeol. Soc.*, **101**, 5–20

Wedlake, W.J., 1958 *Excavations at Camerton, Somerset* (Camerton)

_____, 1982 *The excavation of the shrine of Apollo at Nettleton, Wiltshire, 1956–71*, Rep. Res. Comm. Soc. Antiq. London, **40**

Wheeler, H., 1981 Two Roman bronzes from Brigstock, Northants., *Antiq. J.*, **61**, 309–11

Wheeler, R. E. M., 1943 *Maiden Castle, Dorset*, Rep. Res. Comm. Soc. Antiq. London, **12**

_____, & Wheeler, T.V., 1932 *Report on the prehistoric, Roman and post-Roman site in Lydney Park, Gloucestershire*, Res. Rep. Comm. Soc. Antiq. London, **9**

Wickenden, N.P., 1992 *The temple and other sites in the north-east sector of Caesaromagus*, Counc. Brit. Archaeol. Res. Rep., **75**, Chelmsford Archaeol. Transt. Rep., **7**

Williams, R.J., & Hart, P.J., 1990 *Wavendon Gate, Milton Keynes, Interim Report 1988–1990* (Milton Keynes Archaeol. Unit)

Winbolt, S.E., 1927 Excavations at Farley Heath, Albury, 1926, *Surrey Archaeol. Collect.*, **37**, 180–199

Woodward, A., & Leach, P., 1993 *The Uley Shrines*, English Heritage Archaeol. Rep., **17**

31   A hoard of late Roman ironwork from Sibson, Huntingdonshire

W. H. Manning

The hoard of ironwork from Sibson, Huntingdonshire was discovered in 1958 during a magnetometer survey for Roman pottery kilns undertaken in advance of the widening of the Great North Road (A1) where it passed through the area of the Nene Valley pottery industry (fig. 1). A note in 'Roman Britain in 1958' describes the survey, which was one of the earliest uses of a proton magnetometer in archaeology, but does not refer to the hoard (*J. Roman Stud.*, **49** (1959), 117–18). The objects are now in Peterborough Museum.

Its contents are very mixed, a small group of agricultural tools (nos. 1–5), a few other tools, mostly fragmentary (nos. 6–10), some domestic equipment, again with the larger pieces broken and incomplete (nos. 14–50), and a miscellaneous group of structural fittings and fragments. As an assemblage it can be connected with no one craft or industry, certainly not with the pottery industry. If a single origin has to be sought for such a mixture, the most probable would be a farm. Even the apparently complete tools, such as the hoe (no. 2) and the reaping hooks (nos. 3–4) might have been put to one side because their hafts had broken. But it may have had no single source and simply been a collection of scrap acquired by a smith as raw material.

The date of its burial can be established only in general terms. It had been buried in a shallow pit cut through a rough stone floor; there was no sign of it having had a container. Fragments of weathered 4th-century pottery in the filling of the pit probably indicate a date after *c.*350 (Manning 1972a, 236), and there is nothing in the hoard itself to contradict such a date. Only the cauldron rim (no. 18) might seem out of place in such a late context, for by the end of the 4th-century the type from which it came had apparently been replaced by other forms (Hawkes 1951, 182). But even here certainty is impossible, for the earlier form continued in use until at least the late 3rd century in Germany (Hawkes 1951, 181), and, with the rarity of cauldrons in dated contexts, its survival into the 4th century is not improbable.

Ironwork hoards from Roman Britain were discussed by the writer some years ago (Manning 1972a), and little has been published since then which would radically alter the conclusions arrived at in that paper. Fourth-century hoards form one

of the two main groups of hoards, the other being of late 1st- and early 2nd-century date. The distribution of the two groups is strikingly different; the earlier ones come from the military zone in the north, whilst the later ones are limited to southern England and East Anglia (Manning 1972a, fig. 2). Two others can be added to those listed in 1972, both from East Anglia (Coldham Common, Cambs. and Icklingham, Suffolk (Manning 1985, 181ff.). Thus both in date and location the Sibson hoard conforms with the common pattern. In the quantity and type of its contents it lies in the middle of the group; less spectacular than the large hoards from Great Chesterford and Silchester, but larger and with a wider range of types than many of the others.

The reason for its deposition must remain a subject for speculation. Its only value was as scrap metal, and the frequency with which iron objects are found in the late Roman period suggests that this was not great. Seen in isolation its burial is of little significance, but in the context of the other hoards of the period it becomes of greater interest. This question has been addressed in the paper already mentioned (Manning 1972a), and all that is necessary here is to restate the conclusion reached there, namely that there are good reasons to suggest that many of these hoards were buried as votive offerings rather than for security. In the case of the Sibson hoard, however, such a conclusion can only be suggested on circumstantial grounds, for there is nothing either in the hoard itself or in the circumstances of its burial to support or refute such an idea.

CATALOGUE (figs. 1–10)

1. *Plough coulter* (length 70.3cm) An octagonal-sectioned shaft and triangular blade, now distorted. The blade has an asymmetrical cross-section, but not consistently so, and it is as likely to be the result of wear as the intentional setting of the blade.

Romano-British plough coulters are not uncommon, the majority coming from 4th-century ironwork hoards. A detailed list is given in Rees 1979 (59ff. and 287ff.), and the types of ploughs they were probably used on is discussed in Manning 1964. Their frequent association with bar shares in the

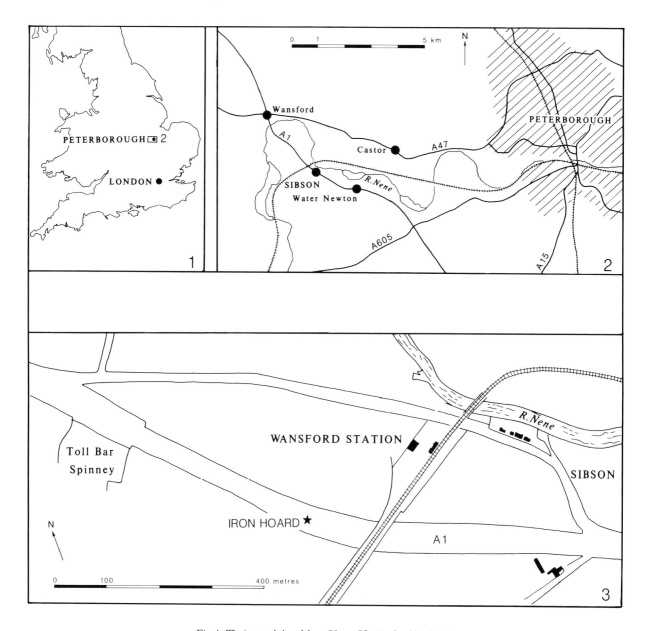

Fig. 1. The ironwork hoard from Sibson, Huntingdonshire: location.

hoards suggests that they were commonly used on some form of bow-ard.

2. *Hoe* (length 15.4cm) A stout socket and a triangular blade with an almost straight edge and concave cross-section. Viewed from the side the blade is at a slight angle to the socket.

The concave blade and strong socket suggests that it is a hoe rather than a plough spud. The differences between the two types are discussed in Manning 1985, 49. Similar tools come from Woodcuts (Pitt Rivers 1887, 81, pl. 26, no. 1), the Coldham Common, Cambs. hoard (Manning 1985, 49, F17) and the River Wandle at Wandsworth (Wheeler 1930, 77, pl. 34, no. 5).

3. *Reaping-hook* (length 25.8cm) A semicircular blade continuing into a triangular tang with an out-turned tip. A nail runs

through the top of the tang. The edge is formed by a chamfer on one face.

This is an example of the common reaping hook of the Iron Age and ancient world, which was pulled through a bunch of stalks held with the left hand, rather than swung as is a sickle. The blade is typical of the type, but the broad tang, with its out-turned tip, is not; most are either socketed or have a narrow tang (Types 2 and 3 of the classification in Manning 1985, 53ff.). It is doubtful if our tang was actually set within the handle, for it is so wide that any handle which completely enclosed it would be uncomfortably large, while the out-turned tip would have extended well beyond the base of the handle, unless this widened at its end. More probably the tang ran along the face of the handle, being held in place by the nail at the top, with the tip of the tang driven into the wood to further secure it. A basically similar arrangement, but with a flanged or open socket replacing the top nail, is found in some small reaping hooks (e.g. Manning 1985, 55, F36, from Cranborne Chase).

Functionally similar tanged hooks come from a number of sites, including Caerwent (Rees 1979, 645, fig. 84a), Newstead (Curle 1911, 283, pl. 77, no. 9), Risingham, Northd. (Manning 1976, 30, no. 85) etc. Examples with tangs similar to ours, including the nail at the top of the tang, come from Irchester, Northants. and Alchester, Oxon., the latter with a more distinctly hooked blade (Rees 1979, 665, fig. 185b; 643, fig. 173b). The relationship of hooks of this type and billhooks is discussed in Manning 1985, 55ff.

4. *Sickle* (length 22.4cm) Strongly hooked blade with a short tang with an upturned tip. The edge extends almost as far as the tang.

Although the hooked blade is balanced about the handle, which would allow it to be swung like a true sickle, the tip is so strongly curved as to block part of the edge if so used. In view of this it is probably best regarded as a hybrid which could be either swung or used with the pulling action of the reaping hook. Its affinities are with the small Iron Age sickle, which continued into the Roman period, rather than with the larger form which first appears in Britain in the Roman period. Both types are discussed in Manning 1985, 51; in terms of the classifications advanced there it is a cross between a Type 1 sickle and a Type 3 reaping hook which also has a strongly hooked blade. A similar tool comes from Ham Hill, Somerset (Rees 1979, fig. 180b). The upturned tip of the tang suggests that it had a surprisingly short handle.

5. *Scythe* (length 38.6cm) A gently curving broken blade, strengthened at the back by a rim on one face, which continues into a short, tapering tang turned up at its tip.

The two main forms of Romano-British scythes are characterised by those from the late 1st-century fort at Newstead (Curle 1911, 284, pl. 62, nos. 3–6) and the 4th-century hoard from Great Chesterford, Essex (Neville 1856, 10, pl. 3.29). The evidence suggests that the Newstead type is usually early, probably not outlasting the 2nd century (Manning 1985, 49), and although the Sibson scythe is fragmentary sufficient remains to make it clear that it was not of that type; the blade is too narrow, while the tang is of a different form and lacks the anchor-shaped rivet found near the junction of the blade and tang on the Newstead scythes. In its relatively narrow blade it resembles the Great Chesterford type, but its tang is markedly shorter and the angle at which tang and blade meet is different, although it does have the slight upturn at the tip of the tang seen on the Great Chesterford scythes. Rees (1979, 475) compares it with a fragment from Irchester, Northants., which has generally similar proportions, and suggests that both come from scythes with blades of a width similar to, but shorter than, those from Great Chesterford. That such scythes did exist in the northern provinces is shown by an example from the German fort at Stockstadt (ORL, B III, Kastell 33 (1914), 55, Taf. 9, no. 7), which has a relatively short, narrow blade and small tang, although in this case with the anchor-shaped rivet seen on the Newstead scythes.

6. *Mason's pick* (length 20.2cm) A narrow chisel-edge at one end and a blunted spike at the other. The round eye is relatively small.

Although it might be taken for a hammer, both its proportions and the spike would be most unusual in a hammer. More probably it is a mason's pick with its blades blunted by use. The long, thin proportions are much more akin to a pick than a hammer, and the combination of spiked and chisel-edged blades is quite common in such tools, which form Type 2 of the classification in Manning 1985. Although the majority of picks tend to have rather wider chisel-edges, a number are known with edges as narrow as this, for example from Hod Hill, Dorset (Manning 1985, 30, C1), the Blackburn Mill, Berwicks. hoard (Piggott 1953, 48, fig. 13, B37), Saalburg (*Saalburg-Jahrbuch*, **1** (1910), 59, Taf. 3, no. 2), Zugmantel (*Saalburg-Jahrbuch*, **2** (1911), 42, Taf. 9, no. 6), and Wiesbaden (ORL, B II 3, Kastell 31 (1915), 101, Taf. 11, no. 47).

7. *Tongs* (length 36.3cm) Part of one arm tapering to a point at its end, with a simple bowed jaw, slightly extended at its tip. The rivet on which the arms pivoted remains.

This form of tongs, with its simple jaw, is the commonest of all Roman types, no doubt because its simplicity made it suitable for a variety of tasks. It is the only type known in the British Iron Age (Manning 1985, 7ff.), and was common in the Roman period. Comparable examples are listed and discussed in Manning 1985, 7. It is possible that the other arm will have been longer than the existing one, for arms of unequal length are a common feature of Roman tongs.

8. *Punch (?)* (length 12.7cm) Tapering, round-sectioned rod.

Although such simple tools can rarely be identified with complete certainty, this is probably a round-sectioned, smith's punch, comparable with others from Woodcuts (Pitt Rivers 1887, 86, pl. 28, no. 13), the Blackburn Mill, Berwicks. hoard (Piggott 1953, 48, fig. 13, B45–47), Shakenoak Farm, Oxon (Brodribb *et al.* 1973, 120, fig. 58, no. 395), Verulamium (Manning 1972b, 163, fig. 60, no. 4) and Feldberg (ORL, B II 1, Kastell 10 (1937), 34, D71, Taf. 8, nos. 54–58) etc.

9. *Fragmentary loop* (length 15.1cm) A loop of flattened rod with out-turned arms, one of which is broken. The other, which tapers to a rolled tip, was probably intended to run parallel with the broken arm to close the loop.

It may be the handle of a tool of some kind; it is unlikely to be a handle from furniture or a utensil. Even so, it is difficult to find a parallel. Another possibility is that it is a cart-fitting such as a rein holder.

10. *Handle ?* (length 72.6cm) Flat-sided head with a hooked loop at its end, and a long stem, apparently cut at its end.

The obvious identification of this piece would be as a poker, but, although these did exist in the Roman period, they are rare, and the form of the head would be ill-suited to such a tool, while the tip is chisel-edged, as if cut, rather than pointed. More probably it was a handle, although the type of tool from which it comes is uncertain. Its size and the form

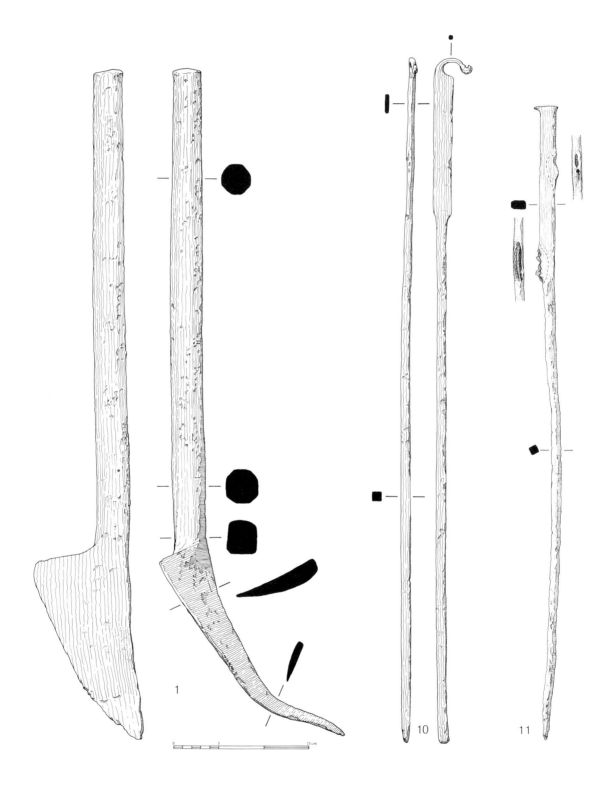

Fig. 2. The Sibson hoard, nos. 1, 10 and 11. Scale 1:4.

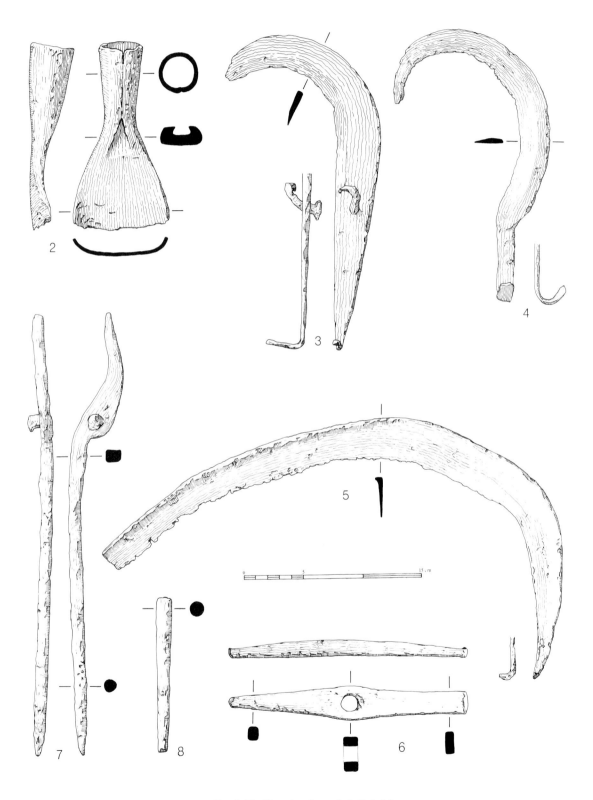

Fig. 3. The Sibson hoard, nos. 2–8. Scale 1:3.

of the head would suggest a fire shovel, but normally these have twisted stems (e.g. from the Carrawburgh Mithraeum (Manning 1976, 39, no. 149, fig. 23)). Another possibility would be that it is part of a smith's rake of the type known in the late Iron Age (Rodwell 1976). These have a spatulate blade set at the end of a long shank, but they are far earlier in date than our piece. It is even possible that it is unfinished, in which case it could be a large latch-lifter as they often have handles of this type (e.g. Manning 1985, 89, O10 etc.).

11. *Steelyard beam* (length 67.2cm) The head has a rectangular cross-section, slightly flanged at its end, with paired, opposed grooves which will have held rings for the fulcrum hooks. The arm has a diamond-shaped cross section and may have lost its tip. None of the gradations are now visible.

Attaching the fulcrum hooks by means of rings set in grooves in the head was normal with large steelyards, and is seen on two very large and fine examples from Dorn, Glos. in the British Museum (Manning 1985, 106, P40 and P41). The load will have hung from a hook at the front of the beam, and the slight projections seen there are probably the remains of the loop which held this hook.

It is too damaged for the original range to be calculated with complete certainty, but the approximate ratios can be found by dividing the distance from the fulcrum to the end of the beam by the distance from the fulcrum to the suspension point.

	Fulcrum 1	Fulcrum 2
a Distance to loading hook	*c.*7cm	*c.*17cm
b Distance to end of beam	*c.*60cm	*c.*50cm
Ratios of *a* to *b*	1:8.6	1:3.0

These figures suggest that the original ratios were 1:9 and 1:3, which means that by using a counterweight of 1 pound loads of up to 3 and 9 pounds could have been weighed. By using other counterweights, of course, the range could have been extended. It is probably significant that one of the Dorn steelyards (P41) has similar ratios.

12. *Steelyard beam* (length 31.0cm) Long, flat head with a round hole at the end for the load hook and two pierced lugs for the fulcrum hooks. The arm has a sub-rectangular section and may have lost the tip which was often knobbed.

Steelyards of this size are more common than the larger ones, although they are functionally identical. Attaching the fulcrum hooks by means of pierced lugs is normal in this type. Similar steelyards are discussed in Manning 1985, 107, where others are cited.

	Fulcrum 1	Fulcrum 2
a Distance to loading hook	*c.*4.5cm	*c.*11.2
b Distance to end of beam	*c.*25.5cm	*c.*18.8cm
Ratios of *a* to *b*	1:5.7	1:1.7

Originally these ratios were probably intended to be 1:6 and 1:2.

It is possible that these two steelyards were a pair, for their ratios complement each other.

13. *Stylus* (length 13.3cm) A plain stem, broken at the point, with a simple, slightly splayed eraser.

A Class I stylus, the simplest form. Cf. Manning 1985, 85, for a discussion of the type.

14. *Knife* (length 16.1cm) The back of the blade continues the line of the tang before turning down towards the broken tip; the straight edge is separated from the tang by a step.

It does not fit easily into any of the types defined in Manning 1985, 107ff. Rather similar knives come from Caerwent, with a rod-handle (Newport Museum), Lydney, Glos. (S. Lysons, *Reliquiae Britannico-Romanae* (1813), pl. 33, no. 2), Woodcuts, Dorset (Pitt Rivers 1887, 71, pl. 23, no. 5) etc.

15. *Knife* (length 17.9cm) A short, symmetrical blade which has a straight edge and back which taper to a point. The tang lies on the mid-line of the blade.

It is an unusually long example of a Type 21 knife as defined in Manning 1985, 17, where others are cited.

16. *Shears* (length 8.0cm) Fragment of one arm, parts of the omega-shaped spring and the blade.

For similar shears from Verulamium cf. Manning 1972, 176, fig. 65, no. 45, where others are cited.

17. *Tripod* (length of leg 18.7cm; width across ring 21.4cm) A ring top and two simple, slightly curved legs, the complete one of which has a small, splayed foot. The third leg is lost, and the whole is much distorted.

Tripods are not common finds either in Britain or abroad, but others of generally similar form are known from the Carlingwark Loch hoard (Piggott 1953, 38, fig. 10, C73), the Brading, I.O.W. villa (*Bull. Institute of Archaeology*, **1** (1958), 67, fig. 11a), and Great Chesterford, Essex (Museum of Archaeology and Ethnology, Cambridge).

18. *Cauldron rim and ring handle* (length 38.2cm) The large handle runs through a broad loop formed by rolling the top of a short strip rivetted to the main bar which originally strengthened the rim of a cauldron. The lower end of this strip may be broken; originally it probably continued below the bar as a short strap, a feature seen on a cauldron from Köngen (F. Behn, *Germania*, **20** (1936), 124, Abb. 1g). Fragments of the metal of the vessel survive at one end of the main bar.

Iron rim-bindings of this type were a feature of many Roman cauldrons (Hawkes 1951, 181), but they are not common finds, and the majority of surviving cauldrons have lost both the binding and the ring-handles. Although a variety of cauldron types had iron rim-bindings (Hawkes 1951; Piggott 1953, 28) there can be little doubt that ours came from a one-piece cauldron, although one cannot be certain of the precise form. Various examples with iron rims are illustrated by Hawkes (1951, figs. 46 and 47). On the Continent the use of

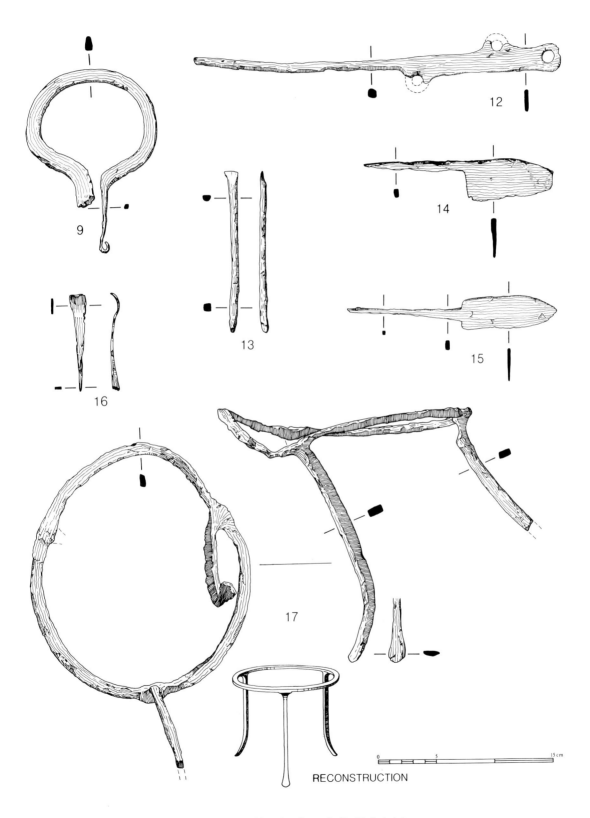

Fig. 4. The Sibson hoard, nos. 9, 12–17. Scale 1:3.

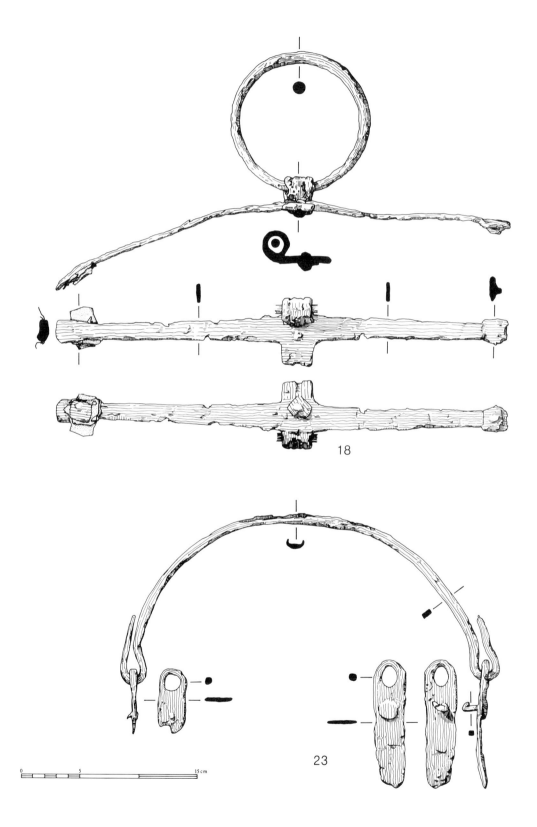

18

23

0   5   15 cm

Fig. 5. The Sibson hoard, nos. 18 and 23. Scale 1:3.

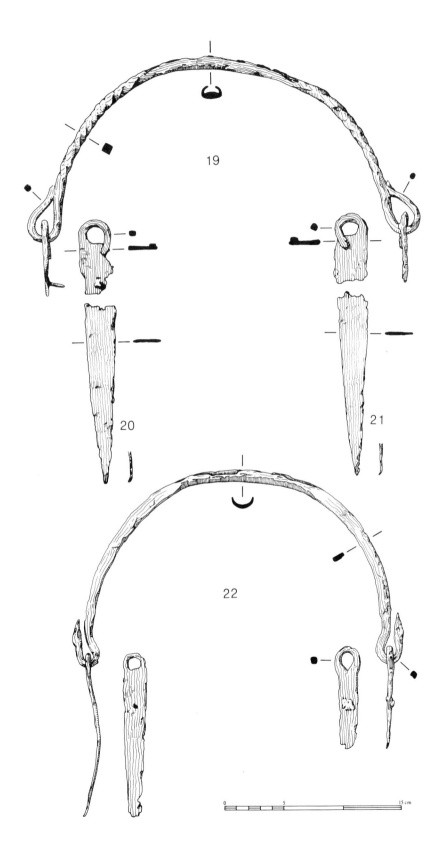

Fig. 6. The Sibson hoard, nos. 19–22. Scale 1:3.

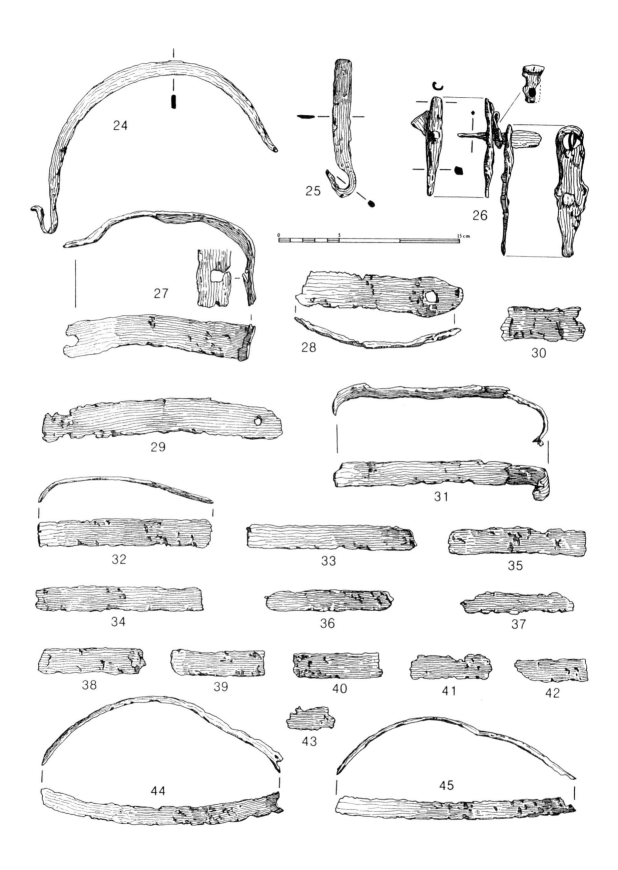

Fig. 7. The Sibson hoard, nos. 24–45. Scale 1:3.

this type of rim survived until at least the mid-3rd century (Hawkes 1951, 181), as examples from Köngen, on the German *Limes*, and Seltz in Alsace show. This is still likely to be some decades before the Sibson hoard was deposited, but there is no reason to suppose that the few surviving datable pieces were necessarily the last ones to be used.

A one-piece cauldron from Thealby, Lincs. still retains much of its iron rim-binding, but not its handles or the mounts by which they were attached (*Antiq. J.*, **15** (1935), 458, fig. 1). However, it is so similar to the Köngen cauldron as to suggest that the missing fittings will have been very similar. Although not identical in all details, our cauldron rim resembles that from Köngen so closely as to leave little doubt that it is an example of the same basic type.

19. *Bucket handle and mounts* (lengths of mounts 6.2cm; 5.5 cm. Width of handle 33.0cm) The handle is formed of square-sectioned rod, with a U-sectioned grip at its centre and spiral twisting on each side. The ends are narrowed and bent into hooks with their ends touching the main bar. Both mounts are broken, but they took the normal form of tapering strips with simple turned-over loops at the top. A single nail survives in the longer one. Nos. 20 and 21 are almost certainly the lower parts of these mounts.

20, 21. *Bucket handle mounts* (lengths 14.8cm; 15.1cm) Tapering fragments now lacking their tops. Probably from the mounts on bucket handle no. 19. The pointed tip is slightly inturned to enable it to be driven into the side of the bucket.

22. *Bucket handle and mounts* (lengths of mounts 13.5cm; 8.5cm. Width of handle 27.8cm) The handle has a U-sectioned grip and slightly open hooks at its ends. The mounts have the normal tapering form with closed loops at their tops; both are broken. The shorter retains a fragment of the nail which secured it to the bucket; the other has a small nail hole. Their tips were probably similar to nos. 20 and 21 above.

23. *Bucket handle and mounts* (lengths of mounts 10.6cm; 5.3cm. Width of handle 31.1cm) Similar to the preceding; both mounts are broken.

24. *Bucket handle* (width 20.8cm) A smaller example of the above type. One hook is missing.

25. *Bucket handle* (length 11.0cm) Fragment of an end-hook and part of the handle.

26. *Bucket handle mount* (overall length 12.7cm) A tapering mount with a closed loop at its head, and the remains of a nail through it just below its midpoint. A spike passes through the loop and through a tapered bar which lies parallel with the mount and 1.0 cm. from it. This bar is placed with its tip just above the nail in the main mount. On the spike between the two is a fragment of the handle. The whole looks like a crudely made modification of a normal mount. The distance between the two main pieces indicates the thickness of the bucket staves.

Discussion

The bucket handles in this group are typical of their type. The U-sectioned grip, although by no means an invariable feature of such handles, is not uncommon, and other examples are cited in Manning 1985, 103, P16.

The mounts seen on no. 19, and probably on no. 22, are examples of one of several forms found. Unfortunately few mounts are complete and, as the head is similar in all cases, it is usually impossible to assign a broken mount to any one type with certainty. For this reason the form of the mounts on no. 23 remains uncertain. To judge by the few relatively complete buckets which survive, the commonest arrangement was to have mounts which ran the full depth of the bucket with their ends either turned under the bucket, as with one from Newstead (Curle 1911, 310, pl. 69, no. 4) and in fragments from the Brampton hoard (Manning 1966, 24, no. 30), or turned out to clasp the bottom hoop, as in an example from the Gadebridge Park villa (Manning 1974, 187, no. 673). All were probably secured by nailing them in place, and quite often by having the bands which bound the bucket placed over them. The Sibson mounts are too short to have done this and they were no doubt nailed to the bucket, probably under the upper hoop, with the tip driven into the side of the bucket. Complete examples of this type of mount are not common but a small group comes from Stockstadt (ORL, B III, Kastell 33 (1914), 55, Taf. 9, nos. 83 and 97, Taf. 10, no. 53).

27–48. *Fragments of bucket hoops (?)* 22 fragments of narrow, curved bindings which can be divided into three groups by width.

Group A Width 2.5–2.8cm.
Lengths - 27: 13.8cm, with a square nail hole in the splayed and tapering tip; 28: 15.9cm, with two nail holes; 29: 20.0cm, with a nail hole; 30: 7.0cm.

Group B Width 1.8–2.2cm. This group probably contains fragments of more than one band, but the range of widths is continuous making any subdivision uncertain. There are 13 fragments, none with nail holes.
Lengths - 31: 17.7cm; 32: 14.5cm; 33: 14.1cm; 34: 14.0cm; 35: 11.3cm; 36: 10.6cm; 37: 9.4cm; 38: 9.0cm; 39: 7.9cm; 40: 7.4cm; 41: 6.8cm; 42: 5.9cm; 43: 4.0cm.

Group C Width 1.4–1.6cm. Five fragments, none with nail holes.
Lengths – 44: 20.1cm; 45: 19.7cm; 46: 8.8cm; 47: 5.0cm; 48: 4.7cm.

49–50. *Fragments of hoops (?)* (lengths 8.1cm; 4.5cm)

Discussion

All of these are probably fragments of hoops from tubs or buckets. Such fragments are common finds (e.g. from the Brampton, Cumb., hoard (Manning 1966, 24, nos. 24–7), complete bands less so, although a group from Borough Hill, Northants., and some others are published in Manning 1985,

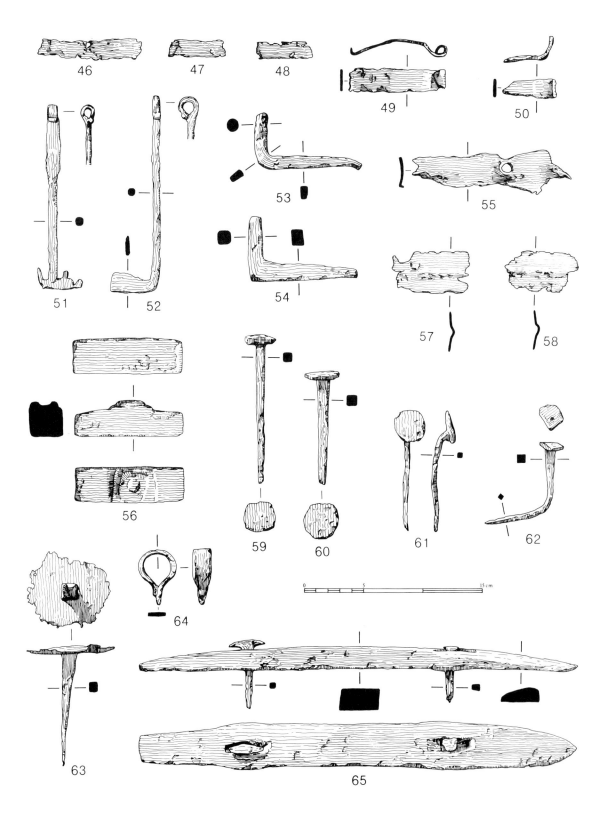

Fig. 8. The Sibson hoard, nos. 46–65. Scale 1:3.

103, P21–P27, and there are other examples in some of the major collections, such as that from Silchester. They also occur on a few complete buckets, such as those from Newstead (Curle 1911, pl. 69, no. 4) and Silchester (*Archaeologia*, **58** (1903), 423), or in complete sets of fittings like those from Woodcuts (Pitt Rivers 1887, 85, pl. 28, nos. 4–6) and the Gadebridge Park villa (Manning 1974, 187, fig. 79). They were normally nailed to the staves in one or two places.

Whether these bands came from the same buckets as the handles discussed above is uncertain. It must seem likely, although only Group B actually contains enough pieces to have formed a hoop large enough to fit a bucket of the diameter indicated by the handles. As each bucket would normally have had two hoops it is clear that not all of the bands from the buckets represented by the handles went into the hoard. None is likely to have been deposited as a complete bucket.

51. *T-shaped lift key* (length 15.2cm) A flat handle with a rolled head, a plain stem and the remains of three teeth on the bit. Originally there may have been four teeth, two on one side of the stem.

52. *L-shaped lift key* (length 16.3cm) A rod-like stem, rolled head and damaged bit which has now lost its teeth.

Discussion

Both of these keys were intended to open simple tumbler-locks. Although lift-keys are common finds (the L-shaped form being the commonest of all Roman key types), T-shaped keys with four teeth are surprisingly rare, the vast majority having but two. However, examples with four teeth come from Fishbourne (Cunliffe 1971, 131, fig. 58, no. 26), Caerleon (*Archaeol. Cambrensis*, **116** (1967), 48, fig. 5, no. 12), and Silchester (Reading Museum). Given its damaged state it probably had four teeth originally, but it is just possible that there were only three, for a three-toothed key of this type is known from Feldberg (ORL, B II 1, Kastell 10 (1937), 38 E 154, Taf. 8, no. 18). By contrast, L-shaped keys with two, three or four teeth are very common. The two types are discussed in some detail in Manning 1985, 90.

53. *L-shaped drop-hinge staple* (length 9.0cm) The shorter arm has a characteristically circular section.
Cf. Manning 1985, 127, R12, for a discussion of the type.

54. *L-shaped drop-hinge staple* (length 9.2cm) Similar to the preceding.

55. *Hinge fragment* (length 13.4cm) A tapering and distorted strip with a nail hole through it and possibly part of a second at the break. At the wider end is a short, broken arm, which is all that remains of a loop if it is part of a loop-hinge , or a U-shaped curve if it comes from a drop-hinge. Of the two the former is the more probable. For the two types cf. Manning 1985, 126.

56. *Object of uncertain function* (length 9.3cm) A heavy rectangular block rising through two steps at its mid-point to a face with a small, circular depression. An unusual piece which may have been the mounting for a spindle.

57–58. *Fragments of water-pipe junction* (lengths 6.2cm; 6.6cm) Fragments of collar with a slight central ridge. For a complete example from London cf. Manning 1985, 128, R19.

59–62. *Nails* (lengths 12.1cm; 9.3cm; 9.9cm; 6.5cm) All are of Type 1B with sub-rectangular or discoidal heads and broken tips. For a discussion of this type of nail, the commonest form used in the Roman period, cf. Manning 1985, 134.

63. *Nail* (length 9.8cm) A large example of a Type 7 nail with a discoidal head. Cf. Manning 1985, 135, for other examples.

64. *Head of a double-spiked loop* (length 4.6cm) A common type. For complete examples and references to others cf. Manning 1985, 130.

65–79. Most of these pieces are structural, using that word in a loose sense, and their precise function remains unclear. Some were probably made for very specific purposes which cannot be known now, but it is possible that the majority came from a cart or carts. Even the heavy hook (no. 70), or the large rings (nos. 73–74) would not be out of place in such a context.

65. *Tie-bar* (length 37.0cm) Heavy bar which thins and tapers towards its ends one of which is pointed; the underside is flat. It is pierced by two countersunk nail holes, both retaining nails: the more complete is of Type 3 with a T-shaped head and the other was probably similar.

The function of this massive piece was probably to bind two pieces of wood, possibly a gate or cart.

66. *Bar* (length 11.1cm) Fragment of heavy bar tapering to a rounded tip; the other end is broken.

At first sight it might be taken for the tip of a plough share, but it lacks the highly characteristic pattern of wear seen on such shares. More probably it is from a tie-bar similar to no. 65, or a large hinge.

67. *Binding* (length 6.5cm) Paired, flat arms which taper to a slightly thickened central bar. There is a single nail hole near the end of each arm.

Although it could have been a U-shaped drop hinge, the use of single nails to hold it in place would mean that it was free to move if so used, and it is more likely to be a distorted binding.

68. *U-fitting* (length 24.4cm) U-shaped bar, broken at its ends, with a nail hole in each arm.

It could have bound a semi-circular object, but the curve of the U probably projected beyond the surface to which the arms were fastened, either to receive a tang of some kind or a rope. Again, a cart fitting seems a likely identification.

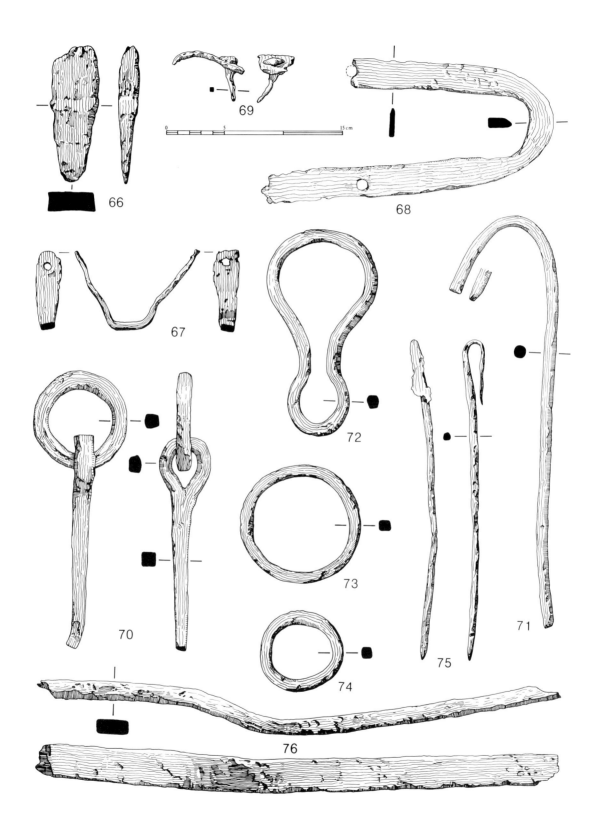

Fig. 9. The Sibson hoard, nos. 66–76. Scale 1:3.

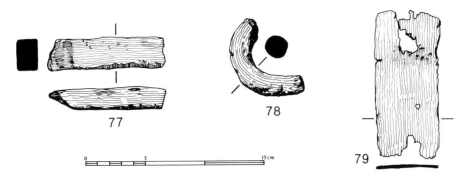

Fig. 10. The Sibson hoard, nos. 77–79. Scale 1:3.

69. *Binding* (length 6.2cm) Fragment of strip with a Class 1 nail through it.

70. *Hook and ring* (length 22.8cm) The heavy ring runs through a slightly pear-shaped eye at the top of a broken stem which almost certainly originally ended in a hook.

This was probably a strong hook of the type used for moving heavy weights. Similar hooks may be cited from Woodcuts (Pitt Rivers 1887, 90, pl. 29, no. 13), London (Museum of London), Saalburg and Zugmantel (*Saalburg-Jahrbuch*, **3** (1912), 21, Taf. 2, no. 18; **7** (1930), 53, Taf. 6, no. 19) etc.

71. *Rod* (length 33.6cm) Round-sectioned rod, now bent; the shorter arm ends in a chisel edge. The bending is probably not significant.

72. *Pear-shaped loop* (length 16.9cm) Sub-rectangular in section; possibly from the end of a chain, although it could have fastened a gate or the like.

A number of large figure-of-eight shaped loops, which could have had a similar function to this piece, are discussed in Manning 1985, 139, S14–S17.

73–74. *Rings* (diameters 10.0cm; 7.0cm) Rings of varying sizes are common site finds and could have had a very wide variety of uses. For others cf. Manning 1985, 140, S18–S48.

75. *Rod* (length 26.3cm) Tapering to a point at one end, and flattened into a damaged plate, which is bent back on itself, at the other. It is possible that this plate was originally welded to another piece, making the surviving fragment a handle or tang.

76. *Fragment of bar* (length 44.4cm) Rectangular in cross-section; cut at each end and bent.

77. *Fragment of bar* (length 9.9cm) Rectangular in cross-section and broken or cut at its ends.

78. *Fragment of curved bar* (length 6.0cm).

79. *Fragment of sheet* (length 12.2cm).

ACKNOWLEDGEMENTS

I would like to thank Dr John Peter Wild and Mr D. F. Mackreth for their help in preparing this paper. The location map was drawn by Mr Howard Mason, and the object drawings by Mr Edward Curry.

Bibliography and abbreviations

Brodribb, A.C.C., Hands, A.R., & Walker, D.R., 1974 *Excavations at Shakenoak Farm, near Wilcote, Oxfordshire*, 4

Cunliffe, B., 1971 *Excavations at Fishbourne 1961–1969, vol. II*, Rep. Res. Comm. Soc. Antiq. London, **27**

Curle, J., 1911 *A Roman frontier post and its people: the fort of Newstead in the Parish of Melrose*

Hawkes, C.F.C., 1951 Bronze-workers, cauldrons and bucket animals in Iron Age and Roman Britain, in Grimes, W.F. (ed.), *Aspects of archaeology in Britain and beyond*, 172–99

Manning, W.H., 1964 The plough in Roman Britain, *J. Roman Stud.*, **54**, 54–65

_____, 1966 A hoard of Romano-British ironwork from Brampton, Cumberland, *Trans. Cumberland Westmorland Antiq. Archaeol. Soc.*, **66**, 1–36

_____, 1972a Ironwork hoards in Iron Age and Roman Britain, *Britannia*, **3**, 224–50

_____, 1972b The iron objects, in Frere, S., *Verulamium excavations, vol. I*, Rep. Res. Comm. Soc. Antiq. London, **28**, 163–95

_____, 1974 Objects of iron, in Neal, D.S., *The excavation of the Roman villa in Gadebridge Park, Hemel Hempstead 1963–8*, Rep. Res. Comm. Soc. Antiq. London, **31**, 157–87

_____, 1976 *Catalogue of Romano-British ironwork in the Museum of Antiquities, Newcastle upon Tyne*

_____, 1985 *Catalogue of the Romano-British iron tools, fittings and weapons in the British Museum*

Neville, R.C., 1856 Description of a remarkable deposit of Roman antiquities of iron, discovered at Great Chesterford, Essex, in 1854, *Archaeol. J.*, **13**, 1–13

ORL *Der obergermanisch-rätische Limes des Römerreiches*

Piggott, S., 1953 Three metalwork hoards of the Roman period from southern Scotland, *Proc. Soc. Antiq. Scotland*, **87**, 1–50

Pitt Rivers, A.H.L., 1887 *Excavations in Cranborne Chase*, **1**

Rees, S. E., 1979 *Agricultural implements in prehistoric and Roman Britain*

Rodwell, W., 1976 Iron pokers of La Tène II-III, *Archaeol. J.*, **133**, 43–9

Wheeler, R.E.M., 1930 *London in Roman times*

32   A sling from Melandra?

John Peter Wild

Newcomers to Brian Hartley's excavations on the Roman fort at Bainbridge in Wensleydale were assured that 'it rains sideways at Bainbridge'. On good days, that was true: on bad days, however, it might be raining upwards. The solid concrete-slab site-hut was not a luxury, but a life-preserver. Much the same conditions were encountered during Brian's rescue excavations in 1968–9 on the vicus of the Roman fort of Slack, now beneath the M62 motorway (Wilson 1970, 281; Fitts & Hartley 1988, 65, fig. 20). There the Wheeler method of box trenching, nowadays often unfairly maligned, proved its worth, for an unexpected reason: each box could be baled out in the morning as required. The rest stayed brim-full of rainwater all day.

Pennine excavations may have their drawbacks; but the concomitant wet conditions underground offer the kind of environment in which some of the more robust categories of organic material can survive. The subject of this note is an object of that class.

The fort of Melandra Castle near Glossop, Derbyshire, sits on the kind of low knoll amid intersecting valleys which was conspicuously popular with Flavian military architects. The site was planted on a complex sandwich of sand and gravel layers, crowned (and underpinned) with a heavy clay (Johnson 1969, 201–2, fig. 4). Since 1973 the fort has been the focus of one of the research and training excavations of Manchester University, and, though the scale of the work has been very modest, a number of new insights have been gained into the structural development of some key site components, notably the defences, the headquarters building and the extramural bath suite.

In 1935 the Excavations Sub-Committee of the Manchester Branch of the Classical Association cut two trenches across the eastern defences of the fort, c. 40' (12m) and 100' (30.5m) respectively south of the centre point of the East Gate (Petch 1943, 50–55, fig. opp. 51). Two – or possibly three – ditches were encountered in the northern trench, and the two innermost ditches were seen to have been revetted with baulks of timber ('a stockade'), still *in situ*. The ditch fillings were waterlogged, and the deep central ditch yielded 'portions of leather sandals and boots … now on loan in the Manchester Museum' (*Manchester Guardian*, 6 October 1937).

In 1973 we followed up the Classical Association's discoveries by cutting a new section across the defences about 25m north of the East Gate (Wilson 1974, 420). We found only one ditch (now c. 1.70m deep and c. 2.80m wide) which may once have been V-shaped; its present shallow, flattened, profile may be the result of later recutting. Its eroded inner lip lay about 1.50m from the outer face of the stone-revetted rampart of Period II. The grey clayey silt on the bottom of the ditch, in what was almost certainly the primary cutting, had lain permanently beneath the local watertable, and in this material rested three oak tent pegs (Wild 1974, 302–5) and a leather artefact which we interpret as a sling. There was no directly associated dating evidence; but the material seems to have accumulated in the ditch silt during the first phase of the fort's occupation, namely between AD 77 or 78 and the upgrading of the defences in stone under Trajan or (more likely) Hadrian. The tent pegs were in pristine condition and, if held in stock, would have been surplus to requirements, once the first timber barracks had been erected.

The leather object (fig. 1) is – or was – lentoid in shape, c. 103mm long and 50mm wide. If originally symmetrical, it would have measured about 112mm long. The full thickness at the better preserved end is c. 3mm, but elsewhere the leather has split into two sheets and begun to fragment. The surviving end, slightly waisted, carries a T-shaped slit, apparently cut through it with a single-edged blade triangular in section; the head of the slit is 4mm, the stem c. 10mm long. The grain side (fig. 1,A) shows slight furrowing; the flesh side (fig. 1,B) is stepped, perhaps reflecting horizontal knife strokes. The outline of the object had been cut in a series of overlapping short strokes with a sharp blade, which had been held sometimes vertically, sometimes obliquely. The material may itself have been an offcut (van Driel-Murray 1993, 7, 16, 26–7, 54). Under the microscope the grain pattern suggests that the leather is cow hide (Reed 1972, 25, fig. 8). There is no sign of wear or stress at the slit or along the edges of the leather, though clearly one end broke away, presumably in antiquity.

At the time of discovery the artefact was almost unanimously identified as a sling. An alternative interpretation, that it was an eye-patch worn by a sufferer from the dreaded 'pink-

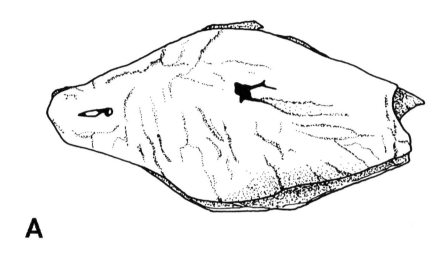

A

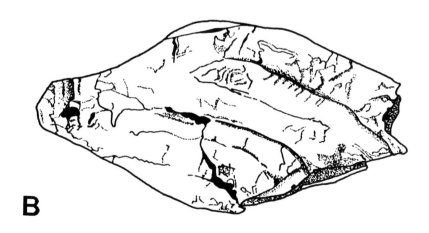

B

cms

Fig. 1. A leather sling (?) from Melandra: **A.** *grain side;* **B.** *flesh side. (Drawing by Christine Barratt (Turnock))*

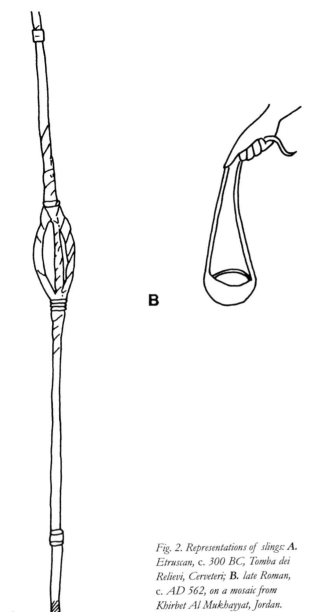

A

B

Fig. 2. Representations of slings: A. Etruscan, c. 300 BC, Tomba dei Relievi, Cerveteri; B. late Roman, c. AD 562, on a mosaic from Khirbet Al Mukhayyat, Jordan.

eye' (*lippitudo*) prevalent at Vindolanda (Bowman & Thomas 1994, 93–4, 98), proved less attractive. What evidence is there in the Roman archaeological, artistic and documentary record for slings and slinging that might support the excavation team's first reaction?

The topic of slings, slingers and sling-shot in the Roman world has been accorded a good deal of attention by scholars in the past decade. Stephen Greep's 1987 study of sling-shot in Roman Britain highlighted the importance of the sling in the later Iron Age and in post-conquest military contexts, and Griffiths (1989) discussed its role in the Roman army in greater depth. More recently, detailed research into the sling's history and capabilities by Thomas Völling and Dietwulf Baatz have led to two comprehensive studies published in the *Saalburg-Jahrbuch* for 1990.

No surviving Roman sling has been securely identified to date (Völling 1990, 26). Griffiths' suggestion (1989) that an elaborate leather thong from Mainz (Göpfrich 1986, Abb. 52,

no. 162) might be a sling is worth considering, but ultimately is not sufficiently convincing. Nor do any representations in provincial Roman art north of the Alps show a sling for certain (Völling 1990, 31).

The best known ancient slingers came from the Balearic Isles; indeed they became a literary *topos* that cannot always be taken literally. Livy explicitly states that their weapon was a simple strap (*habena*) (xxxviii, 29, 3–8). This appears to be the normal Roman form, mentioned in literary sources (Virgil, *Aeneid* xi, 578–580; Statius, *Thebaid* iv, 66) and depicted on monuments such as Trajan's column (Lepper & Frere 1988, 106 scene LXVI, 108 scene LXXX; cf. Griffiths 1989, 268, figs. 6, 7). The standard material employed was leather, but slings of plaited tow (coarse flax) (Virgil, *Georgics* i, 309), hair, sinew and rush (Strabo, iii, 168) are also attested.

In use a missile was placed in the centre of the strap, the ends of which were then brought together and grasped by the slinger in one hand. The weapon was raised aloft, whirled several times round the slinger's head to build up momentum, and then one strap end was released to project the shot towards its target.

In Etruscan art we see a form of sling with a central cup or pocket for the missile (fig. 2,A). But it is an openwork pocket, consisting of three strands of Z-twisted fibre that merge at each end to form the two cords grasped by the slinger (Völling 1990, 29, Abb. 6, 30, Abb. 8; Steingräber 1986, pl. 1, no. 2). As such, it would only be suitable for propelling missiles larger than the recognised types of Roman sling-shot (Greep 1987).

Livy (xxxviii, 29, 3–8) describes another sort of sling favoured among the Achaeans which Völling claims has a central pocket ('Schleudertasche') (1990, 27); but he may be wrong. Livy comments that the Achaean sling 'is not a simple strap, like the sling of the Balearics and other peoples, but is a triple (triple-thickness?) *scutale*, strengthened with close-set lines of stitching'. He is unfortunately the only early Roman writer to use the term *scutale* and so its contemporary meaning can only be gleaned from this passage and one other (xlii, 65, 10) where he observes: 'the sling (*funda*) in the middle had two unequal *scutalia*'. The latter are best construed as thongs of unequal length, and 'thong' may be the right translantion for *scutale* in the first passage, too. The Achaean sling, then, was not like that from Melandra, although its strap may well have been wider in the centre than at the ends.

Indications that the Romans had a sling with a central pocket to which two strings or thongs were attached are in fact hard to find. From later antiquity one may quote a mid-6th-century mosaic from Khirbet Al Mukhayyat in Jordan where a central pocket is depicted quite clearly on the sling in the hunter's right hand (fig. 2,B) (Völling 1990, 33, Abb. 17, 55 Liste 2.11; Piccirillo 1993, 172, pl. 223).

In the first season at Melandra, before the leather sling was uncovered, rounded gritstone pebbles were sometimes over-enthusiastically labelled as sling-stones and registered as small finds. Round stone 'bullets' were certainly used by slingers (Bishop & Coulston 1993, 139; Völling 1990, 39), but only when they turn up in discrete groups, as in the principia at

Lambaesis (Bishop & Coulston 1993, 166), is their function patent. The Roman army preferred lead sling-shot (*glandes*, 'acorns') or terracotta balls – which Caesar called *ex argilla glandes* (*de Bello Gallico* v, 43).

Greep noted two types of cast lead shot from Roman Britain (1987, 191, fig. 7), of which his Type 2 (which *does* resemble an acorn) is confined to this province. Empire-wide, Völling claims to be able to distinguish nine types or sub-types, with overlapping chronologies (1990, 34, Abb. 13). They weigh on average 40–70g each and are about 40mm long. Ubiquitous in military contexts of the 1st century, they are less common in the 2nd century and even rarer thereafter (Bishop & Coulston 1993, 113, 165; Völling 1990, 35–6, 48–54). The round or biconical baked clay 'bullets' which served as sling-shot have a more variable weight (up to 95g) (Völling 1990, 38, Abb. 22). In Britain and northern Gaul they were launched both by the defenders of hillforts and oppida and by the Romans attacking them (Greep 1987).

Neither lead nor clay shot has been recognised yet at Melandra. We know that both legionary and auxiliary troops were trained to use the sling (CIL VII, no. 18042; Greep 1987, 192; Völling 1990, 46–7), but specialist units of *funditores*, 'slingers', were rare and none is attested in Britain.

The identity, origin and particular skills of the garrison at Melandra in Period I are unknown. The centurial stone of the First Cohort of Frisiavones which was recovered in the late 18th century near the north-east corner of the fort (Conway 1906, 122–5, fig. opp. 122; RIB, no. 279) merely suggests that they were involved in the (Period II) rebuilding of the fort defences in stone in the early 2nd century; their real home was Manchester (Holder 1986, 139). A tile stamp of the Third Cohort of Bracaraugustani (Wright & Hassall 1974, 464 no. 14) cannot be assigned to a specific phase of occupation, but it is more likely to stem from Period II than Period I (Holder 1986, 139). (The tiles at Melandra are unusually large and clumsily made, and their production site is likely to have been close to the fort, so the physical presence of Bracaraugustani at *some* juncture seems assured.) At the moment, however, the hunt for slingers among the first garrison at Melandra seems vain.

There is of course no reason to assume that the Melandra sling was a weapon of war. A practised slinger could have hit a moving target with lethal effect at 100m (Baatz 1990, 62, 65) – and that target might well have been something for the pot. Virgil (*Aeneid* xi, 580) speaks of a herdsman knocking down 'Strymonian cranes and white swans', and one remembers the swan, goose and duck potted by members of the Longthorpe garrison (Dannell & Wild 1974, 68). Apicius has a particularly appealing recipe for casseroled crane (vi, II, 3 (Flower & Rosenbaum 1958)): perhaps someone at Melandra knew it.

Bibliography and abbreviations

CIL *Corpus Inscriptionum Latinarum* (Berlin, 1863–)

RIB R.G. Collingwood & R.P. Wright, *The Roman inscriptions of Britain, I: inscriptions on stone* (Oxford, 1965)

Baatz, D., 1990 Schleudergeschoße aus Blei – eine waffentechnische Untersuchung, *Saalburg-Jahrbuch*, **45**, 59–67

Bishop, M.C., & Coulston, J.C.N., 1993 *Roman military equipment from the Punic Wars to the fall of Rome* (London)

Bowman, A.C., & Thomas, J.D., 1994 *The Vindolanda writing tablets (Tabulae Vindolandenses II)* (London)

Conway, R.S., 1906 *Melandra Castle* (Manchester)

Dannell, G.B., & Wild, J.P., 1987 *Longthorpe II: The military works-depot: an episode in landscape history*, Britannia Monograph, **8** (London)

van Driel-Murray, C., 1993 The leatherwork, in R.E. Birley (ed.), *Vindolanda III: The early wooden forts*, 1–75 (Bardon Mill)

Fitts, L., & Hartley, B.R., 1988 *The Brigantes* (Gloucester)

Flower, B., & Rosenbaum, E., 1958 *The Roman cookery book* (London)

Göpfrich, J., 1986 Römische Lederfunde aus Mainz, *Saalburg-Jahrbuch*, **42**, 5–67

Greep, S.J., 1987 Lead sling-shot from Windridge Farm, St Albans, and the use of the sling by the Roman army in Britain, *Britannia*, **18**, 183–200

Griffiths, W.B., 1989 The sling and its place in the Roman imperial army, in C. van Driel-Murray (ed.), *Roman military equipment: the sources of evidence. Proceedings of the fifth Roman Military Equipment Conference*, BAR, **S476**, 255–79 (Oxford)

Holder, P.A., 1986 The Roman garrisons of Manchester, in S.Bryant, M. Morris & J.S.F. Walker (eds), *Roman Manchester: a frontier settlement* 139–40 (Manchester)

Johnson, R.H., 1969 The glacial geomorphology of the area around Hyde, Cheshire, *Proc. Yorkshire Geological Soc.*, **37**, 189–230

Lepper, F., & Frere, S.S., 1988 *Trajan's Column* (Gloucester)

Petch, J.A., 1943 Recent work at Melandra Castle: preliminary report, *Derbyshire Archaeol. J.*, **64**, 49–63

Piccirillo, M., 1993 *The mosaics of Jordan*, American Center of Oriental Research Publication, **1**

Reed, R., 1972 *Ancient skins, parchments and leathers* (London)

Steingräber, S., 1986 *Etruscan painting* (New York)

Völling, T., 1990 Funditores im römischen Heer, *Saalburg-Jahrbuch*, **45**, 24–58

Wild, J.P., 1974 Wooden tent-pegs from the Roman fort at Melandra Castle, Glossop, Derbyshire, *Antiq. J.*, **54**, 302–5

Wilson, D.R., 1970 Roman Britain in 1969, *Britannia*, **1**, 269–305

————, 1974, Roman Britain in 1973, *Britannia*, **5**, 397–460

Wright, R.P., & Hassall, M.W.C., 1974 Roman Britain in 1973: inscriptions, *Britannia*, **5**, 461–70

33   Early occupation at St. Mary's Abbey, York: the evidence of the glass

H.E.M. Cool

The foundation date for the legionary fortress at York is generally accepted to have been about AD 71 or 72, as part of the Flavian advance to the north under the governor Q. Petillius Cerialis (Frere 1987, 83). Many authors have pointed out that the choice of the site showed great insight into its strategic importance (see for example Frere 1987, 83; *Eburacum*, xxix; Ottaway 1993, 19–20), but whether this was because the site was already familiar to the Roman army due to earlier occupation is a matter of debate. The most likely time when this occupation might have taken place is at some point during the struggle for supremacy amongst the Brigantes by their pro-Roman Queen Cartimandua and her husband Venutius. Wenham (1971), in the volume celebrating the nineteenth centenary of the foundation of York, gathered together the literary and archaeological evidence for such a pre-Flavian occupation. In the same volume, however, doubts were cast on the likelihood of such a base from the viewpoints of both the known military dispositions and the samian stamps that had been found at York (Hartley 1971, 56; Dickinson & Hartley 1971, 131). Since then opinion has swung to the view that there was no pre-Flavian military activity at York (Hartley 1988, 154), and the most recent survey of Roman York does not even mention the possibility of such an occupation (Ottaway 1993, 21). Recent re-examination of the Roman vessel glass in the collections of the Yorkshire Museum has brought to light a handful of fragments which have the potential to rekindle this debate, and the aim of this note is to bring them to wider attention.

The fragments come from seven vessels found during the excavations carried out in the ruins of St. Mary's Abbey in the early 1950s by G.F. Willmot. Brief notes have been published about these excavations (Willmot 1952–53; 1953–54; *RB in 1952*, 113; *Eburacum*, 61) but they have never been published in full. Indeed in the literature there seems to be confusion as to when the excavations took place. The Royal Commission suggests 1952–3 (*Eburacum*, 61) and Wenham 1951–4 (1971, 48). The site codes preserved on the fragments, however, continue to 1956. In the brief interim notes published by Willmot (1952–53; 1953–4), he locates the early occupation in the area of the south aisle and adjoining cloister. It

should be noted, however, that three of the fragments to be discussed retain marking that indicate that they were found in 1955 (nos. 1 and 7) and 1956 (no. 5). This indicates that the excavations must have encountered early occupation, or material residual from such early occupation, in later years as well as well as the earlier ones. The area of the excavation (see fig. 1) lies within the enclosure to the north-west of the legionary fortress whose status remains enigmatic. It is known to have contained the area now occupied by the ruins of the Abbey, the Yorkshire Museum, the King's Manor House and the Art Gallery; and in the Royal Commision's survey it is referred to as being of 'uncertain date and purpose' (*Eburacum*, 45). The Roman vessel glass from the St. Mary's Abbey excavations appears to have been preserved in its entirety as it includes many featureless blue/green body fragments as well as material that can be more closely identified. In date the whole assemblage covers the period of the 1st century to the late 2nd to early 3rd century. Fourth-century material does not appear to be present.

The early glass (fig. 2) consists of two polychrome and one monochrome pillar-moulded bowls (nos. 1–3), a mould-blown ribbed cup (no. 4), a *modiolus* (no. 5), a Hofheim cup (no. 6) and a funnel (no. 7). This material can be divided into two categories. The first consists of those vessels which are happiest in a Claudio-Neronian *milieu* (nos 1–3) and which would have been very old-fashioned by the early Flavian period. The other vessels are also Claudio-Neronian forms but are ones which are known to have continued in use into the Flavian period.

Pillar-moulded bowls (Isings 1957, Form 3) were one of the commonest types of 1st-century glass vessel throughout the Roman Empire. They can be divided into three different colour types. There are polychrome ones made from cane segments, monochrome ones made in deliberately coloured bright glass such as deep blue and dark yellow/brown, and ones made in blue/green glass which is the 'natural' colour of early Roman glass which has neither been deliberately coloured or decolourised. The chronological significance of these different colours is well established (see for example Berger 1960, 10–19; Cool & Price 1995, 16). The polychrome

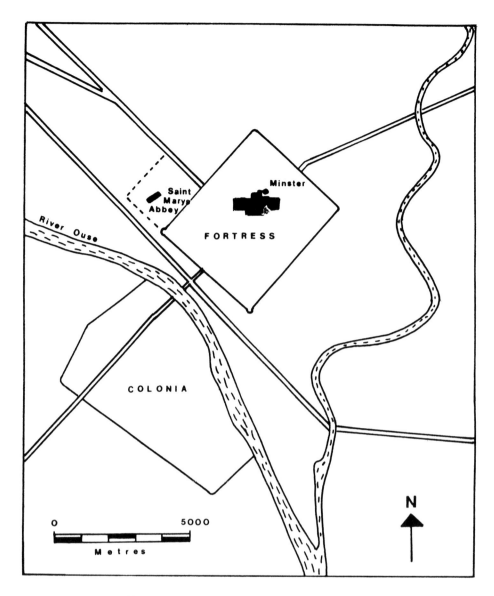

Fig. 1. Roman York showing the location of St. Mary's Abbey.

ones were primarily in use during the first half of the 1st century, the brightly coloured monochrome ones continued in use into the mid-1st century but then declined, and only the blue/green examples were still in common use during the Flavian period.

The value of this observation can be appreciated by comparing the relative proportions of the different types in the assemblages from sites in Roman Britain occupied at different times (for ease of comparison the assemblages are quantified on fragment counts). At the Claudian site at Sheepen, near Colchester, which was destroyed during the Boudican rising in AD 60/1, the pillar-moulded bowl assemblage of 123 fragments consisted of 14% polychrome, 17% monochrome and 67% blue/green (Harden 1947, 288). As examples of sites occupied during the Neronian period we may look at the assemblages from the legionary fortress at Usk, Gwent occupied between AD 52/7 and c.AD 67 and demolished about

AD 72 and from the mid-60s occupation at the fort at Kingsholm, Gloucester. At Usk (106 fragments) the proportions were 7% polychrome, 23% monochrome and 70% blue/green (Price 1993, 68–70), while at Kingsholm the much smaller assemblage of eighteen fragments consisted of three fragments of a polychrome bowl and two from two monochrome bowls with the other fragments coming from blue/green bowls (Price & Cool 1985, 45). For sites founded in the Flavian period the proportion of polychrome and brightly coloured monochrome pillar-moulded bowls declines markedly. At the legionary fortress at Chester founded in the mid-70s (Carrington 1994, 27) I know of 56 fragments of pillar-moulded bowls from sites scattered throughout the fortress (unpublished). The assemblage consists of 3.5% polychrome, 2% monochrome and 94.5% blue/green. At the auxiliary fort and *vicus* at Castleford, West Yorkshire founded c. AD 71–74, 44 fragments were found, eight of which came from one deep blue bowl. All of the others were blue/green and came from a minimum of twelve bowls (unpublished).

At York, therefore, we might expect the occasional fragment of polychrome or monochrome pillar-moulded bowl from a long-treasured vessel, but the bulk of such vessels will have been blue/green. This is the pattern observed at 9 Blake Street in the *praetentura* of the fortress where a large assemblage of pillar-moulded bowls was recovered (90 fragments from a minimum of eleven bowls) all of which were blue/green (Cool *et al.* 1995, 1563). If the assemblage from St. Mary's Abbey is excluded, I know of only three other polychrome or monochrome pillar-moulded bowls from York. One is a small fragment of a deep blue and opaque white bowl found residually at Coppergate (unpublished site code 1979.7, small find 5655), and the others are fragments from a deep blue and a yellow/green bowl now in the Yorkshire Museum but without provenance. At St. Mary's Abbey, by contrast, there are three fragments of polychrome or monochrome bowls compared to seven fragments of blue/green ones. As we have seen, this is a ratio that is typical of a Claudio-Neronian site and not of a Flavian one.

The mould-blown ribbed cup no. 4 belongs to a relatively long-lived type. Examples have been found in late Tiberian to early Claudian contexts on the Continent (Price 1991, 67), and in Britain they are found in Claudio-Neronian contexts and on sites in northern Britain such as Castleford, Binchester, Carlisle and Vindolanda (Price 1991, 70; see also Cool & Price 1995, 52). Like most 1st-century mould-blown vessel types, however, they are uncommon during the last two decades of the 1st century, and probably went out of production during the early Flavian period at the latest.

The rim fragment no. 5 is most likely to have come from a *modiolus* or measuring beaker (Isings 1957, Form 37). Glass examples are very rare in Britain. A ribbed example was found in a pit containing material dated to AD 50–80 at Exeter (*RB in 1952*, 124) and the rim fragment of another (Cool & Price 1995, 101, fig. 6.6, no. 703) was recovered from Culver Street, Colchester from a context dated to between AD 60/1 to *c.* 90/100. The circumstances of the excavation of this area of Culver Street make it very difficult to establish whether or not the fragment might have been residual from the pre-Boudican occupation (Crummy 1992, 71). The rarity of British examples makes it necessary to turn to continental parallels to establish their *floruit*. Many come from contexts which have a *terminus ante quem* of AD 80 (van Lith 1978–79, 64), and this, together with the fact that many are made of strongly-coloured glass, suggests that they are predominantly a mid-1st century form which was going out of use in the early Flavian period.

The Hofheim cup no. 6 is an example of the commonest drinking vessel form of the Claudio-Neronian period (Isings 1957, Form 12). These are very common on sites in the south of England (Cool & Price 1995, 65), but are relatively rare in the north in the area associated with the Flavian advance. Several examples have been found at Chester (unpublished) and single examples are known at Inchtuthil (Price 1985, 305, fig. 93, no.2), at a native settlement in Northumberland (Burgess 1970, 24, fig. 13, nos.2–3) and at Castleford (unpublished). In comparison to the other northern sites, York is relatively prolific. In addition to the cup from St. Mary's Abbey, there are a minimum of five from Blake Street (Cool *et al.* 1995, 1563), an example of the related beaker form (Cool & Price

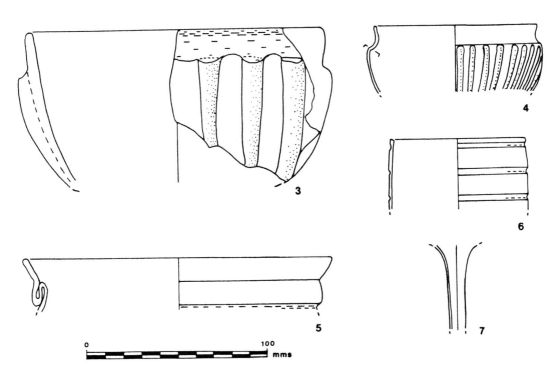

Fig. 2. Vessel glass fragments from St. Mary's Abbey. Scale 1:2.

1995, 68) from Aldwark (Yorkshire Museum Accession no. 1977.55), and a body fragment that could have come from either the cup or beaker form from Fishergate (Hunter & Jackson 1993, 1337).

The final vessel type from St Mary's Abbey that might be indicative of early occupation is the funnel no. 7. Funnels (Isings 1957, Form 74) were in use during the 1st century but are not very common and so are difficult to date precisely. The bulk of the examples from closely dated contexts both in Britain and elsewhere in the western empire are of Claudio-Neronian to very early Flavian date (Cool & Price 1995, 174), but elsewhere in northern Britain they have been found at Watercrook, Cumbria (Charlesworth 1979, 232, no. 170) and Castleford (unpublished).

In summary, therefore, we have a pillar-moulded bowl assemblage that is typical of a Claudio-Neronian rather than a Flavian site, three vessels (nos. 4, 6 and 7) whose main *floruits* are Claudio-Neronian though they are known on early Flavian sites, and the *modiolus* (no. 5) which is a rare form in decline by the early Flavian period. This is a concentration of early forms unmatched elsewhere in York. The much larger assemblage from Blake Street (Cool *et al.* 1995, 1561–5), for example, is more comparable to that from Castleford and other early Flavian assemblages.

This early glass does not stand alone at St. Mary's Abbey. Gallo-Belgic pottery of AD 50 to 85 has also been recovered from the site (Rigby 1993, 726) as well as marbled samian and St. Rémy ware (Wenham 1971, 53, n. 31). Wenham concluded that though the collection of at least thirteen vessels could be Flavian, there were parallels with the pre-Roman native site at North Ferriby, Lincs. Thus the pottery, like the glass, hints at a possible pre-Flavian occupation. It would be unwise to attempt to re-write the early history of York on the basis of a handful of glass fragments but, together with the pottery, they do suggest that the earliest focus of Roman activity at York may not have been within the area of the fortress but within that of the enigmatic 'annexe'.

It gives me great pleasure to dedicate this note to Brian Hartley. No-one who works in the north can remain untouched or unaided by his scholarship and I hope his 'retirement' will be a long and fruitful one.

Catalogue (fig. 2)

1. (Not illustrated) Body fragment of polychrome pillar-moulded bowl. Translucent deep blue ground with opaque white rods. Part of one rib remaining. Dimensions: 15 × 14mm. (SMA55 5TX 208)

2. (Not illustrated) Upper body fragment of polychrome pillar-moulded bowl. Translucent purple ground with opaque white speckles. Part of one rib remaining. Dimensions. 34 × 27mm.

3. Rim fragment of translucent purple pillar-moulded bowl. Exterior of rim bevelled and only lightly wheel-polished. Parts of three ribs remaining with slight tooling marks on upper

surface of each and tooled mark on interior. Rim diameter 160mm, present height 81mm.

4. One rim and one body fragment of blue/green mould-blown ribbed cup. Curved rim, edge cracked off and lightly ground; concave upper body; carination to ribbed body with upper part of one rib remaining. Body fragment retains carination; convex-curved side and parts of five ribs. Rim diameter *c.* 90mm, reconstructed present height 35mm. (SMA 2C 124 (rim fragment); SMA53 2C 49 (body fragment)).

5. Rim fragment of blue/green *modiolus*. Out-turned rim with fire-rounded rim edge; figure-of-eight fold below. Rim diameter 170mm, present height 27mm. (SMA56 4X 103)

6. Rim fragment of blue/green cylindrical Hofheim cup. Vertical rim, edge cracked off and ground; straight side; three wide wheel-cut grooves. Rim diameter 75mm, present height 38mm. (SMA 117 2TC 124)

7. Body fragment of blue/green funnel. Lower body sloping in to cylindrical tapering spout broken at base. Present length 43mm. (SMA55 T5X 208)

Acknowledgements

I would like to thank Mr Brian Hayton, the curator of the Yorkshire Museum, for his permission to publish these items in the collection. I owe a large debt of gratitude to Mrs Elizabeth Hartley, the Keeper of Archaeology at the museum, for all her help and encouragement while I have been studying the glass in her care, and hope that she will forgive me for the slight subterfuge that was necessary to write this note. I am also very grateful to the York Archaeological Trust, the West Yorkshire Archaeological Service and the Chester Archaeological Service for allowing me to study material from their excavations.

Bibliography and abbreviations

Berger, L., 1960 *Römische Gläser aus Vindonissa* (Basel)

Burgess, C. B., 1970 Excavations at the scooped settlement Hetha Burn I, Hethpool, Northumberland, 1969, *Trans. Architect. Archaeol. Soc. Durham Northumberland,* **2,** 1–26

Butler, R.M. (ed.), 1971 *Soldier and civilian in Roman Yorkshire* (Leicester)

Carrington, P., 1994 *English Heritage Book of Chester* (London)

Charlesworth, D., 1979 Glass, beads, armlets, in Potter, T.W., *Romans in northwest England,* Cumberland Westmorland Antiq. Archaeol. Soc. Res. Ser., **1,** 230–34

Cool, H.E.M., Lloyd-Morgan, G., & Hooley, A.D., 1995 *Finds from the fortress,* Archaeology of York, **17/10** (York)

————, & Price, J., 1995 *Roman vessel glass from excavations in Colchester, 1971–85,* Colchester Archaeol. Rep., **8** (Colchester)

Crummy, P., 1992 *Excavations at Culver Street, the Gilberd School, and other sites in Colchester 1971–85,* Colchester Archaeol. Rep., **6** (Colchester)

Dickinson, B.M., & Hartley, K. F., 1971 The evidence of potters' stamps on samian ware and on mortaria for the trading connections of Roman York, in Butler 1971, 127–42

Eburacum: An inventory of the historical monuments in the City of York, Volume 1: Eburacum Roman York, Royal Commision on Historical Monuments England, 1962 (London)

Frere, S., 1987 *Britannia,* 3rd edn (London and New York)

Harden, D.B., 1947 The glass, in Hawkes, C.F.C., & Hull, M.R., *Camulodunum*

First report on the excavations at Colchester 1930–1939, Rep. Res. Comm. Soc. Antiq. London, **14**, 287–307

Hartley, B.R., 1971 Roman York and the northern military command to the third century A.D., in Butler 1971, 55–69

————, 1988 'Plus ça change....., or reflections on the Roman forts of Yorkshire', in Price, J., & Wilson, P.R., *Recent research in Roman Yorkshire*, Brit. Archaeol. Rep. Brit. Ser., **193**, 153–9 (Oxford)

Hunter, J.R., & Jackson, C. M., 1993 Glass, in Rogers, N.S.H., *Anglian and other finds from 46–54 Fishergate,* Archaeology of York, **17/9**, 1331–44 (London)

Isings, C., 1957 *Roman glass from dated finds* (Groningen and Djarkarta)

Ottaway, P., 1993 *English Heritage Book of Roman York* (London)

Price, J., 1985 The Roman glass, in Pitts, L.F., & St. Joseph, J.K., *Inchtuthil, the Roman legionary fortress excavations 1952–65*, Britannia Monograph Ser., **6**, 303–12 (London)

————, 1991 Decorated mould blown tablewares in the first century A.D., in Newby, M., & Painter, K. (eds), *Roman glass: two centuries of art and invention*, Soc. Antiq. London Occas. Papers, **13**, 56–75 (London)

————, 1993 Vessel glass from the Neronian legionary fortress at Usk in South Wales, *Annales du 12e Congrés de l'Association Internationale pour l'Histoire du Verre*, 67–77 (Amsterdam)

————, & Cool, H.E.M., 1985 Glass (including glass from 72 Dean's Way), in Hurst, H.R., *Kingsholm*, Gloucester Archaeol. Rep., **1**, 41–54 (Cambridge)

Rigby, V., 1993 Early Gaulish imports, in Monaghan, J., *Roman pottery from the fortress*, Archaeology of York, **16/7**, 725–8 (London)

RB in 1952 Roman Britain in 1952, *J. Roman Stud.*, **43**, 104–34

van Lith, S.M.E., 1978–79 Römisches Glas aus Valkenburg Z.H., *Oudeid-kundige mededelingen uit het Rijksmuseum van Oudheden te Leiden,* **59–60**, 1–150

Wenham, L.P., 1971 The beginnings of Roman York, in Butler 1971, 45–53

Willmot, G.F., 1952–3 St Mary's Abbey, York, *Yorkshire Architect. York Archaeol. Soc. Annual Rep. & Summary Proc. for 1952–53*, 8

————, 1953–4 Excavations at St Mary's Abbey, *Yorkshire Architect. York Archaeol. Soc. Annual Rep. & Summary Proc. for 1953–54*, 12–3

34   A glass drinking cup with incised decoration from Newton Kyme, North Yorkshire

Jennifer Price

During excavations at the Roman fort at Newton Kyme directed by the late Herman Ramm in 1957, about twenty glass vessel fragments were found, dating from the 2nd to 4th centuries. One of these, from the rim and upper body of a colourless cylindrical cup with incised decoration, is rather unusual, and this short note will explore it and similar finds in Britain and in the north-western provinces.[1]

The fragment is very small (dimensions 15.5 × 21mm, thickness 2.5–5.5mm), and made in good quality colourless glass. The rim is fire-rounded and fire-thickened, and the upper body is vertical. Below the rim, a fish motif facing left, the head and tail portions of which are now missing, has been incised into the outside surface. The outline of the fish has been drawn as a continuous line, using a metal or flint point, and the dorsal fin, gills and other details are shown as shorter lines (fig. 1, no. 1).

When complete, the vessel would have had a thick, fire-rounded rim, a straight or very slightly convex upper body in a more or less vertical alignment, a sharp change of angle to a straight or slightly convex wide lower body, tapering in to a base-ring and slightly concave base (fig. 1, no. 2). Most examples have a double base-ring, the outer being pushed in and tubular, and the inner a thick circular trail set close to the centre of the underside of the base, usually with a pontil mark on it. These vessels are generally accepted as drinking cups. They were produced in various sizes, with rim diameters ranging from less than 80mm to more than 120mm.

Cups of this colour and form are concentrated in the north-west provinces in the later 2nd and early 3rd centuries, and they were undoubtedly produced in the region. This is overwhelmingly the dominant form of drinking cup of the period, occurring both in settlements and in burials, particularly in the Rhineland and in central and northern Gaul. Numerous examples from dated contexts were listed in *Roman glass from dated finds* (Isings 1957, Form 85b), and many others have been recorded since then. Large groups are known from the Rhineland, as at Köln (Fremersdorf & Polónyi-Fremersdorf 1984, 8–10, nos 20–28) and Bonn (Follmann-Schulz 1988, 93–6, nos. 332–46, pl. 41), the Moselle, as at Trier (Goethert-Polaschek 1977, Form 47a, 48–9, nos. 148–153,

pls. 15, 36, 37), Burgundy, as at Nuits St George (Joubeaux 1982, 61–2, nos. C85–98, pl. 17), Normandy (Sennequier 1985, 50–52, nos. 17–22) and elsewhere.

The cups are very common finds in Britain. Their date of introduction is difficult to establish precisely, and has been the subject of some discussion. Fragments found in the latrine drain of the Commandant's House at Housesteads were initially published as part of a group of glass vessels deposited there around AD 139–42 (Charlesworth 1971), but the final excavation report indicated that this drain did not contain a deposit which could be assigned to the second quarter of the 2nd century, as material had accumulated throughout the Antonine period and perhaps into the 3rd century (Charlesworth 1975, 24).

The cups are certainly present in deposits dated to the third quarter of the 2nd century. A rim fragment was found in an Antonine pit at Felmongers, Harlow, a deposit dated by samian pottery to *c.*AD 160–70 (Price 1987, 192–3, 204, no. 19, fig. 2), and others are known from Antonine contexts at Lullingstone (Cool & Price 1987, 112) and Castleford (unpublished). Fragments occur, often in large quantities, at virtually every Romano-British settlement occupied in the last quarter of the 2nd and first quarter of the 3rd century. For example, at least 37 vessels are known from Carlisle, more than 40 from Caerleon (Price 1995a, 164–5), at least 46 from Colchester, and more than 61 from Piercebridge (Cool & Price 1995, 82–5).

They are, however, less common in burials. Three were found in burials in the 3rd-century cemetery at Brougham, Cumbria (Cool 1990, 170, fig. 1, no. 1), four others are known from graves 23, 26, 27 and 30 in the Infirmary Field, Chester (Newstead 1914; 1921), and two or three have come from Scotland beyond the frontier of the Roman province, at Airlie in Grampian, Westray in Orkney and perhaps Kingoldrum in Grampian (Curle 1931–32, 291, 386–7, 395, fig. 3), but otherwise they have not often been noted in funerary contexts.

These cups continued in circulation in Britain until at least the second quarter of the 3rd century. Two pieces in contexts dated to *c.*AD 235 or later came from Vindolanda (Price 1985, 207, nos. 11, 11b, fig. 7), and the cemetery at Brougham already mentioned has been dated to AD 220/30–270/80.

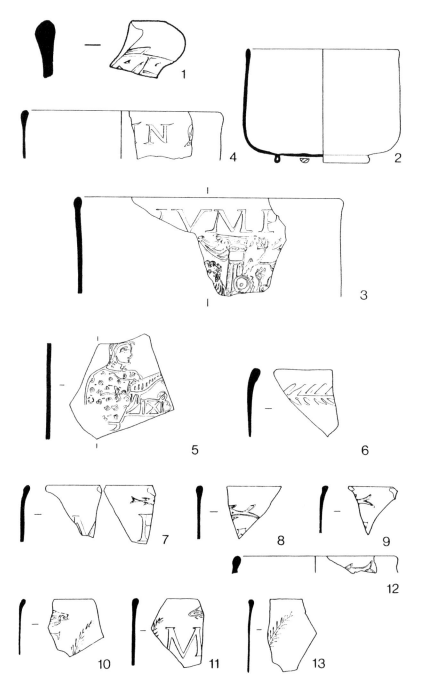

Fig. 1. *Cylindrical glass cups with incised decoration.* **1,** *the Newton Kyme fragment;* **2,** *colourless cylindrical cup (Isings Form 85b);* **3,** *rim fragment, Bishophill, York (after Charlesworth 1978);* **4,** *rim fragment, Pudding Lane, London (after RIB II, 2);* **5,** *body fragment, Great Bulmore, Caerleon (unpublished, drawing from Denise Allen);* **6,** *rim fragment, Rapsley villa, Surrey;* **7,** *two rim fragments, Chesters (after Fremersdorf 1970);* **8,** *rim fragment, Corbridge (after Fremersdorf 1970);* **9,** *rim fragment, Colchester (after Fremersdorf 1970);* **10,** *rim fragment, Silchester (after Fremersdorf 1970);* **11,** *rim fragment, Alstone Cottage, Caerleon;* **12,** *rim fragment, Derby (after Allen 1986);* **13,** *rim fragment, Wood Burcote, Towcester (unpublished, drawing from Denise Allen). Scale: nos. 1, 5–6, 1:1; rest 1:2.*

The vast majority of these cylindrical cups were produced without decoration, but several decorated groups are also known. Cups with colourless horizontal trails on the upper and lower body are found quite frequently in settlements, as in Colchester (Cool & Price 1995, 82, 84, nos. 466–73, fig. 5.12), and at Blake Street, York (Cool *et al.* 1995, 1574–5, nos. 5992–4, fig. 742), and examples have occasionally been found in burials, as at Baldock (Westell 1931, 276, no. 4828, fig. 6). A few fragments have coloured trails, usually opaque white or blue, below the rims and on the bodies and bases, as at Caerleon, Chester, Burgh-by-Sands and Leckie Broch (all unpublished). Another group is decorated with painted scenes. The finds in Britain, the Rhineland and elsewhere within the north-western provinces are very fragmentary, but several complete painted cups are known in burials in northern Germany and Denmark, beyond the Rhine frontier (see Fremersdorf 1970, 63–7, pls. 3, 7–10; Lund Hansen 1987, 74–7, figs. 28, 138, 140).

Cups with incised decoration appear to be less common than the painted versions. Apart from the group with fish and fern or palm-leaf motifs discussed below (to which the Newton Kyme fragment belongs), a few other designs have been recognised. In the Rhineland, a fragmentary cup with handle loops from Köln has decorative panels and four medallions containing human/divine busts (Fremersdorf 1970, 63, no. 20, fig. 5, pl. 6), and fragments from the legionary fortress at Bonn have ivy leaves and tendrils in a band below the rim (Follmann-Schulz 1988, 94, no. 336, pl. 41). Circus scenes are also found; a cup from a burial in Trier has B I B A M V S and an ivy-leaf stop below the rim, and three scenes from the arena on the body (Fremersdorf 1970, 62–3, no. 18, fig. 3, pls. 4–5), and two fragments from Embresin, in Belgium, show running animals (Fremersdorf 1970, 63, no. 19, fig. 4, no. 7).

Figured designs are rare in Britain (see map, fig. 2). The largest piece, found at Bishophill, in the *colonia* at York (fig.1, no. 3), has ... L(?) V M P ... (probably part of Olympus) below the rim, and a scene with a Corinthian column, a draped figure with curly hair holding a disc in the left hand and a tree (Charlesworth 1978, 55–6, no. 169, fig. 30; RIB II.2, no. 2419. 41). No parallels for this are known, but it appears to be a classical cult scene.

Other fragments include the rim fragment from Pudding Lane, London (fig. 1, no. 4) which has ... I N ... below the rim, with part of an ivy-leaf stop pointing down (RIB II.2, no. 2419.55). This might come from a cup with arena scenes, but nothing of the design has survived. A small body fragment from Great Bulmore, near Caerleon (unpublished – information from Denise Allen) is very likely to be from such a cup. It shows part of a male figure with fairly long hair, facing right. He is wearing a spotted garment with short sleeves on his upper body, has a heavily padded left hand and forearm, and his bare right arm is raised diagonally (fig. 1, no. 5). This figure may be a gladiator, and the padded left arm and lack of head or body armour suggests that he is probably a *retiarius*. Exact parallels have not been found, although the left arm padding is generally comparable with that worn by Pulcher, the *retiarius* on the Trier cup. Another small fragment, from

the Roman villa at Rapsley in Surrey (Harden 1968, 69), has a horizontal band of herringbone or fern leaves below the rim (fig. 1, no. 6).

No complete cups with fishes and inscriptions with fern or palm-leaf stops have yet been found, but rim fragments with all or some of these motifs are known at sites in the Rhine and Danube frontier regions, as well as in Britain (see Price 1978, 75, fig. 58, for their distribution, though more pieces are now known). They have not yet been recorded at sites outside the frontiers, in contrast to the painted cups mentioned above.

Pieces have come from at least eight or nine sites in Britain (see map, fig. 2), and the ones with inscribed letters are already well known. The fragments from Chesters, Corbridge, Colchester and Silchester (fig. 1, nos. 7–10) have been discussed by Bulmer (1955, 130–1, fig. 17), Charlesworth (1959, 44, fig. 4), and Fremersdorf (1970, 61, nos. 9–12, fig. 1, nos. 8, 10–12). They, and the Caerleon fragment (fig. 1, no. 11) found in 1970 in Barrack XII, Prysg Field (Price 1995b, 81–3, 87, no. 2, fig. 9), have also been listed in RIB II.2 (nos. 2419. 50, 60–62, 69). The other fragments on which fish or fern/ palm-leaf motifs survive are from Inhumation 104, Derby Racecourse cemetery (fig. 1, no. 12; Allen 1986, 268, fig. 18, no. 1), Wood Burcote, near Towcester (fig. 1, no. 13; unpublished – information from Denise Allen), and Newton Kyme. In addition, a rim fragment from Coventina's Well at Carrawburgh may belong to this group, but the surviving decoration is ambiguous (Allason-Jones & McKay 1985, 39, no. 137, fig.).

In the Rhineland and upper Danube regions, finds have come from Saalburg, Osterburken, Mainz-Weisenau, Butzbach, Deutsch-Altenburg and Bregenz (Fremersdorf 1970, 59–61, 67, fig. 1, nos. 1–7, 9), Straubing (Walke 1965, 49, 144, pl. 75, nos. 38–9), Aalen (Weisshuhn 1984), Kempten (Fasold 1985, 218, fig. 12, no. 3), Chur (Hochuli-Gysel *et al.* 1986, 127, 340, fig. 40, no. 3), Ellingen (Zanier 1992, 272, nos. 19–20, pl. 93), Dambach (cited by Zanier), Bad Wimpfen (information from Ms B. Hoffmann) and elsewhere.

The surviving fragments represent only a very small proportion of the total area of the cups, and it is not possible to recognise their overall designs. The fishes face either left or right, and while there is a little variation in the depictions of the fishes, they are generally uniform in appearance and seem to be representations of the same species of fish. The pointed head and long rounded body with oval patches or scales, and the two dorsal fins, suggest that this may be a Zander or Pikeperch, which is found in the rivers of western and central Europe.

No more than two letters survive on any of the fragments, and the inscriptions have not been deciphered. The British examples have only one letter each, M on the Caerleon piece, one of the Corbridge pieces and probably the Chester piece, T or C or G on the Silchester piece, C or G on the Colchester piece and F or P on the second Corbridge piece. The fragments from the Rhine and upper Danube frontiers have contributed some additional letters, as A, B, I, S and V have been recognised. Two small groups with two letters have been noted: S T below a fish facing right at Osterburken and prob-

310   JENNIFER PRICE

ably also at Deutsch-Altenburg, and B E with a fern or palm leaf stop at Ellingen, plus another from the same site perhaps with the same combination of letters below a fish facing left. Some further fragments found in Britain have a single inscribed letter, without other decoration, and these cannot be assigned to any particular group of cups. Examples are known from Silchester, Verulamium and Springhead, Kent (Fremersdorf 1970, 61–2, nos. 14–16, fig. 2, nos. 3–5 and 7), and Beauport Park, Sussex (RIB II.2, nos. 2419. 52, 55, 64, 67 and 70).

Very few pieces from the decorated groups of cylindrical cups have been recorded in closely dated contexts, and it has sometimes been argued that most of them were produced in the 3rd century. Two of the British fragments with incised decoration, however, provide clear evidence that these cups were already in use in the later 2nd century. The York fragment with the classical cult scene was found in a context predating the construction of a terrace in the late 2nd century (MacGregor 1978, 31, 61), and the fish and leaf fragment from Barrack XII at Caerleon came from a demolition de-

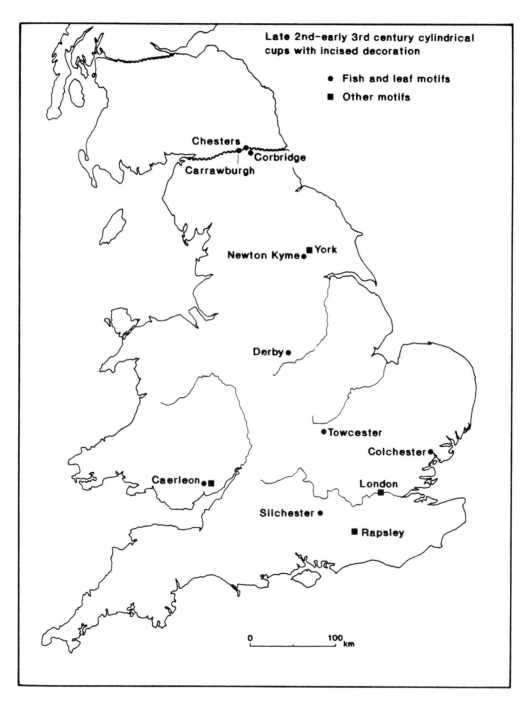

Fig. 2. Distribution of fragments of colourless cylindrical cups with incised decoration in Britain.

posit dateable to the late Antonine period. The Rapsley fragment was found in a deposit belonging to the second decade of the 3rd century.

The presence of the combination of fish and fern/palm-leaf motifs in the designs has often led to assertions that these cups were Christian objects (for example, see Hope 1903, 32; Charlesworth 1959, 46; Boon 1974, 183–4; Thomas 1981, 129–30, and elsewhere). This may, of course, be the correct interpretation, but the supporting evidence does not appear to be very persuasive. The inscribed words or phrases have not yet been deciphered, apart from the two Ellingen fragments which may point to the use of BIBE, so it is not possible to determine whether these have any Christian religious significance, and the use of fern or palm-leaf stops between words or at the end of phrases should not be accepted as Christian without careful consideration, as these frequently occur in contexts without obvious Christian associations. For example, they occur in the inscriptions on various forms of glass vessels, from mould-blown chariot-race cups in the third quarter of the 1st century (for instance from Canterbury and Bricket Wood, near St. Albans; see RIB II.2, nos. 2419.7–8 and 10) to shallow bowls with incised hunting, classical cult and biblical scenes in the mid-4th century (Harden 1960; Harden *et al.* 1987, nos. 126–8).

Similarly, the fishes may have some other symbolic significance, or simply be intended as decorative motifs. Images of fishes occur quite frequently on glass vessels in the ancient world (Newby 1993). They are present in the decorative schemes of Roman glass vessels from the 1st century onwards, and many of these are unlikely to be Christian religious symbols. A few vessels were made in the form of a fish, as in the dark blue cast and carved shallow plate or lid in the Corning Museum of Glass (Harden *et al.* 1987, no. 25), or the pale green mould-blown flask, perhaps from Arles, in the British Museum (Tatton-Brown 1991, fig. 103). Painted depictions of fishes occur on 1st-century hemispherical cups at Winterthur, Vindonissa and Xanten (Rütti 1991, 129–30, fig. 24c, pl. 33b), and on cups of the form under discussion in the late 2nd and early 3rd century at Aachenerstrasse, Köln (Fremersdorf 1970, 125, pl. 10), and Vindolanda (unpublished – information from Mr R. Birley).

In the 3rd and 4th centuries, applied elements in the form of fishes are found on bowls from Köln, Trier, Rome and elsewhere (Harden *et al.* 1987, no. 144), and fishes carved in high relief occur on cage-cups in Pannonia (Barkoczi 1988, 218–20, no. 556, pls. 68 and 107) and Gaul (Grosjean 1985, 145, no. 238b). Polychrome inlays in the form of fishes were occasionally set in mosaic bowls (Weinberg 1962), and cut and engraved fishes are known on various groups of late Roman vessels, such as the shallow bowl with fishing scenes in the Museo Nazionale Romano in Rome and the globular flask with groups of figures in a landscape, perhaps with funerary symbolism, from Amiens (Harden *et al.* 1987, nos. 119 and 132).

Any consideration of the Christian religious significance of these fragments should probably also take account of the character of the settlements in which they have been found.

In Britain, little is known about the precise find-spots of most of the pieces, but some have come from military sites, at Caerleon, Chesters, Carrawburgh and Newton Kyme, or from sites with a strong military presence, at Corbridge. Many of the Rhineland and upper Danube finds have also come from military sites. It is perhaps questionable whether the use of drinking cups making overtly Christian religious statements would be likely to be tolerated in settlements belonging to the Roman state in the later 2nd and early 3rd centuries.

Little is known about the production centres for any of the colourless cylindrical cups. The very large numbers of undecorated examples found throughout the north western provinces might suggest that these were produced by itinerant glassmakers at various glassworking sites at different times, rather than being distributed from one or two large centres, but in the absence of any firm evidence this must remain an open question. The process of adding incised decoration to the cups would be unlikely to leave traces in the archaeological record, so it is unsurprising that there is no evidence to identify the place or places where the process took place. The craftsmen are likely to have been quite distinct from the glass blowers, and they may have worked in close proximity to the glassblowing sites or at some distance away. Indeed, there is no particular reason why the incised decoration should be exactly contemporary with the production of the cups.

The presence of cups with incised designs at sites on or near to the frontiers, and the absence of recorded finds outside the Roman empire, is interesting but not easy to explain. They account for only a minute proportion of the total number of colourless cylindrical cups found in the north-west provinces, and their distribution is patchy within this area; for example, they seem to be largely absent from parts of northern Gaul and the Rhine delta. Their distribution appears to have a strong military bias, though this may in part result from the emphasis on excavation of military, rather than urban or rural, sites. Some pieces have also been found in towns and villas away from the frontier zone, in both Britain and the Rhineland.

To conclude, there is now little doubt that cups with incised decoration were in circulation by the last quarter of the 2nd century, and that they continued in use for much of the same period as their undecorated counterparts, but many other aspects, such as the significance of their designs, where they were produced, how they were distributed and why they occur where they do, remain obscure.

Postscript

C. F. Mawer's book, *Evidence for Christianity in Roman Britain: the small finds* (BAR British Ser. no. **243**, 1995), and S. F. Pfahl's paper, 'Ein gläserner Fischbecher ans Langenhain-Göttingen' (*Heimat- und Altertumsverein Heidenheim an der Brenz Jahrbuch*, 1995/96, 20–36), appeared after this note had been written, so it has not been possible to take account of their discussion of cups with incised fish and leaf motifs.

Note

1.   This note is offered to Brian Hartley in the hope that he will enjoy it,
     and in recognition of his contribution to so many aspects of Roman
     archaeology in Yorkshire and beyond.

     The Newton Kyme excavations are now being prepared for pub-
     lication by members of the Roman Antiquities Section of the York-
     shire Archaeological Society, and the report will appear in a future
     volume of the *Yorkshire Archaeological Journal*. I am grateful to the Roman
     Section for permission to write about the 'fish fragment' in advance
     of the full excavation report.

     I should also like to thank Denise Allen, Sally Cottam and David
     Langridge for assistance while I was preparing this note, and Yvonne
     Beadnell for producing the illustrations.

Bibliography and abbreviations

Allason-Jones, L., & McKay, B., 1985 *Coventina's Well*, Chesters Museum

Allen, D., 1986 Glass, in Dool, J., *et al.*, Roman Derby: excavations 1963–1983, *Derbyshire Archaeol. J.*, **195**, 268–9

Barkóczi, L., 1988 *Pannonische Glasfunde in Ungarn* (Budapest)

Boon, G. C., 1974 *Silchester: the Roman town of Calleva* (Newton Abbot)

Bulmer, W., 1955 Roman glass vessels in the Corstopitum Museum, Corbridge, *Archaeol. Aeliana*, 4 ser., **33**, 116–33

Charlesworth, D., 1959 Roman glass in northern Britain, *Archaeol. Aeliana*, 4 ser., **37**, 33–58

_____, 1971 A group of vessels from the Commandant's House, Housesteads, *J. Glass Stud.*, **13**, 34–7

_____, 1975 The Commandant's House, *Archaeol. Aeliana*, 5 ser., **3**, 17–42

_____, 1978 Glass vessels, in MacGregor, A., 1978, 54–7

_____, 1984 The glass, in Frere, S., *Verulamium excavations, volume III*, 145–73 (Oxford)

Cool, H.E.M. 1990 The problem of 3rd century drinking vessels in Britain, *Annales du 11e Congrès de l'Association Internationale pour l'Histoire du Verre (Bâle 1988)*, 167–75

_____, & Price, J., 1987 The glass, in Meates, G.W., *The Roman villa at Lullingstone, Kent: 2, the wall-paintings and finds*, Kent Archaeol. Soc. Monograph, **3**, 110–42

_____, & _____, 1995 *Roman vessel glass from excavations in Colchester, 1971–85*, Colchester Archaeol. Rep., **8**

_____, Lloyd-Morgan, G., & Hooley, A.D., 1995 *Finds from the fortress*, The archaeology of York. The small finds, **17/10** (York)

Curle, J., 1931–32 Inventory of objects of Roman and provincial Roman origin found on sites in Scotland not definitely associated with Roman constructions, *Proc. Soc. Antiq. Scotland*, **66**, 277–397

Fasold, P., 1985 Die früh- und mittelrömischen Gläser von Kempten-Cambodunum, *Forschungen zur provinzialrömischen Archäologie in Bayerisch-Schwaben*, 193–230 (Augsburg)

Follmann-Schulz, A.B., 1988 *Die römischen Gläser aus Bonn* (Köln)

Fremersdorf, F., 1970 Seltene Varianten steilwandiger römischer Glasbecher des 3.Jh. aus Köln, *Kölner Jahrbuch*, **11**, 59–72

_____, & Polónyi-Fremersdorf, E., 1984 *Die farblosen Gläser der Frühzeit in Köln*, Die Denkmäler des römischen Köln, **9** (Köln)

Goethert-Polaschek, K., 1977 *Katalog der römischen Gläser des Rheinischen Landesmuseums Trier* (Mainz)

Grosjean, B., 1985 La vaiselle en verre, in *Autun Augustodunum: capitale des Eduens*, 143–51 (Autun)

Harden, D.B., 1960 The Wint Hill hunting bowl and related glasses, *J. Glass Stud.*, **2**, 45–81

_____, 1968 The glass, in Hanworth, R., The Roman villa at Rapsley, Ewhurst, *Surrey Archaeol. Collect.*, **65**, 64–9

_____, *et al.*, 1987 *Glass of the Caesars* (Milan)

Hochuli-Gysel, A., *et al.*, 1986 *Chur in römischer Zeit: Ausgrabungen Areal Dosch*, Antiqua, **12** (Basel)

Hope, W.H.St.J., 1902 Excavations on the site of the Roman city of Silchester, Hampshire, in 1901, *Archaeologia*, **58**, 17–36

Isings, C., 1957 *Roman glass from dated finds* (Groningen)

Joubeaux, H., 1982 Verrerie, in Planson, E., *La nécropole gallo-romaine des Bolards, Nuits-St-Georges*, 57–65 (Paris)

Lund Hansen, U., 1987 *Römischer Import im Norden* (København)

MacGregor, A., 1978 *Roman finds from Bishophill and Skeldergate*, The archaeology of York. The small finds, **17/2** (London)

Newby, M., 1993 Ancient of Glaze. Fish imagery in Greek, Roman and Egyptian glass, *Apollo*, **138**, no. 377, 20–24

Newstead, R., 1914 The Roman cemetery in the Infirmary Field, Chester, *Annals Archaeol. Anthropol.*, **6**, 121–67

_____, 1921 The Roman cemetery in the Infirmary Field, Chester, part II, *Annals Archaeol. Anthropol.*, **8**, 49–60

Price, J., 1978 Trade in glass, in du Plat Taylor, J., & Cleere, H. (eds), *Roman shipping and trade: Britain and the Rhine Provinces*, 70–78 (London)

_____, 1985 The glass, in Bidwell, P.T., *The Roman fort of Vindolanda at Chesterholm, Northumberland*, English Heritage Archaeol. Rep., **1**

_____, 1987 Glass from Felmongers, Harlow in Essex: a dated deposit of vessel glass found in an Antonine pit, *Annales du 10e Congrès de l'Association Internationale pour l'Histoire du Verre (Madrid-Segovie 1985)*, 185–206

_____, 1995a Glass vessels, in Manning, W.H., Price, J., & Webster, J., *The Roman small finds*, Excavations at Usk, 1965–1976, 139–91 (Cardiff)

_____, 1995b The glass, in Casey, P.J., & Hoffmann, B., Excavations at Alstone Cottage, Caerleon, in 1970, *Britannia*, **27**, 80–88

RIB II.2 Collingwood, R.G., & Wright, R.P., *The Roman Inscriptions of Britain, Volume II Instrumentum Domesticum, Fascicule 2*, 1991 (Frere, S.S., & Tomlin, R.S.O. (eds))

Rütti, B., 1991 Early enamelled glass, in Newby, M., & Painter, K. (eds), *Roman glass: two centuries of art and invention*, 122–36 (London)

Sennequier, G., 1985 *Verrerie d'époque romaine. Collections des Musées Départementaux de Seine-Maritime* (Rouen)

Tatton-Brown, V., 1991 The Roman empire, in Tait, H. (ed.), *Five thousand years of glass*, 62–97 (London)

Thomas, C., 1981 *Christianity in Roman Britain to AD 500* (London)

Walke, N., 1965 *Das römische Donaukastelle Straubing-Sorviodurum*, Limesforschungen, **3** (Berlin)

Westell, W.P., 1931 A Romano-British cemetery at Baldock, Herts., *Archaeol. J.*, **87**, 247–301

Weinberg, G., 1962 An inlaid glass plate in Athens, *J. Glass Stud.*, **4**, 29–36

Weisshuhn, G., 1984 Aalen, 3, *Fundbericht Baden-Württemberg*, **9**, 666

Zanier, W., 1992 *Das römische Kastell Ellingen*, Limesforschungen, **23** (Berlin)